murach's
ASP.NET 2.0
web programming with
VB 2005

D1614110

Training and Reference

murach's
ASP.NET 2.0
web programming with
VB 2005

Anne Boehm
Doug Lowe

 MIKE MURACH & ASSOCIATES, INC.
1-800-221-5528 • (559) 440-9071 • Fax: (559) 440-0963
murachbooks@murach.com • www.murach.com

Authors:	Anne Boehm
	Doug Lowe
Editor:	Mike Murach
Cover Design:	Zylka Design
Production:	Tom Murach
	Judy Taylor

Books for .NET programmers

Murach's ASP.NET 2.0 Web Programming with VB 2005
Murach's ASP.NET 2.0 Web Programming with C# 2005
Murach's ASP.NET 2.0 Upgrader's Guide: VB Edition
Murach's ASP.NET 2.0 Upgrader's Guide: C# Edition
Murach's ASP.NET Web Programming with VB.NET
Murach's Beginning Visual Basic .NET
Murach's C#
Murach's VB.NET Database Programming with ADO.NET
Murach's SQL for SQL Server

Two books for every Java programmer

Murach's Beginning Java 2, JDK 5
Murach's Java Servlets and JSP

Four books for every IBM mainframe programmer

Murach's OS/390 and z/OS JCL
Murach's Mainframe COBOL
Murach's CICS for the COBOL Programmer
DB2 for the COBOL Programmer, Part 1

Please check www.murach.com
for other books on .NET 2.0 subjects

Printed in the United States of America

10 9 8 7 6 5 4 3 2 1
ISBN: 1-890774-32-4

Contents

Expanded contents

Section 1 The essence of ASP.NET web programming

Section 2 Basic ASP.NET skills

Chapter 18 How to use the login controls to authenticate users

Chapter 19 How to use profiles to personalize a web site

Chapter 20   How to use the MultiView and Wizard controls

Chapter 21   How to use email, custom error pages, and back-button control

Chapter 22   How to use web parts to build portals

Chapter 23   How to configure and deploy a web application

Section 5   Developing reusable code

Chapter 24   How to develop user controls

Chapter 25   How to develop custom server controls

Introduction

As we see it, Microsoft's ASP.NET 2.0 has the potential to help you develop web applications faster and better than ever before. If, for example, you've been using classic ASP or ASP.NET 1.x for developing web applications, you'll soon see that ASP.NET 2.0 has many new and improved features. And if you've been using Java servlets and JSP for developing web applications, you'll see that ASP.NET offers many features that just aren't available on the Java platforms.

Whether or not you're new to web programming, though, this book will get you off to a fast start. In fact, by the end of chapter 4, you'll know how to use Visual Studio to develop and test multi-page database applications. No other ASP.NET book gets you started that fast.

On the other hand, this is much more than a beginning book. By the time you're done, you'll have all the skills you need for developing e-commerce web applications at a professional level. You'll also find that this book does double duty as the best on-the-job reference book that money can buy. No other ASP.NET 2.0 book teaches you so much or so thoroughly.

What this book does

To be more specific about what this book presents, here is a brief description of each of its five sections:

- Section 1 is designed to get you off to a fast start. So the first three chapters show you how to use Visual Studio and ASP.NET to design and code both one-page and multi-page web applications that get data from a database. Then, chapter 4 shows you how to test and debug your web applications. At that point, you're ready to write some serious web applications of your own, and you're ready for rapid progress in the sections that follow.

- Section 2 presents the other skills that you're likely to use in every ASP.NET application that you develop. That includes the essential HTML skills, how to use all of the server and validation controls, and more about managing the state of an application than what's covered in section 1. Then, the last three chapters in this section show you how to use three powerful new ASP.NET 2.0 features: master pages, site navigation, and themes.

- In section 3, you'll learn how to use the data access features of ASP.NET 2.0. That includes a new feature called *data sources*, which can dramatically reduce the amount of data access code that you need for an application. It includes some new bound controls that are designed to work with data sources. And it includes *object data sources*, which make it easier for you to separate presentation code from data access code. This is powerful stuff, so you're going to want to read this section from start to finish.

- Section 4 completes the set of skills that you need for developing professional e-commerce web applications. Here, you'll learn how to secure data transmissions between client and server, authenticate and authorize users, use profiles to personalize your applications, use email within your applications, and much more. Then, the last chapter in this section shows you the best ways to configure and deploy your applications.

- Last, section 5 shows you how to develop user controls, custom server controls, and web services. Those are three different ways that you can write code once and reuse it in more than one web application. And these techniques are commonly used in large development shops.

To get the most from this book, we recommend that you start by reading the first section from start to finish. But after that, you can skip to any of the other sections to get the information that you need, whenever you need it. Since this book has been carefully designed to work that way, you won't miss anything by skipping around.

Why you'll learn faster and better with this book

Like all our books, this one has features that you won't find in competing books. That's why we believe you'll learn faster and better with our book than with any other. Here are just three of those features.

- To make sure that you learn ASP.NET as quickly and easily as possible, all of its features are presented in the context of complete applications. These applications include the web forms, the aspx code, and the Visual Basic code. As we see it, the best way to learn is to study applications like these, even though you won't find them in most competing books.

- Unlike many ASP.NET books, this one shows you how to get the most from Visual Studio 2005 as you develop your applications. Because we've found that this IDE is one of the keys to development productivity, we're surprised that most books still ignore or neglect it.

- If you page through this book, you'll see that all of the information is presented in "paired pages," with the essential syntax, guidelines, and examples on the right page and the perspective and extra explanation on the left page. This not only helps you learn faster by reading less, but is also the best reference format that you'll find anywhere. That's why this book works so well for both training and reference.

What software you need

To develop ASP.NET 2.0 applications, you can use any of the full editions of Visual Studio 2005, including the Standard Edition, Professional Edition, or Team System. All of these come with everything you need to develop ASP.NET 2.0 applications, including the Visual Studio development environment, version 2.0 of the Microsoft .NET Framework, Visual Basic 2005 and C# 2005, a built-in web server that's ideal for testing ASP.NET applications, and a scaled-back version of SQL Server called SQL Server Express.

You can also use the Visual Web Developer 2005 Express Edition plus SQL Server Express to develop ASP.NET 2.0 applications. Together, they provide all of the items listed above, and both can be downloaded from Microsoft's web site. The good news is that SQL Server Express is free, and Web Developer 2005 will be free until November 6, 2006.

Keep in mind, though, that Web Developer 2005 is a scaled-back version of the full editions. That's why you'll find that some of its user interfaces are simpler than the ones in this book, which are all based on the Professional Edition. You may also find that a few of the features in this book aren't available with Web Developer 2005. Nevertheless, Web Developer 2005 is a terrific product for learning how to develop ASP.NET 2.0 applications. And both the applications and skills that you develop will work with any of the full editions.

What you can get from our web site

To help you get the most from this book, you can download the source code and databases for all of the applications presented in this book. Then, you can test and review these applications on your own to see exactly how they work. And you can copy and paste the code that you want to use in your own applications. For more information about downloading and installing these applications, please see appendix A.

Related books

As you read this book, you may discover that your Visual Basic skills aren't as strong as they ought to be. In that case, we recommend that you get a copy of our latest Visual Basic book. It will get you up-to-speed with the language. It will show you how to work with the most useful .NET classes. And as a bonus, it will show you how to develop Windows Forms applications.

Another book that we recommend for all ASP.NET programmers is *Murach's VB.NET Database Programming with ADO.NET*. This book shows you how to write the ADO.NET code that you need for using object data sources. It also gives you insight into what ADO.NET is doing as you use SQL data sources. Although this book is based on ADO.NET 1.x, everything in it still works the same with ADO.NET 2.0. So this is a great book whether you're developing Windows or web applications with ADO.NET 1.x or with ADO.NET 2.0.

A third book that you may be interested in is *Murach's SQL for SQL Server*. To start, it shows you how to write SQL statements in all their variations so you can code the right statements for your data sources. This often gives you the option of having Microsoft SQL Server do more so your applications do less. Beyond that, this book shows you how to design and implement databases and how to use advanced features like stored procedures.

Last, please check our web site periodically for new books. In particular, we will soon be publishing books on Visual Basic 2005 and C# 2005. Before too long, we also intend to publish database programming books for ASP.NET 2.0 developers in both Visual Basic and C# editions.

Please let us know how this book works for you

When we started working with ASP.NET 2.0, we quickly realized that it offered many powerful new features for developing web applications. Some of those features were additions to the ASP.NET 1.x features; some replaced 1.x features. So as we revised the first edition of our ASP.NET book, our goal was to integrate the new features with the old in a way that will help you become a proficient ASP.NET 2.0 programmer as quickly and easily as possible.

Now that we're done, we hope that we've succeeded. So, if you have any comments about our book, we would appreciate hearing from you. If you like our book, please tell a friend. And good luck with your web programming.

Anne Boehm, Author
anne@murach.com

Mike Murach, Publisher
mike@murach.com

Section 1

The essence of ASP.NET web programming

This section presents the essential skills for designing, coding, and testing ASP.NET web applications. After chapter 1 introduces you to the concepts and terms that you need to know for web programming, chapters 2 and 3 teach you the essential skills for designing web forms and writing the Visual Basic code that makes them work. Then, chapter 4 shows you how to use the many features for testing and debugging ASP.NET applications.

When you finish all four chapters, you'll be able to develop real-world applications of your own. You'll have a solid understanding of how ASP.NET works. And you'll be ready to learn all of the other ASP.NET features and techniques that are presented in the rest of this book.

An introduction to ASP.NET web programming

This chapter introduces you to the basic concepts of web programming and ASP.NET. Here, you'll learn how web applications work and what software you need for developing ASP.NET web applications. You'll also see how the HTML code for a web form is coordinated with the Visual Basic code that makes the web form work the way you want it to. When you finish this chapter, you'll have the background you need for developing web applications of your own.

An introduction to web applications

A *web application* consists of a set of *web pages* that are generated in response to user requests. The Internet has many different types of web applications, such as search engines, online stores, auctions, news sites, discussion groups, games, and so on.

Two pages of a Shopping Cart application

Figure 1-1 shows two pages of a simple web application. In this case, the application is for an online store that lets users purchase a variety of Halloween products, including costumes, masks, and decorations. You'll see parts of this application throughout the book, so it's worth taking the time to become familiar with it in this chapter.

The first web page in this figure is used to display information about the various products that are available from the Halloween store. To select a product, you use the drop-down list that's below the banner at the top of the page. Then, the page displays information about the product including a picture, short and long descriptions, and the product's price.

If you enter a quantity in the text box near the bottom of the page and click the Add to Cart button, the second page in this figure is displayed. This page lists the contents of your shopping cart and provides several buttons that let you remove items from the cart, clear the cart entirely, return to the previous page to continue shopping, or proceed to a checkout page.

Of course, the complete Halloween Superstore application also contains other pages. For example, if you click the Checkout button in the second page, you're taken to a page that lets you enter the information necessary to complete a purchase. You'll see how some of these pages are developed as you progress through this book.

An important point to notice about these pages is that they both contain controls that let the user interact with the page, like the drop-down list and buttons on the Order page. A page that contains controls like these is called a *web form*, and an ASP.NET application consists of one web form for each page in the application.

The Order page of a Shopping Cart application

The Cart page of a Shopping Cart application

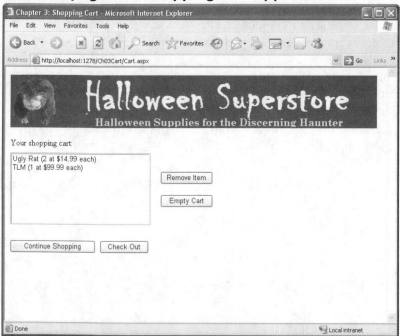

Figure 1-1   Two pages of a Shopping Cart application

The hardware and software components for web applications

Figure 1-2 shows the basic hardware and software components that are required for a web application. To start, a web application is a type of *client/ server application*, which means that the functions of the application are split between a *client* computer and a *server* computer. The client and server computers are connected to one another via the Internet, and they communicate with each other using *HTTP*, or *Hypertext Transfer Protocol*.

To access a web application, you use a *web browser* that runs on a client computer. By far the most popular web browser is Microsoft's Internet Explorer, but two popular alternatives are Netscape's Navigator (or just Netscape) and Mozilla Firefox.

The web application itself is stored on the server computer. This computer runs *web server* software that enables it to send web pages to web browsers. Although many web servers are available, the two most popular are Microsoft's *Internet Information Services* (or *IIS*) and The Apache Software Foundation's *Apache HTTP Server*, which is usually just called *Apache*. For ASP.NET applications, though, the server must run IIS.

Because most web applications work with data that's stored in a database, most server computers also run a *database management system* (or *DBMS*). Two popular database management systems for ASP.NET development are Microsoft SQL Server and Oracle. Note, however, that the database server software doesn't have to run on the same server computer as the web server software. In fact, a separate database server is often used to improve an application's overall performance.

Although this figure shows the client and server computers connected via the Internet, this isn't the only way a client can connect to a server in a web application. If the client and the server are on the same *local area network* (or *LAN*), they can connect via an *intranet*. Since an intranet uses the same protocols as the Internet, a web application works the same on an intranet as it does on the Internet.

Components of a web application

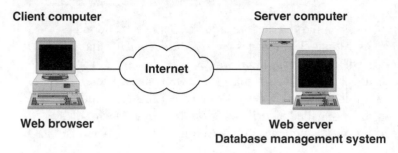

Description

- Web applications are a type of *client/server application*. In that type of application, a user at a *client* computer accesses an application at a *server* computer. In a web application, the client and server computers are connected via the Internet or via an *intranet* (a local area network).

- In a web application, the user works with a *web browser* at the client computer. The web browser provides the user interface for the application. The most popular web browser is Microsoft's Internet Explorer, but other web browsers like Netscape Navigator or Mozilla Firefox may also be used.

- The application runs on the server computer under the control of *web server* software. For ASP.NET web applications, the server must run Microsoft's web server, called *Internet Information Services*, or *IIS*.

- For most web applications, the server computer also runs a *database management system*, or *DBMS*, such as Microsoft's SQL Server. The DBMS provides access to information stored in a database. To improve performance on larger applications, the DBMS can be run on a separate server computer.

- The user interface for a web application is implemented as a series of *web pages* that are displayed in the web browser. Each web page is defined by a *web form* using *HTML*, or *Hypertext Markup Language*, which is a standardized set of markup tags.

- The web browser and web server exchange information using *HTTP*, or *Hypertext Transfer Protocol*.

Figure 1-2   The hardware and software components for web applications

How static web pages work

Many of the web pages on the Internet are *static web pages* that don't change in response to user input. These pages are *HTML documents* that are defined by *HTML*, or *Hypertext Markup Language*.

Figure 1-3 shows how a web server handles static web pages. The process begins when a user at a web browser requests a web page. This can occur when the user enters a web address, called a *URL* (*Uniform Resource Locator*), into the browser's address box or when the user clicks a link that leads to another page.

In either case, the web browser uses HTTP to send an *HTTP request* to the web server. The HTTP request includes information such as the name and address of the web page being requested, the address of the browser making the request, and the address of the web server that will process the request.

When the web server receives an HTTP request from a browser, the server retrieves the requested HTML file from disk and sends the file back to the browser in the form of an *HTTP response*. The HTTP response includes the HTML document that the user requested along with the address of the browser and the web server.

When the browser receives the HTTP response, it formats and displays the HTML document. Then, the user can view the content. If the user requests another page, either by clicking a link or typing another web address in the browser's address box, the process begins again.

Figure 1-3 also shows the components of a URL. The first component is the protocol, in this case, HTTP. In most cases, you can omit the protocol and HTTP is assumed.

The second component is the *domain name*, which identifies your web site. The URL in this figure, for example, includes the domain name for our web site, www.murach.com. The browser uses the domain name to identify the server that's hosting the web site.

After the domain name, you specify the path where the file resides on the server. Notice that front slashes are used to separate the components of a path in a URL. After the path, you specify the name of the file you want to display in the browser. In this case, the file is a static web page named index.htm.

How a web server processes static web pages

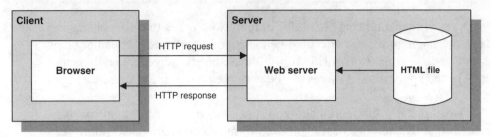

The components of an HTTP URL

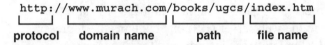

Description

- A *static web page* is an HTML document that is the same each time it's viewed. In other words, a static web page doesn't change in response to user input. Everyone who views a static web page sees exactly the same content.

- Static web pages are usually simple HTML files that are stored on the web server. When a browser requests a static web page, the web server retrieves the file from disk and sends it back to the browser. Static web pages usually have a file extension of .htm or .html.

- A web browser requests a page from a web server by sending the server an HTTP message known as an *HTTP request*. The HTTP request includes, among other things, the name of the HTML file being requested and the Internet address of both the browser and the web server.

- A user working with a browser can initiate an HTTP request in several ways. One way is to type the address of a web page, called a *URL*, or *Uniform Resource Locator*, into the browser's address area and then press the Enter key. Another way is to click a link that refers to a web page.

- A web server replies to an HTTP request by sending a message known as an *HTTP response* back to the browser. The HTTP response contains the addresses of the browser and the server as well as the HTML document that's being returned.

Figure 1-3   How static web pages work

How dynamic web pages work

A web application consists of one or more web pages that are not static, but that can change in some way each time the page is displayed. Instead of being stored on disk in the form of HTML files, these pages are generated dynamically by the application. As a result, the generated pages are often referred to as *dynamic web pages*.

One of the key differences between static web pages and dynamic web pages is that dynamic web pages are web forms that contain one or more *server controls*, such as labels, text boxes, and buttons. Users work with these controls to interact with the application.

Figure 1-4 shows the basic processing for a dynamic web page. To start, the browser sends an HTTP request to the web server (IIS) that contains the address of the web page being requested, along with the information that the user entered into the form. When IIS receives this request, it determines that it's a request for a web form rather than for a static web page. As a result, the web server passes the request on to the *application server* (ASP.NET) for processing. ASP.NET, in turn, manages the execution of the web form that's requested.

To determine if the request is for a static page or a dynamic page, the web server looks up the extension of the requested page in a list of *application mappings*. These mappings indicate what program a file extension is associated with. For example, a static web page typically has an extension of htm or html, while a dynamic ASP.NET page has an extension of aspx. As a result, when the web server receives an HTTP request for an aspx file, it passes this request to ASP.NET, which processes the web form for that page.

When the web form is executed, it processes the information the user entered and generates an HTML document. If, for example, the web form displays data from a database, it queries the database to get the requested information. Then, it generates a page with that information, which is returned by ASP.NET to the web server. The web server, in turn, sends the page back to the browser in the form of an HTTP response, and the browser displays the page. This entire process that begins with the browser requesting a web page and ends with the page being sent back to the client is called a *round trip*.

When a user clicks on a control to start an HTTP request, it is called "posting back to the server," which is referred to as a *postback*. In the Order form in figure 1-1, for example, the user starts a postback by selecting an item in the drop-down list or by clicking on the Add to Cart button. Then, the web form for the Order page is processed using the new values that the user has entered into the page.

Incidentally, the application server for ASP.NET 2.0 can handle requests for web forms that were developed by ASP.NET 1.0 or 1.1 as well as requests for forms that were developed by ASP.NET 2.0. That means that your old 1.x web forms can run right along with your new 2.0 forms, which means that you don't have to convert your old applications to ASP.NET 2.0 (although you do have to configure them to run under ASP.NET 2.0). Then, you can maintain your old web forms with ASP.NET 1.x and develop your new web forms with 2.0.

How a web server processes dynamic pages

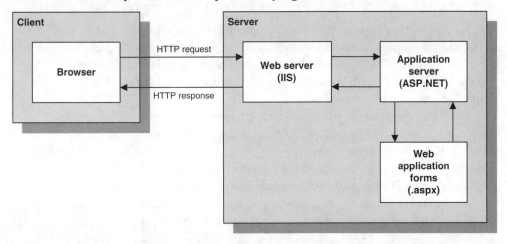

The URL for an ASP.NET web page

`http://msdn.microsoft.com/vs2005/default.aspx`

Description

- A *dynamic web page* is an HTML document that's generated by a web form. Often, the web page changes according to information that's sent to the web form by the browser.

- When a web server receives a request for a dynamic web page, it looks up the extension of the requested file in a list of *application mappings* to find out which application server should process the request. If the file extension is aspx, the request is passed on to ASP.NET for processing.

- When the *application server* receives a request, it runs the specified web form. Then, the web form generates an HTML document and returns it to the application server, which passes it back to the web server and from there to the browser.

- The browser doesn't know or care whether the HTML was retrieved from a static HTML file or generated dynamically by a web form. Either way, the browser simply displays the HTML that was returned as a result of the request.

- After the page is displayed, the user can interact with it using its controls. Some of those controls let the user *post* the page *back* to the server, which is called a *postback*. Then, the page is processed again using the data the user entered.

- The process that begins with the user requesting a web page and ends with the server sending a response back to the client is called a *round trip*.

- If you omit the file name from the URL when you use your browser to request a page, IIS will look for a file with one of four names by default: Default.htm, Default.asp, index.htm, and iisstart.asp. If you want another page to be displayed by default, you can add the name of that page to this list. See appendix A for more information.

Figure 1-4   How dynamic web pages work

How state is handled in ASP.NET applications

Although it isn't apparent in the previous figure, an application ends after it generates a web page. That means that the current status of any data maintained by the application, such as variables or control properties, is lost. In other words, HTTP doesn't maintain the *state* of the application. This is illustrated in figure 1-5.

Here, you can see that a browser on a client requests a page from a web server. After the server processes the request and returns the page to the browser, it drops the connection. Then, if the browser makes additional requests, the server has no way to associate the browser with its previous requests. Because of that, HTTP is known as a *stateless protocol*.

Although HTTP doesn't maintain state, ASP.NET provides several ways to do that, as summarized in this figure. First, you can use *view state* to maintain the values of server control properties. For example, you can use view state to preserve the Text properties of label controls that are changed as a web form is processed or to maintain a list of items in a drop-down list. Because ASP.NET implements view state by default, you don't need to write any special code to use it.

Second, you can use *session state* to maintain data between executions of an application. To make this work, ASP.NET creates a *session state object* that is kept on the server whenever a user starts a new session. This session object contains a unique *session ID*, and this ID is sent back and forth between the server and the browser each time the user requests a page. Then, when the server receives a new request from a user, it can retrieve the right session object for that user. In the code for your web forms, you can add data items to the session object so their previous values are available each time a web form is executed.

Third, you can use an *application state object* to save *application state* data, which applies to all of the users of an application. For example, you can use application state to maintain global counters or to maintain a list of the users who are currently logged on to an application.

Last, ASP.NET 2.0 provides a new *profile* feature that lets you keep track of user data. Although a profile is similar to a session state object, it persists between user sessions because it is stored in a database. When you use profiles, for example, you can keep track of the last three products that a user looked at in his last session. Then, when the user starts a new session, you can display those products in a "Recently viewed items" list.

Why state is difficult to track in web applications

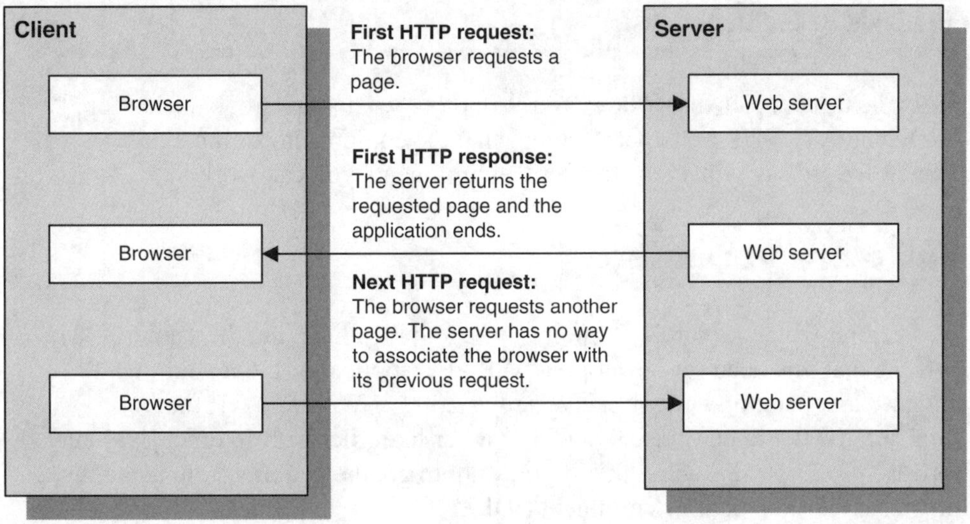

Concepts

- *State* refers to the current status of the properties, variables, and other data maintained by an application for a single user. The application must maintain a separate state for each user currently accessing the application.

- HTTP is a *stateless protocol*. That means that it doesn't keep track of state between round trips. Once a browser makes a request and receives a response, the application terminates and its state is lost.

Three ASP.NET features for maintaining state

- ASP.NET uses *view state* to maintain the value of form control properties that the application changes between executions of the application. Since view state is implemented by default, no special coding is required.

- When a user starts a new session, ASP.NET creates a *session state object* that contains a *session ID*. This ID is passed from the server to the browser and back to the server so the server can associate the browser with an existing session. To maintain *session state*, you can add program values to the session state object.

- When an application begins, ASP.NET creates an *application state object*. To maintain *application state*, you can add program values to the application state object. These values are available to all users of the application until the application ends.

The new profile feature of ASP.NET 2.0

- ASP.NET 2.0 can also maintain a *profile* for each user of an application. Because profiles are stored in a database, the profile data is maintained from one user session to another. This makes it easier to personalize an application.

Figure 1-5   How state is handled in ASP.NET applications

An introduction to ASP.NET application development

In the three topics that follow, you'll find out what software you need for developing ASP.NET web applications, what the components of the .NET Framework are, and what development environments you can work in.

The software you need

The first table in figure 1-6 summarizes both the client and the server software that you need for developing ASP.NET applications. On your own PC, you need an operating system like Windows 2000 or Windows XP, the Microsoft .NET Framework 2.0, and a browser like Microsoft Internet Explorer. You also need Visual Studio 2005 if you want to get the benefits from using that Integrated Development Environment (IDE).

If you're using a server for your development, it will need a server operating system like Windows 2000 Server or later, Microsoft .NET Framework 2.0, and Internet Information Services. If you're going to develop applications from a remote computer, it will also need FrontPage Server Extensions. And if you're going to develop applications for the Internet, it will need an FTP server. In appendix A, you can get information about installing the software for both client and server.

Because most ASP.NET applications require database access, you also need a database server such as Microsoft SQL Server. For development work on your own PC, you can use SQL Server 2005 Express Edition, which is a scaled-back version of SQL Server that comes with Visual Studio 2005. But you'll probably need SQL Server itself on the server for a production application.

If you're developing production applications, you should also download and install other web browsers on your PC including Netscape Navigator and Mozilla Firefox. That way, you can test your applications with a variety of popular browsers.

The second table in this figure shows that Visual Studio 2005 is available in several editions. Most professional developers will work with either the Standard Edition or the Professional Edition. But large development teams may use the Team System edition, which includes features designed for specialized development roles such as architects, developers, and testers.

A less expensive alternative is Visual Web Developer 2005 Express Edition, which retails for around $100 and is available for free until November 2006. This product is designed for individual developers, students, and hobbyists, and most of the features in this book will work with this edition.

The third table in this figure lists some of the most important new features of ASP.NET 2.0. Because each of these features is presented in detail later in this book, I won't describe them here. But this table should show you that ASP.NET 2.0 provides several new features that you'll probably want to use in your new applications.

Software requirements for ASP.NET application development

Client	Server
Windows 2000 or later	Windows 2000 Server or later
Microsoft .NET Framework 2.0	Microsoft .NET Framework 2.0
A browser like Internet Explorer (6.0 or later)	Internet Information Services 5.0 or later (6.0 recommended)
Visual Studio 2005	Microsoft SQL Server or equivalent database
	FrontPage Server Extensions (for remote development only)

Visual Studio 2005 Editions

Edition	Description
Visual Studio 2005 Standard Edition	Supports Windows and Web development using Visual Basic, C#, C++, and J#.
Visual Studio 2005 Professional Edition	Same as Standard Edition with several additional features such as additional deployment options and integration with SQL Server 2005.
Visual Studio 2005 Team System	The top-of-the-line version of Visual Studio, with special features added to support large development teams.
Visual Web Developer 2005 Express Edition	Inexpensive web development in Visual Basic, C#, or J# for hobbyists and novices.

New programming features for ASP.NET 2.0

Feature	Chapters	Description
Master pages	9	Lets you easily create pages with consistent elements such as banners and navigation menus.
Site navigation	10	Provides controls that make it easy to create site navigation menus.
Themes	11	Lets you easily customize formatting elements like fonts and colors.
New data-access features	13-16	New data source controls and bound-data controls drastically reduce the amount of code required for most database applications.
Login and user registration	18	Provides controls to automatically register users and allow them to log in to a web site.
Profiles	19	Uses a database to store data about users between sessions.
Web parts	22	Lets the user choose which elements to include in a web page.

Figure 1-6   The software you need for developing ASP.NET 2.0 applications

The components of the .NET Framework

Because you should have a basic understanding of what the *.NET Framework* does as you develop applications, figure 1-7 summarizes its major components. As you can see, this framework is divided into two main components, the .NET Framework Class Library and the Common Language Runtime, and these components provide a common set of services for applications written in .NET languages like Visual Basic or C#.

The *.NET Framework Class Library* consists of *classes* that provide many of the functions that you need for developing .NET applications. For instance, the ASP.NET classes are used for developing ASP.NET web applications, and the Windows Forms classes are used for developing standard Windows applications. The other .NET classes let you work with databases, manage security, access files, and perform many other functions.

Although it's not apparent in this figure, the classes in the .NET Framework Class Library are organized in a hierarchical structure. Within this structure, related classes are organized into groups called *namespaces*. Each namespace contains the classes used to support a particular function. For example, the System.Web namespace contains the classes used to create ASP.NET web applications, and the System.Data namespace contains the classes used to access data.

The *Common Language Runtime*, or *CLR*, provides the services that are needed for executing any application that's developed with one of the .NET languages. This is possible because all of the .NET languages compile to a common *Intermediate Language* (or *IL*). The CLR also provides the *Common Type System* that defines the data types that are used by all the .NET languages. That way, you can use the same data types regardless of what .NET language you're using to develop your application. Unlike Windows applications, though, all of the forms in a web application must be developed using the same language.

To run an ASP.NET application, the web server must have the .NET Framework installed. However, the client computers that access the web server don't need the .NET Framework. Instead, the client computers can run any client operating system with a modern web browser.

The .NET Framework

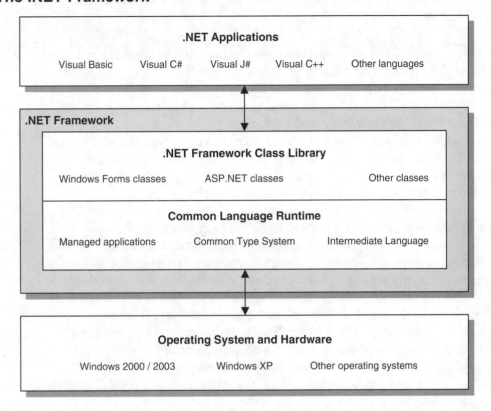

Description

- .NET applications work by using services of the *.NET Framework*. The .NET Framework, in turn, accesses the operating system and computer hardware.

- The .NET Framework consists of two main components: the .NET Framework Class Library and the Common Language Runtime.

- The *.NET Framework Class Library* provides pre-written code in the form of *classes* that are available to all of the .NET programming languages. These classes are organized into groups called *namespaces*. The classes that support ASP.NET web programs are stored in the System.Web namespace.

- The *Common Language Runtime*, or *CLR*, manages the execution of .NET programs by coordinating essential functions such as memory management, code execution, security, and other services.

- The *Common Type System* is a component of the CLR that ensures that all .NET applications use the same data types regardless of what programming languages are used to develop the applications.

- All .NET programs are compiled into *Microsoft Intermediate Language* (*MSIL*) or just *Intermediate Language* (*IL*), which is stored on disk in an assembly. This assembly is then run by the CLR.

Figure 1-7   The components of the .NET Framework

Three environments for developing ASP.NET applications

Figure 1-8 shows three common ways to set up a development environment for coding and testing ASP.NET applications. As you'll see, each setup has its advantages and disadvantages. The environment you choose will depend on your development needs and on the resources that are available to you.

The simplest development environment is a *standalone environment*. In this case, a single computer serves as both the client and the server. Because of that, it must run an operating system that supports ASP.NET development, and it must have the .NET Framework and Visual Studio 2005 installed. Because Visual Studio 2005 comes with its own *development server* for local testing, you don't have to install IIS when you use a standalone environment. Also, since Visual Studio comes with SQL Server 2005 Express Edition (or just *SQL Server Express*), you don't have to install a separate database product.

The second development environment works with separate client and server computers that are connected via a local area network. Here, the client computer has Windows, the .NET Framework, and Visual Studio 2005 installed, while the server runs Windows 2000 Server with the .NET Framework, IIS, and *FrontPage Server Extensions* (*FPSE*). FPSE provides the services that Visual Studio 2005 uses to communicate with a web site on a remote computer. In addition, the server uses SQL Server to handle database access. With this environment, more than one programmer can work on the same application, but all of the programmers are located at the same site.

With the third development environment, the client computers are connected to the server via the Internet rather than a LAN. This makes it possible to work with a web site that's hosted on another server. This environment requires an *FTP server*, which is used to copy the files in a web site between the client computer and the server. The FTP server uses *File Transfer Protocol* (*FTP*) to perform the copy operations, and IIS can be configured to act as an FTP server as well as a web server. So if a web site is hosted on a server that you have access to, you can configure the server so remote users can access it using FTP.

Standalone development

Windows 2000 or later
.NET Framework 2.0
Visual Studio 2005
Optional: IIS, SQL Server

Local area network development

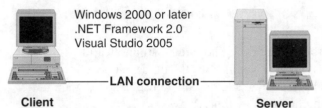

Windows 2000 or later
.NET Framework 2.0
Visual Studio 2005

Windows 2000 Server or later
.NET Framework
IIS 5.0 or later (6.0 recommended)
SQL Server
FrontPage Server Extensions

————LAN connection————

Client   **Server**

Internet development

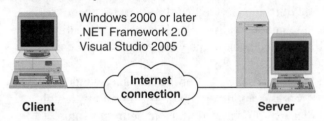

Windows 2000 or later
.NET Framework 2.0
Visual Studio 2005

Windows 2000 Server or later
.NET Framework
IIS 5.0 or later (6.0 recommended)
FTP server
SQL Server

Internet
connection

Client   **Server**

Description

- When you use standalone development, a single computer serves as both the client and the server. Because Visual Studio comes with a scaled-back web server called the ASP.NET Development Server (or just *development server*), you don't need to use IIS for testing web applications on your own PC. However, you do need to use IIS to test certain features of web applications.

- When you use a *local area network* (*LAN*), a client computer communicates with a server computer over the LAN. With this setup, two or more programmers at the same site can work on the same application. This setup requires that *FrontPage Server Extensions* (*FPSE*) be installed on the server.

- When you use Internet development, a client computer communicates with a server computer over the Internet. With this setup, programmers at different locations can work on the same application. This setup requires an *FTP server* on the server. The FTP server uses *File Transfer Protocol* (*FTP*) to transfer files between the client computer and the server.

Figure 1-8   Three environments for developing ASP.NET applications

A quick preview of how an ASP.NET application works

With that as background, you're ready to learn more about how an ASP.NET application works. That's why this topic presents a quick preview of how the Order form in the Shopping Cart application works.

The files used by the Shopping Cart application

Figure 1-9 presents the Order form of the Shopping Cart application as it appears in the Web Forms Designer that you use when you develop web forms with Visual Studio 2005. In chapter 2, you'll learn how to use this Designer, but for now just try to get the big picture of how this form works.

If you look at the Designer window in the middle of the IDE, you can see the table that's used for this form as well as the label controls that are used to display the data for each product. You can also see that the smart tag menu for the drop-down list has been used to enable the AutoPostBack property. This means that the Order form will be posted back to the web server when the user selects an item from the drop-down list.

If you look at the Solution Explorer to the right of the Designer window, you can see the folders and files that this application requires. For now, though, just focus on the six code files that are summarized in the table in this figure. The first two files in this table, which are in the App_Code folder, are two files that represent *business classes* named CartItem and Product. Both of these files have vb as the extension, which means that they're Visual Basic files.

The next four files in the table are for the two web forms, Cart and Order, with two files for each form. The files with aspx as the extension (Cart.aspx and Order.aspx) contain the code that represents the design of the form. This code consists of standard HTML code plus asp tags that define the server controls used on the forms. We refer to this as *aspx code*, because the files that contain the code have the aspx extension.

The other two files, which have aspx.vb as the extension, contain the Visual Basic code that controls the operation of the forms. These are called *code-behind files* because they provide the code behind the web forms. For instance, the Order.aspx.vb file is the code-behind file for the Order form.

Before I go on, you should realize that it isn't necessary to store the aspx and Visual Basic code for a web form in separate files. Instead, ASP.NET lets you combine this code into a single aspx file. However, storing the aspx and Visual Basic code in separate files can simplify application development because it lets you separate the presentation elements for a page from its Visual Basic coding. This also makes it possible for HTML designers to work on the aspx files for an application, and then have Visual Basic programmers develop the code for the code-behind files.

The Order form in Design view

The aspx and Visual Basic files in the Shopping Cart application

Folder	File	Description
App_Code	CartItem.vb	A class that represents an item in the shopping cart.
App_Code	Product.vb	A class that represents a product.
(root)	Cart.aspx	The aspx file for the Cart page.
(root)	Cart.aspx.vb	The code-behind file for the Cart page.
(root)	Order.aspx	The aspx file for the Order page.
(root)	Order.aspx.vb	The code-behind file for the Order page.

Description

- For each web form in an application, ASP.NET 2.0 keeps two files. The file with the aspx extension holds the HTML code and the asp tags for the server controls. The file with the aspx.vb extension is the *code-behind file* that contains the Visual Basic code for the form.

- If an ASP.NET 2.0 application requires other classes like *business classes*, they are kept in the App_Code folder.

Figure 1-9   The files used by the Shopping Cart application

The aspx code for the Order form

To give you some idea of how aspx code works, figure 1-10 shows some of the aspx code for the Order form. All of this code is generated by Visual Studio as you use the Web Forms Designer to design a form, so you don't have to code it. But you still should have a general understanding of how this code works.

The first set of tags for each web form defines a *page directive* that provides four *attributes*. Here, the Language attribute says that the language is Visual Basic, the CodeFile attribute says that the code-behind file is named Order.aspx.vb, and the Inherits attribute specifies the class named Order. In figure 1-12, you'll see how the Order.aspx class inherits the Order class.

The second set of tags defines a DOCTYPE declaration, which tells the browser what version of HTML the HTML document uses. You can ignore this declaration for now, because you'll learn more about it in chapter 5.

The Html tags mark the beginning and end of the HTML document, and the Head tags define the heading for the document. Here, the Title tags define the title that is displayed in the title bar of the browser when the page is run.

The content of the web page itself is defined within the Div tags, which are within the Body and Form tags. Notice that the first Form tag includes a Runat attribute that's assigned a value of "server." That indicates that the form will be processed on the server by ASP.NET. This attribute is required for all ASP.NET web pages and all ASP.NET server controls.

The asp tags within the Div tags define the server controls that appear on the page. For example, the asp:Image tags define an Image control, the asp:Label tags define a label control, the asp:DropDownList tags define a drop-down list, and the asp:Button tags define a button. Since these controls include the Runat attribute with a value of "server," they will be processed on the server by ASP.NET. The last phase of this processing is *rendering* the controls, which means that the asp code is converted to standard HTML so the page can be displayed by a browser.

If you look at the asp code for the drop-down list, you can see that the AutoPostBack attribute has been set to True. That means that a postback will occur whenever the user selects an item from that list. This is the attribute that's checked in the smart tag menu for the list in the previous figure. Note that a postback will also occur whenever the user clicks the Add to Cart button. However, the AutoPostBack attribute isn't required for this control because performing a postback is the default operation of a button.

Another attribute that you should notice is the PostBackUrl attribute for the last button in the aspx code. This attribute provides the path for the Cart.aspx file, which means that the Cart form will be requested when this button is clicked. That's one way to switch from one form to another as an application is run, and you'll see another in the next figure.

Although this has been a quick introduction to the aspx code for a web form, you should begin to see how this code defines a web page. In the next two chapters, though, you'll learn more about this code. And just in case you need it, chapter 5 presents a complete crash course in HTML.

The aspx file for the Order form (Order.aspx)

```
<%@ Page Language="VB" AutoEventWireup="false" CodeFile="Order.aspx.vb"
Inherits="Order" %>

<!DOCTYPE html PUBLIC "-//W3C//DTD XHTML 1.0 Transitional//EN"
"http://www.w3.org/TR/xhtml1-transitional/DTD/xhtml1-transitional.dtd">

<html xmlns="http://www.w3.org/1999/xhtml" >
<head runat="server">
    <title>Chapter 3: Shopping Cart</title>
</head>
<body>
    <form id="form1" runat="server">
    <div>
        <asp:Image ID="Image1" runat="server"
            ImageUrl="~/Images/banner.jpg" /><br /><br />
        <asp:Label ID="Label1" runat="server"
            Text="Please select a product:"></asp:Label>
        <asp:DropDownList ID="ddlProducts" runat="server" Width = "150px"
            DataSourceID="AccessDataSource1" DataTextField="Name"
            DataValueField="ProductID" AutoPostBack="True">
        </asp:DropDownList>
        <asp:AccessDataSource ID="AccessDataSource1" runat="server"
            DataFile="~/App_Data/Halloween.mdb"
            SelectCommand="SELECT [ProductID], [Name], [ShortDescription],
                [LongDescription], [ImageFile], [UnitPrice]
                FROM [Products] ORDER BY [Name]">
        </asp:AccessDataSource>
        <br />
        <table>
            <tr >
                <td style="width: 250px; height: 22px">
                    <asp:Label ID="lblName" runat="server"
                        Font-Bold="false" Font-Size="Larger">
                    </asp:Label>
                </td>
                <td style="width: 20px" rowspan=4>
                </td>
                <td rowspan="4" valign="top">
                    <asp:Image ID="imgProduct" runat="server" Height="200" />
                </td>
            </tr>
                .
                .   (Code for 3 more rows of a table)
                .
        </table>
        <br />
        <asp:Label ID="Label3" runat="server" Text="Quantity:"
            Width="80px" BorderWidth = "0px"></asp:Label>
        <asp:TextBox ID="txtQuantity" runat="server" Width="80px">
        </asp:TextBox>
        <asp:Button ID="btnAdd" runat="server" Text="Add to Cart" /> 
        <asp:Button ID="btnCart" runat="server"
            PostBackUrl="~/Cart.aspx" Text="Go to Cart" />
    </div>
    </form>
</body>
</html>
```

Figure 1-10   The aspx code for the Order form

The Visual Basic code for the Order form

To give you some idea of how the Visual Basic code for a form works, figure 1-11 presents the code-behind file for the Order form. Here, I've highlighted the code that's specific to ASP.NET, and all of the other code is standard Visual Basic code.

The first highlighted line is a Class statement that names the class, which has the same name as the form. Because this statement uses the Partial keyword, which is new with Visual Basic 2005, this is a partial class that must be combined with another partial class when it's compiled. The second line of code in this class indicates that it inherits the System.Web.UI.Page class, which is the .NET class that provides all of the basic functionality of ASP.NET pages.

Each time the page is requested, ASP.NET initializes it and raises the Load event, which is handled by the Page_Load procedure. This procedure uses the IsPostBack property of the page to determine whether the page is being posted back to the server from the same page. If this property isn't True, the DataBind method of the drop-down list is used to bind the products that are retrieved from a database to the list. You will often see the IsPostBack property used like this in a Page_Load procedure to determine whether or not a page is being posted back by the user.

The btnAdd_Click procedure is executed when the user clicks on the Add to Cart button on the Order page, which starts a postback. After this procedure adds the selected item to the cart, it uses the Redirect method of the Response property of the page to transfer to the Cart page. This is a second way to switch from one page to another.

To refer to the session state object, you use the Session property of the page. This is done in the GetCart procedure, which is the last method for the page. Here, if the session state object doesn't already contain a cart, a new sorted list is added to the object. Otherwise, the current cart is retrieved from the session object as a sorted list. Either way, control returns to the calling procedure, which is the AddToCart procedure, and that procedure can add a cart item to the cart. In addition, the Cart page will have access to the cart when the Order page is redirected to the Cart page.

One coding point worth noting is that IsPostBack, Response, and Session are all properties of the page. As a result, you could code them with Page as a qualifier as in

```
Page.IsPostBack
```

However, since Page is the default object within a code-behind file, you can omit this reference.

Although this is just a quick introduction to a code-behind file, I hope it gives you some insight into the way code-behind files are coded. Keep in mind, though, that all of this code will be explained in detail in the next two chapters. For now, you just need a general idea of how the events are processed, how the IsPostBack property is used, how one web page can switch to another page, and how the session state object is used.

The code-behind file for the Order form (Order.aspx.vb)

```vb
Imports System.Data
Partial Class Order
    Inherits System.Web.UI.Page

    Private SelectedProduct As Product

    Protected Sub Page_Load(ByVal sender As Object, _
            ByVal e As System.EventArgs) Handles Me.Load
        If Not IsPostBack Then
            ddlProducts.DataBind()
        End If
        SelectedProduct = Me.GetSelectedProduct()
        lblName.Text = SelectedProduct.Name
        lblShortDescription.Text = SelectedProduct.ShortDescription
        lblLongDescription.Text = SelectedProduct.LongDescription
        lblUnitPrice.Text = FormatCurrency(SelectedProduct.UnitPrice)
        imgProduct.ImageUrl = "Images\Products\" & SelectedProduct.ImageFile
    End Sub

    Private Function GetSelectedProduct() As Product
        Dim dvProduct As DataView = CType(AccessDataSource1.Select( _
            DataSourceSelectArguments.Empty), DataView)
        dvProduct.RowFilter = "ProductID = '" & ddlProducts.SelectedValue & "'"
        Dim Product As New Product
        Product.ProductID = dvProduct(0)("ProductID").ToString
        Product.Name = dvProduct(0)("Name").ToString
        Product.ShortDescription = dvProduct(0)("ShortDescription").ToString
        Product.LongDescription = dvProduct(0)("LongDescription").ToString
        Product.UnitPrice = CDec(dvProduct(0)("UnitPrice"))
        Product.ImageFile = dvProduct(0)("ImageFile").ToString
        Return Product
    End Function

    Protected Sub btnAdd_Click(ByVal sender As Object, _
            ByVal e As System.EventArgs) Handles btnAdd.Click
        Dim CartItem As New CartItem
        CartItem.Product = SelectedProduct
        CartItem.Quantity = CType(txtQuantity.Text, Integer)
        Me.AddToCart(CartItem)
        Response.Redirect("Cart.aspx")
    End Sub

    Private Sub AddToCart(ByVal CartItem As CartItem)
        Dim Cart As SortedList = GetCart()
        Dim sProductID As String = SelectedProduct.ProductID
        If Cart.ContainsKey(sProductID) Then
            CartItem = CType(Cart(sProductID), CartItem)
            CartItem.Quantity += CType(txtQuantity.Text, Integer)
        Else
            Cart.Add(sProductID, CartItem)
        End If
    End Sub

    Private Function GetCart() As SortedList
        If Session("Cart") Is Nothing Then
            Session.Add("Cart", New SortedList)
        End If
        Return CType(Session("Cart"), SortedList)
    End Function
End Class
```

Figure 1-11   The Visual Basic code for the Order form

How an ASP.NET application is compiled and run

The diagram in figure 1-12 shows what actually happens behind the scenes when a user requests a page of an ASP.NET 2.0 application. In step 1, the ASP.NET runtime reads the aspx file for the requested web page and generates a Visual Basic source file that contains two classes. The first generated class is a partial class that contains the declarations for each of the controls contained on the page. This class has the same name as the web page, which is the same name that's used for the partial class for the code-behind file. In step 2, these partial classes are compiled to create a single class that provides all of the event-handling code for the page. The result is stored in a single *assembly* (dll file).

The other class that's generated by the ASP.NET runtime contains the code that actually creates the ASP.NET page. This class gets its name from the aspx file plus _aspx, so its name is Order_aspx in this example. In step 3, this class is compiled and stored in another assembly. Because this class inherits the Order class, an object that is instantiated from the Order_aspx class will contain the code that creates the page, as well as the event-handling code provided by the Order class.

In step 4, after the page classes are compiled, the ASP.NET runtime calls the Visual Basic compiler to compile any class files that are in the application's App_Code folder. For the Shopping Cart application, this means that the CartItem and Product classes are compiled and the result is saved in a single assembly.

After all the files are compiled into assemblies, ASP.NET creates an instance of the page and raises the appropriate events. Then, the events are processed by the event handlers for the page and the HTML for the page is rendered. To complete the round trip, the HTML document for the page is passed back to the web server and on to the user's browser.

Please note that the first four steps are done only the first time an aspx page is accessed. That's because ASP.NET caches the assemblies that are created by these steps. Then, when the page is accessed again, the saved assemblies are reused, so the application doesn't have to be recompiled. However, ASP.NET does compare the time stamps on the source files with the time stamps on the dll files. If any of the source files have been modified since they were last compiled, ASP.NET automatically recompiles them.

You may be interested to know that this method of compiling and running web pages is a significant improvement over the way this worked with ASP.NET 1.x. In particular, the declarations for the controls that you add to a web page are no longer placed in a hidden code region of the code-behind file. Instead, these declarations are generated at runtime and stored in a partial class that's compiled together with the partial class for the code-behind file. That means that the code-behind file can't get out of sync with the page file like it could with ASP.NET 1.x.

How an ASP.NET application is compiled

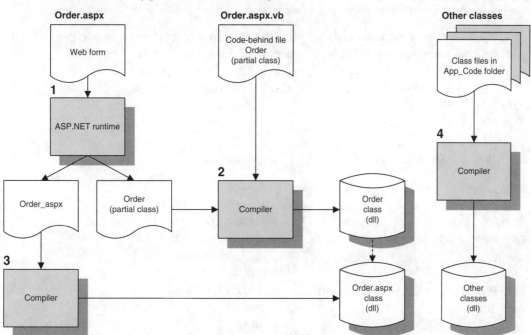

What happens when an ASP.NET page is requested

1. The ASP.NET runtime processes the .aspx file and generates two Visual Basic classes. The first is a partial class that has the same name as the web form (Order); it contains the declarations for each of the controls. The second class has the name of the web form followed by _aspx; it contains the code that will create and render the web page.

2. The Visual Basic compiler compiles the partial class that contains the control declarations and the code-behind partial class into a class (Order) that provides the event-handling code for the requested page. This class is saved as an *assembly* (.dll).

3. The Visual Basic compiler compiles the second generated class (Order_aspx), which inherits the first compiled class (Order). The resulting class is saved as an assembly that's executed when the page is requested.

4. If necessary, the Visual Basic compiler compiles any other class files that are stored in the application's App_Code folder. These classes are saved in a single assembly.

5. ASP.NET creates an instance of the page from the page's final assembly. Then, ASP.NET raises the appropriate events, which are processed by the event handlers for the page, and the page generates the HTML that's passed back to IIS for the response.

Description

*   The first four steps of this process are done only the first time the aspx page is requested. After that, the page is processed directly from the compiled assemblies.

*   For the Default page, the name of the code-behind class is _Default.

Figure 1-12   How an ASP.NET 2.0 application is compiled and run

Perspective

Now that you've read this chapter, you should have a general understanding of how ASP.NET applications work and what software you need for developing these applications. With that as background, you're ready to learn how to develop ASP.NET applications of your own. And that's what you'll learn how to do in the next two chapters.

Terms

web application
web page
web form
client/server application
client
server
HTTP (Hypertext Transfer Protocol)
web browser
web server
IIS (Internet Information Services)
DBMS (database management system)
LAN (local area network)
intranet
static web page
HTML document
HTML (Hypertext Markup Language)
URL (Uniform Resource Locator)
HTTP request
HTTP response
domain name
dynamic web page
server control
application server
application mapping
round trip
postback
state
stateless protocol
view state

session state
session state object
session ID
application state
application state object
profile
.NET Framework
.NET Framework Class Library
class
namespace
CLR (Common Language Runtime)
IL (Intermediate Language)
MSIL (Microsoft Intermediate
    Language)
Common Type System
standalone environment
development server
SQL Server Express
FPSE (FrontPage Server Extensions)
FTP (File Transfer Protocol)
FTP server
business class
aspx code
code-behind file
page directive
attribute
render
assembly

2

How to develop a one-page web application

In the last chapter, you were introduced to the basic concepts of web programming and ASP.NET. Now, this chapter shows you how to develop a one-page web application using Visual Studio 2005. If you've used Visual Studio to develop Windows applications, you'll soon see that you develop web applications in much the same way. As a result, you should be able to move quickly through this chapter.

How to work with ASP.NET web sites

This chapter starts by showing you how to start a new web application, how to work with the Visual Studio IDE, how to add folders and files to an application, and how to close and re-open an application. Once you're comfortable with those skills, you'll be ready to learn how to build your first ASP.NET application.

How to start a new web site

In Visual Studio 2005, a web application is called a *web site*, and figure 2-1 shows the dialog box for starting a new web site. After you open the New Web Site dialog box, you select the language you want to use for the web site and you specify the location where the web site will be created.

The Location drop-down list gives you three options for specifying the location of the web site. The simplest method is to create a *file-system web site*. This type of web site can exist in any folder on your local hard disk, or in a folder on a shared network drive. You can run a file-system web site using either Visual Studio's built-in development server or IIS. You'll learn how to do that later in this chapter.

You use the HTTP option to create a web site that runs under IIS on your local computer or on a computer that can be accessed over a local area network. To use this option, you must specify the IIS server where you want to create the web site. In addition, you must select or create the IIS directory that will contain the files for the web site, or you must select or create a virtual directory for the web site.

The third option, FTP, lets you create a web site on a remote server by uploading it to that server using FTP. To create this type of web site, you must specify at least the name of the FTP server and the folder where the web site resides. You'll learn more about how to use the HTTP and FTP options in chapter 4.

By default, Visual Studio 2005 creates a solution file for your web site in My Documents\Visual Studio 2005\Projects. This solution file is stored in this folder regardless of the location of the web site itself. To change the location where solutions are stored by default, choose Tools→Options. Then, expand the Projects and Solutions node, select the General category, and enter the location in the Visual Studio Projects Location text box.

In the dialog box in this example, I'm starting a new file-system web site named Ch02FutureValue in the ASP.NET 2.0 Web Sites folder on my own PC. Then, when I click the OK button, Visual Studio creates the folder named Ch02FutureValue and puts the starting files for the web site in that folder. It also creates a solution file in the default folder for those files.

The folders and files that are used for developing a web site can be referred to as a *web project*. So in practice, web sites are often referred to as web projects, and vice versa. In a moment, you'll see that Visual Studio often uses the term *project* in the commands for working with web sites.

The New Web Site dialog box

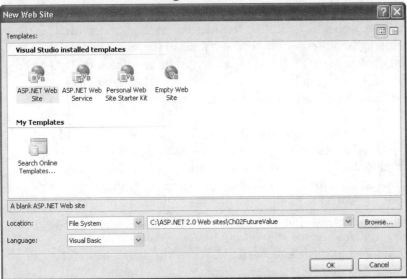

Three location options for ASP.NET web sites

Option	Description
File System	A web site created in a folder on your local computer or in a shared folder on a network. You can run the web site directly from the built-in development server or create an IIS virtual directory for the folder and run the application under IIS.
HTTP	A web site created under the control of an IIS web server. The IIS server can be on your local computer or on a computer that's available over a local area network.
FTP	A web site created on a remote hosting server.

Description

- An ASP.NET web application is called a *web site* under ASP.NET 2.0, so you use the File→New Web Site command to create a new ASP.NET 2.0 web site.

- A *web project* is a project that's used for the development of a web site. In practice, web sites are often referred to as web projects, and vice versa.

- Unlike previous versions of ASP.NET, ASP.NET 2.0 web sites don't use project files. Instead, they use web.config files to store project information.

- When you start a new web site, Visual Studio creates a solution file for the web site in the default location for solution files, which is normally My Documents\Visual Studio 2005\Projects.

Figure 2-1   How to start a new web site

How to work with the Visual Studio IDE

When you start a new web site, ASP.NET provides the starting folders and files for the site, including two files for the first *web form* of the site. The file named Default.aspx contains the HTML and asp code that defines the form, and the file named Default.aspx.vb contains the Visual Basic code that determines how the form works. Then, Visual Studio displays the aspx file for the web form as shown in figure 2-2.

If you've used Visual Studio for building Windows applications, you should already be familiar with the *Toolbox*, *Solution Explorer*, and *Properties window*, as well as the Standard toolbar. They work much the same for web applications as they do for Windows applications. The Solution Explorer, for example, shows the folders and files of the web site. In this example, the Solution Explorer shows one folder named App_Data, plus the two files for the default web form.

To design a web form, you use the *Web Forms Designer* that's in the center of this Integrated Development Environment (IDE). When you start a new web site, this Designer is displayed in *Source view*, which shows the starting HTML code for the first (or only) web form of the application. Normally, though, you'll do most of the design in *Design view*, which you can switch to by clicking on the Design button at the bottom of the Designer window.

If you have your environment settings set to Web Developer, you'll notice that different toolbars are displayed depending on what view you're working in. In Source view, the Standard and HTML Source Editing toolbars are displayed. In Design view, the Standard and Formatting toolbars are displayed. This is typical of the way the Visual Studio IDE works. By the way, to change the environment settings, you use the Tools→Import and Export Settings command.

As you go through the various phases of building a web site, you may want to close, hide, or size the windows that are displayed. You'll see some examples of this as you progress through this chapter, and this figure presents several techniques that you can use for working with the windows.

After you've designed a web form, you'll need to switch to the Code Editor, which replaces the Web Forms Designer in the center of the screen. Then, you can write the Visual Basic code in the code-behind file for the form. One way to switch to the Code Editor is to double-click on the code-behind file in the Solution Explorer. If, for example, you double-click on the file named Default.aspx.vb, you'll switch to the Code Editor and the starting code for that file will be displayed. Later in this chapter, you'll learn other ways to switch between the Web Forms Designer and the Code Editor.

As you work with Visual Studio, you'll see that it commonly provides several ways to do the same task. Some, of course, are more efficient than others, and we'll try to show you the best techniques as you progress through this book. Often, though, how you work is a matter of personal preference, so we encourage you to review and experiment with the toolbar buttons, the buttons at the top of the Solution Explorer, the tabs at the top of the Web Forms Designer or Code Editor, the shortcut menus that you get by right-clicking on an object, and so on.

The starting screen for a new web site

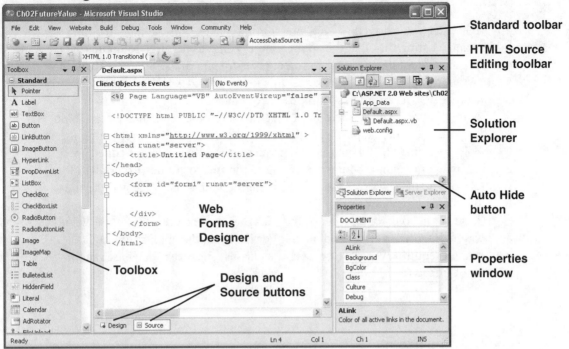

How to work with views and windows

- To change the Web Forms Designer from one view to another, click on the Design or Source button.

- To close a window, click on the close button in the upper right corner. To redisplay it, select it from the View menu.

- To hide a window, click on its Auto Hide button. Then, the window is displayed as a tab at the side of the screen, and you can display it by moving the mouse pointer over the tab. To restore the window, display it and click on the Auto Hide button again.

- To size a window, place the mouse pointer over one of its boundaries and drag it.

Description

- When you start a new web site, the primary window in the Visual Studio IDE is the Web Forms Designer window, or just *Web Forms Designer*. The three supporting windows are the *Toolbox*, the *Solution Explorer*, and the *Properties window*.

- You use the Web Forms Designer to design a *web form*. Later, to write the Visual Basic code for the form, you use the Code Editor as shown in figure 2-14.

- Visual Studio often provides several different ways to accomplish the same task. In this book, we'll try to show you the techniques that work the best.

Figure 2-2   How to work with the Visual Studio IDE

How to add folders and files to a web site

Right after you start a new web site, it often makes sense to add any other folders and existing files that the application is going to require. To do that, you can use the shortcut menus for the project or its folders in the Solution Explorer as shown in figure 2-3. As you can see, this menu provides a New Folder command as well as an Add Existing Item command.

For the Future Value application, I first added a folder named Images. To do that, I right-clicked on the project at the top of the Solution Explorer, chose the New Folder command, and entered the name for the folder. Then, I added an existing image file named MurachLogo.jpg to the Images folder. To do that, I right-clicked on the folder, chose Add Existing Item, and then selected the file from the dialog box that was displayed.

Those are the only other folders and files that I needed for the Future Value application, but often you'll need others. For instance, the application in the next chapter requires two existing business classes, an Access database, and a number of image files.

The Future Value project as a new folder is being added

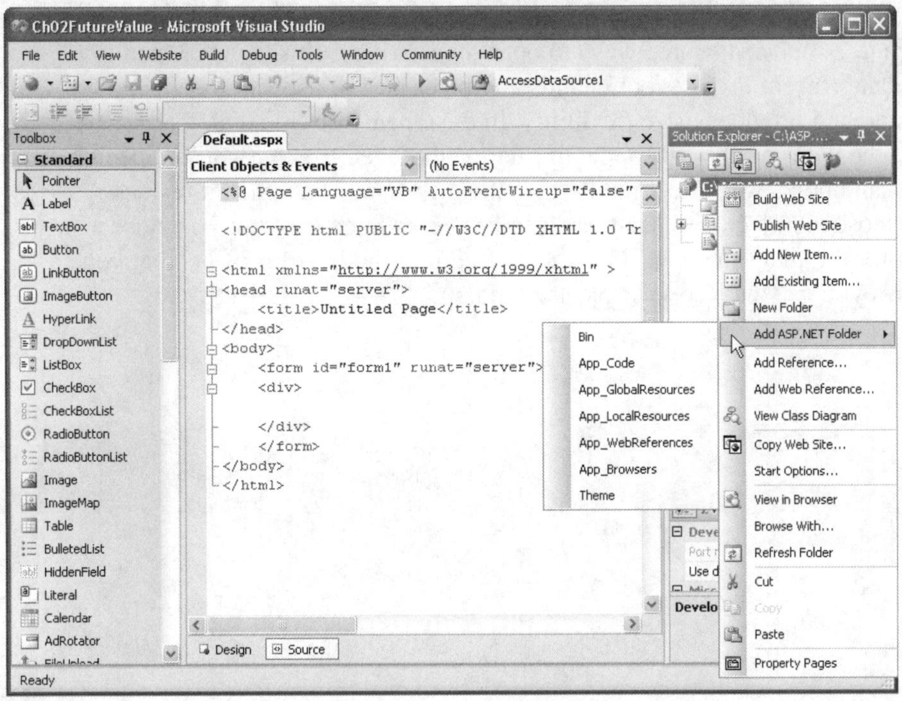

How to add a folder to a web site

- To add a standard folder, right-click on the project or folder you want to add the folder to in the Solution Explorer and choose New Folder. Then, type a name for the folder and press Enter.
- To add a special ASP.NET folder, right-click on the project in the Solution Explorer and choose Add ASP.NET Folder. Then, select the folder from the list that's displayed.

How to add an existing item to a web site

- In the Solution Explorer, right-click on the project or on the folder that you want to add an existing item to. Then, select Add Existing Item and respond to the resulting dialog box.

Description

- When you create a new web form, Visual Studio generates the starting HTML for the form and displays it in Source view of the Web Forms Designer.
- Before you start designing the first web form of the application, you can use the Solution Explorer to add any other folders or files to the web site.

Figure 2-3 How to add folders and files to a web site

How to open or close an existing web site

Figure 2-4 presents three ways to open an existing web site. The Open Project and Recent Projects commands are the easiest to use, but the Open Web Site command provides more flexibility. In the Open Web Site dialog box, you can use the icons on the left to identify the type of web site that you're opening so you can open a web site directly from the web server on which it resides.

To close a project, you use the Close Project command. After you close a project for the first time, you'll be able to find it in the list of projects that you see when you use the Recent Projects command.

The Open Web Site dialog box

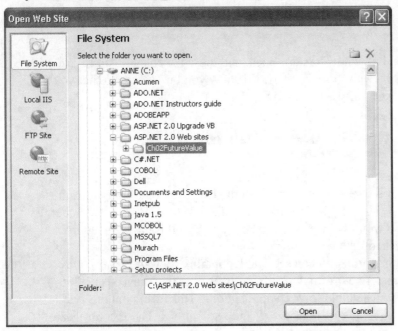

Three ways to open a web site

- Use the File→Open Project command.
- Use the File→Recent Projects command.
- Use the File→Open Web Site command.

How to use the Open Web Site dialog box

- To open a file-system web site, select File System on the left side of the dialog box, then use the File System tree to locate the web site.
- If a web site is managed by IIS on your own computer, you can open it by using the File System tree. Or, if you prefer, you can click Local IIS and select the web site from a list of sites available from IIS.
- The other icons on the left of the Open Web Site dialog box let you open web sites from an FTP site or from a remote IIS site.

How to close a project

- Use the File→Close Project command.

Note

- The Recent Projects list and the Open Project and Open Web Site commands are also available from the Start page.

Figure 2-4   How to open or close an existing web site

How to use Design view to build a web form

Now that you know how to start, open, and close a web site, you're ready to learn how to build a web form. To start, I'll show you the web form that you're going to build. Then, I'll show you how to build it.

The design of the Future Value form

Figure 2-5 presents the design of a Future Value web form that calculates the future value of a fixed monthly investment. This form has enough features to give you a realistic idea of what's involved in the development of a form, but it's so simple that you won't be overwhelmed by detail. In this case, the entire application consists of this single form.

If you study the form, you can see that it contains six *web server controls*. These controls are derived from ASP.NET classes, and they have special features that make them suitable for web applications. This form contains one *drop-down list*, two *text boxes*, one *label*, and two *buttons*. These controls are analogous to the ones that you use for Windows applications.

When you click on a button in a web form, it automatically starts a postback to the server. When you click the Calculate button, for example, the application calculates the future value based on the values in the drop-down list and two text boxes. The result is displayed in the label when the form is returned to the browser. When you click on the Clear button, the text boxes and label are cleared and the value in the drop-down list is reset to 50.

In contrast to the web server controls, the image at the top of this page (the Murach logo) is stored in an *HTML server control*. This is a second type of *server control* that you can use on a web form. The third type is a *validation control*, which you'll learn about later in this chapter.

The arrangement of the web server controls on this web form is done through an HTML table. Above the table, a heading has been entered and formatted. In the first column of the first four rows of the table, text has been entered that describes the data in the second column. The fifth row of the table contains no text or controls. And the six row contains the two buttons.

In the rest of this chapter, you'll learn how to build this web form, how to add validation controls to it, and how to write the code for its code-behind file. Then, you'll learn how to test a web application. At the end of this chapter, you'll find exercises that will walk you through the development of this Future Value application and help you experiment with other features of Visual Studio.

Throughout this chapter, please note that the term *page* is sometimes used to refer to a web form. That's because a web form represents a page that's sent to a browser.

The Future Value web form in a browser

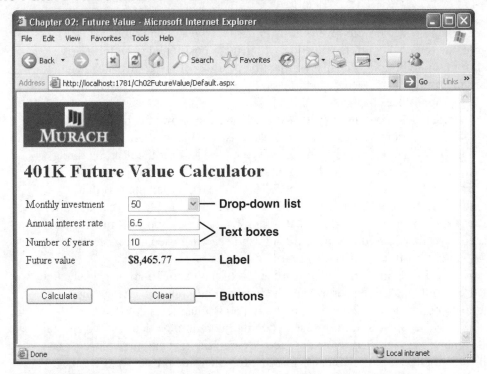

The six web server controls used by the Future Value form

- The *drop-down list* can be used to select a monthly investment value ranging from 50 to 500.

- The two *text boxes* are used to enter values for the annual interest rate and the number of years that the monthly payments will be made.

- The *label* is used to display the future value that is calculated.

- The Calculate and Clear *buttons* are used to post the form back to the server and initiate the processing that needs to be done.

Description

- Besides the *web server controls*, the Future Value form uses an *HTML server control* to display the image at the top of the form, and it uses text to display the heading below the image. It also uses an HTML table to align the text and web server controls below the image and heading.

- When the user clicks on the Calculate button, the future value is calculated based on the three user entries and the results are displayed in the label control.

- When the user clicks on the Clear button, the two text boxes and the label are cleared and the drop-down list is reset to a value of 50.

- To end the application, the user can click the Close button in the upper right corner of the browser window.

Figure 2-5   The design of the Future Value form

How to use flow layout

By default, you develop web forms in *flow layout*. When you use flow layout, the text and controls you add to a form are positioned from left to right and from top to bottom. Because of that, the position of the controls can change when the form is displayed depending on the size of the browser window and the resolution of the display.

To understand how flow layout works, figure 2-6 shows the beginning of a version of the Future Value form that doesn't use a table to align its text and controls. To create this form, I started by typing the text for the heading directly into the form. Then, I pressed the Enter key twice to add space between the heading and the text and controls that follow it. Next, I typed the text that identifies the first control, I pressed the space bar twice to add some space after the text, and I added a drop-down list. When I added the drop-down list, it was placed immediately to the right of the text and spaces. I used similar techniques to enter the remaining text and text box.

Finally, I formatted the heading at the top of the form. To do that, I selected the text and then used the controls in the Formatting toolbar to change the font size to 20 points, to make the heading bold, and to change its color to blue.

You can see the result in the aspx code in this figure. Notice that the special code   was inserted for each space between the text and the controls that follow. In addition, a Br element is inserted for each line break. To apply the formatting to the heading, a Strong element is used, along with a Span element with a Style attribute that specifies the font size and color.

Because you're limited to what you can do with spaces and line breaks, you'll frequently use tables to format a form in flow layout. For example, you can see in this figure that the drop-down list and the text box aren't perfectly aligned. In addition, there's not much space between the line that contains the drop-down list and the line that contains the text box. In the next figure, then, you'll learn how to add a table to a form so you can align the text and controls just the way you want.

The beginning of the Future Value form created using flow layout

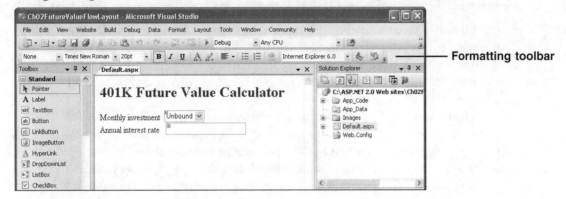

The aspx code for the Future Value form

```
<form id="form1" runat="server">
<div>
    <strong><span style="font-size: 20pt; color: blue">
    401K Future Value Calculator</span></strong><br /><br />
    Monthly investment  
    <asp:DropDownList ID="DropDownList1" runat="server">
    </asp:DropDownList><br />
    Annual interest rate  
    <asp:TextBox ID="TextBox1" runat="server"></asp:TextBox>
</div>
</form>
```

How to use flow layout

- When you add controls to a form in *flow layout*, they will appear one after the other, from left to right and from top to bottom. Flow layout is the default for web forms in Visual Studio 2005.

- To insert a space after a control, use the space bar. The special code   is inserted into the aspx file.

- To insert a line break after a control, press Enter. A <br /> tag is inserted into the aspx file.

- To insert literal text, type it directly into the designer window. Then, you can use the controls in the Formatting toolbar and the commands in the Format menu to change the font or font size; apply bold, italics, or underlining; or apply foreground or background color.

- To align text and controls when you use flow layout, you normally use tables as described in the next figure.

Figure 2-6   How to use flow layout

How to add a table to a form

Figure 2-7 shows how to add a table to a form. In this case, a table of six rows and two columns has already been added to the form, but the Insert Table dialog box is displayed to show what the settings are for that table. Usually, you can keep the dialog box entries that simple, because you can easily adjust the table once it's on the form.

The easiest way to resize a row or column is to drag it by its border. To change the width of a column, drag it by its right border. To change the height of a row, drag it by its bottom border. You can also change the height and width of the entire table by selecting the table and then dragging it by its handles.

You can also format a table in Design view by selecting one or more rows or columns and then using the commands in the Layout menu or the shortcut menu that's displayed when you right-click the selection. These commands let you add, delete, or resize rows or columns. They also let you merge the cells in a row or column. If, for example, you want a control in one row to span two columns, you can merge the cells in that row.

How to add text to the cells of a table

In figure 2-7, you can see that text has been entered into the cells in the first four rows of the first column of the table. To do that, you just type the text into the cells. Then, you can format the text by selecting it and using the controls in the Formatting toolbar or the commands in the Format menu. If, for example, you want to bold the four text entries, you can select the four cells that contain the text and click on the Bold button.

The Future Value form with a table that has been inserted into it

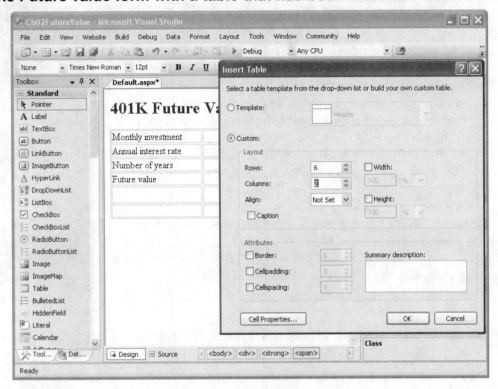

How to add a table to a form

- Use the Layout→Insert Table command to display the Insert Table dialog box. Then, set the number of rows and columns that you want in the table, set any other options that you want, and click OK.

How to format a table after it has been added to a form

- To resize a row, drag it by its bottom border. To resize a column, drag it by its right border. To resize the entire table, select the table and then drag its handles.
- Select rows or columns and then use the commands in the Layout menu or the shortcut menu to add, delete, resize, or merge the rows or columns.

How to add and format text

- To add text to a table, type the text into the cells of the table.
- To format the text in a table, select the text, and then use the controls in the Formatting toolbar or the commands in the Format menu to apply the formatting.

Description

- To control the alignment of the text and controls on a web form in flow layout, you can use tables.

Figure 2-7   How to add a table to a form and text to a table

How to add server controls to a form

Figure 2-8 shows how to add web server controls to a form. To do that, you can just drag a control from the Standard group of the Toolbox and drop it on the form. Or, you can move the cursor where you want a control inserted and then double-click on the control in the Toolbox. This works whether you're placing a control within a cell of a table or outside of a table.

Once you've added the controls to the form, you can resize them by dragging the handles on their sides. If the controls are in a table, you may also want to resize the columns or rows of the table at this time. Keep in mind that you can resize a cell as well as the control within a cell, and sometimes you have to do both to get the formatting the way you want it.

Although you'll typically use web server controls on your web forms, you can also use HTML server controls. These controls appear in the HTML group of the Toolbox, and you can add them to a form the same way that you add web server controls. In addition, you can add an HTML image control to a form by dragging an image from the Solution Explorer. That's how I added the image at the top of the Future Value form.

How to set the properties of the controls

After you have placed the controls on a form, you need to set each control's properties so the control looks and works the way you want it to when the form is displayed. To set those properties, you work in the Properties window as shown in figure 2-8. To display the properties for a specific control, just click on it in Design view.

In the Properties window, you select a property by clicking it. Then, a brief description of that property is displayed in the pane at the bottom of the window. To change a property setting, you change the entry to the right of the property name by typing a new value or choosing a new value from a drop-down list. In some cases, a button with an ellipsis (...) on it will appear when you click on a property. In that case, you can click this button to display a dialog box that helps you set the property.

Some properties are displayed in groups. In that case, a plus sign appears next to the group name. This is illustrated by the Font property in this figure. To display the properties in a group, just click the plus sign next to the group name.

To display properties alphabetically or by category, you can click the appropriate button at the top of the Properties window. At first, you may want to display the properties by category so you have an idea of what the different properties do. Once you become more familiar with the properties, though, you may be able to find the ones you're looking for faster if you display them alphabetically.

As you work with properties, you'll find that most are set the way you want them by default. In addition, some properties such as Height and Width are set interactively as you size and position the controls in Design view. As a result, you usually only need to change a few properties for each control. The only

The Future Value form after six web server controls have been added to it

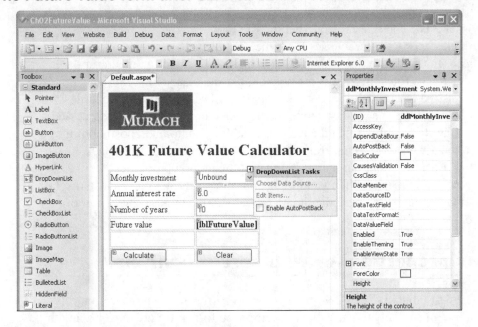

How to add a web server control to a web form

- Drag the control from the Standard group in the Toolbox to the form or to a cell in a table on the form. Or, move the cursor to where you want the control, and then double-click on the control in the Toolbox.

How to set the properties for a control

- Select a control by clicking on it, and all of its properties are displayed in the Properties window. Then, you can select a property in this window and set its value. When you select a property, a brief description is displayed in the pane at the bottom of the window.

- To change the Height and Width properties, you can drag one of the handles on a control. This also changes the Height and Width in the Properties window.

- To change the properties for two or more controls at the same time, select the controls. Then, the common properties of the controls are displayed in the Properties window.

- You can use the first two buttons at the top of the Properties window to sort the properties by category or alphabetically.

- You can use the plus and minus signs that are displayed in the Properties window to expand and collapse the list of properties.

- Many web server controls have a *smart tag menu* that provides options for performing common tasks and setting common properties. To display a smart tag menu, click the Smart Tag icon in the upper right of the control.

Note

- The image on this form was created by dragging the MurachLogo.jpg file from the Solution Explorer to the form. This creates an HTML image control.

Figure 2-8   How to add web server controls to a form and set their properties

property that I set for the drop-down list, for example, is the ID property. This property contains the name that you'll use to refer to the control when you write the Visual Basic code for the code-behind file.

Another way to set properties for some controls is to use the control's *smart tag menu*. In this figure, for example, you can see the smart tag menu for the drop-down list. You can use this menu to choose the data source for the control, which sets the DataSourceID, DataTextField, and DataValueField properties; edit the items in the list, which modifies the collection of items that's accessed through the Items property; and enable or disable the automatic posting of the page when a value is selected from the list, which sets the AutoPostBack property. Because smart tag menus help you set common properties, they're displayed automatically when you drag a control to a form. You can also display a smart tag menu by clicking the Smart Tag icon in the upper right corner of the control.

Common properties for web server controls

The first table in figure 2-9 presents the properties for web server controls that you're most likely to use as you develop web forms. If you've worked with Windows controls, you'll notice that many of the properties of the web server controls provide similar functionality. For example, you use the ID property to name a control that you need to refer to in code, and you can use the Text property to determine what's displayed in or on the control. However, the AutoPostBack, CausesValidation, EnableViewState, and Runat properties are unique to web server controls. Since you already know the purpose of the Runat property, I'll focus on the other three properties here.

The AutoPostBack property determines whether the page is posted back to the server when the user changes the value of the control. Note that this property is only available with certain controls, such as check boxes, drop-down lists, and radio buttons. Also note that this property isn't available with button controls. That's because button controls always post a page back to the server.

The CausesValidation property is available for button controls and determines whether the validation controls are activated when the user clicks the button. This lets you check for valid data before the form is posted back to the server. You'll learn more about validation controls a few figures from now.

The EnableViewState property determines whether a server control retains its property settings from one posting to the next. For that to happen, the EnableViewState property for both the form and the control must be set to True. Since that's normally the way you want this property set, True is the default.

The second table in this figure lists four more properties that are commonly used with drop-down lists and list boxes. However, you don't need to set these at design time. Instead, you use them when you write the Visual Basic code for the code-behind file. For instance, you use the Items collection to add, insert, and remove ListItem objects. And you use the SelectedValue property to retrieve the value of the currently selected item. You'll learn more about these properties when you review the code-behind file for the Future Value form.

Common web server control properties

Property	Description
AutoPostBack	Determines whether the page is posted back to the server when the value of the control changes. Available with controls such as a check box, drop-down list, radio button, or text box. The default value is False.
CausesValidation	Determines whether the validation that's done by the validation controls occurs when you click on the button, link button, or image button. The default value is True. (You'll learn how to use two common validation controls later in this chapter.)
EnableViewState	Determines whether the control maintains its view state between HTTP requests. The default value is True.
Enabled	Determines whether the control is functional. The default value is True.
Height	The height of the control.
ID	The name that's used to refer to the control.
Runat	Indicates that the control will be processed on the server by ASP.NET.
TabIndex	Determines the order in which the controls on the form receive the focus when the Tab key is pressed.
Text	The text that's displayed in the control.
ToolTip	The text that's displayed when the user hovers the mouse over the control.
Visible	Determines whether a control is displayed or hidden.
Width	The width of the control.

Common properties of drop-down list and list box controls

Property	Description
Items	The collection of ListItem objects that represents the items in the control. Although you can set the values for these list items at design time, you normally use code to add, insert, and remove the items in a list or list box.
SelectedItem	The ListItem object for the currently selected item.
SelectedIndex	The index of the currently selected item. If no item is selected in a list box, the value of this property is -1.
SelectedValue	The value of the currently selected item.

Note

- When buttons are clicked, they always post back to the server. That's why they don't have AutoPostBack properties.

Figure 2-9   Common properties for web server controls

How to work in Source view

As you design a form in Design view, HTML and asp tags are being generated in Source view. This is the code that's used to render the web page that's sent to the user's browser. What you see in Design view is just a visual representation of that code. In figure 2-10, you can see some of the tags for the Future Value form after the Designer has been switched to Source view.

How to use Source view to modify the design

As you saw in the last chapter, HTML consists of tags. For instance, the <form> and </form> tags mark the start and end of the HTML code for a web form. And the <table> and </table> tags mark the start and end of the HTML code for a table.

In addition to the HTML tags, ASP.NET adds asp tags for the web server controls that are added to the form. For instance, the <asp:DropDownList> and </asp:DropDownList> tags mark the start and end of the code for a drop-down list. Within these tags, you'll find the code for the property settings of the controls. Note, however, that all of this asp code is converted to HTML before the page can be sent to a browser, because a browser can only interpret HTML.

Because the file that contains the source code for a web form has an aspx extension, we refer to the source code for a form as *aspx code*. This also indicates that the code contains both HTML and asp tags.

In case you need it, chapter 5 presents a crash course in HTML. In the meantime, though, you may be surprised to discover how easy it is to modify the design of a form by adjusting the aspx code using the *HTML Editor*.

To start, you can modify the title of the form that you'll find between the Head tags near the top of the source code. This is the title that's displayed in the title bar of the browser when the form is run (see figure 2-5). In this example, the title has been changed from "Untitled Page" to "Chapter 02: Future Value." As you will see, all of the applications in this book have titles that indicate both the chapter number and the type of application.

You can also use this technique to change the text that has been entered into a form or to change some the settings for HTML elements. If, for example, you want to change the text in the first row of the table from "Monthly investment" to "Investment amount," you can just edit the text in Source view. If you want to change the width of a cell, you can edit that entry. And if you want to modify the color for the heading, you can do that too. As you edit, just follow the syntax of the other entries, which will be easier to do after you read chapter 5.

To change the properties of a server control, you can click in the starting asp tag to select the control. Then, you can use the Properties window just as if you were in Design view. When you change a property, the *attribute* that represents the property in the asp tag for the control is changed. You can also change the attributes directly in the source code whenever the syntax is obvious. That's often the fastest way to make an adjustment.

The design of the Future Value form in Source view

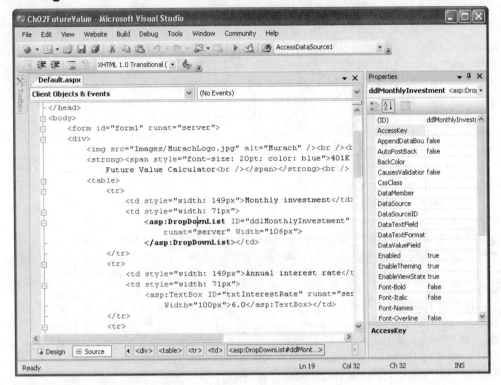

How to change the title of the form

- Change the text between the <title> and </title> tags.

How to change the HTML and text for the form

- Change the source code itself.

How to change the property settings for a control

- To select a control, move the insertion point into the asp tag for the control. Then, use the Properties window to change the property settings for the control. Or, you can modify the property settings in the source code itself.

Description

- Design view presents a visual representation of the code that you see in Source view.
- The source code includes HTML tags and asp tags. Before the form is sent to a browser, the asp tags are converted to HTML because browsers can only run HTML.
- The properties you set for a control appear as *attributes* in the asp tag for the control.
- We refer to the source code as *aspx code*, because the source files have aspx extensions.

Figure 2-10   How to use Source view to modify the design of a form

The aspx code for the Future Value form

Figure 2-11 presents the aspx code for the Future Value form that has been developed thus far (except for the Page and Doctype directives, which you'll learn more about in chapter 5). For now, though, please note that the code for the title that's displayed in the web browser is between the <head> tags, and the code for the form design is between the <div> tags.

Within the <div> tags, I've highlighted the code for the HTML image control and the code for the six web server controls. If you study this code, you can see how the properties are set for each of these controls. For instance, you can see that I set the Width properties of the button controls to 100 pixels so they are both the same width.

You can also see that I set the width of the drop-down list to 106 pixels, even though it appears to be the same width as the text boxes, which are 100 pixels wide. And you can see that I had to set the height of the cells in the fifth row of the table to give that row an adequate height. My point is that the sizing properties in the aspx code aren't always consistent, so you often have to fiddle with these properties to get the design the way you want it.

Before I go on, I want to point out that when you create an HTML image control by dragging the image from the Solution Explorer, it's generated with just a Src property that identifies the name and location of the image. However, the version of HTML that Visual Studio 2005 uses also requires the Alt attribute, which specifies the text that's displayed if for some reason the image can't be displayed. Because of that, I had to add this property to the HTML code for the control.

The aspx code for the Future Value form

```
<html xmlns="http://www.w3.org/1999/xhtml" >
<head runat="server">
    <title>Chapter 02: Future Value</title>
</head>
<body>
    <form id="form1" runat="server">
    <div>
        <img src="Images/MurachLogo.jpg" alt="Murach"/><br /><br />
        <strong><span style="font-size: 20pt; color: blue">401K
            Future Value Calculator<br /></span></strong><br />
        <table>
            <tr>
                <td style="width: 149px">Monthly investment</td>
                <td style="width: 71px">
                    <asp:DropDownList ID="ddlMonthlyInvestment"
                        runat="server" Width="106px">
                    </asp:DropDownList></td>
            </tr>
            <tr>
                <td style="width: 149px">Annual interest rate</td>
                <td style="width: 71px">
                    <asp:TextBox ID="txtInterestRate" runat="server"
                    Width="100px">6.0</asp:TextBox></td>
            </tr>
            <tr>
                <td style="width: 149px">Number of years</td>
                <td style="width: 71px">
                    <asp:TextBox ID="txtYears" runat="server"
                    Width="100px">10</asp:TextBox></td>
            </tr>
            <tr>
                <td style="width: 149px">Future value</td>
                <td style="width: 71px">
                    <asp:Label ID="lblFutureValue" runat="server"
                    Font-Bold="True"></asp:Label></td>
            </tr>
            <tr>
                <td style="width: 149px; height: 25px"></td>
                <td style="width: 71px; height: 25px"></td>
            </tr>
            <tr>
                <td style="width: 149px">
                    <asp:Button ID="btnCalculate" runat="server"
                    BackColor="LightGray" Text="Calculate"
                    Width="100px" /></td>
                <td style="width: 71px">
                    <asp:Button ID="btnClear" runat="server"
                    BackColor="LightGray" Text="Clear"
                    Width="100px" /></td>
            </tr>
        </table>
    </div>
    </form>
</body>
</html>
```

Figure 2-11   The aspx code for the Future Value form

How to add validation controls to a form

A *validation control* is a type of ASP.NET control that's used to validate input data. The topics that follow introduce you to the validation controls and show you how to use two of the commonly used controls. Then, in chapter 7, you can learn all the skills that you need to master the use of these controls.

An introduction to the validation controls

Figure 2-12 shows the Validation group in the Toolbox. It offers five controls that can be called *validators*. These are the controls that you use to check that the user has entered valid data. You can use the last control in this group, the validation summary control, to display all the errors that have been detected by the validators on the form.

The easiest way to add a validation control to a web form is to drag it from the Toolbox. In this example, four validators have been added to the form: two required field validators and two range validators. In this case, the controls have been added below the table so ASP.NET will use flow layout to position the controls. However, these controls could have been added to a third column of the table. Although these controls aren't displayed when the form is displayed, the messages in their ErrorMessage properties are displayed if errors are detected.

In this case, the first required field validator checks to make sure that a value has been added to the text box for the interest rate, and the first range validator checks to make sure that this value ranges from 1 to 20. Similarly, the second required field validator checks to make sure that a value has been entered in the text box for years, and the second range validator checks to make sure that this value ranges from 1 to 45.

Validation tests are typically done on the client before the page is posted to the server. That way, a round trip to the server isn't required to display error messages if any invalid data is detected.

In most cases, client-side validation is done when the focus leaves an input control that has validators associated with it. That can happen when the user presses the Tab key to move to the next control or clicks another control to move the focus to that control. Validation is also done when the user clicks on a button that has its CausesValidation property set to True.

To perform client-side validation, a browser must support *Dynamic HTML*, or *DHTML*. Because most browsers in use today support DHTML, validation can usually be done on the client. However, validation is always done on the server too when a page is submitted. ASP.NET does this validation after it initializes the page.

When ASP.NET performs the validation tests on the server, it sets the IsValid property of each validator to indicate if the test was successful. In addition, after all the validators are tested, it sets the IsValid property of the page to indicate if all the input data is valid. You can test this property in the event handler for the event that causes the page to be posted to the server. You'll see how this works when you review the code-behind file for this form.

The validation controls on the Future Value form

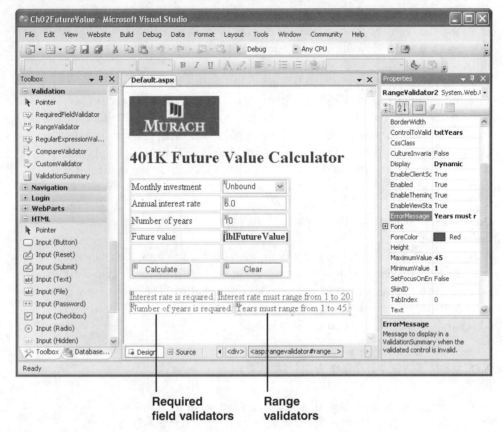

Required   Range
field validators validators

Description

- You can use *validation controls* to test user input and produce error messages. The validation is performed when the focus leaves the control that's being validated and also when the user clicks on a button control whose CausesValidation property is set to True.

- Each validation control is associated with a specific server control, but you can associate one or more validation controls with a single server control.

- The validation controls work by running client-side script. Then, if the validation fails, the page isn't posted back to the server. However, the validation is also performed on the server in case the client doesn't support scripts.

- If the client doesn't support scripts, you can test whether validation has been successful on the server by testing whether the IsValid property of the page is True.

Figure 2-12   An introduction to the validation controls

How to use the required field validator

To use the *required field validator*, you set the properties shown in the table at the top of figure 2-13. These are the properties that are used by all the validators.

To start, you associate the validation control with a specific input control on the form through its ControlToValidate property. Then, when the focus leaves the input control or the user clicks on a button whose CausesValidation property is set to True, the validator checks whether a value has been entered into the input control. If not, the message in the ErrorMessage property is displayed.

When an error occurs, the Display property of the validation control determines how the message in the ErrorMessage property is displayed. When you use flow layout, Dynamic usually works the best for this property. If you use a validation summary control as explained in chapter 7, though, you can change this property to None.

If you look at the aspx code in this figure, you can see how the properties are set for the two required field validators that are shown in the previous figure. The first one validates the text box named txtInterestRate. The second one validates the text box named txtYears. This aspx code will be added after the end tag for the table in the code in figure 2-11.

How to use the range validator

The *range validator* lets you set the valid range for an input value. To use this control, you set the properties in the first table in figure 2-13, plus the properties in the second table. In particular, you set the minimum and maximum values for an input value.

For this control to work correctly, you must set the Type property to the type of data you're testing for. Because the interest rate entry can have decimal positions, for example, the Type property for the first range validator is set to Double. In contrast, because the year entry should be a whole number, the Type property for the second range validator is set to Integer. You can see how all of the properties for the two range validators are set by reviewing the aspx code.

Common validation control properties

Property	Description
ControlToValidate	The ID of the control to be validated.
Display	Determines how an error message is displayed. Specify Static to allocate space for the message in the page layout, Dynamic to have the space allocated when an error occurs, or None to display the errors in a validation summary control.
ErrorMessage	The message that's displayed in the validation control when the validation fails.

Additional properties of a range validator

Property	Description
Maximum	The maximum value that the control can contain.
Minimum	The minimum value that the control can contain.
Type	The data type to use for range checking (String, Integer, Double, Date, or Currency).

The aspx code for the validation controls on the Future Value form

```
<asp:RequiredFieldValidator ID="RequiredFieldValidator1" runat="server"
    ControlToValidate="txtInterestRate" Display="Dynamic"
    ErrorMessage="Interest rate is required.">
</asp:RequiredFieldValidator>
<asp:RangeValidator ID="RangeValidator1" runat="server"
    ControlToValidate="txtInterestRate" Display="Dynamic"
    ErrorMessage="Interest rate must range from 1 to 20."
    MaximumValue="20" MinimumValue="1" Type="Double">
</asp:RangeValidator><br />
<asp:RequiredFieldValidator ID="RequiredFieldValidator2" runat="server"
    ControlToValidate="txtYears" Display="Dynamic"
    ErrorMessage="Number of years is required.">
</asp:RequiredFieldValidator>
<asp:RangeValidator ID="RangeValidator2" runat="server"
    ControlToValidate="txtYears" Display="Dynamic"
    ErrorMessage="Years must range from 1 to 45."
    MaximumValue="45" MinimumValue="1" Type="Integer">
</asp:RangeValidator>
```

Description

- The *required field validator* is typically used with text box controls, but can also be used with list controls.
- The *range validator* tests whether a user entry falls within a valid range.
- If the user doesn't enter a value into the input control that a range validator is associated with, the range validation test passes. Because of that, you should also provide a required field validator if a value is required.

Figure 2-13   How to use the required field and range validators

How to add code to a form

To add the functionality required by a web form, you add Visual Basic code to its code-behind file. This code responds to the events that the user initiates on the form. This code also responds to events that occur as a form is processed.

How to use the Code Editor

To create and edit Visual Basic code, you use the *Code Editor* shown in figure 2-14. The easiest way to display the Code Editor window is to double-click the form or a control in the Web Forms Designer window. That displays the code-behind file for the form.

If you double-click the form in Design view, Sub and End Sub statements for the Load event of the page are generated. If you double-click a control, Sub and End Sub statements for the default event of the control are generated. If you double-click on a button control, for example, an *event procedure* (or *event handler*) for the Click event of that control is created. Then, you can enter the code for that procedure between the generated Sub and End Sub statements.

To create procedures for other events, you can use the drop-down lists at the top of the Code Editor window. The list at the left side of the window includes all of the available objects. When you select one of these objects, the list at the right side of the window lists all the events for that object. When you select an event, Visual Studio generates Sub and End Sub statements for the event handler.

You can also code *general procedures* by entering code directly into the Code Editor window. To create a *Sub procedure*, for example, you enter a Sub statement. And to create a *Function procedure*, or just *function*, you enter a Function statement. When you press the Enter key after entering one of these statements, the End Sub or End Function statement is generated for you. Then, you can enter the code required to implement the procedure between these statements, and you can call the procedure from another procedure.

As you work with the Code Editor, you'll notice that it provides some powerful features that can help you code more quickly and accurately. One of the most useful of these features is the Auto List Members feature provided by IntelliSense. This feature displays a list of members that are available for an object when you type the object name and a period. Then, you can highlight the member you want by clicking on it, typing the first few letters of its name, or using the arrow keys to scroll through the list. In this figure, you can see the members that are listed for a drop-down list after the first character of the member name is entered. When you press the Tab key, the member you select is inserted into your code.

You can also use the Text Editor toolbar to work with code in the Code Editor. You can use it to perform functions such as commenting or uncommenting several lines of code at once, increasing or decreasing the indentation of several lines of code, and working with bookmarks. If you experiment with this toolbar, you should quickly see how it works.

A project with the Code Editor window displayed

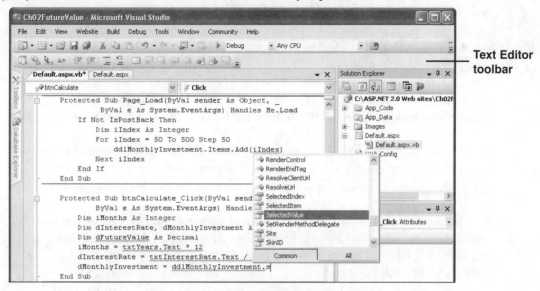

Text Editor toolbar

Three ways to open or switch to a file in the Code Editor window

- Select a web form in the Solution Explorer and click the View Code button at the top of the Solution Explorer. Double-click on a Visual Basic file (.aspx.vb or .vb) in the Solution Explorer. Or, click on a tab at the top of the Web Forms Designer (if the file is already open).

Four ways to start an event procedure

- Double-click on a blank portion of a web form to start an event procedure for the Load event of the page.
- Double-click on a control in the Web Forms Designer to start an event procedure for the default event of that control.
- Select a control in the Web Forms Designer, click the Events button in the Properties window (the button with the lightening bolt), and double-click the event you want to create an event procedure for.
- Select a control from the drop-down list at the top left of the Code Editor window, and select an event from the drop-down list at the top right. To create an event procedure for a page event, select (Page Events) from the first drop-down list.

Description

- The *Code Editor* includes powerful text editing features such as automatic indentation, syntax checking, and statement completion (as shown above).
- To enter a Sub procedure or function, you type the procedure or function from scratch, but Visual Studio will insert the End Sub or End Function statement.

Figure 2-14   How to use the Code Editor

How to use page and control events

The first table in figure 2-15 presents some of the common events for working with web pages. The Init and Load events of a page occur whenever a page is requested from the server. The Init event occurs first, and it's used by ASP.NET to restore the view state of the page and its controls. Because of that, you don't usually create an event handler for this event. Instead, you add any initialization code to the event handler for the Load event. You'll see how this works in the next figure.

In contrast, the PreRender event is raised after all the control events for the page have been processed. It's the last event to occur before a page is rendered to HTML. In later chapters, you'll see a couple of cases in which this event is useful.

The second table in this figure lists some of the common events for web server controls. When the user clicks a button, for example, the Click event of that control is raised. Then, the page is posted back to the server, the event handlers for the Init and Load events of the page are executed, if present, followed by the event handler for the Click event of the control that was clicked.

The TextChanged event occurs when the user changes the value in a text box. In most cases, you won't code an event handler for the TextChanged event. However, you might code an event handler for the CheckedChanged event that occurs when the user clicks a radio button or checks a check box. You might also code an event handler for the SelectedIndexChanged event that occurs when the user selects an item from a drop-down list.

If you want the event handler for one of these events to be executed immediately when the event occurs, you can set the AutoPostBack property of the control to True. Then, the event handler will be executed after the Load and Init event handlers for the page. Note that if you don't set the AutoPostBack property to True, the event is still raised, but the event handler isn't executed until another user action causes the page to be posted to the server. Then, the event handlers for the Load and Init events of the page are executed, followed by the event handlers for the control events in the order they were raised.

In this figure, you can see the event handler for the Click event of the Clear button on the Future Value form. Note that the name for this event handler is btnClear_Click, which is the ID of the button followed by the name of the event. Remember, though, that the Handles clause actually determines what event or events the procedure responds to. In this procedure, the value in the drop-down list is reset to 50, and the text boxes and label are reset to empty strings.

Incidentally, using the Handles clause is the default method for wiring events to their event handlers. However, you can also wire an event to an event handler by naming the event handler on the event attribute of a control. Although you'll learn how this works in chapter 6, there's usually no reason to change from using the Handles clause.

Common ASP.NET page events

Event	Procedure name	Occurs when...
Init	Page_Init	A page is requested from the server. This event is raised before the view state of the page controls has been restored.
Load	Page_Load	A page is requested from the server, after all controls have been initialized and view state has been restored. This is the event you typically use to perform initialization operations such as retrieving data and initializing form controls.
PreRender	Page_PreRender	All the control events for the page have been processed but before the HTML that will be sent back to the browser is generated.

Common ASP.NET control events

Event	Occurs when...
Click	The user clicks a button, link button, or image button control.
TextChanged	The user changes the value in a text box.
CheckedChanged	The user selects a radio button in a group of radio buttons or selects or unselects a check box.
SelectedIndexChanged	The user selects an item from a list box, a drop-down list, a check box list, or a radio button list.

Code for the Click event of the btnClear button

```
Protected Sub btnClear_Click(ByVal sender As Object, _
        ByVal e As System.EventArgs) Handles btnClear.Click
    ddlMonthlyInvestment.Text = 50
    txtInterestRate.Text = ""
    txtYears.Text = ""
    lblFutureValue.Text = ""
End Sub
```

Description

- All of the events associated with an ASP.NET web page and its server controls are executed on the server. Because of that, the page must be posted back to the server to process any event for which you've coded an event handler.

- When a page is posted back to the server, the Init and Load events are always raised so any event handlers for those events are run first. Next, the event handlers for any control events that were raised are executed in the ordered they were raised. When these event handlers finish, the PreRender event is raised and any event handler for that event is run.

Figure 2-15   How to use page and control events

The Visual Basic code for the Future Value form

Figure 2-16 presents the complete Visual Basic code for the code-behind file of the Future Value form. It consists of three event handlers that handle the Load event for the page and the Click events of the Calculate and Clear buttons. This code also includes a function procedure named FutureValue that is called by the event handler for the Click event of the Calculate button.

In this code, I've highlighted the two page properties that are commonly tested in the code for web forms. The first one is the IsPostBack property that's used in the Page_Load procedure. If it is True, it means that the page is being posted back from the user. If it is False, it means that the page is being requested by the user for the first time.

As a result, the statements within the If statement in the Page_Load procedure are only executed if the page is being requested for the first time. In that case, the values 50 through 500 are added to the drop-down list. For all subsequent requests by that user, the IsPostBack property will be True so the values aren't added to the drop-down list.

The other page property that's commonly tested is the IsValid property. It's useful when the user's browser doesn't support the script for the validation controls. In that case, the application has to rely on the validation that's always done on the server. Then, if IsValid is True, it means that all of the input data is valid. But if IsValid is False, it means that one or more controls contain invalid input data so the processing shouldn't be done.

In the btnCalculate_Click procedure, you can see how the IsValid test is used. If it isn't True, the processing isn't done. But otherwise, this procedure gets the years and interest rate values from the text boxes and converts them to monthly units. Then, it uses the SelectedValue property of the drop-down list to get the value of the selected item, which represents the investment amount. Last, it calls the FutureValue function to calculate the future value, uses the FormatCurrency method to format the future value, and puts the formatted value in the label of the form. When this procedure ends, the web form is sent back to the user's browser.

With the exception of the IsPostBack and IsValid properties, this is all standard Visual Basic code so you shouldn't have any trouble following it. But if you do, you can quickly upgrade your Visual Basic skills by getting our latest Visual Basic book.

The Visual Basic code for the Future Value form

```vb
Partial Class _Default
    Inherits System.Web.UI.Page

    Protected Sub Page_Load(ByVal sender As Object, _
            ByVal e As System.EventArgs) Handles Me.Load
        If Not IsPostBack Then
            Dim iIndex As Integer
            For iIndex = 50 To 500 Step 50
                ddlMonthlyInvestment.Items.Add(iIndex)
            Next iIndex
        End If
    End Sub

    Protected Sub btnCalculate_Click(ByVal sender As Object, _
            ByVal e As System.EventArgs) Handles btnCalculate.Click
        Dim iMonths As Integer
        Dim dInterestRate, dMonthlyInvestment As Decimal
        Dim dFutureValue As Decimal
        If IsValid Then
            iMonths = txtYears.Text * 12
            dInterestRate = txtInterestRate.Text / 12 / 100
            dMonthlyInvestment = ddlMonthlyInvestment.SelectedValue
            dFutureValue = FutureValue(iMonths, dInterestRate, dMonthlyInvestment)
            lblFutureValue.Text = FormatCurrency(dFutureValue)
        End If
    End Sub

    Private Function FutureValue(ByVal Months As Integer, _
            ByVal InterestRate As Decimal, _
            ByVal MonthlyInvestment As Decimal) As Decimal
        Dim iIndex As Integer
        Dim dFutureValue As Decimal
        For iIndex = 1 To Months
            dFutureValue = (dFutureValue + MonthlyInvestment) _
                        * (1 + InterestRate)
        Next iIndex
        Return dFutureValue
    End Function

    Protected Sub btnClear_Click(ByVal sender As Object, _
            ByVal e As System.EventArgs) Handles btnClear.Click
        ddlMonthlyInvestment.Text = 50
        txtInterestRate.Text = ""
        txtYears.Text = ""
        lblFutureValue.Text = ""
    End Sub

End Class
```

Figure 2-16   The Visual Basic code for the Future Value form

How to test a web application

After you design the forms and develop the code for a web application, you need to test it to be sure it works properly. Then, if you discover any errors in the application, you can debug it, correct the errors, and test it again.

In chapter 4, you'll learn all the skills you need to test and debug a web application. For now, I just want to show you how to run a web site with the built-in development server so you can test any applications that you develop for this chapter. Then, I'll show you the HTML code that's sent to the browser so you can see how that works.

How to run a web site with the built-in development server

When you run a file-system web site by using one of the techniques in figure 2-17, Visual Studio 2005 compiles the application. If the application compiles without errors, Visual Studio automatically launches the built-in ASP.NET 2.0 Development Server and displays the starting page of the web site in your default browser. Then, you can test the application to make sure that it works the way you want it to.

However, if any errors are detected as part of the compilation, Visual Studio opens the Error List window and displays the errors. These can consist of errors that have to be corrected as well as warning messages. In this figure, all of the errors have been corrected, but 7 warning messages are displayed in the Error List window.

To fix an error, you can double-click on it in the Error List window. This moves the cursor to the line of code that caused the error in the Code Editor. By moving from the Error List window to the Code Editor for all of the messages, you should be able to find the coding problems and fix them.

As you're testing an application with the development server, exceptions may occur. If an exception isn't handled by the application, ASP.NET switches to the Code Editor window and highlights the statement that caused the exception. In this case, you can end the application by clicking on the Stop Debugging button in the Debug toolbar or using the Debug→Stop Debugging command. Then, you can fix the problem and test again.

In chapter 4, you'll learn all of the debugging skills that you'll need for more complex applications. For simple applications, though, you should be able to get by with just the skills you have right now.

An ASP.NET project with the shortcut menu for a web form displayed

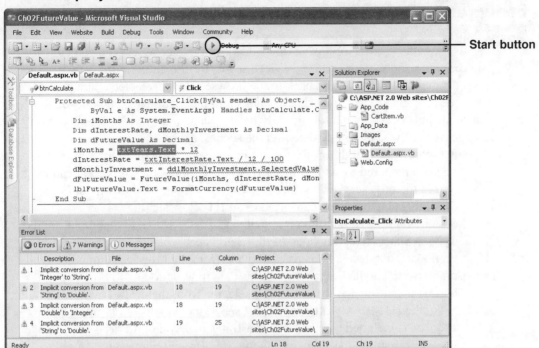

How to run an application

- Click on the Start button in the Standard toolbar or press F5. Then, the project is compiled and the starting page is displayed in your default browser.

- The first time you run an ASP.NET application, a dialog box will appear asking whether you want to modify the web.config file to enable debugging. Click the OK button to proceed.

How to stop an application

- Click the Close button in the upper right corner of the browser. Or, if an exception occurs, click the Stop Debugging button in the Debug toolbar or press Shift+F5.

How to fix build errors

- If any errors are detected when the project is compiled, an Error List window is opened and a list of errors is displayed along with information about each error. To display the source code that caused an error, double-click on the error in the Error List window.

- After you've fixed all of the errors, run the application again, and repeat this process if necessary. Note, however, that you don't have to fix the warnings.

Figure 2-17   How to run a web site with the built-in development server

How to review the HTML that's sent to the browser

To view the HTML for a page that's displayed in a browser, you can use the Source command in your browser's View menu. To illustrate, figure 2-18 presents the HTML that's sent back to the browser after I selected a new value from the drop-down list, entered new values into the text boxes, and clicked the Calculate button. Although you'll rarely need to view this code, it does give you a better idea of what's going on behind the scenes.

First, you'll see that this code doesn't include any asp tags. That's because these tags are rendered to standard HTML so the controls they represent can be displayed in the browser. For instance, the asp tag for the drop-down list in the first row of the table has been converted to an HTML select tag.

Second, you can see that the view state data is stored in a hidden input field named _ViewState. Here, the value of this field is encrypted so you can't read it. Because the data in view state is passed to and from the browser automatically, you don't have to handle the passing of this data in your code.

Third, you can see that the data that I selected from the drop-down list is included in the HTML. Although you can't see it, the data that was entered into the text boxes is included as well. This illustrates that you don't need view state to save the information that's entered by the user. Instead, view state is used to maintain the state of properties that have been set by code. For example, it's used to maintain the values that are loaded into the drop-down list the first time the user requests the form.

Keep in mind that this HTML is generated automatically by ASP.NET, so you don't have to worry about it. You just develop the application by using Visual Studio in the way I've just described, and the rest of the work is done for you.

The HTML for the Future Value form after a post back

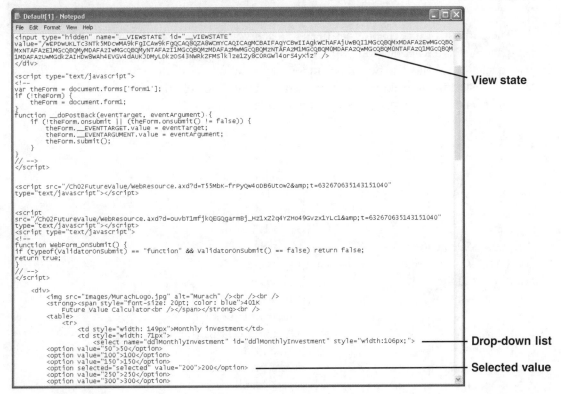

Description

- To view the HTML for a page, use the View→Source command in the browser's menu.

- The HTML that the browser receives consists entirely of standard HTML tags because all of the ASP.NET tags are converted to standard HTML when the page is rendered.

- View state data is stored in a hidden input field within the HTML. This data is encrypted so you can't read it.

- If the page contains validation controls and client scripting is enabled for those controls, the HTML for the page contains script to perform the validation on the client if the client supports DHTML.

- Values that the user enters into a page are returned to the browser as part of the HTML for the page.

Figure 2-18   How to review the HTML that's sent to the browser

Perspective

The purpose of this chapter has been to teach you the basic skills for creating one-page ASP.NET applications with Visual Studio. If you've already used Visual Studio and Visual Basic to develop Windows applications, you shouldn't have any trouble mastering these skills. You just need to get used to HTML and the properties and events for web server controls and validation controls.

Terms

web site	validation control
file-system web site	flow layout
web project	smart tag menu
project	HTML Editor
Web Forms Designer	attribute
Toolbox	aspx code
Solution Explorer	validator
Properties window	required field validator
web form	range validator
Source view	Dynamic HTML (DHTML)
Design view	Code Editor
web server control	event procedure
drop-down list	event handler
text box	general procedure
label	Sub procedure
button	Function procedure
HTML server control	function
server control	

About the book's applications

You can download all of the applications that are presented in this book from our web site (www.murach.com). Then, you can run the applications, review all of their code, and experiment with them on your own system. For more information about downloading and running these applications, please read appendix A.

If you're new to ASP.NET web programming...

If you're new to ASP.NET web programming, we recommend that you practice what you've learned after you finish each chapter in the first section of this book. For instance, you can now use the techniques of chapter 2 to build a Future Value application of your own. To do that, you can page through the figures, use the techniques that are illustrated, and compare your application with the one that you've downloaded. To show you what we mean, exercise 2-1 guides you through the process of building the Future Value application. By the time you complete section 1, though, you should be ready to start building applications of your own.

Exercise 2-1   Build the Future Value application

This exercise demonstrates how you can practice what you've learned after you complete each of the chapters in the first section of this book.

Start, close, and open the application

1. Start a new file-system web site as shown in figure 2-1 named FutureValue in a folder on your own system like C:\Practice Web Sites.

2. Add a folder named Images to your project and add the Murach logo to it, as shown in figure 2-3. You can find the logo in the Images folder of the downloaded FutureValue application.

3. Close the web site using the technique in figure 2-4, and reopen it using one of the three techniques in that figure. Then, switch to Design view.

Use Design view to build the form

4   Drag the logo from the Images folder in the Solution Explorer to the top of the web form. Then, use the techniques in figure 2-6 to enter and format the text for the heading in figure 2-5.

5. Use the techniques in figure 2-7 to add and format a table that provides for the six rows shown in figure 2-5. Then, add the text shown in figure 2-5 to the first four rows in the first column of the table.

6. Use the techniques in figure 2-8 to add the drop-down list, text boxes, label, and buttons shown in figure 2-5 to the table. Then, adjust the size of the columns, rows, and controls, so the table looks the way it does in figure 2-5.

7. Use the techniques of figure 2-8 and the summary in figure 2-9 to set the properties of the controls so they look like the ones in figure 2-5.

Use Source view to modify the aspx code

8. Switch to Source view, and change the title of the form to Future Value using the technique of figure 2-10. In addition, add an Alt attribute with a value of "Murach" to the HTML image control.

9. Press F5 to run the application. When the dialog box asks whether you want to modify the web.config file to enable debugging, click the OK button. Now, test to see what works by clicking on the controls. Also, check to make sure that the web form looks the way it's supposed to when it's displayed in the default browser. (Note that the fifth row of the table is blank.)

10. To end the application, click the Close button in the upper right corner of the browser. Then, adjust the design of the form as necessary by using either Design view or Source view, and test it again.

Add the validation controls

11. Add the validation controls for the interest rate and years text boxes as shown in figure 2-12 and 2-13.

12. Press F5 to run the application. Then, test the field validators by leaving fields blank or entering invalid data. The validation will be done when the focus leaves a text box or when you click on a button.

13. To end the application, click the browser's Close button. Then, fix any problems and test again. If, for example, validation is done when you click the Clear button, you can fix that by setting its CausesValidation property to False.

Add the Visual Basic code and test as you go

14. Use one of the techniques in figure 2-14 to open the Code Editor for the form. Then, use the tab at the top of the window to switch to Design view.

15. Double-click on a blank portion of the form to switch to the Code Editor and start a procedure for the Load event. Next, write the code for this procedure, which should be like the code in figure 2-16. Then, press F5 to compile and test this procedure. If any errors are detected when the application is compiled, use the techniques in figure 2-17 to fix them.

16. Switch back to Design view, and double-click on the Clear button to start a procedure for the Click event of that button. Next, write the code for this procedure, which should be like the code in figure 2-16. Then, compile and test this procedure, and fix any errors.

17. Write the FutureValue function from scratch as shown in figure 2-16. After you enter the signature for the function, Visual Studio should add the End Function line that ends the function.

18. Switch back to Design view, and double-click on the Calculate button to start a procedure for the Click event of that button. Next, write the code for this procedure, which should use the FutureValue function and be like the code in figure 2-16. Then, compile and test, and fix any errors.

Do more testing and experimenting

19. Set the EnableViewState property of the drop-down list to False, and test the application to see what happens. When an exception occurs, click the Stop Debugging button in the Debugging toolbar. Then, reset the property.

20. Set the EnableClientScript property for the validators of the first text box to False so this validation will only be done on the server. Then, test the application to make sure that the validation still works.

21. Run the application again, and use the technique in figure 2-18 to review the HTML that's sent to the browser. When you're through, close the project

3

How to develop a multi-page web application

In the last chapter, you learned how to develop a simple, one-page web application. Now, you'll learn how to develop a multi-page application, which requires several new skills. You'll also learn how to get the data for a web form from a database.

The Shopping Cart application

To illustrate the skills that you're going to learn, this chapter presents two pages of a Shopping Cart application. This application gets product data from a database, stores data in session state, and uses two business classes. So even though this is a simple application, it isn't trivial.

In the four topics that follow, you'll be introduced to the two web forms and the folders and files that this application requires. Then, you'll learn how to add the two business classes to this project.

The Order page

Figure 3-1 presents the first page of the Shopping Cart application. This page, named Order.aspx, includes a drop-down list from which the user can select a product. The products are retrieved from an Access database via an AccessDataSource control, one of the new data source controls provided by ASP.NET 2.0. Since the drop-down list is bound to the data source, the product names are displayed automatically.

Although it isn't apparent in this figure, the product data is retrieved from an Access database named Halloween.mdb. This database includes a table named Products. The Products table has these columns: ProductID, Name, ShortDescription, LongDescription, CategoryID, ImageFile, UnitPrice, and OnHand. All of these columns except CategoryID and OnHand are used by this application.

The AutoPostBack property of the drop-down list is set to True. That way, when the user selects a product, the page is posted back to the server. Then, the code for the page retrieves the data for the selected product from the data source, which has retrieved the data for all of the products from the Access database. The data for the selected product is displayed in several labels. In addition, the ImageUrl property of an Image control is set to the value of the ImageFile column so the product image is displayed in that control.

Once a product is selected, the user can enter a quantity and click the Add to Cart button. However, if the user clicks the Add to Cart button without entering a valid quantity, an error message is displayed. To accomplish that, two validation controls are included on the page. A required field validator makes sure that the user enters a quantity, and a range validator makes sure that the quantity is an integer that ranges from 1 to 500.

If the user enters a valid quantity, a sorted list that contains the user's shopping cart is updated with the product information. If the product isn't already in the shopping cart, a new item is added to the sorted list. But if the product already exists in the shopping cart, the quantity entered is added to the quantity for the product that's in the shopping cart. Because the shopping cart must be retrieved and updated each time a product is added or updated, the sorted list that represents the shopping cart is saved in session state.

The design of the Order page

Description

- The Order page of this application accepts an order for any items in the online store.
- To order an item, the user selects the product from the drop-down list, enters a quantity in the text box, and clicks the Add to Cart button.
- When the user clicks the Add to Cart button, the selected product is added to the shopping cart. If the product is already in the shopping cart, the quantity is added to the quantity in the existing shopping cart item. Then, the Cart page is displayed.
- The product information is retrieved from an Access database by an AccessDataSource control that's bound to the drop-down list.
- The AutoPostBack property of the drop-down list is set to True so the page is posted when the user selects a product. Then, the information for the selected product is displayed.
- The shopping cart information is stored in a SortedList object. This sorted list is saved in session state so it can be retrieved and updated each time a product is ordered.
- Validation controls ensure that the user enters a positive integer for the quantity that ranges from 1 to 500.

Figure 3-1   The Order page of the Shopping Cart application

The Cart page

After the user selects a product from the Order page, enters a quantity, and clicks the Add to Cart button, the Cart page in figure 3-2 is displayed. This page lists all the items currently in the shopping cart in a list box. To do that, it must retrieve the shopping cart from session state.

To work with the items in the shopping cart, the user can use the two buttons to the right of the list box. To remove an item from the shopping cart, the user can select the item and click the Remove Item button. Or, to remove all the items from the shopping cart, the user can click the Empty Cart button.

If the user wants to add items to the shopping cart, he can click the Continue Shopping button to return to the Order page. Then, the user can add additional items to the shopping cart.

Alternatively, the user can click the Check Out button to complete the order. However, the check out function hasn't yet been implemented in this version of the Shopping Cart application. So if the user clicks the Check Out button, a message is displayed to indicate that the check out feature isn't implemented. In a complete application, of course, clicking this button would cause additional pages to be displayed to complete the order.

Like most applications, there are several different ways to implement a shopping cart in ASP.NET. For instance, one design decision is how to save the shopping cart data. For this application, I decided to save the shopping cart data in session state. As an alternative, though, you could save the shopping cart data in a database table. Or, you could use ASP.NET 2.0's new profile feature to save the data. Each approach has its advantages and disadvantages.

A second design decision for a shopping cart application is what type of ASP.NET control to use when you display the shopping cart. To keep this application simple, I used a list box. However, you can create a more advanced shopping cart by using the new GridView control that's presented in chapter 14. With this control, you can display the shopping cart data in neatly arranged columns and include buttons or other controls in each row to let the user delete or modify the cart items.

The design of the Cart page

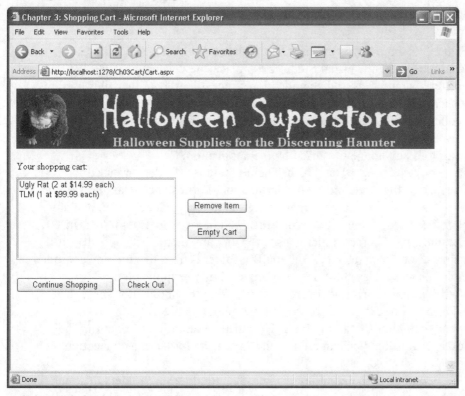

Description

- The Cart page displays the items in the shopping cart in a list box control. To load the list box, it uses the shopping cart information that's saved in session state by the Order page.

- The user can select any item in the shopping cart and then click the Remove Item button to remove the item from the cart. To remove all the items from the cart, the user can click the Empty Cart button.

- After reviewing the cart, the user can click the Continue Shopping button to return to the Order page and order additional products.

- If the user clicks the Check Out button, a message is displayed that indicates that the check out function hasn't been implemented yet.

Figure 3-2   The Cart page of the Shopping Cart application

The files and folders used by the Shopping Cart application

Figure 3-3 summarizes the files and folders used by the Shopping Cart application. By default, Visual Studio 2005 places new web page files and their related code-behind files in the application's root folder, but other files used by the application are placed in special folders. The first table in this figure lists the most commonly used special folders. Besides these folders, though, you can also create your own folders. For example, it's common to create an Images folder to store any image files used by the application.

The App_Code, App_Data, App_Themes, and Bin folders are used for certain types of files required by the application. For instance, class files (other than the class files for web pages) are stored in the App_Code folder, and any database files used by the application are stored in the App_Data folder. In contrast, the App_Themes folder is used to store any theme data, which you'll learn more about in chapter 11. And the Bin folder is used to store any compiled assemblies, such as class libraries, that are used by the application.

Note that the special folders aren't available to the application through normal means. For example, you can't store an image file in the App_Data folder and then refer to it in the ImageUrl attribute of an Image control. The only exception is that you can refer to the App_Data folder in a connection string for an Access database.

The second table in this figure lists the specific files and folders that make up the Shopping Cart application. As you can see, the App_Code folder contains two class files named CartItem.vb and Product.vb that define the CartItem and Product classes required by the application. And the App_Data folder contains an Access database named Halloween.mdb, plus an .ldb file that stores the record locking information for that file.

The Shopping Cart application also includes a folder named Images. This folder includes just one image file, banner.jpg, which provides the banner that's displayed at the top of each page. However, this folder also includes a subfolder named Products, which includes a separate image file for each product in the Products table of the database. Because the Products table includes a column named ImageFile that provides the file name for each product's image, the application can display the correct image for each product.

Finally, the root folder for the application contains two files for each of the application's web pages: one for the page itself, the other for the code-behind file. For example, the Cart.aspx file contains the aspx code that defines the Cart page, and the Cart.aspx.vb file is the code-behind file that contains the Visual Basic code for the Cart page.

Please note that the root folder also contains a web.config file. This file is added automatically when you create an application.

The Solution Explorer for the Shopping Cart application

Special folders used in ASP.NET 2.0 applications

Folder	Description
App_Code	Non-page class files that are compiled together to create a single assembly.
App_Data	Database files used by the application.
App_Themes	Themes used by the application.
Bin	Compiled code used by the application.

Files in the Shopping Cart application

Folder	File	Description
App_Code	CartItem.vb	A class that represents an item in the shopping cart.
App_Code	Product.vb	A class that represents a product.
App_Data	Halloween.mdb	The Access database file that contains the Halloween database.
App_Data	Halloween.ldb	The locking file associated with the Halloween.mdb database file.
Images	Banner.jpg	An image file that displays the banner used at the top of each page.
Images\Products	(multiple)	Contains an image file for each product in the database.
(root)	Cart.aspx	The aspx file for the Cart page.
(root)	Cart.aspx.vb	The code-behind file for the Cart page.
(root)	Order.aspx	The aspx file for the Order page.
(root)	Order.aspx.vb	The code-behind file for the Order page.
(root)	web.config	The application configuration file.

Description

- The Images folder is a custom folder that I created to hold the image files used by this application. The Products subfolder contains the image files for the products in the Products table of the Halloween database.

Figure 3-3   The files and folders used by the Shopping Cart application

How to add a class to a web site

As you just saw in the previous figure, the Shopping Cart application requires two business classes named Product and CartItem. To use these classes with the web site, you can use the techniques presented in figure 3-4.

To add a new class to the web site, you use the Add New Item dialog box shown in this figure. When you display this dialog box, the Class template is selected by default. Then, you can just enter the name for the class and click the Add button to create it. When you do, Visual Studio will create the new class and add Class and End Class statements to it. Then, you can complete the class by coding its properties and methods.

Before you create a new class, you'll typically add the special App_Code folder to the web site so that you can add the class directly to this folder. However, you can also add a new class without first adding the App_Code folder. To do that, just select Add New Item from the shortcut menu for the project. When you do, Visual Studio will display a dialog box that indicates that the class should be placed in an App_Code folder and asks if you want to place the class in that folder. If you click the Yes button in this dialog box, Visual Studio will create the App_Code folder and place the new class in it.

To add an existing class to a web site, you use the Add Existing Item command as described in this figure. Then, the class file that you select is copied to your web site.

If the existing class you want to use is stored in a *class library*, you can use that class by adding a reference to the class library to your web site as described in this figure. One of the advantages of using class libraries is that the source code is stored in a single location. Then, if you need to modify a class, you can just modify the code in the class library and it will be available to any web sites that use that library. In contrast, if you copy a class to each web site that uses it, you have to modify the code in each web site.

The dialog box for adding a new class to the App_Code folder

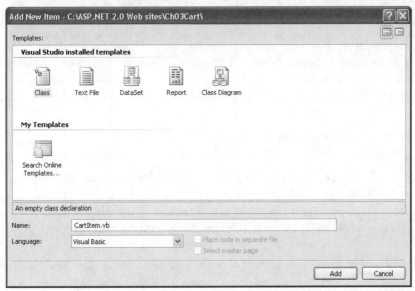

Two ways to open the Add New Item dialog box

- Right-click the App_Code folder in the Solution Explorer if it already exists, and then choose Add New Item from the shortcut menu.
- Click on the App_Code folder in the Solution Explorer to select it, and then choose the Website→Add New Item command.

How to add a new class to a web site

- From the Add New Item dialog box, select the Class template, name the class, and click the Add button. Visual Studio will create the class with Class and End Class statements.
- If you try to add a class directly to the project instead of to the App_Code folder, Visual Studio will warn you that the class should be placed in the App_Code folder and ask you if you'd like to place the class in this folder. If you click the Yes button, Visual Studio will create the App_Code folder if necessary and place the class in this folder.

How to add an existing class to a web site

- To add a class from another project to a web site, right-click the App_Code folder in the Solution Explorer and select Add Existing Item. Then, locate the class file you want to add, select it, and click the Add button. The file is copied to your project.

How to use a class that's part of a class library

- Right-click the project in the Solution Explorer and select Add Reference from the shortcut menu. Click the Browse tab in the dialog box that's displayed, and then locate and select the dll file for the class library you want to use. The class library is added to the project's Bin folder, which is created if it doesn't already exist. To use the classes in the class library without qualification, add an Imports statement for the class library.

Figure 3-4   How to add a class to a web site

Six skills for working with multiple web forms

To create a multi-page web site, you need to learn some new skills like how to add a new web form to a web site, how to rename a web form, how to change the starting page for a web site, and how to transfer from one form to another.

How to add a web form to a web site

To add a new web form to a web site, you use the Add New Item dialog box shown in figure 3-5. When you display this dialog box, the Web Form template is already selected. Then, you enter the name you want to use for the new form and click the Add button to add it to your web site along with the code-behind file.

When you add a new web form, be sure that the language setting is Visual Basic and that the Place Code in Separate File box is checked. These settings are easy to overlook, but difficult to change manually if they're set wrong when you create the page.

To add an existing web form from another web site, you can use the second procedure shown in this figure. You might want to do that if you need to create a form that's similar to a form in another web site. When you add the aspx file for a form, the code-behind file is added too. Then, you can modify the aspx and Visual Basic code so the form works the way you want it to in your new web site.

The Add New Item dialog box for adding a new web form

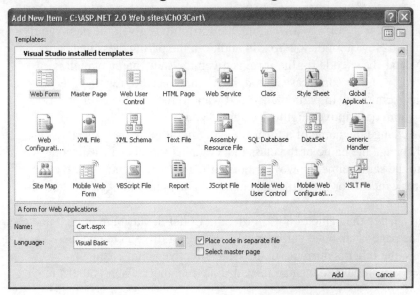

Two ways to open the Add New Item dialog box

- Right-click the project in the Solution Explorer, and then choose Add New Item from the shortcut menu.
- Click on the project in the Solution Explorer to select it, and then choose the Website→Add New Item command.

How to add a new web form to a project

- From the Add New Item dialog box, select the Web Form template, name the form, check the Place Code in Separate File box, and click the Add button.

How to add an existing web form to a project

- In the Solution Explorer, right-click the project and choose Add Existing Item. Then, locate the form you want to add, select it, and click the Add button.

Description

- If there's a form in another application that is like one that you're going to develop, you can copy that form into your web site. That copies both the web form and the code-behind file. Then, you can modify the aspx code and Visual Basic code so the form works the way you want it to.

Figure 3-5   How to add a web form to a web site

How to rename a web form

When you add a web form to a web site, the form file is given the name you specify in the Add New Item dialog box. In addition, the partial class that contains the Visual Basic code for the form is given the same name, which is usually what you want. In some cases, though, you may need to rename the form file or the form class. In particular, you'll want to rename the default form so its name is more descriptive. Figure 3-6 shows you how.

When you change the name of a form file, you might think that Visual Studio would change the name of the class that contains the Visual Basic code for the form to the same name. However, it doesn't. To do that, you have to open the Code Editor window for the form and change the name on the Class statement.

When you change the name of a form file, the CodeFile attribute in the Page directive for the page is changed automatically. However, if you change the name of a class, the Inherits attribute in the Page directive is not changed. Because of that, you'll have to change this attribute manually when you change the name of a class.

How to change the starting web form

If a web site consists of a single form, that form is displayed by default when you run the application. When you add forms to a web site, however, the current form—the one that's selected in the Solution Explorer—is displayed when you run the application. Or, if a form isn't currently selected, the form named Default.aspx is displayed. If the web site doesn't contain a form named Default, a directory listing of the application is displayed.

To make sure that the correct page is displayed when you run an application, you should set the start page for the application. To do that, just right-click on the form in the Solution Explorer and select the Set As Start Page command from the shortcut menu. Note that this only sets the start page that Visual Studio uses when you run an application. It doesn't set the page IIS displays by default when you run the application from a browser outside of Visual Studio. To do that, you have to use IIS. See appendix A for more information.

A web form file being renamed in the Solution Explorer window

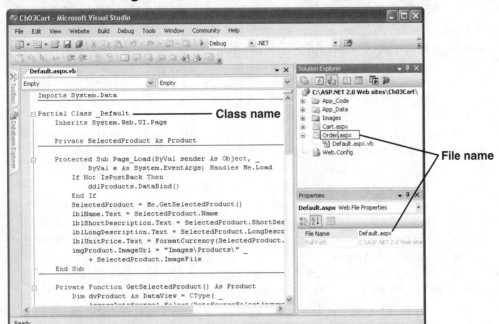

Two ways to rename a web form

- Right-click the form in the Solution Explorer, and then select the Rename command from the shortcut menu. Then, change the name directly in the Solution Explorer window.

- Click on the form in the Solution Explorer to select it. Then, click on it again and change the name directly in the Solution Explorer window.

How to rename the class that contains the Visual Basic code for a web form

- Display the code for the form in the Code Editor window. Then, change the name that's used for the form on the Class statement at the beginning of the file.

- Display the aspx code for the form, and then change the name in the Inherits attribute of the Page directive to the name of the class.

How to change the starting web form for a web site

- Right-click on the web form that you want to use as the starting form in the Solution Explorer. Then, choose Set As Start Page from the shortcut menu.

Note

- In most cases, you'll give a web form an appropriate name when you add it to the project. Since the form that's added by default when you create a web site is named Default, however, you will often want to change this name so it's more descriptive.

Figure 3-6   How to rename a web form and change the starting web form

How to redirect or transfer to another page

When you develop an application with two or more pages, you'll need to know how to display one page from another page. When the user clicks the Add to Cart button on the Order page of the Shopping Cart application, for example, the Cart page should be displayed. Similarly, when the user clicks the Continue Shopping button on the Cart page, the Order page should be displayed. Two ways to do that are presented in figure 3-7.

When you use the Transfer method of the HttpServerUtility class, ASP.NET immediately terminates the execution of the current page. Then, it loads and executes the page specified on the Transfer method and returns it to the browser. The drawback to using this method is that when the new page is sent to the browser, the browser has no way of knowing that the application returned a different page. As a result, the URL for the original page is still displayed in the browser's address box. This can be confusing to the user and prevents the user from bookmarking the page.

The Redirect method of the HttpResponse class works somewhat differently. When this method is executed, it sends a special message called an *HTTP redirect message* back to the browser. This message causes the browser to send a new HTTP request to the server to request the new page. Then, the server processes the page and sends it back to the browser.

Note that because of the way the Redirect method works, it requires an extra round trip to the browser. If this extra round trip will cause a performance problem, you may want to use the Transfer method instead. For most applications, however, the user friendliness of the Redirect method outweighs the small performance gain you get when you use the Transfer method.

The Transfer method of the HttpServerUtility class

Method	Description
`Transfer(URL)`	Terminates the execution of the current page and transfers control to the page at the specified URL.

The Redirect method of the HttpResponse class

Method	Description
`Redirect(URL)`	Redirects the client to the specified URL and terminates the execution of the current page.

Code that transfers control to another page

```
Server.Transfer("Cart.aspx")
```

Code that redirects the client to another page

```
Response.Redirect("Cart.aspx")
```

Description

- The Transfer method is a member of the HttpServerUtility class, which contains helper methods for processing web requests. To refer to this class, you use the Server property of the page.

- The Redirect method is a member of the HttpResponse class, which contains information about the response. To refer to this class, you use the Response property of the page.

- Both the Transfer and Redirect methods cause the page specified by the URL to be displayed in the browser. See figure 3-9 for more information on coding URLs.

- When you use the Transfer method, the current page is terminated and a new page is processed in its place. This processing is efficient because it takes place on the server. However, the browser isn't updated to reflect the address of the new page.

- When you use the Redirect method, the server sends a special message called an *HTTP redirect message* to the browser. When the browser receives this message, it sends an HTTP request to the server to request the new page. The server then processes the new page and sends it back to the browser. Because this involves a round trip to the browser, it's less efficient than the Transfer method.

- In general, you should use the Redirect method to display another web page. You should use the Transfer method only if the application's performance is critical.

Figure 3-7   How to redirect or transfer to another page

How to use cross-page posting

A third way to transfer to a different web page is to use a new feature of ASP.NET 2.0 called *cross-page posting*. It is described in figure 3-8.

To use cross-page posting, you specify the URL of another page in the PostBackUrl property of a button control. Then, when the user clicks the button, an HTTP Post message that contains the URL specified by the PostBackUrl property is sent back to the server. As a result, the page with that URL is loaded and executed instead of the page that was originally displayed.

For example, the Go to Cart button on the Order page uses cross-page posting to go to the Cart page. As a result, the PostBackUrl property of this button is set to Cart.aspx. Then, when the user clicks the Go to Cart button, ASP.NET loads and executes the Cart.aspx page instead of the Order.aspx page.

If the user enters data into one or more controls on a page that uses cross-page posting, you can use the PreviousPage property to retrieve the data entered by the user. As the code example in this figure shows, you should first check to make sure that the PreviousPage property refers to a valid object. If this property doesn't refer to a valid object, it means that either the page isn't being loaded as the result of a cross-page posting, or the request came from another web site. In either case, no previous page is available.

If the PreviousPage property refers to a valid object, you can use the FindControl method to find a control on the previous page. Then, you can use the CType function to cast it to a text box (if the control is a text box). Finally, you can use the Text property to return the data that the text box contains.

Because of the extra programming required to retrieve data entered by the user, cross-page posting is best used when no user input needs to be processed. For instance, since no data needs to be processed when the user clicks the Go to Cart button, I used cross-page posting instead of Response.Redirect or Server.Transfer. However, I used Response.Redirect for the Add to Cart button on the Order page so I could easily retrieve the selected product and the quantity entered by the user.

Incidentally, the Visual Basic example in this figure uses the IsNot keyword that became available with Visual Basic 2005. Otherwise, the If statement would have to start this way:

```
If Not PreviousPage Is Nothing Then
```

Throughout this book, we'll let you know when we use any of the Visual Basic 2005 coding features.

The PostBackUrl property of the Button control

Property	Description
PostBackUrl	Specifies the URL of the page that should be requested when the user clicks the button.

The Page class

Property	Description
PreviousPage	Returns a Page object that represents the previous page.

Method	Description
FindControl(id)	Returns a Control object with the specified id. If the control is a text box, you can cast the Control object to TextBox, then use the Text property to access the data entered by the user.

The aspx code for a button that posts to a different page

```
<asp:Button ID="btnCart" runat="server" Text="Go to Cart"
    CausesValidation="False" PostBackUrl="~/Cart.aspx" />
```

Code that retrieves data from the previous page

```
Protected Sub Page_Load(ByVal sender As Object, _
        ByVal e As System.EventArgs) Handles Me.Load
    If PreviousPage IsNot Nothing Then
        lblQuantity.Text = _
            CType(PreviousPage.FindControl("txtQuantity"), TextBox).Text
    End If
End Sub
```

Description

- *Cross-page posting* lets you use the PostBackUrl property of a button to specify the page that should be requested when the user clicks the button.
- When you post back to another page, the previous page is available via the PreviousPage property. Then, you can use the FindControl method to retrieve data entered by the user.
- In general, cross-page posting is more efficient than the Server.Transfer and Response.Redirect methods. However, cross-page posting makes it more difficult to retrieve data from the original page.
- If you don't need to retrieve data from the original page, cross-page posting is clearly better than the Server.Transfer and Response.Redirect methods.

Figure 3-8   How to use cross-page posting

How to code absolute and relative URLs

In chapter 1, you learned about the basic components of a URL. The URLs you saw in that chapter were all *absolute URLs*. An absolute URL includes the domain name of the web site. When coded within a Transfer or Redirect method, an absolute URL lets you display a page at another web site. For example, the first two statements in figure 3-9 display a page at the web site with the domain name www.murach.com. The first statement displays a page named Default.aspx in the root directory of the web site. The second statement displays a page named Search.aspx in the Books directory of the web site.

To display a page within the same web site, you can use a *relative URL*. This type of URL specifies the location of the page relative to the directory that contains the current page. This is illustrated by the third and fourth statements in this figure. The third statement displays a page that's stored in the same directory as the current page. The fourth statement displays a page in the Login subdirectory of the directory that contains the current page.

The next two statements show how you can use a relative URL to navigate up the directory structure from the current directory. To navigate up one directory, you code two periods followed by a slash as shown in the fifth statement. To navigate up two directories, you code two periods and a slash followed by two more periods and a slash as shown in the sixth statement. To navigate up additional directories, you code two periods and a slash for each directory.

To navigate to the root directory for the host, you code a slash as shown in the seventh statement. You can also navigate to a directory within the root directory by coding the path for that directory following the slash as shown in the eighth statement.

In addition to coding URLs on Transfer and Redirect methods, you can code them for the attributes of some server controls. This is illustrated in the last two examples in this figure. The next to last example shows how you might set the PostBackUrl attribute of a button control. And the last example shows how you might set the ImageUrl attribute of an image control.

Notice that both of these URLs start with a tilde (~) operator. This operator causes the URL to be based on the root directory of the web site. For example, the Cart.aspx file in the first URL is located directly in the root directory, and the banner.jpg file in the second URL is located in the Images subdirectory of the root directory.

Although I could have used relative URLs in these examples, it's easier to maintain URLs that use the tilde operator when you move pages or files from one folder to another. That's because it's easier to maintain a URL that's relative to the root directory of the web site than it is to maintain a URL that's relative to another page. So I recommend you use the tilde operator whenever you code a URL for an attribute of a server control.

Examples of absolute and relative URLs

Statements that use absolute URLs

```
Response.Redirect("http://www.murach.com/Default.aspx")
Response.Redirect("http://www.murach.com/Books/Search.aspx")
```

Statements that use relative URLs that are based on the current directory

```
Response.Redirect("Checkout.aspx")
Response.Redirect("Login/Register.aspx")
```

Statements that use relative URLs that navigate up the directory structure

```
Response.Redirect("../Register.aspx")
Response.Redirect("../../Register.aspx")
Response.Redirect("/Register.aspx")
Response.Redirect("/Login/Register.aspx")
```

Server control attributes that use URLs that are based on the root directory of the current web site

```
PostBackUrl="~/Cart.aspx"
ImageUrl="~/Images/banner.jpg"
```

Description

- When you code an *absolute URL*, you code the complete URL including the domain name for the site. Absolute URLs let you display pages at other web sites.

- When you code a *relative URL*, you base it on the current directory, which is the directory that contains the current page.

- To go to the root directory for the host, you code a slash. Then, you can code one or more directories after the slash.

- To go up one level from the current directory, you code two periods and a slash. To go up two levels, you code two periods and a slash followed by two more periods and a slash. And so on.

- If you're specifying a URL for the attribute of a server control, you can use the web application root operator (~) to base the URL on the root of the web site.

Figure 3-9   How to code absolute and relative URLs

How to create and use data sources

To connect to a database and work with its data, ASP.NET 2.0 offers a new type of control called a *data source*. To illustrate how this works, the following topics show you how to create a data source that connects to a Microsoft Access database and bind it to a drop-down list. Keep in mind, though, that there's much more to working with data sources than these topics let on. That's why section 3 of this book is devoted to the use of data sources and databases.

How to create an Access data source

ASP.NET 2.0 provides several data source controls in the Data group of the Toolbox. The simplest of these controls is AccessDataSource, which is designed to retrieve data from a Microsoft Access database file. Figure 3-10 shows how to create this type of data source.

Before you can use an Access data source, though, you must first create an Access database and add it to the App_Data folder of the web site. As I've mentioned before, the Shopping Cart application for this chapter uses a database named Halloween.mdb.

To create an AccessDataSource control, open the Data group of the Toolbox, drag the AccessDataSource control, and drop it onto the form. Since the data source isn't displayed on the page when the application is run, it doesn't matter where you drop the data source on the page. However, if the data source is going to be bound to a web control, it makes sense to place it near that control.

When you drop the Access data source on the page, a smart tag menu will appear. Then, choose the Configure Data Source command to bring up the first page of the Configure Data Source wizard, which is shown in this figure. From this dialog box, select the Access database file you want to use for the data source.

Once you've selected the database file for the data source, you must configure the data source as described in the next figure. Then, you can bind it to the drop-down list as described in figure 3-12.

The Configure Data Source dialog box

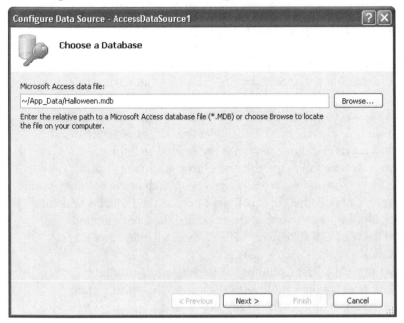

How to create an Access data source

1. In the Web Forms Designer, open the Data group of the Toolbox and drag the AccessDataSource control to the form.

2. Select Configure Data Source from the smart tag menu of the data source control to display the Configure Data Source dialog box.

3. Identify the Access database that you want to use in the App_Data folder and click Next. Then, complete the Configure Data Source wizard as described in the next figure.

Description

*   Before you can create an Access *data source*, you must add the Access database file to the App_Data folder.

*   The Shopping Cart application uses an AccessDataSource control to provide the list of products that's displayed in the drop-down list. This control reads data from a Micro Access database file.

*   Although data source controls are visible in the Web Forms Designer, they don't any HTML to the browser. As a result, they aren't visible when the application

Figure 3-10   How to create an Access data source

How to configure an Access data source

Figure 3-11 shows how to configure an Access data source using the Configure Data Source wizard. After the first page of this wizard lets you select the Access database file you want to use (as in the previous figure), the second page that's shown in this figure lets you specify the query that retrieves data from the database.

To create a query, you can code a SQL SELECT statement. Or, you can choose columns from a single table or view and let the wizard generate the SELECT statement for you. For now, we'll use the second technique.

To select columns from a table, use the Name drop-down list to select the table you want to select the columns from. Then, check each of the columns you want to retrieve in the Columns list. In this figure, I chose the Products table and selected six of the columns. As you check the columns, the Configuration wizard creates a SQL SELECT statement that's shown in the text box at the bottom of the dialog box.

The buttons to the right of the Columns list let you specify additional options for selecting data. If you want to select just rows that meet certain criteria, click the WHERE button, then specify the criteria you want. Or, if you want to specify a sort order, click the ORDER BY button, then choose the columns you want the data sorted by. In this figure, I used this button to specify that the data should be sorted on the Name column, so the SELECT statement includes an ORDER BY clause.

When you've finished specifying the data you want the data source to retrieve, click Next. This takes you to a page that includes a Test Query button. If you click this button, the Wizard immediately retrieves the data that you have specified. You can then look over this data to make sure it's what you expected. If it isn't, click the Back button and adjust the query as needed.

The Configure Data Source wizard

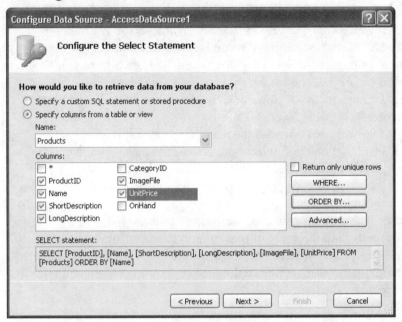

The aspx code for an Access data source control

```
<asp:AccessDataSource ID="AccessDataSource1" runat="server"
    DataFile="~/App_Data/Halloween.mdb"
    SelectCommand="SELECT [ProductID], [Name], [ShortDescription],
        [LongDescription], [ImageFile], [UnitPrice]
        FROM [Products] ORDER BY [Name]">
</asp:AccessDataSource>
```

Description

- The Configure Data Source wizard lets you create a query using SQL. You can specify the SELECT statement for the query directly or you can let the wizard construct the SELECT statement from your specifications.

- You can click the WHERE button to specify one or more conditions that will be used to select the records.

- You can click the ORDER BY button to specify a sort order for the records.

- You can click the Advanced button to include INSERT, UPDATE, and DELETE statements for the data source.

Figure 3-11   How to configure an Access data source

How to bind a drop-down list to a data source

Once you've created a data source, you can bind a drop-down list to it as shown in figure 3-12. To start, select the Choose Data Source command from the smart tag menu for the drop-down list. Then, when the Data Source Configuration Wizard is displayed, choose the data source in the first drop-down list. In this figure, I chose AccessDataSource1, the data source that I created in the previous figures.

Next, select the column that provides the data you want displayed in the drop-down list. The column that you select here is used for the drop-down list's DataTextField property. In this figure, I chose the Name column so the drop-down list displays the name of each product in the data source.

Finally, select the column that you want to use as the value of the item selected by the user. The column you select here is used for the list's DataValueField property, and the value of that column can be retrieved by using the list's SelectedValue property. In this figure, I selected the ProductID column. As a result, the program can use the SelectedValue property to determine the ID of the product selected by the user.

The Data Source Configuration Wizard dialog box

The aspx code for a drop-down list that's bound to a data source

```
<asp:DropDownList ID="ddlProducts" Runat="server" Width="150px"
    AutoPostBack="True"
    DataSourceID="AccessDataSource1"
    DataTextField="Name"
    DataValueField="ProductID" >
</asp:DropDownList>
```

Attributes for binding a drop-down list

Attribute	Description
DataSourceID	The ID of the data source that the drop-down list should be bound to.
DataTextField	The name of the data source field that should be displayed in the drop-down list.
DataValueField	The name of the data source field whose value should be returned by the SelectedValue property of the drop-down list.

Description

- You can bind a drop-down list to a data source so the list automatically displays data retrieved by the data source.
- You can use the Data Source Configuration Wizard dialog box to configure the data binding for a drop-down list. To display this dialog box, select the Choose Data Source command from the list's smart tag menu.
- Alternatively, you can use the Properties window or edit the aspx code directly to set the data binding attributes for a drop-down list.

Figure 3-12   How to bind a drop-down list to a data source

How to use Visual Basic code to get data from a data source

For the Shopping Cart application to work, it must retrieve the data for the product selected by the user from the drop-down list. Although there are several ways to do that, none of them are easy. One way is to create a second data source that queries the database again to retrieve the data for the selected product, and then use a special type of ASP.NET web control called a DetailsView control that is bound to this second data source. You'll learn how to do that in section 3.

A simpler way, though, is to write code that retrieves the product data from the existing Access data source. That's the technique that the Shopping Cart application uses. However, to make this work, you must contend with the classes, methods, and properties that are summarized in figure 3-13.

The example in this figure shows how to retrieve data from a row that matches the ProductID value returned by the SelectedValue property of the drop-down list. First, you use the Select method of the AccessDataSource class with the Empty argument to retrieve all of the rows from the underlying Access database. Then, because the return type of this method is IEnumerable, you must use the CType function to explicitly cast the returned object to a DataView object so you can use the methods of that class.

Once you have the rows in a DataView object, you can use the RowFilter property to filter the rows so only the row selected by the user is available. To do that, you build a simple *filter expression* that lists the column name and value. For example, ProductID='jar01' filters the data view so only the row whose ProductID column contains jar01 is included.

Once you've filtered the DataView object so only the selected row is available, you can use two indexes to retrieve the data for a column. The first index identifies the only row that has been selected, so its value is 0, and this row is returned as a DataRowView object. Then, you can specify the index of the column you want to retrieve from the row, either as a string that provides the column name or as the index position of the column. In this example, column names are used for the columns that need to be retrieved. (Although using an index value is a little more efficient, specifying the column name makes the code more understandable.)

Once you establish the row and column index for each value, all that remains is to cast this value to the appropriate type. In this example, all of the columns except the UnitPrice column are cast to strings using their ToString methods, and the UnitPrice column is cast to a decimal type using the CDec function.

Please note that all six of the values that are retrieved are stored in the Product object that's instantiated by the third statement in this example. If you want to review the code for this class, you can look ahead to figure 3-16. Also note that all of the casting in this example is done explicitly. Although that isn't required, a warning is displayed if you try to perform a narrowing conversion using an implicit cast. Because of that, I recommend that you always use an explicit cast to perform a narrowing conversion.

The Select method of the AccessDataSource class

Method	Description
`Select(selectOptions)`	Returns an IEnumerable object that contains the rows retrieved from the underlying Access database. To get all the rows, the selectOptions parameter should be DataSourceSelectArguments.Empty.

The DataView class

Property	Description
`RowFilter`	A string that is used to filter the rows retrieved from the Access database.
Indexer	**Description**
`(index)`	Returns a DataRowView object for the row at the specified index position.

The DataRowView class

Indexer	Description
`(index)`	Returns the value of the column at the specified index position as an object.
`(name)`	Returns the value of the column with the specified name as an object.

Code that gets product information for the selected product

```
Dim dvTable As DataView = CType(AccessDataSource1.Select( _
    DataSourceSelectArguments.Empty), DataView)
dvTable.RowFilter = "ProductID = '" & ddlProducts.SelectedValue & "'"
Dim drvRow As DataRowView = dvTable(0)
Dim Product As New Product
Product.ProductID = drvRow("ProductID").ToString
Product.Name = drvRow("Name").ToString
Product.ShortDescription = drvRow("ShortDescription").ToString
Product.LongDescription = drvRow("LongDescription").ToString
Product.UnitPrice = CDec(drvRow("UnitPrice"))
Product.ImageFile = drvRow("ImageFile").ToString
```

Description

- The Select method of the AccessDataSource class returns a DataView object that contains the rows retrieved from the Access database. Because the return type of this method is IEnumerable, you must convert the returned object to a DataView object.

- The RowFilter property of the DataView class lets you filter rows in the data view based on a criteria string.

- You can use the indexer of the DataView class to return a specific row as a DataRowView object. Then, you can use the indexer of the DataRowView class to return the value of a specified column. The indexer for the column can be an integer that represents the column's position in the row or a string that represents the name of the column.

Figure 3-13   How to use Visual Basic code to get data from a data source

How to use session state

In chapter 1, you learned that HTTP is a stateless protocol. You also learned that ASP.NET uses *session state* to keep track of each user session and that you can use session state to maintain program values across executions of an application. Now, you'll learn more about how session state works and how you use it.

How session state works

Figure 3-14 shows how session state solves the problem of state management for ASP.NET applications. As you can see, session state tracks individual user sessions by creating a *session state object* for each user's session. This object contains a session ID that uniquely identifies the session. This session ID is passed back to the browser along with the HTTP response. Then, if the browser makes another request, the session ID is included in the request so ASP.NET can identify the session. ASP.NET then matches the session with the session state object that was previously saved.

By default, ASP.NET sends the session ID to the browser as a *cookie*. Then, when the browser sends another request to the server, it automatically includes the cookie that contains the session ID with the request. In chapter 8, you'll learn more about how cookies work. You'll also learn how to implement session state by including the session ID in the URL for a page instead of in a cookie.

Although ASP.NET automatically uses session state to track user sessions, you can also use it to store your own data across executions of an application. This figure lists three typical reasons for doing that. First, you can use session state to maintain information about the user. After a user logs in to an application, for example, you can use the login information to retrieve information about the user from a file or a database. Then, you can store that information in the session state object so it's available each time the application is executed.

Second, you can use session state to save objects that the user is working with. For example, consider a maintenance application that lets the user change customer records. In that case, you can save the customer record that's currently being modified in the session state object so it's available the next time the application is executed.

Third, you can use session state to keep track of the operation a user is currently performing. If a maintenance application lets the user add or change customer records, for example, you can save an item in the session state object that indicates if the user is currently adding or changing a record. That way, the application can determine how to proceed each time it's executed.

How ASP.NET maintains the state of a session

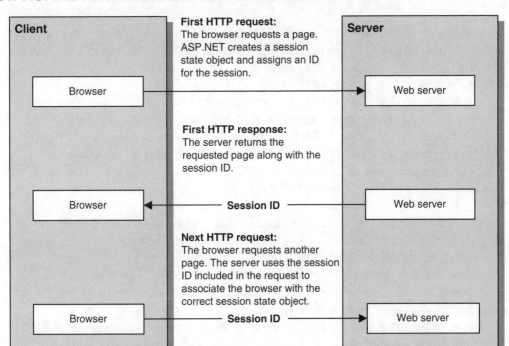

First HTTP request:
The browser requests a page. ASP.NET creates a session state object and assigns an ID for the session.

First HTTP response:
The server returns the requested page along with the session ID.

Next HTTP request:
The browser requests another page. The server uses the session ID included in the request to associate the browser with the correct session state object.

Description

- ASP.NET uses *session state* to track the state of each user of an application. To do that, it creates a *session state object*.

- The session state object includes a session ID that's sent back to the browser as a *cookie*. Then, the browser automatically returns the session ID cookie to the server with each request so the server can associate the browser with an existing session state object.

- If you want your application to work on browsers that don't support cookies, you can configure ASP.NET to encode the session ID in the URL for each page of the application. For more information, see chapter 8.

- You can use the session state object to store and retrieve items across executions of an application.

Typical uses for session state

- **To keep information about the user**, such as the user's name or whether the user has registered.

- **To save objects the user is working with**, such as a shopping cart or a customer record.

- **To keep track of pending operations**, such as what steps the user has completed while placing an order.

Figure 3-14   How session state works

How to work with data in session state

Figure 3-15 shows how you can use the session state object to store application data. To do that, you use the properties and methods of this object, which is created from the HttpSessionState class. To access this object from a web form, you use the Session property of the page.

The session state object contains a collection of items that consist of the item names and their values. One way to add an item to this collection is to use the Item property as shown in the first example. (In this case, since Item is the default property, it is omitted.) Here, an object named Cart is assigned to a session state item named Cart. If the Cart item doesn't exist when this statement is executed, it will be created. Otherwise, its value will be updated.

Another way to add an item to the session state collection is to use the Add method, as illustrated in the second example. Just as when you use the Item property, if the item already exists, it's updated when the Add method is executed. Otherwise, it's added to the collection.

You can also use the Item property to retrieve the value of an item from the session state collection as shown in the third example. Here, the value of the Cart item is retrieved and assigned to the Cart variable. Once again, you don't have to explicitly specify the Item property in this example because the Item property is the default property. However, because the value of a session state item is stored as an Object type, you typically convert it to the appropriate type. In this example, the value of the Cart item is converted to a sorted list because the Cart variable it's assigned to is defined as a sorted list.

Because the session state object uses valuable server memory, you should avoid using it to store large items. Or, if you must store large items in session state, you should remove the items as soon as you're done with them. To do that, you use the Remove method as illustrated in the fourth example in this figure.

The first four examples in this figure use the Session property of the page to access the session state object. Because Session is a property of the System.Web.UI.Page class, however, you can only use this property from a class that inherits the System.Web.UI.Page class. In other words, you can only use it from a code-behind file for a page. To access session state from a class that doesn't inherit the System.Web.UI.Page class, such as a database or business class, you use the Session property of the HttpContext object for the current request. To get this HttpContext object, you use the Current property of the HttpContext class as illustrated in the last example in this figure.

Common properties and methods of the HttpSessionState class

Property	Description
SessionID	The unique ID of the session.
Item(name)	The value of the session state item with the specified name. (Item is the default property of the HttpSessionState class, so you can omit it when you access a session state item.)
Count	The number of items in the session state collection.

Method	Description
Add(name, value)	Adds an item to the session state collection.
Clear	Removes all items from the session state collection.
Remove(name)	Removes the item with the specified name from the session state collection.

A statement that adds or updates a session state item

```
Session("Cart") = Cart
```

Another way to add or update a session state item

```
Session.Add("Cart", Cart)
```

A statement that retrieves the value of a session state item

```
Dim Cart As SortedList = CType(Session("Cart"), SortedList)
```

A statement that removes an item from session state

```
Session.Remove("Cart")
```

A statement that retrieves the value of a session state item from a class that doesn't inherit System.Web.UI.Page

```
Dim Cart As SortedList = CType(HttpContext.Current.Session("Cart"), _
                        SortedList)
```

Description

- The session state object is created from the HttpSessionState class, which defines a collection of session state items.

- To access the session state object from the code-behind file for a web form, use the Session property of the page.

- To access the session state object from a class other than the code-behind file for a web form, use the Current property of the HttpContext class to get the HttpContext object for the current request. This object contains information about the HTTP request. Then, use the Session property of the HttpContext class to get the session state object.

- By default, session state objects are maintained in server memory. As a result, you should avoid storing large items in session state.

Figure 3-15   How to work with data in session state

The code for the Shopping Cart application

Now that you've learned the basic skills for developing a multi-form application, you're ready to see all the aspx and Visual Basic code for the Shopping Cart application. Because you should be able to follow it without much trouble, I'll keep the descriptions to a minimum.

The code for the Product and CartItem classes

Figure 3-16 shows the Visual Basic code for the Product and CartItem classes. The Product class, which represents a product, has public fields for each of the columns in the Products table except CategoryID and OnHand.

The CartItem class, which represents one item in the shopping cart, has two public fields that hold the Product object and quantity for each item. In addition, the Display method returns a string that formats this data so it can be displayed in one line of the list box on the Cart page.

The aspx code for the Order page

Figure 3-17 shows the aspx code for the Order page, which is shown in its rendered form in figure 3-1. Since all of the code for this page is generated by the Web Forms Designer, you don't have to code any of it. To make it easier to follow this code, I highlighted the start tag and ID attribute for each of the server controls that appear on this page.

The first group of four controls defines an image that's used for the banner, a label with the text "Please select a product:", a drop-down list named ddlProducts, and the Access data source that the drop-down list is bound to. Here, the AutoPostBack attribute for the drop-down list is set to True so the page will be posted back to the server when the user selects a product. In addition, the DataSourceID, DataTextField, and DataValueField attributes specify how the drop-down list is bound to the Access data source.

The second group of server controls displays product information using several labels and an image control. A table is used to manage the layout of these controls so the image can be displayed to the right of the labels.

The third group of server controls defines a label with the text "Quantity:" followed by a text box named txtQuantity. Then, two validator controls provide data validation for the text box. Notice that both specify txtQuantity in the ControlToValidate attribute and Dynamic in the Display attribute. The range validator also provides Maximum, Minimum, and Type attributes, which specify that the quantity must be an integer in the range from 1 to 500.

The last group of controls for this page are the two buttons. Here, the btnCart button uses the PostBackUrl property to indicate that when the user clicks the button, the Cart.aspx page should be requested rather than the Order.aspx page. Since the CausesValidation attribute is set to False, the validation controls for the txtQuantity text box won't be executed when this button is clicked.

The code for the Product class

```
Imports Microsoft.VisualBasic

Public Class Product
    Public ProductID As String
    Public Name As String
    Public ShortDescription As String
    Public LongDescription As String
    Public UnitPrice As Decimal
    Public ImageFile As String
End Class
```

The code for the CartItem class

```
Imports Microsoft.VisualBasic

Public Class CartItem
    Public Product As Product
    Public Quantity As Integer

    Public Function Display() As String
        Return Product.Name & " (" & Quantity.ToString() _
            & " at " & FormatCurrency(Product.UnitPrice) & " each)"
    End Function
End Class
```

Description

- The Product class represents a product.
- The CartItem class represents a product that the user has added to the shopping cart plus the quantity ordered.

Figure 3-16   The code for the Product and CartItem classes

The aspx file for the Order page (Order.aspx)   Page 1

```
<%@ Page Language="VB" AutoEventWireup="false" CodeFile="Order.aspx.vb"
Inherits="Order" %>

<!DOCTYPE html PUBLIC "-//W3C//DTD XHTML 1.0 Transitional//EN"
"http://www.w3.org/TR/xhtml1-transitional/DTD/xhtml1-transitional.dtd">

<html xmlns="http://www.w3.org/1999/xhtml" >
<head runat="server">
    <title>Chapter 3: Shopping Cart</title>
</head>
<body>
    <form id="form1" runat="server">
    <div>
        <asp:Image ID="Image1" runat="server"
           ImageUrl="~/Images/banner.jpg" /><br /><br />
        <asp:Label ID="Label1" runat="server"
           Text="Please select a product:"></asp:Label>
        <asp:DropDownList ID="ddlProducts" runat="server" Width = "150px"
           DataSourceID="AccessDataSource1" DataTextField="Name"
           DataValueField="ProductID" AutoPostBack="True">
        </asp:DropDownList>
        <asp:AccessDataSource ID="AccessDataSource1" runat="server"
           DataFile="~/App_Data/Halloween.mdb"
           SelectCommand="SELECT [ProductID], [Name], [ShortDescription],
              [LongDescription], [ImageFile], [UnitPrice]
              FROM [Products] ORDER BY [Name]">
        </asp:AccessDataSource>
        <br />
        <table>
            <tr >
                <td style="width: 250px; height: 22px">
                    <asp:Label ID="lblName" runat="server"
                       Font-Bold="false" Font-Size="Larger">
                    </asp:Label>
                </td>
                <td style="width: 20px" rowspan="4">
                </td>
                <td rowspan="4" valign="top">
                    <asp:Image ID="imgProduct" runat="server" Height="200" />
                </td>
            </tr>
            <tr>
                <td style="width: 250px">
                    <asp:Label ID="lblShortDescription" runat="server">
                    </asp:Label>
                </td>
            </tr>
```

Description

- The Order.aspx page displays a drop-down list that is bound to an Access data source.

- A table is used to specify the layout of the labels and image controls that display information about the product selected by the user.

Figure 3-17   The aspx code for the Order page (part 1 of 2)

The aspx file for the Order page (Order.aspx)   Page 2

```
            <tr>
                <td style="width: 250px">
                    <asp:Label ID="lblLongDescription" runat="server">
                    </asp:Label>
                </td>
            </tr>
            <tr>
                <td style="width: 250px">
                    <asp:Label ID="lblUnitPrice" runat="server"
                        Font-Bold="true" Font-Size="Larger">
                    </asp:Label>
                    <asp:Label ID="Label2" runat="server" Text="each"
                        Font-Bold="true" Font-Size="Larger">
                    </asp:Label>
                </td>
            </tr>
        </table>
        <br />
        <asp:Label ID="Label3" runat="server" Text="Quantity:"
            Width="80px" BorderWidth = "0px"></asp:Label>
        <asp:TextBox ID="txtQuantity" runat="server" Width="80px">
        </asp:TextBox>
        <asp:RequiredFieldValidator ID="RequiredFieldValidator1"
            runat="server" ControlToValidate="txtQuantity" Display="Dynamic"
            ErrorMessage="Quantity is a required field.">
        </asp:RequiredFieldValidator>
        <asp:RangeValidator ID="RangeValidator1" runat="server"
            ControlToValidate="txtQuantity" Display="Dynamic"
            ErrorMessage="Quantity must range from 1 to 500."
            MaximumValue="500" MinimumValue="1" Type="Integer">
        </asp:RangeValidator><br /><br />
        <asp:Button ID="btnAdd" runat="server" Text="Add to Cart" /> 
        <asp:Button ID="btnCart" runat="server" CausesValidation="False"
            PostBackUrl="~/Cart.aspx" Text="Go to Cart" />
    </div>
    </form>
</body>
</html>
```

Description

- The txtQuantity text box lets the user enter the order quantity of the selected item. A RequiredFieldValidator and a RangeValidator are used to ensure that the user enters valid data in this text box.

- The btnCart button uses cross-page posting to post to the Cart.aspx page.

Figure 3-17   The aspx code for the Order page (part 2 of 2)

The Visual Basic code for the Order page

Figure 3-18 presents the code for the Order page's code-behind file, Order.aspx.vb. This code starts by declaring a module-level variable that will hold a Product object that represents the item that the user has selected from the drop-down list. This variable is assigned a Product object by the second statement in the Page_Load procedure, which gets the Product object by calling the GetSelectedProduct function.

The Page_Load procedure starts by calling the DataBind method of the drop-down list if the page is being loaded for the first time (IsPostBack isn't True). This method binds the drop-down list to the Access data source, which causes the data specified in the SelectCommand property of the data source to be retrieved. Then, this procedure calls the GetSelectedProduct function, which gets the data for the selected product from the Access data source and returns a Product object. That object is stored in the SelectedProduct variable, which is available to all of the other procedures in this class. Finally, the Page_Load procedure formats the labels and the image control to display the data for the selected product. At that point, the Order page is sent back to the user's browser.

For many applications, you don't need to call the DataBind method in the Page_Load procedure when you use data binding. Instead, you let ASP.NET automatically bind any data-bound controls. Unfortunately, this automatic data binding doesn't occur until after the Page_Load procedure has been executed. In this case, because the GetSelectedProduct procedure won't work unless the drop-down list has already been bound, I had to call the DataBind method to force the data binding to occur earlier than it normally would.

The code-behind file for the Order page (Order.aspx.vb)   Page 1

```vb
Imports System.Data

Partial Class Order
    Inherits System.Web.UI.Page

    Private SelectedProduct As Product

    Protected Sub Page_Load(ByVal sender As Object, _
            ByVal e As System.EventArgs) Handles Me.Load
        If Not IsPostBack Then
            ddlProducts.DataBind()
        End If
        SelectedProduct = Me.GetSelectedProduct()
        lblName.Text = SelectedProduct.Name
        lblShortDescription.Text = SelectedProduct.ShortDescription
        lblLongDescription.Text = SelectedProduct.LongDescription
        lblUnitPrice.Text = FormatCurrency(SelectedProduct.UnitPrice)
        imgProduct.ImageUrl = "Images\Products\" _
            & SelectedProduct.ImageFile
    End Sub

    Private Function GetSelectedProduct() As Product
        Dim dvTable As DataView = CType(AccessDataSource1.Select( _
            DataSourceSelectArguments.Empty), DataView)
        dvTable.RowFilter = "ProductID = '" & ddlProducts.SelectedValue & "'"
        Dim drvRow As DataRowView = dvTable(0)

        Dim Product As New Product
        Product.ProductID = drvRow("ProductID").ToString
        Product.Name = drvRow("Name").ToString
        Product.ShortDescription = drvRow("ShortDescription").ToString
        Product.LongDescription = drvRow("LongDescription").ToString
        Product.UnitPrice = CDec(drvRow("UnitPrice"))
        Product.ImageFile = drvRow("ImageFile").ToString
        Return Product
    End Function
End Function
```

Description

- The Page_Load procedure binds the drop-down list if the page is not being posted back to itself. Then, it calls the GetSelectedProduct procedure to get a Product object for the selected product. Finally, it sets the label and image controls to display the information for the selected product.
- The GetSelectedProduct procedure extracts the data for the selected product from the data source. Then, it uses this data to create a Product object.

Figure 3-18   The Visual Basic code for the Order page (part 1 of 2)

If the user clicks the Add to Cart button, the btnAdd_Click procedure is executed. It starts by creating a new instance of the CartItem class named CartItem. Next, it sets the item's Product field to the Product object that's stored in the SelectedProduct variable, and it sets the Quantity field to the value entered by the user. Then, it calls the AddToCart procedure to add the CartItem object to the user's shopping cart, which is a SortedList object. Finally, it uses Response.Redirect to go to the Cart.aspx page.

The AddToCart procedure declares a SortedList variable named Cart and calls the GetCart procedure to retrieve the shopping cart from Session state. If you look at the GetCart procedure, you'll see that it first checks to see if a Session state item named "Cart" is equal to Nothing. If it is, which means that a cart hasn't yet been created for the current user, a new shopping cart is created and added to Session state. Then, the GetCart procedure returns the shopping cart to the AddToCart procedure as a SortedList object.

After the shopping cart list has been returned, the AddToCart procedure determines whether the list already contains an entry for the selected product. To do that, it uses the ContainsKey method of a SortedList object to look for a cart entry with the product ID of the product. If an entry is found with this product ID, the quantity the user entered is added to the existing quantity for this item. Otherwise, the Add method for the SortedList object that represents the shopping cart is used to add the cart item to the shopping cart with the product's ID as the key.

The code-behind file for the Order page (Order.aspx.vb)   **Page 2**

```vb
Protected Sub btnAdd_Click(ByVal sender As Object, _
        ByVal e As System.EventArgs) Handles btnAdd.Click
    If Page.IsValid Then
        Dim CartItem As New CartItem
        CartItem.Product = SelectedProduct
        CartItem.Quantity = CType(txtQuantity.Text, Integer)
        Me.AddToCart(CartItem)
        Response.Redirect("Cart.aspx")
    End If
End Sub

Private Sub AddToCart(ByVal CartItem As CartItem)
    Dim Cart As SortedList = GetCart()
    Dim sProductID As String = SelectedProduct.ProductID
    If Cart.ContainsKey(sProductID) Then
        CartItem = CType(Cart(sProductID), CartItem)
        CartItem.Quantity += CType(txtQuantity.Text, Integer)
    Else
        Cart.Add(sProductID, CartItem)
    End If
End Sub

Private Function GetCart() As SortedList
    If Session("Cart") Is Nothing Then
        Session.Add("Cart", New SortedList)
    End If
    Return CType(Session("Cart"), SortedList)

End Function
End Class
```

Description

- The btnAdd_Click procedure is called when the user clicks the Add button. It creates a CartItem object, then calls the AddToCart procedure to add the item to the shopping cart.

- The AddToCart procedure calls the GetCart procedure to get the shopping cart from session state. Then, it checks to see if the shopping cart already contains an item for the selected product. If so, the item's quantity is incremented. If not, the CartItem object is added to the shopping cart.

- The GetCart procedure retrieves the shopping cart from session state. If session state doesn't contain a cart, a cart is created and added to session state.

Figure 3-18   The Visual Basic code for the Order page (part 2 of 2)

The aspx code for the Cart page

Figure 3-19 shows the aspx code for the second page of the Shopping Cart application, Cart.aspx, which is rendered in figure 3-2. Once again, I've highlighted the start of each tag that defines a server control.

Here, the shopping cart is a ListBox control within an HTML table that allows the Remove and Empty buttons to be displayed to the right of the list box. The Continue button uses the PostBackUrl attribute to return to the Order.aspx page. And the lblMessage label is used to display a message when the user clicks the Check Out button. Like the Order page, this page also contains an image control that defines the image that's displayed in the banner.

The Visual Basic code for the Cart page

Figure 3-20 presents the code-behind file for the Cart page. This code starts by declaring a module-level variable that will hold the SortedList object for the shopping cart. Then, each time the page is loaded, the Page_Load procedure calls the GetCart procedure to retrieve the shopping cart from session state and store it in this variable.

If the page is being loaded for the first time, the Page_Load procedure also calls the DisplayCart procedure. This procedure starts by clearing the list box that will display the shopping cart items. Then, it uses a For Each…Next loop to add an item to the list box for each item in the shopping cart list.

To understand this loop, remember that each item in a sorted list is a DictionaryEntry object that consists of a key and a value. Here, the key is the product ID, the value is a CartItem object, and the first line in the body of the loop uses the Value property to retrieve the CartItem object for that entry. However, because the Value property returns an Object type, it must be explicitly cast to CartItem to assign the value to the CartItem variable.

If the user clicks the Remove button, the btnRemove_Click procedure is executed. This procedure begins by making sure that an item in the shopping cart list box is selected and that the cart contains at least one item. If so, the selected item is deleted from the shopping cart. Then, the DisplayCart procedure is called to add the cart items to the list box again, but without the deleted item.

If the user clicks the Empty button, the btnEmpty_Click procedure is executed. This procedure clears the shopping cart and the shopping cart list box. Please note, though, that instead of clearing the list box by calling the Items.Clear method, this procedure could call the DisplayCart procedure. Similarly, the btnRemove_Click procedure could use the Items.Remove method of the list box to remove the item at the selected index instead of calling the DisplayCart procedure. This just shows that there is usually more than one way that procedures like these can be coded.

Note that there is no procedure for the Click event of the Continue button. That's because the Continue button uses the PostBackUrl property to post directly to the Order.aspx page. As a result, the Cart page isn't executed if the user clicks the Continue button.

The aspx file for the Cart page (Cart.aspx)

```
<%@ Page Language="VB" AutoEventWireup="false" CodeFile="Cart.aspx.vb"
Inherits="Cart" %>

<!DOCTYPE html PUBLIC "-//W3C//DTD XHTML 1.0 Transitional//EN"
"http://www.w3.org/TR/xhtml1-transitional/DTD/xhtml1-transitional.dtd">

<html xmlns="http://www.w3.org/1999/xhtml" >
<head runat="server">
    <title>Chapter 3: Shopping Cart</title>
</head>
<body>
    <form id="form1" runat="server">
    <div>
        <asp:Image ID="Image1" runat="server"
            ImageUrl="~/Images/banner.jpg" /><br /><br />
        Your shopping cart:<br />
        <table style="width: 500px" cellspacing="0"
                cellpadding="0" border="0">
            <tr>
                <td style="width: 286px; height: 153px">
                    <asp:ListBox ID="lstCart" runat="server"
                        Width="267px" Height="135px"></asp:ListBox>
                </td>
                <td style="height: 153px">
                    <asp:Button ID="btnRemove" runat="server"
                        Width="100px" Text="Remove Item" /><br /><br />
                    <asp:Button ID="btnEmpty" runat="server"
                        Width="100px" Text="Empty Cart" />
                </td>
            </tr>
        </table>
        <br />
        <asp:Button ID="btnContinue" runat="server"
            PostBackUrl="~/Order.aspx" Text="Continue Shopping" /> 
        <asp:Button ID="btnCheckOut" runat="server" Text="Check Out" /><br />
        <br />
        <asp:Label ID="lblMessage" runat="server"></asp:Label>
    </div>
    </form>
</body>
</html>
```

Description

- The Cart.aspx page uses a list box to display the shopping cart.
- The btnContinue button uses cross-page posting to post back to the Order.aspx page.

Figure 3-19   The aspx code for the Cart page

The code-behind file for the Cart page (Cart.aspx.vb)   **Page 1**

```
Partial Class Cart
    Inherits System.Web.UI.Page

    Private Cart As SortedList

    Protected Sub Page_Load(ByVal sender As Object, _
            ByVal e As System.EventArgs) Handles Me.Load
        Cart = GetCart()
        If Not IsPostBack Then
            Me.DisplayCart()
        End If
    End Sub

    Private Function GetCart() As SortedList
        If Session("Cart") Is Nothing Then
            Session.Add("Cart", New SortedList)
        End If
        Return CType(Session("Cart"), SortedList)
    End Function

    Private Sub DisplayCart()
        lstCart.Items.Clear()
        Dim CartItem As CartItem
        Dim CartEntry As DictionaryEntry
        For Each CartEntry In Cart
            CartItem = CType(CartEntry.Value, CartItem)
            lstCart.Items.Add(CartItem.Display)
        Next
    End Sub
```

Description

- Each time the page is loaded, the Page_Load procedure calls the GetCart procedure to get the shopping cart, which is a SortedList object, from session state. This object is then stored in the SortedList variable named Cart.

- The GetCart procedure retrieves the SortedList object for the shopping cart from session state. But if session state doesn't contain a cart, a cart is created and added to session state.

- If IsPostBack is False in the Page_Load procedure, it calls the DisplayCart procedure to add the shopping cart items to the list box.

- Each item in a SortedList object is a DictionaryEntry object that consists of a key and value. In the DisplayCart procedure, the key is the product ID, the value is a CartItem object, and the first line in the body of the loop uses the Value property of the DictionaryEntry object to retrieve the CartItem object for that entry.

- Because the Value property of a DictionaryEntry object returns an Object type, that object must be converted from an Object type to a CartItem type before it can be stored in the CartItem object. Then, the last line of the loop in the DisplayCart method uses the Display method of the CartItem object to create a string that is added to the list box.

Figure 3-20   The Visual Basic code for the Cart page (part 1 of 2)

The code-behind file for the Cart page (Cart.aspx.vb)   **Page 2**

```
Protected Sub btnRemove_Click(ByVal sender As Object, _
        ByVal e As System.EventArgs) Handles btnRemove.Click
    If lstCart.SelectedIndex > -1 And Cart.Count > 0 Then
        Cart.RemoveAt(lstCart.SelectedIndex)
        Me.DisplayCart()
    End If
End Sub

Protected Sub btnEmpty_Click(ByVal sender As Object, _
        ByVal e As System.EventArgs) Handles btnEmpty.Click
    Cart.Clear()
    lstCart.Items.Clear()
    lblMessage.Text = ""
End Sub

Protected Sub btnCheckOut_Click(ByVal sender As Object, _
        ByVal e As System.EventArgs) Handles btnCheckOut.Click
    lblMessage.Text = "Sorry, that function hasn't been implemented yet."
End Sub
End Class
```

Description

- The btnRemove_Click procedure is called when the user clicks the Remove Item button. It removes the selected item, then calls the DisplayCart procedure to redisplay the shopping cart.

- The btnEmpty_Cart procedure is called when the user clicks the Empty Cart item. It clears the sorted list for the shopping cart as well as the list box.

- The btnCheckOut_Click procedure is called when the user clicks the Check Out button. It displays a message to indicate that the check out function hasn't been implemented yet.

- There isn't any procedure for the Click event of the Continue Shopping button because it uses cross-page posting to go to the Order page.

Figure 3-20   The Visual Basic code for the Cart page (part 2 of 2)

Perspective

The purpose of this chapter has been to get you started with the development of multi-page web applications. Now, if this chapter has worked, you should be able to develop simple multi-page applications of your own. Yes, there's a lot more to learn, but you should be off to a good start.

Frankly, though, much of the Visual Basic code in the Shopping Cart application is difficult, even in a simple application like this one. So if your experience with Visual Basic is limited, you may have trouble understanding some of the code. And you may have trouble writing the same type of code for your new applications.

If that's the case, we recommend that you get our latest Visual Basic book. It will quickly get you up to speed with the Visual Basic language. It will show you how to use dozens of the .NET classes, like the SortedList class. It will show you how to develop Windows applications. It is a terrific on-the-job reference. And it is the perfect companion to this book, which assumes that you already know Visual Basic.

Terms

HTTP redirect message
cross-page posting
absolute URL
relative URL
data source
session state
session state object
cookie

4

How to test and debug an ASP.NET application

If you've done much programming, you know that testing and debugging are often the most difficult and time-consuming phase of program development. Fortunately, Visual Studio includes an integrated debugger that can help you locate and correct even the most obscure bugs. And ASP.NET includes a Trace feature that displays useful information as your ASP.NET pages execute.

In this chapter, you'll learn how to use both of these powerful debugging tools. But first, you'll learn how to create web sites that run under IIS so that you can test them with that web server, and you'll learn how to test an application to determine if it works properly.

How to create ASP.NET web sites that run under IIS

In chapter 2, you learned how to create a file-system web site that runs under the ASP.NET Development Server. If you have access to an IIS web server, though, you may want to create a web site that runs under IIS so you can test the web site in that environment. Or, you may want to create and test a file-system web site with the ASP.NET Development Server first, and then test it under IIS later.

How to create a local IIS web site

A local IIS web site is a web site that resides on your local computer. To create a local IIS web site, then, you must have IIS installed on your computer. Please see appendix A for information on how to install IIS.

Figure 4-1 illustrates how you create a local IIS web site. To start, you select HTTP for the location option in the New Web Site dialog box (see the next figure). Then, you typically click the Browse button to display the Choose Location dialog box shown in this figure.

In the Choose Location dialog box, you can click the Local IIS button at the left side of the dialog box to display the IIS web server. Then, you can select the directory where you want to create your web site. In this case, I selected the ASPNET2005 directory. Then, I clicked the Create New Web Application button to create a new web site named Ch03Cart in that directory.

When you use this technique, the files for the web site are stored within the directory you create. If that's not what you want, you can create a *virtual directory* that points to the directory where the files for the web site will be stored. To do that, just click the Create New Virtual Directory button in the Choose Location dialog box. Then, a dialog box is displayed that lets you enter a name for the virtual directory and the path where the files for the web site should be stored. In the dialog box shown in this figure, for example, the virtual directory will be named Ch03Cart, and the files will be stored in a directory with the same name within the ASP.NET 2.0 Web Sites directory on the C drive.

In addition to using the New Virtual Directory dialog box to create a virtual directory for a new web site, you can also use it to create a virtual directory for a file-system web site you've already created. To do that, just enter the path for the existing web site in this dialog box. Then, when you click the OK button in the New Web Site dialog box, Visual Studio will warn you that there is already a web site at the location you specified. To create a virtual directory that points to the existing web site, select the Open the Existing Web Site option.

Before I go on, you should realize that you can also create a virtual directory for a file-system web site using the IIS Management Console. If you're interested, you can learn how to do that in appendix A. Unless you need to change the default permissions for a virtual directory, though, I recommend that you create the virtual directory from within Visual Studio.

The dialog box for selecting a local IIS web site

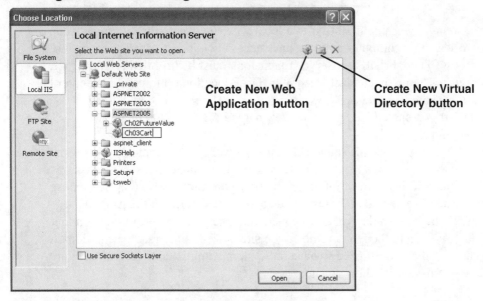

The dialog box for creating a virtual directory

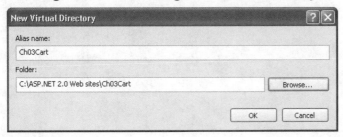

Description

- To create a web site that will run under IIS on your local computer, select HTTP for the location option in the New Web Site dialog box. Then, enter the path of the IIS directory where you want to create the web site, or click the Browse button to display the Choose Location dialog box.

- From the Choose Location dialog box, click the Local IIS button and expand the Default Web Site node. Then, select the directory where you want to create the web site from the default web site and click the Open button, or create a new directory or virtual directory.

- To create a new IIS directory for a web site, click the Create New Web Application button and then enter the name of the directory. The files for the web site will be stored in this directory.

- To create a *virtual directory* for the web site, click the Create New Virtual Directory button to display the New Virtual Directory dialog box. Enter a name for the directory and the path where you want to store the files for the web site. If the path you specify already contains a web site, you can open that web site from the virtual directory.

Figure 4-1   How to create a local IIS web site

How to create a remote IIS web site

A remote web site is similar to a local web site except that a remote web site resides on a computer that you have access to over a LAN. To create this type of web site, FrontPage Server Extensions must be installed on the remote computer. Then, you can just select the HTTP location option and then enter the location of the web site as shown in figure 4-2. Here, a web site named Ch03Cart is being created in a directory named ASPNET2005 on a server named mma1.

Although you use the same techniques to work with a remote web site as you use to work with a local web site, you should realize that the permissions for a remote web site may not be set the way you want. For example, suppose you create a web site that writes to a text file that's stored in the App_Data folder of the site. To do that, the web site must have write permissions on that folder. By default, though, a remote web site is given only read permissions. Because of that, you'll need to have the system administrator assign the appropriate permissions to the web site.

The dialog box for creating a remote IIS web site

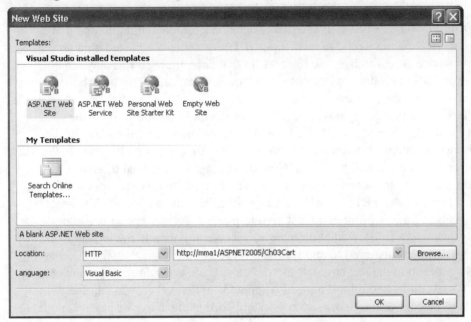

Description

- To create a remote web site, select HTTP from the Location drop-down list. Then, enter the URL of the web site you want to create.

- You can also create a remote web site by clicking the Browse button and then using the Choose Location dialog box that's displayed for a remote site. However, this dialog box doesn't provide any additional options.

- By default, a web application that you create on a remote server doesn't have the permissions needed to change files in the web site at runtime. If an application needs to change a file, then, you'll need to contact the system administrator about giving it the appropriate permissions.

- Visual Studio communicates with a web site on a remote server using HTTP and FrontPage Server Extensions. Because of that, FPSE must be installed on the remote server. For information on how to install FPSE, see appendix A.

Figure 4-2   How to create a remote IIS web site

How to create an FTP web site

An FTP web site is a web site that resides on a remote computer and that supports FTP file transfers. In most cases, FTP web sites are hosted on a server that you have access to over the Internet. In that case, the web site may already be set up for you. If not, you can use the Choose Location dialog box shown in figure 4-3 to create a new web site.

To display this dialog box, select FTP for the location option from the New Web Site dialog box, and click the Browse button. Then, enter the name of the server where you want to create the site and the path to the directory where the files for the web site will be stored. Note that except for the final directory, all the directories in the directory path must already exist. In this example, that means that the Murach directory must already exist. That's because this directory maps to a *virtual root* that must be set up on the server. The virtual root works much like an IIS virtual directory. However, it points to the location where files are transferred to and from the server.

In addition to the server name and directory path, you can specify the port that Visual Studio should use to send commands to the server, you can specify whether the connection to the server is established using active or passive mode, and you can specify whether you're logged in as an anonymous user or an authenticated user. In most cases, you'll leave the port set at 21. However, you may need to change the Passive Mode and Anonymous Login options.

By default, Visual Studio uses *active mode* to establish a connection with the FTP server. To understand how active mode works, you need to realize that two ports are required to use FTP: one to transmit commands and one to transmit data. In active mode, Visual Studio connects to the server using the command port and then passes the address of the data port to be used to the server. Then, the server connects to Visual Studio using the data port.

The problem with using active mode is that if the client computer is behind a firewall, the server probably won't be able to connect to it. In that case, you can connect to the server using *passive mode*. With passive mode, Visual Studio establishes the connections for both the command port and the data port. To use passive mode, just select the Passive Mode option.

In some cases, an FTP server will require that you provide a username and password to connect to the server. Then, you'll need to remove the check mark from the Anonymous Login option and enter the required information in the Username and Password text boxes that become available. Note that because this information is saved until you end Visual Studio, you only need to enter it the first time you connect to the server during a Visual Studio session.

After you enter the required information into the Choose Location dialog box, you click the Open button to return to the New Web Site dialog box. When you do, the location will look something like this:

```
ftp://Murach/Ch03Cart
```

Then, you can just click the OK button to create the web site.

The dialog box for creating an FTP web site

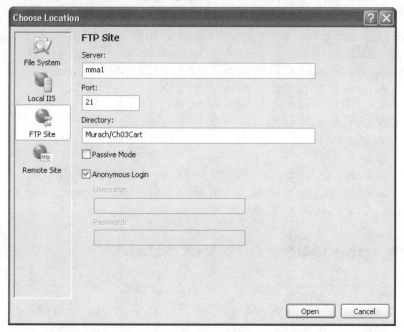

Description

- To create a new FTP web site, select FTP from the Location drop-down list in the New Web Site dialog box. Then, click the Browse button to display the Choose Location dialog box shown above.

- Enter the name of the server and the directory where you want to create the web site. You can typically leave the port set at 21.

- Visual Studio can use either *active mode* or *passive mode* to establish connections to the FTP server. Active mode is the default. If the client is behind a firewall, though, you may need to use passive mode. To do that, select the Passive Mode option.

- By default, Visual Studio logs you in to the FTP server as an anonymous user. However, some FTP servers require you to provide a username and password. In that case, you can deselect the Anonymous Login option and then enter your username and password. The username and password are saved until you end the Visual Studio session.

- If you try to create a new FTP web site by entering a URL in the New Web Site dialog box, Visual Studio will display a dialog box that lets you specify whether you want to use passive mode and whether you want to log in as an anonymous user.

- IIS can be configured to act as an FTP server as well as a web server. For more information, please see appendix A.

Figure 4-3   How to create an FTP web site

How to test an ASP.NET application

To test an ASP.NET application, you typically start by running it from within Visual Studio so that you can locate and correct any errors you encounter. This initial testing uses the default browser and, if you're working with a file-system web site, the ASP.NET Development Server. Next, you test the application with other web browsers to make sure it works with them as well, and you test a file-system web site under IIS. Finally, you run the application from outside of Visual Studio to be sure it will work correctly in a production environment.

You'll learn the techniques for performing all of these types of testing in the topics that follow. In addition, you'll learn how to use the Server Error page that's displayed if an error occurs while you're testing an application.

How to test an application with the default browser

Unless you've changed it, Visual Studio uses Internet Explorer as its default browser. Figure 4-4 presents six different ways you can run a web application with the default browser. Three of these techniques start the debugger so you can use its features to debug any problems that might arise. The other three techniques do not start the debugger.

The first time you run a web application using one of the first three techniques, Visual Studio displays a dialog box indicating that debugging isn't enabled in the web.config file. From this dialog box, you can choose to enable debugging, or you can choose to run the application without debugging. In most cases, you'll enable debugging so that you can use the debugger with your application.

Before I go on, you should realize that before you can run an application with debugging on a remote server, a program called the *Remote Debug Monitor* must be installed and running on the server. For information on how to set up this program, see the help topic "How to: Set Up Remote Debugging."

All of the techniques listed in this figure except the View in Browser command start the application and display the application's designated start page. However, the View in Browser command displays the selected page. For example, if you right-click the Cart page and choose View in Browser, the Cart page will be displayed. This command is most appropriate for making sure that the pages of an application look the way you want them to.

At this point, you should realize that the type of web site you're developing determines the web server that's used to run the application. For example, if you're developing a file-system web site, the ASP.NET Development Server is used to run the application. In that case, the URL for the page that's displayed identifies the server as "localhost:" followed by a number that's assigned by the development server. In contrast, if you're developing an IIS web site, IIS is used

The Order page displayed in the default browser

Three ways to run an application with debugging

- Click the Start Debugging button in the Standard toolbar
- Press F5
- Choose the Debug→Start command

Three ways to run an application without debugging

- Press Ctrl+F5
- Choose Debug→Start Without Debugging
- Right-click a page in the Solution Explorer and choose View in Browser.

Three ways to stop an application that's run with debugging

- Press Shift+F5
- Click the Stop Debugging button in the Debug toolbar
- Choose Debug→Stop Debugging

Description

- If you run an application with debugging, you can use Visual Studio's built-in debugger to find and correct program errors.
- By default, an application is run using Internet Explorer. See figure 4-5 for information on using a different browser. To end the application, close the browser.

Figure 4-4   How to test an application with the default browser

to run the application. Then, the server is identified as just "localhost" for a local web site or by its actual name for a remote or FTP web site.

You should also realize that you can't just run an FTP application from its FTP location. That's because this location is used only to transfer files to and from the server. Instead, a *browse location* must be set up for the web site. A browse location is simply an IIS virtual directory that points to the directory that stores the files for the web site. Then, to access and run the web site, you enter the HTTP URL for the virtual directory. The first time you run an FTP web site, you will be asked to enter this URL. Because the URL is stored as part of the web site, you won't need to enter it again.

How to test an application with a browser other than the default

Once you've thoroughly tested your application with Internet Explorer, you'll want to test it with other browsers to make sure it works as expected. Figure 4-5 describes two ways to do that. First, you can right-click the starting page for the application in the Solution Explorer and choose the Browse With command. This displays a Browse With dialog box like the one shown in this figure. From this dialog box, you can choose the browser you want to use and then click the Browse button.

Notice that the list of browsers in the Browse With dialog box includes the Internal Web Browser. If you choose this browser, the page is displayed in a Browse window within Visual Studio. You can test the application from this browser just as you would from any other browser. Then, when you're done with the browse operation, just close the Browse window.

You can also test an application with another browser by making that browser the default browser. To do that, right-click any page in the Solution Explorer and choose Browse With. Next, select the browser you want to designate as your default browser and click the Set As Default button. Then, click the Cancel button to close the Browse With dialog box. You can then use any of the techniques listed in figure 4-4 to start the application in the browser you selected. Note that setting a browser as the default is the only way to use the debugger with the browser. That's because the Browse With command runs an application without debugging.

Sometimes, the browser you want to test an application with doesn't appear in the Browse With dialog box even though it's installed on your computer. In most cases, that's because you installed the browser after installing Visual Studio. Then, you can add the browser by clicking the Add button in the Browse With dialog box to display the Add Program dialog box. This dialog box lets you locate the executable file for the browser you want to add and enter a "friendly" name that's used for the browser in the Browse With dialog box.

The Browse With dialog box

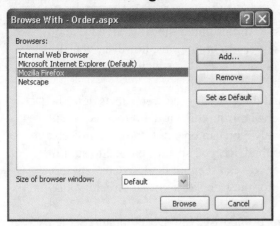

Two ways to test an application with a browser other than the default

- Right-click the starting page for the application in the Solution Explorer and choose Browse With from the shortcut menu. In the Browse With dialog box that's displayed, select the browser you want to use and click the Browse button.

- Select the browser you want to use in the Browse With dialog box and then click the Set as Default button to make that browser the default. The next time you run the application, it will be displayed in the browser you selected.

Description

- It's important to test an ASP.NET application in any browsers that might be used to run the application.

- If a browser isn't included in the list of available browsers, you can add it to the list by clicking the Add button in the Browse With dialog box and then using the Add Program dialog box that's displayed to add the desired browser.

- If you select the Internal Web Browser option, the page is displayed in a Browse window within Visual Studio. To end the browse operation from this window, just close the window.

- You'll need to change the default browser if you want to use the debugger with another browser, since the Browse With command starts the application without debugging.

Figure 4-5   How to test an application with a browser other than the default

How to test a file-system web site with IIS

When you run a file-system web site, it runs under the ASP.NET Development Server by default. Because this server has limitations, however, you'll want to be sure to test a file-system web site under IIS as well as under the development server. Figure 4-6 describes how you do that.

To start, you need to create a virtual directory for the web site as described in figure 4-1. Then, if you open the web site from this virtual directory, it will automatically run under IIS. Alternatively, you can open the file-system web site directly and change its start options so the URL you specify is used to start the application. In this figure, for example, you can see that the Use Custom Server option has been selected and the URL for the web site's virtual directory has been entered in the Base URL text box.

This figure also lists the limitations of the ASP.NET Development Server. The most significant of these limitations is that it always runs under the current user's security context, but your own user account probably has stronger security privileges than the account IIS runs ASP.NET applications under. As a result, when you move the application to a production web server, you may have to contend with security issues that weren't apparent when you tested with the development server, especially if you access files or databases located in folders outside of the application's folder structure.

The dialog box for specifying a web server

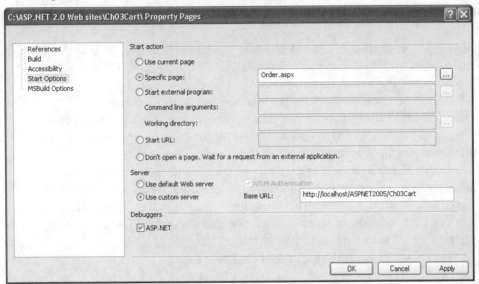

How to test a file-system web site with IIS

- Create a virtual directory for the web site as described in figure 4-1.
- Open the web site from its virtual directory, or open the file-system web site and then use the Property Pages dialog box shown above to specify the URL for the virtual directory.
- Run the application using one of the techniques in figure 4-5.

Limitations of the ASP.NET Development Server

- Can serve pages only to the local computer.
- Runs in current user's security context, so it doesn't accurately test security issues.
- Does not include an SMTP server, so it can't be used to test email applications.
- Uses a randomly chosen port rather than the standard HTTP port 80.

Description

- By default, a file-system web site is run using the ASP.NET Development Server. To run a file-system web site using IIS, you can use one of the techniques above.
- To open the Property Pages dialog box, right-click the project in the Solution Explorer and select Property Pages from the shortcut menu. Then, to change the server that's used to run the web site, click the Start Options node, select the Use Custom Server option, and enter the URL of the virtual directory for the web site.

Figure 4-6   How to test a file-system web site with IIS

How to test an application from outside of Visual Studio

Once you've thoroughly tested and debugged an application from within Visual Studio, you'll want to run it from outside of Visual Studio to make sure it works properly. Figure 4-7 describes how you do that.

To start, you open the browser you want to use. In this example, I used Mozilla Firefox. Then, you enter the URL for the starting page of the application and press Enter. When you do, a request for the page is sent to the server and the resulting page is displayed in the browser.

Note that to run a local IIS web site, you use "localhost" in the URL to identify the server. The URL in this figure, for example, refers to the Order.aspx page of the Ch03Cart web site. This web site is located in the ASPNET2005 directory of the local IIS server. In contrast, to run a remote IIS web site, you specify the actual server name in the URL like this:

```
http://mma1/ASPNET2005/Ch03Cart/Order.aspx
```

And to run an FTP web site, you enter the browse location like this:

```
http://Murach/Ch03Cart/Order.aspx
```

If you haven't already tested an application from within Visual Studio in each browser that might be used to run the application, you should do that from outside Visual Studio. In addition, if the application retrieves and updates data in a database, you'll want to test it simultaneously in two browser windows. To understand why, you need to realize that after an application retrieves data from a database, it closes the connection to the database. Because of that, two or more users can retrieve the same data at the same time. This is called *concurrency*, and it can cause *concurrency errors* when the data is updated.

In section 3 of this book, you'll learn more about concurrency and how you avoid concurrency errors. For now, you should just realize that you'll need to test your applications to be sure that they handle concurrency problems.

The Order page displayed in a Mozilla Firefox browser outside of Visual Studio

Description

- You can run any IIS application from outside of Visual Studio. To do that, open the browser you want to use, enter the URL for the starting page of the application as shown above, and press Enter.

- When you run an application from outside of Visual Studio, you can run it in two or more browser windows simultaneously. That way, you can be sure that the application provides for any *concurrency errors* that can occur.

- If you want to use the debugger while testing for concurrency errors, you can run one instance of the application from within Visual Studio with debugging, and you can run another instance from outside of Visual Studio.

Figure 4-7   How to test an application from outside of Visual Studio

How to use an ASP.NET Server Error page

As you test an ASP.NET application, you may encounter runtime errors that prevent an application from executing. When that happens, an exception is thrown. In many cases, the application anticipates these exceptions and provides code to catch them and process them appropriately. If an exception is not caught, however, ASP.NET terminates the application and sends a Server Error page like the one shown in figure 4-8 back to the browser.

As you can see, the Server Error page indicates the type of exception that occurred and the statement that caused the error. In many cases, this information is enough to determine what caused the error and what should be done to correct it. For example, the Server Error page in this figure indicates that an input string value was not in the correct format. The problem was encountered in line 40 of the source code for the page:

```
CartItem.Quantity = CType(txtQuantity.Text, Integer)
```

Based on that information, you can assume that the Text property of the txtQuantity control contains a value that can't be converted to an integer. This could happen if the application didn't check that the user entered an integer value into this control. (To allow this error to occur, I disabled the range validator for the Quantity text box on the Order page.)

Many of the exceptions you'll encounter will be system exceptions like the one shown here. These exceptions apply to general system operations such as arithmetic operations and the execution of methods and Visual Basic functions. If your applications use ADO.NET, you can also encounter ADO.NET and data provider exceptions. If the connection string for a database is invalid, for example, a data provider exception will occur. And if you try to add a row to a data table with a key that already exists, an ADO.NET error will occur.

In some cases, you won't be able to determine the cause of an error just by analyzing the Server Error page. Then, you can use the Visual Studio debugger to help you locate the problem. You'll learn how to do that next.

An ASP.NET Server Error page

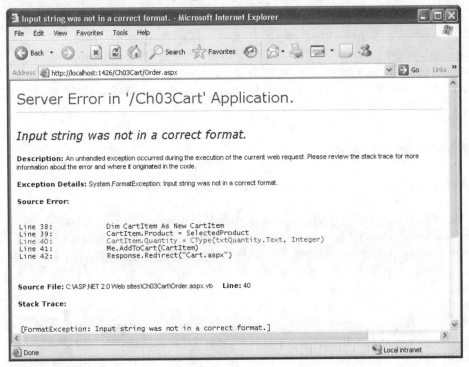

Description

- If an uncaught exception occurs in an ASP.NET application, ASP.NET terminates the application and sends an error page like the one shown above to the browser.

- An ASP.NET Server Error page provides the name of the application, a description of the exception, and the line in the program that caused the error. It also includes a *stack trace* that indicates the processing that led up to the error.

- The information in the Server Error page is often all you need to determine the cause of the error. If not, you should note the line where the error occurred. Then, you can use the debugging techniques presented in this chapter to determine the cause.

Figure 4-8   How to use an ASP.NET Server Error page

How to use the debugger

The topics that follow introduce you to the basic techniques for using the Visual Studio *debugger* to debug an ASP.NET application. Note that these techniques are almost identical to the techniques you use to debug a Windows application. If you've debugged Windows applications, then, you shouldn't have any trouble debugging web applications.

How to use breakpoints

Figure 4-9 shows how to use *breakpoints* in an ASP.NET application. Note that you can set a breakpoint before you run an application or as an application is executing. Remember, though, that an application ends after it generates a page. So if you switch from the browser to Visual Studio to set a breakpoint, the breakpoint won't be taken until the next time the page is executed. If you want a breakpoint to be taken the first time a page is executed, then, you'll need to set the breakpoint before you run the application.

After you set a breakpoint and run the application, the application enters *break mode* before it executes the statement that contains the breakpoint. In this illustration, for example, the application will enter break mode before it executes the statement that caused the exception in figure 4-8 to occur. Then, you can use the debugging features described in the topics that follow to debug the application.

In some cases, you may want to set more than one breakpoint. You can do that either before you begin the execution of the application or while the application is in break mode. Then, when you run the application, it will stop at the first breakpoint. And when you continue execution, the application will execute up to the next breakpoint.

Once you set a breakpoint, it remains active until you remove it. In fact, it remains active even after you close the project. If you want to remove a breakpoint, you can use one of the techniques presented in this figure.

You can also work with breakpoints from the *Breakpoints window*. To disable a breakpoint, for example, you can remove the check mark in front of the breakpoint. Then, the breakpoint isn't taken until you enable it again. You can also move to a breakpoint in the Code Editor window by selecting the breakpoint in the Breakpoints window and then clicking on the Go To Source Code button at the top of this window, or by right-clicking the breakpoint in the Breakpoints window and choosing Go To Source Code from the shortcut menu.

The Order page with a breakpoint

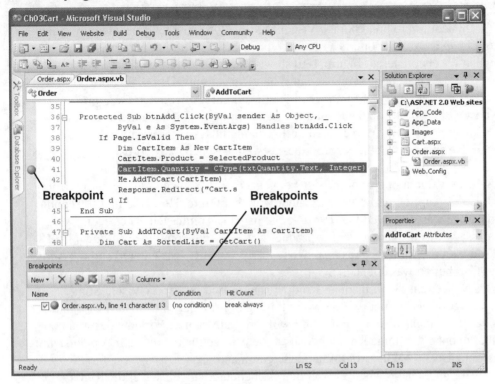

How to set and clear breakpoints

- To set a *breakpoint*, click in the margin indicator bar to the left of the statement where you want the break to occur. The statement will be highlighted and a breakpoint indicator (a large dot) will appear in the margin. You can set a breakpoint before you run an application or while you're debugging the application.

- To remove a breakpoint, click the breakpoint indicator. To remove all breakpoints at once, use the Debug→Clear All Breakpoints command.

- To temporarily disable breakpoints, use the Debug→Disable All Breakpoints command. You can later enable the breakpoints by using Debug→Enable All Breakpoints.

Description

- When ASP.NET encounters a breakpoint, it enters *break mode* before it executes the statement on which the breakpoint is set. From break mode, you can use the debugger to determine the cause of an error.

- The current breakpoints are listed in the *Breakpoints window* (Debug→Windows→ Breakpoints). You can use the toolbar at the top of this window to work with the breakpoints, and you can use the check box next to a breakpoint to enable or disable the breakpoint.

- You can't set breakpoints on blank lines or comments.

Figure 4-9   How to use breakpoints

How to use tracepoints

In addition to breakpoints, Visual Studio 2005 provides a new feature called *tracepoints*. A tracepoint is a special type of breakpoint that performs an action when it's encountered. Figure 4-10 shows how tracepoints work.

To set a tracepoint, you use the When Breakpoint Is Hit dialog box to indicate what you want to do when the tracepoint is encountered or "hit." In most cases, you'll use the Print a Message option to display a message in the *Immediate window*. As indicated in this dialog box, the message can include variable values and other expressions as well as special keywords.

For example, the message shown here will include the value of the SelectedValue property of the ddlProducts control. You can see the output from this tracepoint in the Immediate window in this figure. Here, the first tracepoint message was displayed the first time the page was requested. The second message was displayed when a product was selected from the drop-down list. And the third message was displayed when a quantity was entered and the Add to Cart button was clicked.

Notice that the Immediate window is also used to display Visual Studio messages like the first two shown in this figure. And, as you'll learn later in this chapter, you can also use it to work with program values. For now, just realize that to open the Immediate window so you can see the messages it contains, you use the Debug→Windows→Immediate command.

To run a macro when a tracepoint is encountered, you select the Run a Macro option. Then, the drop-down list becomes available and you can select the macro you want to run from this list.

By default, program execution continues after the tracepoint action is performed. If that's not what you want, you can remove the check mark from the Continue Execution option. Then, the program will enter break mode when the tracepoint action is complete.

After you set a tracepoint on a statement, the statement will be highlighted and a breakpoint indicator will appear in the margin. If program execution will continue after the tracepoint action is performed, the indicator will appear as a large diamond. If the program will enter break mode, however, the same indicator is used as for a standard breakpoint.

The Order page with a tracepoint and the dialog box used to set it

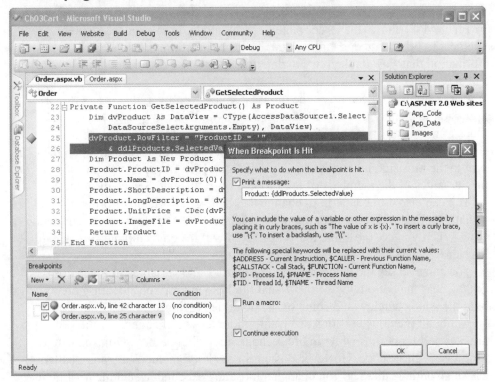

Output from the tracepoint in the Immediate window

```
Immediate Window                                              ▾ ⁴ ×
Auto-attach to process '[2892] aspnet_wp.exe' on machine 'ANNEPC' succeeded.
Warning: Cannot debug script code. Script debugging is disabled for the applicatio
Product: "pow01"
Product: "rat01"
Product: "rat01"
```

Description

- A *tracepoint* is a special type of breakpoint that lets you perform an action. When ASP.NET encounters a tracepoint, it performs the specified action and then continues execution if the Continue Execution option is selected or enters break mode if it isn't.

- You typically use tracepoints to print messages to the *Immediate window*. A message can include text, values, and special keywords. You can also use tracepoints to run macros.

- To set a tracepoint, right-click on the statement where you want it set and choose Breakpoint→Insert Tracepoint. Then, complete the When Breakpoint Is Hit dialog box and click OK. You can also convert an existing breakpoint to a tracepoint by right-clicking on its indicator and choosing When Hit.

- If program execution will continue after the tracepoint action is performed, the tracepoint will be marked with a large diamond as shown above. Otherwise, it will be marked just like any other breakpoint.

Figure 4-10   How to use tracepoints

How to work in break mode

Figure 4-11 shows the Order page in break mode. In this mode, the next statement to be executed is highlighted. Then, you can use the debugging information that's available to try to determine the cause of an exception or a logical error.

For example, you can place the mouse pointer over a variable, property, or expression to display its current value in a *data tip*. You can also display the values of the members of an array, structure, or object. To do that, place the mouse pointer over the array, structure, or object to display its data tip, and then point to the plus sign in that data tip. In this figure, for example, you can see the current values of the members of the Product object named SelectedProduct.

You can also use a data tip to change the value of a variable or property. To do that, just right-click the data tip and then choose Edit Value from the shortcut menu. When you do, the value that's displayed will become editable so you can enter a new value.

You can also see the values of other properties and variables in the Autos window near the bottom left of the Visual Studio window. You'll learn more about the Autos window and some of the other debugging windows in a minute.

Although previous versions of Visual Studio let you change the values of variables and properties while in break mode, they did not let you make changes to the Visual Basic code. However, Visual Studio 2005 includes a feature called Edit and Continue that lets you change almost any executable statement while in break mode. To do that, you just make the change in the Code Editor and then continue program execution using one of the techniques presented in this figure. Note that although you can change executable statements, you are typically not allowed to change declaration statements. For example, you can't add, change, or remove an Imports statement, and you can't change the access modifier for a property or method.

If you make a code change that isn't allowed, Visual Studio marks the change with a purple wavy underline and adds an error to the error list. Then, before you can continue program execution, you must undo the change.

The Shopping Cart application in break mode

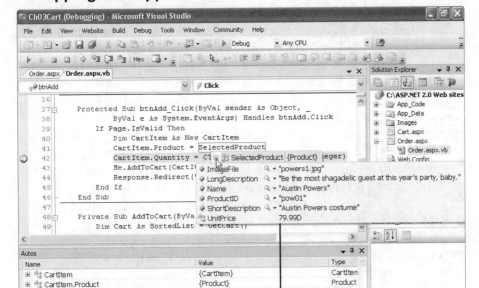

Debugging windows   **Data tip**

Description

- When you enter break mode, the debugger highlights the next statement to be executed.
- You can use the debugging windows and the buttons in the Debug menu and toolbar to control the execution of the program and determine the cause of an exception.
- To display the value of a variable or property in a *data tip,* position the mouse pointer over the variable or property in the Code Editor window. To display a data tip for an expression, highlight the expression and then point to it. The expression must not contain a function call.
- To display the members of an array, structure, or object in a data tip, position the mouse pointer over it to display its data tip, and then point to the plus sign in the data tip.
- To change the value of a variable in a data tip, right-click the data tip, choose Edit Value, and then enter the new value.
- You can also make changes to your code while in break mode. However, you are generally not allowed to change declaration statements. If you make changes, they're applied when you continue program execution.
- To continue program execution, press F5 or click the Continue button in the Standard or Debug toolbar. For more options about controlling program execution, see figure 4-12.

Figure 4-11   How to work in break mode

How to control the execution of an application

Once you're in break mode, you can use a variety of commands to control the execution of the application. These commands are summarized in figure 4-12. As you can see, most of these commands are available from the Debug menu or the Debug toolbar, but three of them are available only from the shortcut menu for the Code Editor window. You can also use shortcut keys to start some of these commands.

To execute the statements of an application one at a time, you use the Step Into command. When you use this command, the application executes the next statement, then returns to break mode so you can check the values of properties and variables and perform other debugging functions. The Step Over command is similar to the Step Into command, but it executes the statements in called procedures without interruption (they are "stepped over").

The Step Out command executes the remaining statements in a procedure without interruption. When the procedure finishes, the application enters break mode before the next statement in the calling procedure is executed.

To skip over code that you know is working properly, you can use the Run To Cursor or Set Next Statement command. You can also use the Set Next Statement command to rerun lines of code that were executed before an exception occurred. And if you've been working in the Code Editor window and have forgotten where the next statement to be executed is, you can use the Show Next Statement command to move to it.

If your application gets caught in a processing loop so it keeps executing indefinitely without generating a page, you can force it into break mode by choosing the Debug→Break All command. This command lets you enter break mode any time during the execution of an application.

Commands in the Debug menu and toolbar

Command	Toolbar	Keyboard	Function
Start/Continue	▶	F5	Start or continue execution of the application.
Break All	‖	Ctrl+Alt+Break	Stop execution and enter break mode.
Stop Debugging	◻	Shift+F5	Stop debugging and end execution of the application.
Restart	↩	Ctrl+Shift+F5	Restart the entire application.
Show Next Statement	⇨		Display the next statement to be executed.
Step Into	⤵	F11	Execute one statement at a time.
Step Over	⤶	F10	Execute one statement at a time except for called procedures.
Step Out	⤴	Shift+F11	Execute the remaining lines in the current procedure.

Commands in the Code Editor window's shortcut menu

Command	Function
Run to Cursor	Execute the application until it reaches the statement that contains the insertion point.
Set Next Statement	Set the statement that contains the insertion point as the next statement to be executed.
Show Next Statement	Move the insertion point to the next statement that will be executed.

Description

- Once the application enters break mode, you can use the Step Into, Step Over, Step Out, and Run To Cursor commands to execute one or more statements and return to break mode.

- To alter the normal execution sequence of the application, you can use the Set Next Statement command. Just place the insertion point in the statement you want to execute next, issue this command, and click the Continue button to continue application execution.

- To stop an application that's caught in a loop, switch to the Visual Studio window and use the Debug→Break All command.

Figure 4-12   How to control the execution of an application

How to use the Autos, Locals, and Watch windows to monitor variables

If you need to see the values of several application variables or properties, you can do that using the Autos, Locals, or Watch windows. By default, these windows are displayed in the lower left corner of the IDE when an application enters break mode. If they're not displayed, you can display them by selecting the appropriate command from the Debug→Windows menu. Note that you can display up to four separate Watch windows.

The content of the Autos, Locals, and Watch windows is illustrated in figure 4-13. The difference between the Autos and Locals windows is in the amount of information they display and the scope of that information.

The *Locals window* displays information about the variables and controls within the scope of the current procedure. Since that includes information about the form and all of the controls on the form if the code in a form is currently executing, that information can be extensive.

In contrast, the *Autos window* displays information about the variables, properties, and constants used in the current statement, the three statements before that statement, and the three statements after that statement. Although the information in this window is more limited than the information shown in the Locals window, the Autos window helps you focus on the variables that are relevant to the current statement.

Unlike the Autos and Locals windows, the *Watch windows* let you choose the values that are displayed. The Watch window shown in this figure, for example, displays the Text property of the txtQuantity and lblUnitPrice controls, the Quantity property of the CartItem object, and the UnitPrice property of the Product object that's stored in the CartItem object. The Watch windows also let you watch the values of expressions you specify. Note that an expression doesn't have to exist in the application for you to add it to a Watch window.

To add an item to a Watch window, you can type it directly into the Name column. Alternatively, if the item appears in the Code Editor window, you can highlight it in that window and then drag it to a Watch window. You can also highlight the item in the Code Editor or a data tip and then right-click on it and select the Add Watch command to add it to the Watch window that's currently displayed.

Besides displaying the values of variables and properties, you can use the Autos, Locals, and Watch windows to change these values. To do that, you simply double-click on the value you want to change and enter a new value. Then, you can continue debugging or continue the execution of the application.

The Autos window

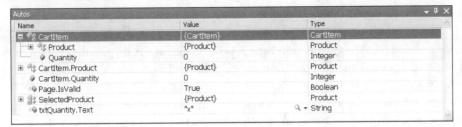

The Locals window

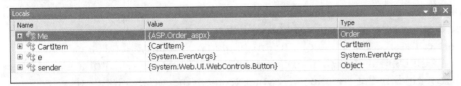

A Watch window

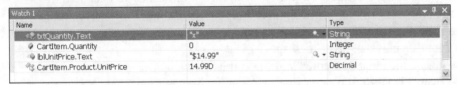

Description

- The *Autos window* displays information about variables, properties, and constants in the current statement and the three statements before and after the current statement.

- The *Locals window* displays information about the variables and controls within the scope of the current procedure.

- The *Watch windows* let you view the values of variables and expressions you specify, called *watch expressions*. You can display up to four Watch windows.

- To add a watch expression, type a variable name or expression into the Name column, highlight a variable or expression in the Code Editor window and drag it to the Watch window, or right-click on a variable or highlighted expression in the Code Editor window or a data tip and choose Add Watch.

- To delete a row from a Watch window, right-click the row and choose Delete Watch. To delete all the rows in a Watch window, right-click the window and choose Select All to select the rows, then right-click and choose Delete Watch.

- To display any of these windows, click on its tab if it's visible or select the appropriate command from the Debug→Windows menu.

- To change the value of a property or variable from any of these windows, double-click on the value in the Value column, then type a new value and press the Enter key.

Figure 4-13   How to use the Autos, Locals, and Watch windows to monitor variables

How to use the Immediate window to work with values

The Immediate window, shown in figure 4-14, is useful for displaying the values of variables or properties that don't appear in the Code Editor window. To display a value, you simply type a question mark followed by the name of the variable or property. The first line of code in this figure, for example, displays the Text property of the item selected from the Categories drop-down list. You can see the result in the second line of this window.

The Immediate window is also useful for executing Visual Basic statements. For example, you can execute an assignment statement to change the value of a variable or property. After I displayed the Text property of the Quantity text box, for example, I assigned a value of 1 to this property. Similarly, you can execute a Sub procedure or function. This can be useful for testing the result of a procedure with different arguments. If you execute a function, you can also preface the function name with a question mark to display the value it returns.

When you enter commands in the Immediate window, they're executed in the same context (or scope) as the application that's running. That means that you can't display the value of a variable that's out of scope. If you try to do that, the debugger displays an error message.

The commands that you enter into the Immediate window remain there until you exit from Visual Studio or explicitly delete them using the Clear All command in the shortcut menu for the window. That way, you can use standard Windows techniques to edit and reuse the same commands from one execution of an application to another without having to reenter them.

To execute a command that you've already entered in the Immediate window, just use the Up and Down arrow keys to scroll through the commands. As you scroll, the commands are displayed at the bottom of the window. Then, you can change a command if necessary and press Enter to execute it.

The Immediate window

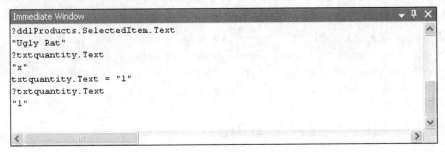

Description

- You can use the Immediate window to display and assign values from a program during execution. To display this window, click on the Immediate Window tab or use the Debug→Windows→Immediate command.

- To display a value in the Immediate window, enter a question mark followed by the expression whose value you want to display. Then, press the Enter key.

- To assign a different value to a variable, property, or object, enter an assignment statement in the Immediate window. Then, press the Enter key.

- To execute a Sub procedure or function from the Immediate window, enter its name and any arguments it requires. Then, press the Enter key. If you want to display the result of a function call, precede the function call with a question mark.

- To reissue a command, use the Up and Down arrow keys to scroll through the commands until you find the one you want. Then, modify the command if necessary and press the Enter key to execute it.

- To remove all commands and output from the Immediate window, use the Clear All command in the shortcut menu for the window.

Figure 4-14   How to use the Immediate window to work with values

How to use the Trace feature

The *Trace feature* is an ASP.NET feature that displays some useful information that you can't get by using the debugger. Because the debugger works so well, you probably won't need to use the Trace feature very much, but you should at least be aware of the information that it can provide.

How to enable the Trace feature

To use the Trace feature, you must first enable tracing. To do that, you add a Trace attribute to the Page directive for the page, and you assign a value of True to this attribute. Then, when you run the page, trace information will be displayed at the end of the page output, as shown in figure 4-15.

When you enable the Trace feature, it is enabled only for the current page, which is usually what you want. To enable tracing for another page, you must modify the Page directive for that page too. Once this feature has been enabled for a page, ASP.NET adds trace output to the page whenever the page is requested.

How to interpret Trace output

In figure 4-15, you can see the start of the output for the Cart page after the user added an item to the shopping cart. After the request details, the trace information provides a list of trace messages that are generated as the application executes. Here, ASP.NET automatically adds Begin and End messages when major page events such as PreInit, Init, and InitComplete occur. If you scroll down to see all of these trace messages, you can see the variety of events that are raised during the life cycle of a page.

After the trace messages, you'll find information about the controls used by the page, the items in the session state object, the cookies that were included with the HTTP request, the HTTP request headers, and the server variables. In this figure, for example, you can see the session state and cookies data for the Cart page of the Shopping Cart application. In this case, an item named Cart has been added to the session state object. And a cookie named ASP.NET_SessionId is used to keep track of the user's session ID so the user's session state object can be retrieved.

The beginning of the trace output for the Cart page

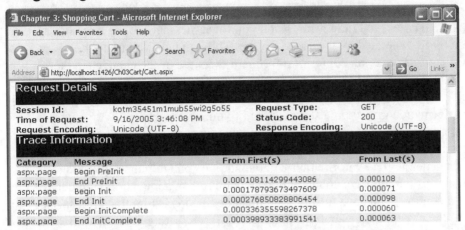

The session and cookies information for the Cart page

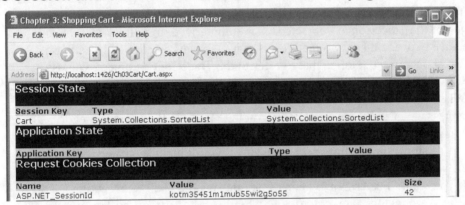

A Page directive that enables tracing for the Cart page

```
<%@ Page Language="VB" AutoEventWireup="false" CodeFile="Cart.aspx.vb"
Inherits="Cart" Trace="True" %>
```

Description

- The ASP.NET *Trace feature* traces the execution of a page and displays trace information and other information at the bottom of that page.

- To activate the trace feature for a page, you add a Trace attribute to the Page directive at the top of the aspx file for the page and set its value to True as shown above.

- The trace information is divided into several tables that provide specific types of trace information. For example, the Trace Information table provides information about how the page request was processed, and the Session State table provides information about the items currently stored in session state.

Figure 4-15   How to enable the Trace feature and interpret Trace output

How to create custom trace messages

In some cases, you may want to add your own messages to the trace information that's generated by the Trace feature. This can help you track the sequence in which the procedures of a form are executed or the changes in the data as the procedures are executed. Although you can also do this type of tracking by stepping through the procedures of a form with the debugger, the trace information gives you a static listing of your messages.

Note, however, that you can also create this type of listing using tracepoints as described earlier in this chapter. The advantage to using tracepoints is that you can generate trace information without adding code to your application. In addition, this output is generated only when you run an application with debugging. In contrast, you have to add program code to add custom trace messages, and the trace output is generated whenever the Trace feature is enabled. Because of that, you may not need to create custom trace messages. But I've included it here in case you do.

To add messages to the trace information, you use the Write or Warn method of the TraceContext object. This is summarized in figure 4-16. The only difference between these two methods is that messages created with the Warn method appear in red. Notice that to refer to the TraceContext object, you use the Trace property of the page.

When you code a Write or Warn method, you can include both a category and a message or just a message. If you include just a message, the category column in the trace output is left blank. If you include a category, however, it appears as shown in this figure. In most cases, you'll include a category because it makes it easy to see the sequence in which the procedures were executed.

If you want to determine whether tracing is enabled before executing a Write or Warn method, you can use the IsEnabled property of the TraceContext object as shown in the example in this figure. Normally, though, you won't check the IsEnabled property because trace statements are executed only if tracing is enabled.

Common members of the TraceContext class

Property	Description
`IsEnabled`	True if tracing is enabled for the page.

Method	Description
`Write(message)`	Writes a message to the trace output.
`Write(category, message)`	Writes a message to the trace output with the specified category.
`Warn(message)`	Writes a message in red type to the trace output.
`Warn(category, message)`	Writes a message in red type to the trace output with the specified category.

Code that writes a custom trace message

```
If Trace.IsEnabled Then
    Trace.Write("Page_Load", "Binding products drop-down list.")
End If
```

A portion of a trace that includes a custom message

Trace Information

Category	Message	From First(s)	From Last(s)
aspx.page	Begin PreInit		
aspx.page	End PreInit	0.000105879378524366	0.000106
aspx.page	Begin Init	0.000174603196775009	0.000069
aspx.page	End Init	0.000298920672878816	0.000124
aspx.page	Begin InitComplete	0.000355911156306179	0.000057
aspx.page	End InitComplete	0.000414019100192902	0.000058
aspx.page	Begin PreLoad	0.000469612758046065	0.000056
aspx.page	End PreLoad	0.000562920706402629	0.000093
aspx.page	Begin Load	0.000620469920059672	0.000058
Page_Load	Binding products drop-down list.	0.00510428001324191	0.004484
aspx.page	End Load	0.103874654460274	0.098770
aspx.page	Begin LoadComplete	0.104021879875794	0.000147
aspx.page	End LoadComplete	0.104087251312667	0.000065
aspx.page	Begin PreRender	0.104144521161209	0.000057
aspx.page	End PreRender	0.104882324429502	0.000738

Custom trace message

Description

- You can use the TraceContext object to write your own messages to the trace output. The TraceContext object is available through the Trace property of a page.

- Use the Write method to write a basic text message. Use the Warn method to write a message in red type.

- Trace messages are written only if tracing is enabled for the page. To determine whether tracing is enabled, you use the IsEnabled property of the TraceContext object.

Figure 4-16   How to create custom trace messages

How to write information directly to the HTTP output stream

Another way to display information as a program executes is to write it directly to the HTTP output stream. To do that, you use the Write method of the HTTP Response object as shown in figure 4-17. When you use this technique, you'll want to be sure to remove any statements you've added when you finish testing your application.

At the top of this figure, you can see a Cart page that includes output that indicates the number of items that are currently in the shopping cart. To generate this output, I added a Response.Write method to the Page_Load procedure of the page. As you can see, this method uses the Count property of the Cart object to determine the number of items that are in the cart.

Notice that the text you include on the Write method can include HTML tags. For example, the Write method shown here includes a <br /> tag so that the item count is followed by a blank line. Also note that the output you write to the output stream is always added to the beginning of the stream. Because of that, it always appears at the top of the browser window.

The Cart page with output generated by Response.Write

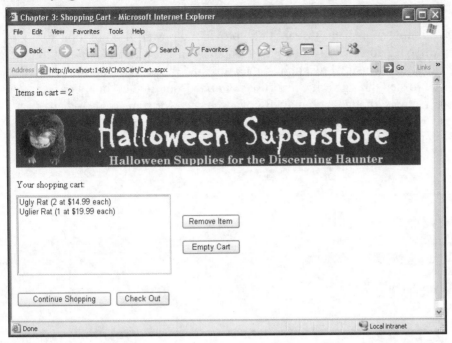

A Page_Load procedure that writes to the HTTP output stream

```
Protected Sub Page_Load(ByVal sender As Object, _
        ByVal e As System.EventArgs) Handles Me.Load
    Cart = GetCart()
    If Not IsPostBack Then
        Me.DisplayCart()
        Response.Write("Items in cart = " & Cart.Count & "<br />")
    End If
End Sub
```

Code that writes HTML output from another class

```
HttpContext.Current.Response.Write("Now updating file.<br />")
```

Description

- The Write method of the HttpResponse object provides a convenient way to write data directly to the HTTP output stream. The output can include any valid HTML.

- To access the HttpResponse object from the code-behind file for a web page, you use the Response property of the page. To access this object from a class that doesn't inherit the Page class, you use the Response property of the HttpContext object for the current request. To access this object, you use the Current property of the HttpContext class.

- The HTML output you add to the HTTP output stream using the Write method of the HttpResponse object appears at the beginning of the output stream. As a result, the output from the Write method always appears at the top of the page in the browser window.

Figure 4-17   How to write information directly to the HTTP output stream

Perspective

As you can now appreciate, Visual Studio provides a powerful set of tools for debugging ASP.NET applications. For simple applications, you can usually get the debugging done just by using breakpoints, data tips, and the Autos window. You may also need to step through critical portions of code from time to time. For complex applications, though, you may discover the need for some of the other features that are presented in this chapter. With tools like these, a difficult debugging job becomes manageable.

Terms

virtual directory
virtual root
active mode
passive mode
Remote Debug Monitor
browse location
concurrency
concurrency error
stack trace
debugger
breakpoint
break mode
Breakpoints window
tracepoint
Immediate window
data tip
Autos window
Locals window
Watch window
watch expression
Trace feature

Section 2

Basic ASP.NET skills

The seven chapters in this section expand upon the essentials that you learned in section 1. To start, chapter 5 presents the essential HTML skills that you will need as an ASP.NET programmer. Then, chapter 6 shows you how to work with the server controls that can be used for developing web pages; chapter 7 shows you how to work with the validation controls; and chapter 8 presents the several ways that you can manage the state of an application or form.

The next three chapters present new features of ASP.NET 2.0. Chapter 9 shows you how to use master pages to create pages with common elements; chapter 10 shows you how to use site navigation to make it easy for users to navigate through your site; and chapter 11 shows you how to use themes to customize the formatting that's applied to the elements on a page.

To a large extent, each of the chapters in this section is an independent unit. As a result, you don't have to read these chapters in sequence. If, for example, you want to know more about state management after you finish section 1, you can go directly to chapter 8. Eventually, though, you're going to want to read all five chapters. So unless you have a compelling reason to skip around, you may as well read the chapters in sequence.

5

A crash course in HTML

When you add ASP.NET controls to a form in Design view, Visual Studio generates the HTML that will be used to render the web page. Although you could work exclusively in Design view, it sometimes makes sense to work directly with the HTML for a form in Source view. In addition, you may occasionally need to include HTML within the Visual Basic coding for a form. To be sure that you have the skills you need to do that, this chapter presents a crash course in HTML.

If you already know how to code HTML, you should be able to go through this chapter quickly. However, you won't want to skip this chapter altogether, because it presents some skills that are specific to Visual Studio.

An introduction to HTML

HTML documents consist of *HTML elements* that define the content and appearance of the page when it's viewed in a web browser. In the topics that follow, you'll learn the basic rules for coding HTML elements, you'll learn how to work with HTML using Visual Studio, and you'll see how some of the basic web server controls are rendered to HTML.

Basic rules for coding HTML elements

Figure 5-1 presents the basic rules for coding HTML elements. To start, each HTML element is coded within a *tag* that starts with an opening bracket (<) and ends with a closing bracket (>). For example, <title>, </h1>, and <hr stylc="color:red"/> are all examples of HTML tags.

Most HTML elements are made up of three parts. First, a *start tag* marks the start of the element. The start tag consists of the element name (such as title or h1) plus one or more optional *attributes* that provide additional information for the tag. After the start tag is the *content*, which is the text or other data that makes up the element. Following the content is the *end tag* that marks the end of the element. The end tag consists of a slash followed by the element's name. This is illustrated by the three lines of code in the first example in this figure.

It's important to realize that the content of an element can contain other elements. For example, consider this HTML code:

```
<h1>This is a <b>bold</b>heading</h1>
```

Here, the H1 element contains the text "This is a bold heading." Within this text, the B element indicates that the word "bold" should be boldfaced. You'll learn about these and other formatting elements later in this chapter.

Not all HTML elements have content and end tags. For example, the line of code in the second example in this figure includes two elements without content or end tags. The first element, <br /> inserts a line break, and the second element, <hr />, inserts a horizontal rule. Notice that the text in this line of code isn't enclosed in tags. That's because, like the <br /> and <hr /> tags, it is content for another tag that's coded at a higher level in the document. You'll learn more about that later.

Notice that all of the tags shown in this figure are lowercase. This will be a requirement of the new XHTML version 1.0 standards. Although ASP.NET 2.0 web pages currently use XHTML version 1.0 Transitional, which allows upper-case tags, you'll want to use lowercase tags so that you won't need to change your HTML in the future.

Notice also that the <br /> and <hr /> tags include a slash before the closing bracket. Although these slashes were optional in earlier XHTML standards, they are required with XHTML version 1.0 Transitional. As a result, you'll want to use them so you won't need to change your HTML in the future.

You can also code *comments* within an HTML document as shown in the third example in this figure. That way, you can document sections of code that

Three HTML elements with start tags, content, and end tags

```
<title>Murach's Halloween Superstore</title>
<h1>About Us</h1>
<b>Choose a product:</b>
```

Two elements that have no content or end tags

```
A red line appears below.<br /><hr style="color:red" />
```

A comment

```
<!-- This text will be ignored. -->
```

A line that has three consecutive spaces

```
Last name:   Wilson
```

Elements and tags

- An *HTML document* includes *HTML elements* that specify the content and appearance of the page when viewed in a web browser.

- Most HTML elements have three parts: a start tag, content, and an end tag. Each *tag* is coded within a set of brackets (< >).

- An element's *start tag* includes the name of the element. The *end tag* includes the element name preceded by a slash. And the *content* includes everything that appears between the start and end tags.

- Some HTML elements have no content or end tag. For example, the <br /> element, which forces a line break, and the <hr /> element, which inserts a horizontal rule, consist of just a start tag.

- You should use the lowercase letters for all your tags.

Attributes

- *Attributes* can appear within a start tag to supply optional values. For example, you can use the Color attribute within an <hr /> element to specify the color of the rule.

- All attribute values should be enclosed in quotation marks.

- Use spaces to separate attributes from one another.

Comments and white space

- A *comment* is text that appears between the <-- and --> characters. Web browsers ignore comments, so you can use them to document sections of your HTML code that might otherwise be confusing.

- *White space*, such as tabs, line returns, and consecutive spaces, is ignored by browsers. As a result, you can use space to indent lines of code and line breaks to separate elements from one another. Used properly, white space can make your HTML code easier to read. However, Visual Studio typically removes white space from the HTML it generates.

- To force the browser to display two or more consecutive spaces, use the special code   for each space.

Figure 5-1   Basic rules for coding HTML elements

might be confusing. In addition, you can use spaces, indentation, and blank lines to make your code easier to read. This is called *white space*, and web browsers ignore it. If you want to include space within a line that the web browser doesn't ignore, you can use the special code   as shown in the last example of figure 5-1.

How to work with HTML using Visual Studio

In chapter 2, you learned how to create a simple web form by dragging ASP.NET controls onto the design surface of the Web Forms Designer. You also learned some basic skills for modifying the design of a form from Source view using the HTML Editor. Now, figure 5-2 reviews some of these skills and presents some additional skills for working in Source view.

When you display a web form in Source view, you'll notice that Visual Studio uses different colors to identify various items of information. For example, element names are displayed in maroon, attribute names are displayed in red, and attribute values are displayed in blue. Visual Studio also makes syntax errors easy to locate by underlining them with a red wavy line.

Visual Studio also provides tools that help you enter and edit HTML code. One of the most useful is the statement completion feature provided by IntelliSense. With this feature, a list of the available elements is displayed when you enter the opening bracket for a start tag. Then, you can select the element you want to add from this list and press the Tab key to add the element name to your document.

After you enter an element name followed by a space, Visual Studio displays a list of the available attributes for that element. In this figure, for example, you can see the list of attributes that's displayed for a Td element. To add an attribute, you just select it from the list and press the Tab key. Then, you can type an equal sign and enter a value for the attribute. To enter additional attributes, type a space to redisplay the list. When you're finished entering the attributes for an element, you enter its closing bracket. Then, the end tag for that element, if it has one, is added automatically.

As you work with the Web Forms Designer, you'll frequently switch back and forth between Source view and Design view. When you make a change to the HTML in Source view, you can quickly switch to Design view to check the results of your editing. Then, you can switch back to Source view to continue editing the HTML.

A web page in Source view with a completion list displayed

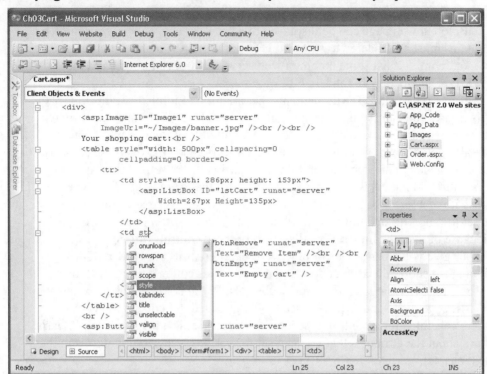

Description

- To edit the HTML for a web page in Visual Studio, display the page in Source view by clicking on the Source button at the bottom of the Web Forms Designer window.

- Visual Studio uses distinctive colors to identify various items in Source view. In addition, it highlights syntax errors with a red wavy underline so they're easy to locate.

- When you enter the opening bracket (<) for a start tag, Visual Studio displays a list of the available elements. To select an element, type one or more letters of the element or scroll to the element, and then press the Tab key.

- When you enter the name of an HTML element followed by a space, Visual Studio displays a list of the attributes you can use with that element. To select an attribute, type one or more letters of the attribute or scroll to the attribute, and then press the Tab key.

- When you enter the closing bracket (>) for a start tag, Visual Studio automatically adds the end tag.

- You can also add or modify element attributes using the Properties window. To do that, move the insertion point into the tag for the element to display its attributes in the Properties window and then change the attribute values as appropriate.

- You can also use Visual Studio's drag-and-drop feature to add server controls to a form in Source view. To do that, just drag the control from the Toolbox to the location where you want it to appear in the HTML document.

Figure 5-2   How to work with HTML using Visual Studio

How web server controls are rendered

Before a web page can be displayed in a browser, any web server controls it contains must be rendered to standard HTML. To help you understand how this works, figure 5-3 list some common web server controls and describes the HTML elements they're rendered to.

If you review the HTML elements that are used to implement the controls in this figure, you can see that the same element can be used to implement more than one control. For example, the text box, button, and image button controls are all implemented by an Input element. The difference in how these controls appear and act, then, depends on how their attributes are set. In this case, the Type attribute indicates the type of input control that's rendered. The Type attribute of a text box, for example, is set to "text," the Type attribute of a button is set to "submit," and the Type attribute of an image button is set to "image." Because of that, the browser handles each of these controls differently.

To give you a better idea of how web server controls are rendered, this figure also shows the aspx code for four web server controls along with the HTML code that's rendered for those controls. If you compare the aspx and HTML code, you should quickly see how it's related. Of course, the HTML that's generated for a control depends on how you set its attributes. You'll learn more about the attributes that you can set for various web server controls in the next chapter.

Some common web server controls and how they're rendered

Name	HTML element	Additional information
Label	\<span>	The \<span> element is typically used to apply special formatting to the text it encloses.
TextBox	\<input>	The type="text" attribute identifies this element as a text box.
Button	\<input>	The type="submit" attribute identifies this element as a button.
ImageButton	\<input>	The type="image" attribute identifies this element as an image button.
LinkButton	\<a>	This control is rendered as an Anchor element whose Href attribute points to a function generated in JavaScript that posts the page back to the server.
HyperLink	\<a>	This control is rendered as an Anchor element that links to another URL.
ListBox	\<select>	Each item in the list is defined by an \<option> element within the \<select> element.
DropDownList	\<select>	Each item in the list is defined by an \<option> element within the \<select> element.
Image	\<img>	Displays the specified image.

The aspx code for four web server controls

```
<asp:Label ID="lblName" runat="server" Font-Bold="True" Font-Size="Larger"
    Text="Murach Books"></asp:Label>
<asp:TextBox ID="txtSearch" runat="server" Width="248px"></asp:TextBox>
<asp:Button ID="btnSearch" runat="server" Text="Search" />
<asp:ListBox ID="lstBooks" runat="server">
    <asp:ListItem Value="UGVB">ASP.NET 2.0 Upgrader's Guide</asp:ListItem>
    <asp:ListItem Value="BVBN">Beginning Visual Basic .NET</asp:ListItem>
    <asp:ListItem Value="SQLS">SQL for SQL Server</asp:ListItem>
</asp:ListBox>
```

How the four web server controls are rendered in HTML

```
<span id="lblName" style="font-size:Larger;font-weight:bold;">Murach
Books</span>
<input name="txtSearch" type="text" id="txtSearch" style="width:248px;"/>
<input type="submit" name="btnSearch" value="Search" id="btnSearch" />
<select size="4" name="lstBooks" id="lstBooks">
    <option value="UGVB">ASP.NET 2.0 Upgrader's Guide</option>
    <option value="BVBN">Beginning Visual Basic .NET</option>
    <option value="SQLS">SQL for SQL Server</option>
</select>
```

Description

- All of the web server controls are *rendered* as standard HTML that can be interpreted by a browser.
- To view the HTML that's rendered for a web page, choose the View→Source command from the browser window. The HTML will be displayed in a separate Notepad window.

Figure 5-3   How web server controls are rendered

How to code HTML documents

Every HTML document for a web form must be structured in a certain way for it to be interpreted properly by ASP.NET. In the topics that follow, you'll learn about the basic structure of an HTML document. You'll also learn how to code some of the common elements that appear within an HTML document.

The basic structure of an HTML document

Figure 5-4 shows the HTML that's generated for a new ASP.NET web page. This HTML illustrates the overall structure of an HTML document. Because the elements that make up this structure are generated for you automatically, you don't have to worry about coding them yourself.

The first two elements are an ASP.NET Page directive and an HTML Doctype declaration. The Page directive supplies the information ASP.NET needs to process the web form, and the Doctype declaration provides information the browser needs to display the page. You'll learn about both of these elements in the next figure.

After the Page directive and the Doctype declaration is an Html element. This element, known as the *root element*, contains all of the document's remaining elements. According to the HTML standards, the start and end tags for the Html element are optional. As a result, you'll sometimes see HTML documents without the <html> and </html> tags.

Within the html section, an HTML document contains two additional sections: a document head and a document body. The document head, defined by a Head element, contains various information about the document. As shown here, one element it contains by default is the Title element. The value of this element determines what's displayed in the title bar of the browser window. Later in this chapter, you'll learn about another element that you can add to the Head element to specify the style sheet you want to use with the page.

The document body, defined by a Body element, contains the HTML content that's displayed when the document is viewed in a browser. For a web form, the document body typically consists of just a single Div element within a Form element. As you've seen in previous chapters, the Div element contains all of the asp and HTML elements for the form. You can use the Div element to apply formatting to all of the elements it contains. Although you can code more than one Div element within a Form element to apply different formatting to different parts of the form, that's unusual.

Because the Head and Body elements are contained with an Html element, the Html element is called a *parent element* and the Head and Body elements are called *child elements*. The Body element is also a parent element because it contains a Form element. And the Form element is a parent element because it contains a Div element. This hierarchy of elements becomes particularly important when you're working with styles, as you'll see later in this chapter.

The HTML generated for a new ASP.NET web page

```
<%@ Page Language="VB" AutoEventWireup="false" CodeFile="Cart.aspx.vb"
Inherits="Cart" %>

<!DOCTYPE html PUBLIC "-//W3C//DTD XHTML 1.0 Transitional//EN"
"http://www.w3.org/TR/xhtml1/DTD/xhtml1-transitional.dtd">

<html xmlns="http://www.w3.org/1999/xhtml" >
<head runat="server">
    <title>Untitled Page</title>
</head>
<body>
    <form id="form1" runat="server">
    <div>

    </div>
    </form>
</body>
</html>
```

HTML elements generated for a new page

Element	Start tag	End tag	Description
Page directive	<%@ page ...>		Identifies various options applied to the web page. See figure 5-5 for details.
Doctype declaration	<!DOCTYPE ...>		Identifies the type of HTML document. See figure 5-5 for details.
Html element	<html>	</html>	Marks the beginning and end of an HTML document.
Head element	<head>	</head>	Marks the beginning and end of the document head.
Title element	<title>	</title>	Provides the title for the page.
Body element	<body>	</body>	Marks the beginning and end of the document body.
Form element	<form>	</form>	Marks the beginning and end of the form.
Div element	<div>	</div>	Marks the beginning and end of a division within the form.

Description

- The Html element contains the content of the document. This element is called the *root element* because it contains all the other elements in the document. Within this element, you code the Head and Body elements.
- The Body element contains the Form element that defines the form.
- The Form element contains a Div element that's used to provide formatting that applies to the entire page. Any elements you add to the page in the Web Forms Designer are inserted within the Div element.
- An element that's contained within another element is called a *child element*. The element that contains a child element is called the child's *parent element*.

Figure 5-4   The basic structure of an HTML document for an ASP.NET web page

The Page directive

Figure 5-5 shows the Page directive that appears at the beginning of all ASP.NET pages. Notice that the Page directive begins with the characters <%@ and ends with the characters %>. These special sequences of characters form a *directive block*. Because directive blocks aren't a part of standard HTML, they aren't included in the final HTML that's sent to the browser when the page is displayed. Instead, directive blocks are processed by ASP.NET when the page is compiled.

As you can see in this figure, the Page directive has several attributes. The first attribute, Language, specifies the programming language that's used for the page's code. For Visual Basic projects, the value of this attribute is VB.

The next attribute is AutoEventWireup. For Visual Basic web forms created in Visual Studio, this attribute is set to False. That causes the event procedures with Handles clauses for page events such as Init and Load to be executed automatically when the events occur. In that case, you can change the names of the procedures since they're associated with the appropriate events through the Handles clause.

You can also associate procedures with these events without using the Handles clause. To do that, you must name the event procedures appropriately. For example, the event procedures for the Init and Load events must be named Page_Init and Page_Load. Then, you set the AutoEventWireup attribute to True.

The CodeFile and Inherits attributes work together to link the ASP.NET web page to the code-behind file. First, the CodeFile attribute provides the name of the code-behind file. Visual Studio uses this attribute to associate the partial class it generates for the page at runtime (the class that contains the control declarations) with the file that contains the Visual Basic code for the page. Then, the Inherits attribute provides the name of the compiled class that the page inherits at runtime. This is the name that's specified on the Class statement within the code-behind file.

Another attribute you can include in the Page directive is Trace. You learned about this attribute in chapter 4. It determines whether or not trace information that you can use for debugging is displayed on the web page.

The Doctype declaration

Figure 5-5 also shows the Doctype declaration. This declaration is used by a web browser to determine which version of HTML the document uses. The Doctype declaration generated by Visual Studio 2005 specifies XHTML version 1.0 Transitional, which includes certain HTML elements that are expected to be phased out in the future. If you use these elements, error or warning messages are displayed in the Error List window.

A typical Page directive

```
<%@ Page Language="VB" AutoEventWireup="false" CodeFile="Cart.aspx.vb"
Inherits="Cart" %>
```

Common attributes of the Page directive

Attribute	Description
Language	Specifies the language used to implement the processing for the page. For Visual Basic applications, this attribute is set to VB.
AutoEventWireup	Indicates whether the event procedures for the page will be called automatically when the events occur for the page (True) or if you must use the Handles keyword to bind procedures to these events (False). The default is True, but Visual Studio sets this attribute to False when it creates a Visual Basic web form.
CodeFile	Specifies the name of the code-behind file. This file defines the partial class that is compiled with the partial class that ASP.NET generates from the page at runtime.
Inherits	Specifies the name of the compiled class (dll) that the page inherits at runtime. This name is typically the same as the name of the partial class defined in the CodeFile attribute.
Trace	Indicates whether tracing is enabled. The default is False.

A typical Doctype declaration

```
<!DOCTYPE html PUBLIC "-//W3C//DTD XHTML 1.0 Transitional//EN"
"http://www.w3.org/TR/xhtml1/DTD/xhtml1-transitional.dtd">
```

Description

- The Page directive is processed by ASP.NET when the page is compiled. It isn't included in the output that's sent to the browser.

- The Doctype declaration specifies that the root element of the document—that is, the first element after the Doctype declaration—is an HTML element.

- The Public attribute of the Doctype declaration and the string that follows it specify the version of HTML that the document complies with.

Figure 5-5   The Page directive and the Doctype declaration

How to code basic text formatting elements

As you know, a web form can contain literal text in addition to server controls. To format literal text like this, you can use the elements shown in figure 5-6.

To use the elements shown in this figure, you enclose the text you want to format in the start and end tags for the element. The exception is the Br tag, which is used to insert a line break. Since this tag doesn't have an end tag, it can be referred to as a *self-closing tag*.

The first three elements listed in this figure are the H1, H2, and H3 heading elements. (Although HTML actually has six levels of headings, it's unlikely that you'll use more than three.) The heading elements are designed to create headings with various formats. For instance, all three of the headings shown in the output in this figure are formatted using H2 elements.

The next two elements, P and Br, let you format paragraphs and force line endings. When you use the P element to create standard text paragraphs, the web browser determines where to break lines based on the width of the browser window and the size of the text. If you want to force a line ending at a particular spot, you need to use a Br element. For instance, the paragraph that describes the P element in this figure is formatted using the P element. Because of that, the text flows to the right side of the browser window. In contrast, the paragraph that describes the Br element contains a Br element that forces a line break.

The last two elements let you create bold or italic text. These elements are typically used within P elements or literal text to format all or part of the text. For instance, the last paragraph shown in the output in this figure illustrates how individual words can be formatted within literal text.

Before I go on, you should realize that the basic appearance of the text in an HTML document is determined by the browser. Because of that, headings and body text may appear differently in one browser than they do in another. Later in this chapter, though, you'll learn how to use styles to control the overall appearance of the elements in a document.

Basic HTML formatting elements

Element	Start tag	End tag	Description
H1	<h1>	</h1>	Level-1 heading
H2	<h2>	</h2>	Level-2 heading
H3	<h3>	</h3>	Level-3 heading
P	<p>	</p>	Standard paragraph
Br	 		Line break
B	<b>	</b>	Bold
I	<i>	</i>	Italic

HTML that uses some basic formatting elements

```
<h2>The P element</h2>
<p>The P element marks a standard paragraph. Note that the
web browser determines where the individual lines within the
paragraph will break.</p>
<h2>The Br element</h2>
In contrast, the Br element lets you force a<br />
line break wherever you wish.
<h2>The B and I elements</h2>
This is <b>bold</b>.  This is <i>italic</i>.
```

The HTML viewed in a browser window

The P element

The P element marks a standard paragraph. Note that the web browser determines where the individual lines within the paragraph will break.

The Br element

In contrast, the Br element lets you force a
line break wherever you wish.

The B and I elements

This is **bold**. This is *italic*.

Description

- The default appearance of heading and body text is determined by the browser. However, you can also use styles to determine the default formatting for various elements.

- The P element formats text as a standard paragraph. The browser determines where line endings occur for the text within the paragraph. If you want to force a line break at a specific location within a paragraph, use the Br element.

Figure 5-6   How to code basic text formatting elements

How to code links to other HTML pages

Most web applications consist of a series of web pages. In chapter 3, you learned how you can display one web page from another by using the Redirect method of the HttpResponse object, the Transfer method of the HttpServerUtility object, or cross-page posting. Another way to display a different page is to code an Anchor, or A, element, often called a link.

Figure 5-7 shows how to use the Anchor element. As you can see, this element typically consists of just the start and end tags, an Href attribute that specifies the URL of the page you want to link to, and the text that's displayed by the browser to identify the link. When viewed in a browser, the text within the Anchor element is usually underlined. In addition, the mouse pointer typically changes to a hand when hovered over the text for the link. Then, when the user clicks on the link, the browser requests the page specified by the Href attribute.

When you code an Href attribute in an Anchor element, you can use either a relative URL or an absolute URL. For instance, the first Anchor element in this figure uses a relative URL to display the Register page in the Login subdirectory of the directory that contains the current page. The second Anchor element uses an absolute URL to display the Index page on the www.murach.com web site.

In the next chapter, you'll learn how to use the hyperlink control to link to another web page. Because this control provides the same functionality as the Anchor element, you'll typically use it in your web forms instead of Anchor elements. However, Anchor elements can be useful in some situations. In particular, they're useful for creating menus in code.

Examples of Anchor elements

An anchor element that uses a relative URL

```
<a href="Login/Register.aspx">Register as a new user</a>
```

An anchor element that uses an absolute URL

```
<a href="http://www.murach.com/Index.aspx">View Murach's web site</a>
```

The Anchor elements viewed in a browser

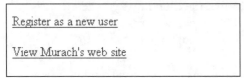

The Anchor element

Start tag	End tag	Description
<a>	</a>	Defines a link to another URL. When the user clicks on the text that's displayed by the element, the browser requests the page that's identified by the Href attribute of the element.

One attribute of an Anchor element

Attribute	Description
href	The URL for the page to be displayed.

Description

- You can code both relative and absolute URLs in the Href attribute. See figure 3-9 in chapter 3 for the details on coding these URLs.
- Because ASP.NET provides a Hyperlink control, you may not use the Anchor element often. However, you may want to assign a series of Anchor elements that are created in code to the Text property of a label or other control to create a menu.

Figure 5-7   How to code links to other HTML pages

How to use styles

With early versions of HTML, the appearance of the HTML elements in a page was determined almost entirely by the browser where the page was displayed. With newer versions of HTML, however, you can use a feature called *cascading style sheets*, or *CSS*, to provide better control over the appearance of your web pages. Like the basic formatting elements you learned about earlier in this chapter, you're most likely to use styles to format the literal text you add to a form. Then, you can use a new feature of ASP.NET 2.0 called skins to apply formatting to the web server controls. As you'll learn in chapter 11, you can store style sheets and skins together in themes.

In the topics that follow, you'll learn about two types of CSS styles: inline styles and external styles. With *inline styles*, you specify style formatting directly in an HTML element. In contrast, *external styles* let you store formatting information in a separate file so you can apply it to all of the pages in a site. When you develop ASP.NET applications, you'll probably work with both types of styles from time to time. However, you should avoid using inline styles whenever possible because they make a web site more difficult to maintain.

How to use inline styles

To use inline styles, you include a Style attribute in the element you want to format. Within this attribute, you specify one or more individual *style properties* that control various style settings. Some of the most common style properties are listed in figure 5-8.

The HTML in this figure illustrates how you can use the Style attribute. Here, the style properties for the H1 element specify that the text it contains should be displayed in a bold, 16-point, white, Arial font against a blue background. Similarly, the style properties for the H2 element specify that the text it contains should be displayed in an italic, 14-point, Times New Roman font.

The three P elements in this figure show how you can use the Text-align property to align text on a page. The first element aligns the text at the left margin, the second element centers the text between the margins, and the third element aligns the text at the right margin. All three of these elements also specify the Courier New font, which is a mono-spaced font. This figure illustrates how these elements and the two heading elements appear in a browser window.

Notice that the syntax for specifying style properties is different from the syntax you use for HTML attributes. Instead of an equals sign, you separate a style name from its value with a colon. And to separate items, you use semicolons.

You should also notice that the Font-family property in each of the Style attributes specifies a specific font plus a generic font style. For example, the Font-family property for the H1 element specifies Arial and sans-serif. That way, if the Arial font isn't installed on the computer where the page is displayed, the

Common properties of the Style attribute

Property	Description
Font-family	A comma-separated list of font names, such as Arial, Times New Roman, and Courier New, and generic font styles, such as serif, sans-serif, and monospace.
Font-size	A specific number of points, a point size relative to the parent element's font size, or a keyword such as small, medium, or large.
Font-style	A keyword that determines how the text is slanted. Possible values are normal, italic, and oblique.
Font-weight	A keyword that determines the boldness of the font. Possible values are normal, bold, bolder, and lighter. Bolder or lighter are relative to the parent element.
Background-color	A color value, such as red, blue, or yellow that controls the background color of an element.
Color	A color value that controls the foreground color of an element.
Text-align	A keyword that determines the alignment of the text in a P element relative to the page margins. Possible values are left, right, center, or justify.

HTML that uses inline styles

```
<h1 style="Font-Weight: bold; Font-Size: 16pt; Color: white; Font-Family:
    Arial, Sans-Serif; Background-Color: blue">The Halloween Store</h1>
<h2 style="Font-Size: 14pt; Font-Style: italic; Font-Family:
    'Times New Roman', Serif">The Halloween Store</h2>
<p style="Font-Size: 10pt; Font-Family: 'Courier New', Monospace;
    Text-Align: left">This text is left-justified and mono-spaced.</p>
<p style="Font-Size: 10pt; Font-Family: 'Courier New', Monospace;
    Text-Align: center">This text is centered and mono-spaced.</p>
<p style="Font-Size: 10pt; Font-Family: 'Courier New', Monospace;
    Text-Align: right">This text is right-justified and mono-spaced.</p>
```

The HTML viewed in a browser window

The Halloween Store

The Halloween Store

```
This text is left-justified and mono-spaced.

            This text is centered and mono-spaced.

                This text is right-justified and mono-spaced.
```

Description

- You can use the Style attribute to create an *inline style* that affects the appearance of a single element in an HTML document and any child elements it contains. If you specify a style for a child element, it overrides the style specified by the parent element.

- Within the Style attribute, you specify one or more *style properties*, such as Font-size and Font-family. The name of each property is separated from its value by a colon, and the properties are separated from one another with semicolons.

Figure 5-8   How to use inline styles

text will be displayed in the default sans-serif font. When you code the Font-family property, you can specify as many different fonts as you want, and the first one that's available will be used. In case none of the fonts you specify are available, however, you should always end the list with a generic font style.

Although it's not illustrated in this figure, you should realize that if an element contains child elements, the style properties for the parent element are also applied to the child elements. For example, if you wanted to display most of the text in the body of a document in 10-point Arial, you could add a Style attribute to the Body element with the appropriate style properties. Then, if you wanted to display a child element within the Body element in a different font, you could add a Style attribute to that element to override the style properties in the Body element.

How to use the Span element to apply styles

When you use inline styles, the style properties you specify apply to the entire element. If you want to apply a style to just a portion of an element, though, you can do that using a Span element. Figure 5-9 illustrates how this works.

The first example in this figure shows how you can use the Span element to format a portion of literal text. Similarly, the second example shows how you can format a portion of the text that's displayed for an Anchor element. If you look at how the literal text and Anchor element appear in a browser, you shouldn't have any trouble understanding how the Span element works.

Examples of Span elements

A Span element used to format a portion of literal text

```
This is the <span style="background-color: blue; color: white">selected
</span> item.
```

A Span element used to format text that's displayed for an Anchor element

```
<a href="inlinestyles.aspx">Click here for a list of
    <span style="FONT-WEIGHT: bold; FONT-SIZE: large; COLOR: red">
    Drastically Reduced</span> items</a>
```

The elements viewed in a browser

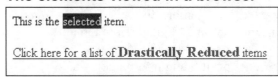

The Span element

Start tag	End tag	Description
<span>	</span>	Delimits HTML content.

One attribute of a Span element

Attribute	Description
Style	Specifies one or more style properties that affect the appearance of the text within the Span element.

Description

- The Span element delimits content within an HTML document. It's typically used to apply styles to all or part of the text within another element.
- When you format selections of text using the controls on the Formatting toolbar, Visual Studio often inserts a Span element to apply the formatting you select.
- See figure 5-8 for some common properties of the Style attribute.

Figure 5-9   How to use the Span element to apply styles

How to use styles to position elements

In most cases, you'll use flow layout to position the elements on the web pages you create. With flow layout, elements are positioned from left to right and from top to bottom on the page. Occasionally, though, you may want to use *two-dimensional positioning* to position an element at a specific location. To do that, you use the properties of the Style attribute presented in figure 5-10.

To start, you use the Position property to indicate how you want an element positioned. If you specify Absolute, the element is positioned at the location specified by the Top and Left properties. In most cases, the top and left values will be relative to the top left corner of the page. For example, the code for the first control in this figure typically positions the control 448 pixels from the left side of the page and 16 pixels from the top of the page. However, if an element is contained within another element that includes positioning information, the element is positioned relative to the top left corner of its containing element.

If you specify Relative for the Position property, the positioning is still based on the values for the Top and Left properties, but the position is relative to where the element appears within the flow of the page. If, for example, the button defined by the second example in this figure appears after a text box, this button will always appear 8 pixels to the right of the text box (unless the browser window isn't wide enough to display it).

In contrast, if you specify Static for the Position property, the element will be positioned using flow layout. You'll typically see this value only if you use the Layout→Position menu to apply absolute or relative positioning to an element and then decide to change the element back to flow layout using this menu. Note, however, that you can also select Not Set from this menu to remove all positioning information from an element.

The last property listed in this figure, Z-index, determines how elements are displayed if their positions cause them to overlap. By default, the first element you position on a form using absolute or relative positioning is given a Z-index value of 100. Then, the Z-index value of each additional element you add that uses absolute or relative positioning is increased by 1. Because elements with higher Z-index values are displayed in front of elements with lower Z-index values, each successive element is displayed in a higher layer on the page. Of course, you can modify the Z-index values if that's not what you want.

Although you can use the Tools→Option command to set up two-dimensional positioning for an entire form (which used to be called *grid layout*), you're usually better off with flow layout because it works better with varying sizes of browser windows. Then, if necessary, you can use two-dimensional positioning to position individual controls exactly where you want them on a page or relative to other controls. And you can use the Z-Index property to overlap elements.

Common Style properties for setting the position of an element

Property	Description
Position	A keyword that determines how an element is positioned on the page. See the table below for possible values.
Top	The position of the top of the element as an absolute value or a value relative to the normal flow of elements, depending on the value of the Position property. The default unit of measure is pixels (px).
Left	The position of the left of the element as an absolute value or a value relative to the normal flow of elements, depending on the value of the Position property. The default unit of measure is pixels (px).
Z-index	Controls the display of overlapped elements. An element with a higher Z-index value is displayed in front of elements with lower Z-index values.

Position values

Value	Description
Absolute	The element is positioned at the location specified by the Top and Left properties within the first parent element that has positioning information. If no parent element has positioning information, the location is based on the Body element.
Relative	The element is positioned at the location specified by the Top and Left properties relative to its flow within the page.
Static	The element is positioned using flow layout.

The aspx code for a control that uses absolute positioning

```
<asp:Image ID="Image1" runat="server" ImageUrl="~/Images/Murach logo.jpg"
    Style="z-index: 100; left: 448px; position: absolute; top: 16px" />
```

The aspx code for a control that uses relative positioning

```
<asp:Button ID="btnSearch" runat="server" Text="Search"
    Style="left: 8px; position: relative; top: 0px; z-index: 101;" />
```

Description

- You can use *two-dimensional positioning* to place an element at a specific location on a page. An element can be placed at an absolute location or at a location relative to its position within the flow of the page.

- To apply absolute or relative positioning to an existing element, select the element in Design view and choose Absolute or Relative from the Layout→Position menu. Then, drag the element to place it on the form.

- To change the positioning of an element back to flow layout, choose Static or Not Set from the Layout→Position menu. Not Set removes all positioning information from the element, and Static changes the value of the Position property to Static.

- The Z-index property lets you layer elements on a page. By default, the first element you add to a form using absolute or relative positioning is given a Z-index value of 100, the next element is given a Z-index value of 101, and so on.

Figure 5-10   How to use styles to position elements

How to use the Style Builder

To simplify the task of creating Style attributes, you can use the Style Builder dialog box shown in figure 5-11. This dialog box lets you select the styles you want to use. Then, it generates a Style attribute with the appropriate style properties for the elements you select.

As you can see in this figure, the Style Builder dialog box separates the style properties into several categories. To display a specific category, you simply click on the category name in the list at the left side of the dialog box. In this figure, for example, you can see the properties in the Font category, which are the ones you'll use most often.

The Style Builder dialog box

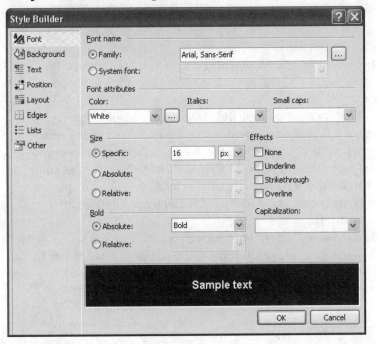

Description

- You can use the *Style Builder* to generate Style attributes for you. The list at the left side of the Style Builder dialog box lets you display different categories of style settings.

- To display the Style Builder dialog box from Design view, select the elements or literal text you want the style to apply to. Then, choose the Format→Style command; right-click the elements or text and choose Style from the shortcut menu that's displayed; or click the Style property in the Properties window and then click the ellipsis button that appears.

- To display the Style Builder dialog box from Source view, place the cursor anywhere in the element you want the style to apply to. Then, click the Style property in the Properties window and click the ellipsis button that appears. However, you can't use the Style Builder to apply styles to literal text in Source view.

- You can use the Style Builder to create inline styles, or you can use it to create style rules for external style sheets as described in figure 5-12.

Figure 5-11   How to use the Style Builder

How to use an external style sheet

Although inline styles are a convenient way to make quick changes to a document's appearance, you'll typically use an external style sheet to define the basic formatting for the elements in a document. Then, if you need to modify that style for a specific element, you can use inline styles. Figure 5-12 shows how to use an external style sheet.

An *external style sheet* contains a set of *style rules* that are stored in a file. Each style rule specifies a list of style properties that are applied to one or more HTML elements. The first style rule shown in this figure, for example, specifies that Body elements should be displayed in the 11-point Times New Roman font. The other style rules specify how H1, H2, H3, and A elements will be displayed. Notice that two different style rules are defined for A elements. You'll learn more about that in the next figure.

To use an external style sheet, a page must include a Link element in its document head. Later in this chapter, you'll learn two techniques you can use to generate a Link element from Visual Studio. For now, you just need to understand the three attributes presented in this figure in case you want to code the Link element yourself.

The first attribute, Href, specifies the URL of the style sheet you want to use. The Link element in this figure, for example, specifies the Murach.css style sheet. The second attribute, Rel, indicates that the link is for a style sheet. And the third attribute, Type, indicates the *MIME type* of the link. For a style sheet, the MIME type should be set to text/css.

The last example in this figure shows how you can create a style rule that applies to more than one element. To do that, you simply code the element names separated by commas at the beginning of the rule. In this example, the style rule applies to both the H2 and H3 elements.

The code for the Murach.css style sheet

```
body  {Font-Family: Times New Roman, Serif; Font-Size: 11pt}

H1 {Font-Family: Arial, Sans-Serif; Font-Size: 14pt; Color: blue;
    Text-Align: center}
H2 {Font-Family: Arial, Sans-Serif; Font-Size: 14pt; Color: blue}
H3 {Font-Family: Arial, Sans-Serif; Font-Size: 12pt; Color: blue}

a {Font-Family: Arial, Sans-Serif; Font-Size: 9pt}
a:hover {Font-Weight: bold}
```

The code in an HTML document that links to the style sheet

```
<head>
    <title>Chapter 5: Shopping Cart</title>
    <link href="Murach.css" rel="stylesheet" type="text/css" />
</head>
```

The Link element

Tag	Description
<link>	Defines the link to an external style sheet.

Attributes of the Link element

Attribute	Description
Href	The URL of the document to be linked. For a style sheet, the document must have a file extension of *css*.
Rel	The relationship between the Link element and the URL specified in the Href attribute. For a style sheet, supply a value of Stylesheet.
Type	The MIME (Multipurpose Internet Mail Extension) type of the Link element. For a style sheet, supply a value of text/css. Required only for email applications.

A style rule for two HTML elements

```
H2, H3 {Font-Family: Arial, Sans-Serif; Font-Size: 14pt; Color: blue}
```

Description

- An *external style sheet* is a file that contains *style rules* for HTML elements. Each style rule associates an HTML element with a list of style properties. Then, the styles are applied automatically whenever an element of the specified type appears in the document.

- To link an HTML document to an external style sheet, you include a Link element that identifies the style sheet within the document's Head element.

- You can create a style rule for two or more elements by coding a comma-separated list of the elements at the beginning of the style rule.

- You can create two or more styles for the same element by using classes. See figure 5-13 for details.

Figure 5-12   How to use an external style sheet

How to use classes in a style sheet

Another feature of style sheets that you may find useful is *style classes*. With *regular classes*, you can define more than one style rule for the same element, or you can define a generic style rule that can be applied to any element. The first set of examples in figure 5-13 illustrates how this works.

The first statement shows how to define a style rule for a class that can be used only with a specific element. To do that, you code the element name, followed by a period and the class name you want to use for the class. Then, you code the style properties just as you would for any other style. To apply a style class to an element, you name the class on the Class attribute for that element as illustrated in the second statement.

The third statement shows how to define a style rule for a class that can be used with any element. To do that, you simply omit the element name from the beginning of the style rule. Then, you can apply the class to any element using its Class attribute.

In addition to the regular classes you define, HTML also provides for *pseudo-classes*. The names of these classes are predefined and, in some cases, can be applied only to specific elements. The Link and Visited classes, for example, can only be applied to an A element, as indicated by the first table in this figure. You can use these classes to specify the style for an A element based on its state. If the user hasn't clicked on the link defined by the element, it's displayed with the style specified by the Link class. Otherwise, it's displayed with the style specified by the Visited class.

Unlike the pseudo-classes you use for A elements, you can apply the Hover, Active, and Focus classes, called *dynamic pseudo-classes*, to any element. In this case, the class that's used is based on a user action. If the user points to the element with the mouse, for example, the element is displayed with the style specified by the Hover class. And if the user moves the focus to the element, it's displayed with the style specified by the Focus class.

The last three style rules in this figure illustrate how you might use pseudo-classes with an A element. Here, the first style rule defines the basic formatting for the element: 9-point Arial. Then, the second style rule specifies that after the user clicks on the link defined by the element, it should be displayed in blue. Finally, if the user points to the link, it should be displayed in bold.

How to use regular classes

A style rule that can be used only with the specified element

```
P.ProductList {Font-Size: X-Large; Font-Family: Arial, Sans-Serif}
```

An element that uses the style rule

```
<p class=ProductList>Ugly Rat</p>
```

A style rule for a generic class

```
.ProductList {Font-Size: X-Large; Font-Family: Arial, Sans-Serif}
```

Pseudo-classes for the Anchor element

Tag	Class	Description
<a>	Link	The style that's applied to links that haven't been visited by the user.
<a>	Visited	The style that's applied to links that have been visited by the user.

Dynamic pseudo-classes

Class	Description
Hover	The style that's applied while the user points to an element with a pointing device (usually the mouse).
Active	The style that's applied while an element is being activated by the user.
Focus	The style that's applied while an element has the focus.

Style rules that include a pseudo-class and a dynamic pseudo-class

```
a {Font-Family: Arial, Sans-Serif; Font-Size: 9pt}
a:visited {Color: blue}
a:hover {Font-Weight: bold}
```

Description

- You can use *style classes* to define two or more styles for the same element. You can define your own *regular classes* or use predefined *pseudo-classes*.

- To define a regular class that can be used only with a specified element, code the name of the element, followed by a period, followed by the class name and style properties. To define a generic class that can be used with any element, omit the element name.

- To use a regular class, name it on the Class attribute of the element you want to apply it to.

- To define a pseudo-class, code the name of the element, followed by a colon, followed by the class name and the style properties. The styles defined by these classes are applied automatically when the specified condition occurs.

- The pseudo-classes you're most likely to use are the ones for the Anchor element and the *dynamic pseudo-classes* shown above. You can use the dynamic pseudo-classes with any element. The style rules for dynamic pseudo-classes must always be coded after any other style rules.

Figure 5-13   How to use classes in a style sheet

Visual Studio features for working with style sheets

Although you can create a style sheet using any text editor, Visual Studio provides some features that make it easy to create and work with style sheets. These features are described in figure 5-14. To create a new style sheet, for example, you can use the Style Sheet template in the Add New Item dialog box.

To work with an existing style sheet, you display it in a Text Editor window. Then, you can add a style rule using the Add Style Rule dialog box shown in this figure. As you can see, this dialog box lets you define a style rule for an element, for a class, or for an element with a specified ID. (ID is an attribute you can use to uniquely identify an element.) Note that if you create a style rule for a class, a generic class is defined by default. To define a class for a specific element, check the Optional Element option and then select the element from the drop-down list. A preview of the style rule appears near the lower right corner of the dialog box. Then, you can click on the add button (>) to create the style rule.

When you create a new style rule, Visual Studio adds the rule without any style properties to the style sheet. After I added the style rule shown in this figure, for example, this code was added to the style sheet:

```
P:ProductList
{
}
```

Then, you can add properties to the style rule using the Style Builder you learned about in figure 5-11. To display the Style Builder dialog box, click anywhere in the style rule and choose the Styles→Build Style command.

You should also notice the CSS Outline window that's displayed at the left side of the Visual Studio window when a style sheet is displayed. This window displays the style rules defined by the style sheet in a tree structure. You can use this tree to navigate to a specific style rule by expanding the folder that contains that rule and then clicking on the rule.

An external style sheet in Visual Studio

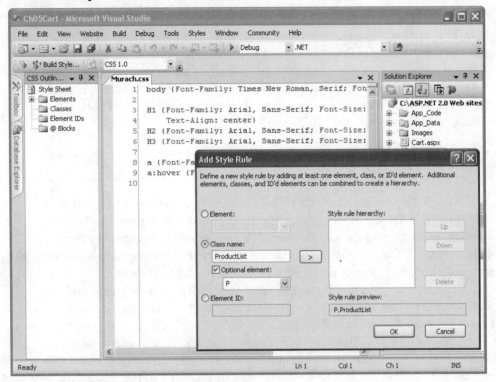

Discussion

- To create an external style sheet, choose the Web Site→Add New Item command. Then, select the Style Sheet template from the list of available templates, type the name you want to use for the new style sheet, and click Add.

- To edit an existing style sheet, double-click on it in the Solution Explorer to display it in a Text Editor window.

- To link a page to a style sheet, display the page in the Web Forms Designer. Then, select DOCUMENT in the drop-down list at the top of the Properties window and set the Stylesheet property to the style sheet you want to use.

- You can also link a page to a style sheet by displaying the page in Source view and then dragging the style sheet from the Solution Explorer to the Head element for the page.

- To add a style rule to a style sheet, use the Add Style Rule dialog box. To display this box, open the style sheet in an editor window, then choose Styles→Add Style Rule.

- To add style properties to a style rule, click anywhere in the rule and choose the Styles→Build Style command to display the Style Builder (see figure 5-11).

- You can use the CSS Outline window (View→Other Windows→Document Outline) that's displayed at the left side of the Visual Studio window to navigate to the style rule you select.

Figure 5-14   Visual Studio features for working with style sheets

How to code tables

HTML *tables* present content in grids of *rows* and *columns*. You can use tables to present tabular information in a way that resembles a spreadsheet. You can also use tables as a way to control the overall layout of page elements such as titles, banners, navigation bars, and content areas. You learned the basic skills for creating tables in chapter 2. Now, you'll learn more about the HTML you can use to code tables.

How to create a table

Figure 5-15 presents the basic HTML elements you use to create a table. To start, you use a Table element to identify the start and end of the table. Within the Table element, you use one or more Tr elements to define each row of the table. (Tr stands for Table Row.) Then, within each Tr element, you use one or more Td elements to create each *cell*. (Td stands for Table Data.)

The code shown in this figure defines a table that contains three rows, each with two cells. Below the code, you can see how the table is displayed in a browser. Tables are frequently used to align form content like this.

Notice that the HTML shown here doesn't specify the size of the table or its cells. Because of that, the sizes will change dynamically depending on the data in each cell. If that's not what you want, you can use some of the formatting attributes you'll learn about in the next figure to control the table and cell sizes.

In this example, the first cell in each row contains literal text, and the second cell in each row contains a text box. You should realize, however, that a cell can store any type of data, including other tables. In fact, it's common for a web page to consist of tables nested within other tables.

The HTML elements for working with tables

Element	Start tag	End tag	Description
Table	\<table>	\</table>	Defines the start and end of a table.
Tr	\<tr>	\</tr>	Defines the start and end of a row.
Td	\<td>	\</td>	Defines the start and end of a cell within a row.

The HTML code for a table

```
<p>Please enter the following information:</p>
<table cellspacing="5" cellpadding="5" border="1">
  <tr>
    <td align="right">First name:</td>
    <td><asp:TextBox id="txtFirstName" runat="server"></asp:TextBox></td>
  </tr>
  <tr>
    <td align="right">Last name:</td>
    <td><asp:TextBox id="txtLastName" runat="server"></asp:TextBox></td>
  </tr>
  <tr>
    <td align="right">Email address:</td>
    <td><asp:TextBox id="txtEmail" runat="server"></asp:TextBox></td>
  </tr>
</table>
```

The table displayed in a browser

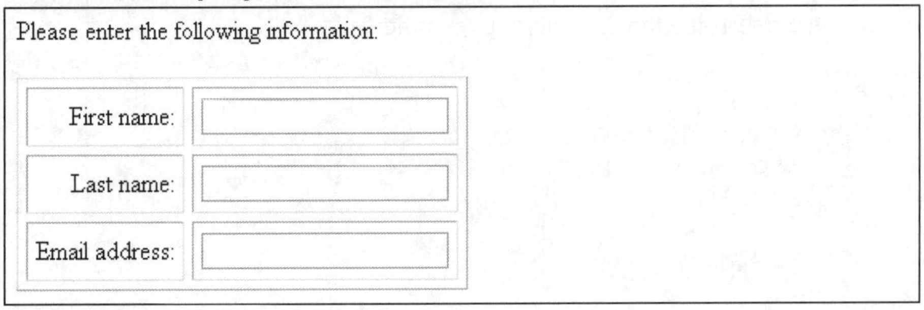

Please enter the following information:

First name:

Last name:

Email address:

Description

- A *table* consists of *rows* and *columns*. The intersection of a row and column is a *cell* that can hold content, such as text, images, controls, or even other tables.
- By default, the height and width of the cells in a table change dynamically depending on their content. However, you can specify static cell sizes as well as other table formatting options using the attributes and style properties presented in figure 5-16.
- Tables are often used to align form content and to control the overall layout of a page.

Figure 5-15   How to create a table

Common table attributes and style properties

Figure 5-16 presents some of the attributes you can use with Table, Tr, and Td elements. To control the border that's displayed around a table and between the cells in a table, for example, you set the Border attribute of the table. Notice that to hide the border, you can set this attribute to 0. To control the amount of space between the cells in a table, you set the Cellspacing attribute of the table. And to control the amount of space between the border and the contents of a cell, you set the Cellpadding attribute of the table.

Two of the attributes shown in this figure, Colspan and Rowspan, are essential when working with complicated table layouts. These attributes let you create cells that span two or more columns or rows. You'll see an example of a table that uses the Colspan attribute in the next figure.

This figure also shows some of the style properties you can use with table elements. You can use the Height and Width properties to set an absolute height or width for the table or for individual rows or cells. These properties are especially useful when you use a table to control page layout. Then, you'll want the total height and width of the table to be less than the total number of pixels for your target resolution. Since many web sites are designed to be viewed best in an 800x600 pixel window, that usually means coding tables with widths less than 780 pixels and heights less than 580 pixels. That leaves an extra 20 pixels for the horizontal and vertical scroll bars. Note that the width of a table includes the width of all of the cells plus the spacing between the cells.

Common attributes of the Table element

Attribute	Description
Border	Specifies the visual border of the table. To turn the border off, specify a value of 0. To specify the width of the border in pixels, specify a value of 1or greater.
Cellspacing	Specifies the number of pixels between cells.
Cellpadding	Specifies the number of pixels between the contents of a cell and the edge of the cell.

Common attribute of the Tr element

Attribute	Description
Valign	Specifies the vertical alignment of the contents of the row. Acceptable values include Top, Bottom, and Middle.

Common attributes of the Td element

Attribute	Description
Align	Specifies the horizontal alignment of the contents of the cell. Acceptable values include Left, Right, and Center.
Colspan	Specifies the number of columns that the cell will span. This attribute is used to create wide cells that span two or more columns.
Rowspan	Specifies the number of rows that the cell will span. This attribute is used to create tall cells that span two or more rows.
Valign	Specifies the vertical alignment of the contents of the cell. Acceptable values include Top, Bottom, and Middle. This value overrides any alignment you specify for the row.

Common style properties for table elements

Property	Description
Height	The height of the element. To specify the height in pixels, use a number such as 60px. To specify the height as a percent of the parent element, use a number followed by the percent sign such as 20%. The height of the parent element must be specified explicitly.
Width	The width of the element. This works like the height property except that you don't have to specify the width of the parent element explicitly if you specify the width of the child element as a percent. You can also specify the width of a table using the Width attribute.
Background-color	The background color for the element. The background color of a row overrides the background color of the table, and the background color of a cell overrides the background color of the row.

Note

- Colors can be specified by using color names or color values, but color values give you more control over the color. To choose a color, use the Color drop-down list in the Background category of the Style Builder dialog box. Or, click on the ellipsis button to the right of the Color drop-down list and then choose the color you want from the Color Picker dialog box that's displayed.

Figure 5-16   Common table attributes and style properties

How to use a table to control the layout of a page

Figure 5-17 shows how to use a table to arrange a page that consists of three areas. A banner area is displayed at the top of the page, a navigation area is displayed at the left side of the page, and a content area occupies the rest of the page. This table consists of two rows. The first one consists of a single cell that contains the banner area. The second one consists of two cells that contain the navigation and content area.

The key to the HTML for this table is the Colspan attribute in the first Td element. It causes the cell in the first row to span both of the columns in that row. Also notice that the Border and Cellspacing attributes of the table are set to 0 so the cells will appear right next to each other. In addition, each cell has a different background color so you can see the area that it occupies. Although this is a relatively simple layout, it should help you begin to see how you can use tables to divide a page into distinct areas.

A table that defines a simple page layout

```
<table style="width: 750px" border="0" cellspacing="0">
    <tr style="height: 75px">
        <td colspan="2" style="background-color: Gray">
            Banner area
        </td>
    </tr>
    <tr style="height: 400px">
        <td style="width: 150px; background-color: Silver" valign="top">
            Navigation area
        </td>
        <td style="width: 600px; background-color: White" valign="top">
            Content area
        </td>
    </tr>
</table>
```

The table viewed in a browser

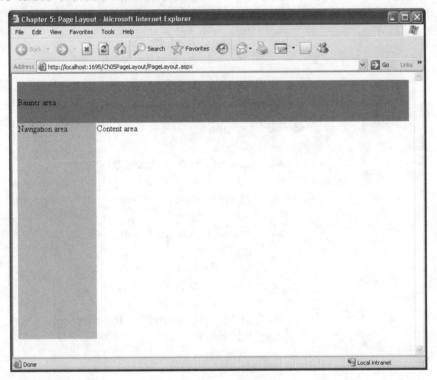

Description

- The Colspan attribute for the cell that makes up the banner area is set to 2 so that it spans both of the columns in the table.
- The Border attribute for the table is set to zero so no border appears around the table or between the cells in the table, and the Cellspacing attribute for the table is set to zero so there is no space between the cells in the table.
- Each cell is defined with a different color so you can see how the layout appears when displayed in the browser.

Figure 5-17   How to use a table to control the layout of a page

Perspective

The goal of this chapter has been to teach you the HTML essentials that you need for ASP.NET programming. So at this point, you should feel qualified to modify the HTML that's generated by Visual Studio so each form looks just the way you want it to. In some cases, you may even find that it's easier to use HTML for creating an element like a table from scratch than it is to use the features of Visual Studio for generating the HTML.

Above all, you should now be able to understand most of the HTML that's generated for a form. You should also understand much of the code that actually gets sent to the browser. Then, to complete your understanding of the code that gets generated for the controls of a form, the next chapter tells you more about asp elements.

Of course, there's a lot more to HTML than what's presented in this chapter. So if you want to learn more about HTML, you can get a book that's dedicated entirely to that topic. When you use Visual Studio to develop your forms, though, that shouldn't be necessary.

Terms

HTML document	column
HTML element	cell
tag	cascading style sheets (CSS)
start tag	inline style
end tag	external style
content	style property
attribute	two-dimensional positioning
comment	grid layout
white space	Style Builder
render a control	external style sheet
root element	style rule
child element	MIME (Multipurpose Internet Mail
parent element	Extension)
directive block	style class
self-closing tag	regular class
table	pseudo-class
row	dynamic pseudo-class

6

How to work with server controls

So far in this book, you've learned the basic skills for working with some of the most common server controls: labels, text boxes, buttons, drop-down lists, and list boxes. Now, this chapter presents some additional skills for working with these controls. It also presents the skills for working with other common controls, like check boxes and radio buttons, and some advanced controls, like the file upload and image map controls. When you complete this chapter, you'll be able to create ASP.NET web forms that use any of the server controls.

An introduction to server controls

In chapter 2, you learned how to add server controls to a web form and set control properties. Now, you'll learn about the different types of server controls and how you use them. You'll also see a summary of the web server controls that are presented in this chapter, you'll learn two ways to handle control events, and you'll learn how to use access keys with web server controls.

Types of server controls

Figure 6-1 describes the seven different types of server controls that you can use in your ASP.NET applications. These seven categories correspond to the groups in the Visual Studio Toolbox. For example, you'll find the standard controls in the Standard group of the Toolbox.

The controls you'll use most often are the standard controls, the data controls, and the validation controls. You'll learn how to use many of the standard controls in this chapter. Then, in chapter 7, you'll learn how to use the validation controls. And you'll learn how to use the data controls in chapters 13 through 16.

You'll use the next three types of controls only for special situations. For example, you can use the navigation controls to provide menus and path maps that let users navigate to various pages within your web site. You can use the login controls to manage access to your site. And you can use the web part controls to build pages that users can customize. You'll learn about these types of controls in later chapters.

Together, the first six types of controls are typically referred to as *web server controls*. As you know, a web server control is implemented by a class that you can use to work with the control from a web application that runs on a web server. In contrast, you can't work with the HTML controls from a web application. That's because these controls map directly to standard HTML elements. For example, the Text control maps directly to an Input element that has its Type attribute set to "Text".

If you want to work with an HTML control from a web application, you can convert it to a server control. To do that, just select the Run As Server Control command from the shortcut menu for the control. This adds a Runat attribute with the value "Server" to the HTML element. This attribute indicates that the element should be processed on the server. Then, you can work with the control using standard object-oriented techniques. Since *HTML server controls* don't provide the same functionality as the web server controls, however, you won't use them often.

Standard

- Commonly used user input controls such as labels, text boxes, and drop-down lists
- Many can be bound to a data source
- The MultiView and Wizard controls will be described in chapter 20

Data

- Databound user-interface controls that display data via a data source control
- Data source controls that access data from a variety of databases, XML data sources, and business objects
- Described in chapters 13 through 16

Validation

- Used to validate user input
- Work by running client-side script
- Can handle most validation requirements
- Described in chapter 7

Navigation

- Controls that provide menus and path maps for navigating a web site
- Described in chapter 10

Login

- Controls that provide user authentication
- Described in chapter 18

WebParts

- Controls that let you create a page from user-selectable components
- Described in chapter 22

HTML

- Standard HTML controls that can be converted to HTML server controls
- Not commonly used in ASP.NET applications

Description

- The Toolbox contains several groups that contain more than 80 different controls. The headings in this figure correspond to the names of the groups in the Toolbox.
- By default, the controls in the HTML group are implemented as standard HTML elements that are processed on the client. To convert an HTML control to a control that can be processed on the server, right-click on the control in Design view and select Run As Server Control from the control's shortcut menu.

Figure 6-1   Types of server controls

The web server controls presented in this chapter

Figure 6-2 summarizes the web server controls that you'll learn about in this chapter. You'll find all of these controls in the Standard group of the Toolbox.

If you've developed Windows applications, you'll notice that many of these controls have Windows counterparts and operate similarly to the Windows controls. Because of that, you shouldn't have much difficulty learning how to use most of these controls. As you'll see in this chapter, however, some of the techniques you use to work with these controls are different from the techniques you use to work with their Windows counterparts. In addition, some of the functionality they provide is different. So you'll want to be sure to read about each control even if you're familiar with Windows controls.

Also, you should realize that there are other standard controls besides the ones shown in this figure. In fact, the Standard group of the Toolbox provides 28 different web server controls. You'll learn about a couple of the controls that aren't listed here in later chapters. And, later in this chapter, you'll learn how to use the Visual Studio documentation to get information about the other controls so you can use them too.

The web server controls presented in this chapter

Control	Name	Suggested prefix	Description
A	Label	lbl	Displays descriptive information.
abl	TextBox	txt	Lets the user enter or modify a text value.
ab	Button	btn	Submits a page for processing.
ab	LinkButton	lbtn	Submits a page for processing.
▣	ImageButton	ibtn	Submits a page for processing.
A	HyperLink	hlnk	Lets the user move to another page in the application.
▤	DropDownList	ddl	Lets the user choose an item from a list that drops down from the control.
▤	ListBox	lst	Lets the user choose one or more items from a list.
☑	CheckBox	chk	Turns an option on or off.
▤	CheckBoxList	cbl	Turns options in a list of options on or off.
◉	RadioButton	rdo	Turns an option on or off. Only one radio button in a group can be on.
▤	RadioButtonList	rbl	Turns an option in a list of options on or off. Only one radio button in the list can be on.
▣	Image	img	Displays an image.
▣	ImageMap	imap	Displays an image with one or more clickable areas that submit the page for processing when clicked.
▤	BulletedList	blst	Displays a bulleted or numbered list.
▦	Calendar	cln	Displays a calendar and lets the user select one or more dates.
▤	FileUpload	upl	Displays a text box and a button that lets the user browse for a file to be uploaded.

Description

- The button, image button, and link button controls all provide the same functionality. They differ only in how they appear on the form.
- The check box list and radio button list controls serve as containers for a collection of check box or radio button items. They're typically used to create a list of check boxes or radio buttons that are bound to a data source. If you need more control over the layout of the check boxes or radio buttons, though, you can use individual controls.
- The image map, bulleted list, and file upload controls are new to ASP.NET 2.0.

Figure 6-2   The web server controls presented in this chapter

Two ways to handle control events

Like other objects, server controls have events that are fired when certain actions are performed on them. When you click on a button control, for example, the Click event is fired. If your application needs to respond to an event, you code a Sub procedure called an *event handler*. Figure 6-3 shows two ways you can do that.

When you generate an event handler from Visual Studio, the Sub procedure for the event includes a Handles clause that names the object and event that it handles. Then, you enter the code you want to be executed when that event occurs within the Sub procedure. This is illustrated by the first example in this figure. Here, the Handles clause of the event handler indicates that the procedure handles the Click event of the control named btnCancel.

You can also create an event handler for a control without using the Handles clause. To do that, you name the event handler on the appropriate event attribute of the control. This is illustrated by the second example in this figure. Here, the asp tag for the control includes an OnClick attribute. This attribute names the Sub procedure that's executed when the Click event of the control is raised.

Regardless of which technique you use, you can use a single event handler to handle more than one event. If you include a Handles clause on the event handler, you simply list the events it will handle on that clause like this:

```
Sub Procedure NavigationButtons_Click _
    Handles btnPrevious.Click, btnNext.Click
```

Here, the event handler will handle the Click event of two buttons named btnPrevious and btnNext. Notice in this example that I changed the name of the procedure to indicate that it processes more than one event. That's possible because the events are associated with the event handler through the Handles clause and not through the procedure name.

To use a single event handler for more than one event when you don't use the Handles clause, you simply name the event handler on the appropriate event attributes. For example, consider these tags:

```
<asp:Button id="btnPrevious" runat="server" Text="Previous"
    OnClick="NavigationButtons_Click">
<asp:Button id="btnNext" runat="server" Text="Next"
    OnClick="NavigationButtons_Click">
```

Here again, the procedure named NavigationButtons_Click will handle the Click event for both buttons.

This figure also lists some of the most common control events and their associated attributes. As I present each of the web server controls in this chapter, I'll illustrate how you can use these events.

Now that you've seen the two techniques for handling control events, you may be wondering which technique is better. In most cases, I recommend you use the Handles clause to create event handlers, since that's the default in Visual Studio. However, you should be familiar with the other technique in case you encounter it in other ASP.NET applications.

Code that handles a Click event using the Handles clause

The asp tag for a button control

```
<asp:Button id="btnCancel" runat="server" Text="Cancel Order">
```

The event handler for the Click event of the control

```
Private Sub btnCancel_Click(ByVal sender As Object,
        ByVal e As System.EventArgs) Handles btnCancel.Click
    Session.Remove("Cart")
    Response.Redirect("Order.aspx")
End Sub
```

Code that handles a Click event using the OnClick attribute

The asp tag for a button control

```
<asp:Button id="btnCancel" runat="server" Text="Cancel Order"
    OnClick="btnCancel_Click">
```

The event handler for the Click event of the control

```
Protected Sub btnCancel_Click(ByVal sender As Object,
        ByVal e As System.EventArgs)
    Session.Remove("Cart")
    Response.Redirect("Order.aspx")
End Sub
```

Common control events

Event	Attribute	Controls
Click	OnClick	Button, image button, link button, image map
Command	OnCommand	Button, image button, link button
TextChanged	OnTextChanged	Text box
SelectedIndexChanged	OnSelectedIndexChanged	Drop-down list, list box, radio button list, check box list
CheckedChanged	OnCheckedChanged	Check box, radio button

Description

- An *event handler* is a Sub procedure that's called when a specified event occurs.
- By default, Visual Studio creates an event handler by including a Handles clause on the Sub procedure. The Handles clause names the control and event that the procedure handles. When you use this technique, you can give the procedure any name you want.
- You can also code an event handler without a Handles clause. Then, you have to name the handler in the appropriate event attribute of the control. For example, you can use the OnClick attribute to name the procedure that's executed when the user clicks a control.
- An event handler that uses the Handles clause can be declared with Public, Protected, or Private scope. Otherwise, it must be declared with Public or Protected scope.
- A single event handler can be used to handle more than one event. If you define the event handler using a Handles clause, you list the controls and events on that clause. Otherwise, you name the handler on each event attribute of each control you want it to handle.

Figure 6-3   Two ways to handle control events

How to use access keys with web server controls

Most Windows applications use *access keys* (also called *accelerator keys*) that let the user select controls by using keyboard shortcuts. If, for example, you designate F as the access key for an input field that accepts a customer's first name, the user can move the focus directly to this field by pressing Alt+F.

As figure 6-4 shows, ASP.NET 2.0 now lets you create access keys for web applications too. To create an access key, you simply add the AccessKey attribute to the control you want to create the keyboard shortcut for. Since the AccessKey attribute is defined by the System.Web.UI.WebControls.WebControl class, you can use it with any web control.

When you use access keys with text boxes and other controls that are identified by literal text, it's common to underline the access key in the literal text. To do that, you can use a Span element with the Text-decoration property set to underline. This is illustrated by the three labels in this figure.

If you use a label to identify a control instead of literal text, you can assign the access key to the label and then underline the appropriate letter of the label. In this case, you should also code the AssociatedControlID attribute to specify the control that should receive the focus when the user uses the access key.

Unfortunately, ASP.NET doesn't provide a way to underline the access key in a button control. That's because buttons are rendered using the <input type=submit> HTML element, which doesn't provide a way to format the text displayed by the button. You can still specify an access key, though, as illustrated by the last line of aspx code in this figure.

How to set the focus on a web server control

ASP.NET 2.0 provides two features that let you set the focus to a specific control on a form. First, you can use the DefaultFocus attribute of the form to determine which control receives the focus when the page is first display. In figure 6-4, for example, this attribute is set to the txtName control.

Second, you can move the focus to a control at runtime. To do that, you use the Focus method of the control. The statement shown in this figure, for example, moves the focus to the txtEmail control.

How to set the default button control

ASP.NET 2.0 also lets you set the button that's activated by default when you press the Enter key. To do that, you set the DefaultButton attribute of the form. In the example in this figure, this attribute is set to the btnNext button. Because of that, the form is posted back to the server when the Enter key is pressed, and the procedure for the Click event of the Next button is executed.

A form that uses access keys and default focus and button attributes

```
Please enter your contact information:

Name:    [                    ]

Email:   [                    ]

[ Previous ]  [ Next ]
```

The aspx code for the form

```
<form id="form1" runat="server" defaultfocus="txtName" defaultbutton="btnNext">
<div>
    Please enter your contact information:<br /><br />
    <table>
        <tr>
            <td style="width: 75px"><span style="text-decoration:
                underline">N</span>ame:</td>
            <td style="width: 100px">
                <asp:TextBox ID="txtName" runat="server"
                    AccessKey="N"></asp:TextBox></td></tr>
        <tr>
            <td style="width: 75px"><span style="text-decoration:
                underline">E</span>mail:</td>
            <td style="width: 100px">
                <asp:TextBox ID="txtEmail" runat="server"
                    AccessKey="E"></asp:TextBox></td></tr></table><br />
    <asp:Button ID="btnPrevious" runat="server" AccessKey="P"
        Text="Previous" /> 
    <asp:Button ID="btnNext" runat="server" AccessKey="N" Text="Next" /><br />
</div>
</form>
```

A statement that moves the focus to a control

```
txtEmail.Focus
```

Description

- In ASP.NET 2.0, you can use the AccessKey attribute on an web server control to specify a keyboard shortcut for the control. To use the keyboard shortcut, the user holds down the Alt key and presses the *access key* to move the focus to the control.

- If you use literal text to identify another control, you can identify the access key used by that control by underlining the appropriate letter in the literal text as shown above.

- If you use a label to identify another control, you can set the AccessKey attribute for the label and then set the AssociatedControlID attribute to the other control. When the user presses the access key for the label, the focus will be moved to the associated control.

- You can set the control that receives the focus when a form is first displayed using the DefaultFocus attribute of the form. To move the focus to a control at runtime, use the Focus method of the control.

- You can set the button that causes a form to be posted back when you press the Enter key using the DefaultButton attribute of the form.

Figure 6-4   How to use access keys with and set form defaults

How to work with button controls

Most web forms have at least one button control that the user can click to submit the form to the server for processing, commonly called a *submit button*. In the topics that follow, you'll learn how to use all three types of button controls that ASP.NET provides: buttons, link buttons, and image buttons.

How to work with buttons, link buttons, and image buttons

Figure 6-5 presents the three types of button controls. These controls differ only in how they appear to the user. This is illustrated by the three buttons shown at the top of this figure. As you can see, a *button* displays text within a rectangular area. A *link button* displays text that looks like a hyperlink. And an *image button* displays an image.

This figure also presents the asp tags for the three buttons that are illustrated. For the button and link button, the Text attribute provides the text that's displayed for the control. For the image button, the ImageUrl attribute provides the URL address of the image that's displayed on the button. In some cases, though, a browser may not be able to display the image. Because of that, you should also code the AlternateText attribute so it provides the text that's displayed if the browser isn't able to display the image.

When a user clicks one of the button controls, ASP.NET raises two events: Click and Command. You can see an event handler for the Click event of a button control in this figure. Notice that this event handler receives two arguments. The sender argument represents the control that was clicked. Because this argument has a type of Object, you'll need to convert it to a button control if you want to access the properties and methods of the control. You might want to do that, for example, if you code a procedure that handles the processing for more than one button. Then, you can use the Id property of the control to determine which button was clicked. An easier way to do that, however, is to use the Command event. You'll see how to use this event in figure 6-7.

The second argument that's passed to the event handler of a Click event, e, contains event-specific information. You're most likely to use this argument with an image button control to determine where the user clicked on the image. You'll learn more about that in the next figure.

Of course, the Click and Command event handlers are executed only if the page posts back to itself. If a value is specified for the PostBackUrl attribute, however, the page at the specified URL is executed and displayed. This is the cross-page posting feature you learned about in chapter 3.

Incidentally, from this point on in this chapter and this book, the figures will often present the asp elements for the controls that are used. By studying the code for these controls, you can quickly see how their attributes are set. Please keep in mind, though, that you usually add a control to a form by using the Designer, and you set the properties for a control by using the Properties window. Then, the code for the asp element in the aspx file is generated automatically.

A button, a link button, and an image button in a browser

The asp tags for the three buttons

```
<asp:Button ID="btnAdd" runat="server" Text="Add to Cart" />
    
<asp:LinkButton ID="lbtnCheckOut" runat="server"
    PostBackUrl="~/CheckOut1.aspx">Check Out</asp:LinkButton>
    
<asp:ImageButton ID="ibtnCart" runat="server" AlternateText="Cart"
    ImageUrl="~/Images/cart.gif" Height="60px" Width="68px"
    PostBackUrl="~/Cart.aspx" />
```

Common button attributes

Attribute	Description
Text	(Button and LinkButton controls only) The text displayed by the button. For a LinkButton control, the text can be coded as content between the start and end tags or as the value of the Text attribute.
ImageUrl	(ImageButton control only) The image to be displayed for the button.
AlternateText	(ImageButton control only) The text to be displayed if the browser can't display the image.
CausesValidation	Determines whether page validation occurs when you click the button. The default is True.
CommandName	A string value that's passed to the Command event when a user clicks the button.
CommandArgument	A string value that's passed to the Command event when a user clicks the button.
PostBackUrl	The URL of the page that should be requested when the user clicks the button.

An event handler for the Click event of a button control

```
Protected Sub btnAccept_Click(ByVal sender As Object, _
        ByVal e As System.EventArgs) Handles btnAccept.Click
    Me.AddInvoice()
    Response.Redirect("Confirmation.aspx")
End Sub
```

Description

- When a user clicks a *button*, *link button*, or *image button*, the page specified in the PostBackUrl attribute is loaded and executed. If this attribute isn't included, the page is posted back to the server and the Click and Command events are raised. You can code event handlers for either or both of these events.

- Two arguments are passed to the Click event handler: sender and e. Sender is the control that the user clicked, and e contains event-specific information. You can use the e argument with the image button control to determine where the user clicked in the image. See figure 6-6 for more information.

- See figure 6-7 for information on coding an event handler for the Command event.

Figure 6-5   How to work with buttons, link buttons, and image buttons

How to use the e argument of an image button control

In some cases, the processing that's performed when the user clicks on an image button will depend on where within the button the user clicks. To illustrate, consider the image button shown at the top of figure 6-6 that represents four navigation buttons. (This image uses the standard icons for First (<<), Previous (<), Next (>), and Last (>>)). This image button could be used to let the user navigate through pages in a section of your web site or to different rows of a data table.

To process an image button like this, you can use the X and Y properties of the e argument that's passed to the Click event handler of the button. These properties indicate the x and y coordinates where the user clicked. The event handler shown in this figure illustrates how this works.

In this example, a Select Case statement is used to determine the value of the X property. If it's between 0 and 23, it indicates that the user clicked the << icon. Then, the event handler executes the GoToFirstRow procedure. If it's between 24 and 47, it indicates that the user clicked the < icon, and the GoToPreviousRow procedure is executed. If it's between 48 and 71, it indicates that the user clicked the > icon, and the GoToNextRow procedure is executed. Last, if it's between 72 and 95, it indicates that the user clicked the >> icon, and the GoToLastRow procedure is executed. Notice that it's not necessary to check the y coordinate in this example. That's because all of the icons have the same y-coordinate range.

An image used for an image button control

The asp tag for the control

```
<asp:ImageButton ID="ibtnNavigate" runat="server"
    ImageUrl="~/Images/navbuttons.gif" Height="24px" Width="112px" />
```

An event handler for the Click event of the control

```
Protected Sub ibtnNavigate_Click(ByVal sender As Object, _
        ByVal e As System.Web.UI.ImageClickEventArgs) _
        Handles ibtnNavigate.Click
    Select Case e.X
        Case 0 To 23
            Me.GoToFirstRow()
        Case 24 To 47
            Me.GoToPreviousRow()
        Case 48 To 71
            Me.GoToNextRow()
        Case 72 To 95
            Me.GoToLastRow()
    End Select
End Sub
```

Properties of the ImageClickEventArgs class

Property	Description
X	An integer that represents the x coordinate where the user clicked the image button.
Y	An integer that represents the y coordinate where the user clicked the image button.

Description

- When the user clicks an ImageButton control, ASP.NET calls the Click event handler for the control and passes the x and y coordinates where the user clicked the image as properties of the e argument.
- You can use the X and Y properties to determine the processing that's performed when the user clicks on a particular part of an image.

Figure 6-6   How to use the e argument of an image button control

How to use the Command event

Figure 6-7 shows how you can use the Command event to process a group of button controls using a single event handler. Like the Click event, this event receives both a sender argument and an e argument. In this case, the e argument represents a CommandEventArgs object.

The two properties of the CommandEventArgs class are shown in this figure. You can use these properties to get the CommandName and CommandArgument properties of a control. When you create a button control, you can set the CommandName and CommandArgument properties to any string value. Then, you can examine them in the Command event handler to determine how the application should respond when the user clicks the button.

The examples in this figure illustrate how this works. The first example shows the asp tags for four button controls. Notice that a different CommandName value is assigned to each one. Although you can also assign CommandArgument values to each control, that's not necessary here.

The second example shows an event handler that processes the Command event of all four controls. To do that, it uses a Select Case statement to test the value of the CommandName property of the e argument. Since this value indicates the control that was clicked, it can be used to determine which procedure to call based on the button that was clicked. This is another way to do the processing you saw in figure 6-6 that used an image button control.

Four button controls that use the CommandName attribute

```
<asp:Button ID="btnFirst" runat="server" Text="<<" Width="25px"
    CommandName="First" />
<asp:Button ID="btnPrevious" runat="server" Text="<" Width="25px"
    CommandName="Previous" />
<asp:Button ID="btnNext" runat="server" Text=">" Width="25px"
    CommandName="Next" />
<asp:Button ID="btnLast" runat="server" Text=">>" Width="25px"
    CommandName="Last" />
```

An event handler for the Command events of the buttons

```
Protected Sub NavigationButtons_Command(ByVal sender As Object, _
        ByVal e As System.Web.UI.WebControls.CommandEventArgs) _
        Handles btnFirst.Command, btnPrevious.Command, _
            btnNext.Command, btnLast.Command
    Select Case e.CommandName
        Case "First"
            Me.GoToFirstRow()
        Case "Previous"
            Me.GoToPreviousRow()
        Case "Next"
            Me.GoToNextRow()
        Case "Last"
            Me.GoToLastRow()
    End Select
End Sub
```

Properties of the CommandEventArgs class

Property	Description
CommandName	The value specified in the CommandName property for the control that generated the Command event.
CommandArgument	The value specified in the CommandArgument property for the control that generated the Command event.

Description

- The Command event is raised whenever a user clicks a button control. It's useful as an alternative to the Click event when you want to code a single event handler for a group of buttons that perform related functions.
- The e argument that's passed to a Command event handler is a CommandEventArgs object. This object includes properties that let you retrieve the values of the CommandName and CommandArgument properties of the control. You can use these values to determine which control raised the Command event.

Note

- If you code an event handler for both the Click event and the Command event, the Click event handler will be executed first.

Figure 6-7   How to use the Command event

How to work with text boxes, labels, check boxes, and radio buttons

Two controls you'll use frequently as you develop web forms are text boxes and labels. As you know, text boxes let you accept input from the user, and labels let you display information to the user. Since you already know the basic skills for working with these controls, the topic that follows presents some additional skills. After that, you'll learn how to use check boxes and radio buttons to let users select from one or more options.

How to work text boxes and labels

At the top of figure 6-8, you can see part of a web page that contains a *text box* and a *label*. Unlike the text boxes you've seen up to this point, the text box shown here lets the user enter multiple lines of text. To accomplish that, the TextMode attribute of the text box is changed from its default of SingleLine to MultiLine. In addition, to indicate the number of lines that can be displayed in the text box at one time, the Rows attribute is set to 5. You can see these attributes in the asp tag for this control.

Another attribute you can use with a multi-line text box is Wrap. By default, this attribute is set to True, which means that text wraps automatically when it reaches the end of the text box. If you set this attribute to False, the user must press the Enter key to start a new line of text.

In addition to SingleLine and MultiLine, you can set the TextMode attribute to Password. Then, the characters the user enters are masked so they aren't displayed. Because ASP.NET 2.0 provides a new Login control that you can use to accept a user name and password from the user, you're not likely to use a text box to accept a password.

Although most text boxes are used to accept data from the user, you may occasionally need to restrict the user from entering data into a text box. To do that, you can set the ReadOnly attribute of the control to True. Then, the user can see the text in the control but can't change it.

You can use the MaxLength attribute to specify the maximum number of characters that can be entered into a text box. This is particularly useful if the data the user enters will be stored in a column of a database table. Then, you can limit the entry to the number of characters that are allowed for that column.

Although the width of a text box is set automatically as you size it in Design view, you can also set the width using the Columns attribute. This attribute specifies the width of the text box in characters. Note, however, that the width is approximate because it's based on the average width of a character for the font that's used.

The label control in this figure is also different from the ones you have seen so far in that it consists of two lines of text. To accomplish that, the text that's assigned to the Text property of the label includes HTML. You'll see the code that assigns this value in just a minute.

A text box and a label displayed in a browser

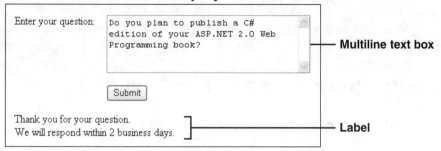

The asp tag for the text box

```
<asp:TextBox ID="txtQuestion" runat="server" Rows="5" TextMode="MultiLine"
    Width="296px"></asp:TextBox>
```

Common text box attributes

Attribute	Description
TextMode	The type of text box. SingleLine creates a standard text box, MultiLine creates a text box that accepts more than one line of text, and Password causes the characters that are entered to be masked. The default is SingleLine.
Text	The text content of the text box.
MaxLength	The maximum number of characters that can be entered into the text box.
Wrap	Determines whether or not text wraps automatically when it reaches the end of a multi-line text box. The default is True.
ReadOnly	Determines whether the user can change the text in the text box. The default value is False, which means that the text can be changed.
Columns	The width of the text box in characters. The actual width is determined based on the font that's used for the text entry.
Rows	The height of a multi-line text box in lines. The default value is 0, which sets the height to a single line.

The asp tag for the label

```
<asp:Label ID="lblConfirm" runat="server"></asp:Label>
```

Common label attribute

Attribute	Description
Text	The text displayed by the label.

Description

- *Text box controls* are typically used to accept input from the user. A text box can accept one or more lines of text depending on the setting of the TextMode attribute.

- *Label controls* provide an easy way to display text that can change from one execution of an ASP.NET page to the next. To display text that doesn't change, you typically use literal text.

Figure 6-8   How to work with text boxes and labels

Before I go on, I want to remind you that you typically use labels only to display text that changes from one execution of the page to the next. To include text that doesn't change, you can use literal text. That's how I entered the text "Enter your question:" in the example shown here.

How to work with check boxes and radio buttons

In addition to entering text into a form, you may want to let users select from one or more options. To do that, you can use *check boxes* or *radio buttons*. The main difference between these two types of controls is that radio buttons in groups are mutually exclusive and check boxes operate independently. In other words, if the user selects one radio button in a group, all of the other radio buttons in the same group are automatically turned off. In contrast, when a user selects a check box, it has no effect on other check boxes.

Figure 6-9 presents part of a web page that includes four check box controls and a group of two radio button controls. The first check box lets the user indicate if he wants to be added to a mailing list. The other check boxes let the user select what he wants to be contacted about. The radio buttons let the user select how he wants to be contacted.

To create a group of radio buttons, you simply specify the same name for the GroupName attribute of each radio button in the group. If you want to create two or more groups of radio buttons on a single form, just use a different group name for each group. Note that if you don't specify a group name for a radio button, that button won't be a part of any group. Instead, it will be processed independently of any other radio buttons on the form.

If you've developed Windows applications, you'll realize that this is in contrast to how Windows radio buttons work. In a Windows application, any radio buttons on a form that aren't specifically included in a group are treated as part of the same group. As a result, if a form has only one group of radio buttons, you can let them default to the same group. Since the Web Server radio button controls don't work that way, however, you'll almost always specify a group name for them.

To determine whether or not a radio button or check box is selected when it's first displayed, you use the Checked attribute. If you look at the aspx code for the check boxes and radio buttons shown in this figure, for example, you'll see that the Checked attributes of the first check box and the first radio button are set to True. When the web page is first displayed, then, these options will be selected as shown. Note that since only one radio button in a group can be selected, you should only set the Checked attribute to True for one button. If you set this property to True for more than one button in a group, the last one will be selected.

Four check boxes and two radio buttons displayed in a browser

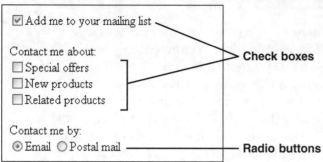

The aspx code for the check box and radio buttons

```
<asp:CheckBox ID="chkMail" runat="server" Checked="True"
    Text="Add me to your mailing list" /><br /><br />

Contact me about:<br />

<asp:CheckBox ID="chkSpecial" runat="server"
    Text="Special offers" /><br />
<asp:CheckBox ID="chkNew" runat="server"
    Text="New products" /><br />
<asp:CheckBox ID="chkRelated" runat="server"
    Text="Related products" /><br /><br />

Contact me by:<br />

<asp:RadioButton ID="rdoEmail" runat="server"
    Checked="True" GroupName="Contact" Text="Email" /> 
<asp:RadioButton ID="rdoPostal" runat="server"
    GroupName="Contact" Text="Postal mail" />
```

Common check box and radio button attributes

Attribute	Description
Text	The text that's displayed next to the check box or radio button.
Checked	Indicates whether the check box or radio button is selected. The default is False.
GroupName	The name of the group that the control belongs to (radio buttons only).

Description

- A *check box* displays a single option that the user can either check or uncheck. *Radio buttons* present a group of options from which the user can select just one option. All of the radio buttons in a group should have the same group name.

- If you want a check box or radio button to be selected when it's initially displayed, set its Checked attribute to True. If you set the Checked attribute of more than one radio button in the same group to True, only the last one will be selected.

Figure 6-9   How to work with check boxes and radio buttons

Visual Basic code for working with these controls

The examples in figure 6-10 show how you can work with text boxes, labels, check boxes and radio buttons in code. First, to retrieve the value the user enters into a text box, you use the Text property. In the example shown here, the Text property is assigned to a String variable. Note, however, that if the text box contains numeric data, you can convert it to the appropriate data type and then assign it to a variable with that data type. To be sure the user enters the correct data type, you can use validation controls as shown in the next chapter.

To assign a value to a label, you use the Text property of the label as shown in the second example in this figure. Notice here that the first line of text ends with an HTML tag for a line break (<br />). That way, the text will be displayed on two lines as you saw in figure 6-8.

The third and fourth examples in this figure show two ways you can process check boxes and radio buttons. First, you can process these controls in the event handler for the Click event of the form's submit button. Then, you just use If statements to test the Checked properties of the check boxes and radio buttons.

You can also process check boxes and radio buttons by writing event handlers for their CheckedChanged events. For a check box, this event is raised whenever the checked status of the control changes. Then, you can use an if statement to test the Checked property of the control just as you do in the event handler for the Click event of a submit button.

The CheckedChanged event works a bit differently for a radio button. Instead of being raised any time the status of the control changes, it's raised only when the status changes to checked. Because of that, there's no need to test the Checked property within the event handler for the CheckedChanged event.

In addition to the check box and radio button controls shown here, ASP.NET provides check box list and radio button list controls. These controls can simplify the task of creating groups of controls. You'll learn about these controls and the other list controls next.

Code that retrieves the text entered by the user in figure 6-8

```
Dim sQuestion As String = txtQuestion.Text
```

Code that changes the Text property of the label in figure 6-8

```
lblConfirm.Text = "Thank you for your question.<br />" _
               & "We will respond within 2 business days."
```

Code that processes the first check box and radio button in figure 6-9

```
Protected Sub btnContinue_Click(ByVal sender As Object, _
        ByVal e As System.EventArgs) Handles btnContinue.Click
    If chkMail.Checked Then
        Customer.Mail = True
    Else
        Customer.Mail = False
    End If
    If rdoEmail.Checked Then
        Customer.MailType = "Email"
    ElseIf rdoPostal.Checked Then
        Customer.MailType = "Postal"
    End If
End Sub
```

Another way to process the check box and radio buttons

```
Protected Sub chkMail_CheckedChanged(ByVal sender As Object, _
        ByVal e As System.EventArgs) Handles chkMail.CheckedChanged
    If chkMail.Checked Then
        Customer.Mail = True
    Else
        Customer.Mail = False
    End If
End Sub

Protected Sub rdoEmail_CheckedChanged(ByVal sender As Object, _
        ByVal e As System.EventArgs) Handles rdoEmail.CheckedChanged
    Customer.MailType = "Email"
End Sub

Protected Sub rdoPostal_CheckedChanged(ByVal sender As Object, _
        ByVal e As System.EventArgs) Handles rdoPostal.CheckedChanged
    Customer.MailType = "Postal"
End Sub
```

Description

- To determine whether a check box or radio button is selected, you test its Checked property.
- For a check box, the CheckedChanged event is raised whenever the checked status of the control changes. For a radio button, this event is raised only when the status of the control changes to checked.
- If you allow the user to select multiple items from a list box, you can use the GetSelectedIndices method to get an array of integer values that correspond with the selected values.

Figure 6-10   Visual Basic code for working with these controls

How to work with list controls

ASP.NET provides several controls that are designed to present lists of information. You'll learn about all five of those controls here: the drop-down list, list box, radio button list, check box list, and bulleted list.

Basic skills for working with list boxes and drop-down lists

Figure 6-11 presents the basic skills for working with *list boxes* and *drop-down lists*. The list box shown here lets the user select from one of four colors. List boxes are typically used in cases like this where there are a small number of items to select from. In contrast, drop-down lists are typically used with larger lists so they don't take up as much space on the page. The drop-down list in this figure, for example, displays a list of the days of the week.

The asp tags for the list box and drop-down list are also shown in this figure. Here, you can see that the ListBox element has four ListItem elements that correspond to the four colors in the list. Similarly, the DropDownList element has seven ListItem elements that correspond to the days of the week. The easiest way to add elements like these to a list is to use the ListItem Collection Editor. You'll see how to do that in figure 6-14.

You can also add items to a list using Visual Basic code. In that case, the aspx code for the form won't include ListItem elements like those shown here. Instead, ASP.NET will generate the elements when the page is rendered. You'll learn two ways to add items to a list in figure 6-13.

A list box displayed in a browser

The asp tag for the list box

```
<asp:ListBox ID="lstColor" runat="server">
    <asp:ListItem Value="Black" Selected="True">Black</asp:ListItem>
    <asp:ListItem Value="Red">Red</asp:ListItem>
    <asp:ListItem Value="Blue">Blue</asp:ListItem>
    <asp:ListItem Value="Green">Green</asp:ListItem>
</asp:ListBox>
```

A drop-down list box displayed in a browser

The asp tag for the drop-down list

```
<asp:DropDownList id="ddlDay" runat="server">
    <asp:ListItem Value="1">Sunday</asp:ListItem>
    <asp:ListItem Value="2">Monday</asp:ListItem>
    <asp:ListItem Value="3">Tuesday</asp:ListItem>
    <asp:ListItem Value="4">Wednesday</asp:ListItem>
    <asp:ListItem Value="5">Thursday</asp:ListItem>
    <asp:ListItem Value="6">Friday</asp:ListItem>
    <asp:ListItem Value="7">Saturday</asp:ListItem>
</asp:DropDownList>
```

Description

- *List boxes* and *drop-down lists* typically contain one or more list items. You can load list items by using Visual Basic code or the ListItem Collection Editor. See figures 6-13 and 6-14 for details.

- A list box lets a user choose one or more items from a list of items. A drop-down list lets a user choose an item from a drop-down list of items.

Figure 6-11   Basic skills for working with list boxes and drop-down lists

Properties for working with list boxes, drop-down lists, and list items

Figure 6-12 presents some common properties for working with list boxes and drop-down lists. As you just saw, these controls contain ListItem objects that define the items in the list. These objects are stored in a collection that you can refer to using the Items property of the control. You'll see examples that use this property in the next figure.

You can also get the selected item using the SelectedItem property of the control, you can get or set the index of the selected item using the SelectedIndex property, and you can get or set the value of the selected item using the SelectedValue property. By default, the SelectedIndex property of a drop-down list is set to zero, which means that the first item is selected. In contrast, the SelectedIndex property of a list box is set to -1 by default, which means that none of the items in the list are selected. Then, you can check if the user has selected an item using code like this:

```
If lstColor.SelectedIndex > -1 Then ...
```

You can also select an item by default by setting the SelectedIndex property to the appropriate index value. And you can clear the selection from a list box by setting this property to -1. Finally, you can select an item by default by setting the SelectedValue property to the appropriate value.

The Rows and SelectionMode properties apply only to list box controls. The Rows property determines how many items are displayed at one time. The SelectionMode property determines whether the user can select more than one item from the list. Note that when multiple selections are allowed, the SelectedItem property gets the first selected item, the SelectedIndex property gets the index of the first selected item, and the SelectedValue property gets the value of the first selected item.

To work with an item in a drop-down list or list box, you use the properties shown in this figure. The Text property specifies the text that's displayed for the item. The Value property specifies a value that's associated with the item. And the Selected property indicates whether the item is selected.

This figure also shows three examples for working with a drop-down list or list box. In the first example, the SelectedValue property of a drop-down list is assigned to an Integer variable. Note that because the SelectedValue property contains a string, it is converted to an integer.

The second example uses the SelectedItem property to retrieve the ListItem object for the selected item. Then, it uses the Text property of the ListItem object to get the text that's displayed for the selected item.

The third example is an event procedure for the SelectedIndexChanged event of the drop-down list. This event occurs any time the item that's selected changes between posts to the server. If you want the page to post immediately when the user selects an item, you should set the AutoPostBack property to True.

Common properties of list box and drop-down list controls

Property	Description
Items	The collection of ListItem objects that represents the items in the control. This property returns an object of type ListItemCollection.
Rows	The number of items that are displayed in a list box at one time. If the list contains more rows than can be displayed, a scroll bar is added automatically.
SelectedItem	The ListItem object for the currently selected item, or the ListItem object for the item with the lowest index if more than one item is selected in a list box.
SelectedIndex	The index of the currently selected item, or the index of the first selected item if more than one item is selected in a list box. If no item is selected in a list box, the value of this property is -1.
SelectedValue	The value of the currently selected item, or the value of the first selected item if more than one item is selected in a list box. If no item is selected in a list box, the value of this property is an empty string ("").
SelectionMode	Indicates whether a list box allows single selections (Single) or multiple selections (Multiple).

Common properties of list item objects

Property	Description
Text	The text that's displayed for the list item.
Value	A string value associated with the list item.
Selected	Indicates whether the item is selected.

Code that retrieves the value of a selected item in a drop-down list

```
Dim iDay As Integer = CType(ddlDay.SelectedValue, Integer)
```

Code that retrieves the text for a selected item in a drop-down list

```
Dim sDay As String = ddlDay.SelectedItem.Text
```

Code that uses the SelectedIndexChanged event of a drop-down list

```
Protected Sub ddlDay_SelectedIndexChanged(ByVal sender As Object, _
        ByVal e As System.EventArgs) Handles ddlDay.SelectedIndexChanged
    Dim iDay as Integer = CType(ddlDay.SelectedValue, Integer)
End Sub
```

Description

- To work with the items in a drop-down list or list box, you use the Items property of the control. This property returns a ListItemCollection object that contains all of the items in the list.
- The SelectedIndexChanged event is raised when the user selects a different item from a drop-down list or list box.

Figure 6-12   Properties for working with drop-down lists, list boxes, and list items

Properties and methods for working with list item collections

Figure 6-13 presents some common properties and methods for working with a collection of list item objects. To get the item at a specific index, for example, you use the Item property. And to get a count of the number of items in the collection, you use the Count property.

All but two of the methods shown here let you add and remove items in the collection. The method you're most likely to use is Add, which adds an item to the end of the collection. The examples in this figure show two different ways you can use this method.

The first example contains the code that's used to load the colors into the list box you saw in figure 6-11. Here, the Add method is used to add an item with the specified string value. When you code the Add method this way, the value you specify is assigned to the both the Text and Value properties of the item.

If you want to assign different values to the Text and Value properties of an item, you use the technique shown in the second example. Here, a new list item object is created with two string values. The first one contains a string that's stored in the Text property, and the second one contains a string that's stored in the Value property. Then, the Add method is used to add the new item to the list item collection of the drop-down list you saw in figure 6-11.

Notice in both of these examples that the Items property is used to refer to the collection of list item objects for the control. You can also use the SelectedIndex property of a control to refer to an item at a specific index. For example, you could use a statement like this to remove the selected item from a drop-down list:

```
ddlDay.Items.RemoveAt(ddlDay.SelectedIndex)
```

The last two methods let you locate a list item based on the value of its Text or Value property. These methods are useful when you need to access a list item and you don't know its index value.

Common properties and methods of list item collection objects

Property	Description
`Item(integer)`	A ListItem object that represents the item at the specified index.
`Count`	The number of items in the collection.

Method	Description
`Add(string)`	Adds a new item to the end of the collection, and assigns the specified string value to the Text property of the item.
`Add(ListItem)`	Adds the specified list item to the end of the collection.
`Insert(integer, string)`	Inserts an item at the specified index location in the collection, and assigns the specified string value to the Text property of the item.
`Insert(integer, ListItem)`	Inserts the specified list item at the specified index location in the collection.
`Remove(string)`	Removes the item from the collection whose Text property is equal to the specified string value.
`Remove(ListItem)`	Removes the specified list item from the collection.
`RemoveAt(integer)`	Removes the item at the specified index location from the collection.
`Clear`	Removes all the items from the collection.
`FindByValue(string)`	Returns the list item whose Value property has the specified value.
`FindByText(string)`	Returns the list item whose Text property has the specified value.

Code that loads items into a list box using strings

```
lstColor.Items.Add("Black")
lstColor.Items.Add("Red")
lstColor.Items.Add("Blue")
lstColor.Items.Add("Green")
```

Code that loads items into a drop-down list using ListItem objects

```
ddlDay.Items.Add(new ListItem("Sunday", "1"))
ddlDay.Items.Add(new ListItem("Monday", "2"))
ddlDay.Items.Add(new ListItem("Tuesday", "3"))
ddlDay.Items.Add(new ListItem("Wednesday", "4"))
ddlDay.Items.Add(new ListItem("Thursday", "5"))
ddlDay.Items.Add(new ListItem("Friday", "6"))
ddlDay.Items.Add(new ListItem("Saturday", "7"))
```

Description

- The ListItemCollection object is a collection of ListItem objects. Each ListItem object represents one item in the list.

- Items in a ListItemCollection object are numbered from 0. So the index for the first item in the list is 0, the index for the second item is 1, and so on.

- When you load items into a list box using strings, both the Text and Value properties of the list item are set to the string value you specify. To set the Text and Value properties of a list item to different values, you must create a list item object and then add that item to the collection.

Figure 6-13   Properties and methods for working with list item collections

How to use the ListItem Collection Editor

In the last figure, you saw how to use the Add method of a list item collection to load items into a drop-down list or list box control. If the items are static, however, you might want to use the ListItem Collection Editor to load them instead. Figure 6-14 shows you how to use this editor.

When you first display the ListItem Collection Editor, the list is empty. Then, you can use the Add button below the Members list to add items to the list. When you do, the item appears in the Members list and its properties appear in the Properties list. The first property lets you disable a list item so that it doesn't appear in the list. The other three properties are the same properties you learned about in figure 6-12. Note, however, that when you set the Text property, the Value property defaults to the same value. If that's not what you want, you can change this value.

The ListItem Collection Editor dialog box

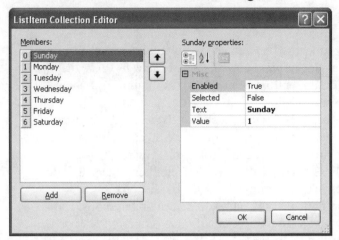

Description

- You can use the ListItem Collection Editor to add items to a drop-down list or list box. You'll typically use it to create a static list of items. Each item you add generates an <asp:ListItem> tag in the aspx file.

- To display the Collection Editor dialog box, select Edit Items from the smart tag menu, or select the control and then click the ellipsis button that appears when you select the Items property in the Properties window.

- To add an item to the list, click the Add button and then enter the properties for the item in the Properties list. The item appears in the Members list.

- By default, the ListItem Collection Editor sets the Value property of a list item to the value you specify for the Text property.

- To remove an item, select it in the Members list and then click the Remove button.

- You can use the up and down arrow buttons to the right of the Members list to move the selected item up or down in the list.

Figure 6-14   How to use the ListItem Collection Editor

How to work with radio button lists and check box lists

Earlier in this chapter, you learned how to use radio buttons and check boxes. But ASP.NET also provides *radio button lists* and *check box lists* that you can use to create lists of radio buttons or check boxes. Figure 6-15 shows you how to use these controls.

As you can see from the asp tags for the check box list and radio button list, each control consists of a collection of ListItem objects. You can refer to this collection through the Items property of the control just as you can for drop-down lists and list boxes. These controls also have SelectedItem, SelectedIndex, and SelectedValue properties just like drop-down lists and list boxes.

Just like a group of radio buttons, only one item in a radio button list can be selected at one time. Then, you can use the SelectedValue property to get or set the value of the selected item, and you can use the SelectedIndex property to get or set the index of the selected item. This is illustrated by the first statement in this figure, which uses the SelectedValue property to get the value of the selected item. Note that this is much simpler than the code you use to get the value of the selected radio button in a group.

Like a list box, you can select more than one item in a check box list. Because of that, you'll usually determine whether an item in the list is selected using the Selected property of the item. This is illustrated in the second example in this figure. Here, the Items property of a check box list is used to get the item at index 0. Then, the Selected property of that item is used to determine if the item is selected. Notice here that you can't refer to individual check boxes by name when you use a check box list. Because of that, your code may not be as readable as it is when you use individual check box controls. That's why I recommend that you use check box lists only when they provide a distinct advantage over using individual controls.

To determine the layout of the items in a radio button or check box list, you use the attributes shown in this figure. The RepeatLayout attribute determines whether ASP.NET aligns the buttons or check boxes in a list using tables or HTML flow. I recommend that you use tables since they're more precise.

The RepeatDirection attribute determines whether the controls are listed horizontally or vertically. For the radio button list in this figure, I set this attribute to Horizontal. In contrast, I left this attribute at its default of Vertical for the check box list.

The RepeatColumns attribute specifies the number of columns in the radio button or check box list. By default, the items are displayed in a single column. If a list contains more than just a few items, however, you may want to display the items in two or more columns to save space. The four check boxes in the list shown in this figure, for example, are displayed in two columns.

A check box list and a radio button list displayed in a browser

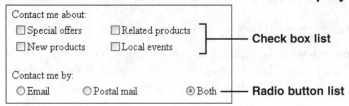

Check box list

Radio button list

The asp tag for the check box list

```
<asp:CheckBoxList id="cblContact" runat="server" Width="305px"
    RepeatColumns="2">
    <asp:ListItem Value="Special">Special offers</asp:ListItem>
    <asp:ListItem Value="New">New products</asp:ListItem>
    <asp:ListItem Value="Related">Related products</asp:ListItem>
    <asp:ListItem Value="Events">Local events</asp:ListItem>
</asp:CheckBoxList>
```

The asp tag for the radio button list

```
<asp:RadioButtonList id="rblMail" runat="server" Width="346px"
    RepeatDirection="Horizontal">
    <asp:ListItem Value="Email">Email</asp:ListItem>
    <asp:ListItem Value="Postal">Postal mail</asp:ListItem>
    <asp:ListItem Value="Both" Selected="True">Both</asp:ListItem>
</asp:RadioButtonList>
```

Attributes for formatting radio button and check box lists

Attribute	Description
RepeatLayout	Specifies whether ASP.NET should use table tags (Table) or normal HTML flow (Flow) to format the list when it renders the control. The default is Table.
RepeatDirection	Specifies the direction in which the controls should be repeated. The available values are Horizontal and Vertical. The default is Vertical.
RepeatColumns	Specifies the number of columns to use when repeating the controls. The default is 0.

A statement that gets the value of the selected item in a radio button list

```
Customer.MailType = rblMail.SelectedValue
```

A statement that checks if the first item in a check box list is selected

```
If cblContact.Items(0).Selected Then ...
```

Description

- A *radio button list* presents a list of mutually exclusive options. A *check box list* presents a list of independent options. These controls contain a collection of ListItem objects that you refer to through the Items property of the control.

- These controls also have SelectedItem, SelectedIndex, and SelectedValue properties. These properties work just like they do for drop-down list and list box controls. See figure 6-12 for more information.

Figure 6-15   How to work with radio button lists and check box lists

How to work with bulleted lists and numbered lists

Figure 6-16 shows how to work with the bulleted list control, which is new with ASP.NET 2.0. In spite of its name, this control can be used to create both *bulleted lists* and *numbered lists*. The type of list that's created depends on the value of the BulletStyle attribute.

Like the other list controls presented in this chapter, a bulleted list control contains a collection of ListItem objects. In this figure, for example, you can see the aspx code for the list items contained in the two controls shown at the top of this figure. Because the BulletStyle attribute of the first control is set to Disc, it's displayed as a bulleted list. In contrast, the BulletStyle attribute of the second control is set to Numbered, so it's displayed as a numbered list.

Unlike the other list controls, the bulleted list control is typically used only to display a list. In other words, it's not used to let the user make a selection. That's the case if the DisplayMode attribute is set to Text. If this attribute is set to Hyperlink, however, the user can click on the link to display the page at the URL specified by the Value attribute of the list item. This is illustrated by the numbered list in this figure.

If the DisplayMode attribute is set to LinkButton, the page is posted back to the server when the user clicks a link. Then, you can respond to the user clicking the link by coding an event procedure for the Click event of the bulleted list control. Within that procedure, you can use the Selected property of a list item to determine if the item was clicked. This is illustrated by the statement in this figure. Alternatively, you can use the value of the e argument's Index property to determine which list item the user clicked.

A bulleted list and a numbered list displayed in a browser

Materials you will need: Select a project type:
- Styrofoam panel   1. Costumes
- Gray and black latex paint   2. Static props
- Stone texture paint   3. Animated props
- Rotary tool

Common attributes of the bulleted list control

Attribute	Description
BulletStyle	Specifies the bullet style. For a bulleted list, allowable values are Disc, Circle, Square, or CustomImage. For a numbered list, allowable values are Numbered, LowerAlpha, UpperAlpha, LowerRoman, or UpperRoman.
BulletImageUrl	Specifies the URL of the image used to display the bullets if the BulletStyle attribute is set to CustomImage.
FirstBulletNumber	Specifies the starting number if numbers are displayed.
DisplayMode	Specifies how the text for each item should be displayed. Allowable values are Text, HyperLink, or LinkButton. Text is the default.

The aspx code for the bulleted list shown above

```
<asp:BulletedList ID="BulletedList1" runat="server" BulletStyle="Disc">
    <asp:ListItem>Styrofoam panel</asp:ListItem>
    <asp:ListItem>Gray and black latex paint</asp:ListItem>
    <asp:ListItem>Stone texture paint</asp:ListItem>
    <asp:ListItem>Rotary tool</asp:ListItem>
</asp:BulletedList>
```

The aspx code for the numbered list shown above

```
<asp:BulletedList ID="BulletedList2" runat="server" BulletStyle="Numbered"
    DisplayMode="HyperLink">
    <asp:ListItem Value="Costumes.aspx">Costumes</asp:ListItem>
    <asp:ListItem Value="StaticProps.aspx">Static props</asp:ListItem>
    <asp:ListItem Value="AnimatedProps.aspx">Animated props</asp:ListItem>
</asp:BulletedList>
```

A statement that checks if the first link button in a bulleted list was clicked

```
If blCategories.Items(0).Selected Then ...
```

Description

- The bulleted list control creates *bulleted lists* or *numbered lists*. This control contains a collection of ListItem objects that you refer to through the Items property of the control.

- If you set the DisplayMode attribute to Hyperlink, you can set the Value attribute of each ListItem object to the URL of the page you want to display when the link is clicked.

- If you set the DisplayMode attribute to LinkButton, you can use the Click event of the bulleted list to respond to the user clicking one of the links.

- Unlike the other list controls, the bulleted list control doesn't have SelectedItem, SelectedIndex, and SelectedValue properties.

Figure 6-16   How to work with bulleted lists and numbered lists

How to use other web server controls

As you learned earlier, ASP.NET provides many other controls besides those you've already seen in this chapter. So in the remaining topics of this chapter, I'll present several of those controls. But first, I want to show you how to get information about using a control that you haven't used before. You can also use this technique to get additional information about controls you have used.

How to get the information you need for using a control

The easiest way to get information about a web server control is to use the Help documentation that comes with Visual Studio. To access this documentation, you can use the commands in the Help menu. The one I've found to be most useful is the Index command. When you select this command, a Help window like the one in figure 6-17 is displayed.

The Index tab in the left pane of this window lets you enter the text you want to look for in the Look For text box. To look for information on a control, for example, you can enter the name of the control. You can also filter the information that's displayed using the drop-down list at the top of the Index tab.

In this figure, I entered "Calendar" and then selected the "about Calendar control" topic under the "Calendar control (Web Forms)" heading. When I did that, some basic information about the Calendar control was displayed in the right pane of the window. This is usually a good place to start when you're learning how to use a control that you haven't used before.

Once you have a basic idea of how a control works, you can display other topics that describe specific features or functions of the control. You can do that by using the links that are available within a topic or by selecting topics from the Index tab.

In addition to the topics that are listed for a control, you may want to review the members of the class that defines the control. In this figure, you can see the Calendar class at the top of the Index tab. You can select the "all members" topic beneath this heading to display all of the members of the class. Or, you can display each type of member separately by selecting the appropriate topic.

Although you can typically find all the information you need using the Index command, you may occasionally need to use other Help features. To access these features, you can use the other commands in the Help menu, or you can use the buttons in the Help window's Standard toolbar if that window is already displayed. If you want to find out how to perform a specific task, for example, you can click the How Do I button. This opens another tab in the right pane of the window that lets you select from predefined tasks. Or, if you want to search for specific information, you can click the Search button. This opens another tab that lets you enter search text and criteria. If you experiment with these and other help features, you'll quickly get a feel for how they work.

Some of the Help documentation for the calendar control

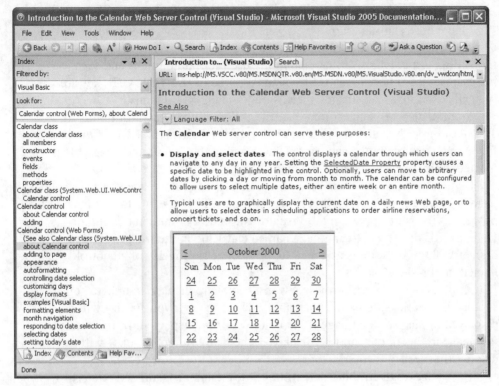

Description

- Visual Studio 2005 provides an abundance of information on the web server controls. The easiest way to display this information is to use the Help→Index command.

- To start, you can review the information about the basic function, usage, and appearance of the control. To do that, just enter the name of the control in the Look For text box and then select the appropriate topic.

- Most controls include an "About" topic like the one shown above that provides basic information about the control along with links to related topics. In addition, you'll find topics that describe specific features of the control.

- To learn more about a control, you can display its properties, methods, events, etc. To do that, enter the name of the control class in the Look For text box. Then, select the "all members" topic to display all of the control's members, or select the appropriate topic to display a specific type of member.

- Once you display the Help documentation, you can use the buttons in the toolbar to switch to a different view of the documentation.

Figure 6-17   How to get the information you need for using a control

How to use the image control

Figure 6-18 shows part of a web page that includes an *image control* that displays a graphic image. In this case, the graphic image is stored in a *JPEG* file. JPEG is a graphics format commonly used for photographs and scanned images. Graphic images are also frequently stored in *GIF* files. GIF files are typically used for small images such as button images and icons.

You can also see some common attributes of an image control in this figure. The most important attribute is ImageUrl, which specifies the URL of the image file. As you can see in the asp tag for the image in this figure, the image file is located in the Images folder of the web site.

If you need to change the image that's displayed in an image control when a page is executed, you can do that by assigning a different value to the ImageUrl property. This is illustrated in the Visual Basic code example in this figure. Here, a URL that refers to an image named cat01.jpg in the Images\Products directory of the web site is assigned to the ImageUrl property of a control named imgProduct.

If you know that some browsers won't be able to display an image, you should also set the AlternateText attribute. Then, the text you specify will be displayed in place of the image if the image can't be displayed. If, for example, the image in this figure can't be displayed, the text "Murach Books" will be displayed instead.

The ImageAlign attribute determines how the image is aligned relative to the web page or other elements on the page. If you set this attribute to Left, for example, the image is aligned at the left side of the page and any text on the page will wrap around the right side of the image. For more information on the available alignment options, see the topic on this attribute in online help.

The last two attributes, Width and Height, let you control the size of the displayed image. If you leave both of these attributes at their defaults, ASP.NET will display the image at its original size. If you specify just one of these attributes, ASP.NET will automatically set the other attribute so that the proportions of the original image are maintained. If you set both attributes, the image will be distorted if necessary to fit the dimensions you specify. Because of that, you'll usually set just one of these attributes.

How to use the hyperlink control

The web page in figure 6-17 also includes a *hyperlink control*. This control navigates to the web page specified in the NavigateUrl attribute when the user clicks the control. If you want to display text for a hyperlink control, you set the Text attribute. Then, the text appears with an underline as shown in this figure. Alternatively, you can display an image for this control. To do that, you set the ImageUrl attribute to the URL of an image you want to display.

An image control and a hyperlink control displayed in a browser

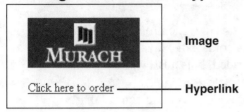 — Image

— Hyperlink

The asp tag for the image control

```
<asp:Image ID="Image1" runat="server" ImageUrl="~/Images/Murach logo.jpg"
    AlternateText="Murach Books" />
```

Code that sets the URL of an image control

```
imgProduct.ImageUrl = "Images/Products/cat01.jpg"
```

Common image attributes

Attribute	Description
ImageUrl	The absolute or relative URL of the image.
AlternateText	The text that's used in place of the image if the browser can't display the image.
ImageAlign	The alignment of the image relative to the web page or other elements on the page.
Width	The width of the image.
Height	The height of the image.

The asp tag for the hyperlink control

```
<asp:HyperLink ID="HyperLink1" runat="server"
    NavigateUrl="http://www.murach.com">Click here to order</
asp:HyperLink>
```

Common hyperlink attributes

Attribute	Description
NavigateUrl	The absolute or relative URL of the page that's displayed when the control is clicked.
Text	The text that's displayed for the control.
ImageUrl	The absolute or relative URL of the image that's displayed for the control.

Description

- An *image control* displays a graphic image, typically in *GIF* (*Graphic Interchange Format*) or *JPEG* (*Joint Photographic Experts Group*) format.

- If you don't specify the Height or Width attributes of an image control, the image will be displayed at full size.

- A *hyperlink control* navigates to another web page when the user clicks the control. You can display either text or an image for the control.

Figure 6-18   How to use the image and hyperlink controls

How to use the file upload control

The *file upload control*, shown in figure 6-19, is designed for applications that let the user upload files to the web site. This control displays a text box that lets the user enter the path for the file to be uploaded, plus a Browse button that displays a dialog box that lets the user locate and select the file.

To upload the selected file, you must also provide a separate control that results in a postback, like the Upload button in this figure. When the user clicks this button, the page is posted and the file selected by the user is sent to the server along with the HTTP request.

The first example in this figure shows the aspx code that declares the file upload control and the Upload button shown at the top of this figure. Note here that the file upload control doesn't include an attribute that specifies where the file should be saved on the server. That's because the file upload control doesn't automatically save the uploaded file. Instead, you must write code that calls the SaveAs method of this control. The second example in this figure shows how to write this code.

Before you call the SaveAs method, you should test the HasFile property to make sure the user has selected a file. If the user has selected a valid file and it was successfully uploaded to the server, the HasFile property will be True. Then, you can use the FileName property to get the name of the selected file, and you can combine the file name with the path where you want the file saved. In this figure, the file is stored in the C:\Uploads directory.

For this code to work, the user account that ASP.NET runs under must have write access to the directory that the file is saved to. To grant that access, use Windows Explorer to navigate to the directory, right-click it, and choose Properties. Then, click the Security tab, click the Add button, add the ASP.NET Machine Account (*machinename*\ASPNET), and grant Modify and Write access to the account.

To illustrate the use of the PostedFile.ContentLength property, the event procedure in this figure uses this property to determine the size of the uploaded file. Then, if this value exceeds the limit set by the iSizeLimit variable, the file isn't saved. Instead, an error message is displayed.

A file upload control displayed in a browser

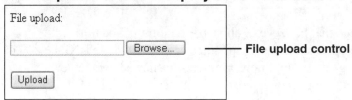

File upload control

The aspx code used to implement the file upload

```
File upload:<br /><br />
<asp:FileUpload ID="uplCustList" runat="server" /><br /><br />
<asp:Button ID="btnUpload" runat="server" Text="Upload" /><br /><br />
<asp:Label ID="lblMessage" runat="server"></asp:Label>
```

The Click event procedure for the Upload button

```
Protected Sub btnUpload_Click(ByVal sender As Object, _
        ByVal e As System.EventArgs) Handles btnUpload.Click
    Dim iSizeLimit As Integer = 5242880      ' 5,242,880 is 5MB
    If uplCustList.HasFile Then
        If uplCustList.PostedFile.ContentLength <= iSizeLimit Then
            Dim sPath As String = "C:\uploads\" & uplCustList.FileName
            uplCustList.SaveAs(sPath)
            lblMessage.Text = "File uploaded to " & sPath
        Else
            lblMessage.Text = "File exceeds size limit."
        End If
    End If
End Sub
```

Properties and methods of the FileUpload class

Property	Description
HasFile	If True, the user has selected a file to upload.
FileName	The name of the file to be uploaded.
PostedFile	The HttpPostedFile object that represents the file that was posted. You can use this object's ContentLength property to determine the size of the posted file.

Method	Description
SaveAs(string)	Saves the posted file to the specified path.

Description

- The *file upload control* displays a text box and a button that lets the user browse the client computer's file system to locate a file to be uploaded.
- Because the file upload control doesn't provide a button to upload the file, you must provide a button or other control to post the page. Then, in the button's Click event procedure, you must call the SaveAs method of the file upload control to save the file on the server.
- To use the SaveAs method, the user must have write access to the specified directory.

Figure 6-19   How to use the file upload control

How to use the image map control

An *image map* is an image that has several clickable regions, called *hot spots*. Although HTML has supported image maps since around 1995, ASP.NET hasn't directly supported image maps until now. Figure 6-20 shows how the new *image map control* provides a simple way to create image maps in ASP.NET 2.0.

The image map control lets you create three types of hot spots: rectangles, circles, and polygons. The example in this figure displays a map of California with two polygon hot spots: one for Northern California, the other for Southern California. Each hot spot is defined by a PolygonHotSpot element, and the polygon shapes are defined on the Coordinates attribute using a list of x and y coordinates that indicate the corners of the hot spot.

You use similar techniques to define rectangle and circle hot spots. To create a rectangle hot spot, you specify the locations of its sides using the Top, Bottom, Left, and Right attributes. To create a circle hot spot, you specify the x and y coordinates of its midpoint and the length of its radius using the X, Y, and Radius attributes.

Unfortunately, Visual Studio doesn't provide a convenient point-and-click editor to define hot spots. As a result, you'll need to use a separate graphics program to determine the x and y coordinates for the map's hot spots, particularly for a polygon hot spot. Once you've determined those coordinates, you can return to Visual Studio to create the hot spot elements for the image map.

The HotSpotMode attribute of an image map indicates whether the page will link to another page (Navigate) or be posted back to the server (PostBack) when the user clicks a hot spot. If you set this attribute to Navigate, you should set the NavigateUrl attribute of each hot spot to the URL of the page you want to be displayed when the hot spot is clicked. If you set this attribute to PostBack, you should set the PostBackValue attribute of each hot spot to the value you want to be passed to the Click event procedure of the image map when the hot spot is clicked. Then, you can use the PostBackValue attribute of the e argument in the Click event procedure to determine which hot spot was clicked. This is illustrated in the code example in this figure.

Note that you can also specify the HotSpotMode attribute for each hot spot rather than for the whole image map. That way, you can perform a postback when some hot spots are clicked and link to other pages when other hot spots are clicked.

The California.gif image

The aspx code for the image map control

```
<asp:ImageMap ID="imapCA" runat="server" ImageUrl="~/Images/California.GIF"
    HotSpotMode="PostBack">
    <asp:PolygonHotSpot Coordinates="76, 228, 177, 158, 121, 111,
        121, 3, 0, 3, 0, 83, 76, 228" PostBackValue="North" />
    <asp:PolygonHotSpot Coordinates="76, 229, 177, 159, 301, 275,
        296, 347, 215, 358, 111, 295, 76, 229" PostBackValue="South" />
</asp:ImageMap>
```

The Click event procedure for the image map

```
Protected Sub imapCA_Click(ByVal sender As Object, _
        ByVal e As System.Web.UI.WebControls.ImageMapEventArgs) _
        Handles imapCA.Click
    Dim sRegion As String
    If e.PostBackValue = "North" Then
        sRegion = "NorthernCalifornia"
    Else
        sRegion = "SouthernCalifornia"
    End If
End Sub
```

Common image map attributes

Attribute	Description
ImageUrl	The URL of the image to be displayed.
HotSpotMode	Sets the behavior for the hot spots. PostBack causes the page to be posted and Navigate links to a different page. This attribute can also be specified for individual hot spot elements.

Description

- The new *image map control* lets you display an *image map* with one or more *hot spots*. The page either posts back or links to another page when the user clicks a hot spot.

- To post the page back when the user clicks a hot spot, set the HotSpotMode attribute to PostBack, and set the PostBackValue attribute of the hot spot to the value you want passed to the Click event procedure.

- To link to another page when the user clicks a hot spot, set the HotSpotMode attribute to Navigate and specify the URL of the page in the NavigateUrl attribute of the hot spot.

- To create a CircleHotSpot element, use the X, Y, and Radius attributes. To create a RectangleHotSpot element, use the Top, Bottom, Left, and Right attributes. To create a PolygonHotSpot element, use the Coordinates attribute.

Figure 6-20   How to use the image map control

How to use the calendar control

The *calendar control* provides an easy way for a user to select a date. Although this control can be used for more sophisticated purposes, this is its most common use. Figure 6-21 shows how you use this control.

The web page at the top of this figure illustrates one way to implement a calendar control. To start, the web page displays two drop-down lists that let the user select a month and day, plus an image button. If the user clicks the image button, the calendar control is displayed and the image button is hidden. Then, the user can use the controls at the top of the calendar to move to the previous or next month if necessary. Finally, when the user selects a date from the calendar, the drop-down lists are set to the selected month and day, the image button is displayed again, and the calendar is hidden.

By default, the calendar control lets the user select a single date. However, you can also let the user select an entire week or month by setting the SelectionMode property to the appropriate value. If you want the user to select entire weeks, set this property to DayWeek. If you want the user to select entire months, set it to DayWeekMonth. If you just want to display a calendar and not let the user make selections, you can set this property to None.

If you review the asp tag for the calendar control in this figure, you'll see that most of the attributes are used to apply styles to the calendar. For example, the BorderStyle and BorderColor attributes display a solid black border around the calendar. The attributes in the TodayDayStyle and TitleStyle elements cause the current date and the month heading to be displayed in white bold text on a blue background. And the ForeColor attribute in the NextPrevStyle element causes the symbols for going to the previous and next page to be displayed in white. The only other attribute used for this control, Visible, causes the control to be hidden when the page is first displayed.

When the user selects a date from the calendar, the SelectionChanged event is raised and the page is posted to the server. Then, you can use the SelectedDate property of the control within the event procedure for this event to determine what date was selected. The procedure shown in this figure, for example, uses this property to select the appropriate values in the drop-down lists so they display the selected date.

If a calendar control lets the user select an entire week or month, you can use the SelectedDates property to retrieve the dates in the week or month the user selects. This property contains a collection of the selected dates, and you can use standard properties to work with this collection. For example, if you want to know how many dates were selected, you can use the Count property of this collection.

A web page with an image button that displays a calendar

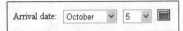

The web page with the calendar displayed

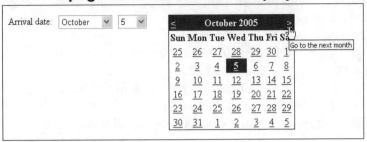

The asp tag for the calendar control

```
<asp:Calendar ID="clnArrival" runat="server" Visible="False"
    BorderColor="Black" BorderStyle="Solid">
    <TodayDayStyle BackColor="Blue" Font-Bold="True" ForeColor="White" />
    <TitleStyle BackColor="Blue" Font-Bold="True" ForeColor="White" />
    <NextPrevStyle ForeColor="White" />
</asp:Calendar>
```

The SelectionChanged event procedure for the calendar control

```
Protected Sub clnArrival_SelectionChanged(ByVal sender As Object, _
        ByVal e As System.EventArgs) Handles clnArrival.SelectionChanged
    ddlMonth.SelectedValue = clnArrival.SelectedDate.Month.ToString
    ddlDay.SelectedValue = clnArrival.SelectedDate.Day.ToString
    clnArrival.Visible = False
    ibtnCalendar.Visible = True
End Sub
```

Common properties of the Calendar class

Property	Description
SelectionMode	Specifies the type of selection that can be made. Acceptable values are Day, DayWeek, DayWeekMonth, and None.
SelectedDate	The currently selected date if a single date was selected, or the first selected date if multiple dates were selected.
SelectedDates	A collection that contains all of the selected dates in sequence. To determine the number of dates that were selected, use the Count property of this collection.

Description

- The *calendar control* is typically used to provide users with an easy way of selecting a date. Entire weeks and months can also be selected.

- When the user makes a selection from a calendar control, the SelectionChanged event is raised and the page is posted to the server.

Figure 6-21   How to use the calendar control

Perspective

In this chapter, you've learned how to use 17 of the standard web server controls that ASP.NET provides. In addition, you've learned how to use the Help documentation that Visual Studio provides to learn about any control. With that as background, you should be able to use any of the server controls.

Keep in mind, though, that you'll learn how to use many of the controls that weren't presented in this chapter later in this book. In the next chapter, for example, you'll learn how to use the validation controls. And in chapters 13 through 16, you'll learn how to use the data controls. If a control is presented in this book, then, you'll want to read about it here before you go to the Help documentation. Then, you can use the Help documentation to learn about any aspects of these controls that we may not present.

Terms

web server control
HTML server control
event handler
access key
accelerator key
submit button
button
link button
image button
text box
label
check box
radio button
list box
drop-down list
radio button list
check box list
bulleted list
numbered list
image control
JPEG (Joint Photographic Experts Group)
GIF (Graphic Interchange Format)
hyperlink control
file upload control
image map
image map control
hot spot
calendar control

7

How to use the validation controls

In chapter 2, you learned the basic skills for using two of the validation controls: the required field validator and the range validator. Now, you'll learn more about using those controls as well as how to use the other validation controls. As you'll see, you can use the validation controls to perform the data validation required by most web forms.

An introduction to the validation controls

ASP.NET provides six *validation controls* that you can use to validate the data on a web form. You'll learn the basic skills for using these controls in the topics that follow.

How to use the validation controls

Figure 7-1 summarizes the validation controls that are available with ASP.NET. As you learned in chapter 2, the first five controls are called *validators*. These are the controls that you use to check that the user has entered valid data into the input controls on a web form. In contrast, you use the validation summary control to display a summary of all the errors on a page.

This figure also illustrates how the validation controls appear in the Web Forms Designer. Here, you can see the Order form for the application that was presented in chapter 3. This form uses two validation controls. The first one is a required field validator that checks that the user entered a value into the Quantity text box, and the second one is a range validator that checks that the user entered an integer that ranges from 1 to 500.

In this example, the required field validator appears directly to the right of the text box, and the range validator appears below it. That's because the compare validator didn't fit on the same line as the required field validator so flow layout pushed it to the next line. As you will see later in this chapter, though, these validators are defined so the error message will be displayed to the right of the text box no matter which validator detects the error.

Validation controls on an Order form

Range validator   Required field validator

The validation controls provided by ASP.NET

Control	Name	Description
	RequiredFieldValidator	Checks that an entry has been made.
	CompareValidator	Checks an entry against a constant value or the value of another control. Can also be used to check for a specific data type.
	RangeValidator	Checks that an entry is within a specified range.
	RegularExpressionValidator	Checks that an entry matches a pattern that's defined by a regular expression.
	CustomValidator	Checks an entry using validation code that you write yourself.
	ValidationSummary	Displays a summary of error messages from the other validation controls.

Description

- You can use the *validation controls* with any of the web server or HTML server input controls.
- Each *validator* is associated with a single input control, but you can associate two or more validators with the same input control.

Figure 7-1   How to use the validation controls

Common validator properties

After you add a validator to a web form, you set its properties to determine which input control it validates and how errors are displayed. Figure 7-2 presents the properties that you use to do that. The most important property is the ControlToValidate property, which associates the validator with an input control on the page.

The Display property determines how the error message for a validator is displayed. The option you choose depends on whether two or more validators are associated with the same input control and whether or not you use a validation summary control. Because the two validators for the form in figure 7-1 have the Display property set to Dynamic, the active error message will print to the right of the text box.

You use the ErrorMessage and Text properties to specify messages that are displayed when the validator detects an error. You can set one or both of these properties depending on whether you use a validation summary control. If you want the same message in both the validator and the validation summary control, just set the ErrorMessage property. But if you want different messages, set the ErrorMessage property to the message you want in the validation summary control and the Text property to the message you want in the validator.

If the Enabled property of a validator is set to True, the validation test for the validator is performed. But if you want to skip the validation that's done by a validator, you can set this property to False. In contrast, the EnableClientScript property determines whether the client-side script for the validation is generated. If this property is set to False, the validation is only done on the server.

When ASP.NET performs the validation test specified by a validator, it sets the IsValid property of the validator to indicate whether or not the data is valid. Then, you can refer to this property in your Visual Basic code to test the result of the validation. In most cases, though, you won't test the result of individual validators. Instead, you'll test that all of the validators on the page passed their validation tests by checking the IsValid property of the page.

Common validator properties

Property	Description
ControlToValidate	The ID of the control to be validated.
Display	Determines how the error message is to be displayed. Specify Static to allocate space for the message in the page layout, Dynamic to have space allocated only when an error occurs, or None to display errors only in a validation summary control. The default is Static.
ErrorMessage	The message that's displayed in the validator and/or the validation summary control when the validation fails. To display one message in the validation summary and another in the validator, use the Text property for the validator message.
Text	The message that's displayed in the validator when you use the ErrorMessage property to display a message in the validation summary control.
Enabled	Indicates whether the validation control is enabled.
EnableClientScript	Indicates whether the validation will be done on the client.
ValidationGroup	Indicates which group the validation control is part of (see figure 7-8).
IsValid	Indicates whether the control specified in the ControlToValidate property passed the validation.

Description

- You typically set the Display property to Dynamic if you use two or more validators to validate the same control. Then, the validators that pass their validation tests don't take up space on the page.

- You can also format the error messages that are displayed by including HTML in the values you assign to the ErrorMessage and Text properties.

- In addition to the properties above, validators have properties that affect the appearance of the message that's displayed. For example, the ForeColor property is set to Red by default so the message is displayed in red.

- Each validator has an IsValid property that indicates whether its validation was successful. You typically use this property in the Visual Basic code-behind files only if you initiate validation manually using the Page.Validate method.

Figure 7-2   Common validator properties

How ASP.NET processes validation controls

To refresh your memory about how validation controls work, figure 7-3 summarizes the key points. To start, you should realize that the validation tests are typically done on the client before the page is posted to the server. That way, a round trip to the server isn't required to display error messages if any invalid data is detected.

In most cases, client-side validation is done when the focus leaves an input control that has validators associated with it. That can happen when the user presses the Tab key to move to the next control or clicks another control to move the focus to that control.

However, the required field validator works a bit differently. When you use this validator, the validation isn't done until the user clicks a button whose CausesValidation property is set to True. The exception is if the user enters a value into an input control and then tries to clear the value. In that case, an error will be detected when the focus leaves the control.

To perform client-side validation, a browser must support *Dynamic HTML*, or *DHTML*. Because most browsers today support DHTML, validation can usually be done on the client. In case the browser doesn't support DHTML, though, validation is always done on the server when a page is submitted. ASP.NET does this validation after it initializes the page.

When ASP.NET performs the validation tests on the server, it sets the IsValid property of each validator to indicate if the test was successful. In addition, it sets the IsValid property of the page to indicate whether all the input data is valid. You usually should test this property in the event handler for the event that caused the page to be posted to the server.

At the top of this figure, for example, you can see how this property is tested in the event handler for the Click event for the Add to Cart button in figure 7-1. You usually do this in case validation wasn't done on the client. That's especially true if the operations within the method perform critical tasks such as updating the database. If the validation is done on the client, of course, the page won't be posted if one or more controls contain invalid data so the IsValid test will always be True.

If you want to bypass client-side validation and just perform the validation on the server, you can set the EnableClientScript property of the validation controls to False. Then, the scripts that are typically used to perform the validation on the client aren't generated, and validation is done only on the server. This is useful in some applications.

Typical code for processing a page that contains validation controls

```
Protected Sub btnAdd_Click(ByVal sender As Object, _
        ByVal e As System.EventArgs) Handles btnAdd.Click
    If Page.IsValid Then
        Dim CartItem As New CartItem
        CartItem.Product = SelectedProduct
        CartItem.Quantity = CType(txtQuantity.Text, Integer)
        Me.AddToCart(CartItem)
        Response.Redirect("Cart.aspx")
    End If
End Sub
```

Description

- If a browser supports *DHTML* (*Dynamic HTML*), the validation controls do their validation on the client using client-side script. That way, the validation is performed and error messages are displayed without the page being posted to the server.

- Validation is always done on the server too, right after the page is initialized, so the validation is done whether or not the browser supports DHTML. Although most browsers support DHTML, your code should still check that a page is valid in case a browser doesn't support DHTML.

- Validation is performed on the server when you click a button whose CausesValidation property is set to True. To create a button that doesn't initiate validation, you can set this property to False.

- Validation is performed on the client when the focus leaves the input control. The exception is a required field validator, which performs its validation only when you click a button whose CausesValidation property is set to True or when you enter a value into a control and then clear and leave the control.

- If a validation control indicates invalid data, the IsValid property of that control is set to False and the IsValid property of the page is set to False. These properties can be tested in your Visual Basic code.

- If you want to perform validation only on the server, you can set the EnableClientScript properties of the validation controls to False. Then, no client-side scripts are generated for validating the data.

Figure 7-3   How ASP.NET processes validation controls

How to use the basic validation controls

In the topics that follow, you'll learn about the three validation controls you'll use most often as you develop web applications. These are the required field validator, the compare validator, and the range validator.

How to use the required field validator

Figure 7-4 shows how to use the *required field validator*. This validator checks that the user entered a value into an input control. If the user doesn't enter a value, the validator's error message is displayed.

The three examples in this figure illustrate how you can use the required field validator. In the first example, this validator is used to check for a required entry in a text box. To do that, its ControlToValidate property is set to the ID property of the text box. Then, if the user doesn't enter anything into the text box, the text in the ErrorMessage property is displayed.

The second and third examples show how you can use the InitialValue property of the required field validator to check that the user changed the initial value of a control. By default, this property is set to an empty string, which is what you want if the input control is empty. If you specify an initial value for an input control, however, you'll want to set the InitialValue property of the required field validator to that value.

In the second example, this technique is used with a text box. Here, the initial value indicates the format for a date entry. If the user doesn't change this value, the validation test will fail.

The third example uses the InitialValue property with a list box. Here, the InitialValue property is set to None, which is the value of the first item in the list. That way, if the user doesn't select another item, the validation test will fail. You can also use this technique with a drop-down list or a radio button list.

Additional property of the required field validator

Property	Description
InitialValue	The initial value of the control that's validated. If this value isn't changed, the validation fails. The default is an empty string.

A required field validator that checks for a required entry

```
<asp:TextBox ID="txtName" runat="server"></asp:TextBox>
<asp:RequiredFieldValidator ID="RequiredFieldValidator1" runat="server"
    ControlToValidate="txtName"
    ErrorMessage="You must enter a name.">
</asp:RequiredFieldValidator>
```

A required field validator that checks that an initial value is changed

```
<asp:TextBox ID="txtBirthDate" runat="server" Width="159px">mm/dd/yyyy
</asp:TextBox> 
<asp:RequiredFieldValidator ID="RequiredFieldValidator2" runat="server"
    ControlToValidate="txtBirthDate"
    InitialValue="mm/dd/yyyy"
    ErrorMessage="You must enter a birth date.">
</asp:RequiredFieldValidator>
```

A required field validator that forces an option to be chosen from a list box

```
<asp:ListBox ID="lstCardType" runat="server" Width="292px">
    <asp:ListItem Selected="True" Value="None">
        —Select a credit card—</asp:ListItem>
    <asp:ListItem Value="Visa">Visa</asp:ListItem>
    <asp:ListItem Value="MC">MasterCard</asp:ListItem>
    <asp:ListItem Value="AmEx">American Express</asp:ListItem>
</asp:ListBox> 
<asp:RequiredFieldValidator ID="RequiredFieldValidator3" runat="server"
    ControlToValidate="lstCardType"
    InitialValue="None"
    ErrorMessage="You must select a credit card type.">
</asp:RequiredFieldValidator>
```

How the input controls are initially displayed in a browser

Description

- The *required field validator* checks that the user entered data into an input control. It's typically used with text box controls, but can also be used with list controls.

Figure 7-4   How to use the required field validator

How to use the compare validator

Figure 7-5 shows how you use the *compare validator*. This validator lets you compare the value entered into an input control with a constant value or the value of another control. You can also use the compare validator to make sure that the value is a particular data type.

To define a compare validator, you use the four additional properties shown in this figure. To compare the input data with a constant value, you specify the value in the ValueToCompare property. Then, you set the Operator property to indicate the type of comparison you want to perform, and you set the Type property to the type of data you're comparing. The first example illustrates how this works. Here, the value entered into a text box is tested to be sure that it's greater than zero. Then, if the user enters a number that isn't greater than zero, or if the user enters a value that isn't an integer, the error message will be displayed.

To test for just a data type, you set the Type property to the type of data you're testing for, and you set the Operator property to DataTypeCheck. This is illustrated by the second example. Here, the value entered into a text box is tested to be sure that it's an integer.

The third example shows how to compare the value of an input control with the value of another control. To do that, you set the Operator and Type properties just as you do when you compare an input value with a constant. Instead of setting the ValueToCompare property, however, you set the ControlToCompare property to the ID of the control whose value you want to compare. This example tests that a date that's entered into one text box is after the date entered into another text box.

When you begin working with compare validators, you'll find that if the user doesn't enter a value into a control, the compare validator associated with that control will pass its validation test. Because of that, you must use a required field validator along with the compare validator if you want to be sure that the user enters a value into the input control.

You should also realize that if you compare the value of a control against the value of another control, the validation test will pass if the user doesn't enter a value into the other control or the value of the other control can't be converted to the correct type. To avoid that problem, you'll want to be sure that the other control is also validated properly.

Additional properties of the compare validator

Property	Description
ValueToCompare	The value that the control specified in the ControlToValidate property should be compared to.
Operator	The type of comparison to perform (Equal, NotEqual, GreaterThan, GreaterThanEqual, LessThan, LessThanEqual, or DataTypeCheck).
Type	The data type to use for the comparison (String, Integer, Double, Date, or Currency).
ControlToCompare	The ID of the control that the value of the control specified in the ControlToValidate property should be compared to.

A compare validator that checks for a value greater than zero

```
<asp:TextBox ID="txtQuantity" runat="server">
</asp:TextBox> 
<asp:CompareValidator ID="CompareValidator1" runat="server"
    ControlToValidate="txtQuantity" Type="Integer"
    Operator="GreaterThan" ValueToCompare="0"
    ErrorMessage="Quantity must be greater than zero.">
</asp:CompareValidator>
```

A compare validator that checks for a numeric entry

```
<asp:TextBox id="txtQuantity" runat="server">
</asp:TextBox> 
<asp:CompareValidator ID="CompareValidator2" runat="server"
    ControlToValidate="txtQuantity"
    Operator="DataTypeCheck" Type="Integer"
    ErrorMessage="Quantity must be an integer.">
</asp:CompareValidator>
```

A compare validator that compares the values of two text boxes

```
<asp:TextBox ID="txtStartDate" runat="server">
</asp:TextBox><br /><br />
<asp:TextBox ID="txtEndDate" runat="server">
</asp:TextBox>

<asp:CompareValidator
    ID="CompareValidator3" runat="server"
    ControlToValidate="txtEndDate"
    Operator="GreaterThan" Type="Date"
    ControlToCompare="txtStartDate"
    ErrorMessage="End Date must be greater than Start Date.">
</asp:CompareValidator>
```

Description

- The *compare validator* compares the value entered into a control with a constant value or with the value entered into another control. You can also use the compare validator to check that the user entered a specific data type.

Figure 7-5   How to use the compare validator

How to use the range validator

The *range validator*, shown in figure 7-6, validates user input by making sure that it falls within a given range of values. To specify the valid range, you set the MinimumValue and MaximumValue properties. You must also set the Type property to the type of data you're checking. The first example in this figure, for instance, checks that the user enters an integer between 1 and 14 into a text box.

The second example in this figure shows how you can set the range for a range validator at runtime. Here, you can see that the MinimumValue and MaximumValue properties aren't set when the range validator is declared. Instead, they're set when the page is loaded for the first time. In this case, the MinimumValue property is set to the current date, and the MaximumValue property is set to 30 days after the current date.

Like the compare validator, you should realize that the range validator will pass its validation test if the user doesn't enter anything into the associated control. Because of that, you'll need to use a required field validator along with the range validator if the user must enter a value.

Additional properties of the range validator

Property	Description
MinimumValue	The minimum value allowed for the control.
MaximumValue	The maximum value allowed for the control.
Type	The data type to use for the comparison (String, Integer, Double, Date, or Currency).

A range validator that checks for a numeric range

```
<asp:TextBox ID="txtDays" runat="server"></asp:TextBox> 
<asp:RangeValidator ID="RangeValidator1" runat="server"
    ControlToValidate="txtDays" Type="Integer"
    MinimumValue="1" MaximumValue="14"
    ErrorMessage="Days must be between 1 and 14.">
</asp:RangeValidator>
```

How to set a range at runtime

A range validator that checks a date range that's set at runtime

```
<asp:TextBox ID="txtArrival" runat="server">01/01/06</asp:TextBox> 
<asp:RangeValidator ID="valArrival" runat="server"
    ControlToValidate="txtArrival" Type="Date"
    ErrorMessage="You must arrive within 30 days.">
</asp:RangeValidator>
```

Code that sets the minimum and maximum values when the page is loaded

```
Protected Sub Page_Load(ByVal sender As Object, _
        ByVal e As System.EventArgs) Handles Me.Load
    If Not IsPostBack Then
        valArrival.MinimumValue = Today.ToShortDateString
        valArrival.MaximumValue = Today.AddDays(30).ToShortDateString
    End If
End Sub
```

Description

- The *range validator* checks that the user enters a value that falls within the range specified by the MinimumValue and MaximumValue properties. These properties can be set when the range validator is created or when the page is loaded.

- If the user enters a value that can't be converted to the correct data type, the validation fails.

- If the user doesn't enter a value into the associated input control, the range validator passes its validation test. As a result, you should also provide a required field validator if a value is required.

Figure 7-6   How to use the range validator

Validation techniques

Now that you're familiar with the basic validation controls, you're ready to learn some additional techniques for validating data. First, you'll learn how to use the validation summary control to display a summary of all the errors on a page. Then, you'll learn how to use validation groups.

How to use the validation summary control

The *validation summary control* lets you summarize all the errors on a page. The summary can be a simple message like "There were errors on the page," or a more elaborate message that includes information about each error. The summary can be displayed directly on the page, or, if validation is being performed on the client, in a separate message box.

Figure 7-7 shows how to use the validation summary control. The most difficult part of using this control is determining how to code the Text and ErrorMessage properties of a validator so the error messages are displayed the way you want. To display the same message in both the validator and the validation summary control, for example, you set the ErrorMessage property to that message.

To display different messages, you set the ErrorMessage property to the message you want to display in the validation summary control, and you set the Text property to the message you want to display in the validator. This technique is illustrated in the example in this figure. Here, the Text properties of two required field validators are set to "*" so those indicators appear next to the controls in error, and the ErrorMessage properties are set to more descriptive error messages. Unlike the ErrorMessage property, the Text property isn't stored in an attribute of the tag for the validator. Instead, it's stored as content between the opening and closing tags for the validator.

If you don't want to display individual error messages in the validation summary control, just set the HeaderText property of the control to the generic message you want to display. Then, leave the ErrorMessage property of each validator blank. Also, to display an error message in the validation summary control but not in a validator, set the Display property of the validator to None.

By default, the error messages displayed by a validation summary control are formatted as a bulleted list as shown in this figure. However, you can also display the errors in a simple list or paragraph format by setting the DisplayMode property accordingly. In addition, you can display the error messages in a message box rather than on the web page by setting the ShowMessageBox property to True and the ShowSummary property to False.

Properties of the validation summary control

Property	Description
DisplayMode	Specifies how the error messages from the validation controls are to be displayed. The available values are BulletList, List, or SingleParagraph. The default is BulletList.
HeaderText	The text that's displayed before the list of error messages.
ShowSummary	A Boolean value that determines whether the validation summary should be displayed on the web page. The default is True.
ShowMessageBox	A Boolean value that determines whether the validation summary should be displayed in a message box (client-side validation only). The default is False.

Two validators and a validation summary control that's displayed on the web page

```
<asp:RequiredFieldValidator ID="RequiredFieldValidator3" runat="server"
    ControlToValidate="lstCardType" InitialValue="None"
    ErrorMessage="You must select a credit card type."
    Display="Dynamic">*</asp:RequiredFieldValidator>

<asp:RequiredFieldValidator ID="RequiredFieldValidator1" runat="server"
    ControlToValidate="txtCardNumber"
    ErrorMessage="You must enter a credit card number."
    Display="Dynamic">*</asp:RequiredFieldValidator>

<asp:ValidationSummary ID="ValidationSummary1" runat="server"
    HeaderText="Please correct the following errors:"/>
```

How the controls appear on the web page

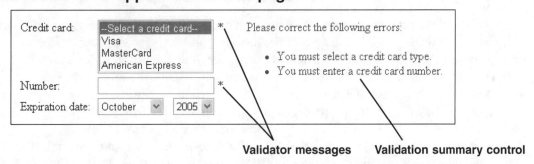

Validator messages   Validation summary control

Description

- The *validation summary control* displays a summary of the error messages that were generated by the page's validators. The summary can be displayed on the web page or in a separate message box.
- The error messages displayed in the validation summary control come from the ErrorMessage property of the page's validators. If you want to display a different message in the validator, set the Text property of the validator.
- If you don't want to display an error message in the validator, set its Display property to None.

Figure 7-7   How to use the validation summary control

How to use validation groups

The new *validation group* feature of ASP.NET 2.0 lets you group validation controls and specify which group should be validated when a page is posted. Figure 7-8 shows how to use these groups.

To illustrate, the web page in this figure provides for a bill-to address and an optional ship-to address, with a check box to indicate whether the ship-to address is the same as the bill-to address. Then, if the check box is checked, the ship-to address isn't required. As a result, the validators for the ship-to fields shouldn't be executed. To implement this type of validation, you can use two validation groups: one for the bill-to fields, the other for the ship-to fields.

The first example in this figure shows just one of the ship-to address text boxes and a validator that's assigned to a validation group named ShipTo. For the purpose of this example, though, you can assume that the other ship-to fields also have validators assigned to the ShipTo group. And you can assume that the bill-to fields have validators assigned to a group named BillTo.

The second example shows the button that submits the page. Here, the button specifies BillTo as its validation group so the bill-to text fields will be validated when the user posts the form, but the ship-to fields won't be.

The third example shows how you can invoke the ShipTo validators in your Visual Basic code if the check box is left unchecked. Here, the Validate method of the Page class is executed with the name of the validation group as its argument, which causes the Validate method of each validator in the ShipTo group to be executed. As a result, the ship-to fields will be validated on the server, but only if the check box isn't checked.

Unfortunately, the fact that validators are executed with client-side script whenever that's possible can complicate the way validation groups work. If, for example, the user leaves the check box unchecked, only the bill-to validations will be executed. That's because those validators are executed on the client side when the user clicks the button. But when they detect that required data is missing, they display their error messages and stop the page from being posted. As a result, the code that calls the validators for the ship-to fields is never executed. (The only way around this limitation is to write your own client-side validation script to validate the ship-to fields if the check box is unchecked.)

Note that any validation controls that don't specify the ValidationGroup attribute are considered part of the *default group*. The validators in this group are executed only when the page is posted with a button or other control that causes validation but doesn't specify a validation group, or when the Page.Validate method is called without specifying a validation group.

Attributes that cause group validation when a button is clicked

Attribute	Description
CausesValidation	Specifies whether validation should be performed when the user clicks the button.
ValidationGroup	Specifies the name of the group to be validated if CausesValidation is True.

A web page that accepts a bill-to and a ship-to address

Bill-to address

Name: George Constantine

Address: 2050 N. Main Street

City, state, zip: Ann Arbor   MI   48103

Ship-to address   ☑ Ship to same address

Name:

Address:

City, state, zip:

[Continue]

A text box with a validator that specifies a validation group

```
<asp:TextBox ID="txtShipToName" runat="server" />
<asp:RequiredFieldValidator ID="RequiredFieldValidator6" runat="server"
    ControlToValidate="txtShipToName"
    ErrorMessage="You must enter a ship-to name."
    ValidationGroup="ShipTo"></asp:RequiredFieldValidator>
```

A button that specifies a validation group

```
<asp:Button ID="btnContinue" runat="server" Text="Continue"
    ValidationGroup="BillTo" />
```

Visual Basic code that conditionally validates the ShipTo group

```
If chkShipToSameAsBillTo.Checked = False Then
    Page.Validate("ShipTo")
End If
```

Description

- A *validation group* is a group of validators that are run when a page is posted.

- To group validators, set the ValidationGroup attribute for each validator. Then, use the ValidationGroup attribute for each control that causes a postback (such as a button or a list box) to specify which group should be executed.

- You can use Visual Basic code to force the execution of a specific validation group by using the Page.Validate method with the validation group name as the argument.

- Any validators that don't specify the ValidationGroup attribute are part of the *default group*. This group is executed when started by a button or control that doesn't specify a validation group or when the Page.Validate method is used without an argument.

Figure 7-8   How to use validation groups

How to use the advanced validation controls

Besides the validation controls you've already learned about, ASP.NET provides two controls that provide advanced functionality. The regular expression validator lets you match data to a pattern you specify, and the custom validator lets you create your own validation routines.

How to use the regular expression validator

A *regular expression* is a string made up of special pattern-matching symbols. You can use regular expressions with the *regular expression validator* to make sure that an input control's data matches a particular pattern, such as a zip code, phone number, or email address. Figure 7-9 shows how to use the regular expression validator.

As you can see, the ValidationExpression property specifies the regular expression the input data must match. For instance, the code for the first regular expression validator in this figure specifies that the input data must contain five decimal digits (\d{5}). And the regular expression for the second validator specifies that the input data must be in the format of a U.S. phone number.

In the next topic, you'll learn how to create your own regular expressions. However, you should know that Visual Studio provides several standard expressions you can choose from. These expressions define patterns for validating phone numbers and postal codes for the U.S., France, Germany, Japan, and China; Social Security numbers for the U.S. and China; and Internet email addresses and URLs.

To use a standard expression, you simply select it from the Regular Expression Editor dialog box. You can also create a custom expression that's based on a standard expression by selecting the standard expression so its definition appears in the text box at the bottom of the Regular Expression Editor dialog box. Then, you can edit the regular expression any way you'd like.

An additional property of the regular expression validator

Property	Description
ValidationExpression	A string that specifies a regular expression. The regular expression defines a pattern that the input data must match to be valid.

A regular expression validator that validates five-digit numbers

```
<asp:TextBox ID="txtZipCode" runat="server"></asp:TextBox>
<asp:RegularExpressionValidator ID="RegularExpressionValidator1"
    runat="server" ControlToValidate="txtZipCode"
    ValidationExpression="\d{5}"
    ErrorMessage="Must be a five-digit U.S. zip code.">
</asp:RegularExpressionValidator>
```

A regular expression validator that validates U.S. phone numbers

```
<asp:TextBox ID="txtPhone" runat="server"></asp:TextBox>
<asp:RegularExpressionValidator ID="RegularExpressionValidator2"
    runat="server" ControlToValidate="txtPhone"
    ValidationExpression="((\(\d{3}\) ?)|(\d{3}-))?\d{3}-\d{4}"
    ErrorMessage="Must be a valid U.S. phone number.">
</asp:RegularExpressionValidator>
```

The Regular Expression Editor dialog box

Description

- The *regular expression validator* matches the input entered by the user with the pattern supplied by the ValidationExpression property. If the input doesn't match the pattern, the validation fails.

- The string you specify for the ValidationExpression property must use *regular expression* notation. For more information, see the next figure.

- ASP.NET provides several standard regular expressions that you can access using the Regular Expression Editor. To display its dialog box, select the validation control, select the ValidationExpression property in the Properties window, and click its ellipsis button.

- You can also use the Regular Expression Editor to create a custom expression that's based on a standard expression. To do that, select the standard expression and then edit it in the Validation Expression text box.

Figure 7-9   How to use the regular expression validator

How to create your own regular expressions

Figure 7-10 presents the basic elements of regular expressions. Although the .NET Framework provides many other elements that you can use in regular expressions, you can create expressions of considerable complexity using just the ones shown here. In fact, all of the standard expressions provided by ASP.NET use only these elements.

To start, you can specify any ordinary character, such as a letter or a decimal digit. If a character must be an A, for example, you just include that character in the expression. To include a character other than an ordinary character, you must precede it with a backslash. For example, \(specifies that the character must be a left parenthesis, \] specifies that the character must be a right bracket, and \\ specifies that the character must be a backslash. A backslash that's used in this way is called an *escape character*.

You can also specify a *character class*, which consists of a set of characters. For example, \d indicates that the character must be a decimal digit, \w indicates that the character must be a *word character*, and \s indicates that the character must be a *whitespace character*. The uppercase versions of these elements—\D, \W, and \S—match any character that is not a decimal digit, word character, or whitespace character.

To create a list of possible characters, you enclose them in brackets. For example, [abc] specifies that the character must be the letter a, b, or c, and [a-z] specifies that the character must be a lowercase letter. One fairly common construct is [a-zA-Z], which specifies that the character must be a lowercase or uppercase letter.

You can also use *quantifiers* to indicate how many of the preceding element the input data must contain. To specify an exact number, you just code it in brackets. For example, \d{5} specifies that the input data must be a five-digit number. You can also specify a minimum number and a maximum number of characters. For example, \w{6,20} specifies that the input data must contain from six to twenty word characters. You can also omit the maximum number to require just a minimum number of characters. For example, \w{6,} specifies that the input data must contain at least 6 word characters. You can also use the *, ?, and + quantifiers to specify zero or more, zero or one, or one or more characters.

If the input data can match one or more patterns, you can use the vertical bar to separate elements. For example, \w+|\s{1} means that the input data must contain one or more word characters or a single whitespace character.

To create groups of elements, you use parentheses. Then, you can apply quantifiers to the entire group or you can separate groups with a vertical bar. For example, (AB)|(SB) specifies that the input characters must be either AB or SB. And (\d{3}-)? specifies that the input characters must contain zero or one occurrence of a three-digit number followed by a hyphen.

To help you understand how you can use each of these elements, this figure presents several examples. If you study them, you'll see the complex patterns that you can provide using these basic elements.

Common regular expression elements

Element	Description
Ordinary character	Matches any character other than ., $, ^, [, {, (, |,), *, +, ?, or \.
\	Matches the character that follows.
\d	Matches any decimal digit (0-9)
\D	Matches any character other than a decimal digit.
\w	Matches any word character (a-z, A-Z, and 0-9).
\W	Matches any character other than a word character.
\s	Matches any white space character (space, tab, new line, etc.).
\S	Matches any character other than a whitespace character.
[abcd]	Matches any character included between the brackets.
[^abcd]	Matches any character that is not included between the brackets.
[a-z]	Matches any characters in the indicated range.
{*n*}	Matches exactly *n* occurrences of the preceding element or group.
{*n*,}	Matches at least *n* occurrences of the preceding element or group.
{*n*,*m*}	Matches at least *n* but no more than *m* occurrences of the preceding element or group.
*	Matches zero or more occurrences of the preceding element.
?	Matches zero or one occurrence of the preceding element.
+	Matches one or more occurrences of the preceding element.
		Matches any of the elements separated by the vertical bar.
( )	Groups the elements that appear between the parentheses.

Examples of regular expressions

Expression	Example	Description
\d{3}	289	A three digit number.
\w{8,20}	Frankenstein	At least eight but no more than twenty word characters.
\d{2}-\d{4}	10-3944	A two-digit number followed by a hyphen and a four-digit number.
\w{1,8}.\w{1,3}	freddy.jpg	Up to eight letters or numbers, followed by a period and up to three letters or numbers.
(AB)|(SB)-\d{1,5}	SB-3276	The letters AB or SB, followed by a hyphen and a one- to five-digit number.
\d{5}(-\d{4})?	93711-2765	A five-digit number, optionally followed by a hyphen and a four-digit number.
\w*\d\w*	arm01	A text entry that contains at least one numeral.
[xyz]\d{3}	x023	The letter x, y, or z, followed by a three-digit number.

Notes

- A regular expression can include elements other than those shown above. For more information, see the *Regular Expression Language Elements* topic in help.
- The standard regular expressions use only the elements shown above.

Figure 7-10   How to create your own regular expressions

How to use a custom validator

If none of the other validators provide the data validation your program requires, you can use a *custom validator*. Then, you can code your own validation routine that's executed when the page is submitted to the server. This technique is frequently used to validate input data that requires a database lookup.

Figure 7-11 shows how you use a custom validator. In this example, a custom validator is used to check that a value entered by the user is a valid product code in a table of products. To do that, the program includes an event handler for the ServerValidate event of the custom validator. This event occurs whenever validation is performed on the server.

When the ServerValidate event occurs, the event handler receives an argument named args that you can use to validate the data the user entered. The Value property of this argument contains the input value. Then, the event handler can perform the tests that are necessary to determine if this value is valid. If so, the event handler assigns a True value to the IsValid property of the args argument so the validator passes its test. If not, the event handler can assign a False value to the IsValid property of this argument so the validator doesn't pass its test. This causes the error message specified by the validator to be displayed.

In this figure, for example, the event handler calls the CheckProductCode method of the HalloweenDB class. Although you haven't seen this class or method before, all you need to know is that it checks the product code by looking it up in a database. If the product code exists, this method returns a value of True. Otherwise, it returns a value of False. In either case, the returned value is assigned to the IsValid property of the args argument.

Properties of the ServerValidateEventArgs class

Property	Description
Value	The text string to be validated.
IsValid	A Boolean property that you set to True if the value passes the validation test or to False otherwise.

Aspx code for a text box and a custom validator

```
<asp:TextBox ID="txtProductCode" runat="server"></asp:TextBox>
<asp:CustomValidator id="valProductCode" runat="server"
    ControlToValidate="txtProductCode"
    ErrorMessage="Product code must be in database.">
</asp:CustomValidator>
```

Visual Basic code for the custom validator

```
Private Sub valProductCode_ServerValidate(ByVal source As Object, _
        ByVal args As System.Web.UI.WebControls.ServerValidateEventArgs) _
        Handles valProductCode.ServerValidate
    args.IsValid = HalloweenDB.CheckProductCode(args.Value)
End Sub
```

Description

- You can use a *custom validator* to validate input data using the validation tests you specify.

- You code the validation tests within an event handler for the ServerValidate event of the custom validator. This event is raised whenever validation is performed on the server. Because of that, the form must be submitted before the validation can be done.

- You can use the properties of the args argument that's passed to the ServerValidate event handler to test the input data (args.value) and indicate whether the data passed the validation test (args.IsValid). If you set the IsValid property of the args argument to False, the error message you specified for the custom validator is displayed.

- If the user doesn't enter a value into the associated input control, the custom validator doesn't perform its validation test. As a result, you should also provide a required field validator if a value is required.

Figure 7-11   How to use a custom validator

A validation routine that validates credit card numbers

To give you a better idea of what you can do with a custom validator, figure 7-12 shows the Visual Basic code for a custom validator that validates credit card numbers. To do that, it checks that the credit card number meets a mod-10 algorithm that all credit card numbers adhere to. This test often catches simple typographic errors before taking the time to actually authorize the card. Please note that this test doesn't establish that an account with the specified number exists or that credit is available on the account. It merely establishes that the number meets the required mod-10 algorithm.

To validate a credit card number, the event handler for the ServerValidate event calls a function named ValidateCreditCard and passes the card number to it. After this function declares three variables, it removes any spaces in the card number by using the Replace method of the String class, and it reverses the digits in the number using the StrReverse function. Next, it uses a For Next loop to double the digits in even-numbered positions. To determine if a digit is in an even-numbered position, it uses the Mod operator to divide the position by 2 to see if there's a remainder. If not, it multiplies the number in that position by 2 and then concatenates it to the variable named sDigits. (Note that because the Substring method that gets the number returns a string, it's coded within a CType function so that an integer value is returned.) Otherwise, it just concatenates the number.

After the digits in the even-numbered positions have been multiplied, the procedure uses another For Next loop to add up all the digits. (Again, a CType function is used to convert the result of the Substring method to an integer.) The Mod operator is then used to determine if the result is evenly divisible by 10. If so, the credit card number is valid and a True value is returned to the calling procedure. Otherwise, a False value is returned and the error message associated with the custom validator is displayed.

Visual Basic code for a credit card validator

```
Private Sub valCreditCardNumber_ServerValidate( _
        ByVal source As Object, _
        ByVal args As System.Web.UI.WebControls.ServerValidateEventArgs) _
        Handles valCreditCardNumber.ServerValidate
    args.IsValid = ValidateCreditCard(args.Value)
End Sub

Private Function ValidateCreditCard(ByVal CardNumber As String) As Boolean
    Dim iDigitSum As Integer
    Dim sDigits As String = ""
    Dim i As Integer
    'Remove spaces and reverse string
    CardNumber = StrReverse(CardNumber.Replace(" ", Nothing))
    'Double the digits in even-numbered positions
    For i = 0 To CardNumber.Length - 1
        If (i + 1) Mod 2 = 0 Then
            sDigits &= CType(CardNumber.Substring(i, 1), Integer) * 2
        Else
            sDigits &= CardNumber.Substring(i, 1)
        End If
    Next
    'Add the digits
    For i = 0 To sDigits.Length - 1
        iDigitSum += CType(sDigits.Substring(i, 1), Integer)
    Next
    'Check that the sum is divisible by 10
    If iDigitSum Mod 10 = 0 Then
        Return True
    Else
        Return False
    End If
End Function
```

What the mod 10 validation algorithm does

1. Removes any spaces from the number.
2. Reverses the number.
3. Doubles the digits in even-numbered positions. If the original digit is 5 or greater, this will insert an additional digit into the number.
4. Adds up the individual digits.
5. Divides the result by 10. If the remainder is 0, the credit card number is valid.

Description

- This code can be used along with a custom validator to ensure that the user enters a credit card number that passes a standard mod-10 algorithm. If the card number passes this test, the program usually continues by checking to make sure that the account is valid and that the customer has available credit.
- The ServerValidate event handler for the custom validator calls a function named ValidateCreditCard and passes the credit card number entered by the user. This function returns a Boolean value that indicates whether the credit card is valid.

Figure 7-12   A validation routine that validates credit card numbers

Perspective

Now that you've completed this chapter, you should be able to create web forms that provide for most of the data validation that your applications will require. Keep in mind, though, that after you add validators to a form, you need to test them thoroughly to be sure that they detect all invalid entries. Although that can be time-consuming, particularly if you use regular expression validators that require complicated expressions or custom validators that require complicated validation routines, it's an essential part of developing professional web applications.

Terms

validation control
validator
DHTML (Dynamic HTML)
required field validator
compare validator
range validator
validation summary control
validation group
default group
regular expression validator
regular expression
escape character
character class
word character
whitespace character
quantifier
custom validator

8

How to manage state

In chapters 2 and 3, you were introduced to the way that view state and session state are used. Now you'll learn more about using these states, and you'll also learn how to use application state. Beyond that, you'll learn how to use cookies and URL encoding to pass data between the server and the client. Because HTTP is a stateless protocol, these are essential skills for every web developer.

How to use view state

For the most part, *view state* is automatic. Because of that, you don't have to set any properties or write any code to use it. Nevertheless, you should at least understand how view state works and how to use it to your advantage. In some cases, you may even want to add your own data to view state.

How to work with view state

As the summary in figure 8-1 says, view state works by saving data in the HTML stream that's sent to the browser when a page is requested. This data is saved as a hidden input field named _VIEWSTATE. Because the field is hidden, it isn't displayed in the browser. And because the field is an input field, it's automatically sent back to the server when the user posts the page.

View state is used to retain the values of the form and control properties that you set in code. In the Future Value application of chapter 2, for example, the values in the drop-down list were set by code. As a result, these values don't need to be reset by code each time the form is posted back to the server. Instead, they're automatically reset by view state.

By default, view state is enabled for each control you add to a form, which is usually what you want. Occasionally, though, you may want to disable view state. One reason for doing that is to get a control to work the way you want it to. Another reason is to improve performance when view state gets so large that it degrades performance.

If, for example, you change the value of a control property in code, but you want the initial value of that property restored each time the page is loaded, you can turn off view state to get the page to work right. Or, if a page is never posted back to itself, you can turn off view state to improve performance. In practice, though, you probably won't turn off view state until you discover that it's creating either a programming or performance problem.

To determine the size of view state, you can enable the ASP.NET Trace feature as described in chapter 4. Then, you can scroll to the Control Tree section of the trace output to see which controls are using view state and how many bytes they're using. That way, you can tell whether it's worth the effort to turn view state off.

View state concepts

- *View state* is an ASP.NET feature that provides for retaining the values of page and control properties that change from one execution of a page to another.

- Before ASP.NET sends a page back to the client, it determines what changes the program has made to the properties of the page and its controls. These changes are encoded into a string that's assigned to the value of a hidden input field named _VIEWSTATE.

- When the page is posted back to the server, the _VIEWSTATE field is sent back to the server along with the HTTP request. Then, ASP.NET retrieves the property values from the _VIEWSTATE field and uses them to restore the page and control properties.

- ASP.NET also uses view state to save the values of the page properties it uses, such as IsPostBack.

- View state is *not* used to restore data entered by a user into a text box or any other input control unless the control responds to change events.

- If view state is enabled for a data-bound control, the control will not be rebound when the page is reposted. Instead, the control's values will be restored from view state.

Two cases when you may want to disable view state

- When restoring the control properties for a page affects the way you want the form to work, you may want to disable view state for one or more controls. Otherwise, you can modify your code so the page works without turning view state off.

- When the size of the view state field gets so large that it affects performance, you may want to disable view state for one or more controls or for an entire page.

How to disable view state

- To disable view state for a control, set the control's EnableViewState property to False.

- To disable view state for an entire page, set the EnableViewState property of the page to False. That disables view state for all the controls on the page.

How to determine the size of view state for a page

- Enable the Trace feature for the page by setting the Trace attribute of the Page directive for the page to True as described in chapter 4. Then, scroll down to the Control Tree section of the trace output to see the number of bytes of view state used by the page and its controls.

Figure 8-1   How to work with view state

How to use view state for your own data

Although view state is designed to automatically save page and control property values across round trips to the browser, you can also add your own data to view state. To do that, you store the data in a *view state object* that's created from the StateBag class as shown in figure 8-2.

Like the session state object, the view state object contains a collection of key/value pairs that represent the items saved in view state. To access this object, you use the ViewState property of the page. Then, you can use the properties and methods listed in this figure to work with the view state object.

To illustrate, the first two examples in this figure show how you can add or update a view state item named TimeStamp. The third example shows how to retrieve that item. And the last example shows how to remove it. Notice in the third example that because the value of a view state item is stored as an Object type, the CType function is used to convert the value to the appropriate data type.

Keep in mind that you usually use session state, not view state, to save data across round trips to the browser. Occasionally, though, it does make sense to use view state for passing small amounts of data, especially when you want to associate the data with a specific page. In chapter 21, you'll see an example of that.

Common properties and methods of the StateBag class

Property	Description
`Item`(name)	The value of the view state item with the specified name. If you set the value of an item that doesn't exist, that item is created. (Item is the default property of the StateBag class, so you can omit it when you access a view state item.)
`Count`	The number of items in the view state collection.
`Keys`	A collection of keys for all of the items in the view state collection.
`Values`	A collection of values for all of the items in the view state collection.

Method	Description
`Add`(name, value)	Adds an item to the view state collection. If the item you name already exists, its value is updated.
`Clear`	Removes all items from the view state collection.
`Remove`(name)	Removes the item with the specified name from the view state collection.

A statement that adds or updates a view state item

```
ViewState.Add("TimeStamp", Now)
```

Another way to add or update a view state item

```
ViewState("TimeStamp") = Now
```

A statement that retrieves the value of a view state item

```
Dim dtTimeStamp As DateTime = CType(ViewState("TimeStamp"), DateTime)
```

A statement that removes an item from view state

```
ViewState.Remove("TimeStamp")
```

Description

- View state is implemented using a *view state object* that's defined by the StateBag class. This class defines a collection of view state items.

- Although the form and control properties are automatically saved in view state, you can also save other data in view state.

- To access the view state object for a page, you use the ViewState property of the page.

Figure 8-2   How to use view state for your own data

How to use session state

In chapter 3, you learned some basic skills for using session state to save data across round trips to the browser. The topics that follow review and expand on that information.

How to work with session state

As you have learned, ASP.NET uses *session state* to track the state of each user of an application. To do that, it creates a *session state object* that contains a unique *session ID* for each user's session. This ID is passed back to the browser as part of the response and then returned to the server with the next request. ASP.NET can then use the session ID to get the session state object that's associated with the request.

To manage a user session, you can store data in the session state object, as shown in figure 8-3. Since you've already seen how session state is used in the Shopping Cart application, you shouldn't have any trouble understanding the first three examples. The first one adds or updates a session state item named EMail. The second one retrieves the value of the EMail item and stores it in a string variable. And the third one removes the EMail item from session state.

All three of these examples assume that session state is being accessed from the code-behind file of a web page. In that case, you refer to the session state object using the Session property of the page. To access session state from outside of a web page, however, you use the Session property of the HttpContext object for the current request as illustrated in the fourth example.

Common properties and methods of the HttpSessionState class

Property	Description
`SessionID`	The unique ID of the session.
`Item(name)`	The value of the session state item with the specified name. If you set the value of an item that doesn't exist, that item is created. (Since Item is the default property of the HttpSessionState class, you can omit it when you access a session state item.)
`Count`	The number of items in the session state collection.

Method	Description
`Add(name, value)`	Adds an item to the session state collection. If the item you name already exists, its value is updated.
`Clear`	Removes all items from the session state collection.
`Remove(name)`	Removes the item with the specified name from the session state collection.

A statement that adds or updates a session state item

```
Session("EMail") = sEmail
```

A statement that retrieves the value of a session state item

```
Dim sEmail As String = Session("EMail").ToString
```

A statement that removes an item from session state

```
Session.Remove("EMail")
```

A statement that retrieves a session state item from a non-page class

```
Dim sEmail As String = HttpContext.Current.Session("EMail").ToString
```

Description

- ASP.NET uses *session state* to track the state of each user of an application. To do that, it creates a *session state object* that contains a *session ID*. This ID is passed to the browser and then back to the server with the next request so the server can identify the session associated with that request.

- Because session state sends only the session ID to the browser, it doesn't slow response time. By default, though, session state objects are maintained in server memory so they can slow performance on the server side.

- To work with the data in session state, you use the HttpSessionState class, which defines a collection of session state items.

- To access the session state object from the code-behind file for a web form, use the Session property of the page.

- To access the session state object from a class other than a code-behind file, use the Current property of the HttpContext class to get the HttpContext object for the current request. Then, use the Session property to get the session state object.

Figure 8-3   How to work with session state

When to save and retrieve session state items

Most ASP.NET developers use session state in a consistent way. First, an application retrieves data from session state and stores it in variables. Then, the application uses these variables when it processes the user events. Finally, the application saves the updated variables back to session state so they can be retrieved the next time the page is posted back to the server.

If an item in session state is used within a single procedure in an application, you can retrieve, process, and save that item within that procedure. However, it's more common for an application to use a session state item in two or more procedures. Because of that, it makes sense to retrieve the item when the application first starts and save it just before it ends. To do that, you can use the Load and PreRender events of the page as shown in figure 8-4.

The example in this figure illustrates how this works. To keep this simple, this application consists of a single page that contains a Post button that the user can click to post the page back to the server. Each time the user clicks this button, the program code updates the label on the page to indicate how many times the button has been clicked.

To implement this application, a session state item named ClickCount is used to maintain a count of the number of times the user clicks the Post button. To start, the Page_Load procedure sets a count variable to zero if the session state item named ClickCount hasn't been created yet. Otherwise, this procedure gets the value of the ClickCount item from the session state object and assigns it to the count variable.

If the user clicked the Post button, the program executes the btnPost_Click procedure. This procedure adds one to the count variable and updates the label on the form to indicate how many times the button has been clicked.

Then, just before ASP.NET renders the HTML for the page, the Page_PreRender procedure is executed. This procedure saves the value of the count variable to session state so it's available the next time the user clicks the Post button. Because PreRender is a page event, it's raised each time the page is executed just like the Load event.

It's important to note that the variable that's used to store the value of the session state item in this example is a value-type variable. That means that the value is actually stored in the variable. Because of that, you have to explicitly update the session state item in the Page_PreRender procedure.

In contrast, if you use a reference-type variable such as a string or other object variable, the session state item is updated automatically when you update the variable that refers to it. That's because the variable contains a pointer to the object, not the data itself. As a result, you don't have to update the session state item explicitly. If you look back to the application in chapter 3, you'll see that the Cart item in the session state object is handled that way.

A Counter application that counts the times the user clicks the button

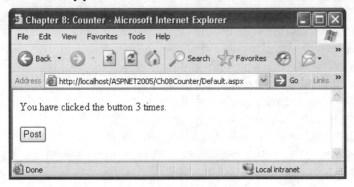

The code for the Counter application

```
Dim iClickCount As Integer

Protected Sub Page_Load(ByVal sender As Object, _
        ByVal e As System.EventArgs) Handles Me.Load
    If Session("ClickCount") Is Nothing Then
        iClickCount = 0
    Else
        iClickCount = CType(Session("ClickCount"), Integer)
    End If
End Sub

Protected Sub btnPost_Click(ByVal sender As Object, _
        ByVal e As System.EventArgs) Handles btnPost.Click
    iClickCount += 1
    lblClickCount.Text = "You have clicked the button " _
        & iClickCount & " times."
End Sub

Protected Sub Page_PreRender(ByVal sender As Object, _
        ByVal e As System.EventArgs) Handles Me.PreRender
    Session("ClickCount") = iClickCount
End Sub
```

Description

- If a session state item is accessed from two or more event handlers, you usually code the application so it retrieves the value of that item in the Load event handler and saves the updated value back to session state in the PreRender event handler.

- Since the Load event is raised before any of the control events for the page, you can use its event handler to retrieve a session state item and store it in a module-level variable. Then, the item is available to all of the other procedures.

- Since the PreRender event is raised after all the control events for the page have been processed, you can use its event handler to update the session state item.

- You only need to update a session state item explicitly if it's stored in a value-type variable. If it's stored in a reference-type variable, the session state item is updated automatically when the variable is updated.

Figure 8-4   When to save and retrieve session state items

Options for storing session state data

By default, ASP.NET stores session state data in server memory and tracks user sessions using cookies. However, as figure 8-5 shows, ASP.NET actually provides four options for storing session state data and two options for tracking session IDs. Although you typically use the default options, you should be familiar with these other options in case you ever need them.

The default for storing session state data is *in-process mode*. With this mode, session state data is stored in server memory within the same process that your ASP.NET application runs. This is the most efficient way to store session state data, but it only works for applications that are hosted on a single web server.

If your application has so many users that a single web server can't carry the load, you can deploy the application on two or more servers. When you do that, you need to store session state data in a location that can be accessed by all of the servers. Session state provides two options for doing that.

State Server mode stores session state data in server memory, but not in the same process as your application. Instead, session state is managed by the ASP.NET state service, which can be accessed by all of the servers that host the application. That's necessary because when two or more servers host an application, a different server can process the application each time it's executed. So if the session state data is stored on the server that processed the application the first time it was executed, that data won't be available if the application is processed by another server the next time it's executed.

Another way to make session state data available to two or more servers is to use *SQL Server mode*. With this mode, session state data is stored in a SQL Server database rather than in server memory. Although SQL Server mode is slower than in-process and State Server mode, it's also the most reliable. That's because if your web server goes down, the session state data will be maintained in the database. In contrast, session state data is lost if the server goes down when you're using in-process or State Server mode.

The last option for storing session state data is *custom mode*. With this mode, you create your own *session state store provider* that saves and retrieves session state data. You might use this option if you want to save session state data in a database, but your shop uses Oracle or some other database instead of Microsoft SQL Server.

Fortunately, the programming requirements for all four session state modes are identical. So you can change an application from one mode to another without changing any of the application's code. If you use the custom mode, however, you'll have to create the session state store provider.

Options for tracking session IDs

By default, ASP.NET maintains session state by sending the session ID for a user session to the browser as a cookie. Then, the cookie is returned to the server with the next request so the server can associate the browser with the

Four options for storing session state data

- *In-process mode* (the default) stores session state data in IIS server memory in the same process as the ASP.NET application. This is the session state model that's used the most, but it's suitable only when a single server is used for the application.
- *State Server mode* stores session state data in server memory under the control of a separate service called the ASP.NET state service. This service can be accessed by other IIS servers, so it can be used when an application is hosted on a web farm that consists of more than one IIS server. In that case, each request for the application can be processed by a different server, so the session state information must be available to all the servers.
- *SQL Server mode* stores session state data in a SQL Server database. Like State Server mode, SQL Server mode is used for applications that require more than one IIS server. Although this mode is slower than In-process mode and State Server mode, it's also the most reliable.
- *Custom mode* lets you write your own *session state store provider* to read and write session state data.

Two options for tracking session IDs

- By default, ASP.NET uses *cookie-based session tracking* to keep track of user sessions. However, if a browser doesn't support cookies, this doesn't work.
- With *cookieless session tracking*, the session ID is encoded as part of the URL. As a result, cookieless session state works whether or not the browser supports cookies.

Description

- The programming requirements for all four session state modes are identical, so you don't have to recode an application if you change the mode. If you use custom mode, however, you do have to create a class that implements the session state store provider.
- Cookieless session tracking introduces security risks because the session ID is visible to the user. It also limits the way URL's can be specified in Response.Redirect and Server.Transfer calls. For these reasons, most developers don't use cookieless sessions.
- You can control how session state data is stored and how session IDs are tracked by setting the attributes of the session state element in the application's web.config file. For more information, see the next figure.
- Custom mode is an advanced mode that isn't covered in this book. To learn more about how to create a session state store provider for use with custom mode, see the "Implementing a Session State Store Provider" topic in the Help documentation.

Figure 8-5   Options for storing session state data and tracking session IDs

session. This is called *cookie-based session tracking*, and this is the most reliable and secure way to track sessions.

If a browser doesn't support cookies, however, session state won't work unless you switch to *cookieless session tracking*. Cookieless session tracking works by adding the session ID to the URL that's used to request the ASP.NET page. Unfortunately, because the URL is visible to the user and isn't encrypted, the use of cookieless session tracking creates a security risk.

Ideally, then, you should use cookie-based session tracking when cookies are supported and cookieless session tracking when they're not. As you can see in figure 8-6, ASP.NET 2.0 lets you do just that.

How to set session state options

As you know, the first time you run an application with debugging, Visual Studio adds a web.config file to your web site. If this file hasn't already been added, however, you can add it by selecting the Website→Add New Item command and then selecting the Web Configuration File template. Then, you can add session state options to this file as shown in figure 8-6.

Although the web.config file is an XML file, you shouldn't have trouble editing it even if you aren't familiar with the details of XML syntax. To edit this file, just double-click on it in the Solution Explorer to display it in a Code Editor window. Then, add a sessionState element within the system.web element as shown in this figure. Within the sessionState element, you can code any of the attributes listed in the table in this figure. In the example shown here, I included the Mode attribute to indicate that in-process mode should be used; I included the Cookieless attribute to indicate that cookies should be used if they're supported, and URLs should be used if they're not; and I included the Timeout attribute to increase the number of minutes that the session should be maintained without activity to 30.

If you use State Server mode, you'll need to set the stateConnectionString attribute to the server name or IP address and port number of the server that hosts the ASP.NET state service. If the name of the server is mma1, for example, the stateConnectionString attribute will look like this:

```
stateConnectionString="tcpip=mma1:42424"
```

Note that the port number is always 42424.

Similarly, if you use SQL Server mode, you'll need to set the sqlConnectionString attribute to the connection string for the instance of SQL Server that contains the database that's used to store the session state data. For instance, if the SQL Server instance is Murach, the attribute might look like this:

```
sqlConnectionString="Data Source=Murach;Integrated
Security=SSPI"
```

Note that the database isn't included in the connection string, which means that the default database named ASPState is used. If you want to use a different database to store session state data, you need to include the name of the database in the connection string, and you need to include the allowCustomSqlDatabase attribute with a value of True.

Attributes of the session state element in the web.config file

Attribute	Description
Mode	The session state mode. Values can be Off, InProc, StateServer, SQLServer, or Custom. The default is InProc.
Cookieless	An HttpCookieMode value that specifies whether cookieless sessions are used. AutoDetect uses cookies if they're supported and a query string if they're not. UseUri uses a query string. The default is UseCookies.
Timeout	The number of minutes a session should be maintained without any user activity. After the specified number of minutes, the session is deleted. The default is 20.
StateConnectionString	The server name or IP address and port number (always 42424) of the server that runs the ASP.NET state service. This attribute is required when State Server mode is used.
SqlConnectionString	A connection string for the instance of SQL Server that contains the database that's used to store the session state data. If the allowCustomSqlDatabase attribute is set to True, the connection string can also include the name of the database. This attribute is required when SQL Server mode is used.
AllowCustomSqlDatabase	A Boolean value that determines if the SqlConnectionString can specify the name of the database used to store state information. The default value is False, in which case the state information is stored in a database named ASPState.
CustomProvider	The name of the custom session state store provider.

A sessionState element in the web.config file that uses in-process mode

```
<?xml version="1.0"?>
<configuration>
  <system.web>
    .
    .
    <sessionState mode="InProc"
      cookieless="AutoDetect"
      timeout="30"
    />
    .
    .
  </system.web>
</configuration>
```

Description

- The web.config file contains settings that affect how an ASP.NET web application operates. To change the default options for session state, you can add a sessionState element to the web.config file and then specify the attributes and values you want to use.
- Before you can use SQL Server mode, you must create the database that will be used to store session state data. For information on how to do that, see the "Session State Modes" topic in the Help documentation.
- If you specify Custom mode, you must include additional information in the web.config file to identify the session state store provider. For more information, see the "Session State Modes" topic in the Help documentation.

Figure 8-6   How to set session state options

How to use application state

In contrast to session state, which stores data for a single user session, application state lets you store data that is shared by all users of an application. In the topics that follow, you'll learn how to use application state.

How application state works

Figure 8-7 presents the concepts you need for working with *application state*. To start, an *application* is made up of all the pages, code, and other files that are located under a single virtual directory in an IIS web server.

The first time a user requests a page that resides in an application's virtual directory, ASP.NET initializes the application. During that process, ASP.NET creates an *application object* from the HttpApplication class. This object is represented by a special class file named global.asax, which you'll learn how to work with in figure 8-9.

The application object can be accessed by any of the application's pages. This object exists until the application ends, which normally doesn't happen until IIS shuts down. However, the application is automatically restarted each time you rebuild the application or edit the application's web.config file.

Each time ASP.NET starts an application and creates an application object, it also creates an *application state object* from the HttpApplicationState class. You can use this object to store data in server memory that can be accessed by any page that's part of the application.

One common use for application state is to store hit counters that track how many times users have retrieved specific pages. For instance, the Counter application at the top of this figure tracks the number of times all of the users of the application have clicked the Post button. This is similar to the application you saw in figure 8-4, but that application used session state to track the count for a single user.

Another common use for application state is to store application-specific data, such as discount terms and tax rates for an ordering system. Although you could retrieve this type of information from a database each time it's needed, it sometimes makes sense to retrieve it just once when the application starts and then store it in application state. That way, the data is more readily accessible as the application executes.

Finally, application state is commonly used to keep track of which users are logged on to the application. That's particularly useful for applications that provide chat rooms or message boards where you can communicate with other users. Then, the application can display a list of the users who are currently in the chat room or who are using the message board.

A Counter application that counts the number of times that all users click the button

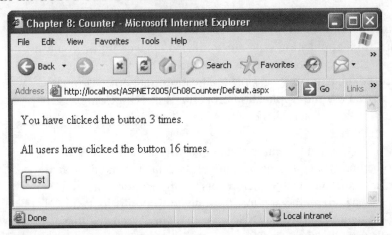

Application concepts

- An ASP.NET *application* is the collection of pages, code, and other files within a single virtual directory on a web server. In most cases, an ASP.NET application corresponds to a single Visual Studio web project.

- An application begins when the first user requests a page that's a part of the application. Then, ASP.NET initializes the application before it processes the request for the page.

- As part of its initialization, ASP.NET creates an *application object* from the HttpApplication class. This object exists for the duration of the application. You can use the global.asax file to work with the application object, as described in figure 8-9.

- Once an application has started, it doesn't normally end until the web server is shut down. If you rebuild the application or edit the web.config file, however, the application will be restarted the next time a user requests a page that's part of the application.

Application state concepts

- If you store items in *application state*, those items are available to all users of the application.

- To provide for the use of application state, ASP.NET creates an *application state object* for each application from the HttpApplicationState class and stores this object in server memory.

Typical uses for application state

- To store hit counters and other statistical data.
- To store global application data such as discount terms and tax rates.
- To track users currently visiting the site by keeping a list of user names or other identifying data.

Figure 8-7   How application state works

How to work with application state data

Figure 8-8 presents the details for working with application state data. As you can see from the first three examples, the techniques you use to add items to and retrieve items from application state are similar to the techniques you use to work with items in session state. The main difference is that you use the Application property of the page to access the application state object from a code-behind file, and you use the Application property of the HttpContext object for the current request to access the application state object from a class other than a code-behind file.

When you're working with application state data, you'll want to lock the application state collection when you modify any of its data. This is illustrated in the last example in this figure, which increments an application state item named ClickCount by one. Here, the application state collection is locked before the ClickCount item is retrieved. Then, after the item is updated, the application state collection is unlocked. To minimize the length of time the application state object is locked, you should do as little processing as possible between the Lock and Unlock methods.

If you don't lock the application state collection while the count is updated, two or more users could access the count at the same time. To illustrate why that's a problem, let's assume that three users access the count item at the same time, and the starting count is 11. Then, when each of those users increment the count it becomes 12, and that's the value that each user stores in the application state collection. In this case, though, the correct count should be 14.

Common properties and methods of the HttpApplicationState class

Property	Description
`Item(name)`	The value of the application state item with the specified name. If you set the value of an item that doesn't exist, that item is created. (Since Item is the default property of the HttpApplicationState class, you can omit it when you access an application state item.)
`Count`	The number of items in the application state collection.

Method	Description
`Add(name, value)`	Adds an item to the application state collection.
`Clear()`	Removes all items from the application state collection.
`Remove(name)`	Removes the item with the specified name from the application state collection.
`Lock()`	Locks the application state collection so only the current user can access it.
`Unlock()`	Unlocks the application state collection so other users can access it.

A statement that retrieves an item from application state

```
Dim iClickCount As Integer = CType(Application("ClickCount"), Integer)
```

A statement that adds an item to application state

```
Application.Add("ClickCount", 0)
```

A statement that retrieves the application state from a non-page class

```
Dim iClickCount As Integer = CType(HttpContext.Current.Application( _
    "ClickCount"), Integer)
```

Code that locks application state while retrieving and updating an item

```
Application.Lock()
Dim iClickCount As Integer = CType(Application("ClickCount"), Integer)
iClickCount += 1
Application("ClickCount") = iClickCount
Application.Unlock()
```

Description

- You can use the application state object to store items that are common to all users of the application.
- To access the application state object from the code-behind file for an ASP.NET web form, use the Application property of the page.
- To access the application state object from a class other than a code-behind file, use the Current property of the HttpContext class to get the HttpContext object for the current request. Then, use the Application property of this object to get the application state object.
- Before you retrieve the value of an application state item that you intend to modify, you should lock the application state object so other users can't modify the application state data at the same time. As soon as you finish modifying the application state data, you should release the application state object so other users can access it.

Figure 8-8   How to work with application state data

How to work with application events

Now that you know how to work with application state data, you may be wondering how to initialize the values of application state items. To do that, you first add a global.asax file to the project as described in figure 8-9. By default, this file contains Sub and End Sub statements for five event handlers as shown in the example in this figure. Then, you can add code to any of these event handlers. This figure summarizes the four events you're most likely to use to work with application state data.

The example in this figure shows how you can initialize and update a session state item named HitCount that keeps track of the number of times a new session is started for an application. In this example, the Application_Start event handler retrieves the current hit count number from a database and adds an application state item named HitCount to the application state object. Similarly, the Application_End event handler saves the HitCount item to the database so it will be accurate when it's retrieved the next time the application starts. Although the HalloweenDB class that includes the methods that are used to retrieve and update the count isn't shown here, all you need to know is that the GetHitCount method retrieves the current hit count from a database as an integer value, and the UpdateHitCount method saves the integer value to the database.

The updating of the HitCount item takes place in the Session_Start event handler, which is raised whenever a new user session begins. This event handler starts by locking the application state object. Then, it increases the HitCount item by 1 and unlocks the application state object.

Four common application events

Event	Description
Application_Start	This event is raised when the first page of an application is requested by any user. It is often used to initialize the values of application state items.
Application_End	This event is raised when an application is about to terminate. It can be used to write the values of critical application state items to a database or file.
Session_Start	This event is raised when a user session begins. It can be used to initialize session state items, update application state items, or authorize user access.
Session_End	This event is raised when a user session is about to terminate. It can be used to free resources held by the user or to log the user off the application. It is raised only when in-process mode is used.

A global.asax file that creates an object in application state

```
<%@ Application Language="VB" %>
<script runat="server">

    Sub Application_Start(ByVal sender As Object, ByVal e As EventArgs)
        ' Code that runs on application startup
        Application.Add("HitCount", HalloweenDB.GetHitCount)
    End Sub

    Sub Application_End(ByVal sender As Object, ByVal e As EventArgs)
        ' Code that runs on application shutdown
        HalloweenDB.UpdateHitCount(Application("HitCount"))
    End Sub

    Sub Application_Error(ByVal sender As Object, ByVal e As EventArgs)
        ' Code that runs when an unhandled error occurs
    End Sub

    Sub Session_Start(ByVal sender As Object, ByVal e As EventArgs)
        ' Code that runs when a new session is started
        Application.Lock
        Application("HitCount") += 1
        Application.Unlock
    End Sub

    Sub Session_End(ByVal sender As Object, ByVal e As EventArgs)
        ' Code that runs when a session ends.
    End Sub

</script>
```

Description

- To create a global.asax file, select the Website→Add New Item command, and then choose the Global Application Class template.
- The global.asax file provides event handlers for application events. The event handlers are coded within a Script element that defines a code declaration block.
- To refer to the application state object from the global.asax file, you use the Application property of the application.

Figure 8-9   How to work with application events

How to use cookies and URL encoding

Earlier in this chapter, you learned that ASP.NET uses cookies to track user sessions. Now, you'll learn how to create and use your own cookies. Then, you'll learn how to use URL encoding as an alternative to the use of cookies.

How to create cookies

A *cookie* is a name/value pair that is stored on the client's computer. For instance, the name of the first cookie in figure 8-10 is ASP.NET_SessionId, and its value is

```
jsswpu5530hcyx2w3jfa5u55
```

This is a typical session ID for a cookie that's generated by ASP.NET to keep track of a session. The other cookie examples are typical of cookies that you create yourself.

To create a cookie, you instantiate an object from the HttpCookie class. Then, you include it in the HTTP response that the server sends back to the browser, and the user's browser stores the cookie either in its own memory or in a text file on the client machine's disk.

A cookie that's stored in the browser's memory is called a *session cookie* because it exists only for that session. When the browser session ends, the contents of any session cookies are lost. Session cookies are what ASP.NET uses to track session ID's. In contrast, *persistent cookies* are written to disk, so they are maintained after the browser session ends. Whether session or persistent, though, once a cookie is sent to a browser, it's automatically returned to the server with each HTTP request.

Besides using cookies for session IDs, you can use cookies to save information that identifies each user so the users don't have to enter that information each time they visit your web site. You can also use cookies to store information that lets you personalize the web pages that are displayed for a user.

When you use cookies to store this type of information, you should keep in mind that some users may have disabled cookies on their browsers. In that case, you won't be able to save cookies on the user's computer. Unfortunately, ASP.NET doesn't provide a way for you to determine whether a user has disabled cookies. As a result, if you use cookies in an application, you may need to notify the user that cookies must be enabled to use it.

This figure also presents some properties of the HttpCookie class. Then, the first example shows how to create a session cookie. Here, both the cookie's name and value are specified on the constructor. Because the Expires property isn't set, it's given a default value of 12:00 a.m. on January 1, 0001. Because this value has already passed, the cookie is deleted when the session ends.

If you don't set the value of a cookie when you create it, you can use the Value property to set it later on. In addition, you can use the Expires property to set the expiration date for a persistent cookie. This is illustrated by the second example in this figure.

Examples of cookies

```
ASP.NET_SessionId=jsswpu5530hcyx2w3jfa5u55
EMail=Anne@Murach.com
user_ID=4993
password=opensesame
```

Two ways to create a cookie

```
cookie = New HttpCookie(name)
cookie = New HttpCookie(name, value)
```

Common properties of the HttpCookie class

Property	Description
Expires	A DateTime value that indicates when the cookie should expire.
Name	The cookie's name.
Secure	A Boolean value that indicates whether the cookie should be sent only when a secure connection is used. See chapter 17 for information on secure connections.
Value	The string value assigned to the cookie.

Code that creates a session cookie

```
Dim NameCookie As New HttpCookie("UserName", sUserName)
```

Code that creates a persistent cookie

```
Dim NameCookie As New HttpCookie("UserName")
NameCookie.Value = sUserName
NameCookie.Expires = Now().AddYears(1)
```

Description

- A *cookie* is a name/value pair that's stored in the user's browser or on the user's disk.
- A web application sends a cookie to a browser via an HTTP response. Then, each time the browser sends an HTTP request to the server, it attaches any cookies that are associated with that server.
- By default, ASP.NET uses a cookie to store the session ID for a session, but you can also create and send your own cookies to a user's browser.
- A *session cookie* is kept in the browser's memory and exists only for the duration of the browser session. A *persistent cookie* is kept on the user's disk and is retained until the cookie's expiration date.
- To create a cookie, you specify its name or its name and value. To create a persistent cookie, you must also set the Expires property to the time you want the cookie to expire.
- Some users disable cookies in their browsers. Browsers can also be configured to limit the number of cookies they will accept from each site, the total number of cookies accepted from all sites, and the maximum size of each cookie. Typical limits are 20 cookies from each site, 300 cookies altogether, and 4K as the maximum cookie size.

Figure 8-10   How to create cookies

How to work with cookies

After you create a cookie, you work with it using the properties and methods of the HttpCookieCollection class shown in figure 8-11. This class defines a collection of HttpCookie objects. To refer to a cookie in a cookies collection, for example, you use the Item property of the collection. And to add a cookie to the collection, you use the Add method of the collection.

The key to working with cookies is realizing that you must deal with two instances of the HttpCookieCollection class. The first one contains the collection of cookies that have been sent to the server from the client. You access this collection using the Cookies property of the HttpRequest object. The second one contains the collection of cookies that will be sent back to the browser. You access this collection using the Cookies property of the HttpResponse object.

To send a new cookie to the client, you create the cookie and then add it to the collection of cookies in the HttpResponse object. This is illustrated in the first example in this figure. Here, a cookie named NameCookie is created and added to the HttpResponse object.

The second example shows you how to retrieve the value of a cookie that's sent from the browser. Here, the Request property of the page is used to refer to the HttpRequest object. Then, the Item property (the default) of the Cookies collection of the request object is used to get the cookie, and the Value property of the cookie is used to get the cookie's value.

The last example in this figure illustrates how you can delete a persistent cookie. To do that, you create a cookie with the same name as the cookie you want to delete, and you set its Expires property to a time in the past. In this example, I set the date to one second before the current time. Then, you add the cookie to the HttpResponse object so it's sent back to the browser. When the browser receives the cookie, it replaces the existing cookie with the new cookie. When the client's system detects that the cookie has expired, it deletes it.

Common properties and methods of the HttpCookieCollection class

Property	Description
`Item(name)`	The cookie with the specified name. (Since Item is the default property of the HttpCookieCollection class, you can omit it when you access a cookie.)
`Count`	The number of cookies in the collection.

Method	Description
`Add(cookie)`	Adds a cookie to the collection.
`Clear`	Removes all cookies from the collection.
`Remove(name)`	Removes the cookie with the specified name from the collection.

A procedure that creates a new cookie and adds it to the HttpResponse object

```
Private Sub AddCookie()
    Dim NameCookie As New HttpCookie("UserName", txtUserName.Text)
    NameCookie.Expires = Now.AddYears(1)
    Response.Cookies.Add(NameCookie)
End Sub
```

A procedure that retrieves the value of a cookie from the HttpRequest object

```
Protected Sub Page_Load(ByVal sender As Object, _
        ByVal e As System.EventArgs) Handles Me.Load
    If Not IsPostBack Then
        If Request.Cookies("UserName") IsNot Nothing Then
            lblUserName.Text = "Welcome back " _
                            & Request.Cookies("UserName").Value _
                            & "."
        End If
    End If
End Sub
```

A procedure that deletes a persistent cookie

```
Private Sub DeleteCookie()
    Dim NameCookie As New HttpCookie("UserName")
    NameCookie.Expires = Now.AddSeconds(-1)
    Response.Cookies.Add(NameCookie)
End Sub
```

Description

- Cookies are managed in collections defined by the HttpCookieCollection class.

- To access the cookies collection for a request or response, use the Cookies property of the HttpRequest or HttpResponse object. To refer to these objects, use the Request and Response properties of the page.

- To delete a persistent cookie, create a cookie with the same name as the cookie you want to delete and set its Expires property to a time that has already passed. Then, when the client's system detects that the cookie has expired, it deletes it.

Figure 8-11   How to work with cookies

How to enable or disable cookies

If an application relies on the use of cookies, you'll want to be sure that cookies are enabled in your browser as you test the application. Conversely, to test an application that's intended to work even if cookies have been disabled, you'll need to disable cookies in your browser. To do that, you can use the techniques presented in figure 8-12.

If you're using Internet Explorer 6.0, you use a slider control to determine what cookies are allowed. The default setting is Medium, which enables both session and persistent cookies. To disable both types of cookies, you can select a privacy setting that blocks all cookies as shown here. Alternatively, you can use the dialog box that's displayed when you click the Advanced button to override the default settings so your browser accepts session cookies but disables persistent cookies.

The technique for using earlier versions of Internet Explorer is similar. The main differences are that you control cookies through the Security tab of the Internet Options dialog box, and you use the Custom tab to modify the defaults so that session cookies are enabled but persistent cookies are disabled.

This figure also describes how to enable or disable cookies if you're using Netscape or Mozilla Firefox. Although these techniques are quite different from the techniques for enabling or disabling cookies with Internet Explorer, you shouldn't have any trouble understanding how to use them.

An Internet Explorer dialog box with disabled cookies

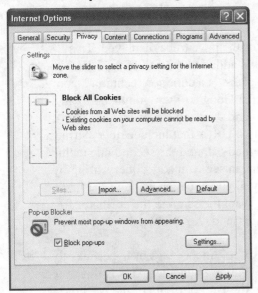

How to enable or disable cookies for Internet Explorer

1. Select the Tools→Internet Options command.
2. For Internet Explorer 6.0, select the Privacy tab. For Internet Explorer 5.5 or earlier, select the Security tab.
3. Use the slider control to set the security level to accept or block cookies.

How to enable or disable cookies for Netscape

1. Select the Edit→Preferences command.
2. For Netscape 7.1, expand the Privacy and Security category and then select Cookies. For Netscape 7.0 or earlier, select the Advanced option.
3. Choose an option to enable or disable cookies.

How to enable or disable cookies for Mozilla Firefox

1. Select the Tools→Options command.
2. Click the Privacy icon and expand the Cookies node.
3. Check or uncheck the Allow Sites to Set Cookies option.

Description

- Internet Explorer also lets you enable or disable persistent cookies and session cookies separately. To do that with Internet Explorer 6.0, click the Advanced button and select from the advanced privacy settings that are displayed. To change these settings from earlier versions of Internet Explorer, select the Custom Level button in the Security tab.

Figure 8-12   How to enable or disable cookies

How to use URL encoding

URL encoding is an alternative to the use of cookies that lets you store information in the URL after the address of the page to be displayed. This information is stored in a *query string* that's added to the end of the URL, as shown in figure 8-13. Since using query strings is a common technique, you've probably seen them used on search sites like Google (www.google.com) and shopping sites like Ebay (www.ebay.com) and Amazon (www.amazon.com).

At the top of this figure, you can see two URLs that include query strings. The first one includes a single attribute named cat, and the second one includes two attributes named cat and prod. As you can see, you add a query string by coding a question mark after the URL. Then, you code the name of the first attribute, an equal sign, and the value you want to assign to the attribute. To include another attribute, you code an ampersand (&), followed by the name and value of the attribute.

In most cases, you'll use query strings with Anchor tags or hyperlinks to pass information from one page of an application to another. This is illustrated in the second example in this figure. Here, the Href attribute of the Anchor tag indicates that it will link to a page named Product.aspx. In addition, the URL includes a query string that contains a category and a product value. The Product page can then use these values to display information for the specified product.

To retrieve the values included in a query string, you use the QueryString property of the Request object as illustrated in the third example. The two statements in this example retrieve the two values passed by the query string in the second example.

The fourth example shows that you can also use query strings in the URLs that you code for Redirect or Transfer methods. Here, the URL contains a query string with a single attribute that contains a category ID. You should also realize that you can code query strings in the PostBackUrl attribute of a button control, although you're not likely to do that.

Two URLs with query strings

```
Order.aspx?cat=costumes
Order.aspx?cat=props&prod=rat01
```

An Anchor tag with a URL that includes a query string

```
<a href='product.aspx?cat=fx&prod=fog01'>Fog machine</a>
```

Statements that retrieve the values of the query string attributes

```
Dim sCategoryID As String = Request.QueryString("cat")
Dim sProductID As String = Request.QueryString("prod")
```

Code that uses a URL with a query string in a Redirect method

```
Response.Redirect("Order.aspx?cat=" & sCategoryID)
```

Description

- When you use *URL encoding*, a *query string* that consists of attribute/value pairs is added to the end of a URL.

- Query strings are frequently used in Anchor tags and hyperlinks to pass information from one page of an application to another or to display different information on the same page.

- Query strings can also be used in the URLs that are specified for Response.Redirect or Server.Transfer calls, and they can be used in the PostBackUrl property of a button control.

- When you use an Anchor tag, a hyperlink, or a Redirect or Transfer method that specifies a URL for the current page, the page is processed as if it's being requested for the first time.

- To code a query string, follow the URL with a question mark, the name of the attribute, an equal sign, and a value. To code two or more attributes, separate them with ampersands (&), and don't include any spaces in the query string.

- To retrieve the value of a query string attribute, use the QueryString property of the HttpRequest object and specify the attribute name. To refer to the HttpRequest object, use the Request property of the page.

- Most browsers impose a limit of 255 characters in a query string.

Figure 8-13   How to use URL encoding

Perspective

If this chapter has succeeded, you should now be able to use view state, session state, and application state whenever they're required by your application. You should also be able to use cookies and URL encoding whenever they're appropriate for your applications. Although this chapter doesn't present a complete application that illustrates the use of all these techniques, you shouldn't have any trouble using them whenever they're called for.

As you work with these techniques, please keep in mind that they aren't exclusive of one another. In fact, you'll often use two or more of these techniques in a single application. Most web applications, for example, use both view state and session state. And many applications also use application state, cookies, and URL encoding.

You should also be aware that ASP.NET 2.0 provides a new feature called *profiles* that presents yet another way to manage the state of a user. This feature has some distinct advantages because it stores its data in a database that's available from one session to another. In chapter 19, you can learn how to use profiles to personalize an application.

Terms

view state
view state object
session state
session state object
session ID
in-process mode
State Server mode
SQL Server mode
custom mode
session state store provider
cookie-based session tracking
cookieless session tracking
application
application object
application state
application state object
cookie
session cookie
persistent cookie
URL encoding
query string

9

How to use master pages

A master page makes it easy for you to create pages that have common elements such as banners and navigation menus. That's why it is one of the most important new features of ASP.NET 2.0. In fact, you may decide that you're going to use one master page for every group of pages that you develop.

How to create master pages

A *master page* is a page that provides a framework within which the content from other pages can be displayed. Master pages make it easy to include banners, navigation menus, and other elements on all of the pages in an application. In the topics that follow, you'll learn how to create master pages in your ASP.NET applications.

An introduction to master pages

Figure 9-1 shows the basics of how master pages work. As you can see, the page that's actually sent to the browser is created by combining elements from a master page and a *content page*. The content page provides the content that's unique to each page in the application, while the master page provides the elements that are common to all pages. In this example, the master page (MasterPage.master) provides a banner at the top of each page, a simple navigation menu at the side of each page, and a message that indicates how many days remain until Halloween at the bottom of each page.

In addition, the master page contains a *content placeholder* that indicates where the content from each content page should be displayed. In this example, the content page is the Order.aspx page, and its content is displayed in the content placeholder in the central portion of the master page.

Notice that the name of the content page is Order.aspx, the same as the Order page that you saw in chapter 3. In other words, when you use master pages, the individual pages of your web application become the content pages. You'll learn how to create content pages or convert existing ASP.NET pages to content pages in figure 9-6.

The Shopping Cart application with a master page

Master page (MasterPage.master)

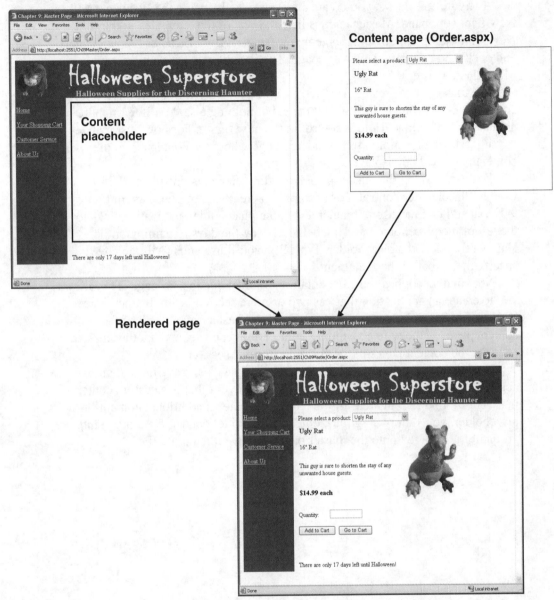

Content page (Order.aspx)

Rendered page

Description

- A *master page* provides a framework in which the content of each page on a web site is presented. Master pages make it easy to create pages that have a consistent look.

- The pages that provide the content that's displayed in a master page are called *content pages*.

- The content of each content page is displayed in the master page's *content placeholder*.

Figure 9-1   An application that uses a master page

How to create a master page

As figure 9-2 shows, you create a master page by using the Website→Add New Item command. Master Page is listed as one of the templates in the Add New Item dialog box. Select this template, select Visual Basic as the language, and click Add to create the master page. The default name for a master page is MasterPage.master.

The master page created from the template includes a ContentPlaceHolder control that will contain the content page, but nothing else. You'll learn more about the ContentPlaceHolder control in the next figure. For now, just realize that it marks the location on the rendered page where the content from the content page will be displayed.

You can develop the master page by adding elements outside of the ContentPlaceHolder control. For example, to create the master page in figure 9-1, you add an image for a banner above the placeholder, navigation links to the left of the placeholder, and a label to display the days remaining until Halloween below the placeholder. Typically, you'll use an HTML table to specify the layout of these elements.

Note that an application can contain more than one master page. This allows you to create an application that has two or more sections with distinct page layouts. For example, you may want to use one master page for all of the content pages in the online shopping section of a web site, and another master page for the content pages in the customer service section.

In addition, you should realize that a master page can have more than one content placeholder. This lets you create a page layout that has custom content in two or more different areas of the page. To create an additional content placeholder, you simply drag the ContentPlaceHolder control from the Standard group of the Toolbox onto the master page and give it a unique ID.

A new master page in Design view

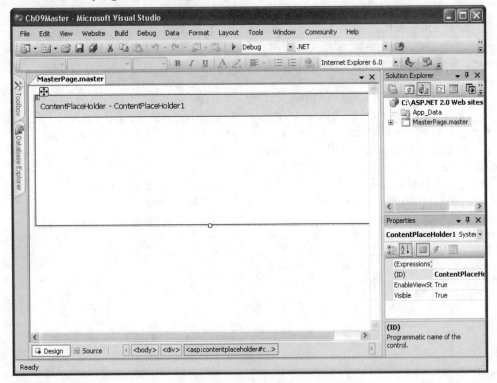

Description

- To add a master page to a project, choose the Website→Add New Item command. Then, in the Add New Item dialog box, select Master Page from the list of templates, specify the name of the master page you want to create in the Name text box (the default is Master Page.master), and select the programming language. Then, click Add.

- The content placeholder appears as a control in the Web Forms Designer. Although you can change the position of the content placeholder, you can't edit its contents from the master page. Instead, you add content to the master page by creating content pages as described later in this chapter.

- Any elements you add to the master page outside of the content placeholder will appear on every content page that uses the master page.

- Although most master pages have just one content placeholder, you can create more than one content placeholder if you need to. In that case, each placeholder displays a portion of the content of each content page.

- An application can have more than one master page, and each content page specifies which master page should be used to display the content page.

- The aspx file for a master page uses the extension .master. The code-behind file uses .master.vb.

Figure 9-2   How to create a master page

The aspx code for a new master page

The listing at the top of figure 9-3 shows the aspx code that's generated when you create a master page using the Master Page template. As you can see, this code is similar to the aspx code generated for a regular ASP.NET web page, with two important differences.

First, instead of a Page directive, the code begins with a Master directive. This indicates that the file contains a master page rather than a regular ASP.NET page. Second, the Div element that normally contains the content for the page now contains a ContentPlaceHolder control.

Notice that the master page file is itself a well-formed HTML document with Html, Head, and Body elements. The Body element includes a Form element, which in turn contains the ContentPlaceHolder control. Any elements you add to the master page should appear within the Form element, but outside of the ContentPlaceHolder control.

The aspx code for a new master page

```
<%@ Master Language="VB" CodeFile="MasterPage.master.vb" Inherits="MasterPage" %>

<!DOCTYPE html PUBLIC "-//W3C//DTD XHTML 1.1//EN" "http://www.w3.org/TR/xhtml11/
DTD/xhtml11.dtd">

<html xmlns="http://www.w3.org/1999/xhtml" >
<head runat="server">
    <title>Untitled Page</title>
</head>
<body>
    <form id="form1" runat="server">
    <div>
        <asp:contentplaceholder id="ContentPlaceHolder1" runat="server">
        </asp:contentplaceholder>
    </div>
    </form>
</body>
</html>
```

Attributes of the Master page directive

Attribute	Description
Language	Specifies the language used for any code required by the page.
CodeFile	Specifies the name of the code-behind file.
Inherits	Specifies the name of the page class defined in the code-behind file.

Attributes of the ContentPlaceHolder control

Attribute	Description
ID	Specifies the name of the content placeholder.
Runat	Specifies that the control is a server-side control.

Description

- A master page must begin with a Master page directive and should include at least one ContentPlaceHolder control.

- Any HTML or aspx elements that you add to the master page will be displayed on every page that uses the master page along with the ContentPlaceHolder control.

Figure 9-3   The aspx code for a new master page

The aspx code for the Halloween Store master page

Figure 9-4 shows the complete aspx code for the master page in figure 9-1. Although this listing fills the entire page, there's nothing complex about it. So you shouldn't have any trouble understanding its elements.

The banner at the top of the page is displayed using an Image control. After the banner, a Table element controls the layout of the rest of the page. The first row of this table specifies a height of 400 pixels. It has three cells. The first cell contains a simple navigation menu built using hyperlinks. The background color for this cell is set to red. The second cell is a small (10 pixel) spacer cell that gives some space between the navigation menu and the content. And the third cell contains the content placeholder.

The second row defines the footer that appears at the bottom of the page. It also has three cells, each the same width as the cells in the first row. However, the height of this row is set to 25 pixels. The third cell in this row contains a label control named lblMessage. This label will be used to display the number of days that remain until Halloween.

The aspx code for the master page

```
<%@ Master Language="VB" CodeFile="MasterPage.master.vb" Inherits="MasterPage" %>

<!DOCTYPE html PUBLIC "-//W3C//DTD XHTML 1.1//EN"
"http://www.w3.org/TR/xhtml11/DTD/xhtml11.dtd">

<html xmlns="http://www.w3.org/1999/xhtml" >
<head runat="server">
    <title>Chapter 9: Master Page</title>
</head>
<body>
    <form id="form1" runat="server">
    <asp:Image ID="Image1" runat="server" ImageUrl="~/Images/banner.jpg" /><br />
    <table cellpadding="2" cellspacing="0">
      <tr style="height:400px">
        <td style="width: 157px; border-color: Red; background-color: Red">
            <br />
            <asp:HyperLink ID="HyperLink1" runat="server" ForeColor="White"
                NavigateUrl="~/Order.aspx">Home</asp:HyperLink>
            <br /><br />
            <asp:HyperLink ID="HyperLink2" runat="server" ForeColor="White"
                NavigateUrl="~/Cart.aspx">Your Shopping Cart</asp:HyperLink>
            <br /><br />
            <asp:HyperLink ID="HyperLink3" runat="server" ForeColor="White"
                NavigateUrl="~/Service.aspx">Customer Service</asp:HyperLink>
            <br /><br />
            <asp:HyperLink ID="HyperLink4" runat="server" ForeColor="White"
                NavigateUrl="~/About.aspx">About Us</asp:HyperLink>
        </td>
        <td style="width: 10px"></td>
        <td style="width: 704px" valign="top">
            <asp:contentplaceholder id="Main" runat="server">
            </asp:contentplaceholder>
        </td>
      </tr>
      <tr style="height:25px">
        <td style="width: 153px; border-color: Red; background-color: Red"
            valign="top"></td>
        <td style="width: 10px"></td>
        <td style="width: 704px" valign="top">
            <asp:Label ID="lblMessage" runat="server"></asp:Label>
        </td>
      </tr>
    </table>
    </form>
</body>
</html>
```

Description

- Most master pages include elements like banners and navigation controls.
- It's common to use tables to provide the layout for the elements on the master page, including the content placeholder.

Figure 9-4   The aspx code for the Halloween Store master page

The code-behind file for the master page

Master pages have events just like regular ASP.NET pages. So it's important to realize that most of these events are raised *after* the corresponding events for the content page are raised. For example, the Load event for the master page will be processed after the Load event for the content page. Likewise, any control events for the content page are processed before any control events for the master page. Note, however, that both the content page and the master page Load events are processed before any of the control events are processed.

Figure 9-5 shows the code-behind file for the master page in figure 9-4. This code-behind file includes a Page_Load procedure that's executed when the master page loads. As you can see, this procedure calls a procedure named DaysUntilHalloween, which calculates and returns the number of days remaining until October 31. Then, an appropriate message is assigned to the Text property of the lblMessage label.

The code-behind file for the master page

```
Partial Class MasterPage
    Inherits System.Web.UI.MasterPage

    Protected Sub Page_Load(ByVal sender As Object, _
            ByVal e As System.EventArgs) Handles Me.Load
        Dim iDaysUntil As Integer = DaysUntilHalloween()
        If iDaysUntil = 0 Then
            lblMessage.Text = "Happy Halloween!"
        ElseIf iDaysUntil = 1 Then
            lblMessage.Text = "Tomorrow is Halloween!"
        Else
            lblMessage.Text = "There are only " & iDaysUntil _
                & " days left until Halloween!"
        End If
    End Sub

    Private Function DaysUntilHalloween() As Integer
        Dim dtmHalloween As Date = New DateTime(DateTime.Today.Year, 10, 31)
        If DateTime.Today > dtmHalloween Then
            dtmHalloween = dtmHalloween.AddYears(1)
        End If
        Dim tsTimeUntil As TimeSpan = dtmHalloween - DateTime.Today
        Return tsTimeUntil.Days
    End Function

End Class
```

Description

- Master pages have events just like regular ASP.NET pages. For this master page, the Load event is used to display the number of days remaining until Halloween.

- Most events for the content page are raised before the corresponding events for the master page. For example, the Load event for the content page is raised before the Load event for the master page. Similarly, events for controls in the content page are raised before events for controls in the master page.

Figure 9-5 The code-behind file for the master page

How to create and develop content pages

Once you create a master page, you can create and develop the content pages for the master page. The topics that follow show how.

How to create a content page

Figure 9-6 shows how to create a content page. In short, you use the same procedure to create a content page that you use to create a regular page, but you check the Select a Master Page check box. Then, you can choose the master page you want to use for the content page from the Select a Master Page dialog box that's displayed.

Alternatively, you can select the master page you want to use in the Solution Explorer. Then, choose the Website→Add Content Page command. This creates a content page for the selected master page. Note that when you use this technique, the content page is automatically named Default.

The code example in this figure shows the code that's generated when you create a new content page named Order for the master page shown in figure 9-4. This code is quite different from the code that's generated when you create a regular ASP.NET page. Although the Page directive includes the same information as a regular ASP.NET page, it also includes a MasterPageFile attribute that specifies the master page you selected. And the rest of the content page is also different from a normal ASP.NET page.

Before I describe the other differences, you should know that the title you specify in the Title attribute of the Page directive of a content page overrides any title you specify in the master page. That way, you can display a different title for each content page. If you want to use the same title for each content page, however, you can specify the title in the master page and then delete the Title attribute from the content pages.

Unlike normal ASP.NET pages, content pages don't include a Doctype directive or any structural HTML elements such as Html, Head, Body, or Form. That's because those elements are provided by the master page. Instead, the content page includes an ASP.NET Content element that indicates which content placeholder the page should be displayed in. Then, you place the content that you want to display on the page between the start and end tags of this element.

This figure also includes a procedure for converting a regular page to a content page. You'll need to follow this procedure if you start a web site without using master pages, and later decide to use master pages. Unfortunately, though, Visual Studio doesn't provide a way to automatically do this. As a result, you'll have to manually edit each of the pages to add the MasterPageFile attribute to the Page directive, remove the Doctype directive and structural HTML elements (Html, Head, Body, and Form), and add a Content element.

The aspx code for a new page that uses the master page in figure 9-4

```
<%@ Page Language="VB" MasterPageFile="~/MasterPage.master"
    AutoEventWireup="false" CodeFile="Order.aspx.vb"
    Inherits="Order" Title="Untitled Page" %>

<asp:Content ID="Content1" ContentPlaceHolderID="Main" Runat="Server">
</asp:Content>
```

How to create a new content page

- One way is to choose the Website→Add New Item command. Then, select Web Form from the list of templates, enter the name for the form, check the Select a Master Page check box, and click Add. When the Select a Master Page dialog box appears, select the master page you want and click OK.

- Another way is to select the master page in the Solution Explorer, then choose the Website→Add Content Page command.

How to convert a regular ASP.NET page to a content page

- First, add a MasterPageFile attribute to the Page directive that specifies the URL of the master page. Next, replace the Div element that contains the actual content of the page with a Content element as shown above. Then, delete everything that's outside this Content element except for the Page directive.

Two other ways to specify the master page

In the web.config file

```
<system.web>
    .
    <pages masterPageFile="MasterPage.master" />
    .
</system.web>
```

In the Page_PreInit procedure

```
Protected Sub Page_PreInit(ByVal sender As Object, _
        ByVal e As System.EventArgs) Handles Me.PreInit
    MasterPageFile = "MasterPage.master"
End Sub
```

Description

- The Page directive in the aspx code for a content page includes a MasterPageFile attribute that specifies the name of the master page.

- The aspx code for a content page includes a Content element that indicates the ID of the content placeholder where the content for the page should be displayed. Any content you create for the page should be placed between the start and end tags for this element.

- You can also specify the master page in the web.config file or in the Page_PreInit procedure. However, the Web Forms Designer doesn't support either of these techniques, so you won't be able to view the content page in Design view.

Figure 9-6   How to create a content page

Because this conversion procedure is error prone, it pays to use master pages for all but the simplest of applications, even if each master page contains only a content placeholder. Then, when you're ready to provide a consistent look to the pages within the application, you can enhance the master pages.

This figure also shows two other ways to specify which master page is used with a content page. First, you can add a Pages element to the web.config file with a MasterPageFile attribute that specifies the master page to be used with all pages that don't specify a master file. Second, you can specify the master page at runtime by setting the MasterPageFile attribute of the page in the Page_PreInit procedure. Note, however, that the Web Forms Designer doesn't support either of these techniques. If you use them, then, you won't be able to view or edit your content pages in Design view.

How to add content to a page

Figure 9-7 shows how a content page appears in Design view. As you can see, the master page is displayed, but it is dimmed, and you can't edit any of the master page elements from this view. However, you can click in the Content control, and then edit the content of the page by adding text or dragging controls from the Toolbox. Later, when you switch to Source view, any elements that you've added will appear between the Content element's start and end tags.

If you work with a master page that has more than one content placeholder, there will be a separate Content control for each placeholder. Then, you can edit the contents for each of those controls.

A content page in Design view

Description

- When you display a content page in Design view, the elements from the master page are dimly displayed so you can see how they will affect the final appearance of the page.

- To add the content for a page, click the content placeholder. Then, you can type text or use the Toolbox to drag controls into the content area of the page. Any text or other elements you add will be placed between the start and end tags of the Content element in the aspx file.

Note

- If you can't edit the contents of the placeholder, click the Smart Tag icon in the upper-right corner of the placeholder and choose Create Custom Content from the menu that appears. This is sometimes necessary, probably due to a bug in Visual Studio.

Figure 9-7   How to add content to a page

How to access master page controls from a content page

In many applications, you need to access one or more of the controls in a master page from one of the application's content pages. For example, the master page shown earlier in this chapter has a label in the footer area that normally displays the number of days remaining until Halloween. But what if you want to display other information in this label when certain content pages are displayed?

For example, when the user is shopping for products with the Order.aspx page, you may want to display the number of items currently in the shopping cart instead of the number of days left until Halloween. To do that, you can expose a master page control as a public property, and then access the property from the content page.

How to expose a master page control as a public property

The easiest way to access a control on a master page from a content page is to create a public property that provides access to the control. Figure 9-8 illustrates a code-behind file for a master page that shows you how to do that.

First, you create a public property in the master page that identifies the control you want to be able to access. In this case, the property is a Label type, and the property is named MessageLabel. Then, you code get and set procedures for the property. Here, the get procedure returns the lblMessage label, and the set procedure assigns the property value to lblMessage.

Please notice that I also added another If statement to the Page_Load procedure for the master page. Now, the lblMessage label is set to the number of days left until Halloween only if the value of the label's Text property is empty. That way, if the content page has assigned a value to this label in its Page_Load procedure, the master page's Page_Load procedure won't overwrite the value. This works because the content page's Page_Load procedure is called before the master page's Page_Load procedure.

The code-behind file for a master page that provides a public property

```
Partial Class MasterPage
    Inherits System.Web.UI.MasterPage

    Public Property MessageLabel() As Label
        Get
            Return lblMessage
        End Get
        Set(ByVal value As Label)
            lblMessage = value
        End Set
    End Property

    Protected Sub Page_Load(ByVal sender As Object, _
            ByVal e As System.EventArgs) Handles Me.Load
        If lblMessage.Text = "" Then
            Dim iDaysUntil As Integer = DaysUntilHalloween()
            If iDaysUntil = 0 Then
                lblMessage.Text = "Happy Halloween!"
            ElseIf iDaysUntil = 1 Then
                lblMessage.Text = "Tomorrow is Halloween!"
            Else
                lblMessage.Text = "There are only " & iDaysUntil _
                    & " days left until Halloween!"
            End If
        End If
    End Sub

    Private Function DaysUntilHalloween() As Integer
        Dim dtmHalloween As Date = New DateTime(DateTime.Today.Year, 10, 31)
        If DateTime.Today > dtmHalloween Then
            dtmHalloween = dtmHalloween.AddYears(1)
        End If
        Dim tsTimeUntil As TimeSpan = dtmHalloween - DateTime.Today
        Return tsTimeUntil.Days
    End Function

End Class
```

Description

- A content page can access a control in the master page if you expose the control as a public property in the master page. To do that, you code a property procedure with get and set procedures.

Figure 9-8   How to expose a master page control as a public property

How to access a public property of the master page from a content page

Figure 9-9 shows how you can access a public property in a master page from a content page. As you can see in the top part of this figure, you use the MasterType directive in the aspx file of the content page to specify the name of the type used for the master page. The value you name in this directive specifies the type of the object returned by the content page's Master property. So in this example, the Master property will return an object of type MasterPage. If you look at the class declaration in the previous figure, you'll see that MasterPage is the name of the class that defines the master page.

The second part of this figure shows two procedures from the code-behind file for the Order.aspx content page. As you can see, the Page_Load procedure calls a procedure named DisplayCartMessage. This procedure determines the number of items currently in the shopping cart and sets the Text property of the label exposed by the master page's MessageLabel property accordingly. But note that no value is assigned to the message label if the shopping cart is empty. In that case, the Page_Load procedure for the master page will set the label to the number of days remaining until Halloween.

Although using the MasterType directive in the content page's aspx file makes it easier to access the properties of the master page, you should realize that this directive isn't necessary. If you don't specify the MasterType directive, the Master property will return an object of type Master. You can then cast this object to the actual type of your master page to access any properties you've created.

For example, you could use code like this to assign text to the MessageLabel property:

```
Dim mp As MasterPage = CType(Me.Master, MasterPage)
If Cart.Count = 1 Then
    mp.MessageLabel.Text = _
        "There is one item in your cart."
ElseIf Cart.Count > 1 Then
    mp.MessageLabel.Text = _
        "There are " & Cart.Count & " items in your cart."
End If
```

Here, the Master object is cast to MasterPage so its MessageLabel property can be accessed. The purpose of the MasterType directive is to avoid this awkward casting.

A portion of the Order.aspx page

```
<%@ Page Language="VB" MasterPageFile="~/MasterPage.master"
AutoEventWireup="false" CodeFile="Order.aspx.vb"
Inherits="Order" %>

<%@ MasterType TypeName="MasterPage" %>

<asp:Content ID="Content1" ContentPlaceHolderID="Main" Runat="server">
.
.
.
</asp:Content>
```

Two procedures from the code-behind file for the Order.aspx page

```
Protected Sub Page_Load(ByVal sender As Object, _
        ByVal e As System.EventArgs) Handles Me.Load
    If Not IsPostBack Then
        ddlProducts.DataBind()
        Me.DisplayCartMessage()
    End If
    SelectedProduct = GetSelectedProduct()
    lblName.Text = SelectedProduct.Name
    lblShortDescription.Text = SelectedProduct.ShortDescription
    lblLongDescription.Text = SelectedProduct.LongDescription
    lblUnitPrice.Text = FormatCurrency(SelectedProduct.UnitPrice)
    imgProduct.ImageUrl = "Images/Products/" _
        & SelectedProduct.ImageFile
End Sub

Private Sub DisplayCartMessage()
    Dim Cart As SortedList = CType(Session("cart"), SortedList)
    If Not Cart Is Nothing Then
        If Cart.Count = 1 Then
            Me.Master.MessageLabel.Text _
                = "There is one item in your cart."
        ElseIf Cart.Count > 1 Then
            Me.Master.MessageLabel.Text _
                = "There are " & Cart.Count & " items in your cart."
        End If
    End If
End Sub
```

Description

- The MasterType directive in an aspx file specifies the name of the master page type. If you include this directive in a content page, you can use the Master property in the code-behind file to access the exposed property of the master page.

Figure 9-9   How to access a public property of the master page from a content page

Perspective

I hope this chapter has illustrated the power of master pages. In fact, I recommend that you use master pages for all but the simplest applications, even if you start out with nothing in your master pages but placeholders. Then, when you're ready to provide a professional look to your content pages, you can enhance the master pages, which will also enhance all of your content pages.

The alternative is to convert regular content pages so they use the master pages that you develop later on. But as figure 9-6 shows, that's a time-consuming and error-prone procedure. How much better it is to think ahead.

You may also be interested to know that you can nest master pages so one master page can be the content page for another master page. We didn't present nested master pages in this book, though, for two reasons. First, you probably won't ever need them. Second, since they aren't supported by the Web Forms Designer in Design View, you have to implement them entirely with aspx code. And that becomes a major impediment to using nested master pages.

New terms

master page
content page
content placeholder

10

How to use the site navigation features

The new ASP.NET 2.0 site navigation features make it easy for users to navigate to the various pages in your site. These features are valuable for both small and large web sites. This chapter shows you how to get the most from these features.

An introduction to site navigation

ASP.NET's *site navigation* features are designed to simplify the task of creating menus and other navigation features that let users find their way around your web site. To implement that, ASP.NET provides a site map data source control and three navigation controls: TreeView, Menu, and SiteMapPath. The following topics introduce you to these controls.

An introduction to the navigation controls

Figure 10-1 shows a page from an ASP.NET 2.0 application called the Navigation application. This application is a variation of the Halloween Store application you saw in the last chapter, but with navigation features added to the master page as well as several new pages, including one that displays a complete site map for the application. All three of the new ASP.NET 2.0 navigation controls are illustrated on this page.

The TreeView control displays the pages in a web site in a tree structure that's similar to a directory tree displayed by Windows Explorer. The user can expand or collapse a node by clicking the + or – icon that appears next to each node that has children. This control is most useful when you want to give users a complete view of the pages in a web site.

The Menu control creates dynamic menus that expand when you hover the mouse over a menu item that contains subitems. For example, if you were to hover the mouse over the Projects item in the menu in this figure, a submenu listing Costumes, Static Props, and Animated Props would appear.

The SiteMapPath control displays a list of links that lead from the web site's home page to the current page. This makes it easy for the user to quickly return to the home page or to a parent of the current page.

The TreeView and the Menu controls must be used with a SiteMapDataSource control, which binds the controls to a file named web.sitemap. This file contains XML that defines the structure of the pages that make up the web site. You'll learn how to create the web.sitemap file in the next two figures.

In most cases, you'll use either the Menu or the SiteMapPath control and possibly a TreeView control in a master page. That way, these navigation controls will be available from any page in the web site. If the site contains a large number of pages, though, you may want to use a separate Site Map page that includes a TreeView control. Then, the user can use the Site Map page to quickly locate any page within the web site.

A page with three site navigation controls

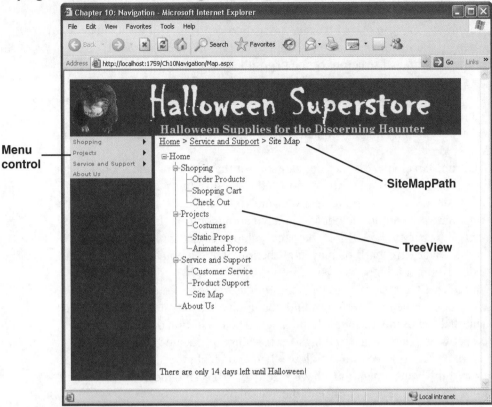

Menu control — SiteMapPath — TreeView

ASP.NET navigation controls

Control	Description
TreeView	Provides a hierarchical view of the site's structure. The user can click + or − icons next to each node to expand or collapse the node. Must be bound to a SiteMapDataSource control. Located in the Navigation group of the Toolbox.
Menu	Creates a horizontal or vertical menu. Must be bound to a SiteMapDataSource control. Located in the Navigation group of the Toolbox.
SiteMapPath	Displays a list of links from the application's root page (the home page) to the current page. Doesn't need to be bound to a SiteMapDataSource control. Located in the Navigation group of the Toolbox.
SiteMapDataSource	Connects a navigation control to the site hierarchy specified by the web.sitemap file. Located in the Data group of the Toolbox.

Description

- ASP.NET 2.0 provides three user-interface controls and a data source control designed to let the user navigate the pages in a web site.

- The navigation structure of a web site is defined by an XML file named web.sitemap located in the application's root folder. You must create this file before you can work with the navigation controls.

Figure 10-1   An introduction to site navigation

How to create a web.sitemap file

Before you can use one of the site navigation controls, you must create a web.sitemap file in the application's root directory. This file uses XML tags to define the hierarchical structure of the pages that make up the application.

As figure 10-2 shows, you can add a web.sitemap file to an application by choosing the Website→Add New Item command and selecting Site Map from the list of templates. Then, you use the Code Editor to edit the contents of this file. The web.sitemap file can contain two types of XML elements: siteMap and siteMapNode.

The siteMap element is the root element for the XML file and should occur only once in the file. You usually don't need to modify this element.

In contrast, you need to create a siteMapNode element for each page in the web site that you want to include in the navigation controls. In the siteMapNode element, you specify the URL of the page (relative to the application's root folder); the page title that's displayed as the link in the menu, tree, or map path; and a description of the page.

To indicate the hierarchy of the pages in the site map, you nest the siteMapNode elements. The file should contain just one top-level siteMapNode element that represents the site's home page. Then, additional elements can be nested between the start and end tags for the home-page siteMapNode.

An important rule you must follow when you create the sitemap file is that each siteMapNode element must have a unique URL. That means each page in the web site can appear only once in the site map.

Another important point is that you don't have to include all of the pages in the web site in the sitemap file. Instead, you should only include those pages that you want to make available via the site's navigation controls. If, for example, the site uses a two-page checkout process, you may not want to include the second check out page in the sitemap file. That way, the user will be able to access the first checkout page from a menu or tree view control, but not the second checkout page.

The web.sitemap file created from the Site Map template

```
<?xml version="1.0" encoding="utf-8" ?>
<siteMap xmlns="http://schemas.microsoft.com/AspNet/SiteMap-File-1.0" >
    <siteMapNode url="" title=""  description="" roles="">
        <siteMapNode url="" title=""  description="" roles="" />
        <siteMapNode url="" title=""  description="" roles="" />
    </siteMapNode>
</siteMap>
```

Attributes of the siteMapNode element

Attribute	Description
Url	The url of the page. Each siteMapNode element must specify a unique value for this attribute.
Title	The text that will appear in the menu for the page.
Description	The tool tip text for the page.
Roles	Indicates which users have access to the page.

Description

- To create a web.sitemap file, choose the Website→Add New Item command, select Site Map from the list of available templates, and click Add. You can then use the Code Editor to edit the web.sitemap file.

- The web.sitemap file contains an XML-based description of the navigation hierarchy of an ASP.NET application.

- Each siteMapNode element defines a page in the web site. You can nest siteMapNode elements within other siteMapNode elements to indicate the hierarchy of pages in the web site. But you don't have to include all of the pages in your web site in the site map.

- The Roles attribute of the siteMapNode element indicates that the page should be made available only to users that have the specified role or roles. For example, if you create a role for administrators called Admin, you can use this attribute to indicate those pages that should be available only to administrators. For more information about user roles, see chapter 18.

Figure 10-2   How to create a web.sitemap file

The web.sitemap file for the Navigation application

Figure 10-3 shows the complete web.sitemap file for the Navigation application. The site navigation structure defined by this file corresponds to the structure shown in the TreeView control in figure 10-1.

If you compare the siteMapNode elements in this file with the items listed in the TreeView control in figure 10-1, you should see how the nesting of the siteMapNode elements specifies the site's hierarchical structure. For example, the siteMapNode elements for the Order.aspx, Cart.aspx, and Checkout1.aspx pages are contained within the start and end elements of the siteMapNode element for the Shopping.aspx page.

In this case, not all of the pages in the Navigation application are listed in the web.sitemap file. For example, there's a second checkout page and an order confirmation page that aren't in the sitemap file. That's because users shouldn't be allowed to navigate directly to these pages.

The web.sitemap file used for the controls in figure 10-1

```xml
<?xml version="1.0" encoding="utf-8" ?>
<siteMap xmlns="http://schemas.microsoft.com/AspNet/SiteMap-File-1.0" >

  <siteMapNode url="Default.aspx" title="Home"
    description="Home page." roles="">

    <siteMapNode url="Shopping.aspx" title="Shopping"
      description="Shop for your favorite products." roles="">
      <siteMapNode url="Order.aspx" title="Order Products"
        description="Order a product." roles="">
      </siteMapNode>
      <siteMapNode url="Cart.aspx" title="Shopping Cart"
        description="View your shopping cart." roles="">
      </siteMapNode>
      <siteMapNode url="Checkout1.aspx" title="Check Out"
        description="Finalize your purchase." roles="">
      </siteMapNode>
    </siteMapNode>

    <siteMapNode url="Projects.aspx" title="Projects"
      description="Do-it-yourself Halloween projects." roles="">
      <siteMapNode url="Costumes.aspx" title="Costumes"
        description="Costume projects." roles="">
      </siteMapNode>
      <siteMapNode url="StaticProps.aspx" title="Static Props"
        description="Static props." roles="">
      </siteMapNode>
      <siteMapNode url="AnimatedProps.aspx" title="Animated Props"
        description="Animated props." roles="">
      </siteMapNode>
    </siteMapNode>

    <siteMapNode url="Service.aspx" title="Service and Support"
      description="Customer service and product support." roles="">
      <siteMapNode url="CustService.aspx" title="Customer Service"
        description="Customer service." roles="">
      </siteMapNode>
      <siteMapNode url="Support.aspx" title="Product Support"
        description="Product support." roles="">
      </siteMapNode>
      <siteMapNode url="Map.aspx" title="Site Map"
        description="A map of all the pages on this web site." roles="">
      </siteMapNode>
    </siteMapNode>

    <siteMapNode url="About.aspx" title="About Us"
      description="All about our company." roles="">
    </siteMapNode>

  </siteMapNode>

</siteMap>
```

Figure 10-3   The web.sitemap file for the Navigation application

How to use the site navigation controls

Once you've created the sitemap file, you're ready to use the site navigation controls. The topics that follow show you how to do that.

How to use the TreeView control

Figure 10-4 shows how to use the TreeView control, which displays the pages in a web site as a hierarchical tree. Each node on the tree is a link that represents a page in the web site. You can click any of these links to go directly to that page. You can also click the + or – icons that appear next to the nodes to expand or collapse the nodes.

The table in this figure lists the attributes you're most likely to use with the TreeView control. The ID attribute provides a name for the TreeView control, and the DataSourceID attribute lists the ID of the data source that provides the site map data. You'll learn how to create a site map data source in the next figure.

The other attributes let you customize the appearance and behavior of the TreeView control. For example, you can use the ExpandDepth attribute to set the number of levels that are initially expanded when the TreeView is first displayed. And you can use the ShowLines attribute to include lines that graphically show the tree's hierarchical structure. The best way to learn how these attributes affect the TreeView control is to experiment with them.

A TreeView control

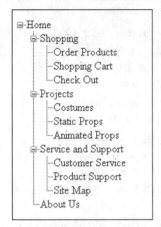

The aspx code for the TreeView control shown above

```
<asp:TreeView ID="TreeView1" runat="server"
              DataSourceID="SiteMapDataSource1"
              ShowLines="True">
</asp:TreeView>
```

Attributes of the TreeView control

Attribute	Description
ID	The ID of the control.
Runat	Must specify Server.
DataSourceID	The ID of the SiteMapDataSource control the tree should be bound to.
ExpandDepth	The number of levels to be automatically expanded when the tree is initially displayed. The default is FullyExpand.
MaxDepthDataBind	Limits the maximum depth of the tree. The default is -1, which places no limit.
NodeIndent	The number of pixels to indent each level. The default is 20.
NodeWrap	Set to True to word-wrap the text of each node. The default is False.
ShowExpandCollapse	Set to False if you want to hide the Expand/Collapse buttons. The default is True.
ShowLines	Set to True to include lines that show the hierarchical structure. The default is False.

Description

- The TreeView control is used to display the site map in a hierarchical tree.
- To display an application's navigation structure, the TreeView control must be bound to a SiteMapDataSource control as described in the next figure.

Figure 10-4   How to use the TreeView control

How to create a SiteMapDataSource control

Figure 10-5 shows two ways to create a SiteMapDataSource control. One way is to drag the SiteMapDataSource control from the Data group of the Toolbox to a page. Then, you can set the properties for the control.

The other way is to click the Smart Tag icon for a TreeView or Menu control, and choose New Data Source from the menu that appears. This brings up the Data Source Configuration Wizard dialog box shown at the top of this figure. Then, you select Site Map and click OK to create a site map data source.

To customize the behavior of the *site map data source*, you can use the attributes listed in this figure. For example, the ShowStartingNode attribute determines whether the highest-level siteMapNode element in the web.sitemap file will be included in the tree or menu. Usually, you'll leave this attribute set to its default of True for TreeView controls and you'll set it to False for Menu controls.

The StartFromCurrentNode and StartingNodeUrl attributes let you bind a TreeView or Menu control to just a portion of the site map. If you specify True for the StartFromCurrentNode attribute, the tree or menu will start from the current page. As a result, only child pages of the current page will appear in the tree or menu. The StartingNodeUrl attribute lets you select any node in the site map as the starting node for the tree or menu.

The Data Source Configuration Wizard dialog box

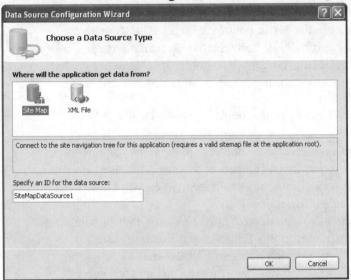

SiteMapDataSource examples

Example 1: A default SiteMapDataSource control

```
<asp:SiteMapDataSource ID="SiteMapDataSource1" runat="server" />
```

Example 2: A SiteMapDataSource control that specifies a starting level

```
<asp:SiteMapDataSource ID="SiteMapDataSource1" runat="server"
    StartingNodeUrl="Projects.aspx" />
```

Common attributes of the SiteMapDataSource control

Attribute	Description
ID	The ID of the control.
Runat	Must specify Server.
StartingNodeUrl	The URL of the node the SiteMapDataSource control should use as its starting node.
ShowStartingNode	Set to False to omit the starting node. The default is True.
StartFromCurrentNode	Set to True to start the navigation from the current node. The default is False, which starts the navigation from the root node specified in the web.sitemap file.

Two ways to create a SiteMapDataSource control

- Drag the control from the Data group of the Toolbox to a page.
- Click the Smart Tag icon in the upper-right corner of a TreeView or Menu control, then select New Data Source in the Choose Data Source drop-down list.

Description

- You use a SiteMapDataSource control to bind a TreeView or Menu control to the navigation structure defined by the web.sitemap file.

Figure 10-5   How to create a SiteMapDataSource control

How to use the Menu control

Figure 10-6 shows how to use the Menu control, which lets you create menus that are arranged either vertically or horizontally. *Vertical menus* are usually used in a sidebar alongside the content placeholder in a master page. In contrast, *horizontal menus* typically appear beneath a banner image and above the content placeholder.

Each item in a menu can contain a submenu that appears when you hover the mouse over the item for a moment. For example, the Service and Support submenu shown in the examples in this figure doesn't appear until you hover the mouse over the Service and Support item. The part of the menu that is always displayed is called the *static menu*. Submenus that appear when you hover the mouse over a menu item are called *dynamic menus*.

Like the TreeView control, the Menu control must be bound to a site map data source. Then, the other attributes in this figure let you customize the appearance of the menu and specify which items will appear in the menu. For example, the Orientation attribute determines whether the menu is arranged vertically or horizontally. And the MaximumDynamicDisplay attribute determines how many layers of dynamic submenus should be displayed.

As you set the properties for a Menu control, you'll see that it includes many style properties that aren't listed in this figure. You can set these properties to control the formatting that's used to display the menu. Alternatively, you can automatically apply a predefined format to the menu by selecting AutoFormat from the Menu control's smart tag menu. When you select an auto format, Visual Studio generates the style properties that apply the formatting that you selected.

A menu with vertical orientation

A menu with horizontal orientation

Typical aspx code for a Menu control

```
<asp:Menu ID="Menu1" Orientation="Horizontal" runat="server"
    DataSourceID="SiteMapDataSource1">
</asp:Menu>
```

Common attributes of the Menu control

Attribute	Description
ID	The ID of the control.
Runat	Must specify Server.
DataSourceID	The ID of the SiteMapDataSource control the menu should be bound to.
ItemWrap	If True, words in the menu items will be word-wrapped if necessary. The default is False.
MaximumDynamicDisplay	The number of levels of dynamic submenus to display.
Orientation	Horizontal or Vertical.
StaticDisplayLevels	The number of levels that should always be displayed. The default is 1.
StaticEnableDefaultPopOutImage	If True, an arrow graphic is displayed next to any menu item that has a pop-out submenu. If false, the arrow graphic is not displayed. The default is True.

Description

- The Menu control displays site navigation information in a menu. Submenus automatically appear when the user hovers the mouse over a menu item that has a submenu.

- To display an application's navigation structure, the Menu control must be bound to a SiteMapDataSource control.

- The Menu control has many formatting attributes that aren't listed in this figure. You can quickly apply a coordinated set of formatting attributes by clicking the Smart Tag icon for the Menu control and choosing AutoFormat from the menu that appears. Then, you can select one of several predefined formats for the menu.

Figure 10-6   How to use the Menu control

How to use the SiteMapPath control

Figure 10-7 shows how to use the SiteMapPath control, which creates a series of links that lead from the application's home page to the current page. These links are sometimes called *bread crumbs* because they let the user find his or her way back to the home page.

Unlike the TreeView and Menu controls, the SiteMapPath control doesn't need to be bound to a data source. Instead, it obtains the site navigation information directly from the web.sitemap file.

The attributes listed in this figure let you customize the appearance of the SiteMapPath control. In particular, you can indicate how many parent nodes to list, which direction the nodes are listed in, what text to use to separate the nodes, and whether the current page should be formatted as a link or just plain text.

Although this figure doesn't show it, the SiteMapPath control includes other style attributes that let you completely customize the appearance of the site map path. And like the Menu control, you can also use the AutoFormat attribute to apply predefined formatting.

A SiteMapPath control

Home > Service and Support > Site Map

Aspx code for a SiteMapPath control

```
<asp:SiteMapPath ID="SiteMapPath1" runat="server">
</asp:SiteMapPath>
```

Common attributes of the SiteMapPath control

Attribute	Description
ID	The ID of the control.
Runat	Must specify Server.
ParentLevelsDisplayed	The maximum number of parent nodes to display. The default is -1, which displays all parent nodes.
PathDirection	Indicates the order in which nodes should be listed. Allowable values are RootToCurrent and CurrentToRoot. The default is RootToCurrent.
PathSeparator	The string displayed between each node of the path. The default is a greater-than sign.
RenderCurrentNodeAsLink	Set to True if you want the node that represents the current page to be rendered as a link. The default is False.

Description

- The SiteMapPath control displays a list of the links for each node in the site map from the root node to the current page.

- Unlike the TreeView and Menu controls, you don't need to bind the SiteMapPath control to a data source. Instead, it automatically uses the web.sitemap file to determine the current page's position within the web site's navigation structure.

Figure 10-7   How to use the SiteMapPath control

A master page for the Navigation application

To show you how the navigation controls work together, figure 10-8 presents the complete listing for a master page that includes both a navigation menu and a site map path. This is the master page that displays the page shown in figure 10-1.

This master page begins with an Image control that displays a banner at the top of the page. Then, a table is used to control the layout of the rest of the page. This table consists of three rows and three columns. Note that the first cell in the first row specifies the RowSpan attribute, which causes the cell to span two rows. That way, the Menu control occupies the first column of both the first and second rows of the table.

Then, the first column that's defined for the first row contains the Menu control (which will also occupy the first column in second row). The second column in the first row provides ten pixels of white space. And the third column in the first row contains the SiteMapPath control.

After that, you can see that the second column in the second row provides ten pixels of white place, and the third column contains the content placeholder. In figure 10-1, a Site Map page is displayed within the content placeholder. You can also see how the message label is defined for the third row.

Notice also that the asp:Menu element includes several style attributes and elements that specify the appearance of the menu. These attributes and elements were generated by Visual Studio when I selected an auto format for the menu.

In addition, this master page uses a code-behind file named MasterPage.master.vb. But since this code-behind file is the same as the one presented in chapter 9, it's not repeated here.

The body of the master page for the Navigation application

```
<body>
    <form id="form1" runat="server">
    <asp:Image ID="Image1" runat="server" ImageUrl="~/Images/banner.jpg" />
    <br />
    <table cellpadding="0" cellspacing="0">
      <tr style="height: 400px">
        <td style="width: 153px; background-color: Red; border-color: Red"
            valign="top" rowspan="2">
        <asp:Menu BackColor="#E3EAEB" DataSourceID="SiteMapDataSource1"
            DynamicHorizontalOffset="2"
            Font-Names="Verdana" Font-Size="0.8em" ForeColor="#666666"
            ID="Menu1" runat="server"
            StaticSubMenuIndent="10px">
          <StaticSelectedStyle BackColor="#1C5E55" />
          <StaticMenuItemStyle HorizontalPadding="5px"
              VerticalPadding="2px" />
          <DynamicMenuStyle BackColor="#E3EAEB" />
          <DynamicSelectedStyle BackColor="#1C5E55" />
          <DynamicMenuItemStyle HorizontalPadding="5px"
              VerticalPadding="2px" />
          <DynamicHoverStyle BackColor="#666666" Font-Bold="True"
              ForeColor="White" />
          <StaticHoverStyle BackColor="#666666" Font-Bold="True"
              ForeColor="White" />
        </asp:Menu>
        <asp:SiteMapDataSource ID="SiteMapDataSource1" runat="server"
            ShowStartingNode="False" />
        </td>
        <td style="width: 10px"></td>
        <td style="width: 704px" valign="top">
            <asp:SiteMapPath ID="SiteMapPath1" runat="server">
            </asp:SiteMapPath>
        </td>
      </tr>
      <tr>
        <td style="width: 10px"></td>
        <td style="width: 704px" valign="top">
            <asp:contentplaceholder id="Main" runat="server">
            </asp:contentplaceholder>
        </td>
      </tr>
      <tr style="height: 25px">
        <td style="width: 153px; background-color: Red; border-color: Red"
            valign="top"></td>
        <td style="width: 10px"></td>
        <td style="width: 704px" valign="top">
            <asp:Label id="lblMessage runat="server">
            </asp:Label>
        </td>
      </tr>
      </table>
    </form>
</body>
```

Figure 10-8   A master page that includes navigation controls

Perspective

This should give you a pretty good idea of how useful the new navigation features can be. If you experiment with them, you should quickly see that they're also easy to use.

You'll also discover that the TreeView, Menu, and SiteMapPath controls include many attributes that weren't described in this chapter. However, most of these attributes are designed to let you alter the appearance of the navigation controls, not their behavior. So once you master the basics of using these controls, you shouldn't have any trouble learning how to tweak their appearance by using the other attributes.

Terms

site navigation
site map data source
vertical menu
horizontal menu
static menu
dynamic menu
bread crumbs

11

How to use themes

When you develop a web site, you usually want to apply consistent formatting to all of its pages so the entire site has a cohesive look and feel. In addition, it's generally considered a good programming practice to separate the formatting of the web pages from the content of the web pages whenever that's possible. That way, web designers can focus on making the site look good, and programmers can focus on making the site work the way it should.

To make this easier and more flexible, ASP.NET 2.0 introduces a new feature known as *themes* that builds upon older formatting technologies such as cascading style sheets (CSS). This new feature allows you to create multiple themes for a web site, and it makes it easy to switch between themes. If you want, you can even write code that allows a user to customize a web site by choosing a preferred theme.

An introduction to themes

When you work with standard HTML, it is a common practice to store the global formatting information for a web site in a file known as a *cascading style sheet (CSS)*. Then, the styles in this sheet are applied to all pages in the application unless they are overridden by individual pages or by individual elements. (To learn more about style sheets, please refer back to chapter 5.)

Although this works well for HTML elements, it can be tricky to get this to work correctly with ASP.NET server controls since this requires the programmer and web designer to understand how server controls are rendered to HTML before being returned to the browser. But now, ASP.NET 2.0 introduces a new feature known as *themes* that allows you to specify the formatting for both HTML elements and server controls. To start, a theme includes a cascading style sheet. In addition, a theme includes information that specifies the formatting for the ASP.NET server controls.

A page before and after a theme has been applied

Figure 11-1 shows the Order page for the Halloween Store application before and after a theme has been applied to it. If you could see these pages in color, you would clearly see the differences between them. In particular, you would see that the second page uses a different font, font color, and font size for all of the elements and controls on the page. In addition, the buttons that are defined on the second page look different than the buttons on the first page because they don't have rounded corners and do use a different background color.

This Order page includes both HTML elements and ASP.NET web server controls. To start, this page includes two HTML tags that define the heading and subheading for the page like this:

```
<h1>Halloween Superstore</h1>
<h4>Halloween supplies for the discerning haunter</h4>
```

The custom formatting for these tags is stored in the cascading style sheet for the theme. Then, this page uses ASP.NET tags to define the server controls that are on the rest of the page. However, the custom formatting for these server controls isn't stored in the Order page. Instead, this formatting is stored in an external file as described in the next figure.

Before: The Order page without a theme

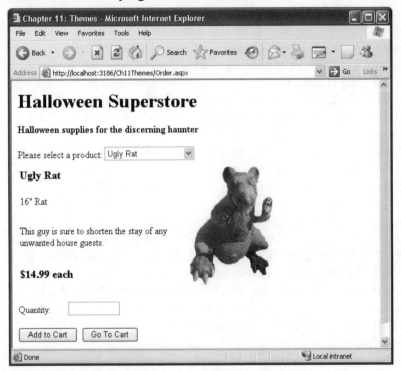

After: The Order page with a theme

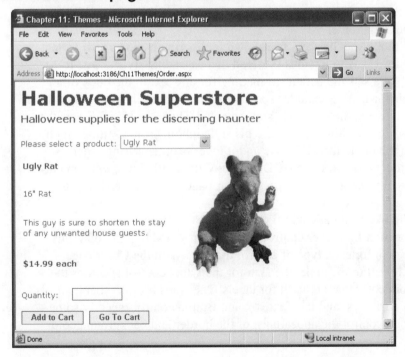

Figure 11-1 A page before and after a theme has been applied

How themes work

Figure 11-2 gives an overview of how themes work. To start, it shows the Solution Explorer for an application that contains an App_Themes folder. This folder can contain multiple subfolders with each subfolder defining one theme.

For example, the App_Themes folder in this figure contains two folders that define themes. The first folder contains the Classic theme. To help identify this folder as a theme folder, Visual Studio adds a paintbrush to the folder icon. The second folder contains the SmokeAndGlass theme.

The SmokeAndGlass folder shows the three types of files that can be contained by a theme. First, a theme folder can contain a file for the cascading style sheet that defines the styles that define the appearance of the HTML elements. This file must have an extension of css. In addition, it typically has the same name as the theme folder, although that's not required.

Second, a theme folder can contain files for the *skins* that define the appearance of the ASP.NET server controls. A skin specifies the formatting attributes for a server control, and a file that contains skins must have an extension of skin. In addition, if the theme only has one skin file, this file typically has the same name as the theme folder, although that's not required. In fact, as you'll see later in this chapter, it's possible to store skin definitions in multiple skin files within a theme folder.

Third, a theme folder can contain the files for any images that are used by the theme. These files can be stored in the theme folder, or they can be stored in any subfolder of the theme folder. In this figure, for example, all of the GIF files that are used by the SmokeAndGlass theme are stored in the Images subfolder of the SmokeAndGlass folder.

The partial SmokeAndGlass.css file shown in this figure shows how formatting information for HTML elements is stored in a cascading style sheet. To start, the BODY style sets the default formatting for any text in the body of an HTML page. This formatting includes specifying the font family, the font size, the line height relative to the font size, and the color. Then, the H1 style sets the formatting for any text within an H1 tag. This style inherits some settings such as font size from the predefined H1 style and it inherits other settings such as font family and font color from the BODY style. With a little bit of experimenting, you can typically set up a css file to get your pages to look the way you want.

The partial SmokeAndGlass.skin file shown in this figure shows how formatting information for server controls is stored in skins. In particular, this file contains one skin for each type of control that's used on the Order page shown in figure 11-1. For example, the skin for the Label control specifies the font name and font color that are used for labels. The skins for the other controls also specify font attributes, and the TextBox and Button controls specify some other attributes that control the appearance of the border and background color.

The directory structure for a theme

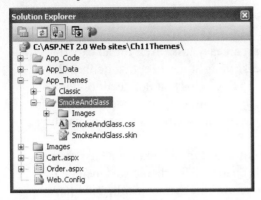

Part of the SmokeAndGlass.css file

```
BODY {
    FONT-FAMILY: Verdana, Geneva, Arial, Helvetica, sans-serif;
    FONT-SIZE: 11pt;
    LINE-HEIGHT: 110%;
    COLOR : #585880;
}

H1 {
    font-family: Verdana, Geneva, Arial, Helvetica, sans-serif;
    COLOR: #585880;
    margin-top: 3px;
}
```

Part of the SmokeAndGlass.skin file

```
<asp:Label    runat="server"           ForeColor="#585880"
              Font-Names="Verdana" />

<asp:DropDownList
              runat="server"           ForeColor="#585880"
              Font-Names="Verdana" />

<asp:TextBox runat="server"            BackColor="#FFFFFF"
             BorderStyle="Solid"       Font-Names="Verdana"
             ForeColor="#585880"       BorderColor="#585880"
             BorderWidth="1pt" />

<asp:Button  runat="server"            BorderColor="#585880"
             Font-Bold="true"          BorderWidth="1pt"
             ForeColor="#585880"       BackColor="#F8F7F4" />
```

Description

- The App_Themes folder can contain multiple subfolders with each subfolder defining one *theme*.
- Each theme folder can contain a file that contains the *cascading style sheet* (CSS) that defines the appearance of the HTML elements, files that define the *skins* that control the appearance of the ASP.NET server controls, and files for any images that are used by the cascading style sheet or the skins.

Figure 11-2   How themes work

How to make an existing theme available to an application

Designing a theme that looks good isn't an easy task, even for an experienced web designer. It requires coding a cascading style sheet that defines the formatting for all of the HTML elements, coding skins that define all of the server controls, and creating any graphics that are used by the style sheets or the skins. As a result, the easiest way to get started with themes is to use an existing theme.

To obtain an existing theme, you can download the SmokeAndGlass theme that's included with the application for this chapter. This theme was included with the Beta 1 version of ASP.NET 2.0 to show how themes work, and I have made some minor modifications to it. Or, you can try to download another theme from the Internet. For example, Microsoft has suggested that they may provide an online theme gallery on www.asp.net that will enable developers to find and share themes for their sites. As more developers began to create themes, the availability and quality of themes available from the Internet should improve.

Once you have a theme folder on your computer that contains the files for a theme, it's easy to make the theme available to an application. To do that, you can use Visual Studio to create the App_Themes folder. Then, you can use Windows Explorer to copy the theme folder into the App_Themes folder as described in figure 11-3. After you do that, you may need to refresh the App_Themes folder before you'll see the new folder.

How to apply a theme to an application

Once the theme has been added to the App_Themes folder, you can apply it to the entire application by editing the web.config file as shown in figure 11-3. To do that, you add a Pages element within the System.web element. Then, you code a Theme attribute within the Pages element that specifies the name of the theme.

For most applications, you'll want to apply a single theme to the entire application as shown in this figure. When you do that, you can't override the formatting that has been specified by the theme for an individual element or control. If, for example, you want to set the color for a label to red, you can't do that because that attribute has already been specified by the theme. However, if an attribute isn't specified by the theme, you can change it for a control. For example, since the theme doesn't specify the Font-Bold attribute for labels, you can apply or remove boldfacing from individual labels.

Most of the time, this is how you want themes to work. However, if you need to apply a different theme to a page or control, if you need to remove a theme from a page or control, or if you want to change the way overriding works, you can learn how to do that later in this chapter.

How to make an existing theme available to an application

1. Create the App_Themes folder. To do that, you can right-click on the root folder, select the Add ASP.NET Folder submenu, and select the Theme item. This creates the App_Themes folder and a subfolder with a default name of Theme1. You can delete this Theme1 folder since you will be using an existing theme.

2. Copy the folder that contains the theme into the App_Themes folder. To do that, you can use the Windows Explorer.

A web.config file that specifies a theme

```
<configuration>
  <system.web>
    <pages theme="SmokeAndGlass" />
  </system.web>
</configuration>
```

Description

- You can get the SmokeAndGlass theme shown in the previous figure by downloading the applications for this book. You may also be able to download themes from the Internet.

- To apply a theme to the current application, you can edit the web.config file for the application. Within the web.config file, you can use the Theme attribute of the Pages element to specify the name of the theme.

- When you use the Theme attribute of the Pages element to apply a theme to a page, you can't override any of the formatting attributes specified by the theme for individual controls. However, you can change attributes that aren't specified by the theme.

- Figures 11-8 and 11-9 show other techniques for applying and removing themes from individual pages and controls.

- Figure 11-10 shows how to allow controls to override attributes that are specified by a theme.

Figure 11-3   How to apply a theme to the entire application

How to create your own themes

In the topics that follow, you'll learn the basic skills for creating your own themes. Even if you never need to create your own themes, you should read through these topics since they show the details of how themes work. In addition, they present skills that you can use to edit an existing theme.

How to use cascading style sheets

In chapter 5, you learned how to store cascading style sheets in an external file. You use the same techniques to create a cascading style sheet that's part of a theme, except that you store the style sheet in the theme folder. Figure 11-4 reviews the basic techniques for creating a cascading style sheet and shows the start of a style sheet named Classic.css. It also presents a simple style sheet and shows how you can use it.

The Body style in this style sheet sets the default color for any text in the body of an HTML page to blue by specifying a value of #000066. As you learned in chapter 5, it's also possible to set the Color attribute to a keyword such as Blue or Navy. However, these keywords limit the number of colors that are available. In addition, they aren't supported by all browsers. As a result, web designers typically use the #000000 format to specify colors.

The H1 and H4 styles in this figure use the Font-Size attribute to specify a font size in points. In addition, the H4 tag uses the Font-Style attribute to specify that the heading should be italicized. The rest of the attributes for the H1 and H4 tags use the default settings, except that they use the Color attribute that's specified by the Body style. If you want to specify a different color, though, you can use the Color attribute of these tags to override the Color attribute of the Body style.

The style sheet in this figure also defines a style class named Highlighted that can be used to change the background color of any HTML element to light gray. To identify this class, a period is coded before the name of the class. Then, the Background-Color attribute is used to set the background to light grey.

To use the styles in a style sheet, you can code the tag as you would normally. However, to use a style class, you must specify the name of the class. To do that, you use the Class attribute for HTML tags and the CssClass attribute for ASP.NET tags.

The start of a cascading style sheet

A .css file that defines three styles and one style class

```
body
{
    color: #000066;
}
h1
{
    font-size: 18pt;
}
h4
{
    font-size: 12pt;
    font-style: italic;
}
.highlighted
{
    background-color: #CCCCCC;
}
```

An HTML tag that uses a style

```
<h1>Halloween Superstore</h1>
```

An HTML tag that specifies a style class

```
<h4 class="highlighted">Halloween supplies for the discerning haunter</h4>
```

An ASP.NET tag that specifies a style class

```
<asp:Label ID="lblName" runat="server" CssClass="highlighted"></asp:Label>
```

Description

- To add a new .css file to a theme, you can right-click on the folder for the theme and select the Add New Item command. Then, you can use the Add New Item dialog box to select the Style Sheet template and enter the name for the .css file.

- When using Visual Studio to work with a css file, you can use IntelliSense to select from lists of HTML elements and attributes. You can also use the Style Builder to edit style attributes.

Figure 11-4   How to use cascading style sheets

How to use skins

Figure 11-5 shows how to create and use a file that contains skins for the controls of an application. As you would hope, this works similarly to cascading style sheets, but it allows you to define styles for ASP.NET server controls. In this figure, for example, you can see a newly created skin file named Classic.skin.

Once you create a skin file, you can add skins to the file by opening the tag, entering the name of the control, entering a RunAt attribute, and closing the tag. For example, you can begin a tag for the Label control like this:

```
<asp:Label runat="server" />
```

Then, you can set other attributes to control the formatting for the control. For example, you can change the ForeColor attribute for a Label control like this:

```
<asp:Label runat="server" ForeColor="#000066" />
```

Since this uses the standard ASP.NET syntax for setting control attributes, you shouldn't have much trouble understanding how this works.

When you use themes, you typically need to define one skin for each type of control that you use in your application. In this figure, for example, you can see the skins for the Label, TextBox, Button, and DropDownList controls. These are all the controls that are used by the Order page shown in figure 11-1. However, for a more robust application, you'd probably need to include skins for many more types of controls. Otherwise, a control that doesn't have a skin probably won't look like the rest of the controls.

The first four skins in this skin file don't include a SkinID attribute. As a result, they're the *default skins* that are used when a control of that type doesn't include a SkinID attribute. For example, the default skin for a label is applied to the Label control that's defined by the first ASP.NET tag shown in this figure.

If you need to supply multiple skins for a control, you can code a *named skin* that includes a SkinID attribute that uniquely identifies the skin. For example, the named skin in this figure provides a second skin for the Label control with a SkinID of Head1. This skin adds boldfacing to the font and sets the font size to large to make the label have the appearance of a heading. To apply this skin to a Label control, you can add a Label control to a form and set its SkinID attribute to Head1 as shown by the second Label control defined in this figure.

All of the skins in this figure specify the color of the font. However, this is already done by the Body style in the cascading style sheet for the Classic theme and is automatically applied to all HTML elements. Since all of the ASP.NET sever controls are eventually rendered as HTML elements before being returned to the client, the color specified in the Body style is automatically applied to the server controls. As a result, you don't need to set the ForeColor attribute for these controls unless you want to make sure that the color specified for these server controls overrides the color that's set by the Body style.

The start of a skin file

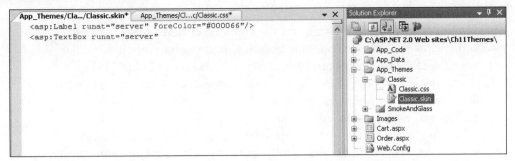

A skin file that defines four default skins and one named skin

```
<asp:Label
    runat="server"          ForeColor="#000066"/>

<asp:DropDownList
    runat="server"          ForeColor="#000066"/>

<asp:TextBox
    runat="server"          ForeColor="#000066"
    BorderStyle="Solid"     BorderWidth="1pt" />

<asp:Button
    runat="server"          ForeColor="#000066"
    Font-Bold="true"        BackColor="#EEEEEE"
    BorderColor="#000066"   BorderWidth="1pt" />

<%-- a named skin for labels --%>
<asp:Label
    runat="server"          ForeColor="#000066"
    Font-Bold="true"        Font-Size="large"
    SkinID="Head1"/>
```

An ASP.NET tag that uses the default skin for a label

```
<asp:Label ID="Label3" Runat="server" Text="Quantity:"></asp:Label>
```

An ASP.NET tag that specifies a named skin for a label

```
<asp:Label ID="lblName" runat="server" SkinID="Head1"></asp:Label>
```

Description

- To add a new skin file to a theme, you can right-click on the folder for the theme, and select the Add New Item command. Then, you can use the Add New Item dialog box to select the Skin File template and enter the name for the skin file.

- To specify a comment within a skin file, you must use the <%-- and --%> tags.

- To create a *default skin*, don't specify the SkinID attribute for the skin. Then, the skin will automatically be applied to any control of that type whose SkinID property isn't set.

- To create a *named skin*, specify the SkinID attribute for the skin. Then, you can use the SkinID attribute to apply the skin to a control of that type.

Figure 11-5   How to use skins

Another way to store skins

In figure 11-5, all of the skins for the application were stored in a single skin file. However, it's also possible to split skins up into multiple files. For example, figure 11-6 shows how you can store the skins in figure 11-5 in separate files. Here, both of the skins for the Label control are stored in a file named Label.skin, the skin for the DropDownList control is stored in a file named DropDownList.skin, and so on.

The choice of how to store your skins depends on your preferences and on the number of skins used by your application. If you have a large number of skins with multiple skins for each type of control, you may find it easier to organize and manage them by splitting them into separate files. This can make it easier to find skins and to copy them from one application to another. On the other hand, you might find that the additional skin files create a file management headache. As a result, you might prefer to keep all skins in a single file even if that file becomes very long.

A theme that uses multiple skin files

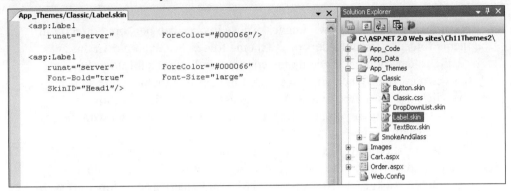

The Label.skin file

```
<asp:Label
    runat="server"         ForeColor="#000066"/>

<asp:Label
    runat="server"         ForeColor="#000066"
    Font-Bold="true"       Font-Size="large"
    SkinID="Head1"/>
```

The DropDownList.skin file

```
<asp:DropDownList
    runat="server"         ForeColor="#000066"/>
```

The TextBox.skin file

```
<asp:TextBox
    runat="server"         ForeColor="#000066"
    BorderStyle="Solid"    BorderWidth="1pt" />
```

The Button.skin file

```
<asp:Button
    runat="server"         ForeColor="#000066"
    Font-Bold="true"       BackColor="#EEEEEE"
    BorderColor="#000066"  BorderWidth="1pt" />
```

Description

- Skins can be stored in a single file as shown in the previous figure or in separate files as shown in this figure.

Figure 11-6   Another way to store skins

How to use images

Each theme can use its own images. These images can be stored directly in the theme folder or in subfolders of the theme folder. For example, in this figure, the folder for the Classic theme contains an Images subfolder that contains two gif files. Once you have added images to a theme, you can use a relative URL to refer to the images from the css and skin files as shown in figure 11-7. That way, if you switch themes, the images associated with the css and skin files will also be switched.

The brownfadetop.gif file can be used as the background for an HTML element or a server control to create a shading effect that isn't possible using a regular colored background. This is an HTML trick that was developed by web designers to get around the limitations of plain HTML, and it's typical of the types of hacks that are often used by web designers. If you look at this image, you can see that it's very narrow. In fact, it's only 5 pixels wide and 100 pixels tall. Although it's difficult to tell from this black-and-white figure, this image contains a brown background that fades to a lighter brown as it nears the top of the image.

The Classic.css style sheet includes a style class named BrownFadeTopBack that sets the BackGround-Image tag to the brownfadetop.gif file in the Images subfolder. As a result, if this style class is used to apply this image to an HTML element or server control, the image will be sized and repeated as necessary to fill the entire background for that HTML element or server control. For example, the H4 tag shown in this figure specifies the BrownFadeTopBack class. As a result, this HTML element's background is shaded accordingly.

The bullet.gif file can be used to customize controls that use bullets. For example, the skin for the BulletedList control uses the BulletImageUrl attribute to specify that this control should use the bullet.gif file stored in the Images subfolder of the current theme. In addition, this skin uses the BulletStyle attribute to specify that the bullet should use a custom image. As a result, the BulletedList control shown in this figure uses this custom bullet.gif image instead of the default bullet style, which is a small black circle.

The images for the Classic theme

The brownfadetop.gif image

A style class that uses this image

```
.brownfadetopback
{
    background-image: url(images/brownfadetop.gif);
}
```

An HTML tag that uses the image

```
<h4 class="brownfadetopback">Halloween supplies for the discerning
haunter</h4>
```

How the H4 tag appears on the page

Halloween supplies for the discerning haunter

The bullet.gif image

The skin for a BulletedList control that uses this image

```
<asp:BulletedList runat="server"
    BulletImageUrl="images/bullet.gif"
    BulletStyle="CustomImage" />
```

An ASP.NET tag that uses the image

```
<asp:BulletedList ID="BulletedList1" runat="server">
    <asp:ListItem Value="Item1">Austin Powers</asp:ListItem>
    <asp:ListItem Value="Item2">Freddy</asp:ListItem>
</asp:BulletedList>
```

How the BulletedList control appears on the page

○ Austin Powers
○ Freddy

Figure 11-7   How to use images

More skills for working with themes

Most of the time, you want to apply a single theme to all pages of an application as described in figure 11-3. However, there may be times when you want to apply a theme to individual pages or controls. For example, you may want to allow each user to select a preferred theme for a page. Conversely, there may be times when you want to remove a theme from individual pages or controls. And there may be times when you want to allow individual controls to override attributes that are specified by the theme.

How to apply a theme to a page

Figure 11-8 starts by showing how you can use the Theme attribute of the Page directive to apply a theme to a single page at design time. Then, it shows how you can use the Theme property of the Page class to apply a theme to a single page at runtime.

At runtime, you must make sure the code that applies the theme is executed before the HTML element or ASP.NET control is added to the page. To do that, you can code an event procedure for the PreInit event of the Page class as shown in this figure. This event procedure is executed before the Init event that adds the controls to the page. As a result, this is a good event to use to apply a theme to a page.

The code within the event procedure for the PreInit event sets the Theme for the Page equal to a string for a theme that has been stored in the Session object. That way, if the user has selected a theme earlier in the session, the theme for this page will be changed to the theme selected by the user. However, unless you store this theme in a persistent data store, this theme will be lost when the user ends the current session.

To make the theme available for future sessions, you can use the profile feature described in chapter 19. To do that, you can configure the profile feature so it includes a Theme property that stores a string for the user's preferred theme. Then, you can use the Profile property to get the theme like this:

```
Page.Theme = Profile.Theme
```

How to apply a skin to a control

In figure 11-5, you saw how to use the SkinID attribute to apply a named skin to a server control at design time. Now, figure 11-8 reviews this skill, and it shows how to use the SkinID property of a server control to apply a named skin at runtime. To do that, you can use the PreInit event of the page to make sure that this skin is applied before the control is added to the page and displayed. This works the same as it does for applying a theme to a page.

How to apply a theme to a page

At design time

```
<%@ Page Language="VB" Theme="SmokeAndGlass" %>
```

At runtime

```
Protected Sub Page_PreInit(ByVal sender As Object, ByVal e As EventArgs) _
        Handles Me.PreInit
    Page.Theme = CType(Session("myTheme"), String)
End Sub
```

How to apply a skin to a control

At design time

```
<asp:Label ID="lblName" runat="server" SkinID="Head1"></asp:Label>
```

At runtime

```
Protected Sub Page_PreInit(ByVal sender As Object, ByVal e As EventArgs) _
        Handles Me.PreInit
    lblName.SkinID = CType(Session("mySkinID"), String)
End Sub
```

Description

- To apply a theme to a single page, you can use the Theme attribute of the Page directive or the Theme property of the Page class.

- To apply a skin to a control, you can use the SkinID attribute or property of the control.

- The code that applies a theme or skin at runtime should be coded in the event procedure for the PreInit event of the Page class so the code is executed before the HTML elements and ASP.NET controls are added to the page.

Figure 11-8   How to apply themes and skins

How to remove a theme from an application

Although it isn't shown in this chapter, it's possible for a web site administrator to set a global theme that applies to all web applications running on the server. In that case, you may want to remove the global theme from all pages of your application. To do that, you can open the web.config file for your application and set the Theme attribute of the Pages element to an empty string as shown in figure 11-9.

How to remove a theme from a page

Figure 11-9 also shows how to remove a theme from a single page. At design time, you can set the Theme attribute of the Page directive to an empty string. At runtime, you can set the Theme property of the Page class to an empty string. To do that, you can use the PreInit event of the page to make sure that this theme is removed before the HTML elements and controls are added to the page and displayed. This works the same as it does for applying a theme to a page.

How to remove a theme from a control

By default, the EnableTheming property is set to True for all controls. As a result, any themes that are applied to a page are applied to all controls on the page. Typically, that's what you want. However, since you can't override an attribute that's set in a skin by setting it at the control level, you may want to remove the theme from the control so you can apply custom formatting to a control. To do that, you can set the EnableTheming attribute for the control to False as shown in figure 11-9. Then, you can use standard ASP.NET formatting techniques to format that control. In this figure, for example, the ForeColor attribute is used to change the color of a label to red.

If you need to set the EnableTheming property at runtime, you can use the PreInit event of the page to make sure that this skin is removed before the HTML elements and controls are added to the page and displayed. This works the same as it does for applying a theme to a page.

How to remove themes from the entire application

At design time

```
<system.web>
  <pages theme="" />
</system.web>
```

How to remove themes from the current page

At design time

```
<%@ Page Language="VB" Theme="" %>
```

At runtime

```
Protected Sub Page_PreInit(ByVal sender As Object, ByVal e As EventArgs) _
        Handles Me.PreInit
    Page.Theme = ""
End Sub
```

How to remove a theme from a control

At design time

```
<asp:Label ID="lblName" runat="server"
    EnableTheming="False" ForeColor="red">
</asp:Label>
```

At runtime

```
Protected Sub Page_PreInit(ByVal sender As Object, ByVal e As EventArgs) _
        Handles Me.PreInit
    lblName.EnableTheming = False
    lblName.ForeColor = System.Drawing.Color.Red
End Sub
```

Description

- To remove a theme from all of the pages in an application, you can set the Theme attribute of the Pages element to an empty string.

- To remove a theme from a single page, you can set the Theme attribute of the Page directive or the Theme property of the Page class to an empty string.

- To remove a theme from a control, you can set the EnableTheming attribute or property to False.

- The code that removes a theme at runtime should be coded in the event procedure for the PreInit event of the Page class so the code is executed before the HTML elements and ASP.NET controls are added to the page.

Figure 11-9   How to remove themes and skins

How to use style sheet themes

When you use the Theme attribute or property to apply a theme, the theme is known as a *customization theme*. So far, all of examples in this chapter have worked with customization themes. When you use a customization theme, you can't override any of attributes that are set by the theme. For example, since the Classic theme sets the color of a label to blue, you can't set the color of an individual label to red unless you remove the theme from the label as shown in figure 11-9. This often isn't ideal because it also removes all other formatting that was applied by the theme.

If you want to be able to override the attributes specified by a theme, you can use the StyleSheetTheme attribute to apply the theme to all pages as shown in figure 11-10. Then, the theme is known as a *style sheet theme*, and you can override any of the attributes specified in this theme by setting them at the control level. For the most part, you can use the same skills for working with style sheet themes that you use for customization themes.

However, to apply a style sheet theme to a single page at runtime, you don't use the PreInit event. Instead, you override the StyleSheetTheme property of the page to get and set the name of the theme. Then, when a page loads, it automatically calls the StyleSheetTheme property to set the style sheet theme. In this figure, for example, the StyleSheetTheme property for the page gets the name of the style sheet theme from the Session object and sets the name of the style sheet theme in the Session object.

To understand how themes work, you need to understand the order in which the attributes of a theme are applied. First, all attributes specified by the style sheet theme are applied. Then, the custom attributes specified for individual controls are applied, overriding the style sheet theme if necessary. Finally, the attributes specified by the customization theme are applied, overriding the style sheet theme if necessary. That's why you can't override a customization theme by setting attributes for a control.

Although it's uncommon, it's possible to apply both types of themes to an application. For example, this figure shows how to apply the SmokeAndGlass theme as the style sheet theme while also applying the Classic theme as the customization theme. As a result, if the same attribute is specified in both themes, the attribute specified in the Classic theme will override the attribute in the SmokeAndGlass theme. However, if an attribute is specified in the SmokeAndGlass theme and it isn't specified in the Classic theme, that attribute will be applied to the page unless, of course, it is overridden by a custom attribute for a control.

How to apply a style sheet theme to all pages in the application

```
<system.web>
  <pages styleSheetTheme="SmokeAndGlass" />
</system.web>
```

How to apply a style sheet theme to a single page

At design time

```
<%@ Page Language="VB" StylesheetTheme="SmokeAndGlass" %>
```

At runtime by overriding the StyleSheetTheme property in the code-behind file

```
Public Overrides Property StyleSheetTheme() As String
    Get
        Return CType(Session("myTheme"), String)
    End Get
    Set(ByVal value As String)
        Session("myTheme") = value
    End Set
End Property
```

How to remove a style sheet theme from a single page

At design time

```
<%@ Page Language="VB" StylesheetTheme="" %>
```

The order in which themes are applied

1. Style sheet theme attributes
2. Control attributes
3. Customization theme attributes

How to apply both a customization theme and a style sheet theme

At design time

```
<%@ Page Language="VB" StylesheetTheme="SmokeAndGlass" Theme="Classic" %>
```

Description

- A *customization theme* can't be overridden by custom settings on controls. A *style sheet theme* can be overridden at the control level.

- To apply or remove a style sheet theme at design time, you can use the StyleSheetTheme property. This works just like the Theme property does for customization themes.

- To apply or remove a style sheet theme at runtime, you can override the StyleSheetTheme property of the page.

Figure 11-10   How to use style sheet themes

Perspective

In this chapter, you learned how themes work and how they can be used to separate the formatting of an application from the code of an application. In addition, you learned enough about creating a theme from scratch to realize that it isn't an easy task, even for an experienced web designer.

Now, you should have all the skills you need to work with a web designer to create a suitable theme for your application. Also, as themes become more widely used, you may be able to download an appropriate theme for your application from the Internet. Either way, once you have the theme you want, you can use the skills of this chapter to get the most from it.

Terms

theme
cascading style sheet (CSS)
skin
default skin
named skin
customization theme
style sheet theme

Section 3

ASP.NET database programming

Since most ASP.NET applications store their data in databases, this section is devoted to the essentials of database programming. When you complete it, you should be able to develop database applications that use *SQL data sources* to access and update the data in the databases that your applications use. In addition, you should have at least a general understanding of how you can use *object data sources* to develop 3-layer database applications.

To start, chapter 12 introduces you to the concepts and terms you need to know for developing database applications. This chapter also presents an overview of the ADO.NET classes that do the database operations when you use SQL data sources. When you use SQL data sources, though, you don't use ADO.NET directly, even though the processing is done by ADO.NET.

Then, chapter 13 shows you how to use SQL data sources and the DataList control to get data from a database. Chapter 14 shows you how to use the new GridView control to create more complex applications. And chapter 15 shows you how to use the new DetailsView and FormView controls. By using SQL data sources and the new controls, you'll be able to develop powerful applications with a minimum of code.

Last, chapter 16 shows you how to use object data sources to develop 3-layer database applications. If you already know how to use ADO.NET directly, you should be able to use object data sources when you complete this chapter. Otherwise, you will at least understand the concepts and recognize the need for learning ADO.NET.

12

An introduction to database programming

This chapter introduces you to the basic concepts and terms that apply to database applications. In particular, it explains what a relational database is and describes how you work with it using SQL. It also presents an overview of the basic ADO.NET classes that are used to access the data in relational databases.

To illustrate these concepts and terms, this chapter presents examples that use *Microsoft SQL Server Express*. This is a scaled-back version of *Microsoft SQL Server 2005*, and SQL Server is the database you're most likely to use as you develop ASP.NET 2.0 database applications. Note, however, that the concepts and terms that you'll learn in this chapter also apply to other databases.

An introduction to relational databases

In 1970, Dr. E. F. Codd developed a model for what was then a new and revolutionary type of database called a *relational database.* This type of database eliminated some of the problems that were associated with standard files and other database designs. By using the relational model, you can reduce data redundancy, which saves disk storage and leads to efficient data retrieval. You can also view and manipulate data in a way that is both intuitive and efficient. Today, relational databases are the de facto standard for database applications.

How a table is organized

The model for a relational database states that data is stored in one or more *tables.* It also states that each table can be viewed as a two-dimensional matrix consisting of *rows* and *columns.* This is illustrated by the relational table in figure 12-1. Each row in this table contains information about a single product.

In practice, the rows and columns of a relational database table are sometimes referred to by the more traditional terms, *records* and *fields.* In fact, some software packages use one set of terms, some use the other, and some use a combination. In this book, we've used the terms *rows* and *columns* for consistency.

If a table contains one or more columns that uniquely identify each row in the table, you can define these columns as the *primary key* of the table. For instance, the primary key of the Products table in this figure is the ProductID column. Here, the primary key consists of a single column. However, a primary key can also consist of two or more columns, in which case it's called a *composite primary key.*

In addition to primary keys, some database management systems let you define additional keys that uniquely identify each row in a table. If, for example, the Name column in the Products table contains a unique name for each product, it can be defined as a *non-primary key.* In SQL Server, this is called a *unique key*, and it's implemented by defining a *unique key constraint* (also known simply as a *unique constraint*). The only difference between a unique key and a primary key is that a unique key can contain a null value and a primary key can't.

Indexes provide an efficient way to access the rows in a table based on the values in one or more columns. Because applications typically access the rows in a table by referring to their key values, an index is automatically created for each key you define. However, you can define indexes for other columns as well. If, for example, you frequently need to sort the rows in the Products table by the CategoryID column, you can set up an index for that column. Like a key, an index can include one or more columns.

The Products table in a Halloween database

Primary key   Columns

ProductID	Name	ShortDescription	LongDescription	CategoryID	ImageFile	UnitPrice	OnHand
arm01	Severed Arm	Bloody Severed ...	A severed arm, ...	props	arm01.jpg	19.9500	200
bl01	Black light (24")	24" black light	Create that cree...	fx	blacklight01.jpg	24.9900	200
cat01	Deranged Cat	20" Ugly Cat	This is one ugly cat.	props	cat01.jpg	19.9900	45
cool01	Cool Ghoul	Cool Ghoul mask	This guy is one c...	props	cool01.jpg	69.9900	25
fog01	Fog Machine	600W Fog Machine	The perfect fog ...	fx	fog01.jpg	34.9900	100
fogj01	Fog Juice (1qt)	1 Qt bottle of Fo...	The drink your f...	fx	nopic.jpg	9.9900	500
frankc01	Frankenstein	Frankenstein cos...	It's alive!	costumes	frank01.jpg	39.9900	100
fred01	Freddie	Freddie Krueger ...	The ultimate in m...	masks	freddy.jpg	29.9900	50
head01	Shrunken Head	Shrunken Head ...	Spikes driven thr...	props	head01.jpg	29.9900	100
head02	Severed Head	Severed Head in...	Incredibly realisti...	props	head02.jpg	29.9900	100
hippie01	Hippie	Ghoulish Hippie ...	This guy did too ...	masks	hippie01.jpg	79.9900	40
jar01	JarJar	Jar Jar Binks	Meesa happy to ...	costumes	jarjar1.jpg	59.9900	25
martian01	Martian	Martian costume	Now includes an ...	costumes	martian1.jpg	69.9900	100
mum01	Mummy	Mummy mask	All wrapped up a...	masks	mummy.jpg	39.9900	30
pow01	Austin Powers	Austin Powers c...	Be the most sha...	costumes	powers1.jpg	79.9900	25
rat01	Ugly Rat	16" Rat	This guy is sure t...	props	rat01.jpg	14.9900	75
rat02	Uglier Rat	20" Rat	Yuch! This one wi...	props	rat02.jpg	19.9900	50
skel01	Life Size Skeleton	Life Size Plastic S...	This blown plasti...	props	skel01.jpg	14.9500	10
skullfog01	Skull Fogger	2,800 Cubic Foo...	This fogger puts ...	fx	skullfog01.jpg	39.9500	50
spider01	Spider	Black widow spider	This spider make...	props	nopic.jpg	12.9900	50
str01	Mini-strobe	Black mini strobe...	Perfect for creati...	fx	strobe1.jpg	13.9900	200
super01	Superman	Superman costume	Look, up in the s...	costumes	superman1.jpg	39.9900	100
tlm01	TLM	Thunder & Light...	Flash! Boom! Cr...	props	tlm1.jpg	99.9900	10
vader01	Darth Vader Mask	The legendary D...	OB1 has taught ...	masks	vader01.jpg	19.9900	100

Rows

Concepts

- A *relational database* uses *tables* to store and manipulate data. Each table consists of one or more *records*, or *rows*, that contain the data for a single entry. Each row contains one or more *fields*, or *columns*, with each column representing a single item of data.

- Most tables contain a *primary key* that uniquely identifies each row in the table. The primary key often consists of a single column, but it can also consist of two or more columns. If a primary key uses two or more columns, it's called a *composite primary key*.

- In addition to primary keys, some database management systems let you define one or more *non-primary keys*. In SQL Server, these keys are called *unique keys*, and they're implemented using *unique key constraints*. Like a primary key, a non-primary key uniquely identifies each row in the table.

- A table can also be defined with one or more *indexes*. An index provides an efficient way to access data from a table based on the values in specific columns. An index is automatically created for a table's primary and non-primary keys.

Figure 12-1   How a table is organized

How the tables in a database are related

The tables in a relational database can be related to other tables by values in specific columns. The two tables shown in figure 12-2 illustrate this concept. Here, each row in the Categories table is related to one or more rows in the Products table. This is called a *one-to-many relationship*.

Typically, relationships exist between the primary key in one table and the *foreign key* in another table. The foreign key is simply one or more columns in a table that refer to a primary key in another table. In SQL Server, relationships can also exist between a unique key in one table and a foreign key in another table.

Although one-to-many relationships are the most common, two tables can also have a one-to-one or many-to-many relationship. If a table has a *one-to-one relationship* with another table, the data in the two tables could be stored in a single table. Because of that, one-to-one relationships are used infrequently.

In contrast, a *many-to-many relationship* is usually implemented by using an intermediate table, called a *linking table*, that has a one-to-many relationship with the two tables in the many-to-many relationship. In other words, a many-to-many relationship can usually be broken down into two one-to-many relationships.

The relationship between the Categories and Products tables

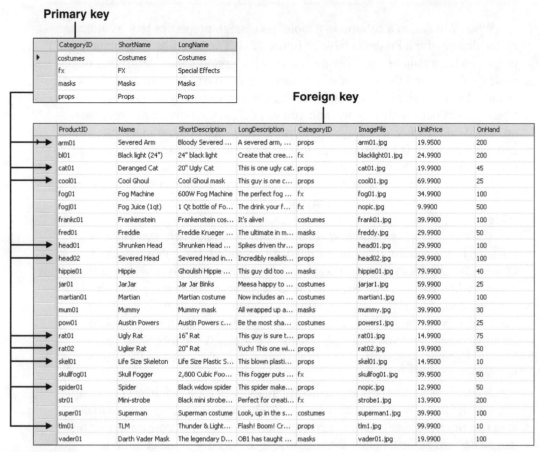

Primary key

CategoryID	ShortName	LongName
costumes	Costumes	Costumes
fx	FX	Special Effects
masks	Masks	Masks
props	Props	Props

Foreign key

ProductID	Name	ShortDescription	LongDescription	CategoryID	ImageFile	UnitPrice	OnHand
arm01	Severed Arm	Bloody Severed ...	A severed arm, ...	props	arm01.jpg	19.9500	200
bl01	Black light (24")	24" black light	Create that cree...	fx	blacklight01.jpg	24.9900	200
cat01	Deranged Cat	20" Ugly Cat	This is one ugly cat.	props	cat01.jpg	19.9900	45
cool01	Cool Ghoul	Cool Ghoul mask	This guy is one c...	props	cool01.jpg	69.9900	25
fog01	Fog Machine	600W Fog Machine	The perfect fog ...	fx	fog01.jpg	34.9900	100
fogj01	Fog Juice (1qt)	1 Qt bottle of Fo...	The drink your f...	fx	nopic.jpg	9.9900	500
frankc01	Frankenstein	Frankenstein cos...	It's alive!	costumes	frank01.jpg	39.9900	100
fred01	Freddie	Freddie Krueger ...	The ultimate in m...	masks	freddy.jpg	29.9900	50
head01	Shrunken Head	Shrunken Head ...	Spikes driven thr...	props	head01.jpg	29.9900	100
head02	Severed Head	Severed Head in...	Incredibly realisti...	props	head02.jpg	29.9900	100
hippie01	Hippie	Ghoulish Hippie ...	This guy did too ...	masks	hippie01.jpg	79.9900	40
jar01	JarJar	Jar Jar Binks	Meesa happy to ...	costumes	jarjar1.jpg	59.9900	25
martian01	Martian	Martian costume	Now includes an ...	costumes	martian1.jpg	69.9900	100
mum01	Mummy	Mummy mask	All wrapped up a...	masks	mummy.jpg	39.9900	30
pow01	Austin Powers	Austin Powers c...	Be the most sha...	costumes	powers1.jpg	79.9900	25
rat01	Ugly Rat	16" Rat	This guy is sure t...	props	rat01.jpg	14.9900	75
rat02	Uglier Rat	20" Rat	Yuch! This one wi...	props	rat02.jpg	19.9900	50
skel01	Life Size Skeleton	Life Size Plastic S...	This blown plasti...	props	skel01.jpg	14.9500	10
skullfog01	Skull Fogger	2,800 Cubic Foo...	This fogger puts ...	fx	skullfog01.jpg	39.9500	50
spider01	Spider	Black widow spider	This spider make...	props	nopic.jpg	12.9900	50
str01	Mini-strobe	Black mini strobe...	Perfect for creati...	fx	strobe1.jpg	13.9900	200
super01	Superman	Superman costume	Look, up in the s...	costumes	superman1.jpg	39.9900	100
tlm01	TLM	Thunder & Light...	Flash! Boom! Cr...	props	tlm1.jpg	99.9900	10
vader01	Darth Vader Mask	The legendary D...	OB1 has taught ...	masks	vader01.jpg	19.9900	100

Concepts

- The tables in a relational database are related to each other through their key columns. For example, the CategoryID column is used to relate the Categories and Products tables above. The CategoryID column in the Products table is called a *foreign key* because it identifies a related row in the Categories table.

- Usually, a foreign key corresponds to the primary key in the related table. In SQL Server, however, a foreign key can also correspond to a unique key in the related table.

- When two tables are related via a foreign key, the table with the foreign key is referred to as the *foreign key table* and the table with the primary key is referred to as the *primary key table*.

- The relationships between the tables in a database correspond to the relationships between the entities they represent. The most common type of relationship is a *one-to-many relationship* as illustrated by the Categories and Products tables. A table can also have a *one-to-one relationship* or a *many-to-many relationship* with another table.

Figure 12-2   How the tables in a database are related

How the columns in a table are defined

When you define a column in a table, you assign properties to it as indicated by the design of the Products table in figure 12-3. The two most important properties for a column are Column Name, which provides an identifying name for the column, and Data Type, which specifies the type of information that can be stored in the column. With SQL Server, you can choose from *system data types* like the ones in this figure, and you can define your own data types that are based on the system data types. As you define each column in a table, you generally try to assign the data type that will minimize the use of disk storage because that will improve the performance of the queries later.

In addition to a data type, you must identify whether the column can store a *null value*. A null represents a value that's unknown, unavailable, or not applicable.

You can also assign a *default value* to each column. Then, that value is assigned to the column if another value isn't provided. If a column doesn't allow nulls and doesn't have a default value, you must supply a value for the column when you add a new row to the table. Otherwise, an error will occur.

Each table can also contain a numeric column whose value is generated automatically by the DBMS. In SQL Server, a column like this is called an *identity column*, and you establish it using the Identity, Identity Seed, and Identity Increment properties. Identity columns are often used as the primary key for a table.

A *check constraint* defines the acceptable values for a column. For example, you can define a check constraint for the Products table in this figure to make sure that the UnitPrice column is greater than zero. A check constraint like this can be defined at the column level because it refers only to the column it constrains. If the check constraint for a column needs to refer to other columns in the table, however, it can be defined at the table level.

After you define the constraints for a database, they're managed by the DBMS. If, for example, a user tries to add a row with data that violates a constraint, the DBMS sends an appropriate error code back to the application without adding the row to the database. The application can then respond to the error code.

Another alternative is to validate the data that is going to be added to a database before the program tries to add it. That way, the constraints shouldn't be needed and the program should run more efficiently. In many cases, both data validation and constraints are used. That way, the programs run more efficiently if the data validation routines work, but the constraints are there in case the data validation routines don't work or aren't coded.

The Server Explorer design view window for the Products table

Column Name	Data Type	Allow Nulls
ProductID	char(10)	☐
Name	varchar(50)	☐
ShortDescription	varchar(200)	☐
LongDescription	varchar(2000)	☐
CategoryID	varchar(10)	☐
ImageFile	varchar(30)	☑
UnitPrice	money	☐
OnHand	int	☐

Column Properties

(Name)	ProductID
Allow Nulls	No
Data Type	char
Default Value or Binding	
Length	10
Table Designer	
Collation	<database default>
⊞ Computed Column Specification	
Condensed Data Type	char(10)
Description	

(General)

Common SQL Server data types

Type	Description
bit	A value of 1 or 0 that represents a True or False value.
char, varchar, text	Any combination of letters, symbols, and numbers.
datetime, smalldatetime	Alphanumeric data that represents a date and time. Various formats are acceptable.
decimal, numeric	Numeric data that is accurate to the least significant digit. The data can contain an integer and a fractional portion.
float, real	Floating-point values that contain an approximation of a decimal value.
bigint, int, smallint, tinyint	Numeric data that contains only an integer portion.
money, smallmoney	Monetary values that are accurate to four decimal places.

Description

- The *data type* that's assigned to a column determines the type of information that can be stored in the column. Depending on the data type, the column definition can also include its length, precision, and scale.

- Each column definition also indicates whether or not the column can contain *null values*. A null value indicates that the value of the column is not known.

- A column can be defined with a *default value*. Then, that value is used for the column if another value isn't provided when a row is added to the table.

- A column can also be defined as an *identity column*. An identity column is a numeric column whose value is generated automatically when a row is added to the table.

- To restrict the values that a column can hold, you define *check constraints*. Check constraints can be defined at either the column level or the table level.

Figure 12-3   How the columns in a table are defined

The design of the Halloween database

Now that you've seen how the basic elements of a relational database work, figure 12-4 shows the design of the Halloween database that's used in the programming examples throughout this book. Although this database may seem complicated, its design is actually much simpler than most databases you'll encounter when you work on actual database applications.

The purpose of the Halloween database is to track orders placed at an online Halloween products store. To do that, the database must track not only invoices, but also products and customers.

The central table for this database is the Invoices table, which contains one row for each order placed by the company's customers. The primary key for this table is the InvoiceNumber column, which is an identity column. As a result, invoice numbers are generated automatically by SQL Server whenever a new invoice is created.

The LineItems table contains the line item details for each invoice. The primary key for this table is a combination of the InvoiceNumber and ProductID columns. The InvoiceNumber column relates each line item to an invoice, and the ProductID column relates each line item to a product. As a result, each invoice can have only one line item for a given product.

The Products and Categories tables work together to store information about the products offered by the Halloween store. The Category table has just three columns: CategoryID, ShortName, and LongName. The CategoryID column is a 10-character code that uniquely identifies each category. The ShortName and LongName columns provide two different descriptions of the category that the application can use, depending on how much room is available to display the category information.

The Products table contains one row for each product. Its primary key is the ProductID column. The Name, ShortDescription, and LongDescription columns provide descriptive information about the product. The ImageFile column provides the name of a separate image file that depicts the product. This column specifies just the name of each image file, not the complete path. The image files are stored in a directory named Images beneath the application's main directory, so the application knows where to find them.

Finally, the Customers table contains a row for each customer who has purchased from the Halloween Store. The primary key for this table is the customer's email address. The other columns in this table contain the customer's name, address, and phone number.

The tables that make up the Halloween database

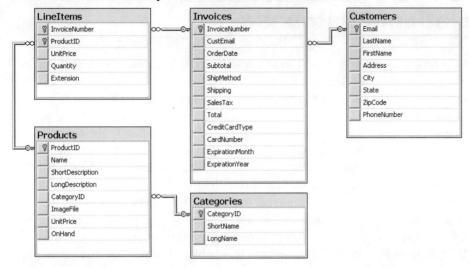

Description

- The Categories table contains a row for each product category. Its primary key is CategoryID, a 10-character code that identifies each category.

- The Products table contains a row for each product. Its primary key is ProductID, a 10-character code that identifies each product. CategoryID is a foreign key that relates each product to a row in the Categories table.

- The Customers table contains a row for each customer. Its primary key is Email, which identifies each customer by his or her email address.

- The Invoices table contains a row for each invoice. Its primary key is InvoiceNumber, an identity field that's generated automatically when a new invoice is created. CustEmail is a foreign key that relates each invoice to a row in the Customers table.

- The LineItems table contains one row for each line item of each invoice. Its primary key is a combination of InvoiceNumber and ProductID. InvoiceNumber is a foreign key that relates each line item to an invoice, and ProductID is a foreign key that relates each line item to a product.

- The relationships between the tables in this diagram appear as links, where the endpoints indicate the type of relationship. A key indicates the "one" side of a relationship, and the infinity symbol (∞) indicates the "many" side.

Figure 12-4   The design of the Halloween database

How to use SQL to work with the data in a relational database

In the topics that follow, you'll learn about the four SQL statements that you can use to manipulate the data in a database: Select, Insert, Update, and Delete. Although you'll learn the basics of coding these statements in the topics that follow, you may want to know more than what's presented here. In that case, we recommend our book, *Murach's SQL for SQL Server*. In addition to the Select, Insert, Update, and Delete statements, that book teaches you how to code the statements you use to define the data in a database, and it teaches you how to use other features of SQL Server that the top professionals use.

Although SQL is a standard language, each DBMS is likely to have its own *SQL dialect*, which includes extensions to the standard language. So when you use SQL, you need to make sure that you're using the dialect that's supported by your DBMS. In this chapter and throughout this book, all of the SQL examples are for Microsoft SQL Server's dialect, which is called *Transact-SQL*.

How to query a single table

Figure 12-5 shows how to use a Select statement to query a single table in a database. In the syntax summary at the top of this figure, you can see that the Select clause names the columns to be retrieved and the From clause names the table that contains the columns. You can also code a Where clause that gives criteria for the rows to be selected. And you can code an Order By clause that names one or more columns that the results should be sorted by and indicates whether each column should be sorted in ascending or descending sequence.

If you study the Select statement below the syntax summary, you can see how this works. Here, the Select statement retrieves three columns from the Products table. It selects a row only if the CategoryID column for the row has a value of "Props." And it sorts the returned rows by UnitPrice, so that the least expensive products are listed first.

This figure also shows the *result table*, or *result set*, that's returned by the Select statement. A result set is a logical table that's created temporarily within the database. When an application requests data from a database, it receives a result set.

Although it's not shown here, you should realize that a result set can include columns that are calculated from other columns in the table. For example, you could create a column for the total value of each product in the Products table by multiplying the OnHand column in that table by the UnitPrice column. This type of column is called a *calculated column*, and it exists only in the results of the query.

Simplified syntax of the Select statement

```
Select column-1 [, column-2]...
From table-1
[Where selection-criteria]
[Order By column-1 [Asc|Desc] [, column-2 [Asc|Desc]]...]
```

A Select statement that retrieves and sorts selected columns and rows from the Products table

```
Select ProductID, Name, UnitPrice
From Products
Where CategoryID = 'Props'
Order By UnitPrice
```

The result set defined by the Select statement

	ProductID	Name	UnitPrice
▶	spider01	Spider	12.9900
	skel01	Life Size Skeleton	14.9500
	rat01	Ugly Rat	14.9900
	arm01	Severed Arm	19.9500
	cat01	Deranged Cat	19.9900
	rat02	Uglier Rat	19.9900
	head01	Shrunken Head	29.9900
	head02	Severed Head	29.9900
	cool01	Cool Ghoul	69.9900
	tlm01	TLM	99.9900

Concepts

- The result of a Select statement is a *result table*, or *result set*, like the one shown above. A result set is a logical set of rows that consists of all of the columns and rows requested by the Select statement.

- A result set can include *calculated columns* that are calculated from other columns in the table.

- To select all of the columns in a table, you can code an asterisk (*) in place of the column names. For example, this statement will select all of the columns from the Products table:

```
Select * From Products
```

Figure 12-5   How to query a single table

How to join data from two or more tables

Figure 12-6 presents the syntax of the Select statement for retrieving data from two tables. This type of operation is called a *join* because the data from the two tables is joined together into a single result set. For example, the Select statement in this figure joins data from the Categories and Products tables into a single result set.

An *inner join* is the most common type of join. When you use an inner join, rows from the two tables in the join are included in the result set only if their related columns match. These matching columns are specified in the From clause of the Select statement. In the Select statement in this figure, for example, rows from the Categories and Products tables are included only if the value of the CategoryID column in the Categories table matches the value of the CategoryID column in one or more rows in the Products table. If there aren't any products for a particular category, that category won't be included in the result set.

Although this figure shows how to join data from two tables, you should know that you can extend this syntax to join data from additional tables. If, for example, you want to include data from the LineItems table in the results shown in this figure, you can code the From clause of the Select statement like this:

```
From Products
    Inner Join Categories
        On Categories.CategoryID = Products.CategoryID
    Inner Join LineItems
        On LineItems.ProductID = Invoices.ProductID
```

Then, in the column list of the Select statement, you can include any of the columns in the LineItems table.

The syntax of the Select statement for joining two tables

```
Select column-list
From table-1
    [Inner] Join table-2
    On table-1.column-1 {=|<|>|<=|>=|<>} table-2.column-2
[Where selection-criteria]
[Order By column-list]
```

A Select statement that joins data from the Products and Categories tables

```
Select ShortName, ProductID, Name, UnitPrice
From Products Inner Join Categories
    On Categories.CategoryID = Products.CategoryID
Order By Categories.CategoryID
```

The result set defined by the Select statement

ShortName	ProductID	Name	UnitPrice
Costumes	frankc01	Frankenstein	39.9900
Costumes	jar01	JarJar	59.9900
Costumes	martian01	Martian	69.9900
Costumes	pow01	Austin Powers	79.9900
Costumes	super01	Superman	39.9900
FX	skullfog01	Skull Fogger	39.9500
FX	str01	Mini-strobe	13.9900
FX	bl01	Black light (24")	24.9900
FX	fog01	Fog Machine	34.9900
FX	fogj01	Fog Juice (1qt)	9.9900
Masks	fred01	Freddie	29.9900
Masks	mum01	Mummy	39.9900
Masks	hippie01	Hippie	79.9900
Masks	vader01	Darth Vader Mask	19.9900
Props	spider01	Spider	12.9900
Props	tlm01	TLM	99.9900
Props	arm01	Severed Arm	19.9500
Props	rat01	Ugly Rat	14.9900
Props	rat02	Uglier Rat	19.9900
Props	skel01	Life Size Skeleton	14.9500
Props	head01	Shrunken Head	29.9900
Props	head02	Severed Head	29.9900
Props	cat01	Deranged Cat	19.9900
Props	cool01	Cool Ghoul	69.9900

Concepts

- A *join* lets you combine data from two or more tables into a single result set.
- The most common type of join is an *inner join*. This type of join returns rows from both tables only if their related columns match.

Figure 12-6   How to join data from two or more tables

How to add, update, and delete data in a table

Figure 12-7 presents the basic syntax of the SQL Insert, Update, and Delete statements. You use these statements to add new rows to a table, to update the data in existing rows, and to delete existing rows.

To add a single row to a table, you use an Insert statement with the syntax shown in this figure. With this syntax, you specify the name of the table you want to add the row to, the names of the columns you're supplying data for, and the values for those columns. In the example, the Insert statement adds a row to the Categories table and supplies a value for each of the three columns in that table. If a table allows nulls or provides default values for some columns, though, the Insert statement doesn't have to provide values for those columns.

To change the values of one or more columns in one or more rows, you use the Update statement. On this statement, you specify the name of the table you want to update, expressions that indicate the columns you want to change and how you want to change them, and a condition that identifies the rows you want to change. In the example, the Update statement changes the ShortName value for just the one row in the Categories table that has a CategoryID value of "food."

To delete one or more rows from a table, you use the Delete statement. On this statement, you specify the table you want to delete rows from and a condition that indicates the rows you want to delete. In the example, the Delete statement deletes just the one Categories row whose CategoryID column is "food."

How to add a single row

The syntax of the Insert statement for adding a single row

```
Insert [Into] table-name [(column-list)]
    Values (value-list)
```

A statement that adds a single row to a table

```
Insert Into Categories (CategoryID, ShortName, LongName)
    Values ("food", "Spooky Food", "The very best in Halloween cuisine")
```

How to update rows

The syntax of the Update statement

```
Update table-name
    Set expression-1 [, expression-2]...
    [Where selection-criteria]
```

A statement that changes the value of the ShortName column for a selected row

```
Update Categories
    Set ShortName = "Halloween cuisine"
    Where CategoryID = "food"
```

How to delete rows

The syntax of the Delete statement

```
Delete [From] table-name
    [Where selection-criteria]
```

A statement that deletes a specified category

```
Delete From Categories
    Where CategoryID = "food"
```

Description

- You use the Insert, Update, and Delete statements to maintain the data in a database table.

- The Insert statement can be used to add one or more rows to a table. Although the syntax shown above is for adding just one row, there is another syntax for adding more than one row.

- The Update and Delete statements can be used for updating or deleting one or more rows in a table using the syntax shown above.

Figure 12-7   How to add, update, and delete data in a table

An introduction to ADO.NET 2.0

ADO.NET 2.0 (*ActiveX Data Objects*) is the primary data access API for the .NET Framework. It provides the classes that are used when you develop database applications. The topics that follow introduce you to the important ADO.NET concepts.

How ADO.NET works

Figure 12-8 presents the primary ADO.NET objects that are used when you develop database applications. To start, the data used by an application is stored in a *dataset* that contains one or more *data tables*. To load data into a data table, you use a *data adapter*.

The main function of the data adapter is to manage the flow of data between a dataset and a database. To do that, it uses *commands* that define the SQL statements to be issued. The command for retrieving data, for example, typically defines a Select statement. Then, the command connects to the database using a *connection* and passes the Select statement to the database. After the Select statement is executed, the result set it produces is sent back to the data adapter, which stores the results in the data table.

To update the data in a database, the data adapter uses a command that defines an Insert, Update, or Delete statement for a data table. Then, the command uses the connection to connect to the database and perform the requested operation.

Although it's not apparent in this figure, the data in a dataset is independent of the database that the data was retrieved from. In fact, the connection to the database is typically closed after the data is retrieved from the database. Then, the connection is opened again when it's needed. Because of that, the application must work with the copy of the data that's stored in the dataset. The architecture that's used to implement this type of data processing is referred to as a *disconnected data architecture*. Although this is more complicated than a connected architecture, the advantages offset the complexity.

One of the advantages of using a disconnected data architecture is improved system performance due to the use of fewer system resources for maintaining connections. Another advantage is that it works well with ASP.NET web applications, which are inherently disconnected.

The ADO.NET classes that are responsible for working directly with a database are provided by the *.NET data providers*. These data providers include the classes you use to create data adapters, commands, and connections. The .NET Framework currently includes data providers for SQL Server, Oracle, OLE DB, and ODBC. Other third-party providers are also available.

Basic ADO.NET objects

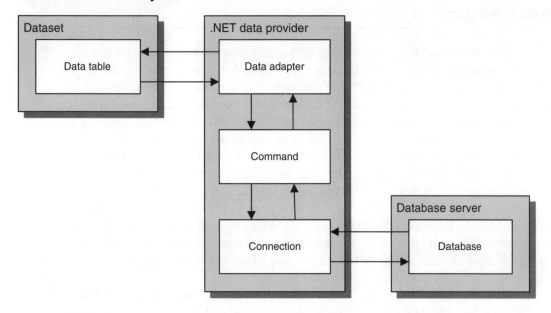

Description

- ADO.NET uses two types of objects to access the data in a database: *datasets*, which can contain one or more *data tables*, and *.NET data provider* objects, which include data adapters, commands, and connections.

- A dataset stores data from the database so it can be accessed by the application. The .NET data provider objects retrieve data from and update data in the database.

- To retrieve data from a database and store it in a data table, a *data adapter* object issues a Select statement that's stored in a *command* object. Next, the command object uses a *connection* object to connect to the database and retrieve the data. Then, the data is passed back to the data adapter, which stores the data in the dataset.

- To update the data in a database based on the data in a data table, the data adapter object issues an Insert, Update, or Delete statement that's stored in a command object. Then, the command object uses a connection to connect to the database and update the data.

- The data provider remains connected to the database only long enough to retrieve or update the specified data. Then, it disconnects from the database and the application works with the data via the dataset object. This is referred to as a *disconnected data architecture*.

- All of the ADO.NET objects are implemented by classes in the System.Data namespace of the .NET Framework. However, the specific classes used to implement the connection, command, and data adapter objects depend on the .NET data provider you use.

Figure 12-8   How ADO.NET works

Concurrency and the disconnected data architecture

Although the disconnected data architecture has advantages, it also has some disadvantages. One of those is the conflict that can occur when two or more users retrieve and then try to update data in the same row of a table. This is called a *concurrency* problem. This is possible because once a program retrieves data from a database, the connection to that database is dropped. As a result, the database management system can't manage the update process.

To illustrate, consider the situation shown in figure 12-9. Here, two users are using the Products table at the same time. These users could be using the same page of a web site or different pages that have accessed the Products table. Now, suppose that user 1 modifies the unit price in the row for a product and updates the Products table in the database. Suppose too that user 2 modifies the description in the row for the same product, and then tries to update the Products table in the database. What will happen? That will depend on the *concurrency control* that's used by the programs.

When you use ADO.NET, you have two choices for concurrency control. By default, a program uses *optimistic concurrency*, which checks whether a row has been changed since it was retrieved. If it has, the update or deletion will be refused and a *concurrency exception* will be thrown. Then, the program should handle the error. For example, it could display an error message that tells the user that the row could not be updated and then retrieve the updated row so the user can make the change again.

In contrast, the *"last in wins"* technique works the way its name implies. Since no checking is done with this technique, the row that's updated by the last user overwrites any changes made to the row by a previous user. For the example above, the row updated by user 2 will overwrite changes made by user 1, which means that the description will be right but the unit price will be wrong. Since errors like this corrupt the data in a database, optimistic concurrency is used by most programs, which means that your programs have to handle the concurrency exceptions that are thrown.

If you know that concurrency will be a problem, you can use a couple of programming techniques to limit concurrency exceptions. If a program uses a dataset, one technique is to update the database frequently so other users can retrieve the current data. The program should also refresh its dataset frequently so it contains the recent changes made by other users.

Another way to avoid concurrency exceptions is to retrieve and work with just one row at a time. That way, it's less likely that two users will update the same row at the same time. In contrast, if two users retrieve the same table, they will of course retrieve the same rows. Then, if they both update the same row in the table, even though it may not be at the same time, a concurrency exception will occur when they try to update the database.

Two users who are working with copies of the same data

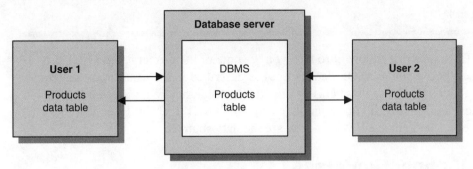

What happens when two users try to update the same row

- When two or more users retrieve the data in the same row of a database table at the same time, it is called *concurrency*. Because ADO.NET uses a disconnected data architecture, the database management system can't prevent this from happening.

- If two users try to update the same row in a database table at the same time, the second user's changes could overwrite the changes made by the first user. Whether or not that happens, though, depends on the *concurrency control* that the programs use.

- By default, ADO.NET uses *optimistic concurrency*. This means that the program checks to see whether the database row that's going to be updated or deleted has been changed since it was retrieved. If it has, a *concurrency exception* occurs and the update or deletion is refused. Then, the program should handle the exception.

- If optimistic concurrency isn't in effect, the program doesn't check to see whether a row has been changed before an update or deletion takes place. Instead, the operation proceeds without throwing an exception. This is referred to as *"last in wins"* because the last update overwrites any previous update. And this can lead to errors in the database.

How to avoid concurrency errors

- For many applications, concurrency errors rarely occur. As a result, optimistic concurrency is adequate because the users will rarely have to resubmit an update or deletion that is refused.

- If concurrency is likely to be a problem, a program that uses a dataset can be designed so it updates the database and refreshes the dataset frequently. That way, concurrency errors are less likely to occur.

- Another way to avoid concurrency errors is to design a program so it retrieves and updates just one row at a time. That way, there's less chance that two users will retrieve and update the same row at the same time.

Figure 12-9   Concurrency and the disconnected data architecture

An introduction to the ADO.NET 2.0 classes

The topics that follow introduce you to some of the primary ADO.NET 2.0 classes. When you use SQL data sources as described in the next three chapters, though, you don't use these classes directly. Instead, they're used behind the scenes. Incidentally, if you're familiar with ADO.NET 1.x, you'll see that these classes haven't changed. What's new are the data sources.

The SqlConnection class

Before you can access the data in a database, you have to create a connection object that defines the connection to the database. To do that, you use the SqlConnection class that's presented in figure 12-10.

The most important property of this class is ConnectionString. A *connection string* is a string that provides the information that's need to connect to a database. That means it includes information such as the name of the database and the database server. It can also contain authentication information such as a user-id and password.

The two methods of this class that are shown in this figure let you open and close the connection. In general, you should leave a connection open only while data is being retrieved or updated. When you use a data adapter, though, the connection is opened and closed for you so you don't need to use these methods.

The SqlCommand class

To execute a SQL statement against a SQL Server database, you create a SqlCommand object that contains the statement. Figure 12-10 presents the SqlCommand class you use to create this object. Notice that the Connection property of this class associates the command with a SqlConnection object, and the CommandText property contains the SQL statement to be executed.

The CommandType property indicates how the command object should interpret the value of the CommandText property. Instead of specifying a SQL statement for the CommandText property, for example, you can specify the name of a stored procedure, which consists of one or more SQL statements that have been compiled and stored with the database. Or you can specify the name of a table.

Earlier in this chapter, you learned that you can use a data adapter to execute command objects. In addition, you can execute a command object directly by using one of the three Execute methods shown in this figure. If, for example, you use ExecuteReader for a Select statement, the results are returned as a DataReader object. If you use ExecuteScalar, only the value in the first column and row of the query results is returned.

If the command contains an Insert, Update, or Delete statement, you'll use the ExecuteNonQuery method to execute it. This method returns an integer value

Common property and methods of the SqlConnection class

Property	Description
ConnectionString	Contains information that lets you connect to a SQL Server database, including the server name, the database name, and login information.

Method	Description
Open	Opens a connection to a database.
Close	Closes a connection to a database.

Common properties and methods of the SqlCommand class

Property	Description
Connection	The SqlConnection object used to connect to the database.
CommandText	The text of the SQL command or the name of a stored procedure or database table.
CommandType	A constant in the CommandType enumeration that indicates whether the CommandText property contains a SQL statement (Text), the name of a stored procedure (StoredProcedure), or the name of a database table (TableDirect).
Parameters	The collection of parameters used by the command.

Method	Description
ExecuteReader	Executes a query and returns the result as a SqlDataReader object.
ExecuteNonQuery	Executes the command and returns an integer representing the number of rows affected.
ExecuteScalar	Executes a query and returns the first column of the first row returned by the query.

Common properties of the SqlParameter class

Property	Description
ParameterName	The name of the parameter.
Value	The value assigned to the parameter.
SqlDbType	The SQL data type for the parameter.

Description

- A SqlConnection object is required to establish a connection to a SQL Server database.
- A SqlCommand object is used to execute a SQL command against a SQL Server database.
- A SqlParameter object is used to pass variable information to a SQL command.

Figure 12-10   The SqlConnection, SqlCommand, and SqlParameter classes

that indicates the number of rows that were affected by the command. If, for example, the command deletes a single row, the ExecuteNonQuery method returns 1.

The SqlParameter class

The SqlParameter class, also shown in figure 12-10, lets you pass parameter values to a SQL command. Parameters are commonly used to limit the number of rows retrieved by a Select statement. For example, you can retrieve the Product row for a specific product by passing the ProductID as a parameter. Or, you can retrieve all of the products for a given category by passing the CategoryID as a parameter. Parameters are also commonly used to pass column values to Insert and Update statements.

The SqlDataReader class

Figure 12-11 lists the most important properties and methods of the SqlDataReader class. You use this class to create a data reader object, which provides an efficient way to read the rows in a result set returned by a database query. In fact, when you use a data adapter to retrieve data, the data adapter uses a data reader to read through the rows in the result set and store them in a dataset.

A data reader is similar to other types of readers you may have encountered in the .NET Framework, such as a TextReader, a StreamReader, or an XmlReader. Like these other readers, a data reader lets you read rows but not modify them. In other words, a data reader is read-only. In addition, it only lets you read rows in a forward direction. Once you read the next row, the previous row is unavailable.

The SqlDataAdapter class

As you have learned, the job of a data adapter is to provide a link between a database and a dataset. The four properties of the SqlDataAdapter class listed in figure 12-11, for example, identify the four SQL commands that the data adapter uses to transfer data from the database to the dataset and vice versa. The SelectCommand property identifies the command object that's used to retrieve data from the database. And the DeleteCommand, InsertCommand, and UpdateCommand properties identify the commands that are used to update the database based on changes made to the data in the dataset.

To execute the command identified by the SelectCommand property and place the data that's retrieved in a dataset, you use the Fill method. Then, the application can work with the data in the dataset without affecting the data in the database. If the application makes changes to the data in the dataset, it can use the data adapter's Update method to execute the commands identified by the DeleteCommand, InsertCommand, and UpdateCommand properties and post the changes back to the database.

Common properties and methods of the SqlDataReader class

Property	Description
Item	Accesses the column with the specified index or name from the current row.
FieldCount	The number of columns in the current row.

Method	Description
Read	Reads the next row. Returns True if there are more rows. Otherwise, returns False.
Close	Closes the data reader.

Common properties and methods of the SqlDataAdapter class

Property	Description
SelectCommand	A SqlCommand object representing the Select statement used to query the database.
DeleteCommand	A SqlCommand object representing the Delete statement used to delete a row from the database.
InsertCommand	A SqlCommand object representing the Insert statement used to add a row to the database.
UpdateCommand	A SqlCommand object representing the Update statement used to update a row in the database.

Method	Description
Fill	Executes the command identified by the SelectCommand property and loads the result into a dataset object.
Update	Executes the commands identified by the DeleteCommand, InsertCommand, and UpdateCommand properties for each row in the dataset that was deleted, added, or updated.

Description

- A data reader provides read-only, forward-only access to the data in a database. Because it doesn't require the overhead of a dataset, it's more efficient than using a data adapter. However, it can't be used to update data.
- When the Fill method of a data adapter is used to retrieve data from a database, the data adapter uses a data reader to load the results into a dataset.

Figure 12-11   The SqlDataReader and SqlDataAdapter classes

Perspective

This chapter has introduced you to the basic concepts of relational databases and described how you use SQL and ADO.NET classes to work with the data in a relational database. With that as background, you're now ready to learn how to develop ASP.NET database applications.

In the next three chapters, then, you'll learn how to use SQL data sources and three of the data controls to build database applications. After that, chapter 16 will show you how to use object data sources to build 3-layer database applications. Although you don't need to use ADO.NET directly when you use SQL data sources, you do need to use ADO.NET directly when you use object data sources.

Terms

Microsoft SQL Server Express	default value
Microsoft SQL Server 2005	identity column
relational database	check constraint
table	SQL dialect
record	Transact-SQL
row	result table
field	result set
column	calculated column
primary key	join
composite primary key	inner join
non-primary key	ADO.NET
unique key	ActiveX Data Objects .NET
unique key constraint	dataset
unique constraint	data table
index	.NET data provider
foreign key	data adapter
foreign key table	command
primary key table	connection
one-to-many relationship	disconnected data architecture
one-to-one relationship	concurrency
many-to-many relationship	concurrency control
linking table	optimistic concurrency
data type	concurrency exception
system data type	last in wins
null value	connection string

13

How to use SQL data sources

The data source controls are one of the most important new features of
ASP.NET 2.0. In this chapter, you'll learn how to use the SqlDataSource
control, which lets you access data from a SQL Server database with little or
no programming. Along the way, you'll also learn how to use the DataList
control, which lets you create lists of data.

How to create a SQL data source

In chapter 3, you learned the basics of using the AccessDataSource control to get data from an Access data source. Now, in the topics that follow, you'll learn how to use a SqlDataSource control, which can be referred to as a *SQL data source,* to get data from a SQL Server database.

A Product List application that uses two SQL data sources

Figure 13-1 shows a simple one-page application that demonstrates the use of two SQL data sources. The drop-down list at the top of the page is bound to a SQL data source that gets the categories for the products that the company offers. Then, when the user selects a category from this list, the products for the selected category are retrieved from a second SQL data source, which is bound to a DataList control that's below the drop-down list. As a result, the products are displayed in the DataList control.

Since this application relies entirely on the data binding that's established in the Web Forms Designer, the code-behind file for this application contains no Visual Basic code. That illustrates one of the major improvements in ASP.NET 2.0: the amount of database handling code that you have to write for a typical database application is drastically reduced. In fact, even complicated applications that insert, update, and delete database data can often be written with little or no code.

That's not to say that most ASP.NET database applications are code-free. In chapters 14 and 15, for example, you'll see applications that require database handling code. In particular, these applications require code to detect database errors and concurrency violations and display appropriate error messages. Also, as you'll learn in chapter 16, you can use object data sources to build 3-layer applications that require extensive amounts of database handling code.

The Product List application displayed in a web browser

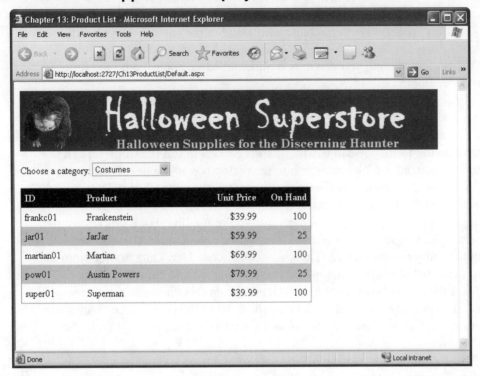

Description

- The Product List application uses two SqlDataSource controls to get category and product data from a SQL Server database and display it in two bound controls.
- The drop-down list near the top of the form displays the product categories. This control is bound to the first data source control.
- The DataList control, which is bound to the second data source control, displays the data for the products that are in the category that's selected in the drop-down list.
- This application requires no Visual Basic code in the code-behind file.

Figure 13-1   The Product List application

How to create a SqlDataSource control

Figure 13-2 shows how to create a SqlDataSource control. As you will see, this process is similar to the one for creating an AccessDataSource control. To get the process started, you can drag a SqlDataSource control onto the form you're developing.

Since a data source control isn't displayed on the page when the application is run, it doesn't matter where you drop this control. But it does make sense to place it near the control that it will be bound to. Once you've got the data source control on the form, you can use its smart tag menu to run the Configure Data Source command, which brings you to the dialog box in the next figure.

You can also create a SqlDataSource control using the Choose Data Source command in the smart tag menu of a bindable control. The exact technique for doing that varies depending on the control you're binding. For a drop-down list, for example, you select the Choose Data Source command to start the Data Source Configuration Wizard. Then, you can choose New Data Source from the drop-down list in the first dialog box that's displayed and click OK. That displays the dialog box shown in this figure. From this dialog box, you can select the Database icon and click OK, which drops the data source control onto the form next to the bindable control and brings you to the dialog box in the next figure.

The technique for creating a SQL data source from a DataList control is similar. The only difference is that the Choose Data Source command in the control's smart tag menu includes a drop-down list that lets you select New Data Source. When you do that, the Data Source Configuration Wizard dialog box shown in this figure is displayed just as it is for a drop-down list.

The starting dialog box of the Data Source Configuration Wizard

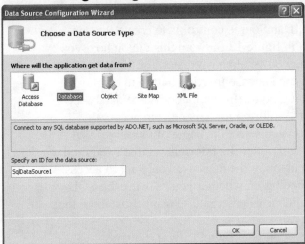

Aspx code generated for a basic SqlDataSource control

```
<asp:SqlDataSource ID="SqlDataSource1" runat="server"
    ConnectionString="<%$ ConnectionStrings:HalloweenConnectionString %>"
    SelectCommand="SELECT [CategoryID], [LongName] FROM [Categories]
        ORDER BY [LongName]">
</asp:SqlDataSource>
```

Basic SqlDataSource control attributes

Attribute	Description
ID	The ID for the SqlDataSource control.
Runat	Must specify "server."
ConnectionString	The connection string. In most cases, you should use a <%$ expression to specify the name of a connection string saved in the web.config file (see figure 13-4).
ProviderName	The name of the provider used to access the database. Values can be System.Data.Odbc, System.Data.Oledb, System.Data.OracleClient, or System.Data.SqlClient. The default is System.Data.SqlClient.
SelectCommand	The SQL Select statement executed by the data source to retrieve data.

Description

- To create a SqlDataSource control, drag the control from the Data group of the Toolbox onto the form. Then, choose Configure Data Source from the control's smart tag menu and proceed from there.
- Once the SqlDataSource control has been configured, you can bind controls to it so they get their data from the SQL data source.
- You can also create a SQL data source using the Choose Data Source command in the smart tag menu of a bindable control. When you use this command, the dialog box shown above is displayed. Then, you can select the Database icon and proceed from there.

Figure 13-2   How to create a SqlDataSource control

How to define the connection

The first step in configuring a SqlDataSource control is to create the connection for the data source, as shown in figure 13-3. From this dialog box, you can select an existing connection (one you've already created for this project or for another project), or you can click the New Connection button to display the Add Connection dialog box. This dialog box helps you identify the database that you want to access and provide the information you need to access it.

In the Add Connection dialog box, you select the name of the server that contains the database you want to access, enter the information that's required to log on to the server, and select the name of the database you want to access. How you do that, though, varies depending on whether you're using the SQL Server Express Edition on your own PC or whether you're using a database that resides on a database server.

If you're using SQL Server Express on your own PC, you can type localhost\sqlexpress for the server name. Alternatively, you can select the server name from the drop-down list, which will include your computer name like this: ANNEPC\SQLEXPRESS. If you will be porting your applications from one computer to another, though, it's best to use localhost. That way, you won't have to change the server name to refer to the correct computer.

For the logon information, you can click on the Use Windows Authentication option. Then, SQL Server Express will use the login name and password that you use for your computer as the name and password for the database too. As a result, you won't need to provide a separate user name and password in this dialog box. Last, you select the name of the database that you want to connect to. When you're done, you can click on the Test Connection button to be sure that the connection works.

In contrast, if you're using a database on a server computer, you need to get the connection information from the network or database administrator. That will include the server name, logon information, and database name. Once you establish a connection to a database, you can use that connection for all of the other applications that use that database.

The dialog boxes for defining a connection

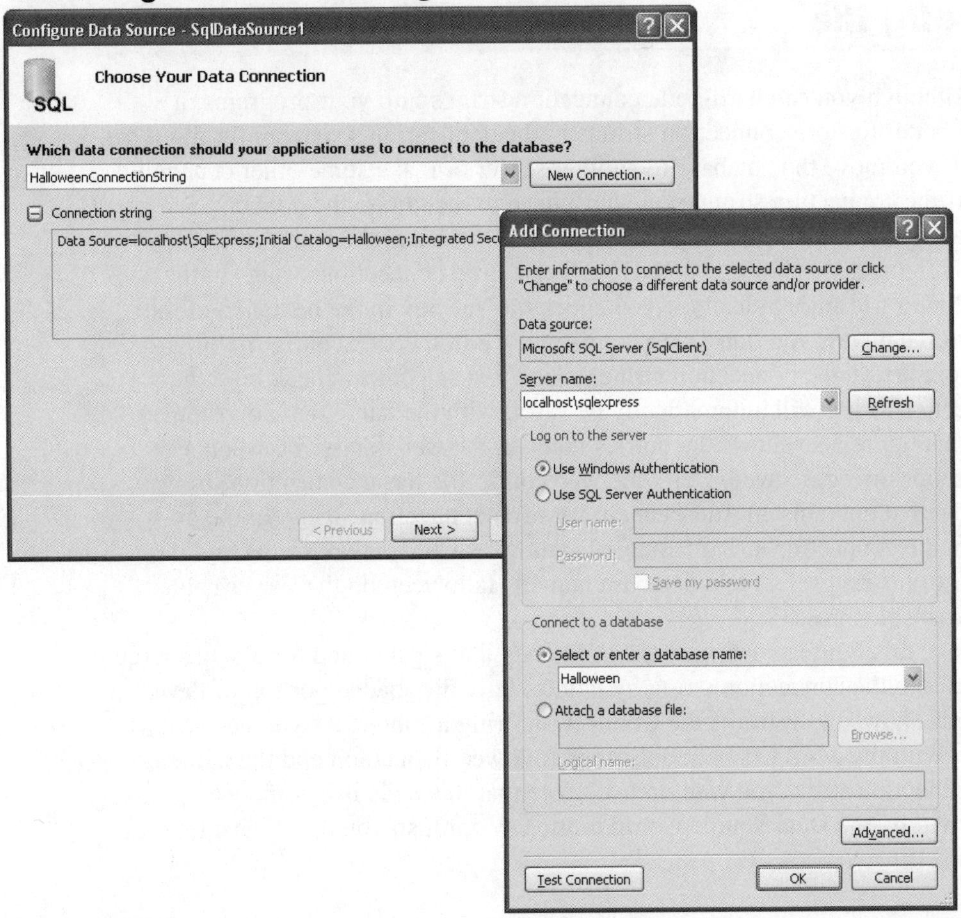

Description

- The Configure Data Source dialog box asks you to identify the data connection for the database you want to use. If you've previously created a connection for that database, you can select it from the drop-down list. To see the connection string for that connection, click the + button below the drop-down list.

- To create a new connection, click the New Connection button to display the Add Connection dialog box. Then, enter the name of the database server in the Server Name text box or select it from the drop-down list. For SQL Server Express, you can use localhost\sqlexpress as the server name.

- After you enter the server name, select the authentication mode you want to use (we recommend Windows Authentication). Then, select the database you want to connect to from the Select or Enter a Database Name drop-down list.

- To be sure that the connection is configured properly, you can click the Test Connection button.

Figure 13-3   How to define the connection

How to save the connection string in the web.config file

Although you can hard-code connection strings into your programs, it's much better to store connection strings in the application's web.config file. That way, if you move the database to another server or make some other change that affects the connection string, you won't have to recompile the application. Instead, you can simply change the connection string in the web.config file.

As figure 13-4 shows, ASP.NET 2.0 can store connection strings in the web.config file automatically if you check the Yes box in the next step of the wizard. That way, you don't have to manually edit the web.config file or write code to retrieve the connection string. When you select this check box, the connection string will automatically be saved with the name that you supply.

This figure also shows the entries made in the web.config file when a connection string is saved. Here, the web.config file has a connectionStrings element that contains an Add element for each connection string. In the example, the connection string is named HalloweenConnectionString. And the connection string refers to a database named Halloween on the server named localhost\sqlexpress.

Last, this figure shows how the aspx code that's generated for a data source can refer to the connection string by name. Here, the shaded portion of the example shows the value of the ConnectionString attribute. As you can see, it begins with the word ConnectionStrings followed by a colon and the name of the connection string you want to use. Note that this code is automatically generated by the Data Source Configuration Wizard, so you don't have to write it yourself.

The dialog box for saving the connection string in the web.config file

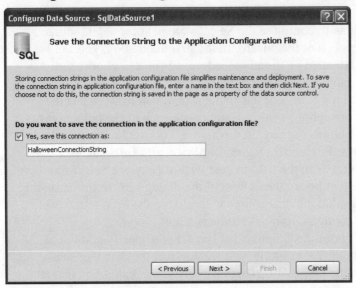

The ConnectionStrings section of the web.config file

```
<connectionStrings>
    <add name="HalloweenConnectionString"
        connectionString="Data Source=localhost\sqlexpress;
        Initial Catalog=Halloween;Integrated Security=True"
        providerName="System.Data.SqlClient" />
</connectionStrings>
```

Aspx code that refers to a connection string in the web.config file

```
<asp:SqlDataSource ID="SqlDataSource1" runat="server"
    ConnectionString="<%$ ConnectionStrings:HalloweenConnectionString %>"
    SelectCommand="SELECT [CategoryID], [LongName] FROM [Categories]
        ORDER BY [LongName]">
</asp:SqlDataSource>
```

Description

- ASP.NET 2.0 applications can store connection strings in the web.config file.
- If you choose to save the connection string in the web.config file, the ConnectionString attribute of the data source control will include a special code that retrieves the connection string from the web.config file.
- If you choose not to save the connection string in the web.config file, the ConnectionString attribute of the data source control will specify the actual connection string.
- We recommend that you always save the connection string in the web.config file. Then, if the location of the database changes, you can change the connection string in the web.config file rather than in each page that uses the connection.

Figure 13-4   How to save the connection string in the web.config file

How to configure the Select statement

Figure 13-5 shows how to configure the Select statement for a data source as you proceed through the steps of the wizard. In the first dialog box, you can specify a custom SQL statement or stored procedure, or you can choose the columns for the query from a single table or view.

To select columns from a table, use the Name drop-down list to select the table you want to select the columns from. Then, check each of the columns you want to retrieve in the Columns list box. In this figure, I chose the Products table and selected four columns: ProductID, Name, UnitPrice, and OnHand.

As you check the columns in the list box, the wizard creates a Select statement that's shown in the text box at the bottom of the dialog box. In this case, the Select statement indicates that the data source will retrieve the ProductID, Name, UnitPrice, and OnHand columns from the Products table.

The buttons to the right of the Columns list box let you specify additional options for selecting data. If, for example, you want to sort the data that's retrieved, you can click on the ORDER BY button to display a dialog box that lets you select up to three sort columns. If you want to select specific types of records, you can click on the WHERE button to display the dialog box that's described in the next figure. And if you want to use an advanced feature, you can click on the Advanced button to display the dialog box that's described in figure 13-16.

When you finish specifying the data you want the data source to retrieve, click Next. This takes you to a page that includes a Test Query button. If you click this button, the wizard immediately retrieves the data that you specified. You can then look over this data to make sure the query retrieves the data you expected. If it doesn't, click the Back button and adjust the query as needed.

The second dialog box in this figure is the one that you use to specify a custom SQL statement or stored procedure. As you can see, this dialog box includes tabs that also let you enter Update, Insert, and Delete statements for the data source. You can also click on the Query Builder button to open the Query Builder, which lets you visually create advanced Select statements that include joins and other features. You'll learn more about the Query Builder in figure 13-8.

The dialog box for defining the Select statement

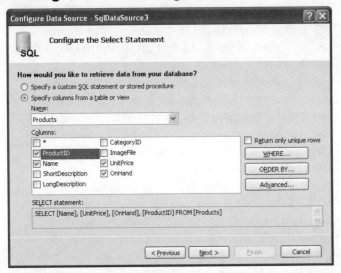

The dialog box for entering a custom Select statement

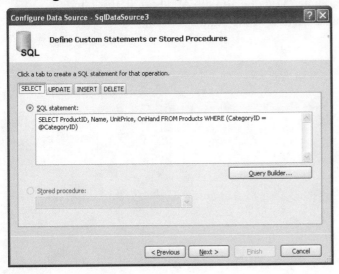

Description

- To configure the Select statement, you choose whether you want to use custom SQL statements or specify the columns from a table or view in the database.

- If you choose to select the columns from a table or view, you can choose the table or view and columns you want retrieved. You can click the ORDER BY button to specify how the records should be sorted. And you can click the WHERE button to specify the selection criteria as shown in figure 13-6.

- If you choose to use custom SQL statements, the next dialog box lets you enter the SQL statements or click the Query Builder button to build the query as shown in figure 13-8.

Figure 13-5   How to configure the Select statement

How to create a Where clause

If you click on the WHERE button shown in the first dialog box in figure 13-5, the Add WHERE Clause dialog box in figure 13-6 is displayed. It lets you create a Where clause and parameters for the Select statement.

A Where clause is made up of one or more conditions that limit the rows retrieved by the Select statement. To create these conditions, the Add WHERE Clause dialog box lets you compare the values in the columns of a database table with several different types of data, including a literal value, the value of another control on the page, the value of a query string passed via the page's URL, a profile property (see chapter 19), or a cookie.

For example, the Select statement for the data source that's bound to the DataList control in the Product List application uses a Where clause that compares the CategoryID column in the Products table with the category selected from the drop-down list. To create this Where clause, select CategoryID in the Column drop-down list, the equals operator in the Operator drop-down list, and Control in the Source drop-down list. Next, select ddlCategory in the Control ID drop-down list. When you do, the SelectedValue property of the control is automatically selected. Then, when you click on the Add button, this condition is shown in the WHERE clause section of the dialog box.

The Add WHERE Clause dialog box

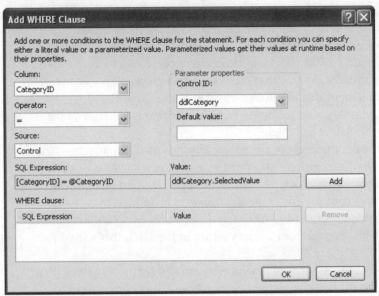

The WHERE clause section after a condition has been added

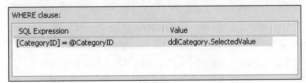

Description

- The Add WHERE Clause dialog box lets you specify a Where clause for the Select statement.

- The Where clause consists of one or more conditions that you construct by using the controls in this dialog box. To create a condition, you select the column you want to compare, the operator you want to use for the comparison, and the source of the data to use for the comparison. Then, you must click Add to add the condition to the list of Where clause conditions.

- The source of the data for the comparison can be a literal value, the value of another control on the form, a cookie, an HTML form field, a profile property, a query string in the URL for the page, or a value stored in session state.

Remember

- After you select the column, operator, and source for the comparison, be sure to click the Add button to add the condition to the generated Where clause. Otherwise, the condition won't be added to the Where clause.

Figure 13-6   How to create a Where clause

How select parameters work

When you create a Where clause as described in the previous figure, the wizard creates one or more *select parameters* that provide the values used by the Where clause. Figure 13-7 shows how these select parameters work. As you can see, each SqlDataSource control that includes select parameters is defined by a SqlDataSource element that includes a child element named SelectParameters. Then, this element contains a child element for each of the parameters used by the Select statement.

The select parameters themselves are defined by one of the elements listed in the first table. Each of these elements specifies a parameter whose value is obtained from a different type of source. For example, if the parameter's value is obtained from a form control, this *control parameter* is defined by a ControlParameter element. Similarly, the QueryStringParameter element defines a parameter whose value comes from a query string in the URL that's used for the page.

The second table in this figure lists the attributes used by the ControlParameter element to define a parameter whose value comes from a form control. As you can see, these attributes provide the name of the parameter, the SQL data type used for the parameter, the ID of the form control that provides the value, and the name of the property used to obtain the value.

The code example at the top of this figure shows the aspx code generated for the second SqlDataSource control used by the Product List application. Here, the Select statement uses one parameter named CategoryID. This parameter is defined by a ControlParameter element whose Name attribute is set to CategoryID. The SQL data type for this parameter is String, and the parameter's value is obtained from the SelectedValue property of the form control whose ID is ddlCategory.

Please note that the code in this example is generated by the Web Forms Designer when you configure the data source using the Data Source Configuration Wizard. As a result, you don't have to write this code yourself.

The aspx code for a SqlDataSource control that includes a select parameter

```
<asp:SqlDataSource
    ConnectionString="<%$ ConnectionStrings:HalloweenConnectionString %>"
    ID="SqlDataSource2" runat="server"
    SelectCommand="SELECT [ProductID], [Name], [UnitPrice], [OnHand]
        FROM [Products]
        WHERE ([CategoryID] = @CategoryID)
        ORDER BY [ProductID]">
    <SelectParameters>
        <asp:ControlParameter Name="CategoryID" Type="String"
            ControlID="ddlCategory" PropertyName="SelectedValue" />
    </SelectParameters>
</asp:SqlDataSource>
```

Elements used to define select parameters

Element	Description
SelectParameters	Contains a child element for each parameter used by the data source's Select statement.
ControlParameter	Defines a parameter that gets its value from a control on the page.
QueryStringParameter	Defines a parameter that gets its value from a query string in the URL used to request the page.
FormParameter	Defines a parameter that gets its value from an HTML form field.
SessionParameter	Defines a parameter that gets its value from an item in session state.
ProfileParameter	Defines a parameter that gets its value from a property of the user's profile.
CookieParameter	Defines a parameter that gets its value from a cookie.

The ControlParameter element

Attribute	Description
Name	The parameter name.
Type	The SQL data type of the parameter.
ControlID	The ID of the web form control that supplies the value for the parameter.
PropertyName	The name of the property from the web form control that supplies the value for the parameter.

Description

- The SelectParameters element defines the *select parameters* that are used by the Select statement of a data source. The aspx code that defines these parameters is generated automatically when you use the Add WHERE Clause dialog box to create parameters.

- A *control parameter* is a parameter whose value is obtained from another control on a web form, such as the value selected by a drop-down list. Control parameters are defined by the ControlParameter element.

- Once you understand how to use control parameters, you shouldn't have any trouble learning how to use the other types of parameters on your own.

Figure 13-7   How select parameters work

How to use the Query Builder

You may have used the *Query Builder* with previous versions of Visual Studio. If so, you'll be glad to know that the Query Builder is still available, although it's a little harder to get to now. The topics that follow explain how to use it.

How to create a Select statement with the Query Builder

To use the Query Builder, you tell the wizard that you want to specify a custom SQL statement or stored procedure in the first dialog box shown in figure 13-5. Then, when the next dialog box appears, you click the Query Builder button to display the dialog box shown in figure 13-8.

When the Query Builder window opens, the Add Table dialog box is displayed. This dialog box, which isn't shown in this figure, lists all of the tables and views in the database that the data source is connected to. You can use this dialog box to add one or more tables to the *diagram pane* of the Query Builder window so you can use them in your query. In this figure, for example, the Products table has been added to the diagram pane.

In the *grid pane*, which appears beneath the diagram pane, you can see the columns that will be included in the query. To add columns to this pane, you just check the boxes before the column names in the diagram pane. You can also enter an expression in the Column column of the grid pane to create a calculated column, and you can enter a name in the Alias column to give the calculated column a name.

Once the columns have been added to the grid pane, you can use the Sort Type column to identify any columns that should be used to sort the returned rows and the Sort Order column to give the order of precedence for the sort if more than one column is identified. The Query Builder uses these specifications to build the Order By clause for the Select statement.

You can use the Filter column to establish the criteria to be used to select the rows that will be retrieved by the query. For the query in this figure, a parameter named @CategoryID is specified for the CategoryID column. As a result, only the products whose CategoryID field matches the value of the @CategoryID parameter will be retrieved.

The Query Builder dialog box

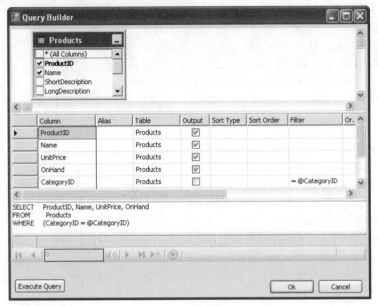

Description

- The *Query Builder* is displayed if you choose to enter a custom Select statement, and then click the Query Builder button in the dialog box that follows.

- The Query Builder lets you build a Select statement by choosing columns from one or more tables and views and specifying the sort order and filter criteria for each column.

- When you first start the Query Builder, a dialog box is displayed that lets you select the database tables you want to include in the query. Each table you select is displayed in the *diagram pane* at the top of the Query Builder window.

- If you add two related tables to the diagram pane, the Query Builder automatically joins the two tables by including a Join phrase in the From clause. You can also create a join by dragging a column from one table to a column in another table.

- To include a column from a table, use the check box that appears next to the column in the diagram. This adds the column to the *grid pane* that appears beneath the diagram pane. Then, you can specify any sorting or filtering requirements for the column.

- You can use a parameter in an expression in the Filter column to create a parameterized query. If you use one or more parameters in the query, the Data Source Configuration Wizard lets you specify the source of the parameter values, as described in figure 13-9.

- As you select columns and specify sort and selection criteria, the Query Builder builds the Select statement and displays it in the *SQL pane*.

- To display the results of the query, click the Execute Query button. If the query includes parameters, you will be asked to enter the value of each parameter.

Figure 13-8   How to create a Select statement with the Query Builder

How to define the parameters

If you specify one or more parameters when you create a Select statement with the Query Builder, the next dialog box lets you define those parameters as shown in figure 13-9. Here, the list box on the left side of the dialog box lists each of the parameters you created in the Query Builder. To define the source for one of these parameters, you select the parameter in this list box. Then, you can use the controls on the right side of the dialog box to select the parameter's source.

In this example, the source of the CategoryID parameter is set to the SelectedValue property of the control named ddlCategory. When I selected the ddlCategory control, the SelectedValue property was selected by default. If you want to use a different property as the source for a parameter, however, you can click the Show Advanced Properties link to display a list of the parameter properties. Then, you can set the PropertyName property to the control property you want to use.

The dialog box for defining parameters

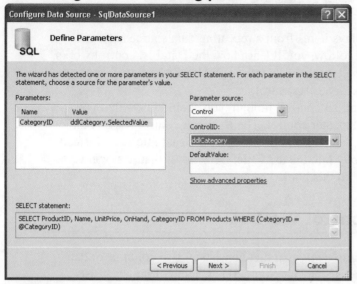

Parameter sources

Source	Description
Control	The parameter's value comes from a control on the page.
QueryString	The parameter's value comes from a query string in the URL used to request the page.
Form	The parameter's value comes from an HTML form field.
Session	The parameter's value comes from an item in session state.
Profile	The parameter's value comes from a property of the user's profile.
Cookie	The parameter's value comes from a cookie.

Description

- If you specify one or more parameters when you use the Query Builder to define a Select statement, the next dialog box lets you define those parameters.
- To define a parameter, you specify the source of the value for each parameter.

Figure 13-9   How to define the parameters

How to use the DataList control

A DataList control displays items from a repeating data source such as a data table. In the topics that follow, you'll learn how the DataList control works, you'll learn how to create the templates that define a DataList control, and you'll learn how to format a DataList control.

Before I present the DataList control, though, you should know that you can also create a list using the Repeater control. The Repeater control has one major drawback, however. That is, you can't define it using a visual interface. Instead, you have to enter code directly into the aspx file. Because of that, we won't present the Repeater control in this book.

How the DataList control works

Figure 13-10 shows a simple *data list* that consists of two columns of data. To create a list like this, you use the DataSourceID attribute of the DataList control to bind the control to a data source. Then, you define one or more *templates* within the control that define the content and format of the list.

In the aspx code shown in this figure, you can see that the source of data for the data list is a SQL data source control named SqlDataSource2. You can also see that a single Item template is used to create this list. This template includes two label controls that are bound to the Name and UnitPrice columns of the data source. You'll learn about the expressions you use to accomplish this binding later in this chapter.

A simple list displayed by a DataList control

```
Austin Powers $79.99
Frankenstein $39.99
JarJar $59.99
Martian $69.99
Superman $39.99
```

The asp tag for the DataList control

```
<asp:DataList ID="DataList1" runat="server" DataSourceID="SqlDataSource2">
    <ItemTemplate>
        <asp:Label ID="lblName" runat="server"
            Text='<%# Eval("Name") %>'></asp:Label>
        <asp:Label ID="lblUnitPrice" runat="server"
            Text='<%# Eval("UnitPrice", "{0:c}") %>'></asp:Label>
    </ItemTemplate>
</asp:DataList>
```

Basic attributes of the DataList control

Attribute	Description
ID	The ID for the DataList control.
Runat	Must specify "server."
DataSourceID	The ID of the data source to bind the data list to.

Description

- A *data list* displays a list of items from the data source that it's bound to. To bind a data list to a data source, use the Choose Data Source command in the control's smart tag menu.

- To define the information to be displayed in a data list, you create one or more *templates*. Visual Studio provides a designer interface you can use to create the templates as shown in the next figure.

- To display the data from a column in the data source in a data list, you add a control to a template and then bind that control. See figure 13-14 for more information.

- You can use a DataList control for edit operations as well as display operations. However, you're more likely to use the GridView, DetailsView, and FormView controls for edit operations.

Figure 13-10   How the DataList control works

How to define the templates for a data list

Figure 13-11 shows you how to define the templates for a data list. The table in this figure lists the templates you're most likely to use. Although you can also create templates that let the user select and edit items in the list, you're not likely to use a DataList control for these functions. Instead, you'll use the GridView, DetailsView, or FormView controls as described in the next two chapters.

The only template that's required for a data list is the Item template, which defines how each item in the data source is displayed. Depending on the requirements of your application, though, you may need to use one or more of the other templates as well. For example, you'll typically use a Header template to create headings that are displayed in the first row of the data list.

To define the templates for a data list, you work in *template-editing mode*. At the top of this figure, for example, you can see the Item template for a list that includes four columns. This template is displayed by default when you enter template-editing mode. To display a different template, you can use the Display drop-down list in the smart tag menu for the control. You can also display a group of related templates by selecting the group name from this list. For example, you can display both the Header and Footer templates by selecting the Header and Footer Templates item.

If a data list consists of two or more columns, you'll want to place the text and controls in each template within a table. That way, you can set the width of each column in the data list by setting the widths of the columns in the table. In addition, if you add two or more templates to a data list, you can align the columns in the templates by setting the widths of the corresponding table columns to the same values. In this illustration, for example, I set the Width attributes of the corresponding columns in the Item template and the Header template to the same values.

Before I go on, you should realize that you use templates to define the content of a data list and not its appearance. For example, you use the AlternatingItem template to display different content for every other row in a data list, not to shade or highlight every other row. To format a data list, you use styles as shown in the next figure.

The Item template in template-editing mode

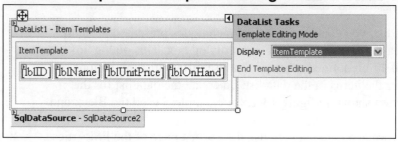

A Header template

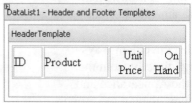

Common template elements for a data list

Element	Description
HeaderTemplate	Displayed before the first item in the data source.
FooterTemplate	Displayed after the last item in the data source.
ItemTemplate	Displayed for each item in the data source.
AlternatingItemTemplate	Displayed for alternating items in the data source.
SeparatorTemplate	Displayed between items.

Description

* The templates you define for a data list specify what content to display and what controls to use to display it. At the least, you must create an Item template that defines the items from the data source that you want to display.

* To create a template, choose Edit Templates from the smart tag menu for the control to display the control in *template-editing mode*. Then, select the template or group of templates you want to edit from the smart tag menu.

* To add text to a template, click in the template and begin typing. To add a control to a template, drag the control from the Toolbox onto the template, then use the Properties window or the control's smart tag menu to set its properties. When you're finished, choose End Template Editing from the smart tag menu.

* To line up the text and controls in two or more templates, place them in tables within the templates and set the column widths to the same values.

* When you set the data source for a DataList control, Visual Studio creates a default Item template. This template includes a text box for each column in the data source preceded by text that identifies the column.

Figure 13-11   How to define the templates for a data list

How to format a data list

To format a data list, you can use one of the techniques presented in figure 13-12. The easiest way is to use the Auto Format dialog box. This dialog box lets you select one of 17 predefined schemes that use different combinations of colors and borders for the items in the data list. To create the data list for the Product List application shown in figure 13-1, for example, I used the Black and Blue 1 scheme.

Another way to format a data list is to use the Format page of the Properties dialog box shown in this figure. This dialog box lets you set the colors, fonts, alignment, and other formatting options for the data list and each of its templates. Note that you can use this dialog box to customize an Auto Format scheme or to design your own scheme.

The Auto Format and Properties dialog boxes provide convenient ways to format a data list. However, you can also apply formatting directly from the Properties window. To do that, you use the properties in the Appearance and Style sections of this window, which are available when you display the properties by category. The properties in the Appearance section apply to the data list as a whole, and the properties in the Style section apply to the templates that make up the data list. To set the properties for the Item template, for example, you can expand the ItemStyle group, and to set the properties for the Header template, you can expand the HeaderStyle group.

This figure also presents the five style elements you're most likely to use with a data list. When you use one of the techniques in this figure to format the templates in a data list, the appropriate style elements are generated for you. In this figure, for example, you can see the HeaderStyle element that was generated when I applied the Black and Blue 1 scheme to the product list in figure 13-1. Of course, you can also format a data list by entering style elements directly into the aspx code. That's not usually necessary, however.

The Format page of the Properties dialog box

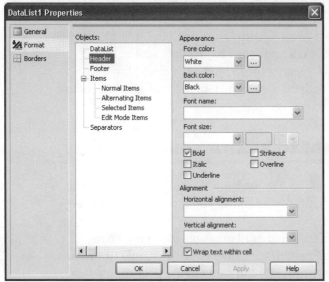

Common style elements for a data list

Element	Description
HeaderStyle	The style used for the header.
FooterStyle	The style used for the footer.
ItemStyle	The style used for each item in the data source.
AlternatingItemStyle	The style used for alternating items in the data source.
SeparatorStyle	The style for the separator.

The asp tag for a Header style

```
<HeaderStyle BackColor="Black" Font-Bold="True" ForeColor="White" />
```

Description

- You can format a data list by applying a predefined scheme, by using the Properties dialog box, by using the Properties window, or by editing the aspx code.

- To apply a scheme, choose AutoFormat from the control's smart tag menu and then select the scheme you want to apply.

- To use the Properties dialog box, choose Property Builder from the control's smart tag menu and then set the properties for the data list and its templates.

- To use the Properties window to format a template, expand the style property for that template and then set its properties.

Figure 13-12   How to format a data list

How to use data binding

Once you've configured a data source control, you can bind it to a web form control to automatically display the data retrieved by the data source on the page. In the following topics, you'll learn how to bind a list control to a data source and how to bind controls defined within the templates of another control like a DataList control.

How to bind a list control to a data source

In chapter 6, you learned about the five list controls that you can use in an ASP.NET 2.0 application. Now, figure 13-13 shows you how you can bind any of these controls to a data source.

The table in this figure shows the three attributes you use to bind a list control to a data source. The DataSourceID attribute provides the ID of the data source. The DataTextField attribute provides the name of the data source field that's displayed in the list. And the DataValueField attribute provides the name of the data source field that is returned by the SelectedValue property when the user selects an item from the list.

You can set these attributes manually by using the Properties window or by directly editing the aspx code. Or, you can use the Data Source Configuration Wizard shown at the top of this figure to set these properties. To do that, display the smart tag menu for the list and select Choose Data Source. Then, use the wizard's controls to set the data source, display field, and value field.

The code example in this figure shows a drop-down list that's bound to a data source named SqlDataSource1. The field named LongName provides the values that are displayed in the drop-down list, and the field named CategoryID supplies the value that's returned by the SelectedValue property when the user selects an item from the list.

The Data Source Configuration Wizard for binding a drop-down list

List control attributes for data binding

Attribute	Description
DataSourceID	The ID of the data source to bind the list to.
DataTextField	The name of the data source field that should be displayed in the list.
DataValueField	The name of the data source field whose value should be returned by the SelectedValue property of the list.

The aspx code for a drop-down list that's bound to a SQL data source

```
<asp:DropDownList ID="ddlCategory" runat="server"
    AutoPostBack="True" Width="130px"
    DataSourceID="SqlDataSource1"
    DataTextField="LongName"
    DataValueField="CategoryID" />
```

Description

- You can bind any of the controls that inherit the ListControl class to a data source. That includes the list box control, the drop-down list control, the check box list control, the radio button list control, and the bulleted list control.

- You can use the Data Source Configuration Wizard to select the data source for a list control, the data field to display in the list, and the data value to return for the selected item.

- You can also use the DataTextFormatString attribute of a list control to specify a format string you want to apply to the text that's displayed in the control.

Figure 13-13   How to bind a list control to a data source

How to bind the controls in a template

Figure 13-14 shows how you can bind the controls in a template to columns of a data source. This technique can be used with any control that uses templates and specifies a data source. In the application presented in this chapter, these binding techniques are used for the DataList control.

To bind a control to a column of the data source, you use the DataBindings dialog box. From this dialog box, you can select the Field Binding option and then select the field you want to bind to from the first drop-down list. If you want to format the bound data, you can also select a format from the second drop-down list.

By default, you bind the Text property of a control so that the bound data is displayed in the control. However, you may occasionally want to bind to another property. For example, you might want to bind the Enabled or Visible property of a control to a Boolean field. To do that, you simply select the property you want to bind from the Bindable Properties list.

As you make selections in the DataBindings dialog box, Visual Studio generates an Eval method that contains the data binding expression that's used to bind the control. You can see the syntax of the Eval method in this figure along with two examples. If you compare these examples with the binding options in the DataBindings dialog box, you shouldn't have any trouble understanding how this method works.

Although the drop-down lists in the DataBindings dialog box make it easy to create a data binding expression, you can also create your own custom binding expressions. To do that, you just select the Custom Binding option and then enter the binding expression in the Code Expression text box. You might want to do that, for example, if you need to apply a custom format to the data. Or, you might want to code a custom expression that uses the Bind method instead of the Eval method.

Unlike the Eval method, which only provides for displaying bound data, the Bind method provides for both displaying and updating data. This method implements a new feature of ASP.NET 2.0 called *two-way binding*. You'll see an application that uses two-way binding in chapter 15.

By the way, if you're familiar with earlier versions of ASP.NET, you may notice that the Eval method of ASP.NET 2.0 is much simpler than the Eval method you used with earlier versions. To start, this method doesn't explicitly refer to the DataBinder class. In addition, it doesn't specify the data source. Instead, it assumes that the data source is specified by the containing control's DataSourceID attribute.

The DataBindings dialog box for binding a control

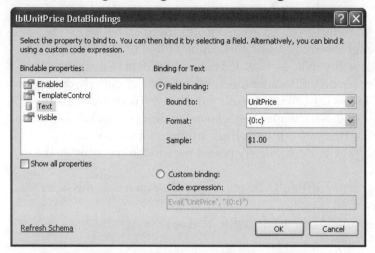

The syntax of the Eval and Bind methods

```
<%# {Eval|Bind}(NameString [,FormatString]) %>
```

Code examples

```
<%# Eval("Name") %>
<%# Eval("UnitPrice", "{0:c}") %>
<%# Bind("UnitPrice", "{0:c}") %>
```

Description

- To bind a control in a template, select the Edit DataBindings command from the smart tag menu for the control to display the DataBindings dialog box. Then, select the property you want to bind to (usually Text), select the Field Binding option, and select the field you want to bind to from the Bound To drop-down list.

- If you want to apply a format to the bound data, select a format from the Format drop-down list.

- As you specify the binding for a control, Visual Studio generates a data binding expression that uses the Eval method. You can see this method in the Code Expression box at the bottom of the DataBindings dialog box.

- You can also create a custom binding expression by selecting the Custom Binding option and then entering the expression in the Code Expression text box.

- The Eval method provides only for displaying data from a data source in a control. In contrast, the Bind method provides for *two-way binding*, which means that it can be used to display as well update data from a data source.

Note

- If the Field Binding option isn't enabled, you can click the Refresh Schema link and then click the OK button in the dialog box that's displayed to enable it.

Figure 13-14   How to bind the controls in a template

The aspx file for the Product List application

To show you how everything you've learned works together, figure 13-15 presents the aspx code for the Product List application of figure 13-1. To make it easier for you to follow this code, I've shaded parts of the data source controls and the controls they're bound to. Because this application relies entirely on the data binding declared in this aspx file, it doesn't require any Visual Basic code.

The first control is the drop-down list that's bound to the first SqlDataSource control, SqlDataSource1. Here, the AutoPostBack attribute for the drop-down list is set to True so the page is automatically posted back to the server when the user selects a category.

The second control is the first SqlDataSource control, which uses this Select statement to get the required data:

```
SELECT [CategoryID], [LongName] FROM [Categories]
    ORDER BY [LongName]
```

As a result, this data source gets the CategoryID and LongName columns for each row in the Categories table and sorts the result based on the LongName column. Then, these columns are used by the drop-down list that's bound to this data source.

The third control is a DataList control that's bound to the second SqlDataSource control, SqlDataSource2. The Header template for this control provides for a row of headings that are defined within a row of a table. Then, the Item template defines the table rows that display the data in the rows that are retrieved by the data source. As you can see, each column in the table contains a label whose Text attribute is bound to a column in the data source. Also notice that the widths of the columns in the Item template are the same as the widths of the columns in the Header template so that these columns are aligned. In addition, the last two columns in each template are right aligned since they contain numeric data.

The last two elements for the DataList control define the styles for alternating items and for the header. You saw the Header style earlier in this chapter. It indicates that the header text should be displayed in a white, boldface font on a black background. The AlternatingItem style indicates that every other row in the data list should be displayed on a light gray background. Since no Item style is included, the other rows will be displayed on a white background.

The fourth control, SqlDataSource2, uses this Select statement:

```
SELECT [ProductID], [Name], [UnitPrice], [OnHand]
    FROM [Products]
    WHERE ([CategoryID] = @CategoryID)
    ORDER BY [ProductID]
```

Here, the Where clause specifies that only those rows whose CategoryID column equal the value of the CategoryID parameter should be retrieved. To make this work, the ControlParameter element specifies that the value of the CategoryID parameter is obtained from the SelectedValue property of the ddlCategory control.

Default.aspx (ProductList application)

```
<body>
    <form id="form1" runat="server">
    <div>
        <asp:Image ID="Image1" runat="server"
            ImageUrl="~/Images/banner.jpg" /><br /><br />Choose a category:
        <asp:DropDownList ID="ddlCategory" runat="server" AutoPostBack="True"
            Width="130px" DataSourceID="SqlDataSource1" DataTextField="LongName"
            DataValueField="CategoryID"></asp:DropDownList>
        <asp:SqlDataSource ID="SqlDataSource1" runat="server"
            ConnectionString="<%$ ConnectionStrings:HalloweenConnectionString %>"
            SelectCommand="SELECT [CategoryID], [LongName] FROM [Categories]
                ORDER BY [LongName]"></asp:SqlDataSource><br /><br />
        <asp:DataList ID="DataList1" runat="server" DataSourceID="SqlDataSource2"
            BackColor="White" BorderColor="#999999" BorderStyle="Solid"
            BorderWidth="1px" CellPadding="3" ForeColor="Black"
            GridLines="Vertical">
            <HeaderTemplate>
                <table><tr>
                    <td style="width: 100px">ID</td>
                    <td style="width: 200px">Product</td>
                    <td style="width: 80px" align="right">Unit Price</td>
                    <td style="width: 80px" align="right">On Hand</td></tr>
                </table>
            </HeaderTemplate>
            <ItemTemplate>
                <table><tr>
                    <td style="width: 100px">
                        <asp:Label ID="lblID" runat="server"
                            Text='<%# Eval("ProductID") %>'></asp:Label></td>
                    <td style="width: 200px">
                        <asp:Label ID="lblName" runat="server"
                            Text='<%# Eval("Name") %>'></asp:Label></td>
                    <td style="width: 80px" align="right">
                        <asp:Label ID="lblUnitPrice" runat="server"
                            Text='<%# Eval("UnitPrice", "{0:c}") %>'>
                        </asp:Label></td>
                    <td style="width: 80px" align="right">
                        <asp:Label ID="lblOnHand" runat="server"
                            Text='<%# Eval("OnHand") %>'></asp:Label></td></tr>
                </table>
            </ItemTemplate>
            <AlternatingItemStyle BackColor="#CCCCCC" />
            <HeaderStyle BackColor="Black" Font-Bold="True" ForeColor="White" />
        </asp:DataList>
        <asp:SqlDataSource ID="SqlDataSource2" runat="server"
            ConnectionString="<%$ ConnectionStrings:HalloweenConnectionString %>"
            SelectCommand="SELECT [ProductID], [Name], [UnitPrice], [OnHand]
                FROM [Products]
                WHERE ([CategoryID] = @CategoryID)
                ORDER BY [ProductID]">
            <SelectParameters>
                <asp:ControlParameter  Name="CategoryID" Type="String"
                    ControlID="ddlCategory" PropertyName="SelectedValue"  />
            </SelectParameters>
        </asp:SqlDataSource>
    </div>
    </form>
</body>
```

Figure 13-15   The aspx file for the Product List application

How to use the advanced features of a SQL data source

The SqlDataSource control provides several advanced features that you may want to use in your applications. These features are explained in the topics that follow.

How to create a data source that can update the database

Much like ADO.NET 1.x data adapters, a SQL data source can include Insert, Update, and Delete statements that let you automatically update the underlying database based on changes made by the user to bound data controls. To automatically generate these statements, you can check the first box in the dialog box shown in figure 13-16, which is displayed when you click on the Advanced button in the first dialog box shown in figure 13-5. You can also check the box for optimistic concurrency, which enhances the generated statements so they check whether updated or deleted rows have changed since the data source retrieved the original data.

The code in this figure shows the aspx elements that are generated when you request Insert, Update, and Delete statements without using optimistic concurrency. Here, the InsertCommand, UpdateCommand, and DeleteCommand attributes provide the statements, and the InsertParameters, UpdateParameters, and DeleteParameters child elements define the parameters used by these statements. Because optimistic concurrency isn't used, these statements will update the database whether or not the data has changed since it was originally retrieved, which could lead to corrupt data.

If you check the Use Optimistic Concurrency check box, though, the update and delete commands will include Where clauses that compare the value of each column with the value originally retrieved. Because these values are passed as parameters, the generated aspx code will include additional elements that define these parameters. The SqlDataSource element will also include two additional attributes that indicate the format that should be used for the names of the parameters that will hold the original column values. Then, if the value of any column has changed since it was originally retrieved, the update or delete operation will be refused, and your application needs to provide code that handles that situation. You'll see how that works in chapter 14.

The Advanced SQL Generation Options dialog box

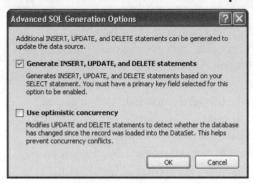

The aspx code for a SqlDataSource control that uses action queries

```
<asp:SqlDataSource ID="SqlDataSource1" runat="server"
    ConnectionString="<%$ ConnectionStrings:HalloweenConnectionString %>"
    SelectCommand="SELECT [ShortName], [CategoryID] FROM [Categories]"
    InsertCommand="INSERT INTO [Categories] ([ShortName], [CategoryID])
                   VALUES (@ShortName, @CategoryID)"
    UpdateCommand="UPDATE [Categories] SET [ShortName] = @ShortName
                   WHERE [CategoryID] = @CategoryID"
    DeleteCommand="DELETE FROM [Categories]
                   WHERE [CategoryID] = @CategoryID" >

    <DeleteParameters>
        <asp:Parameter Name="CategoryID" Type="String" />
    </DeleteParameters>

    <UpdateParameters>
        <asp:Parameter Name="ShortName" Type="String" />
        <asp:Parameter Name="CategoryID" Type="String" />
    </UpdateParameters>

    <InsertParameters>
        <asp:Parameter Name="ShortName" Type="String" />
        <asp:Parameter Name="CategoryID" Type="String" />
    </InsertParameters>
</asp:SqlDataSource>
```

Description

- To automatically generate Insert, Update, and Delete statements for a data source, check the first box in the dialog box that you get by clicking on the Advanced button in the first dialog box in figure 13-5. To generate enhanced versions of the Insert, Update, and Delete statements that use optimistic concurrency, check the second box too.

- The InsertCommand, UpdateCommand, and DeleteCommand attributes in the aspx code define the Insert, Update, and Delete statements used by a data source. If these statements require parameters, the InsertParameters, UpdateParameters, and DeleteParameters elements specify those parameters.

Figure 13-16   How to create a SQL data source that can update the database

How to change the data source mode

As you may remember from chapter 12, ADO.NET provides two basic ways to retrieve data from a database. You can either retrieve the data into a dataset, which retains a copy of the data in memory so it can be accessed multiple times and updated if necessary. Or, you can retrieve the data using a data reader, which lets you retrieve the data in forward-only, read-only fashion.

In figure 13-17, you can see how you can use the DataSourceMode attribute to set the mode for a SQL data source. If the data will be read just once and not updated, you can usually improve the application's performance by changing this attribute to DataReader mode. Otherwise, you can leave it at the default DataSet mode.

How to use caching

ASP.NET's caching feature lets you save the data retrieved by a data source in cache memory on the server. That way, the next time the data needs to be retrieved, the cached data is used instead of getting it from the database again. Since this reduces database access, it often improves an application's overall performance.

In ASP.NET 1.x, you had to write code that explicitly saved and retrieved the data in cache memory. But with ASP.NET 2.0, you can automatically cache the data that has been retrieved by using a data source control as shown in figure 13-17.

To enable caching, you simply set the EnableCaching attribute for a SQL data source to True. Then, you can use the CacheDuration attribute to specify how long data should be kept in the cache. If, for example, the cached data rarely changes, you can set a long cache duration value such as 30 minutes or more. Or, if the data changes frequently, you can set a short cache duration value, perhaps just a few seconds.

But what if the data in the database changes before the duration expires? In that case, the user will view data that is out of date. Sometimes, that's okay so you don't have to worry about it. Otherwise, you can minimize the chance of this happening by setting a shorter duration time.

The DataSourceMode attribute

Attribute	Description
DataSourceMode	DataSet or DataReader. The default is DataSet, but you can specify DataReader if the data source is read-only.

A SqlDataSource control that uses a data reader

```
<asp:SqlDataSource ID="SqlDataSource1" runat="server"
    ConnectionString="<%$ ConnectionStrings:HalloweenConnectionString %>"
    DataSourceMode="DataReader"
    SelectCommand="SELECT [CategoryID], [LongName]
        FROM [Categories]
        ORDER BY [LongName]"
</asp:SqlDataSource>
```

SqlDataSource attributes for caching

Attribute	Description
EnableCaching	A Boolean value that indicates whether caching is enabled for the data source. The default is False.
CacheDuration	The length of time in seconds that the cached data should be saved in cache storage.
CacheExpirationPolicy	If this attribute is set to Absolute, the cache duration timer is started the first time the data is retrieved and is not reset to zero until after the time has expired. If this attribute is set to Sliding, the cache duration timer is reset to zero each time the data is retrieved. The default is Absolute.
CacheKeyDependency	A string that provides a key value associated with the cached data. If you provide a key for the cached data, you can use the key value to programmatically expire the cached data at any time.

A SqlDataSource control that uses caching

```
<asp:SqlDataSource ID="SqlDataSource1" runat="server"
    ConnectionString="<%$ ConnectionStrings:HalloweenConnectionString %>"
    EnableCaching="True" CacheDuration="60"
    SelectCommand="SELECT [CategoryID], [LongName]
        FROM [Categories]
        ORDER BY [LongName]"
</asp:SqlDataSource>
```

Description

- The DataSourceMode attribute lets you specify that data should be retrieved using a data reader rather than a dataset. For read-only data, a data reader is usually more efficient.

- The data source caching attributes let you specify that data should be stored in cache storage for a specified period of time. For data that changes infrequently, caching can improve performance.

Figure 13-17   How to change the data source mode and use caching

Perspective

In this chapter, you've learned how to use ASP.NET 2.0's SqlDataSource control. However, we've only scratched the surface of what this data source can do. As you will see, the real power of a SQL data source lies in what it can do in combination with data controls like GridView, DetailsView, and FormView. As a result, all this chapter has really done is set the foundation for what you'll learn in chapters 14 and 15.

I also want to point out what many developers feel is a weakness of the SQL data source control. Because this control can directly specify the SQL statements used to access and update a database, it violates one of the basic principles of good application design. That is, that the code that's used to manage the application's user interface should be separated from the code that's used to access the application's database and perform its business logic. Clearly, when you use the SqlDataSource control, the database code is mixed with the presentation code.

Fortunately, ASP.NET 2.0 provides two ways to minimize or eliminate this problem. First, the SqlDataSource control can use stored procedures rather than SQL statements. That way, the SQL statements that access and update the database are placed in the database itself, separate from the presentation code. Second, you can use ObjectDataSource controls rather than SqlDataSource controls. When you use ObjectDataSource controls, you can create and use separate database access classes, so the database access code isn't in the aspx file at all. In chapter 16, you'll learn how that works.

Terms

SQL data source
select parameter
control parameter
Query Builder
diagram pane
grid pane
SQL pane
data list
template
template-editing mode
two-way binding

14

How to use the GridView control

In this chapter, you'll learn how to use the GridView control. This control is new with ASP.NET 2.0 and replaces the ASP.NET 1.x DataGrid control. The GridView control lets you display the data from a data source in the rows and columns of a table. It includes many advanced features, such as automatic paging and sorting. It lets you update and delete data with minimal Visual Basic code. And its appearance is fully customizable.

How to customize the GridView control

The GridView control is one of the most powerful user interface controls available in ASP.NET 2.0. It provides many options that let you customize its appearance and behavior. In the following topics, you'll learn how to define fields, customize the contents and appearance of those fields, enable sorting, and provide for custom paging.

How the GridView control works

As figure 14-1 shows, the GridView control displays data provided by a data source in a row and column format. In fact, the GridView control renders its data as an HTML table with one Tr element for each row in the data source, and one Td element for each field in the data source.

The GridView control at the top of this figure displays the data from the Categories table of the Halloween database. Here, the first three columns of the control display the data from the three columns of the table.

The other two columns of this control display buttons that the user can click to edit or delete a row. In this example, the user has clicked the Edit button for the masks row, which placed that row into edit mode. In this mode, text boxes are displayed in place of the labels for the short and long name columns, the Edit button is replaced by Update and Cancel buttons, and the Delete button is removed.

The table in this figure lists some of the basic attributes of the GridView control, and the aspx code in this figure is the code that creates the GridView control above it. By default, this control automatically creates columns for each of the columns in the data source. But you'll almost always want to override that behavior by setting the AutoGenerateColumns attribute to False. Then, you can provide a Columns element to define your own columns. The Columns element, in turn, contains the child elements that define the fields to be displayed. In this code example, the Columns element includes three BoundField elements and two CommandField elements. Notice also that the three BoundField elements contain ItemStyle elements that define the styles used to display the data in the columns.

Most of the aspx code for a GridView control is created automatically by Visual Studio when you drag the control from the Toolbox onto the form and when you use the configuration wizard to configure the data source. However, you commonly work with the aspx code directly so you can have more control over the appearance and behavior of this control.

A GridView control that provides for updating a table

ID	Short Name	Long Name		
costumes	Costumes	Costumes	Edit	Delete
fx	FX	Special Effects	Edit	Delete
masks	Masks	Masks	Update Cancel	
props	Props	Props	Edit	Delete

The aspx code for the GridView control shown above

```
<asp:GridView ID="GridView1" runat="server" AutoGenerateColumns="False"
         DataSourceID="SqlDataSource1" DataKeyNames="CategoryID" >
    <Columns>
        <asp:BoundField DataField="CategoryID" HeaderText="ID"
                    ReadOnly="True" SortExpression="CategoryID">
            <ItemStyle Width="100px" />
        </asp:BoundField>
        <asp:BoundField DataField="ShortName" HeaderText="Short Name"
                    SortExpression="ShortName">
            <ItemStyle Width="150px" />
        </asp:BoundField>
        <asp:BoundField DataField="LongName" HeaderText="Long Name"
                    SortExpression="LongName">
            <ItemStyle Width="200px" />
        </asp:BoundField>
        <asp:CommandField ButtonType="Button" ShowEditButton="True"
                    CausesValidation="False" />
        <asp:CommandField ButtonType="Button" ShowDeleteButton="True"
                    CausesValidation="False" />
    </Columns>
</asp:GridView>
```

Basic attributes of the GridView control

Attribute	Description
ID	The ID of the control.
Runat	Must specify "server."
DataSourceID	The ID of the data source to bind to.
DataKeyNames	The names of the primary key fields separated by commas.
AutoGenerateColumns	Specifies whether the control's columns should be automatically generated.
SelectedIndex	Specifies the row to be initially selected.

Description

- The GridView control displays data from a data source in a row and column format. The data is rendered as an HTML table.
- To create a GridView control, drag the GridView icon from the Data group of the Toolbox.
- To bind a GridView control to a data source, use the smart tag menu's Choose Data Source command.

Figure 14-1   How the GridView control works

How to define the fields in a GridView control

By default, a GridView control displays one column for each column in the data source. If that's not what you want, you can choose Edit Columns from the control's smart tag menu to display the Fields dialog box shown in figure 14-2. Then, you can use this dialog box to delete fields you don't want to display, change the order of the fields, add additional fields like command buttons, and adjust the properties of the fields.

The Available Fields list box lists all of the available sources for GridView fields, while the Selected Fields list box shows the fields that have already been added to the GridView control. To add an additional field to the GridView control, select the field you want to add in the Available Fields list box and click Add. To change the properties for a field, select the field in the Selected Fields list, and use the Properties list.

The table in this figure lists some of the properties you're most likely to want to change. For example, the HeaderText property determines the text displayed for the field's header row, and the ItemStyle.Width property sets the width for the field.

If you want to format fields that contain numbers or dates, you can use the DataFormatString property to specify the type of formatting. For example, for a field that contains a decimal value, you can specify a string of "{0:c}" to apply standard currency formatting to the value. However, this formatting won't be applied unless you set the HtmlEncode property to False. This turns off HTML encoding, which allows the format to be applied to the data. Although HTML encoding makes your application more secure by preventing the database from returning an unsafe script to the browser, it typically isn't necessary, especially if you're confident that no unsafe scripts have been stored in your database.

The Fields dialog box

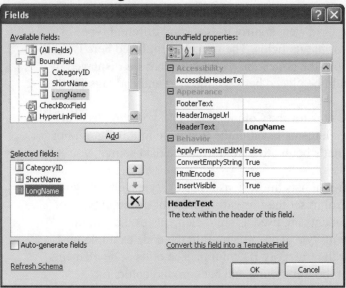

Commonly used field properties

Property	Description
DataField	For a bound field, the name of the column in the underlying data source that the field should be bound to.
DataFormatString	A format string used to format the data. For example, use {0:c} to format a decimal value as currency.
HtmlEncode	Determines if values are HTML-encoded before they're displayed in a bound field. Set this property to False if you use the DataFormatString property.
ItemStyle.Width	The width of the field.
ReadOnly	True if the field is used for display only.
NullDisplayText	The text that's displayed if the data field is null.
ConvertEmptyStringToNull	If True (the default), empty strings are treated as nulls when data is updated in the database. Set this property to False if the underlying database field doesn't allow nulls.
HeaderText	The text that's displayed in the header row for the field.
ShowHeader	True if the header should be displayed for this field.

Description

- By default, the GridView control displays one column for each column in the data source.

- To define the fields that you want to display in the GridView control, display the Fields dialog box by selecting the Edit Columns command in the control's smart tag menu.

- You can also add columns by choosing the Add New Column command from the smart tag menu. This technique is illustrated for the DetailsView control in the next chapter, but it works just as well for the GridView control.

Figure 14-2   How to define the fields in a GridView control

Elements used to create and format fields

As figure 14-3 shows, the GridView control uses several different types of child elements to create and format its fields. The first element listed here is the Columns element, which defines the collection of columns that are displayed by the control. This element should be placed between the start and end tags for the GridView control.

Between the start and end tags for the Columns element, you can place any combination of the remaining elements listed in the first table in this figure. For example, to create a column that's bound to a field from the data source, you use the BoundField element.

The second table in this figure lists the various types of style elements you can use with a GridView control to set the formatting used for different parts of the control. Some of these elements are used as child elements of the column elements. For example, the ItemStyle element is used in the code example in this figure to set the width for the Category ID column. The other style elements in this example are used to set the foreground and background colors for different types of rows displayed by the GridView control.

Note that you don't have to create all of these elements yourself. These elements are created automatically when you use the Fields dialog box as described in the previous figure, when you use the Properties window to specify the styles for an element, or when you apply an AutoFormat to the GridView control.

Column field elements

Element	Description
Columns	The columns that are displayed by a GridView control.
asp:BoundField	A field bound to a data source column.
asp:ButtonField	A field that displays a button.
asp:CheckBoxField	A field that displays a check box.
asp:CommandField	A field that contains Select, Edit, Delete, Update, or Cancel buttons.
asp:HyperlinkField	A field that displays a hyperlink.
asp:ImageField	A field that displays an image.
asp:TemplateField	Lets you create a column with custom content.

Style elements

Element	Description
RowStyle	The style used for data rows.
AlternatingRowStyle	The style used for alternating data rows.
SelectedRowStyle	The style used when the row is selected.
EditRowStyle	The style used when the row is being edited.
EmptyDataRowStyle	The style used when the data source is empty.
ItemStyle	The style used for an individual field.
HeaderStyle	The style used to format the header row.
FooterStyle	The style used to format the footer row.
PagerStyle	The style used to format the GridView's pager row.

The aspx code for a control that uses field and style elements

```
<asp:GridView ID="GridView1" runat="server" AutoGenerateColumns="False"
              DataKeyNames="CategoryID" DataSourceID="SqlDataSource1">
  <Columns>
    <asp:BoundField DataField="CategoryID" HeaderText="ID" readOnly="true" >
      <ItemStyle Width="100px" />
    </asp:BoundField>
     .
     .
  </Columns>
  <HeaderStyle BackColor="LightGray" ForeColor="White"
              Font-Bold="True" />
  <RowStyle BackColor="White" ForeColor="Black" />
  <SelectedRowStyle BackColor="Gray" ForeColor="White"
                   Font-Bold="True" />
  <FooterStyle BackColor="LightGray" ForeColor="Blue" />
  <PagerStyle BackColor="LightGray" ForeColor="Blue"
             HorizontalAlign="Center" />
</asp:GridView>
```

Description

- The GridView control uses several child elements to define the column fields in a row and the styles used to format the data.

Figure 14-3   Elements used to create and format fields

How to enable sorting

The GridView control has a built-in ability to let the user sort the rows based on any or all of the columns displayed by the control. As figure 14-4 shows, all you have to do to enable sorting is set the AllowSorting attribute to True and provide a SortExpression attribute for each column you want to allow sorting for. When sorting is enabled for a column, the user can sort the data by clicking the column header.

Note that a SortExpression attribute is automatically generated for each column that you create with the Fields dialog box. As a result, instead of adding SortExpression attributes for the columns you want to allow sorting for, you must remove the SortExpression attributes for the columns you don't want to allow sorting for. You can use the Fields dialog box to do that by clearing the SortExpression properties. Or, you can use the HTML Editor to delete the SortExpression attributes.

The code example in this figure allows sorting for three of the five fields displayed by the GridView control. For the first two fields, the SortExpression attribute simply duplicates the name of the data source column the field is bound to. If, for example, the user clicks the header of the ProductID column, the data is sorted on the ProductID field.

In some cases, though, you may want the sort expression to be based on two or more columns. To do that, you just use commas to separate the sort field names. In this example, the sort expression for the Category ID column is "CategoryID, Name". That way, any rows with the same Category ID will be sorted by the Name column.

It's important to note that the GridView control doesn't actually do the sorting. Instead, it relies on the underlying data source to sort the data. As a result, sorting will only work if the data source provides for sorting. For a SqlDataSource or AccessDataSource, this means that you need to use the default DataSet mode.

A GridView control with sorting enabled

ID	Name	Category	Unit Price	On Hand
pow01	Austin Powers	costumes	$79.99	25
frankc01	Frankenstein	costumes	$39.99	100
jar01	JarJar	costumes	$59.99	25
martian01	Martian	costumes	$69.99	100
super01	Superman	costumes	$39.99	100
bl01	Black light (24")	fx	$24.99	200
fogj01	Fog Juice (1qt)	fx	$9.99	500
fog01	Fog Machine	fx	$34.99	100
str01	Mini-strobe	fx	$13.99	200
skullfog01	Skull Fogger	fx	$39.95	50
vader01	Darth Vader Mask	masks	$19.99	100
fred01	Freddie	masks	$29.99	50

The aspx code for the control shown above

```
<asp:GridView ID="GridView1" runat="server" AllowSorting="True"
    AutoGenerateColumns="False" DataKeyNames="ProductID"
    DataSourceID="SqlDataSource1">
    <Columns>
        <asp:BoundField DataField="ProductID" HeaderText="ID"
            ReadOnly="True" SortExpression="ProductID">
            <HeaderStyle HorizontalAlign="Left"  />
            <ItemStyle Width="75px" />
        </asp:BoundField>
        <asp:BoundField DataField="Name" HeaderText="Name"
            SortExpression="Name">
            <HeaderStyle HorizontalAlign="Left" />
            <ItemStyle Width="200px" />
        </asp:BoundField>
        <asp:BoundField DataField="CategoryID" HeaderText="Category"
            SortExpression="CategoryID, Name" />
        <asp:BoundField DataField="UnitPrice" DataFormatString="{0:c}"
            HtmlEncode="False" HeaderText="Unit Price">
            <ItemStyle Width="85px" HorizontalAlign="Right" />
            <HeaderStyle HorizontalAlign="Right"  />
        </asp:BoundField>
        <asp:BoundField DataField="OnHand" HeaderText="On Hand">
            <ItemStyle Width="85px" HorizontalAlign="Right" />
            <HeaderStyle HorizontalAlign="Right"  />
        </asp:BoundField>
    </Columns>
    <HeaderStyle BackColor="LightGray" />
</asp:GridView>
```

Description

- To enable sorting, set the AllowSorting attribute to True. Then, add a SortExpression attribute to each column you want to allow sorting for.

- For sorting to work, the DataSourceMode attribute of the data source must be set to DataSet mode.

Figure 14-4   How to enable sorting

How to enable paging

Paging refers to the ability of the GridView control to display bound data one page at a time, along with paging controls that let the user select which page of data to display next. Although the old DataGrid control provided some basic support for paging, you had to write a lot of code to support it. But as figure 14-5 shows, the GridView control lets you enable paging simply by setting the AllowPaging attribute to True.

When you enable paging, an additional row is displayed at the bottom of the GridView control to display the paging controls. If you want, you can provide a PagerStyle element to control how this row is formatted. In the example in this figure, the PagerStyle element specifies that the background color for the pager row should be light gray and the pager controls should be horizontally centered.

Unlike sorting, the GridView control doesn't delegate the paging function to the underlying data source. Like sorting, however, paging works only for data sources that are in DataSet mode.

A GridView control with paging enabled

ID	Name	Category	Unit Price	On Hand
arm01	Severed Arm	props	$19.95	200
bl01	Black light (24")	fx	$24.99	200
cat01	Deranged Cat	props	$19.99	45
cool01	Cool Ghoul	props	$69.99	25
fog01	Fog Machine	fx	$34.99	100
fogj01	Fog Juice (1qt)	fx	$9.99	500
frankc01	Frankenstein	costumes	$39.99	100
fred01	Freddie	masks	$29.99	50
head01	Shrunken Head	props	$29.99	100
head02	Severed Head	props	$29.99	100

1 2 3

The code for the GridView control shown above

```
<asp:GridView ID="GridView1" runat="server" AllowPaging="True"
    AutoGenerateColumns="False" DataKeyNames="ProductID"
    DataSourceID="SqlDataSource1">
    <Columns>
        <asp:BoundField DataField="ProductID" HeaderText="ID"
            ReadOnly="True">
            <HeaderStyle HorizontalAlign="Left"  />
            <ItemStyle Width="75px" />
        </asp:BoundField>
        <asp:BoundField DataField="Name" HeaderText="Name">
            <HeaderStyle HorizontalAlign="Left" />
            <ItemStyle Width="200px" />
        </asp:BoundField>
        <asp:BoundField DataField="CategoryID" HeaderText="Category" />
        <asp:BoundField DataField="UnitPrice" DataFormatString="{0:c}"
            HtmlEncode="False" HeaderText="Unit Price">
            <ItemStyle Width="85px" HorizontalAlign="Right" />
            <HeaderStyle HorizontalAlign="Right"  />
        </asp:BoundField>
        <asp:BoundField DataField="OnHand" HeaderText="On Hand">
            <ItemStyle Width="85px" HorizontalAlign="Right" />
            <HeaderStyle HorizontalAlign="Right"  />
        </asp:BoundField>
    </Columns>
    <HeaderStyle BackColor="LightGray" />
    <PagerStyle BackColor="LightGray" HorizontalAlign="Center" />
</asp:GridView>
```

Description

- To enable *paging*, set the AllowPaging attribute to True. Then, add a PagerStyle element to define the appearance of the pager controls. You can also add a PagerSettings element as described in the next figure to customize the way paging works.

- For paging to work, the DataSourceMode attribute of the data source must be set to DataSet mode.

Figure 14-5 How to enable paging

How to customize paging

Figure 14-6 shows how you can customize the way paging works with a GridView control. To start, the two attributes in the first table let you enable paging and specify the number of data rows that will be displayed on each page. The default setting for the second attribute is 10.

You can also customize the appearance of the pager area by including a PagerSettings element between the start and end tags of a GridView control. Then, you can use the attributes in the second table for the customization. The most important of these attributes is Mode, which determines what buttons are displayed in the pager area. If, for example, you set the mode to NextPrevious, only Next and Previous buttons will be displayed.

If you specify Numeric or NumericFirstLast for the Mode attribute, individual page numbers are displayed in the pager area so the user can go directly to any of the listed pages. You can then use the PageButtonCount attribute to specify how many of these page numbers should be displayed in the pager area. Note that if you specify NumericFirstLast, the first and last buttons are displayed only if the total number of pages exceeds the value you specify for the PageButtonCount attribute and the first or last page number isn't displayed.

The remaining attributes in this table let you control the text or image that's displayed for the various buttons. By default, the values for the First, Previous, Next, and Last buttons use less-than and greater-than signs, but the example shows how you can change the text for these buttons.

Attributes of the GridView control that affect paging

Attribute	Description
AllowPaging	Set to True to enable paging.
PageSize	Specifies the number of rows to display on each page. The default is 10.

Attributes of the PagerSettings element

Attribute	Description
Mode	Controls what buttons are displayed in the pager area. You can specify NextPrevious, NextPreviousFirstLast, Numeric, or NumericFirstLast.
FirstPageText	The text to display for the first page button. The default is <<, which displays as <<.
FirstPageImageUrl	The URL of an image file used to display the first page button.
PreviousPageText	The text to display for the previous page button. The default is <, which displays as <.
PreviousPageImageUrl	The URL of an image file used to display the previous page button.
NextPageText	The text to display for the next page button. The default is >, which displays as >.
NextPageImageUrl	The URL of an image file used to display the next page button.
LastPageText	The text to display for the last page button. The default is >>, which displays as >>.
LastPageImageUrl	The URL of an image file used to display the last page button.
PageButtonCount	The number of page buttons to display if the Mode is set to Numeric or NumericFirstLast.
Position	The location of the pager area. You can specify Top, Bottom, or TopAndBottom.
Visible	Set to False to hide the pager controls.

Example

A PagerSettings element

```
<PagerSettings Mode="NextPreviousFirstLast"
               NextPageText="Next" PreviousPageText="Prev"
               FirstPageText="First" LastPageText="Last" />
```

The resulting pager area

First Prev Next Last

Description

- You can use the PageSize attribute of the GridView element to specify the number of rows to display on each page.
- You can also add a PagerSettings element to control the appearance of the pager area.

Figure 14-6   How to customize paging

A list application that uses a GridView control

Now that you've learned the basics of working with a GridView control, the following topics present the design and code for an application that uses a GridView control to list the rows of a data source. As you'll see, this application provides for sorting and paging and doesn't require a single line of Visual Basic code.

The Product List application

Figure 14-7 presents the Product List application. Here, the data from the Products table of the Halloween database is displayed in a GridView control. The data is displayed 8 rows at a time, and numeric page buttons are displayed at the bottom of the GridView control so the user can navigate from page to page. In addition, the user can sort the data by clicking the column headings for the ID, Name, and Category columns.

The Product List application

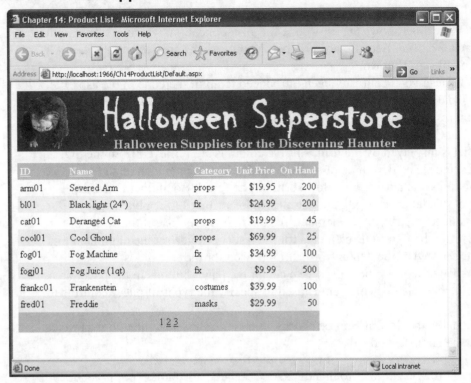

Description

- The Product List application uses a GridView control to display a list of all the products in the Products table. The GridView control is bound to a SqlDataSource control that works in DataSet mode.

- Sorting is enabled for the first three columns. That way, the user can sort the product data by ID, Name, or Category.

- Paging is enabled with 8 products displayed on each page.

- Currency formatting is applied to the Unit Price column.

Figure 14-7   The Product List application

The aspx file

Figure 14-8 shows the aspx code for this application, which is stored in the Default.aspx file. Because no code-behind procedures are needed, the code-behind file isn't shown.

Because you've already been introduced to all of the code in the aspx file, you should be able to follow it without much trouble. So I'll just point out a few highlights.

The Columns element contains five BoundField child elements that define the fields displayed by the grid. All five columns are retrieved from the SQL data source. The first three of these BoundField elements include the SortExpression attribute to allow sorting. The fourth BoundField element includes DataFormatString and HtmlEncode attributes to apply currency formatting. The ItemStyle elements for the first two fields set the width of the fields, and the ItemStyle elements for the last two fields set the alignment to right. Otherwise, the default formatting is used for the five fields.

A PagerStyle element is used to center the pager buttons in the pager area. Then, a PagerSettings element is used to specify the types of pager controls to display.

Finally, the SqlDataSource control uses this Select statement to retrieve data from the Halloween database:

```
SELECT [ProductID], [Name], [CategoryID],
    [UnitPrice], [OnHand] FROM [Products] ORDER BY [ProductID]
```

Because the DataSourceMode attribute isn't set, the default of DataSet mode is used, which means that sorting and paging can be enabled.

The Default.aspx file

```
<%@ Page Language="VB" AutoEventWireup="false" CodeFile="Default.aspx.vb"
Inherits="_Default" %>

<!DOCTYPE html PUBLIC "-//W3C//DTD XHTML 1.1//EN"
"http://www.w3.org/TR/xhtml11/DTD/xhtml11.dtd">

<html xmlns="http://www.w3.org/1999/xhtml" >
<head runat="server">
    <title>Chapter 14: Product List</title>
</head>
<body>
    <form id="form1" runat="server">
    <div>
        <asp:Image ID="Image1" runat="server" ImageUrl="~/Images/banner.jpg" />
        <br /><br />
        <asp:GridView ID="GridView1" runat="server"
            AllowSorting="True"
            AllowPaging="True" PageSize="8"
            DataKeyNames="ProductID" DataSourceID="SqlDataSource1"
            AutoGenerateColumns="False"
            CellPadding="4" GridLines="None" ForeColor="Black">
            <Columns>
                <asp:BoundField DataField="ProductID" HeaderText="ID"
                    ReadOnly="True" SortExpression="ProductID">
                    <HeaderStyle HorizontalAlign="Left" />
                    <ItemStyle Width="75px" />
                </asp:BoundField>
                <asp:BoundField DataField="Name" HeaderText="Name"
                    SortExpression="Name">
                    <HeaderStyle HorizontalAlign="Left" />
                    <ItemStyle Width="200px" />
                </asp:BoundField>
                <asp:BoundField DataField="CategoryID" HeaderText="Category"
                    SortExpression="CategoryID, Name" />
                <asp:BoundField DataField="UnitPrice" DataFormatString="{0:c}"
                    HtmlEncode="False" HeaderText="Unit Price">
                    <ItemStyle HorizontalAlign="Right" />
                </asp:BoundField>
                <asp:BoundField DataField="OnHand" HeaderText="On Hand">
                    <ItemStyle HorizontalAlign="Right" />
                </asp:BoundField>
            </Columns>
            <HeaderStyle BackColor="Silver" Font-Bold="True"
                ForeColor="White" />
            <RowStyle BackColor="White" ForeColor="Black" />
            <AlternatingRowStyle BackColor="WhiteSmoke" ForeColor="Black" />
            <FooterStyle BackColor="Silver" Font-Bold="True" ForeColor="White" />
            <PagerStyle BackColor="Silver" ForeColor="Blue"
                HorizontalAlign="Center" />
            <PagerSettings Mode="NumericFirstLast" />
        </asp:GridView>
        <asp:SqlDataSource ID="SqlDataSource1" runat="server"
            ConnectionString="<%$ ConnectionStrings:HalloweenConnection %>"
            SelectCommand="SELECT [ProductID], [Name], [CategoryID],
                [UnitPrice], [OnHand] FROM [Products] ORDER BY [ProductID]">
        </asp:SqlDataSource>
    </div>
    </form>
</body>
</html>
```

Figure 14-8   The aspx file of the Product List application

How to update GridView data

Another impressive feature of the GridView control is its ability to update data in the underlying data source with little additional code. Before you can set that up, though, you must configure the data source with Update, Delete, and Insert statements, as described in the last chapter. Once you've done that, you can set up a GridView control so it calls the Update and Delete statements, which you'll learn how to do next.

How to work with command fields

A *command field* is a GridView column that contains one or more command buttons. Figure 14-9 shows five of the command buttons that you can include in each row of a GridView control. Please note, however, that the Update and Cancel buttons are displayed only when a user clicks the Edit button to edit a row. You can't display these buttons in separate command fields.

When the user clicks a Delete button, the GridView control calls the data source control's Delete method, which deletes the selected row from the underlying database. Then, the GridView control redisplays the data without the deleted row.

When the user clicks the Edit button, the GridView control places the selected row in *edit mode*. In this mode, the labels used to display the editable bound fields are replaced by text boxes so the user can enter changes. Also, the row is formatted using the style attributes provided by the EditRowStyle element. Finally, the Edit button itself is replaced by Update and Cancel buttons. Then, if the user clicks the Update button, any changes are sent back to the data source, which in turn updates the underlying database. But if the user clicks Cancel, any changes made by the user are discarded and the original values are redisplayed.

The Select button lets the user select a row. Then, the selected row is displayed with the settings in the SelectedRowStyle element. Also, the SelectedIndex and SelectedRow properties are updated to reflect the selected row. The Select button is most often used in combination with a FormView or DetailsView control to create pages that show the details for an item selected from the GridView control. You'll learn how this works in chapter 15.

The two tables in this figure show the attributes of a CommandField element. For instance, you can set the ShowEditButton attribute to True to display an Edit button in a command field. And you can use the EditText attribute to set the text that's displayed on that button.

Although a single command field can display more than one button, it's common to create separate command fields for Select, Edit, and Delete buttons. It's also common to set the CausesValidation attribute of the Select and Delete buttons to False since these buttons don't cause any data to be sent to the server. On the other hand, you'll usually leave the CausesValidation attribute of the Edit button set to True so that validation is performed when the user clicks the Update button. Later in this chapter, you'll learn how to use validation controls with the Edit button by creating template fields.

The Fields dialog box for working with a command field

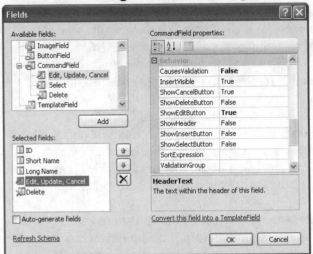

Typical code to define command fields

```
<asp:CommandField ButtonType="Button" ShowEditButton="True"
    CausesValidation="False" />
<asp:CommandField ButtonType="Button" ShowDeleteButton="True"
    CausesValidation="False" />
```

Attributes of the CommandField element

Attribute	Description
ButtonType	Specifies the type of button displayed in the command field. Valid options are Button, Link, or Image.
CausesValidation	Specifies whether validation should be performed if the user clicks the button.
ValidationGroup	Specifies the name of the group to be validated if CausesValidation is True.

Attributes that show buttons and set the text or images they display

Button	Show	Text	Image
Cancel	ShowCancelButton	CancelText	CancelImage
Delete	ShowDeleteButton	DeleteText	DeleteImage
Edit	ShowEditButton	EditText	EditImage
Select	ShowSelectButton	SelectText	SelectImage
Update	n/a	UpdateText	UpdateImage

Description

- A *command field* adds buttons that let the user edit, delete, or select data in a GridView control.
- The CommandField element also provides for an Insert button, but the GridView control doesn't directly support insert operations.

Figure 14-9   How to work with command fields

How to use events raised by the GridView control

Although the GridView control provides many features automatically, you still must write some code to handle such things as data validation, database exceptions, and concurrency errors. As figure 14-10 shows, most of this code will be in the form of event handlers that respond to one or more of the events raised by the GridView control.

If you look at the list of events in the table in this figure, you'll see that several of them come in pairs, with one event raised before an action is taken and the other after the action completes. For example, when the user clicks the Delete button in a GridView row, two events are raised. The RowDeleting event is raised before the row is deleted, and the RowDeleted event is raised after the row has been deleted.

The most common reason to handle the before-action events is to provide data validation. For example, when the user clicks the Update button, you can handle the RowUpdating event to make sure the user has entered correct data. If not, you can set the e argument's Cancel property to True to cancel the update.

In contrast, the after-action events give you an opportunity to make sure the database operation completed successfully. In most applications, you should test for two conditions. First, you should check for any database exceptions by checking the Exception property of the e argument. If this property refers to a valid object, an exception has occurred and you can notify the user with an appropriate error message.

Second, if optimistic concurrency is used, you should check to see if a concurrency violation has occurred. To do that, you can check the AffectedRows property of the e argument. If this property is zero, which means no rows have been changed, a concurrency error has probably occurred, and you can notify the user with an appropriate error message.

When you use optimistic concurrency, remember that the Where clause in an Update or Delete statement tries to find a row that has the same values as when the row was originally retrieved. If that row can't be found, which means that another user has updated one of the columns, the update or delete operation never takes place so no rows are affected.

When you try to update a row, one of the most common exceptions is caused by an attempt to store a null value in a database column that doesn't allow null values. This occurs when the user doesn't enter a value in one of the columns that's being updated. In this case, you can display an appropriate error message and set the e argument's ExceptionHandled property to True to suppress further processing of the exception. You can also set the KeepInEditMode property to True to leave the GridView control in edit mode. This is illustrated by the event procedure that's coded in this figure.

Events raised by the GridView control

Event	Raised when ...
RowCancelingEdit	The Cancel button of a row in edit mode is clicked.
RowDataBound	Data binding completes for a row.
RowDeleted	A row has been deleted.
RowDeleting	A row is about to be deleted.
RowEditing	A row is about to be edited.
RowUpdated	A row has been updated.
RowUpdating	A row is about to be updated.
SelectedIndexChanged	A row has been selected.
SelectedIndexChanging	A row is about to be selected.

An event handler for the RowUpdated event

```
Protected Sub GridView1_RowUpdated(ByVal sender As Object,_
        ByVal e As System.Web.UI.WebControls.GridViewUpdatedEventArgs) _
        Handles GridView1.RowUpdated
    If e.Exception IsNot Nothing Then
        lblError.Text = "An exception occurred. " _
            & e.Exception.Message
        e.ExceptionHandled = True
        e.KeepInEditMode = True
    ElseIf e.AffectedRows = 0 Then
        lblError.Text = "No rows were updated. " _
            & "Another user may have updated that category. " _
            & "Please try again."
    End If
End Sub
```

Description

- The GridView control raises various events that can be handled when data is updated.

- The RowUpdating and RowDeleting events are often used for data validation. You can cancel the update or delete operation by setting the e argument's Cancel property to True.

- You can handle the RowUpdated and RowDeleted events to ensure that the row was successfully updated or deleted.

- To determine if a SQL exception has occurred, check the Exception property of the e argument. If an exception has occurred, the most likely cause is a null value for a column that doesn't accept nulls. To suppress the exception, you can set the ExceptionHandled property to True. And to keep the control in edit mode, you can set the KeepInEditMode property to True.

- To determine how many rows were updated or deleted, check the AffectedRows property of the e argument. If this property is zero and an exception has *not* been thrown, the most likely cause is a concurrency error.

Figure 14-10   How to use events raised by the GridView control

How to insert a row in a GridView control

You may have noticed that although the GridView control lets you update and delete rows, it has no provision for inserting new rows. When you use the GridView control in concert with a FormView or DetailsView control, though, you can provide for insert operations with a minimum of code. You'll learn how to do that in chapter 15. Another alternative is to create a page that lets you insert data into a GridView control by using the techniques described in figure 14-11.

To provide for insertions, you must first create a set of input controls such as text boxes in which the user can enter data for the row to be inserted. Next, you must provide a button that the user can click to start the insertion. Then, in the event handler for this button, you can set the insert parameter values to the values entered by the user and call the data source's Insert method to add the new row.

This is illustrated by the code in this figure. Here, if the insertion is successful, the contents of the text boxes are cleared. But if an exception is thrown, an error message is displayed. This message indicates that an exception has occurred and uses the Message property of the Exception object to display the message that's stored in the Exception object.

Method and properties of the SqlDataSource class for inserting rows

Method	Description
Insert	Executes the Insert command defined for the data source.

Property	Description
InsertCommand	The Insert command to be executed.
InsertParameters("name")	The parameter with the specified name.

Property of the Parameter class for inserting rows

Property	Description
DefaultValue	The default value of a parameter. This value is used if no other value is assigned to the parameter.

Code that uses a SqlDataSource control to insert a row

```
Protected Sub btnAdd_Click(ByVal sender As Object, _
        ByVal e As System.EventArgs) Handles btnAdd.Click
    SqlDataSource1.InsertParameters("CategoryID").DefaultValue _
        = txtID.Text
    SqlDataSource1.InsertParameters("ShortName").DefaultValue _
        = txtShortName.Text
    SqlDataSource1.InsertParameters("LongName").DefaultValue _
        = txtLongName.Text
    Try
        SqlDataSource1.Insert()
        txtID.Text = ""
        txtShortName.Text = ""
        txtLongName.Text = ""
    Catch ex As Exception
        lblError.Text = "An exception occurred. " _
            & ex.Message
    End Try
End Sub
```

Description

- The GridView control doesn't support insert operations, but you can use the GridView's data source to insert rows into the database. When you do, the new row will automatically be shown in the GridView control.

- To provide for inserts, the page should include controls such as text boxes for the user to enter data and a button that the user can click to insert the data.

- To use a SqlDataSource control to insert a database row, first set the DefaultValue property of each insert parameter to the value you want to insert. Then, call the Insert method.

- The Insert method may throw a SqlException if a SQL error occurs. The most likely cause of the exception is a primary key constraint violation.

Figure 14-11   How to insert a row in a GridView control

A maintenance application that uses a GridView control

To give you a better idea of how you can use a GridView control to update, delete, and insert data, the following topics present an application that maintains the Categories table in the Halloween database.

The Category Maintenance application

Figure 14-12 introduces you to the Category Maintenance application. It lets the user update, delete, and insert rows in the Categories table of the Halloween database. Here, a GridView control is used to display the rows in the Categories database along with Edit and Delete buttons. In this figure, the user has clicked the Edit button for the third data row, placing that row in edit mode.

Beneath the GridView control, three text boxes let the user enter data for a new category. Then, if the user clicks the Add New Category button, the data entered in these text boxes is used to add a category row to the database. Although it isn't apparent from this figure, required field validators are used for each text box. Also, there's a label control beneath the GridView control that's used to display error messages when an update, delete, or insert operation fails.

The Category Maintenance application

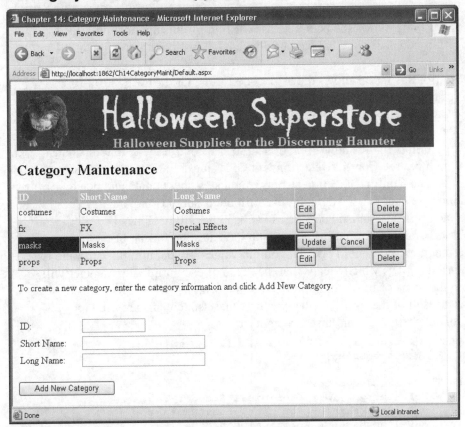

Description

- The Category Maintenance application uses a GridView control to let the user update or delete rows in the Categories table.
- To edit a category, the user clicks the Edit button. This places the GridView control into edit mode. The user can then change the ID, Short Name, or Long Name and click Update. Or, the user can click Cancel to leave edit mode.
- To delete a category, the user clicks the Delete button.
- The user can add a category to the table by entering data into the text boxes beneath the GridView control and clicking the Add New Category button.
- If the user attempts to update or add a row with a column that is blank, an error message is displayed. In addition, an error message is displayed if the user tries to insert a category with an ID that's already in use.

Figure 14-12 The Category Maintenance application

The aspx file

Figure 14-13 shows the complete aspx listing for this application. Since most of this code has already been introduced, I'll just point out a few highlights.

Part 1 of this figure shows the aspx code for the GridView control. It specifies that the data source is SqlDataSource1 and the primary key for the data is CategoryID. The five columns defined in the Columns element display the three columns from the data source, an Edit button, and a Delete button.

Part 2 of this figure shows the SqlDataSource control. Note that this data source includes the ConflictDetection and OldValuesParameterFormatString attributes. The ConflictDetection attribute indicates how update and delete operations are handled. By default, this attribute is set to CompareAllValues, which means that optimistic concurrency checking will be done. The OldValuesParameterFormatString attribute indicates the format of the parameter names that are used to hold original column values. By default, this attribute is set to original_{0}, which means that the name of each original parameter will include the name of the column prefixed with "original_".

As a result of these two attribute values, these statements are used to retrieve, delete, update, and insert category rows:

```
SELECT [CategoryID], [ShortName], [LongName]
   FROM [Categories]

DELETE FROM [Categories]
   WHERE [CategoryID] = @original_CategoryID
     AND [ShortName] = @original_ShortName
     AND [LongName] = @original_LongName

UPDATE [Categories]
   SET [ShortName] = @ShortName,
       [LongName] = @LongName
   WHERE [CategoryID] = @original_CategoryID
     AND [ShortName] = @original_ShortName
     AND [LongName] = @original_LongName

INSERT INTO [Categories]
     ([CategoryID], [ShortName], [LongName])
     VALUES (@CategoryID, @ShortName, @LongName)"
```

Here, the Where clauses implement optimistic concurrency by looking for rows that have the values originally retrieved. Then, the DeleteParameters, UpdateParameters, and InsertParameters elements in the aspx code define the parameters used by these statements.

Finally, part 3 of this figure shows the input controls used to enter the data for a new category. As you can see, each text box is validated by a required field validator that makes sure the user has entered data for the field. This validation is performed when the user clicks the Add New Category button.

The Default.aspx file

```
<%@ Page Language="VB" AutoEventWireup="false" CodeFile="Default.aspx.vb"
Inherits="_Default" %>

<!DOCTYPE html PUBLIC "-//W3C//DTD XHTML 1.1//EN"
"http://www.w3.org/TR/xhtml11/DTD/xhtml11.dtd">

<html xmlns="http://www.w3.org/1999/xhtml" >
<head runat="server">
    <title>Chapter 14: Category Maintenance</title>
</head>
<body>
    <form id="form1" runat="server">
    <div>
        <asp:Image ID="Image1" runat="server" ImageUrl="~/Images/banner.jpg" />
        <br /><br />
        <h2>Category Maintenance</h2>
        <asp:GridView ID="GridView1" runat="server"
            AutoGenerateColumns="False" DataKeyNames="CategoryID"
            DataSourceID="SqlDataSource1" ForeColor="Black">
            <Columns>
                <asp:BoundField DataField="CategoryID" HeaderText="ID"
                ReadOnly="True">
                    <HeaderStyle HorizontalAlign="Left" />
                    <ItemStyle Width="100px" />
                </asp:BoundField>
                <asp:BoundField DataField="ShortName" HeaderText="Short Name">
                    <HeaderStyle HorizontalAlign="Left" />
                    <ItemStyle Width="150px" />
                </asp:BoundField>
                <asp:BoundField DataField="LongName" HeaderText="Long Name">
                    <HeaderStyle HorizontalAlign="Left" />
                    <ItemStyle Width="200px" />
                </asp:BoundField>
                <asp:CommandField ButtonType="Button" ShowEditButton="True"
                    CausesValidation="False" />
                <asp:CommandField ButtonType="Button" ShowDeleteButton="True"
                    CausesValidation="False" />
            </Columns>
            <HeaderStyle BackColor="Silver" Font-Bold="True"
                ForeColor="White" />
            <RowStyle BackColor="White" ForeColor="Black" />
            <AlternatingRowStyle BackColor="WhiteSmoke" ForeColor="Black" />
            <EditRowStyle BackColor="Blue" ForeColor="White" />
        </asp:GridView>
```

Notes

- The GridView control is bound to the data source SqlDataSource1.
- The Columns element includes child elements that define five columns. Three are for the bound fields, the other two for the command buttons.

Figure 14-13   The aspx file of the Category Maintenance application (part 1 of 3)

The Default.aspx file

```
<asp:SqlDataSource ID="SqlDataSource1" runat="server"
    ConflictDetection="CompareAllValues"
    ConnectionString="<%$ ConnectionStrings:HalloweenConnection %>"
    OldValuesParameterFormatString="original_{0}"
    SelectCommand="SELECT [CategoryID], [ShortName], [LongName]
        FROM [Categories]"
    DeleteCommand="DELETE FROM [Categories]
        WHERE [CategoryID] = @original_CategoryID
          AND [ShortName] = @original_ShortName
          AND [LongName] = @original_LongName"
    UpdateCommand="UPDATE [Categories] SET [ShortName] = @ShortName,
        [LongName] = @LongName
        WHERE [CategoryID] = @original_CategoryID
          AND [ShortName] = @original_ShortName
          AND [LongName] = @original_LongName"
    InsertCommand="INSERT INTO [Categories]
        ([CategoryID], [ShortName], [LongName])
        VALUES (@CategoryID, @ShortName, @LongName)">
    <DeleteParameters>
        <asp:Parameter Name="original_CategoryID" Type="String" />
        <asp:Parameter Name="original_ShortName" Type="String" />
        <asp:Parameter Name="original_LongName" Type="String" />
    </DeleteParameters>
    <UpdateParameters>
        <asp:Parameter Name="ShortName" Type="String" />
        <asp:Parameter Name="LongName" Type="String" />
        <asp:Parameter Name="original_CategoryID" Type="String" />
        <asp:Parameter Name="original_ShortName" Type="String" />
        <asp:Parameter Name="original_LongName" Type="String" />
    </UpdateParameters>
    <InsertParameters>
        <asp:Parameter Name="CategoryID" Type="String" />
        <asp:Parameter Name="ShortName" Type="String" />
        <asp:Parameter Name="LongName" Type="String" />
    </InsertParameters>
</asp:SqlDataSource><br />
```

Notes

- The Select statement retrieves all rows in the Categories table.
- The Where clauses in the Delete and Update statements provide for optimistic concurrency.

Figure 14-13   The aspx file of the Category Maintenance application (part 2 of 3)

The Default.aspx file   **Page 3**

```
            To create a new category, enter the category information
            and click Add New Category.<br />
            <asp:Label ID="lblError" runat="server" EnableViewState="False"
                ForeColor="Red"></asp:Label><br /><br />
            <table>
             <tr>
               <td style="width: 100px">ID:</td>
               <td style="width: 100px">
                 <asp:TextBox ID="txtID" runat="server"
                     EnableViewState="False" Width="100px"></asp:TextBox></td>
               <td style="width: 195px">
                 <asp:RequiredFieldValidator ID="RequiredFieldValidator1"
                     runat="server" ControlToValidate="txtID"
                     ErrorMessage="ID is a required field.">
                 </asp:RequiredFieldValidator></td>
             </tr>
             <tr>
               <td style="width: 100px">Short Name:</td>
               <td style="width: 100px">
                 <asp:TextBox ID="txtShortName" runat="server"
                     EnableViewState="False" Width="200px"></asp:TextBox></td>
               <td style="width: 195px">
                 <asp:RequiredFieldValidator ID="RequiredFieldValidator2"
                     runat="server" ControlToValidate="txtShortName"
                     ErrorMessage="Short Name is a required field.">
                 </asp:RequiredFieldValidator></td>
             </tr>
             <tr>
               <td style="width: 100px">Long Name:</td>
               <td style="width: 100px">
                 <asp:TextBox ID="txtLongName" runat="server"
                     EnableViewState="False" Width="200px"></asp:TextBox></td>
               <td style="width: 195px">
                 <asp:RequiredFieldValidator ID="RequiredFieldValidator3"
                     runat="server" ControlToValidate="txtLongName"
                     ErrorMessage="Long Name is a required field.">
                 </asp:RequiredFieldValidator></td>
             </tr>
            </table>
            <br />
            <asp:Button ID="btnAdd" runat="server" Text="Add New Category" />
        </div>
        </form>
</body>
</html>
```

Notes

- The text boxes are used to enter data for a new row.
- The required field validators ensure that the user enters data for each column of a new row.

Figure 14-13   The aspx file of the Category Maintenance application (part 3 of 3)

The code-behind file

Although it would be nice if you could create a robust database application without writing any Visual Basic code, you must still write code to insert data into a GridView control and to catch and handle any database or concurrency errors that might occur. Figure 14-14 shows this code for the Category Maintenance application.

As you can see, this code-behind file consists of just three procedures. The first, btnAdd_Click, sets the value of the three insert parameters to the values entered by the user. Then, it calls the Insert method of the data source control. If an exception is thrown, an appropriate error message is displayed.

The second procedure, GridView1_RowUpdated, is called after a row has been updated. This procedure checks the Exception property of the e argument to determine if an exception has been thrown. If so, an error message is displayed, the ExceptionHandled property is set to True to suppress the exception, and the KeepInEditMode property is set to True to leave the GridView control in edit mode. If an exception hasn't occurred, the e argument's AffectedRows property is checked. If it's zero, it means that a concurrency error has occurred and an appropriate message is displayed.

The third procedure, GridView1_RowDeleted, is called after a row has been deleted. This procedure checks the e argument's AffectedRows property and displays an appropriate error message if a concurrency error has occurred.

The Default.aspx.vb file

```vb
Partial Class _Default
    Inherits System.Web.UI.Page

    Protected Sub btnAdd_Click(ByVal sender As Object, _
            ByVal e As System.EventArgs) Handles btnAdd.Click
        SqlDataSource1.InsertParameters("CategoryID").DefaultValue _
            = txtID.Text
        SqlDataSource1.InsertParameters("ShortName").DefaultValue _
            = txtShortName.Text
        SqlDataSource1.InsertParameters("LongName").DefaultValue _
            = txtLongName.Text
        Try
            SqlDataSource1.Insert()
            txtID.Text = ""
            txtShortName.Text = ""
            txtLongName.Text = ""
        Catch ex As Exception
            lblError.Text = "An exception occurred. " _
                & ex.Message
        End Try
    End Sub

    Protected Sub GridView1_RowUpdated(ByVal sender As Object, _
            ByVal e As System.Web.UI.WebControls.GridViewUpdatedEventArgs) _
            Handles GridView1.RowUpdated
        If e.Exception IsNot Nothing Then
            lblError.Text = "An exception occurred. " _
                & e.Exception.Message
            e.ExceptionHandled = True
            e.KeepInEditMode = True
        ElseIf e.AffectedRows = 0 Then
            lblError.Text = "No rows were updated. " _
                & "Another user may have updated that category. " _
                & "Please try again."
        End If
    End Sub

    Protected Sub GridView1_RowDeleted(ByVal sender As Object, _
            ByVal e As System.Web.UI.WebControls.GridViewDeletedEventArgs) _
            Handles GridView1.RowDeleted
        If e.Exception IsNot Nothing Then
            lblError.Text = "An exception occured. " _
                & e.Exception.Message
            e.ExceptionHandled = True
        ElseIf e.AffectedRows = 0 Then
            lblError.Text = "No rows were deleted. " _
                & "Another user may have updated this category. " _
                & "Please try again."
        End If
    End Sub

End Class
```

Figure 14-14   The code-behind file of the Category Maintenance application

How to work with template fields

Although using bound fields is a convenient way to include bound data in a GridView control, the most flexible way is to use template fields. A *template field* is simply a field that provides one or more templates that are used to render the column. You can include anything you want in these templates, including labels or text boxes, data binding expressions, and validation controls. In fact, including validation controls for editable GridView controls is one of the main reasons for using template fields.

How to create template fields

Figure 14-15 shows how to create template fields. The easiest way to do that is to first create a regular bound field and then convert it to a template field. This changes the BoundField element to a TemplateField element and, more importantly, generates ItemTemplate and EditItemTemplate elements that include labels and text boxes with appropriate binding expressions. In particular, each EditItemTemplate element includes a text box that uses the new Bind method to implement two-way binding (please see figure 13-14 for more information about this method).

Once you've converted the bound field to a template, you can edit the template to add any additional elements you want to include, such as validation controls. In the code example in this figure, you can see that I added a RequiredFieldValidator control to the EditItem template for the CategoryID field. That way, the user must enter data into the txtGridCategory text box. I also changed the names of the label and the text field generated for the EditItem template from their defaults (Label1 and TextBox1) to lblGridCategory and txtGridCategory.

You can also edit the templates from Design view. To do that, you use the same basic techniques that you use to work with the templates for a DataList control. The main difference is that each bound column in a GridView control has its own templates. In this figure, for example, you can see the EditItem template for the first column in the control.

How to edit templates

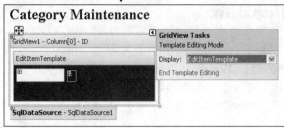

GridView template elements

Element	Description
ItemTemplate	The template used for an individual field.
AlternatingItemTemplate	The template used for alternate rows.
EditItemTemplate	The template used when the row is being edited.
HeaderTemplate	The template used for the header row.
FooterTemplate	The template used for the footer row.

A template field that includes a validation control

```
<asp:TemplateField HeaderText="ID">
    <ItemTemplate>
        <asp:Label ID="lblGridCategory" runat="server"
            Text='<%# Bind("CategoryID") %>'></asp:Label>
    </ItemTemplate>
    <EditItemTemplate>
        <asp:TextBox ID="txtGridCategory" runat="server"
            Text='<%# Bind("CategoryID") %>'></asp:TextBox>
        <asp:RequiredFieldValidator runat="server"
            ID="RequiredFieldValidator4"
            ControlToValidate="txtGridCategory"
            ErrorMessage="ID is a required field."
            ValidationGroup="Edit">*</asp:RequiredFieldValidator>
    </EditItemTemplate>
    <HeaderStyle HorizontalAlign="Left" />
    <ItemStyle Width="100px" />
</asp:TemplateField>
```

Description

- *Template fields* provide more control over the appearance of the columns in a GridView control. A common reason for using template fields is to add validation controls.

- To create a template field, first use the Fields dialog box to create a bound field. Then, click the Convert This Field into a TemplateField link.

- To edit a template, choose Edit Templates from the smart tag menu for the GridView control. Then, select the template you want to edit in the smart tag menu and edit the template by adding text or other controls. You may also want to change the names of the labels and text fields that were generated when you converted to a template field. When you're finished, choose End Template Editing in the smart tag menu.

Figure 14-15   How to create template fields

The template version of the Category Maintenance application

Figure 14-16 shows a version of the Category Maintenance application that uses templates instead of bound fields in the GridView control. Then, each edit template includes a required field validator. In addition, the page uses a validation summary control to display any error messages that are generated by the required field validators.

The aspx code for the template version

Figure 14-17 shows the aspx code for the template version of the Category Maintenance application. Because most of this file is similar to the file shown in figure 14-13, this figure shows only the portions that are different. In particular, it shows the code for the GridView control and the ValidationSummary control. Because you've already been introduced to most of this code, I'll just point out a few highlights.

First, the GridView control uses template fields that include required field validators to validate the text box input fields. Here, each validator is assigned to a validation group named Edit. Then, in the CommandField element for the Edit button, the CausesValidation attribute is set to True and the ValidationGroup attribute is set to Edit. As a result, when a row is displayed in edit mode, just the validators that belong to the Edit group will be invoked when the Update button is clicked.

Second, the ErrorMessage attribute of each of the Edit validators provides the error message that's displayed in the ValidationSummary control. For this control, you can see that the ValidationGroup is set to Edit so the right messages will be displayed. In addition, the content of each validator specifies that an asterisk will appear to the right of each field in the GridView control. If you look closely at the screen in the last figure, you can see that these asterisks are displayed in white on the dark column dividers.

Please note that there is one other difference between this version of the application and the previous version that isn't shown in this figure. Because this version uses a validation group for the validators in the GridView control, it must also use a validation group for the validators that are outside of the GridView control. As a result, the three validators for the text boxes as well as the Add New Category button all have a ValidationGroup attribute that assigns them to the New group.

The Category Maintenance application with template fields

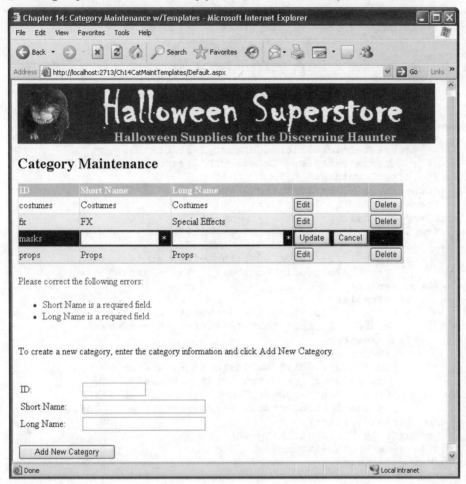

Description

- This version of the Category Maintenance application uses template fields in the GridView control, and the edit template for each field includes a required field validator.

- A ValidationSummary control is used to display the error messages generated by the required field validators.

Figure 14-16   The template version of the Category Maintenance application

The Default.aspx file

```
<asp:GridView ID="GridView1" runat="server"
    AutoGenerateColumns="False" DataKeyNames="CategoryID"
    DataSourceID="SqlDataSource1" ForeColor="Black">
    <Columns>
        <asp:TemplateField HeaderText="ID">
            <ItemTemplate>
                <asp:Label id="lblGridCategory" runat="server"
                    Text='<%# Bind("CategoryID") %>'></asp:Label>
            </ItemTemplate>
            <EditItemTemplate>
                <asp:Label id="lblGridCategory" runat="server"
                    Text='<%# Bind("CategoryID") %>'></asp:Label>
            </EditItemTemplate>
            <HeaderStyle HorizontalAlign="Left" />
            <ItemStyle Width="100px" />
        </asp:TemplateField>
        <asp:TemplateField HeaderText="Short Name">
            <ItemTemplate>
                <asp:Label ID="lblGridShortName" runat="server"
                    Text='<%# Bind("ShortName") %>'></asp:Label>
            </ItemTemplate>
            <EditItemTemplate>
                <asp:TextBox ID="txtGridShortName" runat="server"
                    width = "125px" Text='<%# Bind("ShortName") %>'>
                </asp:TextBox>
                <asp:RequiredFieldValidator
                    ID="RequiredFieldValidator5" runat="server"
                    ControlToValidate="txtGridShortName"
                    ErrorMessage="Short Name is a required field."
                    ValidationGroup="Edit">*</asp:RequiredFieldValidator>
            </EditItemTemplate>
            <HeaderStyle HorizontalAlign="Left" />
            <ItemStyle Width="150px" />
        </asp:TemplateField>
```

Figure 14-17   The aspx code for the template version of the Category Maintenance application
(part 1 of 2)

The Default.aspx file   **Page 2**

```
        <asp:TemplateField HeaderText="Long Name">
            <ItemTemplate>
                <asp:Label ID="lblGridLongName" runat="server"
                    Text='<%# Bind("LongName") %>'></asp:Label>
            </ItemTemplate>
            <EditItemTemplate>
                <asp:TextBox ID="txtGridLongName" runat="server"
                    width = "180px" Text='<%# Bind("LongName") %>'>
                </asp:TextBox>
                <asp:RequiredFieldValidator
                    ID="RequiredFieldValidator6" runat="server"
                    ControlToValidate="txtGridLongName"
                    ErrorMessage="Long Name is a required field."
                    ValidationGroup="Edit">*</asp:RequiredFieldValidator>
            </EditItemTemplate>
            <HeaderStyle HorizontalAlign="Left" />
            <ItemStyle Width="200px" />
        </asp:TemplateField>
        <asp:CommandField ButtonType="Button" ShowEditButton="True"
            CausesValidation="True" ValidationGroup="Edit" />
        <asp:CommandField ButtonType="Button" ShowDeleteButton="True"
            CausesValidation="False" />
    </Columns>
    <HeaderStyle BackColor="Silver" Font-Bold="True"
        ForeColor="White" />
    <RowStyle BackColor="White" ForeColor="Black" />
    <AlternatingRowStyle BackColor="WhiteSmoke" ForeColor="Black" />
    <EditRowStyle BackColor="Blue" ForeColor="White" />
</asp:GridView>
.
.
.
<asp:ValidationSummary ID="ValidationSummary1" runat="server"
    HeaderText="Please correct the following errors:"
    ValidationGroup="Edit"/>
.
.
.
```

Description

- This figure shows the aspx code for just the GridView control and the ValidationSummary control. The other elements are identical to the listing in figure 14-13.

- The three template fields include required field validators, which are assigned to a validation group named Edit. This group is also referenced in the code for the Edit button and the ValidationSummary control so only the validators in this group are included.

Figure 14-17   The aspx code for the template version of the Category Maintenance application
(part 2 of 2)

Perspective

The GridView control is one of the most significant improvements of ASP.NET 2.0. This control is ideal for any application that displays a list of items retrieved from a database, and nearly all applications have that need. For instance, the Shopping Cart application of chapter 3 can easily be implemented with a GridView control if the database is enhanced so it supports shopping cart items. The GridView control is also ideal for displaying search results, such as product searches for an online catalog or document searches in an online customer support site.

In the next chapter, you'll build on your knowledge of the GridView control by learning how to use it in combination with the new FormView and DetailsView controls. Both are designed to display the details for an item that's selected from a GridView control or a list control. And the combination of a GridView control and a FormView or DetailsView control can be powerful.

Terms

paging
command field
edit mode
template field

15

How to use the DetailsView and FormView controls

In this chapter, you'll learn how to use the DetailsView and FormView controls, which are new with ASP.NET 2.0. Although both of these controls are designed to work with the GridView control to display the details of the item selected in that control, they can also be used on their own or in combination with other types of list controls such as drop-down lists or list boxes.

How to use the DetailsView control

The following topics present the basics of working with the DetailsView control. However, much of what you'll learn in these topics applies to the FormView control as well.

An introduction to the DetailsView control

As figure 15-1 shows, the DetailsView control is designed to display the data for a single item of a data source. To use this control effectively, you must provide some way for the user to select which data item to display. The most common way to do that is to use the DetailsView control in combination with another control such as a GridView control or a drop-down list. At the top of this figure, you can see how the DetailsView control works with a drop-down list, and you'll see how it works with a GridView control later in this chapter.

Alternatively, you can enable paging for the DetailsView control to allow the user to select the data item to be displayed. Then, a row of paging controls appears at the bottom of the DetailsView control to allow the user to select the item. You'll learn how this works in figure 15-4.

As the code example in this figure shows, you use the DataSourceID attribute to specify the data source that a DetailsView control should be bound to. Then, the Fields element contains a set of child elements that define the individual fields to be displayed by the DetailsView control. This is similar to the way the Columns element for a GridView control works.

A DetailsView control can be displayed in one of three modes. In ReadOnly mode, the data for the current data source row is displayed but can't be modified. In Edit mode, the user can modify the data for the current row. And in Insert mode, the user can enter data that will be inserted into the data source as a new row.

A DetailsView control that displays data for a selected product

```
Choose a product: Skull Fogger    ▼

Product ID:          skullfog01
Name:                Skull Fogger
Short Description:   2,800 Cubic Foot Fogger
                     This fogger puts out a whopping 2,800
Long Description:    cubic feet of fog per minute. Comes with
                     a 10-foot remote control.
Category ID:         fx
Image File:          skullfog01.jpg
Unit Price:          39.9500
On Hand:             50
```

The aspx code for the DetailsView control shown above

```
<asp:DetailsView ID="DetailsView1" runat="server" AutoGenerateRows="False"
    DataKeyNames="ProductID" DataSourceID="SqlDataSource2"
    ForeColor="Black" GridLines="Horizontal" Width="400px">
    <Fields>
        <asp:BoundField DataField="ProductID" HeaderText="Product ID:" >
            <HeaderStyle Width="150 px" />
            <ItemStyle Width="250px" />
        </asp:BoundField>
        <asp:BoundField DataField="Name" HeaderText="Name:" />
        <asp:BoundField DataField="ShortDescription"
            HeaderText="Short Description:"/>
        <asp:BoundField DataField="LongDescription"
            HeaderText="Long Description:"/>
        <asp:BoundField DataField="CategoryID" HeaderText="Category ID:"/>
        <asp:BoundField DataField="ImageFile" HeaderText="Image File:"/>
        <asp:BoundField DataField="UnitPrice" HeaderText="Unit Price:"/>
        <asp:BoundField DataField="OnHand" HeaderText="On Hand:"/>
    </Fields>
</asp:DetailsView>
```

Three modes of the DetailsView control

Mode	Description
ReadOnly	Used to display an item from the data source.
Edit	Used to edit an item in the data source.
Insert	Used to insert a new item into a data source.

Description

- The DetailsView control displays data for a single row of a data source. It is usually used in combination with a drop-down list or GridView control that is used to select the item to be displayed.
- The DetailsView element includes a Fields element that contains a BoundField element for each field retrieved from the data source.
- You can edit the fields collection by choosing Edit Fields from the smart tag menu of a DetailsView control.

Figure 15-1   An introduction to the DetailsView control

Attributes and child elements for the DetailsView control

The tables in figure 15-2 list the attributes and child elements you can use to declare a DetailsView control. The first table lists the attributes you're most likely to use for this control. You can use the DataKeyNames attribute to list the names of the primary key fields for the data source. And you'll usually set the AutoGenerateRows attribute to False to prevent the DetailsView control from automatically generating data fields. That way, you can define the data fields you want to appear in the DetailsView control by using the Fields element.

By the way, there are many other attributes you can use on the DetailsView element to specify the control's layout and formatting. For example, you can include attributes like Height, Width, BackColor, and ForeColor. To see all of the attributes that are available, you can use the HTML Editor's IntelliSense feature.

The second table in this figure lists the child elements that you can use between the start and end tags of the DetailsView element. Most of these elements provide styles and templates that control the formatting for the different parts of the DetailsView control.

The Fields element can contain any of the child elements listed in the third table of this figure. These elements describe the individual data fields that are displayed by the DetailsView control. You can use the HTML Editor to create these elements manually. You can use the Fields dialog box as described in the previous chapter by choosing Edit Fields from the smart tag menu. Or, you can use the Add Field dialog box as described in the next figure.

Although this figure doesn't show it, the child elements in the third table can themselves include child elements to specify formatting information. For example, you can include HeaderStyle and ItemStyle as child elements of a BoundField element to control the formatting for the header and item sections of a bound field. Here again, you can use the HTML Editor's IntelliSense feature to see what child elements are available and what attributes they support.

DetailsView control attributes

Attribute	Description
ID	The ID of this control.
Runat	Must specify "server".
DataSourceID	The ID of the data source to bind the DetailsView control to.
DataKeyNames	A list of field names that form the primary key for the data source.
AutoGenerateRows	If True, a row is automatically generated for each field in the data source. If False, you must define the rows in the Fields element.
DefaultMode	Sets the initial mode of the DetailsView control. Valid options are Edit, Insert, or ReadOnly.
AllowPaging	Set to True to allow paging.

DetailsView child elements

Element	Description
Fields	The fields that are displayed by a DetailsView control.
RowStyle	The style used for data rows in ReadOnly mode.
AlternatingRowStyle	The style used for alternate rows.
EditRowStyle	The style used for data rows in Edit mode.
InsertRowStyle	The style used for data rows in Insert mode.
CommandRowStyle	The style used for command rows.
EmptyDataRowStyle	The style used for data rows when the data source is empty.
EmptyDataTemplate	The template used when the data source is empty.
HeaderStyle	The style used for the header row.
HeaderTemplate	The template used for the header row.
FooterStyle	The style used for the footer row.
FooterTemplate	The template used for the footer row.
PagerSettings	The settings used to control the pager row.
PagerStyle	The style used for the pager row.
PagerTemplate	The template used for the pager row.

Fields child elements

Element	Description
BoundField	A field bound to a data source column.
ButtonField	A field that displays a button.
CheckBoxField	A field that displays a check box.
CommandField	A field that contains command buttons.
HyperlinkField	A field that displays a hyperlink.
ImageField	A field that displays an image.
TemplateField	A column with custom content.

Figure 15-2   Attributes and child elements for the DetailsView control

How to add fields to a DetailsView control

Figure 15-3 shows how to add fields to a DetailsView control by using the Add Field dialog box. To display this dialog box, choose Add Field from the control's smart tag menu. Next, select the type of field you want to add. Then, set any other settings required by the field. If, for example, you select BoundField as the field type, you'll need to enter the text to display as a heading and identify the data source field you want to bind to.

Each time you use the Add Field dialog box, a child element is added to the Fields element of the DetailsView control. As you can see in the code example in this figure, each BoundField element includes a ReadOnly attribute that's set to True as well as a SortExpression attribute. However, since the sort expression is only meaningful if you enable paging, you can safely delete this attribute if you're not using paging.

Remember that, by default, the DetailsView control automatically generates a bound field for each field in the data source. You can prevent that, though, by setting the AutoGenerateRows attribute to False. Then, you'll have complete control over the fields that are displayed in the DetailsView control.

The Add Field dialog box

Aspx code generated by the Add Field dialog box

```
<asp:BoundField DataField="ProductID" HeaderText="Product ID:"
    ReadOnly="True" SortExpression="ProductID" />
```

Description

- The DetailsView control supports the same field types as the GridView control.
- You can add a field to a DetailsView control by choosing Add Field from the smart tag menu. Then, you can use the Add Field dialog box to add the field.
- You can also choose Edit Fields from the smart tag menu to bring up the Fields dialog box that's shown in figure 14-2 of chapter 14.
- By default, the DetailsView control will automatically generate a field for each field in the data source. To prevent this, set the AutoGenerateRows attribute for the control to False.

Figure 15-3   How to add fields to a DetailsView control

How to enable paging

Like the GridView control, the DetailsView control supports paging. As figure 15-4 shows, a row of paging controls is displayed at the bottom of the DetailsView control when you set the AllowPaging attribute to True. Then, you can specify the paging mode by including a PagerSettings element, and you can include PagerStyle and PagerTemplate elements to specify the appearance of the pager controls.

Note that if the data source contains more than a few dozen items, paging isn't a practical way to provide for navigation. In most cases, then, a DetailsView control is associated with a list control that is used to select the item to be displayed. You'll learn how to create pages that work this way in the next figure.

A DetailsView control that allows paging

ProductID	bl01
Name	Black light (24")
Short Description:	24" black light
Long Description:	Create that creepy glow-in-the-dark effect with this powerful black light.
Category ID:	fx
Image File:	blacklight01.jpg
Unit Price:	24.9900
On Hand:	200

<< < > >>

The aspx code for the DetailsView control shown above

```
<asp:DetailsView ID="DetailsView1" runat="server" AllowPaging="True"
    AutoGenerateRows="False"
    DataKeyNames="ProductID" DataSourceID="SqlDataSource1"
    Height="50px" Width="420px">
    <PagerSettings Mode="NextPreviousFirstLast" />
    <Fields>
        <asp:BoundField DataField="ProductID" HeaderText="ProductID"
            ReadOnly="True">
            <HeaderStyle Width="150px" />
            <ItemStyle Width="300px" />
        </asp:BoundField>
        <asp:BoundField DataField="Name" HeaderText="Name:" />
        <asp:BoundField DataField="ShortDescription"
            HeaderText="Short Description:" />
        <asp:BoundField DataField="LongDescription"
            HeaderText="Long Description:" />
        <asp:BoundField DataField="CategoryID"
            HeaderText="Category ID: " />
        <asp:BoundField DataField="ImageFile" HeaderText="Image File:" />
        <asp:BoundField DataField="UnitPrice" HeaderText="Unit Price:" />
        <asp:BoundField DataField="OnHand" HeaderText="On Hand:" />
    </Fields>
</asp:DetailsView>
```

Description

- The DetailsView control supports paging. Then, you can move from one item to the next by using the paging controls. This works much the same as it does for a GridView control, except that data from only one row is displayed at a time.

- For more information about paging, please refer to figure 14-6 in chapter 14.

Figure 15-4   How to enable paging

How to create a Master/Detail page

As figure 15-5 shows, a *Master/Detail page* is a page that displays a list of data items from a data source along with the details for one of the items selected from the list. The list of items can be displayed by any control that allows the user to select an item, including a drop-down list or a GridView control. Then, you can use a DetailsView control to display the details for the selected item. The page shown in figure 15-1 is an example of a Master/Detail page in which the master list is displayed as a drop-down list and a DetailsView control is used to display the details for the selected item.

A Master/Detail page typically uses two data sources. The first retrieves the items to be displayed by the control that contains the list of data items. For efficiency's sake, this data source should retrieve only the data columns neces- sary to display the list. For example, the data source for the drop-down list in figure 15-1 only needs to retrieve the ProductName and ProductID columns from the Products table in the Halloween database.

The second data source provides the data for the selected item. It usually uses a parameter to specify which row should be retrieved from the database. In the example in this figure, the data source uses a parameter that's bound to the drop-down list. That way, this data source automatically retrieves the data for the product that's selected by the drop-down list.

A Master/Detail page typically contains:

- A control that lets the user choose an item to display, such as a drop-down list or a GridView control.

- A data source that retrieves all of the items to be displayed in the list. The control that contains the list of data items should be bound to this data source.

- A DetailsView control that displays data for the item selected by the user.

- A data source that retrieves the data for the item selected by the user. The DetailsView control should be bound to this data source. To retrieve the selected item, this data source can use a parameter that's bound to the SelectedValue property of the control that contains the list of data items.

A SqlDataSource control with a parameter that's bound to a drop-down list

```
<asp:SqlDataSource ID="SqlDataSource2" runat="server"
    ConnectionString="<%$ ConnectionStrings:HalloweenConnection %>"
    SelectCommand="SELECT [ProductID], [Name], [ShortDescription],
        [LongDescription], [CategoryID], [ImageFile], [UnitPrice], [OnHand]
        FROM [Products]
        WHERE ([ProductID] = @ProductID)">
    <SelectParameters>
        <asp:ControlParameter ControlID="ddlProducts" Name="ProductID"
            PropertyName="SelectedValue" Type="String" />
    </SelectParameters>
</asp:SqlDataSource>
```

Description

- A *Master/Detail page* is a page that displays a list of items from a database along with the details of one item from the list. The DetailsView control is often used to display the details portion of a Master/Detail page.

- The list portion of a Master/Detail page can be displayed by any control that contains a list of data items, including a drop-down list or a GridView control.

- A Master/Detail page usually includes two data sources, one for the master list and the other for the DetailsView control.

Figure 15-5   How to create a Master/Detail page

How to update DetailsView data

Besides displaying data for a specific item from a data source, you can also use a DetailsView control to edit, insert, and delete items. You'll learn how to do that in the following topics.

An introduction to command buttons

Much like the GridView control, the DetailsView control uses command buttons to let the user edit and delete data. Thus, the DetailsView control provides Edit, Delete, Update, and Cancel buttons. In addition, the DetailsView control lets the user insert data so it provides for two more buttons. The New button places the DetailsView control into Insert mode, and the Insert button accepts the data entered by the user and writes it to the data source. These command buttons are summarized in figure 15-6.

There are two ways to provide the command buttons for a DetailsView control. The easiest way is to use the AutoGenerate*xxx*Button attributes, which are listed in the second table and illustrated in the code example. However, when you use these attributes, you have no control over the appearance of the buttons. For that, you must use command fields as described in the next figure.

A DetailsView control with automatically generated command buttons

Product ID:	arm01
Name:	Severed Arm
Short Description:	Bloody Severed Arm
Long Description:	A severed arm, complete with protruding bones and lots of blood.
Category ID:	props
Image File:	arm01.jpg
Unit Price:	19.9500
On Hand:	200
Edit Delete New	

Command buttons

Button	Description
Edit	Places the DetailsView control in Edit mode.
Delete	Deletes the current item and leaves the DetailsView control in ReadOnly mode.
New	Places the DetailsView control in Insert mode.
Update	Displayed only in Edit mode. Updates the data source, then returns to ReadOnly mode.
Insert	Displayed only in Insert mode. Inserts the data, then returns to ReadOnly mode.
Cancel	Displayed in Edit or Insert mode. Cancels the operation and returns to ReadOnly mode.

Attributes that generate command buttons

Attribute	Description
AutoGenerateDeleteButton	Generates a Delete button.
AutoGenerateEditButton	Generates an Edit button.
AutoGenerateInsertButton	Generates a New button.

A DetailsView element that automatically generates command buttons

```
<asp:DetailsView ID="DetailsView1" runat="server"
    DataSourceID="SqlDataSource2" DataKeyNames="ProductID"
    AutoGenerateRows="False"
    AutoGenerateDeleteButton="True"
    AutoGenerateEditButton="True"
    AutoGenerateInsertButton="True">
```

Description

- The DetailsView control supports six different command buttons.
- You can use the AutoGenerateDeleteButton, AutoGenerateEditButton, and AutoGenerateInsertButton attributes to automatically generate command buttons.
- To customize command button appearance, use command fields instead of automatically generated buttons, as described in the next figure.

Figure 15-6   An introduction to command buttons

How to add command buttons

Like the GridView control, the DetailsView control lets you use CommandField elements to specify the command buttons that should be displayed by the control. One way to do that is to use the Add Field dialog box shown in figure 15-7 to add a command field to a DetailsView control. Of course, you can also use the Edit Fields dialog box to add command fields, or you can use the HTML Editor to code the CommandField element manually.

When you select CommandField as the field type, four check boxes appear that let you select which command buttons you want to show in the command field. In addition, a drop-down list lets you choose whether the command buttons should be displayed as buttons or hyperlinks.

Note that the CommandField element includes attributes that let you specify the text or image to be displayed and whether the button causes validation. For more information about using these attributes, please refer back to chapter 14.

The Add Field dialog box for adding a command field

Code generated by the above dialog box

```
<asp:CommandField ButtonType="Button"
    ShowDeleteButton="True"
    ShowEditButton="True"
    ShowInsertButton="True" />
```

Description

- You can add command buttons to a DetailsView control to let the user update, insert, and delete data.

- The command buttons for a DetailsView control are similar to the command buttons for a GridView control. However, the DetailsView control doesn't provide a Select button, and it does provide New and Insert buttons. For more information about command buttons, please refer to figure 14-9 in chapter 14.

- To display the Add Field dialog box, choose Add Fields from the smart tag menu of the DetailsView control.

Figure 15-7   How to add command buttons

How to handle DetailsView events

Figure 15-8 lists the events that are raised by the DetailsView control. As you can see, these events are similar to the events raised by the GridView control. Most of these events come in pairs, one that's raised before an operation occurs, and another that's raised after the operation completes. For example, the ItemDeleting event is raised before an item is deleted, and the ItemDeleted event is raised after an item has been deleted.

As with the GridView control, the most common reason to handle the before events for the DetailsView control is to provide data validation. For example, when the user clicks the Update button, you can handle the ItemUpdating event to make sure the user has entered correct data. Then, you can set the e argument's Cancel property to True if the user hasn't entered correct data. This cancels the update.

The after-action events let you check that database operations have completed successfully. To do that, you need to check for two types of errors. First, you should check for database exceptions by testing the Exception property of the e argument. If it refers to an object, a database exception has occurred. Then, you should display an appropriate error message to let the user know about the problem.

If the data source uses optimistic concurrency, you should also check to make sure there hasn't been a concurrency error. You can do that by testing the AffectedRows property of the e argument. If a concurrency error has occurred, this property will be set to zero meaning that no rows have been changed. Then, you can display an appropriate error message.

If no errors occurred during the update operation, the ItemUpdated event shown in this figure ends by calling the DataBind method for the drop-down list control. This is necessary because view state is enabled for this control. As a result, this control will continue to display the old data unless you call its DataBind method to refresh its data. If view state were disabled for this control, the DataBind call wouldn't be necessary.

Unfortunately, there is a bug in the way ASP.NET 2.0 data sources handle optimistic concurrency when null values are involved. For more information about this bug and how to work around it, see the next figure.

Events raised by the DetailsView control

Event	Description
ItemCommand	Raised when a button is clicked.
ItemCreated	Raised when an item is created.
DataBound	Raised when data binding completes for an item.
ItemDeleted	Raised when an item has been deleted.
ItemDeleting	Raised when an item is about to be deleted.
ItemInserted	Raised when an item has been inserted.
ItemInserting	Raised when an item is about to be inserted.
ItemUpdated	Raised when an item has been updated.
ItemUpdating	Raised when an item is about to be updated.
PageIndexChanged	Raised when the index of the displayed item has changed.
PageIndexChanging	Raised when the index of the displayed item is about to change.

An event handler for the ItemUpdated event

```
Protected Sub DetailsView1_ItemUpdated(ByVal sender As Object, _
        ByVal e As System.Web.UI.WebControls.DetailsViewUpdatedEventArgs) _
        Handles DetailsView1.ItemUpdated
    If e.Exception IsNot Nothing Then
        lblError.Text = "Invalid data. Please correct and try again."
        e.ExceptionHandled = True
    ElseIf e.AffectedRows = 0 Then
        lblError.Text = "Another user has updated that product. " _
            & "Please try again."
    Else
        ddlProducts.DataBind()
    End If
End Sub
```

Description

- Like the GridView control, the DetailsView control raises events that can be handled when data is updated. At the minimum, you should use these events to test for database exceptions and concurrency errors.

- To determine if a SQL exception has occurred, test the Exception property of the e argument. If an exception has occurred, you can set the ExceptionHandled property to True to suppress the exception. You can also set the KeepInEditMode property to True to keep the DetailsView control in edit mode.

- If the AffectedRows property of the e argument is zero and an exception has not been thrown, a concurrency error has probably occurred.

- If the DetailsView control is used on a Master/Detail page, you should call the DataBind method of the master list control after a successful insert, update, or delete.

Figure 15-8   How to handle DetailsView events

How to fix the optimistic concurrency bug

Optimistic concurrency works by using a Where clause that compares each column in the database row with the values saved when the row was originally retrieved. If that row can't be found, it means that another user has updated the row and changed one of the columns. Then, the row isn't updated or deleted.

Unfortunately, there's a bug in the way ASP.NET 2.0 generates the Where clauses for columns that allow nulls. This bug, along with a workaround for it, is described in figure 15-9. In short, the problem is that when a database column allows nulls, the comparisons generated for the Where clauses don't work. That's because SQL defines the result of an equal comparison between a null and a null as False. (Since a null represents an unknown value, no value–even another null–can be considered equal to a null.)

The Halloween database illustrates this problem because it allows nulls for the ImageFile column in the Products table. But look at the Where clause that's generated for the first Delete statement in this figure:

```
[ImageFile] = @original_ImageFile
```

In this case, if the original value of the ImageFile column is null, this comparison will never test true, so the row will never be deleted.

The workaround to this bug is to modify the generated Delete and Update statements for any database table that allows nulls in any of its columns. For the ImageFile column, you can modify the Delete statement so it looks like this:

```
( [ImageFile] = @original_ImageFile
  OR [ImageFile] IS NULL AND @original_ImageFile IS NULL )
```

Then, the comparison will test true if both the ImageFile column and the @original_ImageFile parameter are null.

A generated Delete statement that handles concurrency errors

```
DELETE FROM [Products]
      WHERE [ProductID] = @original_ProductID
        AND [Name] = @original_Name
        AND [ShortDescription] = @original_ShortDescription
        AND [LongDescription] = @original_LongDescription
        AND [CategoryID] = @original_CategoryID
        AND [ImageFile] = @original_ImageFile
        AND [UnitPrice] = @original_UnitPrice
        AND [OnHand] = @original_OnHand"
```

How to modify the Delete statement for a column that allows nulls

```
DELETE FROM [Products]
      WHERE [ProductID] = @original_ProductID
        AND [Name] = @original_Name
        AND [ShortDescription] = @original_ShortDescription
        AND [LongDescription] = @original_LongDescription
        AND [CategoryID] = @original_CategoryID
        AND ( [ImageFile] = @original_ImageFile
         OR ImageFile IS NULL AND @original_ImageFile IS NULL )
        AND [UnitPrice] = @original_UnitPrice
        AND [OnHand] = @original_OnHand"
```

Description

- When you select optimistic concurrency for a data source in the Data Source Configuration Wizard, the wizard adds code to the Update and Delete statements that prevents concurrency errors.

- Unfortunately, the generated code for Update and Delete statements doesn't work properly for database columns that allow nulls because two nulls aren't treated as equal.

- To fix this error, you can edit the Update and Delete statements so they include an Is Null test for each column that allows nulls.

Known bug

- This is a known bug in the final release of this product.

Figure 15-9   How to fix the optimistic concurrency bug

The Product Maintenance application

The following topics present an application that uses a GridView and a DetailsView control in a Master/Detail page to maintain the Products table in the Halloween database.

The operation of the application

Figure 15-10 shows the operation of the Product Maintenance application. This application uses a GridView control to list the product records on the left side of the page. This control uses paging to allow the user to scroll through the entire Products table.

When the user clicks the Select button for a product, the details for that product are displayed in the DetailsView control on the right side of the page. Then, the user can use the Edit or Delete buttons to edit or delete the selected product. The user can also click the New button to insert a new product.

The aspx file

Figure 15-11 shows the complete Default.aspx file for the Product Maintenance application. This file uses a table to control the overall layout of the page. In part 1, you can see the GridView control that displays the products as well as the data source for this control. Notice that the SelectedIndex attribute of the GridView control is set to 0. That way, the information for the first product will be displayed in the DetailsView control when the page is first displayed.

The DetailsView control is shown in parts 2 and 3 of the listing. Here, the DetailsView element includes the attributes that control the overall appearance of the control. I generated most of these attributes by applying an AutoFormat to the DetailsView control, then editing the attributes to change the colors. You can also see that the AutoFormat added HeaderStyle and ItemStyle attributes to each of the BoundField elements in the Fields collection. And you can see that I added a CommandField element to provide the Edit, Delete, and New buttons.

Note that this DetailsView control doesn't provide for data validation for insert and update operations. Instead, it relies on the data source to throw database exceptions if the user tries to enter incorrect data. To provide data validation in Insert or Edit mode, you could convert the bound fields to template fields and add data validators as shown in figure 14-15 in chapter 14.

Also notice that the DataFormatString and HtmlEncode attributes apply currency formatting to the Unit Price field. This works the same for the DetailsView control as it does for the GridView control. For more information, please refer to figure 14-2 in chapter 14.

The rest of this listing is filled mostly with the data source that the DetailsView control is bound to. This data source includes Delete, Insert, and Update commands that use optimistic concurrency. If you look at the Where clauses for the Delete and Update commands, you can see the modifications that I made to correctly handle nulls for the ImageFile column.

The Product Maintenance application

Description

- The Product Maintenance application uses a GridView and a DetailsView control to let the user update the data in the Products table.
- To select a product, the user locates the product in the GridView control and clicks the Select button. This displays the details for the product in the DetailsView control. Then, the user can click the Edit button to change the product data or the Delete button to delete the product.
- To add a new product to the database, the user clicks the New button in the DetailsView control. Then, the user can enter the data for the new product and click the Insert button.

Figure 15-10   The Product Maintenance application

The Default.aspx file

```
<%@ Page Language="VB" AutoEventWireup="false" CodeFile="Default.aspx.vb"
Inherits="_Default" %>

<!DOCTYPE html PUBLIC "-//W3C//DTD XHTML 1.1//EN"
"http://www.w3.org/TR/xhtml11/DTD/xhtml11.dtd">

<html xmlns="http://www.w3.org/1999/xhtml" >
<head runat="server">
    <title>Chapter 15: Product List</title>
</head>
<body>
  <form id="form1" runat="server">
  <div>
    <asp:Image ID="Image1" runat="server" ImageUrl="~/Images/banner.jpg" />
    <br /><br />
    <table>
      <tr>
        <td style="width:300px" valign="top">
          <asp:GridView ID="GridView1" runat="server"
              AllowSorting="True" AllowPaging="True"
              DataKeyNames="ProductID" DataSourceID="SqlDataSource1"
              AutoGenerateColumns="False" SelectedIndex="0"
              CellPadding="4" GridLines="None" ForeColor="Black" >
            <Columns>
              <asp:BoundField DataField="ProductID" HeaderText="ID"
                  ReadOnly="True">
                <HeaderStyle HorizontalAlign="Left" />
                <ItemStyle Width="75px" />
              </asp:BoundField>
              <asp:BoundField DataField="Name" HeaderText="Name">
                <HeaderStyle HorizontalAlign="Left" />
                <ItemStyle Width="200px" />
              </asp:BoundField>
              <asp:BoundField DataField="CategoryID" HeaderText="Category" />
              <asp:CommandField ButtonType="Button" ShowSelectButton="True" />
            </Columns>
            <HeaderStyle BackColor="Silver" Font-Bold="True"
                ForeColor="White" />
            <RowStyle BackColor="White" ForeColor="Black" />
            <AlternatingRowStyle BackColor="WhiteSmoke" ForeColor="Black" />
            <SelectedRowStyle BackColor="Blue" ForeColor="White" />
            <FooterStyle BackColor="Silver" Font-Bold="True"
                ForeColor="White" />
            <PagerStyle BackColor="Silver" ForeColor="Blue"
                HorizontalAlign="Center" />
            </asp:GridView>

          <asp:SqlDataSource ID="SqlDataSource1" runat="server"
              ConnectionString="<%$ ConnectionStrings:HalloweenConnection %>"
              SelectCommand="SELECT [ProductID], [Name], [CategoryID]
                  FROM [Products] ORDER BY [ProductID]">
          </asp:SqlDataSource>
        </td>
```

Figure 15-11   The aspx file for the Product Maintenance application (part 1 of 4)

The Default.aspx file   Page 2

```
<td style="width:400px" valign="top">
  <asp:DetailsView ID="DetailsView1" runat="server"
    DataSourceID="SqlDataSource2" DataKeyNames="ProductID"
    Height="50px" Width="400px" AutoGenerateRows="False"
    BackColor="White" BorderColor="White" BorderStyle="Ridge"
    BorderWidth="2px" CellPadding="3" CellSpacing="1"
    GridLines="None">
  <RowStyle BackColor="#DEDFDE" ForeColor="Black" />
  <Fields>
    <asp:BoundField DataField="ProductID"
        HeaderText="Product ID:"
        ReadOnly="True" SortExpression="ProductID">
      <HeaderStyle HorizontalAlign="Left" Width="150px" />
      <ItemStyle Width="250px" />
    </asp:BoundField>
    <asp:BoundField DataField="Name" HeaderText="Name:">
      <HeaderStyle HorizontalAlign="Left" Width="150px" />
      <ItemStyle Width="250px" />
    </asp:BoundField>
    <asp:BoundField DataField="ShortDescription"
        HeaderText="Short Description:">
      <HeaderStyle HorizontalAlign="Left" Width="150px" />
      <ItemStyle Width="250px" />
    </asp:BoundField>
    <asp:BoundField DataField="LongDescription"
        HeaderText="Long Description:">
      <HeaderStyle HorizontalAlign="Left" Width="150px" />
      <ItemStyle Width="250px" />
    </asp:BoundField>
    <asp:BoundField DataField="CategoryID"
        HeaderText="Category ID:">
      <HeaderStyle HorizontalAlign="Left" Width="150px" />
      <ItemStyle Width="250px" />
    </asp:BoundField>
    <asp:BoundField DataField="ImageFile"
        HeaderText="Image File:" SortExpression="ImageFile">
      <HeaderStyle HorizontalAlign="Left" Width="150px" />
      <ItemStyle Width="250px" />
    </asp:BoundField>
    <asp:BoundField DataField="UnitPrice"
        HeaderText="Unit Price:" DataFormatString="{0:c}"
        HtmlEncode="False">
      <HeaderStyle HorizontalAlign="Left" Width="150px" />
      <ItemStyle Width="250px" />
    </asp:BoundField>
    <asp:BoundField DataField="OnHand" HeaderText="On Hand:">
      <HeaderStyle HorizontalAlign="Left" Width="150px" />
      <ItemStyle Width="250px" />
    </asp:BoundField>
```

Figure 15-11   The aspx file for the Product Maintenance application (part 2 of 4)

The Default.aspx file

```
            <asp:CommandField ButtonType="Button"
                ShowDeleteButton="True"
                ShowEditButton="True"
                ShowInsertButton="True" />
        </Fields>
        <HeaderStyle BackColor="Silver" Font-Bold="True"
            ForeColor="Black" />
        <EditRowStyle BackColor="Blue" Font-Bold="True"
            ForeColor="White" />
    </asp:DetailsView>

    <asp:SqlDataSource ID="SqlDataSource2" runat="server"
        ConflictDetection="CompareAllValues"
        ConnectionString="<%$ ConnectionStrings:HalloweenConnection %>"
        OldValuesParameterFormatString="original_{0}"
        SelectCommand="SELECT [ProductID], [Name], [ShortDescription],
            [LongDescription], [CategoryID], [ImageFile],
            [UnitPrice], [OnHand]
          FROM [Products]
          WHERE ([ProductID] = @ProductID)"
        DeleteCommand="DELETE FROM [Products]
          WHERE [ProductID] = @original_ProductID
            AND [Name] = @original_Name
            AND [ShortDescription] = @original_ShortDescription
            AND [LongDescription] = @original_LongDescription
            AND [CategoryID] = @original_CategoryID
            AND ( [ImageFile] = @original_ImageFile
             OR ImageFile IS NULL AND @original_ImageFile IS NULL )
            AND [UnitPrice] = @original_UnitPrice
            AND [OnHand] = @original_OnHand"
        InsertCommand="INSERT INTO [Products] ([ProductID], [Name],
            [ShortDescription], [LongDescription], [CategoryID],
            [ImageFile], [UnitPrice], [OnHand])
          VALUES (@ProductID, @Name, @ShortDescription,
                @LongDescription, @CategoryID, @ImageFile,
                @UnitPrice, @OnHand)"
        UpdateCommand="UPDATE [Products] SET [Name] = @Name,
            [ShortDescription] = @ShortDescription,
            [LongDescription] = @LongDescription,
            [CategoryID] = @CategoryID,
            [ImageFile] = @ImageFile,
            [UnitPrice] = @UnitPrice,
            [OnHand] = @OnHand
          WHERE [ProductID] = @original_ProductID
            AND [Name] = @original_Name
            AND [ShortDescription] = @original_ShortDescription
            AND [LongDescription] = @original_LongDescription
            AND [CategoryID] = @original_CategoryID
            AND ( [ImageFile] = @original_ImageFile
             OR ImageFile IS NULL AND @original_ImageFile IS NULL )
            AND [UnitPrice] = @original_UnitPrice
            AND [OnHand] = @original_OnHand">
```

Figure 15-11   The aspx file for the Product Maintenance application (part 3 of 4)

The Default.aspx file   **Page 4**

```
        <SelectParameters>
          <asp:ControlParameter ControlID="GridView1" Name="ProductID"
             PropertyName="SelectedValue" Type="String" />
        </SelectParameters>
        <DeleteParameters>
          <asp:Parameter Name="original_ProductID" Type="String" />
          <asp:Parameter Name="original_Name" Type="String" />
          <asp:Parameter Name="original_ShortDescription" Type="String" />
          <asp:Parameter Name="original_LongDescription" Type="String" />
          <asp:Parameter Name="original_CategoryID" Type="String" />
          <asp:Parameter Name="original_ImageFile" Type="String" />
          <asp:Parameter Name="original_UnitPrice" Type="Decimal" />
          <asp:Parameter Name="original_OnHand" Type="Int32" />
        </DeleteParameters>
        <UpdateParameters>
          <asp:Parameter Name="Name" Type="String" />
          <asp:Parameter Name="ShortDescription" Type="String" />
          <asp:Parameter Name="LongDescription" Type="String" />
          <asp:Parameter Name="CategoryID" Type="String" />
          <asp:Parameter Name="ImageFile" Type="String" />
          <asp:Parameter Name="UnitPrice" Type="Decimal" />
          <asp:Parameter Name="OnHand" Type="Int32" />
          <asp:Parameter Name="original_ProductID" Type="String" />
          <asp:Parameter Name="original_Name" Type="String" />
          <asp:Parameter Name="original_ShortDescription" Type="String"
          <asp:Parameter Name="original_LongDescription" Type="String" />
          <asp:Parameter Name="original_CategoryID" Type="String" />
          <asp:Parameter Name="original_ImageFile" Type="String" />
          <asp:Parameter Name="original_UnitPrice" Type="Decimal" />
          <asp:Parameter Name="original_OnHand" Type="Int32" />
        </UpdateParameters>
        <InsertParameters>
          <asp:Parameter Name="ProductID" Type="String" />
          <asp:Parameter Name="Name" Type="String" />
          <asp:Parameter Name="ShortDescription" Type="String" />
          <asp:Parameter Name="LongDescription" Type="String" />
          <asp:Parameter Name="CategoryID" Type="String" />
          <asp:Parameter Name="ImageFile" Type="String" />
          <asp:Parameter Name="UnitPrice" Type="Decimal" />
          <asp:Parameter Name="OnHand" Type="Int32" />
        </InsertParameters>
      </asp:SqlDataSource><br />

      <asp:Label ID = "lblError" runat="server" ForeColor="Red"
          EnableViewState="False"></asp:Label>
    </td>
   </tr>
  </table>
 </div>
 </form>
</body>
</html>
```

Figure 15-11   The aspx file for the Product Maintenance application (part 4 of 4)

The code-behind file

Figure 15-12 shows the code-behind file for the Default page of the Product Maintenance application. Even though this application provides complete maintenance for the Products table, only four procedures are required. These procedures respond to events raised by the DetailsView control. The first three handle database exceptions and concurrency errors for updates, deletions, and insertions.

Note that the error-handling code for the insert procedure is simpler than the error-handling code for the update and delete procedures. That's because optimistic concurrency doesn't apply to insert operations. As a result, there's no need to check the AffectedRows property to see if a concurrency error has occurred.

The last procedure, DetailsView1_ItemDeleting, handles a problem that can occur when you apply a format to a bound field. In this case, the currency format is applied to the unit price field. Because this application uses optimistic concurrency, the original values of each field are passed to the Delete statement as parameters to make sure that another user hasn't changed the product row since it was retrieved. Unfortunately, the DetailsView control sets the value of the unit price parameter to its formatted value, which includes the currency symbol. If you allow this value to be passed on to the Delete statement, an exception will be thrown because the parameter value is in the wrong format.

Before the Delete statement is executed, then, the DetailsView1_ItemDeleting procedure is called. This procedure removes the currency symbol from the parameter value so the value will be passed to the Delete statement in the correct format. Note that a similar procedure isn't required when you update a row because the DetailsView control doesn't use the format string in Edit mode by default.

The Default.aspx.vb file

```vb
Partial Class _Default
    Inherits System.Web.UI.Page

    Protected Sub DetailsView1_ItemUpdated(ByVal sender As Object, _
            ByVal e As System.Web.UI.WebControls.DetailsViewUpdatedEventArgs) _
            Handles DetailsView1.ItemUpdated
        If e.Exception IsNot Nothing Then
            lblError.Text = "Invalid data. Please correct and try again."
            e.ExceptionHandled = True
        ElseIf e.AffectedRows = 0 Then
            lblError.Text = "Another user has updated that product. " _
                & "Please try again."
        Else
            GridView1.DataBind()
        End If
    End Sub

    Protected Sub DetailsView1_ItemDeleted(ByVal sender As Object, _
            ByVal e As System.Web.UI.WebControls.DetailsViewDeletedEventArgs) _
            Handles DetailsView1.ItemDeleted
        If e.Exception IsNot Nothing Then
            lblError.Text = "A database error has occurred. " _
                & "Please try again."
            e.ExceptionHandled = True
        ElseIf e.AffectedRows = 0 Then
            lblError.Text = "Another user has updated that product. " _
                & "Please try again."
        Else
            GridView1.DataBind()
        End If
    End Sub

    Protected Sub DetailsView1_ItemInserted(ByVal sender As Object, _
            ByVal e As System.Web.UI.WebControls.DetailsViewInsertedEventArgs) _
            Handles DetailsView1.ItemInserted
        If e.Exception IsNot Nothing Then
            lblError.Text = "Invalid data. Please correct and try again."
            e.ExceptionHandled = True
        Else
            GridView1.DataBind()
        End If
    End Sub

    Protected Sub DetailsView1_ItemDeleting(ByVal sender As Object, _
            ByVal e As System.Web.UI.WebControls.DetailsViewDeleteEventArgs) _
            Handles DetailsView1.ItemDeleting
        e.Values("UnitPrice") _
            = e.Values("UnitPrice").ToString().Substring(1);
    End Sub

End Class
```

Figure 15-12   The code-behind file for the Product Maintenance application

How to use the FormView control

Besides the DetailsView control, ASP.NET 2.0 also provides a new FormView control. Like the DetailsView control, the FormView control is designed to display data for a single item from a data source. However, as you'll see in the following topics, the FormView control uses a different approach to displaying its data.

An introduction to the FormView control

Figure 15-13 presents an introduction to the FormView control. Although the FormView control is similar to the DetailsView control, it differs in several key ways. Most importantly, the FormView control isn't restricted by the HTML table layout of the DetailsView control, in which each field in the data source is rendered as a table row. Instead, the FormView control uses templates to specify how the data item is rendered. This gives you complete control over the layout of the data.

Another important difference is that the FormView control doesn't include a Fields collection like the DetailsView control. As a result, data binding for a FormView control is done with binding expressions rather than BoundField elements.

The easiest way to create a FormView control is to drag the FormView control icon from the Toolbox onto the page. Then, you can use the smart tag menu to bind the FormView control to a data source. When you do that, the Web Forms Designer will automatically create the FormView control's templates for you, as shown in the first image in this figure.

You can then edit the templates to achieve the layout you want. To do that, choose Edit Templates from the smart tag menu. This places the control in template-editing mode, as shown in the second image in this figure. The drop-down list in this figure shows the various templates that are used by the FormView control. For most applications, you'll use just the Item, EditItem, InsertItem, and EmptyData templates.

A FormView control after a data source has been assigned

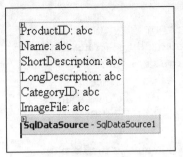

A FormView control in template-editing mode

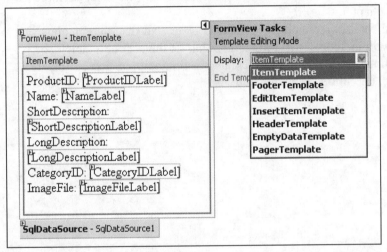

How the FormView control differs from the DetailsView control

- The DetailsView control is easier to work with, but the FormView control provides more formatting and layout options.
- The DetailsView control renders each data source item as a table row, but the FormView control uses a template to render each item.
- The DetailsView control uses BoundField elements to define bound data fields, but the FormView control uses data binding expressions in its templates to display bound data.

Description

- A FormView control is similar to a DetailsView control, but it uses templates that give you more control over how its data is displayed.
- To create a FormView control, you drag its icon from the Data group of the Toolbox onto the page, and you assign a data source to the control. Then, you edit the control's templates so the data is displayed the way you want.

Figure 15-13   An introduction to the FormView control

How to work with the Item template

When you use the Web Forms Designer to create a FormView control and bind it to a data source, the Web Forms Designer automatically generates basic templates for the FormView control. For instance, the code in figure 15-14 shows a typical Item template that has been generated. As you can see, it consists of a literal header and a label control for each field in the data source. The Text attribute of each label control uses either the ASP.NET 2.0 Bind or Eval method for data binding.

To control the format and layout of the item data, you can edit the Item template. In fact, it's common to include an HTML table in the Item template to control the layout of the individual fields in the template. You'll see an example of this later in this chapter.

Note that if the data source includes Update, Delete, and Insert commands, the Item template will include command buttons that let the user edit, delete, or add new rows. Although these buttons are created as link buttons, you can easily change them to regular buttons or image buttons.

The Item template generated for a FormView control

```
<asp:FormView ID="FormView1" runat="server" DataKeyNames="ProductID"
    DataSourceID="SqlDataSource1">
    <ItemTemplate>
        ProductID:
        <asp:Label ID="ProductIDLabel" runat="server"
            Text='<%# Eval("ProductID") %>'></asp:Label><br />
        Name:
        <asp:Label ID="NameLabel" runat="server"
            Text='<%# Bind("Name") %>'></asp:Label><br />
        ShortDescription:
        <asp:Label ID="ShortDescriptionLabel" runat="server"
            Text='<%# Bind("ShortDescription") %>'></asp:Label><br />
        LongDescription:
        <asp:Label ID="LongDescriptionLabel" runat="server"
            Text='<%# Bind("LongDescription") %>'></asp:Label><br />
        CategoryID:
        <asp:Label ID="CategoryIDLabel" runat="server"
            Text='<%# Bind("CategoryID") %>'></asp:Label><br />
        ImageFile:
        <asp:Label ID="ImageFileLabel" runat="server"
            Text='<%# Bind("ImageFile") %>'></asp:Label><br />
    </ItemTemplate>
    .
    .
    .
</asp:FormView>
```

Description

- When you bind a FormView control to a data source, templates are created with heading text, bound labels, and text boxes for each column in the data source.

- The Item template is rendered whenever the FormView control is bound in ReadOnly mode.

- The generated templates use the new Eval and Bind methods to create binding expressions for each of the fields in the data source (see figure 13-14 in chapter 13).

- If the data source includes Update, Delete, and Insert statements, the generated Item template will include Edit, Delete, and New buttons.

- The Web Forms Designer also generates an EditItem template and an InsertItem template, even if the data source doesn't include an Update or Insert command. For more information, see the next figure.

- You can add a table to a generated template to control the layout of the data that's rendered for that template.

Figure 15-14   How to work with the Item template

How to work with the EditItem and InsertItem templates

As figure 15-15 shows, the Web Forms Designer also generates an EditItem and InsertItem template when you bind it to a data source. These templates are generated even if the data source doesn't have an Update or Insert command. As a result, you can delete these templates if your application doesn't allow for edits and inserts. Although this figure only shows an EditItem template, the InsertItem template is similar.

One drawback to using the FormView control is that once you edit the Item template so the data is arranged the way you want, you must provide similar layout code in both the EditItem template and the InsertItem template. If, for example, you create a table in the Item template to arrange the fields in a certain way, you'll need to create similar tables in the EditItem and InsertItem templates so the layout is the same in all three templates. And if you later decide to change that layout, you'll have to make the change to all three templates. Unfortunately, there's no escaping this duplication of effort.

A generated EditItem template as displayed in a browser window

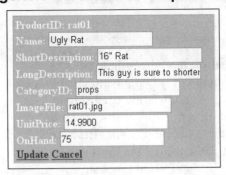

The aspx code for the edit item template shown above

```
<EditItemTemplate>
    ProductID:
    <asp:Label ID="ProductIDLabel1" runat="server"
        Text='<%# Eval("ProductID") %>'></asp:Label><br />
    Name:
    <asp:TextBox ID="NameTextBox" runat="server" Text='<%# Bind("Name") %>'>
    </asp:TextBox><br />
    ShortDescription:
    <asp:TextBox ID="ShortDescriptionTextBox" runat="server"
        Text='<%# Bind("ShortDescription") %>'>
    </asp:TextBox><br />
    .
    .
    .
    .
    .
```

> The code generated for the LongDescription, CategoryID, ImageFile, UnitPrice, and OnHand columns is similar to the code generated for the ShortDescription column.

```
    <asp:LinkButton ID="UpdateButton" runat="server" CausesValidation="True"
        CommandName="Update" Text="Update">
    </asp:LinkButton>
    <asp:LinkButton ID="UpdateCancelButton" runat="server"
        CausesValidation="False" CommandName="Cancel" Text="Cancel">
    </asp:LinkButton>
</EditItemTemplate>
```

Description

- The EditItem template determines how the FormView control is rendered in Edit mode. It includes a text box for each bound column in the data source. The Text attribute for each text box uses a binding expression that binds the text box to its data source column.

- The EditItem template also includes Update and Cancel buttons.

- The InsertItem template is similar to the EditItem template. It determines how the FormView control is rendered in Insert mode.

Figure 15-15   How to work with the EditItem and InsertItem templates

A Shopping Cart application that uses a FormView control

To show the versatility of the FormView control, the following topics present a version of the Order page from the Shopping Cart application that was originally presented in chapter 3. That version of the application used simple label and image controls to display the information for the product selected by the user. Because data binding didn't work for those controls, Visual Basic code was required in the Page_Load procedure to set the values of the label and image controls. In contrast, this new version of the application takes advantage of the data binding ability of the FormView control, so no Page_Load procedure is required.

Because this application doesn't allow the user to update, delete, or insert product information, it doesn't illustrate the use of the EditItem or InsertItem templates or the use of command buttons with a FormView control. If you want to see an application that does use those features, though, you can download a FormView version of the Product Maintenance application from our web site, www.murach.com.

The operation of the application

To refresh your memory, figure 15-16 shows the Order page displayed by the Shopping Cart application. As you can see, this page lets the user select a product from a drop-down list. When the user selects a product, the page displays the name, description, price, and an image of the selected product. Then, the user can order the product by entering a quantity and clicking the Add to Cart button.

This time, the product information is displayed within a FormView control, and the Item template includes a simple HTML table that displays the text information on the left and the image on the right. This demonstrates the layout flexibility of the FormView control. With a DetailsView control, it wouldn't be possible to display the image to the right of the text data, because the DetailsView control displays each column of the data source in a separate table row.

The Order page as viewed in the Web Forms Designer

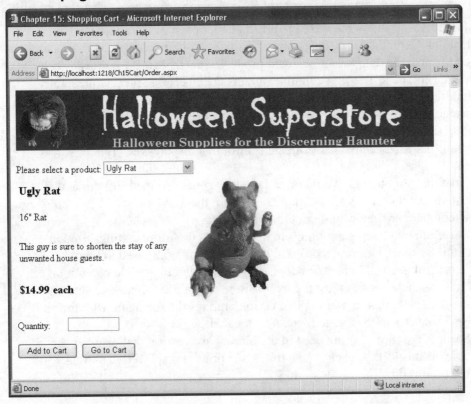

Description

- This is the Shopping Cart application that was originally presented in chapter 3, but this time it's implemented with a FormView control that displays the data for the selected product.
- The Item template for the FormView control includes an HTML table with cells that contain labels that are bound to the columns in the data source. It also includes an Image control whose ImageUrl property is bound to the ImageFile column in the data source.

Figure 15-16   The Shopping Cart application with a FormView control

The aspx file for the Order page

Figure 15-17 shows the aspx file for the Order page of the Shopping Cart application. Here, the FormView control includes an Item template that uses a table to format the data for the selected product. This table has four rows, each with three columns. The first column contains the labels that present the name, short description, long description, and price for the selected product. The second column (which spans all four rows) is a small spacer column to provide some space between the text and the image. And the third column (which also spans all four rows) contains the image control that displays the product's image.

Note that although the Web Forms Designer generated the EditItem and InsertItem templates, this application doesn't use them. As a result, I deleted those templates so they wouldn't clutter the listing.

There are two interesting things to notice about the format strings used in the binding expressions on this page. First, the format string used to bind the image control is this: "Images/Products/{0}". Since the ImageFile column in the Products table contains just the name of the image file for each product, not its complete path, this formatting expression prefixes the file name with the path Images/Products/ so the image file can be located.

Second, the format string used in the binding expression that displays the unit price is this: "{0:c} each". As a result, the price is displayed in currency format, followed by the word "each."

The code-behind file for the Order page

Figure 15-18 shows the code-behind file for the Order page. This code is almost identical to the code for the original version of this program that was presented back in chapter 3. In fact, there are only two substantial differences. First, this version doesn't include a Page_Load procedure because it doesn't need to do any data binding.

Second, the GetSelectedProduct procedure in this version is simpler than the one in the original version. Because the new application uses two data sources, a select parameter can be used to retrieve the selected product in the second data source. Then, because the second data source retrieves just a single row, a row filter isn't required. Instead, the index value 0 is used to retrieve data from the first and only row of the data source.

The Order.aspx file   **Page 1**

```
<%@ Page Language="VB" AutoEventWireup="false" CodeFile="Order.aspx.vb"
Inherits="Order" %>

<!DOCTYPE html PUBLIC "-//W3C//DTD XHTML 1.1//EN"
"http://www.w3.org/TR/xhtml11/DTD/xhtml11.dtd">

<html xmlns="http://www.w3.org/1999/xhtml" >
<head runat="server">
    <title>Chapter 15: Shopping Cart w/FormView</title>
</head>
<body>
    <form id="form1" runat="server">
    <div>
        <asp:Image ID="Image1" runat="server"
            ImageUrl="~/Images/banner.jpg" /><br /><br />
        <asp:Label ID="Label1" runat="server"
            Text="Please select a product:"></asp:Label>
        <asp:DropDownList ID="ddlProducts" runat="server" Width="150px"
            AutoPostBack="True" DataSourceID="SqlDataSource1"
            DataTextField="Name" DataValueField="ProductID">
        </asp:DropDownList>
        <asp:SqlDataSource ID="SqlDataSource1" runat="server"
            ConnectionString="<%$ ConnectionStrings:HalloweenConnection %>"
            SelectCommand="SELECT [ProductID], [Name] FROM [Products]
                ORDER BY [Name]">
        </asp:SqlDataSource>
        <br />
        <asp:FormView ID="FormView1" runat="server"
            DataSourceID="SqlDataSource2">
          <ItemTemplate>
            <table>
              <tr>
                <td style="height: 22px; width: 250px">
                  <asp:Label ID="lblName" runat="server"
                      Font-Bold="True" Font-Size="Larger"
                      Text='<%# Bind("Name") %>' >
                  </asp:Label>
                </td>
                <td style="width: 20px" rowspan="4" valign="top"></td>
                <td rowspan="4" valign="top">
                  <asp:Image ID="imgProduct" runat="server" Height="200px"
                      ImageUrl='<%# Bind("ImageFile", "Images/Products/{0}") %>' />
                </td>
              </tr>
              <tr>
                <td style="width: 250px">
                  <asp:Label ID="lblShortDescription" runat="server"
                      Text='<%# Bind("ShortDescription") %>'>
                  </asp:Label>
                </td>
              </tr>
```

Figure 15-17   The aspx file for the Order page of the Shopping Cart application (part 1 of 2)

The Order.aspx file

```
      <tr>
        <td style="width: 250px">
          <asp:Label ID="lblLongDescription" runat="server"
              Text='<%# Bind("LongDescription") %>'>
          </asp:Label>
        </td>
      </tr>
      <tr>
        <td style="width: 250px">
          <asp:Label ID="lblUnitPrice" runat="server"
              Font-Bold="True" Font-Size="Larger"
              Text='<%# Bind("UnitPrice", "{0:c} each") %>'>
          </asp:Label>
        </td>
      </tr>
    </table>
  </ItemTemplate>
</asp:FormView>
<asp:SqlDataSource ID="SqlDataSource2" runat="server"
    ConnectionString="<%$ ConnectionStrings:HalloweenConnection %>"
    SelectCommand="SELECT [ProductID], [Name], [ShortDescription],
        [LongDescription], [ImageFile], [UnitPrice]
      FROM [Products]
      WHERE ([ProductID] = @ProductID)">
    <SelectParameters>
        <asp:ControlParameter ControlID="ddlProducts" Name="ProductID"
            PropertyName="SelectedValue" Type="String" />
    </SelectParameters>
</asp:SqlDataSource><br />
<asp:Label ID="Label2" runat="server" BorderWidth="0px" Text="Quantity:"
    Width="80px"></asp:Label>
<asp:TextBox ID="txtQuantity" runat="server" Width="80px"></asp:TextBox>
<asp:RequiredFieldValidator
    ID="RequiredFieldValidator1" runat="server"
    ControlToValidate="txtQuantity" Display="Dynamic"
    ErrorMessage="Quantity is a required field.">
</asp:RequiredFieldValidator>
<asp:CompareValidator ID="CompareValidator1" runat="server"
    ControlToValidate="txtQuantity" Display="Dynamic"
    ErrorMessage="Quantity must be greater than zero."
    Operator="GreaterThan" ValueToCompare="0">
</asp:CompareValidator><br /><br />
<asp:Button ID="btnAdd" runat="server" Text="Add to Cart" /> 
<asp:Button ID="Button1" runat="server"  Text="Go to Cart"
    CausesValidation="False" PostBackUrl="~/Cart.aspx" />
    </div>
    </form>
</body>
</html>
```

Figure 15-17   The aspx file for the Order page of the Shopping Cart application (part 2 of 2)

The Order.aspx.vb file

```vb
Imports System.Data

Partial Class Order
    Inherits System.Web.UI.Page

    Protected Sub btnAdd_Click(ByVal sender As Object, _
            ByVal e As System.EventArgs) Handles btnAdd.Click
        If Page.IsValid Then
            Dim CartItem As New CartItem
            CartItem.Product = GetSelectedProduct()
            CartItem.Quantity = CType(txtQuantity.Text, Integer)
            Me.AddToCart(CartItem)
            Response.Redirect("Cart.aspx")
        End If
    End Sub

    Private Function GetSelectedProduct() As Product
        Dim dvProduct As DataView = CType( _
            SqlDataSource2.Select(DataSourceSelectArguments.Empty), DataView)
        Dim Product As New Product
        Product.ProductID = dvProduct(0)("ProductID").ToString
        Product.Name = dvProduct(0)("Name").ToString
        Product.ShortDescription = dvProduct(0)("ShortDescription").ToString
        Product.LongDescription = dvProduct(0)("LongDescription").ToString
        Product.UnitPrice = CDec(dvProduct(0)("UnitPrice"))
        Product.ImageFile = dvProduct(0)("ImageFile").ToString
        Return Product
    End Function

    Private Sub AddToCart(ByVal CartItem As CartItem)
        Dim Cart As SortedList = GetCart()
        Dim sProductID As String = CartItem.Product.ProductID
        If Cart.ContainsKey(sProductID) Then
            CartItem = CType(Cart(sProductID), CartItem)
            CartItem.Quantity += CType(txtQuantity.Text, Integer)
        Else
            Cart.Add(sProductID, CartItem)
        End If
    End Sub

    Private Function GetCart() As SortedList
        If Session("cart") Is Nothing Then
            Session.Add("cart", New SortedList)
        End If
        Return CType(Session("cart"), SortedList)
    End Function

End Class
```

Figure 15-18   The code-behind file for the Order page of the Shopping Cart application

Perspective

The DetailsView and FormView controls are ideal for any application that displays bound data one row at a time. The choice of whether to use a DetailsView or a FormView control depends mostly on how much control you want over the layout of the data. If you want to present a simple list of fields, choose the DetailsView control because it can automatically present data in that format. But if you need more control over the data layout, choose the FormView control.

Up to this point, all of the database applications presented in this book have relied heavily on data binding that's defined in the aspx code, using Visual Basic code only for data validation and exception handling. However, ASP.NET 2.0 also has powerful new features for working with data access classes written with custom code. In the next chapter, then, you'll learn how the new ObjectDataSource control lets you use data bound controls such as the GridView, DetailsView, and FormView controls with custom data access classes.

Term

Master/Detail page

16

How to use object data sources

This chapter is designed to introduce you to the use of object data sources as an alternative to the Access or SQL data sources that you've already learned about. The benefit of using object data sources is that they let you use a three-layer design in which the data access code is kept in data access classes. This lets you separate the presentation code from the data access code, but still lets you use the data binding features of ASP.NET 2.0.

To write the data access classes that are used with object data sources, you need to be able to use ADO.NET, which isn't presented in this book. But even if you don't understand ADO.NET, this chapter will show you how to use object data sources with existing data access classes. Then, you'll be able to decide whether you want to use object data sources in your applications and whether you want to learn how to use ADO.NET.

An introduction to object data sources

The following topics introduce you to object data sources and the 3-layer architecture that they let you implement.

How 3-layer applications work in ASP.NET 2.0

As you probably know, most development experts recommend a *3-layer architecture* for web applications that separates the presentation, business rules, and data access components of the application. The *presentation layer* includes the web pages that define the user interface. The *middle layer* includes the classes that manage the data access for those objects, and it may also include classes that implement business rules such as data validation requirements or discount policies. The *database layer* consists of the database itself.

Unfortunately, using the 3-layer architecture in previous versions of ASP.NET meant that you couldn't take advantage of ASP.NET's powerful data binding features. That's because data binding with ASP.NET 1.x required that you place the data access components in the application's presentation layer.

But now, as figure 16-1 shows, ASP.NET 2.0 addresses that problem by providing *object data sources*. To make that work, the ObjectDataSource control serves as an interface between the data-bound controls in the presentation layer and the *data access classes* in the middle layer. This means that you can use data binding in the presentation layer without placing the data access code in that layer.

When you use an ObjectDataSource control, you must create a data access class to handle the data access for the control. This class provides at least one method that retrieves data from the database and returns it in a form that the ObjectDataSource control can handle. It can also provide methods to insert, update, and delete data. The data access class should be placed in the application's App_Code folder.

When you code a data access class, you can use any techniques you want to access the database. In this chapter, for example, you'll see data access classes that use the ADO.NET classes that were introduced with .NET 1.0. These classes can be used to get data from a SQL Server database, from other types of databases such as Oracle or MySQL databases, or from other sources such as XML or plain text files.

If you have already developed data access classes for the database used by your application, you may be able to use those classes with an object data source. Often, though, it's better to develop the data access classes specifically for the ObjectDataSource controls that you're going to use. That way, you can design each class so it works as efficiently as possible.

Incidentally, Microsoft uses both the term *business object class* and the term *data object class* to refer to a class that provides data access for an object data source. In this chapter, though, I used the term *data access class* for this type of class because if you use shared methods to provide the data access functions, an object is never instantiated from the class.

The 3-layer architecture in ASP.NET 2.0

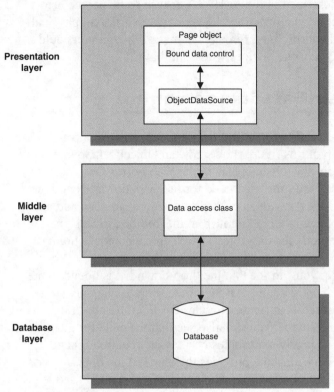

The three layers

- The **presentation layer** consists of the ASP.NET 2.0 pages that manage the appearance of the application. This layer can include bound data controls and ObjectDataSource objects that bind the data controls to the data.

- The **middle layer** contains the *data access classes* that manage the data access for the application. This layer can also contain business objects that represent business entities such as customers, products, or employees and that implement business rules such as credit and discount policies.

- The **database layer** consists of the database that contains the data for the application. Ideally, the SQL statements that do the database access should be saved in stored procedures within the database, but the SQL statements are often stored in the data access classes.

Description

- An *object data source* is implemented by the new ObjectDataSource control, which lets you use data binding with the *3-layer architecture* for a database application.

- An object data source is similar to a SQL data source. However, instead of directly accessing a database, the object data source gets its data through a data access class that handles the details of database access.

Figure 16-1   How 3-layer applications work in ASP.NET 2.0

Also, you may be accustomed to using the term *3-tier architecture* for the *3-layer architecture* that's described in figure 16-1. Because some people use *3-tier* to refer to an architecture that puts the 3 layers on three different physical devices, though, I've used the term *3-layer* in this chapter. Although you could put each of the 3 layers on 3 separate devices, you don't have to.

How to use the ObjectDataSource control

Figure 16-2 presents the basics of working with the ObjectDataSource control. The image at the top of this figure shows how an ObjectDataSource control that's bound to a drop-down list appears in the Web Forms Designer. Then, the first code example shows the aspx code for the drop-down list and the object data source it's bound to. As with any other data source, you can add an object data source to a web page by dragging it from the Toolbox in Design view or by entering the aspx code for the ObjectDataSource element in Source view.

In the first code example, you can see that the drop-down list is bound to the object data source just as if it were bound to a SQL data source. The only difference is that the DataSourceID attribute provides the ID of an object data source rather than a SQL data source. You can also see that the code for the ObjectDataSource control has just two attributes besides the required ID and Runat attributes. The TypeName attribute provides the name of the data access class, and the SelectMethod attribute provides the name of the method used to retrieve the data. In this case, the data access class is ProductDB and the select method is GetAllCategories.

The second code example in this figure shows the GetAllCategories method of the ProductDB data access class. This method uses straightforward ADO.NET code to retrieve category rows from the Categories table and return a data reader that can be used to read the category rows. Notice, though, that the return type for this method is IEnumerable. Because the SqlDataReader class implements the IEnumerable interface, a data reader is a valid return object for this method. (You'll learn more about the return types that are acceptable for a select method in figure 16-8.)

A drop-down list bound to an ObjectDataSource control

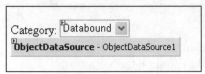

The code for the drop-down list and the ObjectDataSource control

```
<asp:DropDownList ID="ddlCategories" runat="server" AutoPostBack="True"
    DataSourceID="ObjectDataSource1"
    DataTextField="ShortName"
    DataValueField="CategoryID">
</asp:DropDownList>
<asp:ObjectDataSource ID="ObjectDataSource1" runat="server"
    TypeName="ProductDB"
    SelectMethod="GetAllCategories">
</asp:ObjectDataSource>
```

The GetAllCategories method of the ProductDB class

```
<DataObjectMethod(DataObjectMethodType.Select)> _
Public Shared Function GetAllCategories() As IEnumerable
    Dim sel As String = "SELECT CategoryID, ShortName " _
        & "FROM Categories ORDER BY ShortName"
    Dim cmd As SqlCommand = _
        New SqlCommand(sel, New SqlConnection(GetConnectionString))
    cmd.Connection.Open()
    Return cmd.ExecuteReader(CommandBehavior.CloseConnection)
End Function
```

Basic attributes of the ObjectDataSource control

Attribute	Description
ID	The ID of the control.
Runat	Must specify "server."
TypeName	The name of the data access class.
SelectMethod	The name of the method that retrieves the data.
UpdateMethod	The name of the method that updates the data.
DeleteMethod	The name of the method that deletes the data.
InsertMethod	The name of the method that inserts the data.
DataObjectTypeName	The name of a class that provides properties that are used to pass parameter values.
ConflictDetection	Specifies how concurrency conflicts will be detected. CompareAllValues uses optimistic concurrency checking. OverwriteValues, which is the default, does no concurrency checking.

Description

- The ObjectDataSource control specifies the name of the data access class and the methods used to select, update, delete, and insert data.

Figure 16-2 How to use the ObjectDataSource control

How to configure an ObjectDataSource control

Figure 16-3 shows how you can use the Data Source Configuration Wizard to configure an object data source control. As you can see, the first step of the wizard lets you choose the business object that will be associated with this object data source. The selection you make here will be used in the TypeName attribute of the ObjectDataSource control. (Notice that Microsoft refers to the data access class as a *business object* in this wizard. In other contexts, though, Microsoft refers to the data access class as a *data object* or a *data component*.)

The drop-down list in the first step of the wizard lists all of the classes that are available in the App_Code folder. If you check the "Show Only Data Components" box, only those classes that identify themselves as data components will be listed. In figure 16-10, you'll learn how to mark classes this way.

When you select a data access class and click Next, the Define Data Methods step of the configuration wizard is displayed. Here, you can select the method you want to use to retrieve data for the object data source. The one you select is specified in the SelectMethod attribute of the ObjectDataSource control. (In this step, the wizard uses a new .NET 2.0 feature called *reflection* to determine all of the available methods, and you'll learn more about reflection in a moment.)

If you select a select method that requires parameters, the Define Parameters step lets you specify the source for each of the required parameters. Then, the wizard generates the elements that define the parameters required by the ObjectDataSource control.

As you can see in this figure, the Data Source Configuration Wizard also provides tabs that let you specify the methods for update, insert, and delete operations. Later in this chapter, you'll see an application that uses these methods. But for now, I'll just focus on how you can use an ObjectDataSource control to retrieve data.

The Data Source Configuration Wizard

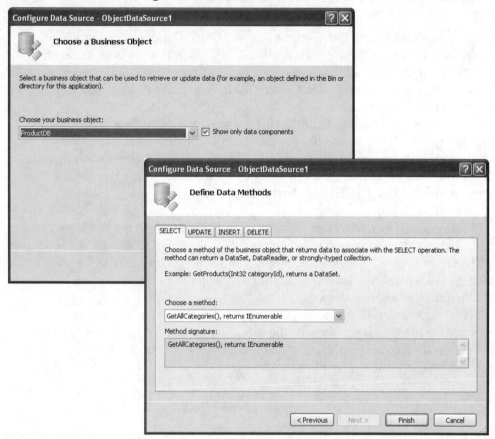

Description

- You can use the Data Source Configuration Wizard to configure an ObjectDataSource control by choosing Configure Data Source from its smart tag menu.
- The Choose a Business Object step of the wizard lets you select the data access class you want to use.
- The Define Data Methods step of the wizard includes tabs that let you choose the methods you want to use for select, update, insert, and delete operations.
- If you choose a method that requires parameters, a Define Parameters step will appear. This step will let you choose the source of each parameter required by the method. For example, you can specify that a drop-down list should be used as the source for a parameter.

Figure 16-3   How to configure an ObjectDataSource control

A Product List application

To illustrate the basics of working with the ObjectDataSource control, figure 16-4 presents a Product List application. This application is identical in appearance to the Product List application that was presented in chapter 13. However, instead of using SqlDataSource controls to retrieve the data, it uses ObjectDataSource controls.

This figure also lists the methods that are provided by the data access class named ProductDB that is used by this application. The first method, GetAllCategories, returns an IEnumerable object (actually, a data reader) that contains the data for all of the categories in the Categories table. This data includes just the category ID and short name for each category.

The second method, GetProductsByCategory, returns an IEnumerable object (again, a data reader) that includes all of the products in the Products table that have the category ID that's supplied by a parameter. This parameter will be bound to the SelectedValue property of the drop-down list. As a result, the ID of the category selected by the user will be passed to the GetProductsByCategory method.

This application illustrates how the use of object data sources lets you separate the presentation code from the data access code. As you will see, all of the presentation code is in the aspx file. And all of the data access code is in the data access class that's named ProductDB.

The Product List application

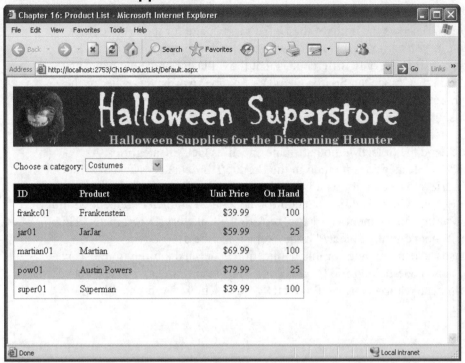

Methods of the ProductDB class

Method	Description
GetAllCategories() As IEnumerable	Returns an IEnumerable object with the ID and short name of all the categories in the Categories table.
GetProductsByCategory(CategoryID As String) As IEnumerable	Returns an IEnumerable object with the ID, name, unit price, and on-hand quantity for all products in the Products table for the specified category.

Description

- The Category drop-down list is bound to an ObjectDataSource control that receives a list of categories from the Categories table.

- The DataList control is bound to a second ObjectDataSource control that uses a parameterized query to retrieve the products for a selected category. The CategoryID for the parameter is taken from the SelectedValue property of the drop-down list.

- Both ObjectDataSource controls use a data access class named ProductDB that contains the shared methods that return a list of categories and the products for a specific category.

Figure 16-4   The Product List application

The aspx file

Figure 16-5 shows the body of the Default.aspx page for the Product List application. If you compare this listing with the listing shown in figure 13-15, you'll discover that the only difference is that the SqlDataSource elements have been replaced by ObjectDataSource elements. In other words, the code for the drop-down list and DataList controls is identical whether the application uses a SQL data source or an object data source.

In the first ObjectDataSource control, the TypeName attribute specifies ProductDB, and the SelectMethod attribute specifies GetAllCategories. As a result, the GetAllCategories method in the ProductDB data access class will be called to retrieve the category data when the drop-down list is bound.

In the second ObjectDataSource control, a ControlParameter element within the SelectParameters element is used to declare the CategoryID parameter. This parameter is bound to the SelectedValue property of the drop-down list.

Because the data binding for this application is defined entirely in the aspx file, there is no code-behind file for this page. As a result, the only Visual Basic code for this application is in the ProductDB class, which is presented in the next figure.

The body of the Default.aspx file

```
<body>
    <form id="form1" runat="server">
    <div>
        <asp:Image ID="Image1" runat="server"
            ImageUrl="~/Images/banner.jpg" /><br /><br />Choose a category:
        <asp:DropDownList ID="ddlCategory" runat="server" AutoPostBack="True"
            DataSourceID="ObjectDataSource1" DataTextField="LongName"
            DataValueField="CategoryID" Width="130px">
        </asp:DropDownList>
        <asp:ObjectDataSource ID="ObjectDataSource1" runat="server"
            TypeName="ProductDB" SelectMethod="GetAllCategories">
        </asp:ObjectDataSource><br /><br />
        <asp:DataList ID="DataList1" runat="server"
            DataSourceID="ObjectDataSource2" GridLines="Vertical"
            BackColor="White" BorderColor="#999999" BorderStyle="Solid"
            BorderWidth="1px" CellPadding="3" ForeColor="Black">
            <HeaderTemplate>
                <table><tr>
                    <td style="width: 100px">ID</td>
                    <td style="width: 200px">Product</td>
                    <td style="width: 80px" align="right">Unit Price</td>
                    <td style="width: 80px" align="right">On Hand</td></tr>
                </table>
            </HeaderTemplate>
            <ItemTemplate>
                <table><tr>
                    <td style="width: 100px">
                        <asp:Label ID="lblID" runat="server"
                            Text='<%# Eval("ProductID") %>'></asp:Label></td>
                    <td style="width: 200px">
                        <asp:Label ID="lblName" runat="server"
                            Text='<%# Eval("Name") %>'></asp:Label></td>
                    <td style="width: 80px" align="right">
                        <asp:Label ID="lblUnitPrice" runat="server"
                            Text='<%# Eval("UnitPrice", "{0:c}") %>'>
                        </asp:Label></td>
                    <td style="width: 80px" align="right">
                        <asp:Label ID="lblOnHand" runat="server"
                            Text='<%# Eval("OnHand") %>'></asp:Label></td></tr>
                </table>
            </ItemTemplate>
            <AlternatingItemStyle BackColor="#CCCCCC" />
            <HeaderStyle BackColor="Black" Font-Bold="True" ForeColor="White" />
        </asp:DataList>
        <asp:ObjectDataSource ID="ObjectDataSource2" runat="server"
            TypeName="ProductDB" SelectMethod="GetProductsByCategory" >
            <SelectParameters>
                <asp:ControlParameter ControlID="ddlCategory"
                    Name="CategoryID" PropertyName="SelectedValue"
                    Type="String" />
            </SelectParameters>
        </asp:ObjectDataSource>
    </div>
    </form>
</body>
```

Figure 16-5   The aspx file for the Product List application

The ProductDB class

Figure 16-6 presents the Visual Basic code for the ProductDB class. To create this class, I used the Website→Add New Item command to add a class file to the App_Code folder. Then, I added the code for the public GetAllCategories and GetProductsByCategory methods. I also created a private method named GetConnectionString. This method is used by both of the public methods to retrieve the connection string for the Halloween database.

Before I explain the details of how these methods work, I want to point out the DataObject and DataObjectMethod attributes that appear in this class. These attributes are used to identify the class and methods as data objects, and you'll learn how to use them in figure 16-10. For now, just realize that they're used by the Data Source Configuration Wizard to determine which classes and methods to display when you configure an object data source.

The GetAllCategories method uses a standard ADO.NET SqlCommand object to retrieve data from the Halloween database using this Select statement:

```
SELECT CategoryID, LongName
FROM Categories
ORDER BY LongName
```

The SqlCommand object is instantiated using a string that contains the above Select statement and the connection string returned by the GetConnectionString method. Then, the command is opened by calling the connection's Open method. Finally, the ExecuteReader method is called, which returns a data reader that contains the requested data.

The GetProductsByCategory method is slightly more complicated because it uses a parameter in its Select statement:

```
SELECT ProductID, Name, UnitPrice, OnHand
FROM Products
WHERE CategoryID = @CategoryID
ORDER BY ProductID
```

Here again, a SqlCommand object is created using this Select statement and the connection string returned from the GetConnectionString method. Then, a parameter named CategoryID is added to the command's Parameters collection before the connection is opened, and the command is executed so it returns a data reader with the requested data.

The GetConnectionString method uses the ConfigurationManager class to retrieve the connection string named "HalloweenConnection" from the web.config file. As a result, the connection string for the Halloween database must be stored in web.config. To refresh your memory about how to store it, please refer to figure 13-4 in chapter 13.

The ProductDB class

```
Imports Microsoft.VisualBasic
Imports System.ComponentModel
Imports System.Data
Imports System.Data.SqlClient

<DataObject(True)> _
Public Class ProductDB

    <DataObjectMethod(DataObjectMethodType.Select)> _
    Public Shared Function GetAllCategories() As IEnumerable
        Dim sel As String = "SELECT CategoryID, LongName " _
            & "FROM Categories ORDER BY LongName"
        Dim cmd As SqlCommand = _
            New SqlCommand(sel, New SqlConnection(GetConnectionString))
        cmd.Connection.Open()
        Dim rdr As SqlDataReader = _
            cmd.ExecuteReader(CommandBehavior.CloseConnection)
        Return rdr
    End Function

    <DataObjectMethod(DataObjectMethodType.Select)> _
    Public Shared Function GetProductsByCategory(ByVal CategoryID As String) _
            As IEnumerable
        Dim sel As String = "SELECT ProductID, Name, UnitPrice, OnHand " _
            & "FROM Products " _
            & "WHERE CategoryID = @CategoryID " _
            & "ORDER BY ProductID"
        Dim cmd As SqlCommand = _
            New SqlCommand(sel, New SqlConnection(GetConnectionString))
        cmd.Parameters.AddWithValue("CategoryID", CategoryID)
        cmd.Connection.Open()
        Dim rdr As SqlDataReader = _
            cmd.ExecuteReader(CommandBehavior.CloseConnection)
        Return rdr
    End Function

    Private Shared Function GetConnectionString() As String
        Return ConfigurationManager.ConnectionStrings _
            ("HalloweenConnection").ConnectionString
    End Function

End Class
```

Note

- The DataObject and DataObjectMethod attributes are described in figure 16-10.

Figure 16-6   The ProductDB class for the Product List application

How to create a data access class

The most challenging aspect of using object data sources is developing the data access classes that they require. So the topics that follow explain how to design and implement these classes.

How to design a data access class

As figure 16-7 shows, the data access class used by an ObjectDataSource control can have four different types of methods that are used to select, insert, update, and delete data. You can use any method names that you want for these methods, and you can design the class so that it has more than one of each of these types of methods. For example, the ProductDB class used in the previous figure has two select methods that are named GetAllCategories and GetCategoriesByProduct.

The data access methods can be shared methods or instance methods. If you define them as instance methods, the ObjectDataSource control will create an instance of the data access class before it calls the method, and then destroy the object after the method has been executed. For this to work, the data access class must provide a parameterless constructor. In Visual Basic, though, a parameterless constructor is provided by default if the class has no constructors.

Because creating and destroying a data access object can be time consuming, I suggest that you use shared methods for the select, insert, update, and delete methods whenever possible. That way, the ObjectDataSource control won't have to create an instance of the data access class when it calls one of the data access methods.

Although you provide the name of the methods called by the ObjectDataSource control by using the SelectMethod, InsertMethod, UpdateMethod, and DeleteMethod attributes, the ObjectDataSource control needs more than just the method names to know what methods to call. In addition, the ObjectDataSource control needs to know what parameters those methods are designed to accept. Because the parameters aren't specified at design time, the ObjectDataSource control must determine them at runtime. To do that, it uses a .NET feature called *reflection*.

In case you haven't encountered reflection before, it's a .NET feature that provides information about compiled classes at runtime. For example, reflection can determine what methods are provided by a particular class. In addition, it can determine what parameters each method requires and the type returned by the method.

The ObjectDataSource control uses reflection to determine the parameters that are expected by the data access class methods. That way, the ObjectDataSource control can pass the correct parameters when it calls the select, insert, update, or delete method. It also uses reflection to determine the return type of each data access class method. As you'll see in the next figure, this lets you design a select method that can return the selected data in a variety of forms.

Types of methods in a data access class

Method type	Description
Select	Retrieves data from a database and returns it as an IEnumerable object or a dataset.
Insert	Inserts data for one row into the underlying database. The values are passed via parameters.
Update	Updates the data for one row in the underlying database. The values are passed via parameters.
Delete	Deletes a row from the underlying database. The key or keys for the row to be deleted are passed via parameters.

How an object data source determines which method to call

- The name of the method used for select, insert, update, and delete operations is specified by the SelectMethod, InsertMethod, UpdateMethod, or DeleteMethod attribute.
- The ObjectDataSource control determines what parameters need to be passed to the data access class methods based on the data fields to be inserted, updated, or deleted.
- The ObjectDataSource control then uses reflection to determine the parameter signatures for the insert, update, and delete methods provided by the data access class.
- At runtime, if the class doesn't provide a method with the correct name and parameters, an exception is thrown.

Description

- A data access class can declare public methods that select, insert, update, and delete data. These methods can be instance methods or shared methods.
- You can use any method names you want for the select, insert, update, and delete methods.
- If the select, insert, update, and delete methods are shared methods, the methods are used without creating an instance of the data access class.
- If the select, insert, update, and delete methods are instance methods, an instance of the data access class is created and destroyed for each data access operation. In this case, the data access class must provide a parameterless constructor.
- You can use parameters to pass selection criteria or other data to the select, insert, update, and delete methods. For more information, see figure 16-9.
- *Reflection* is a .NET feature that provides information about compiled classes and methods at runtime.

Figure 16-7   How to design a data access class

How to create a select method

Figure 16-8 shows how to design and code a select method that can be used with an ObjectDataSource control. The table at the top of this figure lists the four different types of values that a select method can return. The simplest is the IEnumerable interface, which can return a data reader because a data reader implements the IEnumerable interface. Also, the IEnumerable object can be a strongly-typed collection that's created by using the new generics feature of Visual Basic.

The select method can also return a DataTable or DataSet object. Because a dataset can contain more than one table, the ObjectDataSource control simply uses the first table in the dataset. As a result, you must design the select method so the first table in the dataset contains the data you want to access.

The main advantage of returning a dataset rather than a table is that the object data source can cache a dataset. Then, to enable caching, you can set the EnableCaching attribute to True for the ObjectDataSource control. In that case, the select method will be called only the first time the data is requested. For more information on caching, which works the same as it does for a SqlDataSource control, please refer back to chapter 13.

You can also pass parameters to the select method. But if you do, you should provide a SelectParameters collection for the ObjectDataSource control. Then, you can use a ControlParameter element to bind a parameter to a control such as a drop-down list. You saw an example of this in figure 16-5.

Allowable return types for a select method

Return type	Description
IEnumerable	A collection such as an ArrayList or HashTable or a strongly-typed collection such as System.Collections.Generic.List. (Because the DataReader class implements IEnumerable, the select method can also return a data reader.)
DataTable	If the select method returns a data table, the ObjectDataSource control automatically extracts a data view from the table and uses the view for data binding.
DataSet	If the select method returns a dataset, the ObjectDataSource control extracts a data view from the first data table in the dataset and uses the view for data binding.
Object	If the select method returns a single object, the ObjectDataSource control wraps the object in an IEnumerable collection with just one item, then does the data binding as if the method returned an IEnumerable.

A select method that returns a data reader

```
Public Shared Function GetAllCategories() As IEnumerable
    Dim sel As String = "SELECT CategoryID, LongName " _
        & "FROM Categories ORDER BY LongName"
    Dim cmd As SqlCommand = _
        New SqlCommand(sel, New SqlConnection(GetConnectionString))
    cmd.Connection.Open()
    Return cmd.ExecuteReader(CommandBehavior.CloseConnection)
End Function
```

A select method that returns a dataset

```
Public Shared Function GetAllCategories() As DataSet
    Dim sel As String = "SELECT CategoryID, LongName " _
        & "FROM Categories ORDER BY LongName"
    Dim da As SqlDataAdapter = New SqlDataAdapter(sel, GetConnectionString)
    Dim dsCategories As DataSet = New DataSet
    da.Fill(dsCategories, "Categories")
    Return dsCategories
End Function
```

Description

- The select method returns data retrieved from the underlying database.
- The select method can return the data in several forms, including a data reader or a dataset.
- If the select method returns a dataset, the object data source can cache the data.
- The select method can also return a strongly-typed collection using Visual Basic's new generics feature. For more information on using generics, see the Help documentation.
- If the select method accepts parameters, the parameters must be declared within the SelectParameters collection of the ObjectDataSource control. Within this collection, you can use the ControlParameter element to declare a parameter that's bound to another control on the page.

Figure 16-8   How to create a select method

How to create update, delete, and insert methods

Besides select methods, the data access class used by an object data source can provide methods that update, delete, and insert data in the underlying database. Figure 16-9 presents some guidelines that you should follow when you create these methods.

Undoubtedly the most difficult aspect of working with object data sources is determining how the parameters for update, delete, and insert methods are passed to them from the data source. The reason for this difficulty is that these parameters aren't determined until runtime. Then, the ObjectDataSource control creates a collection of parameters that are passed to the data access class method based on several factors, including (1) the bound fields that are used by the control that the object data source is bound to, (2) the DataKeyNames attribute of the bound control, (3) whether the object data source uses optimistic concurrency checking, and (4) whether the key fields are read-only or updatable.

Once the ObjectDataSource control has determined what parameters need to be passed, it uses the new reflection feature to determine whether the data access class has a method that accepts the required parameters. If so, the method is called using these parameters. If not, an exception is thrown. This means that you must anticipate the parameters that will be passed to your method so you can code them correctly. Fortunately, though, if you guess wrong, you can use the message displayed by the exception that occurs to determine what parameters were expected and then correct your code.

If the object data source is bound to a GridView or DetailsView control, the parameter names are determined by the DataField attributes of the BoundField elements that are used to create the bound data fields. In contrast, if the object data source is bound to a FormView control, the parameter names are determined by the names specified in the Bind methods of the bound controls. As a result, the parameter names you use in your data access class methods must be the same as the names you use on the DataField attributes or in the Bind methods.

Note, however, that the order of the parameters doesn't matter. Instead, the object data source control uses reflection to determine the names and order of the parameters expected by the data access methods. Then, when it calls those methods, the object data source passes the parameters in the expected order.

The most confusing aspect of how the ObjectDataSource control generates parameters has to do with the cases that require two sets of values to be passed to an update method. That happens if you use optimistic concurrency or if the primary key column is updatable. For optimistic concurrency, both values are needed so the update statement can make sure the data hasn't been changed before it applies the update. And if optimistic concurrency isn't used but the key column is updatable, the update statement needs the original key value so it can properly retrieve the row to be updated.

If you create an ObjectDataSource control that uses optimistic concurrency, Visual Studio will automatically add an OldValuesParameterFormatString

A typical Update method

```
Public Shared Sub UpdateCategory(ByVal CategoryID As String, _
        ByVal ShortName As String, ByVal LongName As String)
    Dim up As String = "UPDATE Categories " _
        & "SET ShortName = @ShortName, " _
        & "LongName = @LongName " _
        & "WHERE CategoryID = @CategoryID"
    Dim cmd As SqlCommand = _
        New SqlCommand(up, New SqlConnection(GetConnectionString))
    cmd.Parameters.AddWithValue("CategoryID", CategoryID)
    cmd.Parameters.AddWithValue("ShortName", ShortName)
    cmd.Parameters.AddWithValue("LongName", LongName)
    cmd.Connection.Open()
    cmd.ExecuteNonQuery()
End Sub
```

How parameters are generated

- Parameters are automatically generated when an ObjectDataSource control is bound to a control that lets you update a row in a data source, including the GridView, DetailsView, and FormView controls.

- One parameter is generated for each bound column using the name specified in the DataField attribute or the Bind method.

- If the ObjectDataSource control uses optimistic concurrency, an additional parameter is generated for each bound column when you call the update method. These parameters hold the original values of the columns.

- If optimistic concurrency isn't used but the key column of the data source is updatable, an additional parameter is generated for the key column when you call the update method. This parameter holds the original value of the key column.

- When you call the delete method, a parameter is always generated to hold the original value of the key column.

- If you create an ObjectDataSource control that uses optimistic concurrency, Visual Studio automatically adds an OldValuesParameterFormatString property with a value of original_{0}. That way, the names of the parameters for the original column values will be different from the names of the parameters for the new column values.

- If you don't use optimistic concurrency but the key column is updatable, you'll need to add the OldValuesParameterFormatString property manually.

Description

- To properly design an update, delete, or insert method, you must be aware of how the ObjectDataSource control generates the parameters passed to these methods.

- Although the order in which the parameters appear in your update, delete, and insert methods doesn't matter, your parameter names must match the names generated by the ObjectDataSource control.

- If your methods don't use the parameter names that the object data source expects, you can use the exception messages that occur at runtime to correct your parameter names.

Figure 16-9   How to create update, delete, and insert methods

attribute with a value of original_{0}. That way, the names of the parameters that are generated for an update operation will consist of the column names prefixed with "original_". That means that if the new value of a field named ShortName is passed via a parameter named ShortName, the original value will be passed via a parameter named original_ShortName. Without the OldValuesParameterFormatString attribute, the names of both parameters would be ShortName. That's because the default value of the OldValuesParameterFormatString attribute is {0}.

If the key column is updatable and the ObjectDataSource control doesn't use optimistic concurrency, Visual Studio doesn't generate the OldValuesParameterFormatString attribute. That means that the name of the parameter that holds the original value of the column will be the same as the name of the parameter that holds the new value of the column. To avoid that, you'll need to set the value of this property yourself.

The name of the parameter that's passed to a delete method also depends on whether the ObjectDataSource control is created with optimistic concurrency. If optimistic concurrency isn't used, the parameter name is simply the name of the key column. But if optimistic concurrency is used, the delete parameter will begin with original_.

How to use attributes to mark a data access class

Figure 16-10 shows how you can use *Visual Basic attributes* to identify a data access class and its methods. In case you haven't worked with attributes before, they are simply a way to provide declarative information for classes, methods, properties, and so on. Although some of these attributes have meaning at runtime, the attributes in this figure are used at design time. In particular, the Data Source Configuration Wizard uses these attributes to determine which classes in the App_Code folder are data access classes and which methods in the data access class are select, insert, update, and delete methods.

Note, however, that you don't need to use these attributes. The only reason to use them is to help the Data Source Configuration Wizard recognize the data access classes and methods. If you haven't marked your data access classes with these attributes, you can still access them from the wizard by clearing the Show Only Data Components checkbox in the Choose a Business Object step of the wizard (see figure 16-3).

Attributes for marking data access classes

To mark an element as...	Use this attribute...
A data object class	`<DataObject(True)>`
A Select method	`<DataObjectMethod(DataObjectMethodType.Select)>`
An Insert method	`<DataObjectMethod(DataObjectMethodType.Insert)>`
An Update method	`<DataObjectMethod(DataObjectMethodType.Update)>`
A Delete method	`<DataObjectMethod(DataObjectMethodType.Delete)>`

A marked data access class

```
Imports Microsoft.VisualBasic
Imports System.ComponentModel
Imports System.Data
Imports System.Data.SqlClient

<DataObject(True)> _
Public Class ProductDB

    <DataObjectMethod(DataObjectMethodType.Select)> _
    Public Shared Function GetAllCategories() As IEnumerable
        Dim sel As String = "SELECT CategoryID, LongName " _
            & "FROM Categories ORDER BY LongName"
        Dim cmd As SqlCommand = _
            New SqlCommand(sel, New SqlConnection(GetConnectionString))
        cmd.Connection.Open()
        Return cmd.ExecuteReader(CommandBehavior.CloseConnection)
    End Function

End Class
```

Description

- You can use DataObject and DataObjectMethod attributes to mark data access classes and methods. Visual Studio uses these attributes to determine which classes and methods to list in the drop-down boxes of the Data Source Configuration Wizard.
- The DataObject and DataObjectMethod attributes are in the System.ComponentModel namespace.

Figure 16-10   How to use attributes to mark a data access class

A Category Maintenance application

To give you a better idea of how you can use an object data source to update, delete, and insert data, the following topics present an application that maintains the Categories table in the Halloween database. This application is a variation of the Category Maintenance application that was presented in chapter 14.

The design

Figure 16-11 presents the design for this version of the Category Maintenance application. It uses a GridView control to let the user update and delete category rows and a DetailsView control below the GridView control to insert new category rows. Both the GridView and DetailsView controls are bound to a single ObjectDataSource control. But the DetailsView control is used only in insert mode so it isn't used to display, update, or delete existing category records.

The table in this figure shows the public methods that are provided by the CategoryDB class. These four methods provide the select, update, delete, and insert functions. Since all of these methods are defined as shared, an instance of the CategoryDB class doesn't have to be created to access the database.

The aspx file

The two parts of figure 16-12 show the Default.aspx file for this application. In part 1, you can see the aspx code for the GridView control that displays the category rows. Its Columns collection includes three BoundField columns, named CategoryID, ShortName, and LongName.

In part 2, you can see the aspx code for the ObjectDataSource control. It names CategoryDB as the data access class, then provides the names of the select, insert, update, and delete methods that will be used to access the data. Notice that the ConflictDetection attribute is set to CompareAllValues so optimistic concurrency will be used. You'll see one way to implement optimistic concurrency with an object data source when you see the Visual Basic code for this application.

You can also see the aspx code for the DetailsView control in part 2. Here, I set the DefaultMode attribute to Insert so this control is always displayed in Insert mode.

The Category Maintenance application

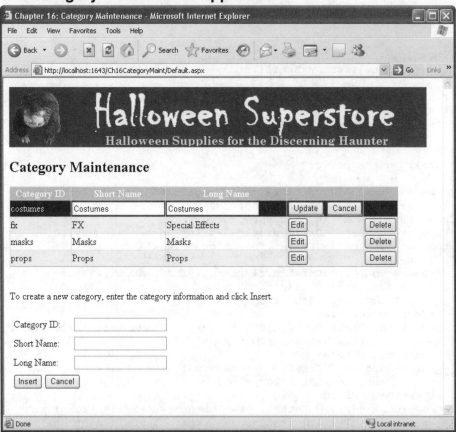

Methods of the CategoryDB class

Method type	Signature
Select	`Public Shared Function GetCategories() As IEnumerable`
Update	`Public Shared Sub UpdateCategory(ByVal CategoryID As String, _` `    ByVal ShortName As String, ByVal LongName As String)`
Delete	`Public Shared Sub DeleteCategory(By Val CategoryID As String)`
Insert	`Public Shared Sub InsertCategory(ByVal CategoryID As String, _` `    ByVal ShortName As String, ByVal LongName As String)`

Description

* This version of the Category Maintenance application uses a GridView control to update and delete rows and a DetailsView control to insert rows. These controls are bound to an ObjectDataSource control that accesses the Categories table of the Halloween database.

* The data access class named CategoryDB provides the select, insert, update, and delete methods.

Figure 16-11   The Category Maintenance application

The Default.aspx file

```
<%@ Page Language="VB" AutoEventWireup="false" CodeFile="Default.aspx.vb"
Inherits="_Default" %>

<!DOCTYPE html PUBLIC "-//W3C//DTD XHTML 1.1//EN"
"http://www.w3.org/TR/xhtml11/DTD/xhtml11.dtd">

<html xmlns="http://www.w3.org/1999/xhtml" >
<head runat="server">
    <title>Chapter 16: Category Maintenance</title>
</head>
<body>
    <form id="form1" runat="server">
    <div>
        <asp:Image ID="Image1" runat="server" ImageUrl="~/Images/banner.jpg" />
        <br /><br /><h2>Category Maintenance</h2>
        <asp:GridView ID="GridView1" runat="server"
            DataSourceID="ObjectDataSource1" DataKeyNames="CategoryID"
            AutoGenerateColumns="False" ForeColor="Black" >
            <Columns>
                <asp:BoundField DataField="CategoryID" ReadOnly="True"
                    HeaderText="Category ID" >
                    <ItemStyle Width="100px" />
                </asp:BoundField>
                <asp:BoundField DataField="ShortName" HeaderText="Short Name" >
                    <ItemStyle Width="150px" />
                </asp:BoundField>
                <asp:BoundField DataField="LongName" HeaderText="Long Name" >
                    <ItemStyle Width="200px" />
                </asp:BoundField>
                <asp:CommandField ButtonType="Button" ShowEditButton="True" />
                <asp:CommandField ButtonType="Button" ShowDeleteButton="True" />
            </Columns>
            <HeaderStyle BackColor="Silver" Font-Bold="True"
                ForeColor="White" />
            <RowStyle BackColor="White" ForeColor="Black" />
            <AlternatingRowStyle BackColor="WhiteSmoke" ForeColor="Black" />
            <EditRowStyle BackColor="Blue" ForeColor="White" />
        </asp:GridView>
```

Note

- If you use the designer to bind fields defined by an object data source to controls like the GridView control, you should realize that the fields won't be listed by name. That's because the fields are defined in the data access class and not directly in the data source. Because of that, you'll have to enter the names of the fields you want to bind manually.

Figure 16-12   The aspx file of the Category Maintenance application (part 1 of 2)

The Default.aspx file   **Page 2**

```
<asp:ObjectDataSource ID="ObjectDataSource1" runat="server"
    TypeName="CategoryDB"
    SelectMethod="GetCategories"
    InsertMethod="InsertCategory"
    DeleteMethod="DeleteCategory"
    UpdateMethod="UpdateCategory"
    ConflictDetection="CompareAllValues"
    OldValuesParameterFormatString="original_{0}" >
    <UpdateParameters>
        <asp:Parameter Name="CategoryID" Type="String" />
        <asp:Parameter Name="ShortName" Type="String" />
        <asp:Parameter Name="LongName" Type="String" />
    </UpdateParameters>
    <InsertParameters>
        <asp:Parameter Name="CategoryID" Type="String" />
        <asp:Parameter Name="ShortName" Type="String" />
        <asp:Parameter Name="LongName" Type="String" />
    </InsertParameters>
</asp:ObjectDataSource><br />

<asp:Label ID="lblError" runat="server" EnableViewState="False"
    ForeColor="Red">
</asp:Label><br />
To create a new category, enter the category information
and click Insert.<br /><br />

<asp:DetailsView ID="DetailsView1" runat="server"
    AutoGenerateRows="False" DataSourceID="ObjectDataSource1"
    DefaultMode="Insert" Height="50px" Width="300px"
    GridLines="None" BorderStyle="None" CellSpacing="5" >
    <Fields>
        <asp:BoundField DataField="CategoryID"
            HeaderText="Category ID:" />
        <asp:BoundField DataField="ShortName"
            HeaderText="Short Name:" />
        <asp:BoundField DataField="LongName"
            HeaderText="Long Name:" />
        <asp:CommandField ButtonType="Button"
            ShowInsertButton="True" />
    </Fields>
</asp:DetailsView>
    </div>
    </form>
</body>
</html>
```

Figure 16-12   The aspx file of the Category Maintenance application (part 2 of 2)

The code-behind file

Figure 16-13 shows the code-behind file for the Default.aspx page of the Category Maintenance application. This file consists of five procedures that handle the exceptions that might be raised and the concurrency errors that might occur when the object data source's update, delete, or insert methods are called.

The first procedure is executed after the data source is updated. This procedure retrieves the return value from the update method using the ReturnValue property of the e argument and assigns it to the AffectedRows property of the e argument. This is necessary because the AffectedRows property isn't set automatically like it is for a SQL data source. For this to work, of course, the update method must return the number of rows that were updated. You'll see the code that accomplishes that in the next figure.

The second procedure is executed after a row in the GridView control is updated, which happens after the data source is updated. This procedure checks the Exception property of the e argument to determine if an exception has been thrown. If so, an error message is displayed, the ExceptionHandled property is set to True to suppress the exception, and the KeepInEditMode property is set to True to leave the GridView control in edit mode.

If an exception didn't occur, this procedure continues by checking the AffectedRows property of the e argument. The value of this property is passed forward from the AffectedRows property of the object data source's Updated event. If the value of this property is zero, the row was not updated, most likely due to the concurrency checking code that was added to the SQL Update statement. As a result, an appropriate error message is displayed.

The next two procedures are similar, except they handle the Deleted event of the ObjectDataSource control and the RowDeleted event of the GridView control. Like the Updated event handler of the ObjectDataSource control, the Deleted event handler sets the AffectedRows property of the e argument. And, like the RowUpdated event handler of the GridView control, the RowDeleted event handler checks for exceptions and concurrency errors.

The last procedure is executed after a row is inserted using the DetailsView control. It checks whether an exception has occurred and responds accordingly. Note that currency checking isn't necessary here because a concurrency error can't occur for an insert operation.

By the way, this code illustrates just one way that you can provide for concurrency errors. Another way is to write the update and delete methods so they throw an exception if a concurrency error occurs. Then, the RowUpdated and RowDeleted event handlers can test the e.Exception property to determine if this exception has been thrown. I prefer the technique illustrated here, though, because the code for the RowUpdated and RowDeleted event handlers is the same as it is when you use a SQL data source.

The Default.aspx.vb file

```vb
Partial Class _Default
    Inherits System.Web.UI.Page

    Protected Sub ObjectDataSource1_Updated(ByVal sender As Object, _
    ByVal e As System.Web.UI.WebControls.ObjectDataSourceStatusEventArgs) _
    Handles ObjectDataSource1.Updated
        e.AffectedRows = CType(e.ReturnValue, Integer)
    End Sub

    Protected Sub GridView1_RowUpdated(ByVal sender As Object, _
    ByVal e As System.Web.UI.WebControls.GridViewUpdatedEventArgs) _
    Handles GridView1.RowUpdated
        If e.Exception IsNot Nothing Then
            lblError.Text = "Invalid data. Please correct and try again."
            e.ExceptionHandled = True
            e.KeepInEditMode = True
        ElseIf e.AffectedRows = 0 Then
            lblError.Text = "The row was not updated. " _
                & "Another user may have updated that category. " _
                & "Please try again."
        End If
    End Sub

    Protected Sub ObjectDataSource1_Deleted(ByVal sender As Object, _
    ByVal e As System.Web.UI.WebControls.ObjectDataSourceStatusEventArgs) _
    Handles ObjectDataSource1.Deleted
        e.AffectedRows = CType(e.ReturnValue, Integer)
    End Sub

    Protected Sub GridView1_RowDeleted(ByVal sender As Object, _
    ByVal e As System.Web.UI.WebControls.GridViewDeletedEventArgs) _
    Handles GridView1.RowDeleted
        If e.Exception IsNot Nothing Then
            lblError.Text = "The category cound not be deleted."
            e.ExceptionHandled = True
        ElseIf e.AffectedRows = 0 Then
            lblError.Text = "The row was not deleted. " _
                & "Another user may have updated that category. " _
                & "Please try again."
        End If
    End Sub

    Protected Sub DetailsView1_ItemInserted(ByVal sender As Object, _
    ByVal e As System.Web.UI.WebControls.DetailsViewInsertedEventArgs) _
    Handles DetailsView1.ItemInserted
        If e.Exception IsNot Nothing Then
            lblError.Text = "Invalid data. Please correct and try again."
            e.ExceptionHandled = True
        End If
    End Sub

End Class
```

Figure 16-13   The code-behind file for the Category Maintenance application

The CategoryDB class

The two parts of figure 16-14 present the CategoryDB class that's used as the data access class for this application. This class uses the DataObject and DataObjectMethod attributes to mark the class as a data object class and to mark the methods as data object methods.

The four public methods in this class provide for the select, insert, delete, and update operations performed by this application. These methods use standard ADO.NET code to access the database. Since this code is straightforward, you shouldn't have any trouble understanding how it works. So I'll just describe it briefly here.

The GetCategories method retrieves all of the rows and columns from the Categories table in the Halloween database. This data is then returned as a data reader, and the object data source uses it to populate the GridView control.

To get a connection to the Halloween database, the GetCategories method calls the private GetConnectionString method. This connection is stored in the web.config file. The GetConnectionString method is also called by the other public methods.

When the user clicks the Insert button in the DetailsView control, the object data source executes the InsertCategory procedure. This procedure is declared with three parameters that correspond to the three columns in the Categories table. When the object data source executes this procedure, it passes the values that the user entered into the DetailsView control. Then, the procedure creates and executes a command that uses these parameter values to insert a new row.

The CategoryDB.vb file   **Page 1**

```vb
Imports Microsoft.VisualBasic
Imports System.Data
Imports System.Data.SqlClient
Imports System.ComponentModel

<DataObject(True)> _
Public Class CategoryDB

    <DataObjectMethod(DataObjectMethodType.Select)> _
    Public Shared Function GetCategories() As IEnumerable
        Dim sel As String = "SELECT CategoryID, ShortName, LongName " _
            & "FROM Categories ORDER BY ShortName"
        Dim cmd As SqlCommand = _
            New SqlCommand(sel, New SqlConnection(GetConnectionString))
        cmd.Connection.Open()
        Return cmd.ExecuteReader(CommandBehavior.CloseConnection)
    End Function

    Private Shared Function GetConnectionString() As String
        Return ConfigurationManager.ConnectionStrings _
            ("HalloweenConnection").ConnectionString
    End Function

    <DataObjectMethod(DataObjectMethodType.Insert)> _
    Public Shared Sub InsertCategory(ByVal CategoryID As String, _
            ByVal ShortName As String, ByVal LongName As String)
        Dim ins As String = "INSERT INTO Categories " _
            & "(CategoryID, ShortName, LongName) " _
            & "VALUES(@CategoryID, @ShortName, @LongName)"
        Dim cmd As SqlCommand = _
            New SqlCommand(ins, New SqlConnection(GetConnectionString))
        cmd.Parameters.AddWithValue("CategoryID", CategoryID)
        cmd.Parameters.AddWithValue("ShortName", ShortName)
        cmd.Parameters.AddWithValue("LongName", LongName)
        cmd.Connection.Open()
        cmd.ExecuteNonQuery()
    End Sub
```

Figure 16-14   The CategoryDB class for the Category Maintenance application (part 1 of 2)

When the user clicks the Delete button in the GridView control, the object data source executes the DeleteCategory method. This procedure accepts three parameters: the original category ID, short name, and long name. The values of the parameters are used within the Where clause of the Delete statement that's executed by this procedure to identify the row to be deleted and to perform concurrency checking.

Notice that this procedure is written as a function that returns an integer value. Then, when the command that contains the Delete statement is executed, the result is stored in an integer variable, which is returned to the object data source. Because this value indicates the number of rows that were deleted, it can be used as shown in the previous figure to check for a concurrency error.

The last procedure, UpdateCategory, is executed when the user clicks the Update button in the GridView control. It's declared with five parameters: the new short name and long name and the original category ID, short name, and long name. The values of the new short name and long name parameters are used to update the category, and the values of the original parameters are used to perform concurrency checking.

Like the DeleteCategory method, the UpdateCategory method returns an integer value that indicates the number of rows that were affected by the update operation. Then, this value can be used to check for a concurrency error.

The CategoryDB.vb file

```vb
<DataObjectMethod(DataObjectMethodType.Delete)> _
Public Shared Function DeleteCategory( _
        ByVal original_CategoryID As String, _
        ByVal original_ShortName As String, _
        ByVal original_LongName As String) _
        As Integer
    Dim del As String = "DELETE FROM Categories " _
        & "WHERE CategoryID = @original_CategoryID " _
        & "AND ShortName = @original_ShortName " _
        & "AND LongName = @original_LongName "
    Dim cmd As SqlCommand = _
        New SqlCommand(del, New SqlConnection(GetConnectionString))
    cmd.Parameters.AddWithValue("original_CategoryID", _
        original_CategoryID)
    cmd.Parameters.AddWithValue("original_ShortName", original_ShortName)
    cmd.Parameters.AddWithValue("original_LongName", original_LongName)
    cmd.Connection.Open()
    Dim i As Integer = cmd.ExecuteNonQuery()
    cmd.Connection.Close()
    Return i
End Function

<DataObjectMethod(DataObjectMethodType.Update)> _
Public Shared Function UpdateCategory(ByVal ShortName As String, _
        ByVal LongName As String, ByVal original_CategoryID As String, _
        ByVal original_ShortName As String, _
        ByVal original_LongName As String) As Integer
    Dim up As String = "UPDATE Categories " _
        & "SET ShortName = @ShortName, " _
        & "LongName = @LongName " _
        & "WHERE CategoryID = @original_CategoryID " _
        & "AND ShortName = @original_ShortName " _
        & "AND LongName = @original_LongName"
    Dim cmd As SqlCommand = _
        New SqlCommand(up, New SqlConnection(GetConnectionString))
    cmd.Parameters.AddWithValue("ShortName", ShortName)
    cmd.Parameters.AddWithValue("LongName", LongName)
    cmd.Parameters.AddWithValue("original_CategoryID", _
        original_CategoryID)
    cmd.Parameters.AddWithValue("original_ShortName", original_ShortName)
    cmd.Parameters.AddWithValue("Original_LongName", original_LongName)
    cmd.Connection.Open()
    Dim i As Integer = cmd.ExecuteNonQuery()
    cmd.Connection.Close()
    Return i
End Function

End Class
```

Figure 16-14   The CategoryDB class for the Category Maintenance application (part 2 of 2)

Perspective

In this chapter, you've learned the basics of working with object data sources, one of the major new features of ASP.NET 2.0. Many ASP.NET experts are excited about this feature because it provides a way to take advantage of the time-saving data binding features of ASP.NET without sacrificing the basic principle of separating presentation code from data access code.

However, it remains to be seen how well the object data sources will deliver on their promise because of two shortcomings. First, this feature's reliance on reflection means that it must resolve method calls at runtime rather than at compile time, which adds overhead (albeit small) to every data access. Second, the way this feature uses parameters often leaves developers guessing at what parameters the ObjectDataSource control is going to pass to your data access methods, which makes it more difficult to code and test them.

If you decide that you do want to use object data sources in your applications, you will of course need to learn how to use ADO.NET in code. For that, we recommend our ADO.NET book for Visual Basic programmers, which provides a complete course in ADO.NET database programming. When you finish it, you'll be able to use ADO.NET with or without data sources.

Terms

3-layer architecture
presentation layer
middle layer
database layer
object data source
data access class
business object class
data object class
3-tier architecture
reflection
Visual Basic attribute

Section 4

Professional ASP.NET skills

This section consists of seven chapters that present ASP.NET skills that are often used in professional web applications. To start, chapter 17 shows you how to use a secure connection for an application, and chapter 18 shows you how to use the new login controls to authenticate the users of an application. These are essential skills for e-commerce applications.

Next, chapter 19 shows you how you can use profiles to personalize an application, and chapter 20 shows you how to use two of the new multi-page server controls. Then, chapter 21 shows you how to use email and custom error pages as well as how to deal with the problems that can occur when users click the Back buttons in their browsers. These are useful skills for most professional applications.

In chapter 22, you'll learn how to use web parts to develop portals that the user can customize. Although you may never need this feature, it sure comes in handy when you do need it. Then, chapter 23 shows you how to configure and deploy an application, which you'll need to do for every application that you develop. At that point, you'll be able to develop and deploy e-commerce applications at a thoroughly professional level.

Because each of the chapters in this section is written as an independent module, you can read these chapters in whatever sequence you prefer. If, for example, you want to learn how to use profiles as an alternative to session state, you can skip directly to chapter 19. Or, if you want to learn how to send email from a web application, you can skip to chapter 21. Eventually, though, you'll want to read all of the chapters because you should at least be aware of the capabilities that they offer.

17

How to secure a web site

Security is one of the most important concerns for any developer of e-commerce web sites. To secure a web site, you must make sure that private data that's sent between the client and the server can't be intercepted. To accomplish that, this chapter shows you how to use an Internet protocol called SSL.

An introduction to SSL

To prevent others from reading data that's transmitted over the Internet, you can use the *Secure Sockets Layer*, or *SSL*. SSL is an Internet protocol that lets you transmit data over the Internet using data encryption. The topics that follow explain how SSL works.

How secure connections work

Figure 17-1 shows a web page that uses SSL to transfer data between the server and the client over a *secure connection*. To determine if you're transmitting data over a secure connection, you can read the URL in the browser's address bar. If it starts with HTTPS rather than HTTP, then you're transmitting data over a secure connection. In addition, a small lock icon appears in the lower right corner of the browser window.

With a regular HTTP connection, all data is sent as unencrypted plain text. As a result, if a hacker intercepts this data, it is easy to read. With a secure connection, however, all data that's transferred between the client and the server is encrypted. Although a hacker can still intercept this data, he won't be able to read it without breaking the encryption code.

Note that to test an application that uses a secure connection, you must run the application under IIS. Because of that, if you created the application as a file-system web site, you'll need to use one of the techniques described in chapter 4 to run it under IIS.

A page that was requested with a secure connection

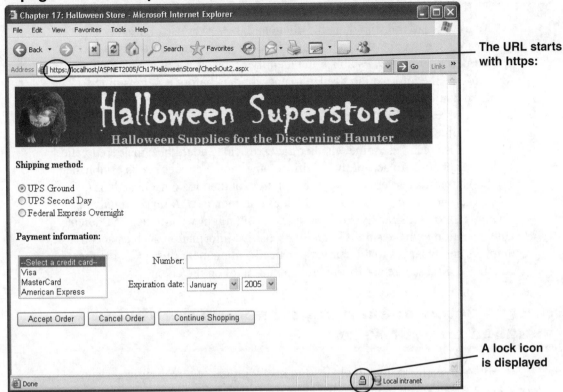

The URL starts
with https:

A lock icon
is displayed

Description

- The *Secure Sockets Layer*, or *SSL*, is the protocol used by the World Wide Web that allows clients and servers to communicate over a *secure connection*.
- With SSL, the browser encrypts all data that's sent to the server and decrypts all data that's received from the server. Conversely, the server encrypts all data that's sent to the browser and decrypts all data that's received from the browser.
- SSL is able to determine if data has been tampered with during transit.
- SSL is also able to verify that a server or a client is who it claims to be.
- The URL for a secure connection starts with HTTPS instead of HTTP.
- A web browser that is using a secure connection displays a lock in the lower right corner.

Note

- To test an application that uses SSL, you must run the application under the control of IIS. For information on how to do that, see chapter 4.

Figure 17-1   How secure connections work

How digital secure certificates work

To use SSL to transmit data, the client and the server use *digital secure certificates* like the one shown in figure 17-2. Digital secure certificates serve two purposes. First, they establish the identity of the server or client. Second, they provide the information needed to encrypt data before it's transmitted.

By default, browsers are configured to accept certificates that come from trusted sources. If a browser doesn't recognize a certificate as coming from a trusted source, however, it informs the user and lets the user view the certificate. Then, the user can determine whether the certificate should be considered valid. If the user chooses to accept the certificate, the secure connection is established.

Sometimes, a server may want the client to authenticate itself with *SSL client authentication*. Although this isn't as common as *SSL server authentication*, it is used occasionally. For example, a bank might want to use SSL client authentication to make sure it's sending sensitive information such as account numbers and balances to the correct person. To implement this type of authentication, a digital secure certificate must be installed on the client.

How to determine if a digital secure certificate is installed on your server

Before you learn how to obtain and install digital secure certificates and trial certificates, you may want to check if a certificate is already installed on your server. If IIS is running on your local machine, chances are that a certificate hasn't been installed. But if IIS is running on a server on a network, you can use the procedure in figure 17-2 to determine if a certificate has been installed and to view the certificate.

How you start IIS depends on whether you're using Windows XP or Windows 2000. Either way, find Administrative Tools in the program menus. Then, choose Internet Information Services for Windows XP or Internet Services Manager for Windows 2000.

The Certificate dialog box for a digital secure certificate

Types of digital secure certificates

Certificate	Description
Server certificate	Issued to trusted servers so client computers can connect to them using secure connections.
Client certificate	Issued to trusted clients so server computers can confirm their identity.

Concepts

- *Authentication* determines whether a server or client is who it claims to be.
- When a browser makes an initial attempt to communicate with a server over a secure connection that uses SSL, the server authenticates itself by sending its *digital secure certificate* to the browser.
- In some instances, the server may also request that a browser authenticate itself by presenting its own digital secure certificate. This is uncommon, however.

How to determine if a digital secure certificate is installed on your server

1. Start the Internet Information Services program.
2. Expand the node for the server and the Web Sites node and then right-click on the Default Web Site node and select Properties to display the Properties dialog box.
3. Click the Directory Security tab. If a digital secure certificate is installed, the View Certificate button will be enabled. Click this button to display the dialog box shown above.

Figure 17-2   How digital secure certificates work

How to get and use a digital secure certificate

In the topics that follow, you'll first learn how to get a digital secure certificate or at least a trial certificate that you can use for testing. Then, you'll learn how to use IIS's Web Server Certificate Wizard to manage certificates.

How to get a digital secure certificate

If you want to develop an ASP.NET application that uses SSL to secure client connections, you must first obtain a digital secure certificate from a trusted source such as those listed in figure 17-3. These *certification authorities*, or *CAs*, verify that the person or company requesting the certificate is a valid person or company by checking with a *registration authority*, or *RA*. To obtain a digital secure certificate, you'll need to provide a registration authority with information about yourself or your company. Once the registration authority approves the request, the certification authority can issue the digital secure certificate.

A digital secure certificate from a trusted source isn't free, and the cost of the certificate will depend on a variety of factors such as the level of security. As a result, when you purchase a digital certificate, you'll want one that fits the needs of your web site. In particular, you'll need to decide what *SSL strength* you want the connection to support. SSL strength refers to the level of encryption that the secure connection uses when it transmits data.

Most certificates sold today provide for up to 128-bit SSL strength. It's nearly impossible to break the encryption code provided by this SSL strength, and the most popular browsers support it. If a browser doesn't support it, however, the browser will use the maximum strength it does support, which is either 40-bit or 56-bit. Some CAs also sell certificates that provide for 256-bit SSL strength, but this strength isn't currently supported by IIS.

In addition to SSL strength, you should consider whether a certificate is a single root certificate or a chained root certificate. A *single root certificate* is a certificate from a trusted source that has already been added to the most popular browsers. These certificates are stable and easy to install. In contrast, a *chained root certificate* is a certificate that inherits a certificate that browsers recognize. Although chained root certificates can be less expensive than single root certificates, they are less stable and more difficult to install.

Common certification authorities that issue digital secure certificates

```
www.verisign.com
www.geotrust.com
www.entrust.com
www.thawte.com
```

SSL strengths

Strength	Pros and Cons
40-bit	Most browsers support it, but it's relatively easy to break the encryption code.
56-bit	It's thousands of times stronger than 40-bit strength and most browsers support it, but it's still possible to break the encryption code.
128-bit	It's over a trillion times a trillion times stronger than 40-bit strength, which makes it extremely difficult to break the encryption code, but it's more expensive and not all browsers support it.

Description

- To use SSL in your web applications, you must first purchase a digital secure certificate from a trusted *certification authority*, or *CA*. Once you obtain the certificate, you send it to the people who host your web site so they can install it on the server.

- A certification authority is a company that issues and manages security credentials. To verify information provided by the requestor of the secure certificate, a CA must check with a *registration authority*, or *RA*. Once the registration authority verifies the requestor's information, the certification authority can issue a digital secure certificate.

- Since SSL is built into all major browsers and web servers, installing a digital secure certificate enables SSL.

- *SSL strength* refers to the length of the generated key that is created during the encryption process. The longer the key, the more difficult it is to break the encryption code.

- The SSL strength that's used depends on the strength provided by the certificate, the strength supported by the web server, and the strength supported by the browser. If a browser isn't able to support the strength provided by the certificate, a lesser strength is used.

- Most certificates are issued by trusted certification authorities who own and use their own certificates. These CAs are known to browser vendors, and their certificates have been added to many of the most popular browsers. This type of certificate is called a *single root certificate*.

- A *chained root certificate* is one that inherits the recognition of a trusted certification authority. This type of certificate is more difficult to install and some web servers and web applications can't use them.

Figure 17-3 How to get a digital secure certificate

How to get a trial certificate for testing

Most certification authorities will provide you with a free trial certificate that you can use for testing purposes. The trial certificate typically expires after a relatively short period of time, such as two weeks or a month. Although you can continue to use the trial certificate after the testing period expires, the dialog box shown at the top of figure 17-4 will appear each time you enter a secure connection. This dialog box simply informs you that the certificate has expired and shouldn't be trusted.

Of course, you shouldn't run an ASP.NET application in a production environment using an expired certificate. When you're ready to deploy your application, then, you should contact the certification authority to obtain a valid certificate.

Another way to obtain certificates for testing purposes is to set up your own certification authority using Microsoft Certificate Services, which comes with Windows 2000 Server and Windows Server 2003. You can then use the certificate server to issue certificates for testing purposes. To learn more about Microsoft Certificate Services, you can review the online help for Windows 2000 Server or Windows Server 2003 or you can visit Microsoft's web site.

The dialog box that's displayed when your trial certificate has expired

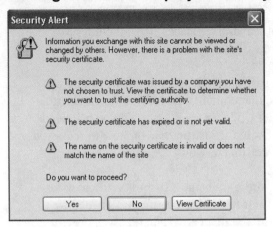

Description

- To test SSL connections in a local environment, you can request a free trial certificate from an established certification authority. The certificate typically expires in 14 to 30 days.

- After the certificate expires, you can still use it for testing purposes. When you switch to a secure connection and the certificate has expired, the dialog box shown above will be displayed. Then, you can click Yes to proceed with the secure connection even though the certificate has expired.

- The certification authority's web site will have detailed instructions you can follow to request, download, and install a trial certificate.

- An alternative to requesting a trial certificate from a certification authority is to become your own certification authority. To do that, you need to install Microsoft Certificate Services on a separate server computer on your network. Then, you can use the certificate server to create certificates you can use for testing.

- Certificates issued by a certification authority on a local network won't be trusted outside of your network, but they will be adequate for testing ASP.NET applications that use SSL.

Figure 17-4   How to get a trial certificate for testing

How to use the IIS Certificate Wizard

Microsoft's web server, Internet Information Services (IIS), includes a Certificate Wizard you can use to manage digital certificates. Figure 17-5 describes how you use this wizard.

If your IIS server doesn't have a certificate installed, the wizard walks you through the steps needed to create a file that contains the information a certification authority needs to issue a certificate. Once you create this file, you'll need to go to the certification authority's web site for instructions on how to request a certificate. Then, when you receive the certificate, you can return to the Certificate Wizard to install it.

You can also use the Certificate Wizard to manage existing certificates for your IIS server. For example, you can use it to remove certificates or renew expired certificates. You can also use it to assign a certificate that was previously installed but has been removed or to import a certificate used by another server.

The Certificate Wizard options for an IIS server that doesn't have a certificate installed

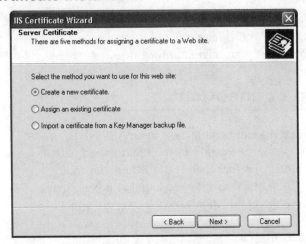

How to start the IIS Certificate Wizard

1. Display the Properties dialog box for the Default Web Site node of the server as described in figure 17-2 and display the Directory Security tab.

2. Click the Server Certificate button to display the first Certificate Wizard dialog box. This dialog box indicates whether a certificate is installed or a request is pending and summarizes the functions the wizard can help you perform.

Description

- The IIS Certificate Wizard manages the process of requesting certificates from certification authorities and installing certificates in IIS.

- If a certificate is already installed on your IIS server, the wizard lets you renew the certificate if it's expired, remove the certificate, or replace it with another certificate.

- If no certificate is installed, the wizard lets you create a certificate file that you can use to request a certificate from a certification authority, assign a certificate that was previously installed, or import a certificate from a copy exported from another server.

- If you have requested a certificate from a certification authority but haven't installed the resulting certificate, the wizard lets you complete the request and install the certificate or cancel the request.

Note

- When you request a certificate from a certification authority, it's usually sent to you as an email attachment. Then, you can save the attachment on your hard drive and use the Wizard to install it. If the certificate is sent as text within the email instead, you'll need to copy and paste it into a file using a program such as WordPad and then save it with the extension *cer*.

Figure 17-5   How to use the Web Server Certificate Wizard

How to use a secure connection

In the topics that follow, you'll first learn how to request secure connections for the pages of your applications. Then, you'll learn how to force a page to use a secure connection when a user bypasses your navigation features.

How to request a secure connection

Figure 17-6 shows how to request a secure connection in an ASP.NET application. To do that, you simply execute a Response.Redirect method with a URL that specifies HTTPS as the protocol rather than HTTP. Then, depending on how the user's browser is configured, the user may see a dialog box similar to the one shown in this figure before the application enters the secure connection.

To request a secure connection using HTTPS, you must use an absolute URL. That means that the URL must include the complete application path, including the web server's domain name and the directory path that leads to the application. For example, the first URL in this figure specifies //localhost as the web server's domain name and /ASPNET2005/Ch17HalloweenStore as the directory path.

Rather than coding this information into each URL, you may want to store the application path in the web.config file as shown in the second coding example in this figure. As you can see, you store this information as an element within the appSettings section of this file. Then, you can use the AppSettings property of the ConfigurationManager class to retrieve the value of the element that contains the path. This is illustrated in the third coding example. If you use this technique, you'll only need to change the application path in the web.config file if you deploy the application to a different location.

Once your application has established a secure connection, it can navigate to other pages using relative URLs while maintaining the secure connection. To close the secure connection, the application must navigate to another page by specifying an absolute URL with HTTP rather than HTTPS as the protocol. This is illustrated in the last coding example in this figure.

A dialog box that may be displayed for secure connections

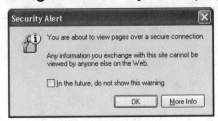

A URL that requests a secure connection

```
https://localhost/ASPNET2005/Ch17HalloweenStore/CheckOut1.aspx
```

A web.config file that defines the AppPath setting

```
<?xml version="1.0"?>
<configuration xmlns="http://schemas.microsoft.com/.NetConfiguration/v2.0">
    <appSettings>
        <add key="AppPath"
            value="//localhost/ASPNET2005/Ch17HalloweenStore/" />
    </appSettings>
    <system.web>
    .
    .
```

Code that retrieves the application path from the web.config file

```
Dim sURL As String = "https:" _
    & ConfigurationManager.AppSettings("AppPath") _
    & "CheckOut1.aspx"
Response.Redirect(sURL)
```

Code that returns to an unsecured connection

```
Dim sURL As String = "http:" _
    & ConfigurationManager.AppSettings("AppPath") _
    & "Order.aspx"
Response.Redirect(sURL)
```

Description

- To request a secure connection, you must use an absolute URL that specifies HTTPS as the protocol. Once you establish a secure connection, you can use relative URLs to continue using the secure connection.
- To return to an unsecured connection after using a secure connection, you must code an absolute URL that specifies the HTTP protocol.
- Instead of coding the application's path into each URL, you can store it in the appSettings section of the web.config file. That way, if the path changes, you can change it in just one location.
- You can use the AppSettings property of the ConfigurationManager class within the application to access the elements in the appSettings section of the web.config file.
- Depending on the security settings in your browser, a dialog box may be displayed before a secure connection is established or before a secure connection is closed.

Figure 17-6   How to request a secure connection

How to force a page to use a secure connection

When you build a complete web application, you usually include navigation features such as menus or hyperlinks that guide the user from page to page. Unfortunately, users sometimes bypass your navigation features and access pages in your application directly. For example, a user might bookmark a page in your application and return to it later. Other users might simply type the URL of individual pages in your application into their browser's address bar. Some users do this innocently; others do it in an attempt to bypass your application's security features.

Because of that, a page that should use SSL to send or receive sensitive information shouldn't assume that a secure connection has been established. Instead, it should check for a secure connection and establish one if necessary. To do that, you can use the properties of the HttpRequest class shown in figure 17-7.

To check for a secure connection, you use the IsSecureConnection property. Then, if the connection isn't secure, you can use the Url property to retrieve the URL for the page and modify that URL so it uses the HTTPS protocol. After you do that, you can use the Redirect method to redirect the browser using the new URL. Notice that you typically include this code at the beginning of the Load procedure for the page. That way, you can be sure that no other code is executed until a secure connection is established.

Another way to force a page to use a secure connection is by setting a property of the page from IIS. You can also use this technique to change the minimum SSL strength that's required from 40-bit to 128-bit. When you use this technique, a user won't be able to access the page without using a secure connection. In other words, he won't be able to bypass the navigation features provided by your application. For more information on how to use this technique, please see appendix A.

Properties of the HttpRequest class for working with secure connections

Property	Description
IsSecureConnection	Returns True if the current connection is secure. Otherwise, returns False.
Url	The URL of the current request.

A Page_Load procedure that forces the page to use a secure connection

```
Protected Sub Page_Load(ByVal sender As Object, _
        ByVal e As System.EventArgs) Handles Me.Load
    If Not Request.IsSecureConnection Then
        Dim sURL As String
        sURL = Request.Url.ToString.Replace("http:", "https:")
        Response.Redirect(sURL)
    End If
End Sub
```

Discussion

- If a page requires the user to enter sensitive information, such as passwords or credit card data, it should make sure that it's operating on a secure connection. To do that, the page should check the IsSecureConnection property of the HttpRequest object in its Load procedure.

- If the page isn't using a secure connection, it should switch to a secure connection to protect the privacy of the user's data. To do that, it can replace the HTTP protocol in the URL to HTTPS and then redirect the browser to the new URL.

- You can also prevent a user from accessing a page without a secure connection by setting a property of the page from the Internet Information Services program. When you use this technique, you can also set the default SSL strength to 128-bit. For more information, see appendix A.

Figure 17-7   How to force a page to use a secure connection

A Halloween Store application that uses SSL

To show how secure connections are used in a typical application, the next two topics present a version of the Halloween Store application that uses SSL.

The operation of the Halloween Store application

Figure 17-8 shows the five pages of the Halloween Store application. As you can see, the application lets the user select products and display the shopping cart without establishing a secure connection. When the user clicks the Check Out button from the Cart page, however, a secure connection is established. The secure connection is then maintained while the two Check Out pages and the Confirmation page are displayed. When the user clicks the Return to Order Page button, however, the Order page is redisplayed with an unsecured connection.

The code for the Halloween Store application

Figure 17-9 presents the code for using SSL in the Halloween Store application. At the top of the first page of this figure, you can see the code for the Click event of the Check Out button on the Shopping Cart page. (The code for the Click event of the Check Out button on the Order page is identical.) This code creates a URL that uses the HTTPS protocol and the path that's specified in the appSettings section of the web.config file. Then, it redirects the browser to the first Check Out page using a secure connection.

In the code for the first Check Out page, you can see that the Load event procedure checks if a secure connection has been established. If not, the URL is retrieved from the request and the HTTP protocol is replaced with HTTPS. Then, the browser is redirected to that URL, which uses a secure connection.

If the user clicks the Continue Checkout button, a relative URL is used to display the second Check Out page, which means that the secure connection is maintained. If the user clicks the Cancel or Continue Shopping button, however, the browser is redirected to the Order page with an unsecured connection.

The code for the second Check Out page is shown in part 2 of this figure. Like the first Check Out page, its Load event procedure makes sure that a secure connection is established before proceeding. In addition, if the user clicks the Cancel or Continue Shopping button, the Order page is redisplayed with an unsecured connection. If the user clicks the Accept Order button, however, the secure connection is maintained and the Confirmation page is displayed.

The code for the Confirmation page is also shown in this figure. As you can see, if the user clicks the Return to Order Page button on this page, the Order page is redisplayed with an unsecured connection.

How security is used by the Halloween Store application

Cart.aspx

CheckOut1.aspx

CheckOut2.aspx

Secure

Order.aspx

Confirmation.aspx

Unsecure

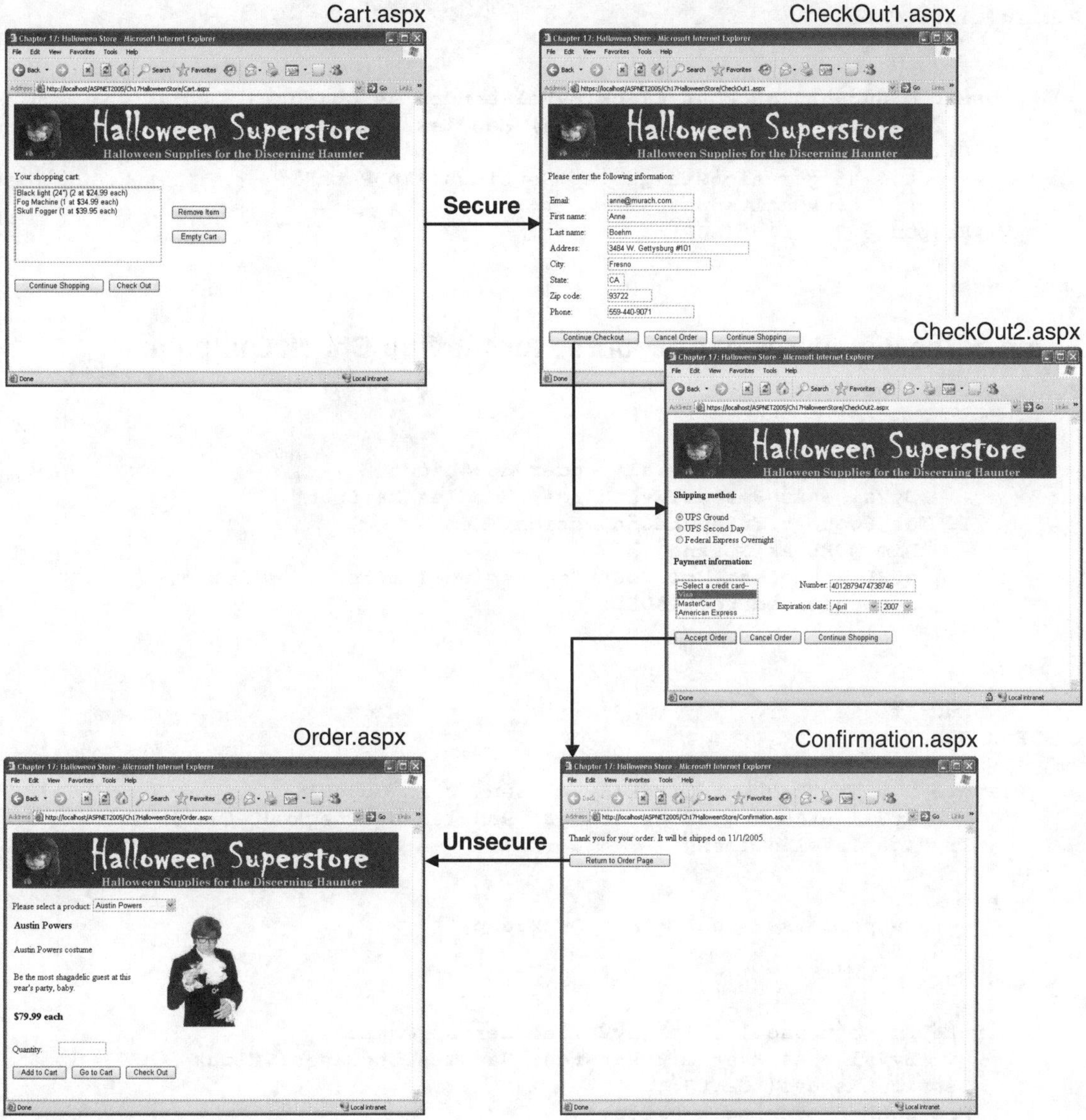

Description

- When the user clicks the Check Out button from the Shopping Cart page (or the Order page), the browser is redirected to the first Check Out page using a secure connection.
- When the user clicks the Continue Checkout button from the first Check Out page, the browser is redirected to the second Check Out page and remains in the secure connection.
- When the user clicks the Accept Order button from the second Check Out page, the browser is redirected to the Confirmation page and remains in the secure connection.
- When the user clicks the Return to Order Page button from the Confirmation page, the browser is redirected to the Order page in an unsecured connection.

Figure 17-8   The operation of the Halloween Store application with SSL

Some of the Visual Basic code for the Cart page

```
Public Class Cart
        .
        .
    Protected Sub btnCheckOut_Click(ByVal sender As Object, _
            ByVal e As System.EventArgs) Handles btnCheckOut.Click
        Dim sURL As String = "https:" _
            & ConfigurationManager.AppSettings("AppPath") _
            & "CheckOut1.aspx"
        Response.Redirect(sURL)
    End Sub
End Class
```

Some of the Visual Basic procedures for the first Check Out page

```
Public Class CheckOut1
        .
        .
    Protected Sub Page_Load(ByVal sender As Object, _
            ByVal e As System.EventArgs) Handles Me.Load
        If Not Request.IsSecureConnection Then
            Dim sURL As String
            sURL = Request.Url.ToString.Replace("http:", "https:")
            Response.Redirect(sURL)
        Else
            .
            .
        End If
    End Sub

    Private Sub btnCheckOut_Click(ByVal sender As Object, _
            ByVal e As System.EventArgs) Handles btnCheckOut.Click
        If Page.IsValid Then
            .
            .
            Response.Redirect("CheckOut2.aspx")
        End If
    End Sub

    Private Sub btnCancel_Click(ByVal sender As Object, _
            ByVal e As System.EventArgs) Handles btnCancel.Click
        Session.Remove("Cart")
        Dim sURL As String = "http:" _
                & ConfigurationManager.AppSettings("AppPath") _
                & "Order.aspx"
        Response.Redirect(sURL)
    End Sub

    Private Sub btnContinue_Click(ByVal sender As Object, _
            ByVal e As System.EventArgs) Handles btnContinue.Click
        Dim sURL As String = "http:" _
                & ConfigurationManager.AppSettings("AppPath") _
                & "Order.aspx"
        Response.Redirect(sURL)
    End Sub
End Class
```

Figure 17-9   The code for the Halloween Store application (part 1 of 2)

Some of the Visual Basic procedures for the second Check Out page

```
Public Class CheckOut2
    .
    .
    .
    Private Sub Page_Load(ByVal sender As Object, _
            ByVal e As System.EventArgs) Handles Me.Load
        If Not Request.IsSecureConnection Then
            Dim sURL As String
            sURL = Request.Url.ToString.Replace("http:", "https:")
            Response.Redirect(sURL)
        Else
            .
            .
            .
        End If
    End Sub

    Private Sub btnAccept_Click(ByVal sender As Object, _
            ByVal e As System.EventArgs) Handles btnAccept.Click
        If Page.IsValid Then
            .
            .
            .
            Response.Redirect("Confirmation.aspx")
        End If
    End Sub

    Private Sub btnCancel_Click(ByVal sender As Object, _
            ByVal e As System.EventArgs) Handles btnCancel.Click
        Session.Remove("Cart")
        Dim sURL As String = "http:" _
                & ConfigurationManager.AppSettings("AppPath") _
                & "Order.aspx"
        Response.Redirect(sURL)
    End Sub

    Private Sub btnContinue_Click(ByVal sender As Object, _
            ByVal e As System.EventArgs) Handles btnContinue.Click
        Dim sURL As String = "http:" _
            & ConfigurationManager.AppSettings("AppPath") _
            & "Order.aspx"
        Response.Redirect(sURL)
    End Sub
End Class
```

Some of the Visual Basic code for the Confirmation page

```
Public Class Confirmation
    .
    .
    .
    Private Sub btnReturn_Click(ByVal sender As Object, _
            ByVal e As System.EventArgs) Handles btnReturn.Click
        Dim sURL As String = "http:" _
          & ConfigurationManager.AppSettings("AppPath") _
          & "Order.aspx"
        Response.Redirect(sURL)
    End Sub
End Class
```

Figure 17-9   The code for the Halloween Store application (part 2 of 2)

Perspective

Now that you've completed this chapter, you should be able to use SSL encryption to secure the data transmissions between client and server. That's one part of securing an application. The other part is making sure that only authorized users are able to use your application, and you'll learn how to provide for that in the next chapter.

By the way, if you're interested in seeing the rest of the code for the Halloween Store application in this chapter looks like, you should know that you can download all of the applications in this book from our web site (www.murach.com).

Terms

Secure Sockets Layer (SSL)
secure connection
authentication
server authentication
client authentication
digital secure certificate
certification authority (CA)
registration authority (RA)
SSL strength
single root certificate
chained root certificate

18

How to use
the login controls
to authenticate users

In the last chapter, you learned how to secure the transmission of data between client and server. Now, you'll learn how to restrict access to some of the pages of an application, but let authorized users access those pages. To provide this functionality without writing a single line of code, you can use the new Web Site Administration Tool and the new login controls.

An introduction to authentication

If you want to limit access to all or part of your ASP.NET application to certain users, you can use *authentication* to verify each user's identity. Then, once you have authenticated the user, you can use *authorization* to check if the user has the appropriate privileges for accessing a page. That way, you can prevent unauthorized users from accessing pages that they shouldn't be able to access.

Three types of authentication

Figure 18-1 describes the three types of authentication you can use in ASP.NET applications. The first, called *Windows-based authentication*, requires that you set up a Windows user account for each user. Then, you use standard Windows security features to restrict access to all or part of the application. When a user attempts to access the application, Windows displays a login dialog box that asks the user to supply the username and password of the Windows account.

To use *forms-based authentication*, you add a login page to your application that typically requires the user to enter a username and password. Then, ASP.NET displays this page automatically when it needs to authenticate a user who's trying to access the application. One of the new features of ASP.NET 2.0 is that it automatically creates a database to store user data such as usernames and passwords. In addition, it includes new login controls that automatically generate code that reads data from and writes data to this database. As a result, you can implement forms-based authentication without having to write a single line of code. That makes this type of authentication easy to use, and you'll see how this works as you progress through this chapter.

Passport authentication relies on the *Microsoft Passport* service to authorize users. Passport is a centralized account management service that lets users access multiple web applications with a single user account. Unfortunately, you must pay Microsoft a hefty fee for the right to use Passport in your applications. In addition, Passport has had some problems with security flaws that have caused several major web sites to stop supporting it. As a result, it hasn't become as widely used as Microsoft had originally hoped.

Windows-based authentication

- Causes the browser to display a login dialog box when the user attempts to access a restricted page.
- Is supported by most browsers.
- Is configured through the IIS management console.
- Uses Windows user accounts and directory rights to grant access to restricted pages.

Forms-based authentication

- Lets developers code a login form that gets the username and password.
- The username and password entered by the user are encrypted if the login page uses a secure connection.
- Doesn't rely on Windows user accounts. Instead, the application determines how to authenticate users.

Passport authentication

- *Passport* is a centralized authentication service offered by Microsoft.
- Passport lets users maintain a single user account that lets them access any web site that participates in Passport. The advantage is that the user only has to maintain one username and password.
- Passport authentication isn't free. You must sign up for Passport authentication and pay a significant fee to use it in your applications. For more information about Passport authentication, visit www.passport.net.

Description

- *Authentication* refers to the process of validating the identity of a user so the user can be granted access to an application. A user must typically supply a username and password to be authenticated.
- After a user is authenticated, the user must still be authorized to use the requested application. The process of granting user access to an application is called *authorization*.

Figure 18-1   Three types of authentication

How forms-based authentication works

To help you understand how forms-based authentication works, figure 18-2 shows a typical series of exchanges that occur between a web browser and a server when a user attempts to access a page that's protected by forms-based authentication. The authentication process begins when a user requests a page that is part of a protected application. When the server receives the request, it checks to see if the user has already been authenticated. To do that, it looks for a cookie that contains an *authentication ticket* in the request for the page. If it doesn't find the ticket, it redirects the browser to the login page.

Next, the user enters a user name and password and posts the login page back to the server. Then, if the username and password are found in the database, which means they are valid, the server creates an authentication ticket and redirects the browser back to the original page. Note that the redirect from the server sends the authentication ticket to the browser as a cookie. As a result, when the browser requests the original page, it sends the cookie back to the server. This time, the server sees that the user has been authenticated and the requested page is sent back to the browser.

By default, the authentication ticket is sent as a session cookie. In that case, the user is authenticated only for that session. However, you also can specify that the ticket be sent as a persistent cookie. Then, the user will be authenticated automatically for future sessions, until the cookie expires.

HTTP requests and responses with forms-based authentication

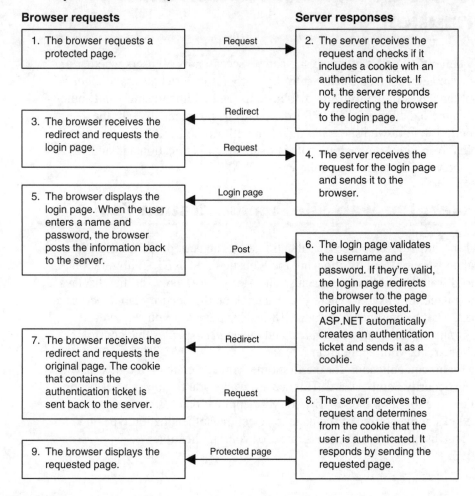

Browser requests

1. The browser requests a protected page.

3. The browser receives the redirect and requests the login page.

5. The browser displays the login page. When the user enters a name and password, the browser posts the information back to the server.

7. The browser receives the redirect and requests the original page. The cookie that contains the authentication ticket is sent back to the server.

9. The browser displays the requested page.

Server responses

2. The server receives the request and checks if it includes a cookie with an authentication ticket. If not, the server responds by redirecting the browser to the login page.

4. The server receives the request for the login page and sends it to the browser.

6. The login page validates the username and password. If they're valid, the login page redirects the browser to the page originally requested. ASP.NET automatically creates an authentication ticket and sends it as a cookie.

8. The server receives the request and determines from the cookie that the user is authenticated. It responds by sending the requested page.

(arrows labeled: Request, Redirect, Request, Login page, Post, Redirect, Request, Protected page)

Discussion

- When ASP.NET receives a request for a page that's protected from a user who has not been authenticated, the server redirects the user to the login page.

- To be authenticated, the user's computer must contain an *authentication ticket*. By default, this ticket is stored as a session cookie.

- ASP.NET automatically creates an authentication ticket when the application indicates that the user should be authenticated. ASP.NET checks for the presence of an authentication ticket any time it receives a request for a restricted page.

- The authentication ticket cookie can be made persistent. Then, the user will be authenticated automatically in future sessions, until the cookie expires.

Figure 18-2   How forms-based authentication works

How to set up authentication and authorization

By default, all pages of a web site can be accessed by all users whether or not they are authenticated. As a result, if you want to restrict access to all or some of the pages of the web site, you need to set up authentication and authorization. In the old days of ASP.NET 1.0, you needed to manually edit the web.config file for a web site to do that. But with ASP.NET 2.0, you can use the ASP.NET Web Site Administration Tool to set up authentication and authorization as shown in the topics that follow.

How to start the Web Site Administration Tool

When you're developing an application, you can start the ASP.NET Web Site Administration Tool by choosing the Website→ASP.NET Configuration command from Visual Studio's menus. This starts a web browser that displays the home page for this tool. Then, you can click on the Security tab to access a web page like the one shown in figure 18-3. This page lets you set up users, create groups of users known as *roles*, and create *access rules* that control access to parts of your application.

To set up authentication for the first time, you can click on the link that starts the Security Setup wizard. This wizard walks you through several steps that allow you to set up the security for your application. Alternatively, you can use the links at the bottom of the page to select the authentication type and manage the users, roles, and access rules for your application.

The Security tab of the Web Site Administration Tool

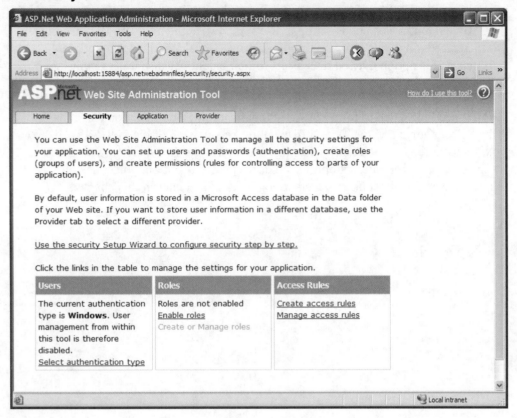

Description

- When developing an application, you can start the ASP.NET Web Site Administration Tool by choosing the Website→ASP.NET Configuration command.

- You can use the ASP.NET Web Site Administration Tool to set up users, roles, and access rules.

Figure 18-3   How to start the Web Site Administration Tool

How to enable forms-based authentication

By default, a web site is set up to use Windows authentication. If all users will be accessing your web site through a private local Windows network (an intranet), this option may be the easiest to implement because it uses built-in Windows dialog boxes to allow users to log in.

However, if any of your users will access your web site from the Internet, you'll need to switch to forms-based authentication. To do that, you can click on the Select Authentication Type link from the Security tab of the Web Site Administration Tool to display the page shown in figure 18-4. Then, you can select the From the Internet option. When you use this option, you'll need to create a web form that allows users to log in as shown later in this chapter.

How to enable forms-based authentication

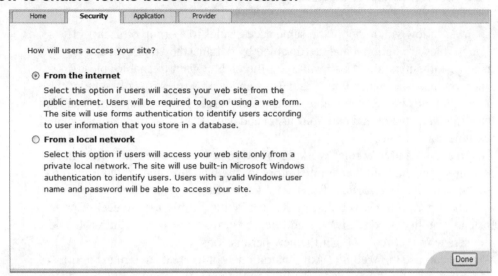

Description

- By default, a web site is set up to use Windows authentication. However, this option is only appropriate for accessing a web site through a local intranet.

- To switch to forms-based authentication, select the From the Internet option. This is the option that you'll need to use if you intend to deploy the application so it's available from the Internet.

Figure 18-4   How to enable forms-based authentication

How to create and manage roles

Roles allow you to apply the same access rules to a group of users. Although roles are optional and are disabled by default, they make it easy to manage authentication. As a result, you'll typically want to enable roles. And since you use roles when you create users and access rules, it's often helpful to set up the roles before you create the users and access rules. That way, you don't have to go back later and edit your users and access rules so they are associated with the correct roles.

To understand how roles work, let's say you create a role named admin for all employees that will be administrators for the web site, and you assign this role to multiple users. Later, if you want to give all users in the admin role additional permissions, you don't have to give the permissions to each user. Instead, you just need to give the additional permissions to the admin role and all users with that role will get the new permissions.

You can use the Web Site Administration Tool to create and manage roles. To do that, you need to click on the link on the Security tab to enable roles. Then, you can click on the Create or Manage Roles link to display a page like the one in figure 18-5.

The first two controls on this page allow you to add roles. To do that, you just enter a name for the role and click on the Add Role button, and the role will appear in the table at the bottom of the page. Then, you can click on the Manage link for the role to add users to the role or to remove users from the role. Or, you can click the Delete link for the role to delete the role entirely.

Usernames and roles

```
Username     Roles
anne         admin
joel         admin, custserv
kelly        custserv
```

How to create and manage roles

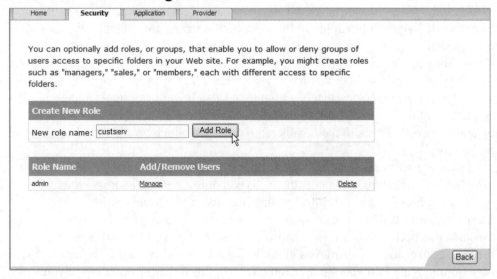

Description

- A *role* allows you to apply the same access rules to a group of users.
- Each user may be associated with one or more roles.
- By default, roles are disabled. To enable them, you need to click on the link in the Security tab that enables roles.
- Once you enable roles, you can use the page shown above to add roles, to manage all users associated with the role, or to delete the role.

Figure 18-5   How to create and manage roles

How to create and manage users

The first page displayed in figure 18-6 shows how to use the Web Site Administration Tool to create users. To do that, you start by entering all of the required information for a user. This information includes a username, a password, an email address, and a security question and answer. If you want to associate the user with one or more roles, you can select the check box next to each role that you want to apply to the user. In this figure, for example, the user is associated with the admin role. When you're done, you can click on the Create User button to create the user.

The default password policy for an ASP.NET 2.0 application requires that you enter at least seven characters with one of them being a non-alphanumeric character. If that's too strict for your web site, though, you can relax this policy by adding two attributes to the membership provider, which you'll learn how to do in figure 18-8.

Once you've created one or more users, you can use the second screen displayed in this figure to manage them. To edit a user's email address, you can click on the Edit User link. (However, this link doesn't let you edit the username, password, or security question and answer.) To change the roles assigned to a user, you can select the Edit Roles link for the user and work with the check boxes that are displayed in the Roles column of the table. To prevent a user from logging into your application but retain his or her information in your database, you can set the status to inactive by clearing the Active check box to the left of the username.

If your application contains many users, you may need to use the Search For Users table to search for users. When you use this table, you can search by username or email address. For example, to search by email address, you can select the email address option from the Search By combo box, enter the email address in the For text box, and click on the Find User button. If necessary, you can use the asterisk (*) wildcard for multiple characters, and you can use the question mark (?) wildcard for a single character. Alternatively, you can click on the letters displayed on this page to display all users whose username or email address begins with the specified letter. Either way, you should be able to quickly find the user that you're looking for.

How to create a user

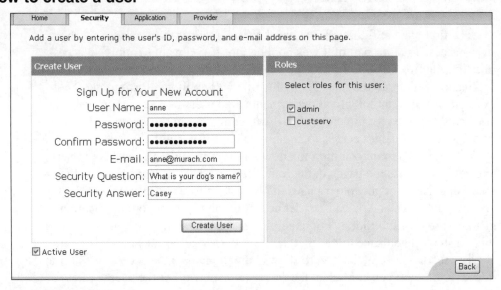

How to manage users

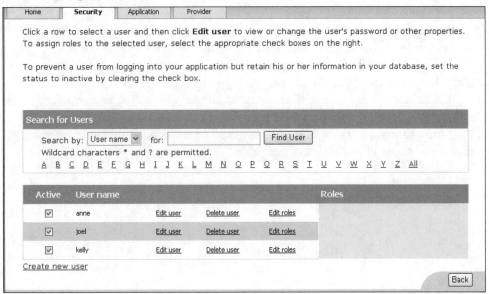

Figure 18-6   How to create and manage users

How to create and manage access rules

The first page in figure 18-7 shows how to create an *access rule* that restricts access to all or part of a web application. If you want to apply an access rule to the entire web application, you can select the root directory for the web application and apply the rule. Then, this rule will apply to all subfolders. For example, if you want to only allow authenticated users to access your web site, you can select the root directory (Ch18Authentication in this example), and create a rule that denies access to anonymous users.

However, it's more common to allow all users including anonymous users to be able to access the pages in the root directory. That way, all users can view your home page and any other pages that you want to make available to the general public. Then, you can restrict access to the pages in your application that are stored in subfolders. For example, this screen shows how to create a rule for the Maintenance folder that denies access to all users.

The second page in this figure shows how to manage the access rules for a folder. To do that, you can select the folder to display all of the access rules for the folder. Then, you can move rules up or down, which is important since they're applied in the order in which they're displayed. Or, you can delete any rules that you no longer want to apply.

On the second page, you can see the rules that restrict access to the Maintenance folder. Here, the bottom rule (which is dimmed) is the rule that's automatically applied to all pages of a web site if you don't create new rules. This rule allows access to all users including anonymous users. Then, the middle rule overrides the bottom rule and denies access to all users including authenticated users. However, the top rule overrides the middle rule and allows access to users in the admin role. As a result, only authenticated users in the admin role are able to access the pages in the Maintenance folder.

How to create an access rule

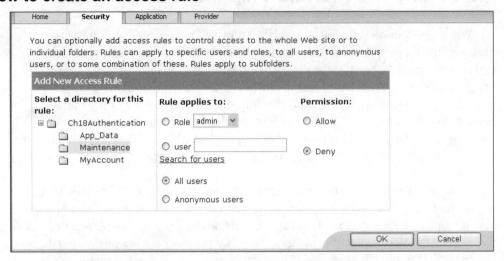

How to manage access rules

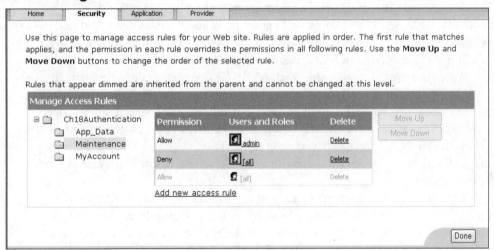

Description

- An *access rule* determines which users have access to portions of a web site.
- Each rule overrides the rules below it. As a result, for the Maintenance directory shown above, users in the admin role are allowed and all other users are denied.

Figure 18-7   How to create and manage access rules

How to modify the membership and role provider

When you add roles and users, a class known as a *data provider* contains the code that reads and writes the data for the users and roles. A data provider that works with membership data is often called a *membership provider*, and a data provider that works with roles data is often called a *role provider*. By default, a data provider named AspNetSqlProvider is used to store both membership and role data in a SQL Server Express database named AspNetDb.mdf that's stored in the App_Data folder of your web site. This database is created for you automatically, and it usually works the way you want, at least for prototyping.

However, the data provider architecture lets you use different data providers if you want to. If, for example, you want to use one data provider for the membership data and another for role data, you can use the Provider tab shown in figure 18-8 to select separate providers. The only provider for membership data is AspNetSqlMembershipProvider. Two providers are available for role data: AspNetSqlRoleProvider and AspNetWindowsTokenRoleProvider. If you use the Windows token provider, the role information will be based on Windows accounts. Because of that, you won't create roles and users as described in the previous topics. In addition, you won't use forms-based authentication. Instead, you'll need to use Windows-based authentication.

If the data providers that ship with ASP.NET 2.0 aren't adequate for your application, you may need to write a custom data provider. If, for example, you need to store membership data in an Oracle database, a MySQL database, or even on a midrange or mainframe computer, you can write a custom membership provider to do that. Or, if you need to work with existing membership data that's stored in a SQL Server database, you can write a custom provider to work with that data.

To write a membership provider, you need to code a class that implements the abstract MembershipProvider class. To write a role provider, you need to code a class that implements the abstract RoleProvider class. After you implement all of the necessary properties and methods of these classes, you can edit the machine.config or web.config file to add the providers to the list for all applications or the list for one application. Then, you can use the Provider tab to select the data providers for memberships and roles. Once you do that, the rest of the authentication features should work as described in this chapter.

This figure also shows how you can modify the attributes of a data provider to change the way that the data provider behaves. In particular, it shows how you can relax the strict password requirements for an application. To do that, you can copy the Membership element from the machine.config file (which applies to all web applications) to the web.config file (which applies to your application). Then, you can edit the Name attribute of the Add element to create a unique name for the modified provider, and you can add and set the minRequiredPasswordLength and minRequiredNonAlphanumericCharacters attributes. In this case, these attributes are set so each password requires 6 characters and zero special characters. Last, you can add the defaultProvider attribute to the Membership element so your application uses this provider.

The Provider tab of the Web Site Administration Tool

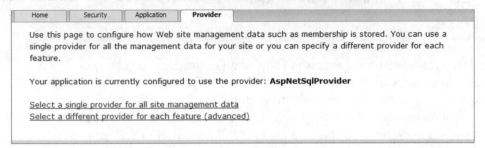

Elements in the web.config file that relax the default password policy

```
<membership defaultProvider="AspNetSqlMembershipProviderRelaxed">
  <providers>
    <add name="AspNetSqlMembershipProviderRelaxed"
        type="System.Web.Security.SqlMembershipProvider,
              System.Web, Version=2.0.0.0, Culture=neutral,
              PublicKeyToken=b03f5f7f11d50a3a"
        connectionStringName="LocalSqlServer"
        enablePasswordRetrieval="false"
        enablePasswordReset="true"
        requiresQuestionAndAnswer="true"
        applicationName="/"
        requiresUniqueEmail="false"
        passwordFormat="Hashed"
        maxInvalidPasswordAttempts="5"
        passwordAttemptWindow="10"
        passwordStrengthRegularExpression=""
        minRequiredPasswordLength="6"
        minRequiredNonalphanumericCharacters="0"/>
  </providers>
</membership>
```

Description

- By default, a *data provider* named AspNetSqlProvider is used to store both membership and role data in a SQL Server Express database named AspNetDb.mdf. However, you can use separate membership and role providers, and you can write your own custom providers.
- The definitions for the default membership and role providers can be found in the machine.config file. This file is stored in the Config folder subordinate to the .NET Framework installation folder.
- To relax the password restrictions for a provider, you can change the attributes for password length and non-alphanumeric characters in the web.config file for an application.

Figure 18-8   How to modify the membership and role provider

How to use the ASP.NET 2.0 login controls

Once you've restricted access to some or all of the pages of your web application, you need to allow users with the proper permissions to log in and access the restricted pages. In addition, you may want to provide other features such as allowing users to log out, to create an account by themselves, to recover a forgotten password, or to change a password. With ASP.NET 2.0, you can use the controls in the Login group of the Toolbox to automatically handle these tasks.

How to use the Login control

Figure 18-9 shows how to create a login page that contains a Login control. When you create a login page, you should name it Login.aspx. That's because ASP.NET looks for a page with this name when it attempts to authenticate a user. Also, since this page is used for the entire application, you usually want to use a simple format so it works equally well for all parts of the application.

Once you've created a page named Login.aspx, you can add all of the login functionality just by adding a Login control to the page. To do that, drag the Login control that's in the Login group of the Toolbox onto the page.

Like most login pages, the Login control includes two text boxes that let the user enter a username and a password. In addition, it includes a check box that lets the users indicate whether or not they want to be logged in automatically the next time the application is accessed. If the user selects this check box, the application can create a persistent cookie that contains the authentication ticket.

When the user clicks the Log In button within the Login control, the code for the control tries to authenticate the user. It does that by checking to see whether the username and password are in the membership provider. Then, if the user is authenticated, the code checks the role provider to see whether the user has the proper authorization for the requested page. If so, this code continues by redirecting the browser to that page.

If you want to automatically apply formatting to the Login control, you can right-click on the control and select the AutoFormat command. Then, you can use the resulting Auto Format dialog box to select a scheme that you like. When you do, Visual Studio will change many of the control's formatting properties. This feature works similarly for the CreateUserWizard, PasswordRecovery, and ChangePassword controls described in the pages that follow.

Although it's not shown in this figure, a login page should always force the page to use a secure connection. Then, if a hacker manages to intercept a user's username and password, your application won't be compromised.

A Login control in the Web Forms Designer

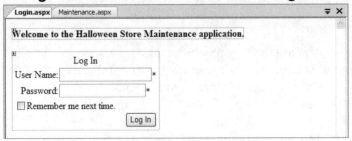

The aspx code for the Login control

```
<asp:Login ID="Login1" runat="server">
</asp:Login>
```

Common attributes of the Login control

Attribute	Description
RememberMeSet	Determines whether the RememberMe check box is displayed. By default, this is set to True.
RememberMeText	The text for the label of the RememberMe text box.
FailureText	The text that's displayed when a login attempt fails.

The AutoFormat dialog box for a Login control

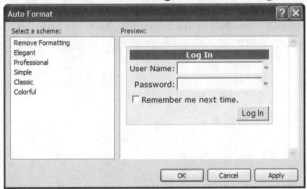

Description

- When a user attempts to access a page that requires authentication, ASP.NET automatically redirects the user to the application's login page. This page must be named Login.aspx.
- To automatically apply formatting to the Login control, right-click on it and select the AutoFormat command.

Figure 18-9   How to use the Login control

How to use the LoginStatus and LoginName controls

Figure 18-10 shows how you can use the LoginStatus and LoginName controls. In the page at the top of this figure, you can see that the LoginName control provides the name of a logged in user. In contrast, the LoginStatus control provides a Login link if a user hasn't logged in yet, and a Logout link if the user has logged in. Notice that this page also includes a hyperlink that the user can click if the username that's displayed is incorrect. This hyperlink is not part of the LoginName or LoginStatus control.

To use these controls, you just drag them onto the form from the Login group of the Toolbox. Then, you can change the properties as needed. For instance, you can use the LoginText and LogoutText attributes of the LoginStatus control to change the text that's displayed by the links. And you can use the FormatString attribute of the LoginName control to add text before or after the placeholder for the username.

When the user clicks on the Login link of a LoginStatus control, the user will be redirected to the login page and required to enter a username and password. Then, after the user has been authenticated, the user will be redirected to the original page. Conversely, when the user clicks the Logout link, the user will be redirected to the login page (Login.aspx).

When a user has been authenticated, the LoginName control will display the user name. Otherwise, the control won't display the user name. However, it will display any other text that has been specified in the FormatString attribute.

The LoginName and LoginStatus controls displayed in a browser

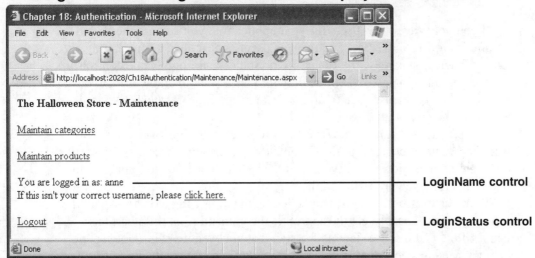

LoginName control

LoginStatus control

The LoginName and LoginStatus controls in the Web Forms Designer

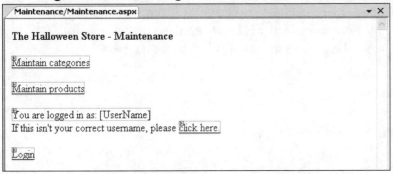

The aspx code for the LoginName and LoginStatus controls

```
<asp:LoginName ID="LoginName1" runat="server"
    FormatString="You are logged in as: {0}" /><br />

<asp:LoginStatus ID="LoginStatus1" runat="server" />
```

Common attributes of the LoginName control

Attribute	Description
FormatString	The text that's displayed with the username. This string uses "{0}" to identify the UserName parameter, and you can add text before or after this parameter.

Common attributes of the LoginStatus control

Attribute	Description
LoginText	The text that's displayed for the login link.
LogoutText	The text that's displayed for the logout link.

Figure 18-10   How to use the LoginStatus and LoginName controls

How to use the CreateUserWizard control

If you only have a few users for your application, you can use the Web Site Administration Tool to create and manage users as described earlier in this chapter. Then, you can use the Login, LoginStatus, and LoginName controls to allow users to log in and out. Often, though, you'll want to allow users to create user accounts for themselves. To do that, you can use the CreateUserWizard control as shown in figure 18-11.

By default, the CreateUserWizard control uses two steps to create a new user: the Create User step and the Complete step. Usually, these steps work like you want them to. However, if you need to modify their behavior, you can do that by changing the properties of the control.

To do that, select the control and click on the Smart Tag icon to display the smart tag menu. Then, select the appropriate command from the smart tag menu. Often, that means selecting the step that you want to edit. For example, you may need to select the Complete step so you can modify its properties. In particular, you may need to set the PostBackUrl property of the Continue button so the user is redirected to the appropriate page.

When you use the pages that result from the CreateUserWizard control, you should realize that the membership provider is being used to write the data to the appropriate data source. This works the same as it does for the Web Site Administration Tool.

The CreateUserWizard control with the smart tag menu shown

The two steps of the CreateUserWizard control in a browser

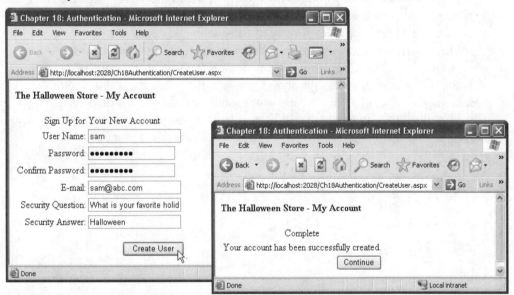

Description

- If you select the CreateUserWizard control in the Web Forms Designer, you can use the smart tag menu to switch between its two steps and reset or customize either step.

- In the Complete step, you need to set the PostBackUrl property of the Continue button so the user is directed to the appropriate page.

Figure 18-11   How to use the CreateUserWizard control

How to use the PasswordRecovery control

It's inevitable that some users will forget their passwords. Fortunately, the PasswordRecovery control makes it easy to automate the process of recovering forgotten passwords. This process is described in figure 18-12, and it's especially useful if you are managing a site with a large number of users.

When you use the PasswordRecovery control, the password is sent to the user via email. As a result, you need to make sure that your system is set up so it can send email before you test this control. By default, an application will try to send email to an SMTP server set to localhost on port 25.

The most important element of the PasswordRecovery control is the MailDefinition element. In particular, you must set the From attribute of the MailDefinition element to the email address that's sending the email message or an error will occur when your system attempts to send the email. Typically, the From email address is set to the email address that's used by the web site administrator. If you set this attribute correctly, a standard message will be sent to the user. To customize the subject line and message body, you can edit the other attributes of the MailDefinition element.

The PasswordRecovery control uses three views. In the Web Forms Designer, you can switch between these three views by using the smart tag menu, and you can edit the properties for any of these views as necessary.

When you display this control in a browser, the first view asks the user to enter a username. Then, the second view requires the user to answer the security question. If the answer to this question is correct, the password is emailed to the address that's associated with the username, and the third view is displayed. This view displays a message that indicates that the password recovery was successful and that the password has been sent to the user via email.

The PasswordRecovery control in the Web Forms Designer

The first two views of the PasswordRecovery control

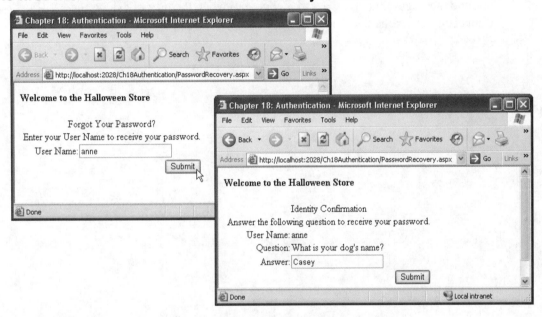

The aspx code for the PasswordRecovery control

```
<asp:PasswordRecovery ID="PasswordRecovery1" runat="server">
    <MailDefinition From="anne@murach.com">
    </MailDefinition>
</asp:PasswordRecovery>
```

Description

- After the second view is completed, the password is emailed to the user. For this to work, you need to edit the From attribute of the MailDefinition element to supply the from address for this email. In addition, the web server that you're using must be configured to work with an SMTP server.

- By default, an application will try to send email to an SMTP server set to localhost on port 25. For information on how to change these settings, see chapter 21.

Figure 18-12   How to use the PasswordRecovery control

How to use the ChangePassword control

Another common task associated with the authentication process is allowing users to change their passwords. To make that easy for you, ASP.NET 2.0 provides the ChangePassword control, and figure 18-13 shows how to use it.

The ChangePassword control uses two views. The first view lets the user enter the current password and the new password twice. Then, if the old password is correct and the two new passwords match, the second view is displayed. This view tells the user that the password has been successfully changed.

Once you've placed the PasswordControl on the form, it usually works the way you want it to. However, you may need to edit the Url attributes so they point to the pages that you want to navigate to when the user clicks on the Cancel and Continue buttons.

The first view of the ChangePassword control in the Web Forms Designer

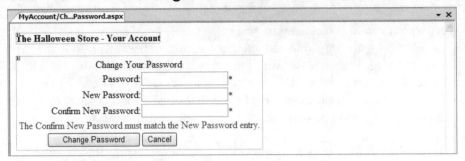

The second view of the ChangePassword control

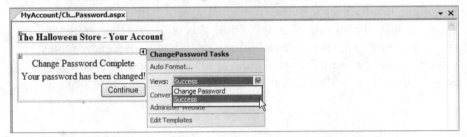

The aspx code for the ChangePassword control

```
<asp:ChangePassword ID="ChangePassword1" runat="server"
    CancelDestinationPageUrl="MyAccount.aspx"
    ContinueDestinationPageUrl="MyAccount.aspx">
</asp:ChangePassword>
```

Description

- The ChangePassword control uses two views to allow users to change their passwords. The first view lets the user change the password. The second view is displayed when the change has been successful.
- The CancelDestinationPageUrl and ContinueDestinationPageUrl attributes provide the URLs that are navigated to when the Cancel or Continue buttons are clicked.

Figure 18-13   How to use the ChangePassword control

How to use the LoginView control

If your web site uses authentication, you often to need to display one message to users who are logged in and another message to users who aren't logged in. For example, when a user isn't logged in, you may want to display a message that asks the user to log in. Conversely, if a user is logged in, you may want to display a message that welcomes the user back and allows the user to log out. Figure 18-14 shows how to use the LoginView control to accomplish these tasks.

The LoginView control uses two views. The first view contains the controls that are displayed to users who aren't logged in (*anonymous users*). The second view contains the controls that are displayed to users who are logged in (*authenticated users*). In this figure, each view of the LoginView control contains a Label control followed by a LoginStatus control. This is a fairly typical use of the LoginView control. However, the LoginView control can store entire tables if that's necessary. Then, the height and width of the LoginView control will be adjusted automatically to accommodate the controls that you place inside of it.

The LoginView control in the Web Forms Designer

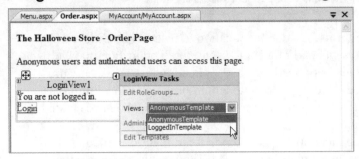

The aspx code for the LoginView control

```
<asp:LoginView ID="LoginView1" runat="server">
    <LoggedInTemplate>
        <asp:Label ID="Label2" runat="server"
            Text="You are logged in." Width="155px"></asp:Label><br />
        <asp:LoginStatus ID="LoginStatus2" runat="server" />
    </LoggedInTemplate>
    <AnonymousTemplate>
        <asp:Label ID="Label1" runat="server"
            Text="You are not logged in." Width="175px"></asp:Label><br />
        <asp:LoginStatus ID="LoginStatus1" runat="server" />
    </AnonymousTemplate>
</asp:LoginView>
```

The LoginView control displayed in a browser

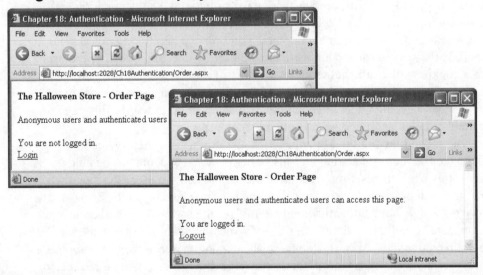

Description

- The LoginView control lets you change what's on the web page depending on whether the user isn't logged in (an *anonymous user*) or is logged in (an *authenticated user*).

Figure 18-14   How to use the LoginView control

The Authentication application

To show how to use forms-based authentication to restrict access to a web application, this topic presents part of a Halloween Store application that we'll refer to as the Authentication application. This application restricts access to all pages in the Maintenance folder to users with admin privileges. In addition, it restricts access to all pages in the MyAccount folder to users who have created an account and logged in.

As you review this application, please keep in mind that the authentication and authorization features don't require any code. That's why the figures that follow show only the pages, the directory structure, the access rules, and the web.config files.

The pages

Figure 18-15 shows just four pages of the Authentication application, but you can also think of the pages in figures 18-11 through 18-13 as part of this application. For instance, the Forgot Your Password link on the Login page goes to the page in figure 18-12, and the Need to Create a New Account link goes to the page in figure 18-11. Also, the Change Password link on the MyAccount page goes to a ChangePassword page like the one in figure 18-13.

To start this application, the Menu page in figure 18-15 contains three links that allow you to perform some tests to make sure that the authentication and authorization features are working correctly. The first link on this page lets the user access an Order page to begin placing an order. When the user clicks on this link, the system tries to authenticate the user by checking whether the user has a cookie with a valid authentication ticket. If so, the user will be authenticated automatically. If not, the user can view the Order page as an anonymous user. Either way, the Order page will be displayed. In other words, this page is available to both anonymous and authenticated users.

The second link on the Menu page lets the user access the MyAccount page where the user can edit settings for his or her personal account. To be able to access this page, the user must be authenticated. When the user clicks on this link, the system attempts to authenticate the user by checking if the browser has a cookie with a valid authentication ticket. If so, the user will be authenticated automatically and allowed to access the MyAccount page. If not, the user will be redirected to the Login page so he or she can log in. Once the user supplies a valid username and password to the Login page, the browser will be redirected to the MyAccount page.

The Menu page

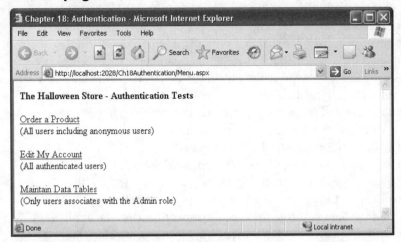

The Login page

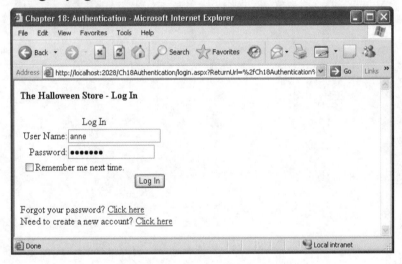

Description

- The Menu page contains three links. The first lets anonymous users or authenticated users access the Order page. The second lets authenticated users access the MyAccount page. The third lets authenticated users who are associated with the Admin role access the Maintenance page.

- The Login page is only displayed if the user clicks on the second or third link and the browser doesn't contain a cookie that authenticates the user.

- If the user clicks on the Forgot your Password link on the Login page, the PasswordRecovery page in figure 18-12 is displayed. If the user clicks on the Need to Create a New Account link, the CreateUser page in figure 18-11 is displayed.

Figure 18-15   The pages of the Authentication application (part 1 of 2)

The third link on the Menu page lets users access the Maintenance page that can be used to manage data that's stored in the Categories and Products tables of the database for the web site. To be able to access this page, the user must be authenticated and the user must be associated with the admin role. When the user clicks on this link, the system attempts to authenticate the user by checking if the browser has a cookie with a valid authentication ticket. If so, the user will be authenticated automatically and allowed to access the Maintenance page. If not, the user will be redirected to the Login page so he or she can log in. Once the user supplies a valid username and password for a user with admin privileges, the browser will be redirected to the Maintenance page.

When you're using the MyAccount and Maintenance pages, the LoginStatus control on these pages allows the users to log out when they're done. This removes the authentication ticket from the browser. As a result, the application won't remember the user the next time the user attempts to access the application, even if the user has selected the Remember Me check box to store the authentication ticket in a persistent cookie.

The MyAccount page

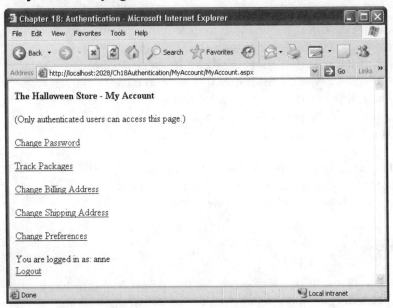

The Maintenance page

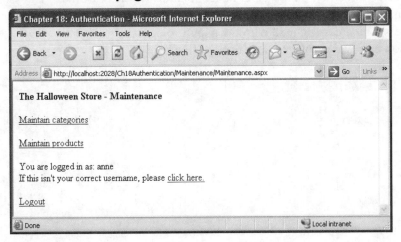

Description

- The MyAccount page lets a user edit account data. The user must be authenticated, but need not be associated with any role. When the user clicks on the Change Password link, a page like the one in figure 18-13 is displayed.

- The Maintenance page lets a user maintain data in the Categories and Products tables. The user must be authenticated and must be associated with the admin role.

- The LoginStatus control on these pages lets the user log out when done. This removes the authentication ticket from the browser. As a result, the application won't be able to remember the user the next time the user attempts to access the application.

Figure 18-15   The pages of the Authentication application (part 2 of 2)

572 Section 4 Professional ASP.NET skills

The directory structure

Figure 18-16 shows the directory structure for the Authentication application. This shows the App_Data folder that stores the SQL Server Express database that's used to store the data about the web site's registered users and their roles. In addition, it shows two directories that store web pages that have restricted access. First, it shows the Maintenance directory, which contains the Maintenance page shown in the previous figure. Second, it shows the MyAccount directory, which contains the MyAccount page shown in the previous figure.

In addition, there are three web.config files for this application: one for the root directory, one for the Maintenance directory, and one for the MyAccount directory. The complete listings for these files are shown in figure 18-17.

The access rules

Figure 18-16 also shows the one access rule for the MyAccount directory. This rule denies access to anonymous users. As a result, only users who are authenticated can access the MyAccount directory.

The Maintenance directory, on the other hand, contains two access rules. The first rule denies access to all users. Then, the second rule allows access to authenticated users who are associated with the admin role. To refresh your memory about how this works, please refer back to figure 18-7.

The directory structure for the Authentication application

The access rules for the Maintenance directory

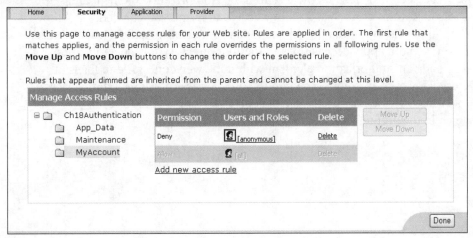

Description

- The MyAccount page lets a user edit personal account data. The user must be authenticated, but doesn't need to be associated with any role.

Figure 18-16   The directory structure and access rules for the Authentication application

The web.config files

Figure 18-17 shows the three web.config files for the Authentication application. When you use the Web Site Administration Tool to create access rules, it automatically creates and modifies these web.config files. As a result, you don't need to be able to manually edit these files. However, it's good to have an idea of what's going on under the hood as you use the Web Site Administration Tool.

In addition, once you become familiar with these files, you may find that you prefer to manually edit or review these files. But first, you need to understand the XML code that's used by these files to store configuration settings.

To enable forms-based authentication, you can use the Mode attribute of the Authentication element. This attribute is set to "Windows" by default to use Windows authentication, but you can set it to "Forms" to enable forms-based authentication.

Once you've enabled forms-based authentication, you can use the Authorization element to deny or allow access to specified users. To deny access to users, you can code a Deny element within the Authorization element and set the Users and Roles attributes. To allow access to users, you can code an Allow element within the Authorization element and set the Users and Roles attributes.

If you want to apply access rules to the root directory for the application, you can code an Authorization element within the web.config file in the root directory. However, it's more common to apply access rules to subdirectories of the root directory. In that case, you can code a web.config file for each directory as shown in this figure.

The web.config files for the Authentication application

For the root directory

```xml
<?xml version="1.0"?>
<configuration>
    <system.web>
        <roleManager enabled="True"/>
        <authentication mode="Forms" />
        <compilation debug="true"/>
    </system.web>
</configuration>
```

For the MyAccount directory

```xml
<?xml version="1.0" encoding="utf-8"?>
<configuration>
    <system.web>
        <authorization>
            <deny users="?" />
        </authorization>
    </system.web>
</configuration>
```

For the Maintenance directory

```xml
<?xml version="1.0" encoding="utf-8"?>
<configuration>
    <system.web>
        <authorization>
            <allow roles="admin" />
            <deny users="*" />
        </authorization>
    </system.web>
</configuration>
```

Wildcard specifications in the users attribute

Wildcard	Description
*	All users, whether or not they have been authenticated.
?	All unauthenticated users.

Discussion

- When you use the Web Site Administration Tool to create access rules, it automatically creates and modifies the web.config files for an application.

- If you prefer, you can manually edit these files and you can read them to quickly review the settings for an application.

- To enable forms-based authentication, set the Mode attribute of the Authentication element to "Forms." This attribute is set to "Windows" by default.

- To deny access to users, you can code a Deny element within the Authorization element and set the Users and Roles attributes.

- To allow access to users, you can code an Allow element within the Authorization element and set the Users and Roles attributes.

Figure 18-17   The web.config files for the Authentication application

How to use code to work with authentication

For most web applications, you can use the Web Site Administration Tool to create users, roles, and access rules. Then, you can use the login controls to allow authorized users to access the restricted pages. And you can do all of this without having to write any code.

However, if you do need to write code to work with authentication, ASP.NET 2.0 provides three new classes that make it easy to do that: the Membership, MembershipUser, and Roles classes. These classes work well with the FormsAuthentication class that was widely used with ASP.NET 1.x. All of these classes are stored in the System.Web.Security namespace.

How to use the Membership class

If you need to work with user data, you can use the Membership class as shown in figure 18-18. This class uses the membership provider that's specified for the application to read and write data from the data store. For more information about how this works, see figure 18-8.

All methods of the Membership class are static. As a result, you never need to create an instance of this class to use its methods. To give you an idea of the types of methods that are available from the Membership class, some of the most commonly used methods are summarized in this figure. However, for a full list of methods, you should consult the documentation for the Membership class.

You can use these methods to create or delete a user. When you use some of these methods, you may need to catch the exceptions that are thrown by them. For example, when you create a user, you need to catch the MembershipCreateUserException that's thrown when the user can't be created.

You can also use these methods to retrieve and update the data that's stored for a user. To do that, you must work with an object created from the MembershipUser class. For example, the GetUser method returns a MembershipUser object that contains the data for the user such as the username, password, email address, security question, and security answer. For more information about working with this class, see the next figure.

If you create a custom login page that doesn't use the Login control shown earlier in this chapter, you can use the ValidateUser method of the Membership class to authenticate the user. Then, if the specified username and password exist in the database and the user has the proper authorization, this method will return a true value. In that case, you can safely redirect the request to the original page that caused the custom login page to be displayed. You can see an example of how this works in figure 18-20.

Common methods of the Membership class

Method	Description
ValidateUser(username, password)	Returns a Boolean value that indicates whether the user is authenticated and authorized.
CreateUser(username, password)	Creates a user with the specified username and password.
CreateUser(username, password, email)	Creates a user with the specified username, password, and email address.
GetUser()	Returns a MembershipUser object that contains data about the currently logged-on user. Updates the last activity date-time stamp.
GetUser(username)	Returns a MembershipUser object that contains data about the user with the specified username. Updates the last activity date-time stamp.
GetUserNameByEmail(email)	Returns a string that contains the username that corresponds with the specified email address.
GetAllUsers()	Returns a MembershipUserCollection object that contains MembershipUser objects.
DeleteUser(username)	Deletes the user with the specified username.
UpdateUser(membershipUser)	Updates the user with the data that's stored in the specified MembershipUser object.

A statement that checks if a user is valid

```
Dim bIsValidUser As Boolean
bIsValidUser = Membership.ValidateUser(txtUserName.Text, txtPassword.Text)
```

A statement that creates a user

```
Try
    Membership.CreateUser(txtUserName.Text, txtPassword.Text)
Catch eCreateUser As MembershipCreateUserException
    lblStatus.Text = eCreateUser.Message
End Try
```

A statement that gets the current user and updates the last activity timestamp

```
Dim User As MembershipUser = Membership.GetUser
```

A statement that deletes a user

```
Membership.DeleteUser(txtUsername.Text)
```

Description

- All methods of the Membership class are static.
- For more information about the MembershipUser class, see the next figure.
- The Membership class is in the System.Web.Security namespace.

Figure 18-18   How to use the Membership class

How to use the MembershipUser class

Figure 18-19 shows how to use the MembershipUser class. To start, you typically use a method of the Membership class to retrieve a MembershipUser object from the data source that's used for authentication. Then, you can use the properties and methods of the MembershipUser object to get or modify the data that's stored in this object.

For example, you might want to use the Email property to get the email address from the MembershipUser object. Or, you might want to set the IsApproved property to False if the user is unsuccessful at logging in a given number of times. Then, the user would not be allowed to log in until the password question was answered correctly, at which time the IsApproved property could be reset to True.

You might also want to use the ChangePassword method to change the password for the object. When you use this and other methods from the MembershipUser object, it updates the data in the MembershipUser object and it updates the data in the membership data store. As a result, you don't need to use the UpdateUser method of the Membership class to update the data in the data store.

Common properties of the MembershipUser class

Property	Description
Username	The username for the membership user.
Email	The email address for the membership user.
PasswordQuestion	The password question for the membership user.
CreationDate	The date and time when the user was added to the membership data store.
LastLoginDate	The date and time when the membership user was last authenticated.
LastActivityDate	The date and time when the membership user was last authenticated or accessed the application.
IsApproved	A boolean value that indicates whether the membership user can be authenticated.

Common methods of the MembershipUser class

Method	Description
GetPassword()	Gets the password for the membership user from the membership data store.
ChangePassword(oldPassword, newPassword)	Updates the password for the membership user in the membership data store.
ResetPassword()	Resets a user's password to a new, automatically generated password.
ChangePasswordQuestionAndAnswer(password, question, answer)	Updates the password question and answer for the membership user in the membership data store.

Code that changes a user's password

```
Dim User As MembershipUser = Membership.GetUser
Try
    User.ChangePassword(txtOldPassword.Text, txtNewPassword.Text)
Catch eHttp As HttpException
    lblStatus.Text = "An exception occurred. Unable to change password."
End Try
```

Description

- The MembershipUser class is in the System.Web.Security namespace.
- The methods shown here update the MembershipUser object and the data that's stored in the membership data store.

Figure 18-19   How to use the MembershipUser class

How to use the FormsAuthentication class

If you don't want to use the Login control described earlier in this chapter, you can create a login form that includes text boxes that allow the user to enter a username and password. Then, you can write code that authenticates the user and redirects the user from the login page to the page that was originally requested. To do that, you can use the ValidateUser method of the Membership class with the RedirectFromLoginPage method of the FormsAuthentication class as shown in figure 18-20.

When a login page has established that a user has entered a correct username and password, it can use the RedirectFromLoginPage method to create an authentication ticket for the user and redirect the browser to the page that the user originally tried to access. The two arguments for this method specify the username and whether or not the authentication ticket should be saved in a persistent cookie. Because the example in this figure specifies false for the second argument, the authentication ticket will be saved in a session cookie.

Whether the authentication ticket is saved in a session cookie or a persistent cookie, you can use a SignOut method like the one shown in the second statement to log a user off your application. This method removes the authentication ticket from the user's computer. Then, the user will have to be authenticated again the next time the application is accessed.

Common methods of the FormsAuthentication class

Method	Description
RedirectFromLoginPage(username, createPersistentCookie)	Issues an authentication ticket for the user and redirects the browser to the page it was attempting to access when the login page was displayed. If the createPersistentCookie argument is True, the cookie that contains the authentication ticket is persistent across browser restarts. Otherwise, the cookie is only available for the current session.
SignOut()	Logs the user off by removing the cookie that contains the authentication ticket.

A statement that redirects the browser to the originally requested page

```
If Membership.ValidateUser(txtUserName.Text, txtPassword.Text) Then
    FormsAuthentication.RedirectFromLoginPage(txtUserName.Text, False)
Else
    lblStatus.Text = "Invalid user! Try again."
End If
```

A statement that logs a user off

```
FormsAuthentication.SignOut()
```

Discussion

* After you authenticate a user, you can use the RedirectFromLoginPage method of the FormsAuthentication class to redirect the browser to the page that was originally requested. This method creates an authentication ticket that's passed as a cookie to the browser.

* The FormsAuthentication class is in the System.Web.Security namespace.

Figure 18-20   How to use the FormsAuthentication class

How to use the Roles class

The Roles class in figure 18-21 works similarly to the Membership class. First, all methods of the Roles class are static methods. Second, you can use the Roles class to read data from and write data to the role provider that's specified for the application.

Although you can use the Roles class to add and delete roles from the roles data store, you probably won't need to do that. However, you might need to provide some custom code that works with roles in another way. To illustrate, let's say you've used the Web Site Administration Tool to define a role named premium. Then, when users pay a small fee, they can access the premium pages of the web site. In that case, you might need to write code that adds the current user to the premium role after the user has paid for the premium subscription. To do that, you can use the AddUserToRole method of the Roles class as shown in this figure.

Common methods of the Roles class

Method	Description
CreateRole(rolename)	Adds a new role to the data source.
GetAllRoles()	Gets a string array containing all the roles for the application.
AddUserToRole(username, rolename)	Adds the specified user to the specified role.
GetRolesForUser(username)	Gets a string array containing the roles that a user is in.
GetUsersInRole(rolename)	Gets a string array containing users in the specified role.
IsUserInRole(username, rolename)	Gets a Boolean value indicating whether a user is in the specified role.
RemoveUserFromRole(username, rolename)	Removes the specified user from the specified role.
DeleteRole(rolename)	Removes a role from the data source.

Code that creates a role

```
Try
    Roles.CreateRole(txtRoleName.Text)
Catch ex As Exception
    sMessage = "Error creating role: " + ex.Message
End Try
```

Code that gets all roles in the system

```
Dim sRoles As String() = Roles.GetAllRoles
```

A statement that adds a user to a role

```
Roles.AddUserToRole(currentUsername, "premium")
```

A statement that removes a user from a role

```
Roles.RemoveUserFromRole(txtUsername.Text, cboRoles.SelectedValue)
```

Description

- The Roles class is in the System.Web.Security namespace.
- All methods of the Roles class are static.

Figure 18-21   How to use the Roles class

Perspective

This chapter has presented the skills that you need for using forms-based authentication to restrict access to a web application. When you combine these skills with those of the previous chapter, you should have all of the skills you need for providing the security that an e-commerce application needs.

Terms

authentication
authorization
Windows-based authentication
forms-based authentication
Passport authentication
Microsoft Passport
authentication ticket
role
access rule
data provider
membership provider
role provider
anonymous user
authenticated user

19

How to use profiles
to personalize a web site

In the last chapter, you learned how to work with authentication. In particular, you learned how to create user accounts that include information about a user such as username, password, and email address. Once you understand how authentication works, you're ready to learn how to use profiles.

You can use the profile feature to store additional information about a user such as the user's mailing address or the preferences that a user has for working with your web application. You can also use it as an easier way to store and retrieve session data like a shopping cart. By default, the profile feature is designed to work with authenticated users, but you can also use it to work with anonymous users.

An introduction to profiles

The *profile feature* is new to ASP.NET 2.0. It is part of the *personalization feature* that includes the forms-based authentication you learned about in the last chapter and the web parts feature you'll learn about in chapter 22. As you will see, the use of profiles has several advantages, along with a few potential pitfalls.

Profiles compared with session state

The profile feature lets you use the ProfileCommon class to store and retrieve data that's associated with a user, which can be referred to as a *profile*. This works similarly to storing user data in session state, but the profile feature has several advantages over the Session class. Figure 19-1 describes three of these advantages.

First, the profile feature is designed to store data in a persistent data store that's available for future sessions. In contrast, session state is designed to work with temporary data that's available for only the current session.

Second, the ProfileCommon class uses strongly typed data. As a result, you can use IntelliSense to discover the properties that are stored in a profile, and you typically don't need to use casting when retrieving profile data. In contrast, session state uses keys to retrieve objects of the Object type. As a result, you must know the name of the key to be able to access an object, and then you must cast the object to its appropriate type when you retrieve it.

Third, the profile feature works more efficiently than session state because it only retrieves data when the data is requested. In contrast, all values of the session state object are retrieved on each request, whether or not they're used.

This figure also describes some of the difficulties of working with the profile feature. These difficulties are mainly due to the complexities that are brought on by the challenges of storing persistent data.

First, if you have an existing data store that you want to use, you have to write a significant amount of code to get the profile feature to be able to work with this data. That's because, by default, the profile feature uses a data provider to store profile data in a SQL Server Express database named AspNetDb.mdf. This type of provider is called a *profile provider*. To change the way this works, you need to write a custom profile provider that will use your existing data store, but this is a significant undertaking.

Second, if you decide to use the profile feature to store data about anonymous users, the amount of data in your database can quickly grow so that it contains stale and redundant data that isn't useful and will eventually slow the performance of your site. That's especially true if you have a high volume site with a large number of anonymous users. As a result, you'll need to implement a strategy for managing this data. For example, you'll need to find a way to delete data when it becomes stale or redundant.

Advantages of using the profile feature

Persistent data storage

Unlike session state, which only stores data for the current session, the profile feature stores data in a persistent data store. As a result, you can retrieve the data in later sessions.

Strongly typed data access

Unlike session state, which requires you to use keys and casting to retrieve data, the profile feature uses properties that have data types. This allows you to use the IntelliSense feature to display the properties that are stored in the profile, and it allows you to retrieve data without casting.

Efficient data retrieval

Unlike session state, which retrieves data each time a page is posted, the profile feature only retrieves data when necessary.

Disadvantages of using the profile feature

Difficulty accessing legacy data

By default, the profile feature creates and lets you work with the data in a SQL Server Express database. However, if you have data that's stored in an existing database and want to use the profile feature to work with that data, you need to write a custom profile provider and configure your web application to use that profile provider.

Data that's stale and redundant

Since the profile feature stores data persistently about each user, it's easy for your database to become full of stale and redundant data. This is especially true if you store data about anonymous users. If this begins to slow the performance of your site, you'll need to develop a strategy for managing this data.

Description

- The *profile feature* is used to persistently store data associated with a user such as first name, birth date, shopping cart, and so on. This data can be referred to as a *profile*.
- To implement the profile feature, ASP.NET 2.0 uses a data provider called a *profile provider*.

Figure 19-1   Profiles compared with session state

An overview of how profiles work

Figure 19-2 gives an overview of how the profile feature works. To start, you define the properties of the ProfileCommon class in the web.config file for the application. Then, when you run the application, ASP.NET generates the ProfileCommon class based on the properties you defined. It also creates an instance of that class that you can refer to using the Profile property of the HttpContext object.

If you take a closer look at the web.config file in this figure, you can see that it uses the Profile, Properties, and Add elements to define the profile properties. Within each Add element, you must use the Name attribute to specify the name for the property. Then, if you want to specify a data type besides the String type, you can use the Type attribute to specify the data type. In addition, you can use other attributes to specify other behaviors for the profile property. As you progress through this chapter, you'll learn the details for working with the attributes that are available from the Add element.

By default, the data that's stored by the profile feature can only be read by authenticated users. As a result, the user must log in or submit a cookie with a valid authentication ticket before retrieving or storing profile data. However, it's possible to use the profile feature with another new ASP.NET 2.0 feature known as *anonymous identification* that allows anonymous users to use the profile feature. Anonymous identification lets ASP.NET identify users by storing a unique identifier for each user, usually as a cookie within the user's browser.

In this figure, the web.config file allows anonymous identification by setting the Enabled attribute of the anonymousIdentification element to True. Then, to allow the Cart property to use anonymous identification, the AllowAnonymous attribute of the Cart property is set to True. As a result, users can persistently store items in their cart even if they don't log in.

Once you've defined the profile properties in the web.config file, you can use the Profile property of the application to get and set these properties. Since the properties are strongly typed, you don't need to use casting when you retrieve data from the profile. However, if you want to display non-string data in a text box, you need to use a ToString method to convert the data type to a string. For example, since the LastActivityDate property is of the DateTime type, the ToShortDateString method is used to convert the property to a string that can be displayed in a text box. Conversely, you may sometimes need to convert a value that's entered as a string to a data type before you can store it in a profile.

A web.config file that configures a profile

```
<system.web>

  <anonymousIdentification enabled="true" />

  <profile>
    <properties>

      <add name="FirstName"/>

      <add name="LastActivityDate"
           type="System.DateTime"/>

      <add name="Cart"
           type="Cart"
           serializeAs="Binary"
           allowAnonymous="true"/>

    </properties>
  </profile>
</system.web>
```

Visual Basic code that stores profile data

```
Protected Sub btnSave_Click(ByVal sender As Object, _
      ByVal e As System.EventArgs) Handles btnSave.Click
    Profile.FirstName = txtFirstName.Text
    Profile.LastActivityDate = DateTime.Now
    Profile.Cart = Cart
End Sub
```

Visual Basic code that retrieves profile data

```
Dim Cart As ShoppingCart

Protected Sub Page_Load(ByVal sender As Object, _
      ByVal e As System.EventArgs) Handles Me.Load
    If Not IsPostBack Then
        txtFirstName.Text = Profile.FirstName
        txtLastActivityDate.Text = Profile.LastActivityDate.ToShortDateString()
        Cart = Profile.Cart
    End If
End Sub
```

Description

- After you define the properties of a profile in the web.config file, you can use the Profile property of the HttpContext object to store and retrieve the data.
- By default, the profile feature only allows you to access data for users who have been authenticated. However, it's also possible to store data about anonymous users.

Figure 19-2   An overview of how profiles work

How the default profile provider works

The machine.config file sets the defaults for all web applications on the current machine. In figure 19-3, you can see the elements that set the default profile provider.

To start, this figure shows the default connection string. This connection string is named LocalSqlServer, and it connects to a SQL Server Express database named AspNetDb.mdf that's stored in the data directory of the application. This is the same connection string and database that's used for the membership and role providers that are described in chapter 18.

Then, this figure shows the code that configures the profile feature so it uses a profile provider named AspNetSqlProfileProvider. This provider uses the LocalSqlServer connection string to connect to the AspNetDb.mdf database using the SqlProfileProvider class that's stored in the System.Web.Profile namespace.

If you're developing a web application from scratch, you may want to use this default provider as is. It works well for prototyping and may be acceptable for some small to medium-sized web applications. Then, since the database is automatically created and configured, you can use the ProfileCommon class to store and retrieve data without having to write any data access code.

However, if you need to work with an existing data store, or if you need to gain control over low-level data access details, the default profile provider won't work for your application. If, for example, you need to access data that's stored in an existing SQL Server database that uses a different database schema, the default provider won't work. Or, if you need to access data that's stored in an Oracle database, the default provider won't work.

In that case, one option is to avoid the profile feature altogether. After all, if you have an existing database, you may already have existing classes that read and write profile data to and from the database. If not, you can write this data access code yourself. Typically, that means storing temporary profile data in the session state object. Although this alternative may not be as slick as using the profile feature, it will give you more control over when and how profile data is stored.

Another option is to implement a custom profile provider. To do that, you need to write a class that implements all of the abstract methods of the abstract ProfileProvider class. Then, you need to modify the web.config file for your application so it uses this custom profile provider.

The elements of the machine.config file that are used by the profile feature

The default connection string for SQL Server Express

```
<connectionStrings>
  <add name="LocalSqlServer"
      connectionString="data source=.\SQLEXPRESS;Integrated
          Security=SSPI;AttachDBFilename=|DataDirectory|aspnetdb.mdf;User
          Instance=true"
      providerName="System.Data.SqlClient" />
</connectionStrings>
```

The default profile provider

```
<system.web>

  <profile>
    <providers>
      <add name="AspNetSqlProfileProvider"
          connectionStringName="LocalSqlServer"
          applicationName="/"
          type="System.Web.Profile.SqlProfileProvider,
                System.Web, Version=2.0.0.0, Culture=neutral,
                PublicKeyToken=b03f5f7f11d50a3a" />
    </providers>
  </profile>

</system.web>
```

Description

- To store data, the profile feature uses a *profile provider*.

- By default, the profile feature uses a profile provider named AspNetSqlProfileProvider to store and retrieve data from a SQL Server Express database named AspNetDb.mdf.

- To use the ProfileCommon class with data that's stored in an existing database, you must write and configure a custom profile provider.

Figure 19-3   How the default profile provider works

How to use profiles with authenticated users

By default, the profile feature only works for authenticated users. Most of the time, this makes sense. For example, you typically want a user to create an account and log in before you allow the user to read or write personalized data such as first name, last name, or preferences for the web application. The topics that follow show you how to use profiles, but they assume that the user has been authenticated before accessing the specified web pages.

How to define profile properties

Figure 19-4 shows the details of how to define and use a profile property for a String data type. To start, you must code a Profile element and a Properties element within the System.web element of the web.config file. Within the Properties element, you can code one or more Add elements to add profile properties. Then, you can use the Name attribute of the Add element to specify the name of the property. In this figure, the web.config file contains two properties named FirstName and LastName. Since the Add elements don't specify a data type, the String data type is used by default.

Once you have defined profile properties in the web.config file, you can write code that uses the Profile property of the HttpContext object to store and retrieve the profile properties. Remember, though, that these properties can only be accessed for a user after the user has been authenticated. In this figure, for example, let's assume that the code that stores profile data is in the code-behind file for a page named MyAccount.aspx that can only be accessed by an authenticated user. As a result, the user must log in or submit a cookie with a valid authentication ticket before being allowed to access the MyAccount page.

When the user accesses this page, the code that's in the Load event procedure for the page uses the Profile property to read the user's first and last name from the data store. Since this data is stored as the String type, it can be loaded directly into a text box without any casting or conversions. Then, the MyAccount page will be displayed with the data for the current authenticated user displayed in the text boxes for the FirstName and LastName properties. If no data exists for the current user, though, the FirstName and LastName properties will return nulls. In that case, you should leave the text boxes at their default values of empty strings.

At this point, the user can enter or edit his or her first or last name in these text boxes. Then, the user can click on the Save button to execute the event handler for the Click event of the button. This event procedure saves the data that's in the text boxes for the first and last names to the FirstName and LastName properties of the profile. Again, since these properties are of the String type, no casting or conversion is needed.

How to define profile properties in the web.config file

```
<system.web>

  <profile>
    <properties>

      <add name="FirstName"/>
      <add name="LastName"/>

    </properties>
  </profile>

</system.web>
```

Visual Basic code that retrieves profile data

```
Protected Sub Page_Load(ByVal sender As Object, _
        ByVal e As System.EventArgs) Handles Me.Load
    If Not IsPostBack Then
        txtFirstName.Text = Profile.FirstName
        txtLastName.Text = Profile.LastName
    End If
End Sub
```

Visual Basic code that stores profile data

```
Protected Sub btnSave_Click(ByVal sender As Object, _
        ByVal e As System.EventArgs) Handles btnSave.Click
    Profile.FirstName = txtFirstName.Text
    Profile.LastName = txtLastName.Text
End Sub
```

Description

- To define the properties that can be used by a profile in the web.config file, you code an Add element within the Profile and Properties elements. The only attribute that's required within an Add element is the Name attribute, which specifies the name that's used to access the property.

- By default, all profile properties are stored with the String data type.

- By default, the user must be authenticated before the profile properties can be accessed. If the user isn't authenticated, the property will return an empty string.

Figure 19-4   How to define profile properties

How to specify data types

Figure 19-5 shows how to use the Type attribute of a profile property to specify a data type other than the String type. To start, this figure shows the XML code for the FirstName property displayed in the last figure. Then, it shows the XML code for a property named BirthDate that uses the DateTime data type. Last, it shows the XML code for a property named AccessCount that uses an integer data type.

When you specify a .NET data type, you must qualify it by including the namespace. For example, you must use System.DateTime for the Date data type, and you must use System.Int32 for the Integer type. In contrast, you can use Visual Basic data types like Date and Integer without any qualification.

In addition, if you use a custom data type and that data type is stored within the application's App_Code folder, you only need to include the namespace if the custom data type is stored in a namespace. For example, let's assume that you store a class named Customer within the App_Code folder. Let's also assume that this class isn't coded within a namespace. In that case, you can specify the Customer type like this:

```
<add name="Customer" type="Customer">
```

However, if this class is coded within the Business namespace, you must specify the Customer type like this:

```
<add name="Customer" type="Business.Customer">
```

You'll learn more about working with custom data types later in this chapter.

When you work with profile properties that use data types, you need to convert these properties to a different data type so they can be displayed in a control. For example, the BirthDate property in this figure (which is of the DateTime type) is stored in a text box (which takes a String type). That's why the code in this figure uses the ToShortDateString method to convert the BirthDate property to a string, and that's why the ToDateTime method of the Convert class is used to convert the string that's stored in the text box to a valid DateTime object.

However, if you don't need to convert a profile property to get it to work with a control, you can often work with it directly. For example, the last statement in this figure shows how you can update the AccessCount property (which is an Integer type). To do this, you just use the += operator to add 1 to the property. This updates AccessCount and causes the updated count to be stored in the data source.

How to specify data types for profile properties in the web.config file

```
<!-- System.String is the default type -->
<add name="FirstName" />

<add name="BirthDate"
     type="System.DateTime" />

<add name="AccessCount"
     type="System.Int32" />
```

Visual Basic code that retrieves typed profile data

```
txtFirstName.Text = Profile.FirstName

txtBirthDate.Text =
    Profile.BirthDate.ToShortDateString

lblCount.Text =
    Profile.AccessCount.ToString
```

Visual Basic code that stores typed profile data

```
Profile.FirstName = txtFirstName.Text

Profile.BirthDate =
    Convert.ToDateTime(txtBirthDate.Text)

Profile.AccessCount += 1        ' updates and stores the access count
```

Description

- You can use the Type attribute of the Add element to specify the data type for a profile property in the web.config file.
- By default, all profile properties are stored with the String data type.
- To specify the Type attribute for a .NET data type, you must include the namespace.
- To specify the Type attribute for a custom data type that's in the App_Code folder, you only need to include the namespace if the data type is stored in a namespace (see figure 19-8).

Figure 19-5   How to use data types with profile properties

How to group profile properties

Figure 19-6 shows how to group profile properties. To do that, you code a Group element within the Profile and Properties elements. Within this Group element, you must code a Name attribute that specifies the name of the group. In this figure, for example, the Name attribute creates a group named Preferences.

Within the Group element, you can code one or more Add elements to specify the properties for the group. In this figure, for example, the Preferences group contains two properties of the Boolean type named SendPromotions and SendNewProducts. These properties can be used to determine whether to send a user emails about special product promotions or announcements for new products. Please note, however, that you can't nest one group within another.

Once you've defined a group and its properties within the web.config file, you can access them just as you would any other property. The only difference is that you need to specify the name of the group before the name of the property. To illustrate, the examples in this figure show how to use the SendPromotions and SendNewProducts properties with the Checked property of a check box. Since the Checked property expects a Boolean value, no casting or conversion is required to synchronize the check box with the profile property.

This figure also shows that the IntelliSense feature works with groups just as it does for regular properties. To access it, you just type "Profile" followed by a period to display a list that includes all of the groups that are available from the ProfileCommon class. Then, you can select a group by typing the first few letters of the group's name and pressing the Tab key. Finally, you can enter a period and then select a property within the group.

How to group profile properties

```
<group name="Preferences">

    <add name="SendPromotions"
        type="System.Boolean" />

    <add name="SendNewProducts"
        type="System.Boolean" />

</group>
```

Visual Basic code that retrieves grouped profile properties

```
chkPromotions.Checked = Profile.Preferences.SendPromotions
chkNewProducts.Checked = Profile.Preferences.SendNewProducts
```

Visual Basic code that stores grouped profile properties

```
Profile.Preferences.SendPromotions = chkPromotions.Checked
Profile.Preferences.SendNewProducts = chkNewProducts.Checked
```

How IntelliSense makes it easy to work with profile properties

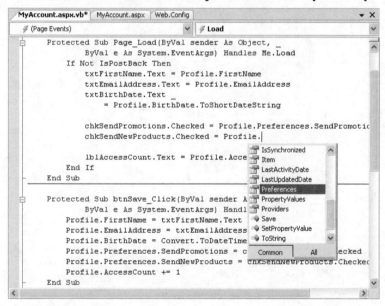

Description

- To group properties, you can code a Group element around any Add elements within the Profile and Properties elements in the web.config file. The only attribute that's required within a Group element is the Name attribute, which specifies the name for the group.

- You can't nest a second Group element within the first Group element.

Figure 19-6   How to group profile properties

How to specify default values

The first example in figure 19-7 shows how to use the DefaultValue attribute of the Add element to specify a default value for a profile property. Here, the default value for the Boolean SendPromotions property is set to True. As a result, the first time you use the ProfileCommon class to retrieve this property it will be a True value. If you don't code a default value, a blank value will be displayed for this property.

How to specify read-only properties

By default, you can read and write all profile properties. However, if you want to make a profile property read-only, you can set the ReadOnly attribute of the Add element to True. This is shown in the second example in this figure.

How to specify default values for profile properties

```
<add name="SendPromotions"
     type="System.Boolean"
     defaultValue="true" />
```

How to specify read-only profile properties

```
<add name="DisplayName"
     readOnly="true" />
```

Description

- You can use the DefaultValue attribute of the Add element to initialize the value of a property.
- You can set the ReadOnly attribute of the Add element to True to prevent the application from writing to that property.

Figure 19-7 How to specify two more profile property attributes

How to use custom types

Figure 19-8 shows how to use a custom data type named Customer. To start, this figure shows the Customer class, which specifies the types of data that are stored within a Customer object. The Serializable attribute at the start of the class lets the .NET Framework know that it's OK to convert this class to the specified format. You'll see how to specify the format that's used in just a moment.

In this example, each of the eight public fields of the Customer class store string data. However, you can use any of the data types for a class like this. If, for example, you want to store a Date data type, you can do that. Or, if you want to store a custom data type named Address to store street address information, you can do that as long as you mark that data type as serializable too.

To specify the format you want to use to store a custom data type, you use the SerializeAs attribute of the Add element for a profile property. The default value of this attribute is String, which stores all the public fields and properties of a data type as plain text. For many data types, this setting is adequate. Note that you don't need to mark a data type as serializable to use this setting. However, we recommend that you mark all your custom data types as serializable in case you decide to save the data in a different format later on.

If a custom data type contains a reference to another object, or if you need to save the private fields of the data type, you'll need to set the SerializeAs attribute to binary. Although neither of these conditions apply to the Customer data type, I used binary serialization here for illustrative purposes. Because of that, a Customer object will be converted to binary data before it's saved to a column in the database. Conversely, the binary data will be converted to a Customer object when the column is retrieved from the database.

The Visual Basic code in the examples shows how to work with the Customer data type. To start, you can retrieve the Customer object for a user just as you would retrieve any other type of profile property for a user. But note that if you try to retrieve a Customer object and no object exists, one is created using the default constructor. Conversely, you can save the Customer object for a user just as you would save any other type of profile property.

Since the profile property named Customer is of the Customer data type, you can use it to directly access any of the properties stored within the Customer object. For example, to retrieve the Email property of the Customer object for the user, you can use this statement:

```
txtEmail.Text = Profile.Customer.Email
```

This retrieves the Customer object for the user, accesses the Email property, and stores it in the email text box. Conversely, to store a change that's made in the email text box, you can use this statement:

```
Profile.Customer.Email = txtEmail.Text
```

Although you can also set the SerializeAs attribute to XML or ProviderSpecific, you probably won't need to use these settings unless you create a custom profile provider. In that case, you may want to set the SerializeAs attribute to ProviderSpecific so the profile provider can determine how to store and retrieve each object.

The Customer class in the App_Code folder

```
<Serializable()> _
Public Class Customer
    Public Email As String
    Public LastName As String
    Public FirstName As String
    Public Address As String
    Public City As String
    Public State As String
    Public ZipCode As String
    Public Phone As String
End Class
```

How to specify a custom data type for a profile property

```
<add name="Customer"
    type="Customer"
    serializeAs="Binary"/>
```

Possible values for the SerializeAs attribute

Value	Description
String	Converts the object to plain text and stores it within the specified data store for the application. This is the default setting.
Binary	Converts the object to binary data and stores it within the specified data store for the application. For this to work, the .NET Framework must be able to serialize the object.
XML	Converts the object to XML and stores it in the specified data store for the application.
ProviderSpecific	Allows a custom profile provider to decide how to store the object.

Visual Basic code that retrieves typed data

```
Dim Customer As Customer = Profile.Customer
```

Visual Basic code that stores profile data

```
Dim Customer As Customer = Profile.Customer
Customer.Email = txtEmail.Text
Customer.LastName = txtLastName.Text
Customer.FirstName = txtFirstName.Text
    .
    .
    .
Profile.Customer = Customer
```

Description

- To specify the Type attribute of the Add element for a custom data type that's in the App_Code folder, you can code just the name of the class. However, if the class is coded within a namespace, you must include the name of the namespace.

- To store a custom data type as binary data, you need to mark it as serializable by coding the Serializable attribute just before the declaration of the class. Then, you can set the SerializeAs attribute of the Add element to binary to specify that the data should be stored as binary data.

Figure 19-8   How to use custom data types

How to use profiles with anonymous users

By default, the profile feature only works with authenticated users. However, there are times when you may want to use profiles with anonymous users. For example, you probably don't want to force a user to log in before he or she can add items to a shopping cart. Fortunately, the new *anonymous identification* feature that came with ASP.NET 2.0 lets you use profiles with anonymous users.

How to enable anonymous identification

Before you can identify anonymous users, you need to enable the anonymous identification feature as shown in figure 19-9. To do that, you just code an anonymousIdentification element with an Enabled attribute set to True. Once you do that, a cookie will be stored for each user that visits your web site. This cookie will be named .ASPXANONYMOUS, and it will be stored on the user's machine for 100,000 minutes, which is almost 70 days. That way, each time an anonymous user visits your site, the user's browser passes a cookie to the site that contains an identifier that uniquely identifies the user.

Most of the time, that's all you need to do to enable anonymous identification. However, if you want to change the name of the cookie, you can use the CookieName attribute. Or, if you want to shorten or lengthen the amount of time that the cookie is stored on the user's system, you can use the CookieTimeout attribute. Or, if you need to make sure that this works even if the user's browser doesn't support cookies (which is rare), you can use the Cookieless attribute. In that case, you typically set the Cookieless attribute to AutoDetect so cookies can be used if they're available.

How to allow anonymous users to access profile properties

Once you've enabled anonymous identification, you must specify which profile properties can be accessed by an anonymous user. To do that, you can set the AllowAnonymous attribute of the Add element to True. In this figure, for example, the Cart property can be accessed by anonymous users, but the Customer property can't. Note that the Cart property uses a ShoppingCart data type that's defined by the ShoppingCart class shown in figure 19-12.

How to use profile properties with anonymous users

```
<system.web>

    <anonymousIdentification enabled="true" />

    <profile>
      <properties>

        <add name="Customer"
             type="Customer"
             serializeAs="Binary"/>

        <add name="Cart"
             type="ShoppingCart"
             serializeAs="Binary"
             allowAnonymous="true"/>

      </properties>
    </profile>

</system.web>
```

Attributes of the anonymousIdentification element

Attribute	Description
Enabled	Enables or disables anonymous identification. The default setting is False.
CookieName	Sets the name of the cookie that's stored for each anonymous user. The default setting is .ASPXANONYMOUS.
CookieTimeout	Sets the length of time that the cookie will be stored on the user's machine in minutes. The default setting is 100,000 minutes, which is almost 70 days.
Cookieless	Specifies how to identify anonymous users. You can use one of the four values shown below.

Possible values for the Cookieless attribute

Value	Description
UseCookies	Uses cookies to store the anonymous identifier. This is the default setting.
UseUrl	Stores the anonymous identifier in the URL.
AutoDetect	Allows ASP.NET to detect whether the browser can support cookies. If so, it uses cookies to store the anonymous identifier. If not, it uses the URL.
UseDeviceProfile	Configures the anonymous identifier for the device or browser.

Description

- Once you've enabled *anonymous identification*, you can set the AllowAnonymous attribute of any Add element to True to allow anonymous users to access the specified profile property.

Figure 19-9   How to enable anonymous identification

How to migrate data from anonymous to authenticated users

Once you begin storing personalized data for anonymous users, you need to develop a strategy for what to do if the anonymous user creates an account and authenticates. To illustrate, let's assume an anonymous user has added items to his or her cart and that this cart has been saved to the data store. Then, the anonymous user decides to purchase the items in the cart. At this point, the user must get authenticated by creating an account or by logging in, and you must decide what to do with the data that's stored in the anonymous user's cart.

Figure 19-10 shows how you can use the Profile_MigrateAnonymous event procedure to handle this situation. To start, you can create a global.asax file for your application if one doesn't already exist. Then, you can code the Profile_MigrateAnonymous event procedure in this file. Because Profile_MigrateAnonymous is an application-wide event, it will be called whenever a user authenticates. In fact, unless you remove the cookie that contains the anonymous identifier as shown in the second example in this figure, this method may be called twice each time the user authenticates.

One way to migrate data is to copy the data that's stored in the Cart property for the anonymous user to the Cart property for the authenticated user as shown in the first example in this figure. Here, the first statement retrieves the profile for the anonymous user and stores it in a ProfileCommon object named ProfileCommon. To accomplish this, this statement uses the AnonymousId property of the ProfileMigrateEventsArg object to retrieve the unique identifier for the user, and it uses the static GetProfile method of the ProfileCommon class. Then, the second statement copies the Cart property from the anonymous user's profile to the Cart property for the newly authenticated user's profile. This will replace any items in the authenticated user's cart with the items in the anonymous cart.

At this point, the data for the ShoppingCart object is stored for both the anonymous user and the authenticated user. As a result, if the user logs out and becomes anonymous again, the user's cart will still contain all of the same items. On the other hand, if the user logs in and becomes authenticated, the user's cart will be replaced by whatever items are stored in the anonymous cart.

Although this solution works, it doesn't provide for an anonymous user that already has stored items in the cart for his authenticated account. In that case, you may not want to replace the authenticated Cart property with the anonymous Cart property. Instead, you may want to merge the items in the two carts as shown in the second example. In this case, if the same item is in both carts, the AddItem method of the ShoppingCart class increases the quantity for the item appropriately.

After the items in the two carts have been merged, this code uses a method of the ProfileManager class to delete the anonymous profile from the data store. Then, it uses a method of the AnonymousIdentificationModule class to clear the cookie that stores the anonymous identifier from the client's browser. This reduces the size of the data store, it deletes all items from the anonymous cart, and it prevents the Profile_MigrateAnonymous event procedure from being run twice each time a user authenticates.

Code that copies the data for an anonymous user to an authenticated user

```
Public Sub Profile_MigrateAnonymous(ByVal sender As Object, _
        ByVal e As ProfileMigrateEventArgs)
    Dim AnonProfile As ProfileCommon = Profile.GetProfile(e.AnonymousID)
    Profile.Cart = AnonProfile.Cart
End Sub
```

Code that merges data for an anonymous user with data for an authenticated user

```
Public Sub Profile_MigrateAnonymous(ByVal sender As Object, _
        ByVal e As ProfileMigrateEventArgs)

    ' get the anonymous profile
    Dim ProfileCommon As ProfileCommon = Profile.GetProfile(e.AnonymousID)

    If AnonProfile.Cart.Count > 0 And Profile.Cart.Count = 0 Then
        ' swap carts
        Profile.Cart = AnonProfile.Cart
    ElseIf Profile.Cart.Count > 0 And AnonProfile.Cart.Count > 0 Then
        ' put all anonymous items in the authenticated cart
        Dim Item As CartItem
        For Each Item In AnonProfile.Cart.GetItems
            If Not Item Is Nothing Then
                Profile.Cart.AddItem(Item)
            End If
        Next Item
    End If

    ' delete the anonymous profile data from the data store
    ProfileManager.DeleteProfile(e.AnonymousID)

    ' clear the cookie that identifies the anonymous user
    AnonymousIdentificationModule.ClearAnonymousIdentifier()
End Sub
```

Description

- Since the Profile_MigrateAnonymous event procedure may be called from multiple web pages, it is often stored in the global.asax file. This event procedure is executed whenever a user is authenticated.

- If you don't delete the profile data for the anonymous user and remove the anonymous identifier after the data for an anonymous user has been migrated to the authenticated user, the Profile_MigrateAnonymous procedure will be executed twice each time a user is authenticated.

- The code for the GetItems and AddItem procedures of the ShoppingCart class is shown in figure 19-12.

Figure 19-10   How to migrate data from anonymous to authenticated users

The Cart Profile application

Now that you've seen the details for how to use profiles to work with authenticated users and anonymous users, you're ready to see how these details fit together within an application. In particular, you're ready to see how the Halloween Store application can use profiles to provide for a shopping cart that persists across sessions for both anonymous and authenticated users, and you're ready to see how this application can use profiles to store other user data for authenticated users. We'll call this the Cart Profile application.

The pages

Part 1 of figure 19-11 shows how the Cart page of this application can be displayed for an anonymous user or an authenticated user. The first Cart page contains a single item, and you can tell that the user is an anonymous user because the Login control at the bottom of the page says, "Login."

The second Cart page shows that the user is an authenticated user because the Login control at the bottom of the page says, "Logout." In addition, you can tell that this authenticated user has previously saved first name data because the page displays "Anne's shopping cart" instead of "Your shopping cart" above the list box that's used for the shopping cart. Last, the cart for the authenticated user contains two items instead of one because the application has merged the anonymous cart with the authenticated cart.

The Cart page before the user logs in

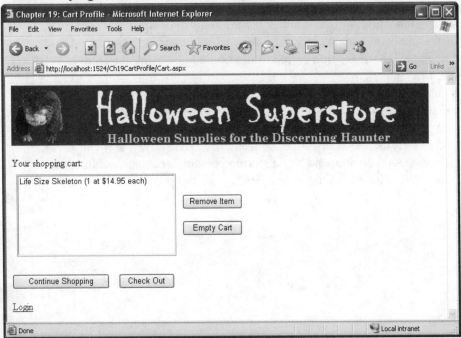

The Cart page after the user logs in

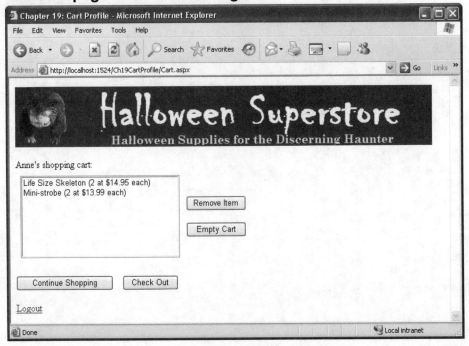

Figure 19-11   The pages of the Cart Profile application (part 1 of 2)

Part 2 of figure 19-11 shows the CheckOut1 page that's displayed when the user clicks on the Check Out button on the Cart page. This page can only be accessed by an authenticated user, which is appropriate since this page allows the user to enter and edit personalized customer data. If an anonymous user tries to access this page, the user is transferred to the Login page using the techniques of the last chapter.

In this application, you can only display the CheckOut1 page by clicking on the Check Out button from the Cart page. However, in a more full-featured application, you might want to add a "My Account" link that allows a user to edit this type of information at his or her convenience. That way, a user can create an account, authenticate, and begin storing personalized data like the data shown in this figure without having to begin the check out process.

The CheckOut1 page

Description

- The Cart page can display the cart for an anonymous user or an authenticated user. When an anonymous user logs in, all items in the anonymous user's cart are copied into the authenticated user's cart, adding to the quantity as necessary for duplicate items.

- The CheckOut1 page can only be accessed by an authenticated user. This page allows the user to enter or edit personalized user data.

- If an anonymous user clicks on the Check Out button on the Cart page, the Login page is automatically displayed by using the techniques presented in chapter 18.

Figure 19-11   The pages of the Cart Profile application (part 2 of 2)

The code

Part 1 of figure 19-12 shows the code for the ShoppingCart class. Since this is a typical business class, you shouldn't have any trouble understanding it. However, there are a few points to notice.

First, the Serializable attribute is coded at the top of this class to mark it as serializable. This allows the profile feature to store and retrieve ShoppingCart objects from the data store. However, the ShoppingCart class uses the CartItem and Product classes that were presented in chapter 3. As a result, for the ShoppingCart class to be serialized successfully, the CartItem and Product classes must also be marked as serializable.

Second, the AddItem method contains all of the logic that's used to add an item to the cart. In particular, if the item already exists in the cart, the quantity of that item is increased appropriately. As a result, you can access this code from any point in the application. For example, the Order page calls this method to add an item to the cart, and the global.asax file calls this method to migrate items from the anonymous cart to the authenticated cart.

Third, the ShoppingCart class works with strongly typed data. For example, the AddItem method only accepts objects of the CartItem type. As a result, it's impossible for a programmer to accidentally add another type of object to the cart (which could cause a nasty debugging problem). Conversely, the GetItems method returns an array of CartItem objects. As a result, you don't need to use casting to retrieve the CartItem objects.

The code for the ShoppingCart class

```
Imports Microsoft.VisualBasic

<Serializable()> _
Public Class ShoppingCart

    Private Cart As SortedList = New SortedList()

    Public ReadOnly Property Count() As Integer
        Get
            Return Cart.Count
        End Get
    End Property

    Public Sub AddItem(ByVal Item As CartItem)
        Dim sProductID As String = Item.Product.ProductID
        If (Cart.ContainsKey(sProductID)) Then
            Dim ExistingItem As CartItem
            ExistingItem = CType(Cart.Item(sProductID), CartItem)
            ExistingItem.Quantity += Item.Quantity
        Else
            Cart.Add(sProductID, Item)
        End If
    End Sub

    Public Function GetItems() As CartItem()
        Dim Items(Cart.Count) As CartItem
        Dim i As Integer
        If (Cart.Count > 0) Then
            For i = 0 To Cart.Count - 1
                Items(i) = CType(Cart.GetByIndex(i), CartItem)
            Next
        End If
        Return Items
    End Function

    Public Sub Clear()
        Cart.Clear()
    End Sub

    Public Sub RemoveAt(ByVal i As Integer)
        Cart.RemoveAt(i)
    End Sub

End Class
```

Description

- The ShoppingCart class uses the CartItem and Product classes that were presented in chapter 3. The only difference is that the Serializable attribute has been added to these classes to mark them as serializable.

Figure 19-12   The code for the Cart Profile application (part 1 of 3)

Part 2 of figure 19-12 presents a partial listing of the code for the Cart page. To start, when the page is loaded, the Page_Load event procedure sets the title for the cart. First, this procedure declares the default title that's displayed for anonymous users and for authenticated users who have not saved their first names in the data store. Then, this procedure uses the Profile property of the application to check if the FirstName property of the Customer object contains a null value or an empty string. If not, the first name data is used to personalize the title for the cart. Finally, the DisplayCart procedure is called to load all items in the cart into the list box for the cart.

The DisplayCart procedure begins by clearing any existing items from the list box. Then, it uses a For Each…Next loop to add each item in the cart to the list box. To do that, it uses the GetItems method of the Cart property of the profile to get an array of CartItem objects.

The btnRemove_Click and the btnEmpty_Click procedures both use the Cart property of the profile to update the items that are stored in the cart. These updates are automatically made to the data store as soon as the statements are executed. If, for example, you click the Empty Cart button, the code that's in the btnEmpty_Click procedure will clear all items from the Cart property of the profile, which will delete all cart items from the data store.

The code for the Cart page

```
Partial Class Cart
    Inherits System.Web.UI.Page

    Protected Sub Page_Load(ByVal sender As Object, _
            ByVal e As System.EventArgs) Handles Me.Load
        If Not IsPostBack Then
            Dim sTitle As String = "Your shopping cart:"
            Dim sFirstName As String = Profile.Customer.FirstName
            If Not sFirstName Is Nothing And Not sFirstName = "" Then
                sTitle = sFirstName & "'s shopping cart:"
            End If
            lblCartTitle.Text = sTitle
            Me.DisplayCart()
        End If
    End Sub

    Private Sub DisplayCart()
        lstCart.Items.Clear()
        Dim CartItem As CartItem
        For Each CartItem In Profile.Cart.GetItems
            If Not CartItem Is Nothing Then
                lstCart.Items.Add(CartItem.Display)
            End If
        Next CartItem
    End Sub

    Protected Sub btnRemove_Click(ByVal sender As Object, _
            ByVal e As System.EventArgs) Handles btnRemove.Click
        If lstCart.SelectedIndex > -1 And Profile.Cart.Count > 0 Then
            Profile.Cart.RemoveAt(lstCart.SelectedIndex)
            Me.DisplayCart()
        End If
    End Sub

    Protected Sub btnEmpty_Click(ByVal sender As Object, _
            ByVal e As System.EventArgs) Handles btnEmpty.Click
        Profile.Cart.Clear()
        lstCart.Items.Clear()
    End Sub

    Protected Sub btnCheckOut_Click(ByVal sender As Object, _
            ByVal e As System.EventArgs) Handles btnCheckOut.Click
        Response.Redirect("~/CheckOut/CheckOut1.aspx")
    End Sub

End Class
```

Description

- Within the Page_Load event procedure, the Profile.Customer property is used to display a different title for the cart if the user is authenticated and has stored a first name in the database.

- Within the other procedures, the Profile.Cart property is used to work with the items that are stored in the cart for the current user. Since this property is of the ShoppingCart type, you can use the methods defined in the ShoppingCart class to work with it.

Figure 19-12   The code for the Cart Profile application (part 2 of 3)

Part 3 of figure 19-12 presents a partial listing of the code for the CheckOut1 page. To start, when this page loads, it binds the states data to the State combo box. Then, it uses the Profile property to return a Customer object and display the properties of the Customer object within the text boxes on the page. Remember that the first statement shown here will create a Customer object if one doesn't already exist. Because of that, you need to check this object to be sure it isn't null before you assign its properties to the text boxes. If you don't, an error will occur because the properties of the object will be null.

On the CheckOut1 page, if the user clicks the Continue Checkout or Continue Shopping button, the UpdateCustomer procecure is called. This procedure begins by creating a new Customer object. Then, it sets the properties of this Customer object to the string values that are stored in the text boxes on the page. Last, it saves the updated Customer object in the profile.

If, on the other hand, the user clicks on the Cancel button, the UpdateCustomer procedure isn't called. As a result, the customer data on the CheckOut1 page isn't saved. Instead, the Cart property of the user's authenticated profile is cleared, and the user is redirected to the Order page.

The code for the CheckOut1 page

```
Partial Class CheckOut1
    Inherits System.Web.UI.Page

    Protected Sub Page_Load(ByVal sender As Object, _
            ByVal e As System.EventArgs) Handles Me.Load
        If Not IsPostBack Then

            ' Code that binds data to the State combo box goes here

            Dim Customer As Customer = Profile.Customer
            If Not Customer Is Nothing Then
                txtLastName.Text = Customer.LastName
                txtFirstName.Text = Customer.FirstName
                txtAddress.Text = Customer.Address
                txtCity.Text = Customer.City
                ddlState.SelectedValue = Customer.State
                txtZipCode.Text = Customer.ZipCode
                txtPhone.Text = Customer.Phone
                txtEmail.Text = Customer.Email
            End If
        End If
    End Sub

    Protected Sub UpdateCustomer()
        Dim Customer As New Customer
        Customer.LastName = txtLastName.Text
        Customer.FirstName = txtFirstName.Text
        Customer.Address = txtAddress.Text
        Customer.City = txtCity.Text
        Customer.State = ddlState.SelectedValue
        Customer.ZipCode = txtZipCode.Text
        Customer.Phone = txtPhone.Text
        Customer.Email = txtEmail.Text
        Profile.Customer = Customer
    End Sub

    Protected Sub btnContinue_Click(ByVal sender As Object, _
            ByVal e As System.EventArgs) Handles btnContinue.Click
        UpdateCustomer()
        Response.Redirect("~/Order.aspx")
    End Sub

    Protected Sub btnCheckout_Click(ByVal sender As Object, _
            ByVal e As System.EventArgs) Handles btnCheckout.Click
        UpdateCustomer()
        lblMessage.Text = "Sorry, that function hasn't been implemented yet."
    End Sub

    Protected Sub btnCancel_Click(ByVal sender As Object, _
            ByVal e As System.EventArgs) Handles btnCancel.Click
        Profile.Cart.Clear()

Response.Redirect("~/Order.aspx")
    End Sub

End Class
```

Description

- This page uses the Profile.Customer property to store and retrieve Customer objects.

Figure 19-12   The code for the Cart Profile application (part 3 of 3)

Perspective

This chapter has presented the skills you need for using the profiles feature to store data for authenticated and anonymous users. Now, you should be able to use profiles to quickly prototype a new application without writing any of the data access code. That is one of the strengths of this feature. Then, once you get the prototype working, you can decide whether you need to write a custom profile provider to gain control of how this feature stores your data.

Terms

profile feature
personalization feature
profile
profile provider
anonymous identification

20

How to use the MultiView and Wizard controls

The MultiView and Wizard controls are new ASP.NET 2.0 controls. These controls provide two ways to divide a page into multiple views or steps. Both of these controls let you navigate between views or steps without writing any Visual Basic code, and they make it easy to work with the data that's stored within these views or steps.

How to use the MultiView control

In the topics that follow, you'll see how a MultiView control can be used as part of a Checkout application. Of course, the MultiView control can also be used for any application that lets the user navigate between related pages.

How the MultiView control works

Figure 20-1 shows a Checkout application that uses three *views* of a MultiView control. Although each of these views appears to be a separate page, each view is actually on the same page (the Checkout.aspx page). When the user clicks on any of the buttons within a MultiView control, the page requires a postback. As a result, all of the data on the page is posted each time the user clicks on a navigation button to switch views. For example, when the user clicks on the Next button in the first view, the data that's stored in all three views is posted. Although this isn't as efficient as coding three separate pages, the MultiView control makes it easier to develop and maintain these pages.

The first view of a MultiView control

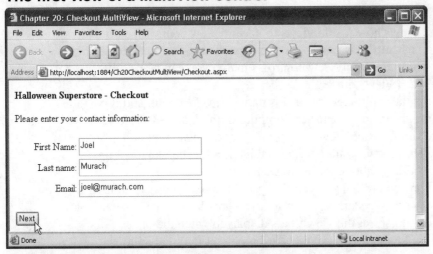

The second view of a MultiView control

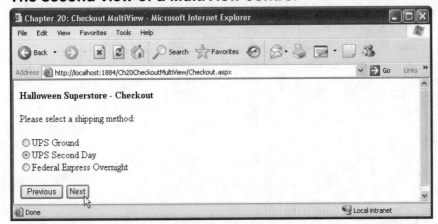

The third view of a MultiView control

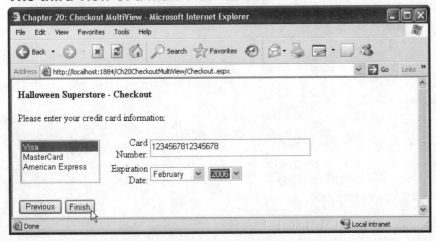

Figure 20-1   How the MultiView control works

How to add views

Figure 20-2 shows how to add views to a MultiView control. To do that, you begin by placing a MultiView control on the form. Then, you can add multiple View controls within the MultiView control. Finally, you can place other controls within each View control.

In this figure, the MultiView control is named mvCheckout, and it contains three View controls named vContact, vShippingMethod, and vCreditCard. To keep this figure simple, each view only contains some plain text and a Button control or two. This allows you to get the navigation for the views set up correctly before adding other controls to each view.

The MultiView control allows you navigate between views without writing any Visual Basic code. To start, you can set the ActiveViewIndex attribute of the MultiView control to select the view that's displayed when the page is first loaded. For example, in this figure, this attribute is set to 0 to display the first view. Then, you can set a button's CommandName attribute to one of the commands that work with the MultiView control. For example, in this figure, the CommandName attribute of the Next button is set to NextView, and the CommandName attribute of the Previous button is set to PrevView. This is all the code that's needed to get these buttons to work! For more information about using the CommandName attribute, see figure 20-4.

A MultiView control with three View controls

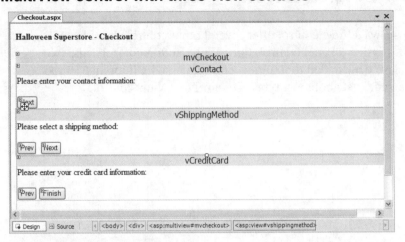

The aspx code for these controls

```
<asp:MultiView ID="mvCheckout" runat="server" ActiveViewIndex="0">
    <asp:View ID="vContact" runat="server">
        Please enter your contact information:<br /><br />
        <asp:Button ID="Button1" runat="server"
            CommandName="NextView" Text="Next" />
    </asp:View>
    <asp:View ID="vShippingMethod" runat="server">
        Please select a shipping method:<br /><br />
        <asp:Button ID="Button2" runat="server"
            CommandName="PrevView" Text="Prev" /> 
        <asp:Button ID="Button3" runat="server"
            CommandName="NextView" Text="Next" />
    </asp:View>
    <asp:View ID="vCreditCard" runat="server">
        Please enter your credit card information:<br /><br />
        <asp:Button ID="Button4" runat="server"
            Text="Prev" CommandName="PrevView" />
        <asp:Button ID="btnFinish" runat="server"
            Text="Finish" PostBackUrl="~/Completion.aspx" />
    </asp:View>
</asp:MultiView>
```

Description

- Once you add a MultiView control to a page, you can add one or more View controls within the MultiView control, and you can add other controls such as labels, text boxes, and buttons within the View control.

- To display the first view when the page is loaded, set the ActiveViewIndex attribute of the MultiView control to 0.

- To use commands to navigate to the next or previous view, you can add any control that has a CommandName attribute such as a Button control. Then, you can set the CommandName attribute to NextView or PrevView.

Figure 20-2   How to add views

How to add controls to a view

Figure 20-3 shows a View control after several other controls have been added to it. In this figure, a Panel control, three RadioButton controls, and two Button controls have been added to the View control named vShippingMethod. However, you can add just about any type of control to a View control.

The second view of figure 20-1

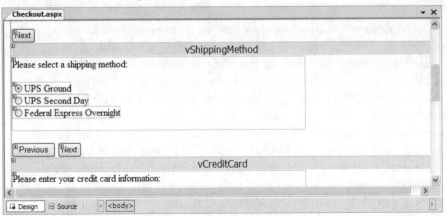

The aspx code for the second View control

```
<asp:MultiView ID="mvCheckout" Runat="server" ActiveViewIndex="0">

    <asp:View ID="vContactInfo" Runat="server">
        <!-- code for the first view goes here -->
    </asp:View>

    <asp:View ID="vShippingMethod" Runat="server">
        <asp:Panel ID="Panel1" Runat="server" Width="492">
            Please select a shipping method:<br /><br />
            <asp:RadioButton ID="rdoUPSGround" Runat="server"
                Text="UPS Ground" GroupName="ShipVia"
                Checked="True" /><br />
            <asp:RadioButton ID="rdoUPS2Day" Runat="server"
                Text="UPS Second Day" GroupName="ShipVia" /><br />
            <asp:RadioButton ID="rdoFedEx" Runat="server"
                Text="Federal Express Overnight" GroupName="ShipVia" /><br />
        </asp:Panel><br />
        <asp:Button ID="Button2" runat="server"
            CommandName="PrevView" Text="Previous" />
        <asp:Button ID="Button3" runat="server"
            CommandName="NextView" Text="Next" />
    </asp:View>

    <asp:View ID="vCreditCard" Runat="server">
        <!-- code for the third view goes here -->
    </asp:View>

</asp:MultiView>
```

Description

- Within a View control, you can add any other controls including controls such as panels and tables that contain other controls such as labels, text boxes, radio buttons, check boxes, combo boxes, buttons, and so on.

Figure 20-3   How to add controls to a view

How to navigate between views with commands

For most MultiView controls, you can navigate between the views by adding one or more buttons to each view and then setting the CommandName attribute of each button to NextView or PrevView as shown in figure 20-2. However, in some cases, you'll need to be able to navigate to any view on the page. To do that, you can use the CommandName and CommandArgument attributes of a button as shown in figure 20-4.

If you need to navigate to a view with a specified index, you can set the CommandName attribute to SwitchViewByIndex. Then, you can set the CommandArgument attribute to the appropriate index (where 0 is the first view, 1 is the second view, and so on).

If you prefer to navigate to a view with a specified ID, you can set the CommandName attribute to SwitchViewByID. Then, you can set the CommandArgument attribute to the ID.

Within a MultiView control, you can use any control that has CommandName and CommandArgument attributes to navigate between the views. All button controls (Button, ImageButton, and LinkButton) have both of these attributes. That's why this figure can use LinkButton controls instead of the Button controls that were used in figure 20-2.

A view that allows you to navigate to other views

How to navigate by index

```
<asp:View ID="vNavigate" runat="server">
    <asp:LinkButton ID="LinkButton1" runat="server"
        CommandName="SwitchViewByIndex" CommandArgument="0" >
        View 1: Contact Info</asp:LinkButton><br />
    <asp:LinkButton ID="LinkButton2" runat="server"
        CommandName="SwitchViewByIndex" CommandArgument="1" >
        View 2: Shipping Method</asp:LinkButton><br />
    <asp:LinkButton ID="LinkButton3" runat="server"
        CommandName="SwitchViewByIndex" CommandArgument="2" >
        View 3: Credit Cart Info</asp:LinkButton>
</asp:View>
```

How to navigate by ID

```
<asp:View ID="vNavigate" runat="server">
    <asp:LinkButton ID="LinkButton1" runat="server"
        CommandName="SwitchViewByID" CommandArgument="vContact" >
        View 1: Contact Info</asp:LinkButton><br />
    <asp:LinkButton ID="LinkButton2" runat="server"
        CommandName="SwitchViewByID" CommandArgument="vShippingMethod" >
        View 2: Shipping Method</asp:LinkButton><br />
    <asp:LinkButton ID="LinkButton3" runat="server"
        CommandName="SwitchViewByID" CommandArgument="vCreditCart" >
        View 3: Credit Cart Info</asp:LinkButton>
</asp:View>
```

Description

- If a control within a MultiView control has CommandName and CommandArgument attributes, you can use those attributes to navigate between the available views. For example, both the Button and LinkButton controls have CommandName and CommandArgument attributes.

- To navigate to the next or previous view, you can set the CommandName attribute to NextView or PrevView as shown in figure 20-2.

- To navigate to the view with the specified index, you can set the CommandName attribute to SwitchViewByIndex, and you can set the CommandArgument attribute to the appropriate index where 0 is the first view, 1 is the second view, and so on.

- To navigate to the view with the specified ID, you can set the CommandName attribute to SwitchViewByID, and you can set the CommandArgument attribute to the ID.

Figure 20-4   How to navigate between views with commands

How to access the data stored in a MultiView control

To show how to access the data that's stored within a MultiView control, figure 20-5 presents a fourth and final view that displays all of the data that's entered in the three views shown in figure 20-1. This final view is displayed when the user clicks on the Finish button that's available from the third view. Since the data for each of the previous views is automatically stored in the view state of the page, the code for this final view can access that data. In other words, the state of these controls is automatically maintained. And since all of the controls are on the same page, you can directly access them just as you would any control.

For example, the code in the DisplayMessage procedure begins by getting the shipping type from the radio buttons that are in the second view. Then, this code builds a string that contains the data that's stored in the first three views. To do that, it directly accesses the text box, list box, and drop-down list controls from the first and third views. Finally, it displays this message in the multi-line text box of the fourth and final view.

In this figure, the code only converts the text to a string and displays it in a text box. However, this code could store this data in the session state object so it's available to other pages within the current session. Or, this code could store this data in a database so it's available for future sessions. Regardless, this figure shows how the MultiView control makes it easy to access the data that's stored within any of its views.

A view that displays the data of the MultiView control

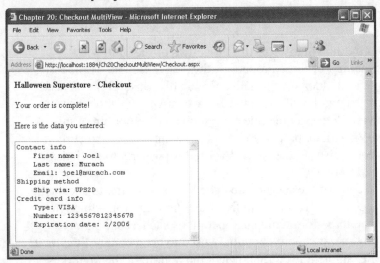

Code that accesses the data that's stored in the MultiView control

```
Protected Sub btnFinish_Click(ByVal sender As Object, _
        ByVal e As System.EventArgs) Handles btnFinish.Click
    Me.DisplayMessage()
End Sub

Protected Sub DisplayMessage()
    Dim sShipVia As String = ""
    If (rdoUPSGround.Checked) Then
        sShipVia = "UPSG"
    ElseIf (rdoUPS2Day.Checked) Then
        sShipVia = "UPS2D"
    ElseIf (rdoFedEx.Checked) Then
        sShipVia = "FEDEX"
    End If
    Dim sMessage As String
    sMessage = _
        "Contact info" & ControlChars.CrLf & _
        "    First name: " & txtFirstName.Text & ControlChars.CrLf & _
        "    Last name: " & txtLastName.Text & ControlChars.CrLf & _
        "    Email: " & txtEmail.Text & ControlChars.CrLf & _
        "Shipping method" & ControlChars.CrLf & _
        "    Ship via: " & sShipVia & ControlChars.CrLf & _
        "Credit card info" & ControlChars.CrLf & _
        "    Type: " & lstCardType.SelectedValue & ControlChars.CrLf & _
        "    Number: " & txtCardNumber.Text & ControlChars.CrLf & _
        "    Expiration date: " & ddlExpirationMonth.SelectedValue & "/" & _
                            ddlExpirationYear.SelectedValue
    txtMessage.Text = sMessage
End Sub
```

Description

- Because the state of each control in the MultiView and View controls is stored in view state, it's easy to access the data for the controls from the code-behind file.

Figure 20-5   How to access the data stored in a MultiView control

Properties and events of the MultiView and View controls

Figure 20-6 starts by showing two useful properties of the MultiView control. You can use the first of these properties, the ActiveViewIndex property, to get or set the zero-based index for the active view. This is useful if you need to write code to display the index of the active view or if you need to write code to change the active view. For example, the code shown at the bottom of this figure uses the ActiveViewIndex property to display the number of the current view. However, you could also set the ActiveViewIndex property to the index of the view you want to display.

You can use the second of these properties, the Views property, to access the collection of View objects that are stored in the MultiView control. Although this property allows you to perform complex operations such as adding or removing a view at runtime, it's more commonly used to get a count of the total number of views. For example, the code shown at the bottom of this figure uses the Count property of the Views collection to display the total number views.

For a MultiView control like the one presented in figure 20-1, you don't usually need to use the events of the MultiView or View controls. However, if you add controls outside of the MultiView control that need to be synchronized with the MultiView control, you may need to code event procedures for the events shown in this figure. For example, the code shown at the bottom of this figure is an event procedure for the ActiveViewChanged event of the MultiView control. The code within this event procedure changes the text that's displayed in a label that's placed outside of the MultiView control. This causes the label to display a message for each view like this:

```
View 1 of 4
```

Since this event procedure is executed every time the active view changes, the text within this label will always be synchronized with the view that's displayed.

Properties of the MultiView control

Property	Description
ActiveViewIndex	Gets or sets the index for the active view where 0 is the first view, 1 is the second view, and so on. By default, this is set to -1 so no view is selected as the active view.
Views	Gets the collection of View objects contained within the MultiView control. The Count property of this collection can be used to determine the total number of View controls in the MultiView control.

Button properties that work with the MultiView control

Property	Description
CommandName	Sets the navigation command for the button. This property can be set to NextView, PrevView, SwitchViewByIndex, or SwitchViewByID. For more information, see figure 20-2 and figure 20-4.
CommandArgument	Sets the arguments required by the SwitchViewByIndex and SwitchViewByID commands. For more information, see figure 20-4.

An event of the MultiView control

Event	Description
ActiveViewChanged	Fires every time the active view changes.

Events of the View control

Event	Description
Activate	Fires every time the view is activated.
Deactivate	Fires every time the view is deactivated.

Code that uses the ActiveViewChanged event of the MultiView control

```
Protected Sub mvCheckout_ActiveViewChanged(ByVal sender As Object, _
        ByVal e As System.EventArgs) Handles mvCheckout.ActiveViewChanged
    Dim iViewNumber As Integer = mvCheckout.ActiveViewIndex + 1
    lblStatus.Text = "View " & iViewNumber & " of " & mvCheckout.Views.Count
End Sub
```

Figure 20-6   Properties and events of the MultiView and View controls

How to use the Wizard control

In the topics that follow, you'll see how a Wizard control can be used to code a Checkout application that's similar to the one presented earlier in this chapter. This will help you compare the MultiView control to the Wizard control.

How the Wizard control works

Figure 20-7 shows a Checkout application that uses three *steps* of a Wizard control. Although each of these steps appears to be a separate page, each step is actually part of the same page (Checkout.aspx). This works like the views within a MultiView control. The main difference is that, by default, the Wizard control includes a *side bar* on the left side of the control, which provides links to each step in the control. As a result, you can easily navigate to any step in the wizard.

In addition, by default, the Wizard control automatically includes the Next, Previous, and Finish buttons shown on these steps. As a result, if you want to include these features, you may prefer using a Wizard control over a MultiView control.

Step 1 of a Wizard control

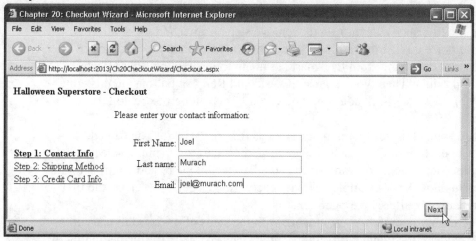

Step 2 of a Wizard control

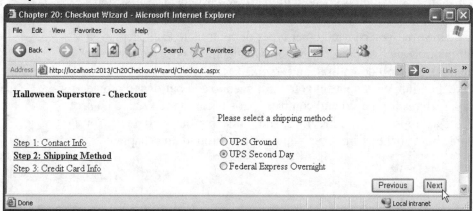

Step 3 of a Wizard control

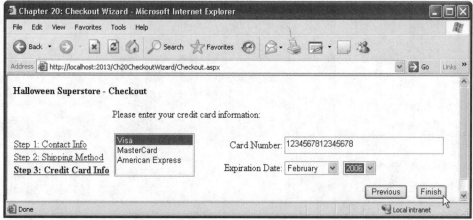

Figure 20-7 How a Wizard control works

How to add or remove steps

Figure 20-8 shows how to add or remove steps from a Wizard control. To start, you place a Wizard control on a page. Next, you select the Add/Remove WizardSteps command from the smart tag menu to display the WizardStep Collection Editor. Then, you can use the Add and Remove buttons on this editor to add or remove steps. In addition, you can use this dialog box to edit the properties for each step.

Once you get the correct number of steps for your wizard, you can add controls to each step. To do that, you can use the smart tag menu to select and display the step. Then, you can use any standard technique to add controls to the step. In this figure, for example, a TextBox control has been placed on the first step immediately after some plain text.

Whenever you prefer, you can work with the steps of a wizard directly in the aspx code. For example, this figure shows the aspx code for the beginning of a Wizard control with three steps. Here, three WizardStep tags are coded within the WizardSteps tag, which is coded within the Wizard tag. The first step contains some plain text and a text box, and the next two steps contain only plain text. However, you can add other types of controls to each step, even container controls such as panels and tables that contain other controls such as labels, text boxes, drop-down lists, and so on.

Unlike the MultiView control, you don't need to add buttons to provide for navigation features for the Wizard control. That's because the Wizard control displays the appropriate Next, Previous, and Finish buttons by default. You'll learn more about how this works as you progress through this chapter.

A wizard with three steps

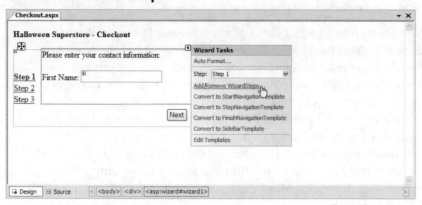

The WizardStep Collection Editor

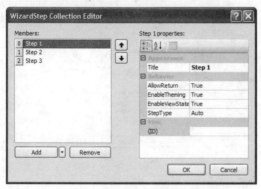

The aspx code for a Wizard control

```
<asp:Wizard ID="Wizard1" runat="server" ActiveStepIndex="0" Width="344px">
    <WizardSteps>
        <asp:WizardStep runat="server" Title="Step 1">
            Please enter your contact information:<br /><br />
            First Name: <asp:TextBox ID="txtFirstName" runat="server">
                </asp:TextBox><br /><br />
        </asp:WizardStep>
        <asp:WizardStep runat="server" Title="Step 2">
            Please select a shipping method:</asp:WizardStep>
        <asp:WizardStep runat="server" Title="Step 3">
            Please enter your credit card information:</asp:WizardStep>
    </WizardSteps>
</asp:Wizard>
```

Description

- To access the WizardStep Collection Editor, you can select the Add/Remove WizardSteps command from the smart tag menu for the Wizard control.

- To add or remove steps or to edit the properties for a step, you can edit the aspx code, or you can use the WizardStep Collection Editor.

Figure 20-8   How to add or remove steps

How to add a Cancel button

Figure 20-9 shows how to add a Cancel button to each step in a Wizard control. To do that, you set the DisplayCancelButton property of the wizard to True. Once you display the Cancel button, you can code an event procedure to handle the CancelButtonClick event that occurs when the user clicks this button. You can see an example of this in the event procedure in this figure.

The code within this event procedure displays the first step and clears all of the text from the text box controls on this page. To display the first step, this code sets the ActiveStepIndex property of the wizard to 0. Then, it sets the Text property of the three text box controls on this page to an empty string. This shows that you can directly access all of the controls within the wizard from the code-behind file for the page.

A wizard with a Cancel button

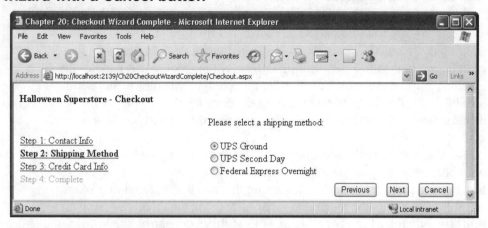

A Wizard tag that displays a Cancel button

```
<asp:Wizard ID="wizCheckout" runat="server" Width="739px"
    DisplayCancelButton="true">
```

Visual Basic code that works with the Cancel button

```
Protected Sub wizCheckout_CancelButtonClick(ByVal sender As Object, _
        ByVal e As System.EventArgs) Handles wizCheckout.CancelButtonClick
    wizCheckout.ActiveStepIndex = 0
    txtFirstName.Text = ""
    txtLastName.Text = ""
    txtEmail.Text = ""
End Sub
```

Description

- You can display a Cancel button for each step of a wizard by setting the DisplayCancelButton property of the Wizard control to True. By default, this property is set to False.

- You can use the CancelButtonClick event of the Wizard control to respond to the user clicking on the Cancel button.

- You can use the ActiveStepIndex property of the Wizard control to get or set the active step where 0 is the first step, 1 is the second step, and so on.

Figure 20-9   How to add a Cancel button

How to add a completion step

Figure 20-10 shows how to add a fourth and final step to the wizard that's displayed in figure 20-7. This step is displayed when the user clicks on the Finish button in the third step. But first, the event procedure that handles the FinishButtonClick event of the wizard is executed. In this figure, this event procedure calls the DisplayMessage procedure, which displays all of the data that's been entered in the first three steps in the multiline text box of the fourth step.

The DisplayMessage procedure called by this event procedure contains the same code as the DisplayMessage procedure that was presented in figure 20-5. This shows that the technique for accessing the data that's stored in a Wizard control is the same as the technique for accessing the data that's stored in a MultiView control. That's because, like the MultiView control, the Wizard control stores its data in the view state for the page.

The primary difference between the fourth step and the first three steps is that it doesn't have a side bar or navigation buttons. That's because the StepType attribute for this step has been set to Complete. This attribute is left at the default setting of Auto for the first three steps. As a result, the first step only contains a Next button, the second step contains Previous and Next buttons, and the third step contains Previous and Finish buttons. That's usually what you want, but if it isn't, you can use the StepType attribute to change it.

A wizard with a completion step

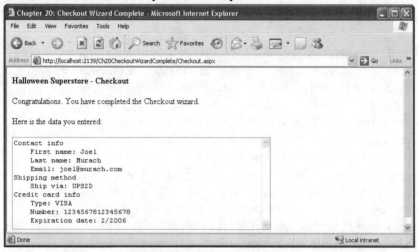

A WizardStep tag that defines a completion step

```
<asp:WizardStep runat="server"
    StepType="Complete" Title="Step 4: Complete">
        Congratulations. You have completed the Checkout wizard.<br /><br />
    <asp:Label ID="Label1" runat="server"
        Text="Here is the data you entered:"></asp:Label><br />
    <asp:TextBox ID="txtMessage" runat="server" Height="166px"
        TextMode="MultiLine" Width="489px"></asp:TextBox>
</asp:WizardStep>
```

Visual Basic code that displays a message on the completion page

```
Protected Sub wizCheckout_FinishButtonClick(ByVal sender As Object, _
        ByVal e As System.Web.UI.WebControls.WizardNavigationEventArgs) _
        Handles wizCheckout.FinishButtonClick
    Me.DisplayMessage()
End Sub
```

Possible values for the StepType attribute

Value	Description
Auto	Automatically sets the first step to Start, the last step to Finish, and any intermediate steps to Step. This is the default.
Start	Defines a step that doesn't have a Previous button.
Step	Defines a step that has Previous and Next buttons.
Finish	Defines a step that has Previous and Finish buttons.
Complete	Defines a step that doesn't have a side bar or any buttons. This step is typically used to display a completion message.

Description

- To add a completion step, you can add a final WizardStep tag and set its StepType attribute to Complete.

Figure 20-10   How to add a completion step

Properties and events of the Wizard and WizardStep controls

Figure 20-11 starts by summarizing three useful properties of the Wizard control. First, you can use the ActiveStepIndex property to get or set the active step. For example, the event procedure for the Cancel button shown in figure 20-9 sets this property to 0 to display the first step. Second, you can set the DisplayCancelButton property to True to display a Cancel button for each step of the wizard as described in figure 20-9. Third, if you don't want to display the side bar, you can set the DisplaySideBar property to False.

Besides these properties, there are many other properties of the Wizard control that you can use to control the appearance and function of the wizard. For example, you can edit the text that's displayed on the navigation buttons. Or, you can edit the type of button that's used for the navigation buttons. By default, the wizard uses regular Button controls, but it's also possible to use ImageButton or LinkButton controls. If you use the AutoFormat command that's available from the smart tag menu for a wizard, you can automatically change many of these properties.

In a typical wizard, you only need to handle the FinishButtonClick event that's fired when the user clicks on the Finish button. An example of this is shown in figure 20-10. Within this event procedure, you can store the data that has been gathered by the wizard and redirect the application to the next page. However, if you add a Cancel button, you'll probably want to add an event procedure for the CancelButtonClick event of the wizard that's executed when the Cancel button is clicked as shown in figure 20-9. And, if necessary, you can write event procedures for any of the other events shown in this figure. For example, you may want to write an event procedure for the ActiveStepChanged event to synchronize any controls that are placed outside of the Wizard control with the wizard's current step.

This figure finishes by presenting two properties of the WizardStep control that can be used to control the types of buttons that are displayed on the step. First, you can set the StepType property to any of the values shown in figure 20-10. Second, you can set the AllowReturn property to False to remove the Previous button from the step. However, the user can still return to the previous step by clicking the browser's Back button or by clicking on the links in the side bar if it's displayed. As a result, if it's critical to your application to prevent the user from returning to the previous step, you'll need to remove the side bar and disable the browser's Back button.

Properties of the Wizard control

Property	Description
ActiveStepIndex	Gets or sets the index for the active page where 0 is the first page, 1 is the second page, and so on. By default, this property is set to the page that's selected in Design view.
DisplayCancelButton	To show a Cancel button on every step, you can set this property to True. The default is False.
DisplaySideBar	To hide the side bar, you can set this property to False. The default is True.

Events of the Wizard control

Event	Description
ActiveStepChanged	Fires every time the active step changes.
NextButtonClick	Fires every time a Next button is clicked.
PreviousButtonClick	Fires every time a Previous button is clicked.
CancelButtonClick	Fires every time a Cancel button is clicked.
FinishButtonClick	Fires every time the Finish button is clicked.
SideBarButtonClick	Fires every time one of the side bar links is clicked.

Properties of the WizardStep control

Property	Description
StepType	Changes the types of buttons (Previous, Next, Finish) that are available for the step (see figure 20-10).
AllowReturn	To remove the Previous button from the step, you can set this property to False. The default is True.

Description

- You can use other properties of the Wizard control to control the formatting options for a wizard.
- You can use the AutoFormat command that's available from the smart tag menu for a wizard to automatically apply many formatting options for the wizard.

Figure 20-11   Properties and events of the Wizard and WizardStep controls

How to use templates and styles with wizards

Figure 20-12 shows how you can use templates and styles to customize the default controls and formatting for your wizard. For example, you can use templates to override the default controls for the parts of a wizard. Or, you can use styles to change the formatting for the parts of a wizard.

To begin working with templates, you can select the Edit Templates command from the wizard's smart tag menu to enter template-editing mode. In template-editing mode, you can select the template that you want to edit from the smart tag menu. In this figure, for example, you can see the start navigation template that contains the navigation buttons for the start step.

Once you've displayed a template, you can use standard techniques to add controls to the template. In this figure, for example, the LinkButton control has been added to the StartNavigationTemplate. This causes the LinkButton control on this template to override the Button control that's used by default.

When you're done modifying the templates, you can select the End Template Editing command from the smart tag menu. Then, you can run the application and see how the new template works.

Once you understand how to modify one template, you shouldn't have much trouble modifying the other ones. You can use the three navigation templates to modify the navigation buttons for the start, step, and finish steps. You can use the side bar template to modify the links displayed in the side bar. And you can use the header template to add a header to the wizard control. By default, the header template doesn't contain any controls, so adding controls to this template activates a new part of the wizard.

To work with styles, you can begin entering the tag for the style in the HTML Editor. Then, you can use the IntelliSense feature to select the style and attributes that you want to modify. In this figure, for example, the first style tag uses the navigation style to set the horizontal alignment for all navigation buttons to left. Then, the second style tag uses the side bar style to make the font size smaller for the links in the side bar. As a result, the side bar will use a smaller font and won't take up as much horizontal space.

Although it might seem like a lot of extra work to set up templates and styles for an application, the extra work might pay off in certain situations. For example, you might want to use templates and styles if you have an application where you need to develop multiple wizards with custom formatting. Then, you can apply a consistent format to all of these wizards by copying the tags for the templates and styles to all pages that contain a wizard.

A Wizard control in template-editing mode

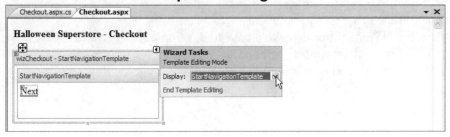

Aspx code for wizard templates and styles

```
<asp:Wizard ID="wizCheckout" runat="server" >

    <StartNavigationTemplate>
        <asp:LinkButton ID="LinkButton1" runat="server" >Next
        </asp:LinkButton>
    </StartNavigationTemplate>

    <NavigationStyle HorizontalAlign="Left" />
    <SideBarStyle Font-Size="Small" />

    <WizardSteps>
        <!-- wizard steps go here -->
    </WizardSteps>
</asp:Wizard>
```

Wizard templates and styles

Template	Style
HeaderTemplate	HeaderStyle
StartNavigationTemplate	StartNextButtonStyle
StepNavigationTemplate	StepNextButtonStyle
	StepPreviousButtonStyle
FinishNavigationTemplate	FinishCompleteButtonStyle
	FinishPreviousButtonStyle
SideBarTemplate	SideBarButtonStyle
	SideBarStyle
	CancelButtonStyle
	NavigationButtonStyle
	NavigationStyle

Description

- You can use templates and styles to customize the default controls and formatting for your wizard.

Figure 20-12   How to use templates and styles with wizards

Perspective

The MultiView and Wizard controls make it easy to develop a set of related views or steps that gather or display information. They also make it easy to access the data that's gathered by these views or steps. That's why you're going to want to use these controls whenever you find the need for them.

Terms

view
step
side bar

21

How to use email, custom error pages, and back-button control

Once you've got an application working the way it's supposed to, you can add enhancements that make it work even better. In this chapter, you'll learn how to add three of the most useful enhancements. First, you'll learn how to send email from an ASP.NET application. Then, you'll learn how to create and use custom error pages. And last, you'll learn how to handle the problems that can occur when the user uses the Back button to access a page that has already been posted.

How to send email

When you create a web application, you often need to send email messages from the application. For instance, when a user makes a purchase from an e-commerce site, a web application usually sends an email to the customer that confirms the order. Or, if a serious error occurs, the web application often sends an email message to the support staff that documents the error. In the topics that follow, you'll learn how to send email from your ASP.NET applications.

An introduction to email

You're probably familiar with *mail client* software such as Microsoft Outlook or Outlook Express that allows you to send and retrieve email messages. This type of software communicates with a *mail server* that actually sends and retrieves your email messages. Most likely, your mail server software is provided by your Internet Service Provider (ISP) or through your company.

The diagram in figure 21-1 shows how this works. The two protocols that are commonly used to send email messages are *SMTP* and *POP*. When you send an email message, the message is first sent from the mail client software on your computer to your mail server using the SMTP protocol. Then, your mail server uses SMTP to send the mail to the recipient's mail server. Finally, the recipient's mail client uses the POP protocol to retrieve the mail from the recipient's mail server.

A third protocol you should know about is *MIME*, which stands for *Multi-purpose Internet Mail Extension*. Unlike SMTP or POP, MIME isn't used to transfer email messages. Instead, it defines how the content of an email message and its attachments are formatted. In this chapter, you'll learn how to send messages that consist of simple text as well as messages that use HTML format.

How email works

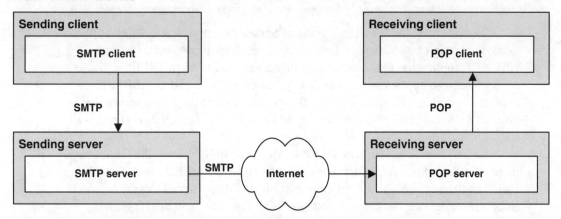

Three email protocols

Protocol	Description
SMTP	*Simple Mail Transfer Protocol* is used to send a message from one mail server to another.
POP	*Post Office Protocol* is used by mail clients to retrieve messages from mail servers. Currently, POP is in version 3 and is known as POP3.
MIME	The *Multipurpose Internet Mail Extension* specifies the type of content that can be sent as a message or attachment.

Three common reasons for sending email from an ASP.NET application

- **To confirm receipt of an order.** When the user completes an order, the application can email a confirmation of the order to the user.

- **To remind a registered user of a forgotten password.** If the user forgets his or her password, the application can email the password to the email address that's on file for the user. You can also accomplish this using the PasswordRecovery control presented in chapter 18.

- **To notify support personnel of a problem.** If a problem like an unhandled exception occurs, the application can email a message that summarizes the problem to the appropriate support person.

Description

- When an email message is sent, it goes from the sender's *mail client* to the sender's *mail server* to the receiver's mail server to the receiver's mail client.

- *SMTP* and *POP* are the protocols that are commonly used for sending and retrieving email messages. *MIME* is the protocol for defining the format of an email message.

Figure 21-1   An introduction to email

How to configure the SMTP service in IIS

If you're using the Web Development Server to test your ASP.NET applications, they won't be able to send email. As a result, before you can test an ASP.NET application that sends email messages, you must install IIS and use it to run your web applications. In addition, before you can test an ASP.NET application that sends email messages, you must enable the email server that's built into IIS and configure it to send mail from your application. Figure 21-2 shows how to do that.

The first step is to start the SMTP service. You do that from the IIS management console, which you can reach in Windows XP by opening the Control Panel, and then opening Administrative Tools and double-clicking the Internet Information Services icon. (In Windows 2000, this icon is named Internet Services Manager.) Once you've opened the IIS management console, you can expand the tree to display the Default SMTP Virtual Server node. Then, you can start the SMTP service by selecting it in the tree and clicking the Start button in the toolbar.

Once you've started the SMTP service, you must configure it so that it allows your ASP.NET applications to send mail. To do that, you enable relaying for the local computer. This allows the mail server to accept mail from a specified computer and deliver it to the intended recipient. To configure the SMTP service to relay mail from the local computer, open the Relay Restrictions dialog box as described in this figure and add the localhost address (127.0.0.1) to the list of computers that the SMTP server will relay mail for.

How to make sure SMTP is running on your local server

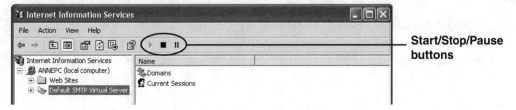

1. Click the Start button in the Windows task bar, then select All Programs→Administrative Tools→Internet Information Services (Windows XP) to open the IIS management console shown above.

2. Expand the tree to display your local computer's IIS server and the services running under it.

3. Select the Default SMTP Virtual Server service.

4. If the SMTP service is *not* running, the Stop button (■) will be disabled. In that case, click the Start button (▶) to start the SMTP service.

How to allow relaying for the local host

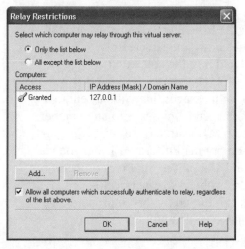
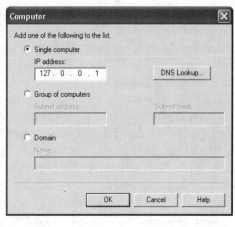

1. In the IIS management console, right-click the Default SMTP Virtual Server node and choose the Properties command.

2. Click the Access tab, then click the Relay button. This displays the Relay Restrictions dialog box shown above.

3. Click the Add button to display the Computer dialog box shown above. Then, select Single Computer, type 127.0.0.1 into the IP address field, click OK to close the Computer dialog box, and click OK again to close the Relay Restrictions dialog box.

Figure 21-2   How to configure the SMTP service in IIS

How to create an email message

Figure 21-3 shows the constructors and properties of the MailMessage class that you use to create email messages. It also shows the constructors of the MailAddress class. This class is used to create the addresses that are stored in the From, To, Cc, and Bcc properties of a mail message.

The first example in this figure illustrates how you can use these classes to create a mail message that includes a carbon copy (cc). Here, all of the values needed to create the email message are passed to the procedure as arguments. Then, the first three statements of the procedure create MailAddress objects for the from, to, and cc addresses. Notice that the MailAddress object for the from address includes both an email address and a display name. When a display name is included, it's displayed in the mail client's email list instead of the email address.

The fourth statement in this procedure creates a MailMessage object using the to and from MailAddress objects. Then, the next two statements set the Subject and Body properties of the message. Finally, the last statement adds the cc MailAddress object to the collection of objects in the Cc property.

The second example in this figure shows how to send the same email as in the first example without setting the display name for the sender. To do that, you simply create the MailMessage object using the from and to addresses and the subject and body. This example also illustrates how you can create a MailAddress object for the carbon copy and add it to the collection of objects using a single statement.

Although the examples in this figure create messages that will be sent to a single recipient, you should realize that you can send a message to any number of recipients. To do that, you need to use the first constructor for the MailMessage class shown here to create an empty mail message. Then, you can create a MailAddress object for the sender and assign it to the From property of the message. And you can create a MailAddress object for each recipient and add it to the collection of MailAddress objects returned by the To property of the mail message. For example, to create a message that will be sent to two people, your code will look something like this:

```
Dim msg As New MailMessage()
msg.From = New MailAddress("anne@murach.com")
msg.To.Add(New MailAddress("joel@murach.com"))
msg.To.Add(New MailAddress("kelly@murach.com"))
```

Constructors and properties of the MailMessage class

Constructor	Description
`MailMessage()`	Creates an empty mail message.
`MailMessage(from, to)`	Creates a mail message with the to and from addresses specified as strings or MailAddress objects.
`MailMessage(from, to, subject, body)`	Creates a mail message with the to address, from address, subject, and body specified as strings.

Property	Description
`From`	A MailAddress object for the message sender.
`To`	A collection of MailAddress objects for the message recipients.
`Cc`	A collection of MailAddress objects for the copy recipients.
`Bcc`	A collection of MailAddress objects for the blind copy recipients.
`Subject`	The subject line for the message.
`Body`	The body of the message.
`IsBodyHtml`	A Boolean value that indicates if the body of the message contains HTML. The default is False.
`Attachments`	A collection of Attachment objects.

Constructors of the MailAddress class

Constructor	Description
`MailAddress(address)`	Creates an email address with the specified address string.
`MailAddress(address, displayname)`	Creates an email address with the specified address and display strings.

Code that creates an email message with a carbon copy

```
Private Sub SendTextMessageCC(ByVal FromAddress As String, _
ByVal FromName As String, ByVal ToAddress As String, _
ByVal Subject As String, ByVal Body As String, ByVal CCAddress As String)
    Dim fromAdd As New MailAddress(FromAddress, FromName)
    Dim toAdd As New MailAddress(ToAddress)
    Dim ccAdd As New MailAddress(CCAddress)
    Dim msg As New MailMessage(fromAdd, toAdd)
    msg.Subject = Subject
    msg.Body = Body
    msg.Cc.Add(ccAdd)
End Sub
```

Another way to create a message

```
Dim msg As New MailMessage(FromAddress, ToAddress, Subject, Body)
msg.Cc.Add(New MailAddress(CCAddress))
```

Description

- To create an email message, you use the MailMessage and MailAddress classes that are in the System.Net.Mail namespace.

- To add an address to a collection of MailAddress objects, you use the Add method of the collection.

Figure 21-3 How to create an email message

How to send an email message

After you create an email message, you use the SmtpClient class shown in figure 21-4 to send the message. The technique you use to do that depends on the message you're sending and on whether you have set the SMTP configuration settings for the application. To set the SMTP configuration settings, you use the Web Site Administration Tool as shown in this figure. Then, these settings are saved in the web.config file.

To illustrate, the first example in this figure shows you how to send a message using settings in the web.config file. When you use this technique, you don't have to specify the name or port for the SMTP server when you create the SmtpClient object. Instead, these settings are taken from the Smtp section of the web.config file.

The first example also illustrates how to send a message that's been stored in a MailMessage object. To do that, you simply name the MailMessage object on the Send method.

If you haven't set the SMTP configuration options, or if you want to override these options, you can specify the domain name of the server when you create the SmtpClient object. This is illustrated in the second example in this figure. Here, the name "localhost" is specified so that the SMTP server that's built into the local IIS server will be used. Notice that when you use the local IIS server, you don't have to specify a port number. That's because the default port number is 25, which is also the default port for the IIS server. If you use a server at a different port, though, you'll have to specify the port number.

The second example also illustrates how you can send a mail message without creating a MailMessage object. To do that, you just pass the from and to addresses and the subject and body text to the Send method. Then, the Send method creates the MailMessage object for you and sends it. You can use this format of the Send method if the message is in simple text format, you don't need to send the message to more than one person, you don't need to send copies of the message to anyone, and you don't need to send attachments with the message.

If you've read chapter 18, you know that another way to send an email is to use the PasswordRecovery control. This control sends an email to a user that includes the user's password. Because you don't specify the server that's used to send the message when you use this control, you must set the server name (and port if necessary) in the web.config file for it to work. In addition, you should set a from address to appear in the email that's sent by this control.

How to set the SMTP configuration settings

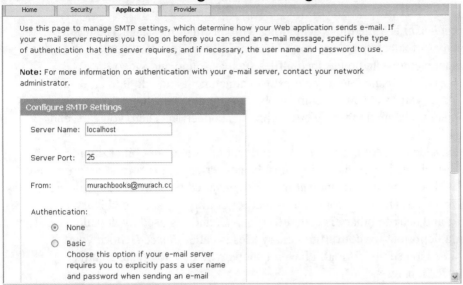

Constructors and methods of the SmtpClient class

Constructor	Description
`SmtpClient()`	Creates a client using the settings specified in the web.config file.
`SmtpClient(name)`	Creates a client that can send email to the specified SMTP server.
`SmtpClient(name, port)`	Creates a client that can send email to the specified SMTP server and port.

Method	Description
`Send(message)`	Sends the specified MailMessage object.
`Send(from, to, subject, body)`	Creates and sends an email message using the specified from, to, subject, and body strings.

Code that sends a message using settings in the web.config file

```
Dim client As New SmtpClient()
client.Send(msg)
```

Code that creates and sends a message to a named server

```
Dim client As New SmtpClient("localhost")
client.Send(FromAddress, ToAddress, Subject, Body)
```

Description

- To send an email message, you use the SmtpClient class in the System.Net.Mail namespace.
- You can use the Web Site Administration Tool to specify the settings that will be used to send email messages. To do that, select the Website→ASP.NET Configuration command, display the Application tab, click the Configure SMTP E-mail Settings link, and enter the values on the page that's displayed.

Figure 21-4   How to send an email message

How to add an attachment to an email message

An *attachment* is a file that's sent along with an email message. The most common types of attachments are text files, word processing documents, spreadsheets, pictures, and other media files such as sound and video files.

Figure 21-5 shows how you can create an attachment and add it to an email message. After you create an attachment object using the Attachment class, you add the object to the mail message's Attachments collection. Then, you can send the message.

Since SMTP protocol is designed to send text messages, not binary files, any email attachment for a binary file must be converted to text format before it can be sent. Then, the text attachment must be converted back to a binary file when it's received. The most common format for converting attached binary files to text and back to binary is called *UUEncode*, and it's used by default. The other available format for converting binary files is called *Base64*. Since you shouldn't need to use this format, I haven't shown you how to create an attachment that uses it here.

The syntax for creating an attachment

```
New Attachment(filename)
```

One way to create a new attachment and add it to a message

```
Dim sFileName As String
sFileName = "C:\HalloweenStore\Attachments\ReturnPolicy.doc"
Dim attach As New Attachment(sFileName)
Dim msg As New MailMessage(FromAddress, ToAddress, Subject, Body)
msg.Attachments.Add(attach)
```

Another way to create a new attachment and add it to a message

```
Dim sFileName As String
sFileName = "C:\HalloweenStore\Attachments\ReturnPolicy.doc"
msg.Attachments.Add(New Attachment(sFileName))
```

Description

- An *attachment* is a file that is sent along with an email message. When the recipient receives the email message, he or she can open or save the attachment.

- To add an attachment to an email message, you create the attachment using the Attachment class. Then, you add the attachment to the message using the Add method of the Attachments collection of the MailMessage class.

- If an email attachment contains a binary file, it must be converted to text before it can be sent, and it must be converted back to binary when it's received. By default, binary files are converted to a format called *UUEncode*. However, you can also use a format called *Base64*.

Figure 21-5   How to add an attachment to an email message

How to create an HTML message

By default, email messages consist of plain text with no formatting. However, you can create a formatted message by using HTML as the MIME type as described in figure 21-6. When you set the IsBodyHtml property of the MailMessage object to True, you can use HTML formatting tags in the body of the message.

The example in this figure calls a private function named ConfirmationMessage that formats the HTML for the body of an order confirmation message. This function uses basic HTML formatting tags to create a message that includes an image and some text. Note that if you refer to an image in the body by including an <img> tag, you must include the image file as an attachment as shown here. Otherwise, the recipient won't be able to see the image.

How an HTML message appears in an email client

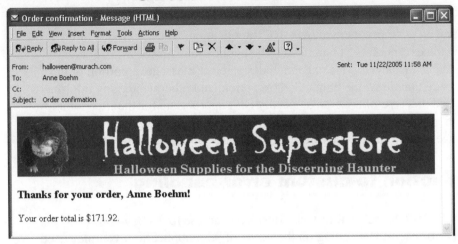

A procedure that creates and sends a simple HTML message

```
Private Sub SendConfirmation()
    Dim msg As New MailMessage("halloween@murach.com", sEmail)
    msg.Subject = "Order Confirmation"
    msg.Body = Me.ConfirmationMessage
    msg.IsBodyHtml = True
    Dim sFile As String _
        = "C:\ASP.NET 2.0 Web sites\Ch21HalloweenStore\Images\banner.jpg"
    msg.Attachments.Add(New Attachment(sFile))
    Dim client As New SmtpClient("localhost")
    client.Send(msg)
End Sub

Private Function ConfirmationMessage() As String
    Dim sMsg As String
    sMsg = "<HTML><head><title>Order confirmation</title></head>" _
        & "<body><img src='banner.jpg' alt='Halloween Store' />" _
        & "<br /><br /><h3>Thanks for your order, " _
        & dvCustomer(0)("FirstName").ToString & " " _
        & dvCustomer(0)("LastName").ToString & "!</h3>" _
        & "<p>Your order total is " & FormatCurrency(dInvoiceTotal) _
        & ".</p></body></HTML>"
    Return sMsg
End Function
```

Description

- To create an email message in HTML format, set the IsBodyHtml property to True. Then, you can use HTML in the message that you assign to the Body property.

- An HTML email message can include links to your web site. However, you should avoid sending HTML that includes scripts or web form controls. Many mail servers will reject them because they might be malicious.

- If the HTML includes <img> tags, you should include the image files as attachments. Otherwise, users won't be able to see the images in your email.

Figure 21-6   How to create an HTML message

How to use custom error handling

When an error occurs in an ASP.NET application, an exception is thrown. Then, if the exception isn't handled by the application, an ASP.NET Server Error page is displayed. This page includes an error message, a portion of the source code that threw the unhandled exception, and other debugging information. Since this type of error page usually isn't appropriate for the users of an application, you typically replace the generic error pages with your own custom error pages after you're done testing the web site but before you go live with it.

An introduction to custom error handling

Figure 21-7 describes four techniques you can use to display your own custom error pages. Depending on the needs of your application, you may need to use one or more of these techniques.

The first technique is to enclose code that might generate exceptions in a Try...Catch block. Then, you can redirect to a custom error page if an exception does occur.

The second technique is to code a Page_Error procedure in the code-behind file for a page. This procedure is called whenever an unhandled exception occurs on the page. Then, in the Page_Error procedure, you redirect the user to a custom error page.

The third technique is to code an Application_Error procedure in the global.asax file. This procedure is called whenever an unhandled exception occurs on a page that doesn't have a Page_Error procedure. Then, the Application_Error procedure can redirect the user to a custom error page.

The fourth technique is to use the customErrors element in the web.config file to designate custom error pages. This technique is used to display custom error pages when common HTTP errors such as a 404 – Not Found error occur.

A custom error page in a browser

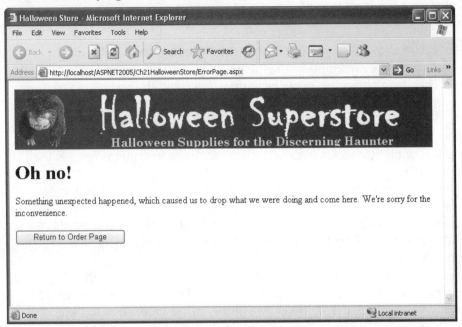

Four ways to display a custom error page when an exception occurs

- Use Try...Catch statements to catch exceptions as they occur, then redirect or transfer to a custom error page.
- Use the Page_Error procedure in a code-behind file to catch unhandled exceptions at the page level, then redirect or transfer to a custom error page.
- Use the Application_Error procedure in the global.asax file to catch unhandled exceptions at the application level, then redirect or transfer to a custom error page.
- Use the customErrors element of the web.config file to specify custom error pages that are displayed for specific types of HTTP errors.

Description

- If an unrecoverable error occurs, most applications display a custom error page to inform the user that a problem has occurred.
- Behind the scenes, the custom error page may also record the error in a log or send an email message to the application's support staff to notify them of the error.
- Custom error pages often use an Exception object to display a detailed message that describes the error.

Figure 21-7   An introduction to custom error handling

How to get and use the Exception object for an error

Figure 21-8 shows how you can use the properties and methods of the Exception and HttpServerUtility classes to get and use the Exception object for an error. This is the object that contains information about the exception that has occurred. The examples in this figure show how this works.

The first example shows how you can use a Try...Catch statement to get the Exception object. As you should know, the Catch clause catches the Exception object if any of the statements in the Try clause throw an exception. You can use this technique in any procedure of a code-behind file.

The second example shows how to get the Exception object within the Page_Error procedure. This procedure is executed automatically if an exception isn't handled by the other procedures of a code-behind file. Here, you use the GetLastError method of the Server object, which you access using the Server property of the page.

The third example shows how to get the Exception object within the Application_Error procedure of the global.asax file. This procedure is executed automatically if an exception isn't handled by any of the procedures in the code-behind file including the Page_Error procedure. In the Application_Error procedure, however, the GetLastError method doesn't return the correct Exception object. That's because a second exception called HttpUnhandledException is thrown if an exception occurs and the exception isn't handled by a Try...Catch statement or a Page_Error procedure. As a result, the GetLastError method returns the HttpUnhandledException exception, not the exception that originally caused the error. To access the original exception, you must use the InnerException property of the Exception object that's returned by the GetLastError method.

Although you might think that you could use the ClearError method to clear the HttpUnhandledException exception and then use GetLastError to get the original exception, that won't work. That's because you can only use GetLastError to get the Exception object for the last exception that occurred. In this case, that's the HttpUnhandledException exception.

The fourth example shows how you might use the properties of an Exception object as you test an application. Here, the Write method of the HttpResponse object is used to display the Message and Source properties on the page. Notice that before this method is executed, the ClearError method of the Server object is used to clear the error. That way, the ASP.NET Server Error page won't be displayed.

Common properties of the Exception class

Property	Description
Message	A message that describes the error.
Source	The name of the application or object that caused the error.
InnerException	The Exception object that caused the exception at the application level.

Methods of the HttpServerUtility class for working with exceptions

Method	Description
GetLastError	Gets the most recent exception.
ClearError	Clears the most recent exception.

Code that gets the Exception object at the procedure level

```
Try
    statements that could throw an exception
Catch ex As Exception
    statements that use the Exception object named ex
End Try
```

Code that gets the Exception object at the page level

```
Dim ex As Exception
ex = Server.GetLastError
```

Code that gets the Exception object at the application level

```
Dim ex As Exception
ex = Server.GetLastError.InnerException
```

Code that displays the error message and source of the Exception object

```
Server.ClearError()
Response.Write(ex.Message & "<br />" & ex.Source)
```

Description

- You can use a Try...Catch statement in any procedure of a code-behind file to get the Exception object for an error.
- The Page_Error event procedure is executed when an unhandled exception occurs. Within this procedure, you use the GetLastError method of the Server object to get the Exception object for the error.
- If you don't handle an exception with a Try...Catch statement or a Page_Error event procedure, an HttpUnhandledException is thrown. Then, you can use the Application_Error procedure in the global.asax file to handle the exception. To do that, you use the GetLastError method of the Server object to get the Exception object for the HttpUnhandledException, and you use the InnerException property of that exception to get the Exception object that caused the error.
- During testing, you may want to use the Write method of the HttpResponse object to write information about the exception to the page. Before you do that, you need to clear the error from the Server object so that the ASP.NET Server Error page isn't displayed.

Figure 21-8   How to get and use the Exception object for an error

How to code procedures that redirect to a custom error page

Figure 21-9 shows three ways to redirect to a custom error page when an exception occurs in an ASP.NET application. The first example shows how you can redirect to a custom error page from a Try...Catch statement. Here, a call to the Insert method of a SQL data source is placed in a Try clause so any database exceptions can be handled in the Catch clause. If an exception occurs, the Catch clause adds the Exception object to session state and redirects to the error page. Then, the error page can use the Exception object to get information about the exception.

The second example shows how you can use a Page_Error procedure to catch all unhandled exceptions for a page and redirect to a custom error page. Here, the GetLastError method is used to get the Exception object. Then, the procedure adds the Exception object to session state and redirects to the custom error page.

The third example shows how you can use an Application_Error procedure in the global.asax file to catch all unhandled exceptions for an entire application. Here, the GetLastError method is used to get the Exception object, and the InnerException property of the Exception object is used to get the exception that caused the error. Then, the procedure adds the Exception object to session state and redirects to the custom error page.

A Try...Catch statement that redirects to a custom error page if an exception occurs during a database operation

```
Try
    SqlDataSource1.Insert()
Catch ex As Exception
    Session("Exception") = ex
    Response.Redirect("ErrorPage.aspx")
End Try
```

A Page_Error event procedure that redirects to a custom error page

```
Protected Sub Page_Error(ByVal sender As Object, _
        ByVal e As System.EventArgs) Handles Me.Error
    Dim ex As Exception
    ex = Server.GetLastError
    Session("Exception") = ex
    Response.Redirect("ErrorPage.aspx")
End Sub
```

An Application_Error event procedure in the global.asax file that redirects to a custom error page

```
Sub Application_Error(ByVal sender As Object, ByVal e As EventArgs)
    ' Code that runs when an unhandled error occurs
    Dim ex As Exception
    ex = Server.GetLastError.InnerException
    Session("Exception") = ex
    Response.Redirect("ErrorPage.aspx")
End Sub
```

Description

- You can redirect to a custom error page from a Try...Catch statement, a Page_Error procedure, or an Application_Error procedure in the global.asax file.

- Before redirecting to a custom error page, the Exception object should be added to session state so it can be used by the error page.

- If you run an application with debugging and an exception occurs, Visual Studio enters break mode and displays a dialog box that describes the error and provides links you can use to get additional information on the error. To continue program execution when this dialog box is displayed, click the Continue button.

Figure 21-9   How to code procedures that redirect to a custom error page

The code for a custom error page

Figure 21-10 shows the aspx code and the code-behind file for the custom error page that's shown in figure 21-7. Here, the aspx code should be self-explanatory because it simply displays a message and provides a button for returning to the Order page.

The code-behind file for the error page is more interesting, though, because it sends an email message to the support personnel that describes the error that has occurred. This assumes that the Try...Catch statement, Page_Error procedure, or Application_Error procedure that redirects to the error page has added the Exception object to session state. Then, the Load procedure for the error page gets the Exception object from session state and passes it to the SendEmail procedure, which sends the email message. After that, the Load procedure removes the Exception object from session state.

The aspx code for the body of the Error page

```
<body>
    <form id="form1" runat="server">
    <div>
        <asp:Image ID="Image1" runat="server"
            ImageUrl="~/Images/banner.jpg" /><br />
        <h2>Oh no!</h2>
        Something unexpected happened, which caused us to drop what we were
        doing and come here. We're sorry for the inconvenience.<br /><br />
        <asp:Button ID="btnReturn" runat="server"
            Text="Return to Order Page" PostBackUrl="~/Order.aspx" />
    </div>
    </form>
</body>
```

The Visual Basic code for the Error page

```
Imports System.Net.Mail

Partial Class ErrorPage
    Inherits System.Web.UI.Page

    Protected Sub Page_Load(ByVal sender As Object, _
            ByVal e As System.EventArgs) Handles Me.Load
        If Not IsPostBack Then
            Me.SendEmail(Session("Exception"))
            Session.Remove("Exception")
        End If
    End Sub

    Private Sub SendEmail(ByVal ex As Exception)
        Dim sBody As String
        sBody = "An exception occurred at " & Now.ToLongTimeString _
            & " on " & Now.ToLongDateString & "<br />" & ex.Message
        Dim msg As New MailMessage("halloween@murach.com", _
            "support@murach.com")
        msg.Subject = "Exception in Halloween application"
        msg.Body = sBody
        msg.IsBodyHtml = True
        Dim client As New SmtpClient("localhost")
        client.Send(msg)
    End Sub

End Class
```

Note

- This code assumes that the Exception object has been placed in session state.

Figure 21-10   The code for a custom error page

How to handle HTTP errors with the web.config file

Not all unrecoverable errors cause ASP.NET to throw an exception. As figure 21-11 shows, some error conditions result in HTTP errors that are handled by the web server itself. For these errors, you can use the customErrors element in the web.config file to specify custom error pages.

Although there are many different types of HTTP errors that can occur, the common types are listed in this figure. Of these, the most common is the 404 error. This error occurs when a user attempts to retrieve a page that doesn't exist. In some cases, a 404 error is caused by a missing page or a page that has been renamed. In other cases, a 404 error is caused by an error in your application's navigation controls, such as a hyperlink that uses an incorrect URL.

As this figure shows, you include an Error element in the web.config file for each HTTP error that you want to redirect to a custom error page. In the example, this is done for two types of errors. The first Error element specifies that the page named E404.aspx should be displayed if a 404 error occurs. The second element specifies that the page named E500.aspx should be displayed if a 500 error occurs.

You can also specify a default error page that's displayed if an HTTP error that isn't specifically listed in an Error element occurs. In the example in this figure, the defaultRedirect attribute specifies that a page named DefaultError.aspx should be displayed if a HTTP error other than 404 or 500 occurs.

A customErrors element in the web.config file that designates custom error pages

```
<customErrors mode="On" defaultRedirect="DefaultError.aspx">
    <error statusCode="404" redirect="E404.aspx" />
    <error statusCode="500" redirect="E500.aspx" />
</customErrors>
```

Common HTTP error codes

Code	Description
401	Unauthorized request. The client must be authorized to access the resource.
403	Forbidden request. The client is not allowed to access the resource.
404	File Not Found. The resource could not be located.
500	Internal Server Error. This is usually the result of an unhandled exception.

Description

- The customErrors element in the web.config file lets you designate custom error pages that are automatically displayed when unrecoverable HTTP errors occur. You don't have to write any code to redirect or transfer to these pages.

- To enable custom error pages, add a customErrors element to the web.config file. Then, set the Mode attribute to "On," and set the defaultRedirect attribute to the name of the generic error page.

- To associate a custom error page with an HTTP error, add an Error element that specifies the HTTP error code in the statusCode attribute and the name of the custom error page in the Redirect attribute.

- You can also add a customErrors element to the web.config file using the Web Site Administration Tool. To do that, select the Website→ASP.NET Configuration command, display the Application tab, click the Define Default Error Page link, and then select the appropriate settings.

Figure 21-11   How to handle HTTP errors with the web.config file

How to handle the back-button problem

If the user clicks the Back button in the browser window to return to a previous ASP.NET form and then posts the form, the application's session state may not correspond to that form. In some cases, this can result in a problem that we refer to as the *back-button problem*. The topics that follow show you how to deal with this problem.

An introduction to the back-button problem

Figure 21-12 illustrates the back-button problem in a shopping cart application. Here, the contents of the user's shopping cart are stored in session state and displayed on the page. The user then deletes one of the two items, which changes the data in session state. At that point, the user changes his mind and clicks the Back button, which displays both items again, even though session state only includes one item.

If the user now proceeds to check out, the order is likely to show one item when the user thinks he has ordered two items. But that depends upon how the application is coded. In the worst cases, the back-button problem may cause an application to crash. In the best cases, clicking on the Back button won't cause a problem at all.

In general, there are two ways to handle the back-button problem. The first is to try to prevent pages from being saved in the browser's cache. Then, when the user clicks the Back button, the old page can't be retrieved. As you will see in the next figure, ASP.NET provides four methods for doing that, but they don't work if the user's browser ignores the page cache settings that are sent with a response.

The second way is to code critical web forms so they detect when the user attempts to post a page that isn't current. To do that, a form can use timestamps or random numbers to track the use of pages. Because there's no reliable way to prevent a page from being cached and retrieved via the Back button, you should use this second technique whenever possible.

An example of a back-button problem in the Cart page of the Halloween Store application

1. The user adds two products to the shopping cart. The shopping cart data is stored in session state and currently contains two items: one Cool Ghoul at $69.99 and one Deranged Cat at $19.99. The shopping cart displayed in the browser window looks like this:

2. The user selects the first product and clicks the Remove Item button to delete it. The first line item is deleted from the shopping cart in session state and the updated page is sent to the browser:

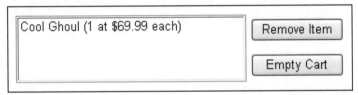

3. The user decides that he or she wants to purchase the Deranged Cat after all and clicks the browser's Back button, thinking this will undo the Delete action. The browser retrieves the previous page from its local cache:

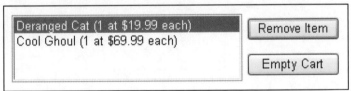

Because the browser redisplayed this page directly from its cache, the first line item was not added back to the shopping cart in session state. As a result, session state contains only one item even though the web page displays two items.

Two ways to handle the back-button problem

- Disable browser page caching for user input forms.
- Use timestamps or random numbers to track pages so you can detect when a page isn't current.

Description

- When a user clicks the browser's Back button, the browser retrieves a locally cached copy of the previous page without notifying the server. As a result, the information stored in session state can become out of sync with the data displayed in the browser window.

Figure 21-12   An introduction to the back-button problem

How to disable browser page caching

Figure 21-13 shows how you can use four ASP.NET methods to prevent a user's browser from caching pages. All of these methods work by adding information to the HTTP headers that are sent to the browser along with the page.

Unfortunately, some browsers ignore these headers, so these techniques don't guarantee that a page won't be cached. Still, it's not a bad idea to add the code in this figure to the Page_Load procedure of any ASP.NET page that gets important data like customer or product information.

The warning message that's displayed if the user returns to a page and caching is disabled

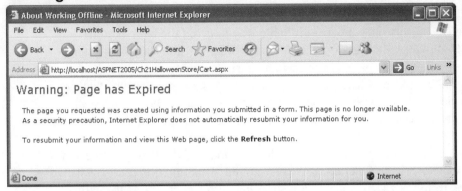

Methods that set page caching options

Method	Description
`Response.Cache.SetCacheability`	Indicates how the page should be cached. Specify HttpCacheability.NoCache to suppress caching.
`Response.Cache.SetExpires`	Specifies when the cached page should expire. Specify Now().AddSeconds(-1) to mark the page as already expired.
`Response.Cache.SetNoStore`	Specifies that the browser should not cache the page.
`Response.AppendHeader`	Adds a header to the HTTP response object. Specifying "Pragma" for the key and "no-cache" for the value disables caching.

Code that disables caching for a page

```
Response.Cache.SetCacheability(HttpCacheability.NoCache)
Response.Cache.SetExpires(Now.AddSeconds(-1))
Response.Cache.SetNoStore()
Response.AppendHeader("Pragma", "no-cache")
```

Description

- You can limit the effect of the Back button by directing the browser to not cache pages that contain state-sensitive data. Then, when the user attempts to return to a page using the Back button, the warning message at the top of this figure is displayed.

- You can place the code to disable browser page caching in the procedure that handles the Load event of the page. This code should be executed each time the page is loaded.

- Unfortunately, the technique described in this figure doesn't ensure that the user's browser won't cache the page because the user's browser may ignore the page cache settings. As a result, you should use the technique in the next figure to prevent back-button problems.

Figure 21-13   How to disable browser page caching

How to use timestamps to avoid the back-button problem

Figure 21-14 illustrates the most reliable way to avoid the back-button problem. Here, you see the code for a web page that uses timestamps to determine whether the posted page is current. The basic technique is to record a timestamp in two places when a page is posted: view state and session state. Then, the view state stamp is sent back to the browser and cached along with the rest of the information on the page, while the session state stamp is saved on the server.

Later, when the user posts a form for the second time, the Page_Load event procedure calls a private function named IsExpired. This function retrieves the timestamps from view state and session state and compares them. If they are identical, the page is current and IsExpired returns False. But if they are different, it indicates that the user has posted a page that was retrieved from the browser's cache via the Back button. In that case, the IsExpired function returns True. Then, the Page_Load procedure redirects to a page named Expired.aspx, which in turn displays a message indicating that the page is out of date and can't be posted.

Notice that before comparing the timestamp items in session state and view state, the IsExpired function checks that both of these items exist. If not, the function returns False so that current timestamps can be saved in both session state and view state.

Incidentally, this technique can also be used to deal with problems that occur when the user clicks the Refresh button. This posts the page to the server and gets a new response, which refreshes the page, so it has nothing to do with the browser's cache. However, this can cause problems like a user ordering a product twice without realizing it. Because most users tend to click the Back button far more than the Refresh button, though, the Refresh button causes far fewer errors. That's why most web developers ignore this problem.

A page that checks timestamps to avoid the back-button problem

```
Partial Class Cart
    Inherits System.Web.UI.Page

    Private Cart As SortedList

    Protected Sub Page_Load(ByVal sender As Object, _
            ByVal e As System.EventArgs) Handles Me.Load
        If IsExpired() Then
            Response.Redirect("Expired.aspx")
        Else
            Me.SaveTimeStamps()
        End If
        Cart = GetCart()
        If Not IsPostBack Then
            Me.DisplayCart()
        End If
    End Sub

    Private Function IsExpired() As Boolean
        If Session("Cart_TimeStamp") Is Nothing Then
            Return False
        ElseIf ViewState("TimeStamp") Is Nothing Then
            Return False
        ElseIf ViewState("TimeStamp").ToString _
            = Session("Cart_TimeStamp").ToString Then
            Return False
        Else
            Return True
        End If
    End Function

    Private Sub SaveTimeStamps()
        Dim dtm As DateTime = Now
        ViewState.Add("TimeStamp", dtm)
        Session.Add("Cart_TimeStamp", dtm)
    End Sub
    .
    .
    .
End Class
```

Description

- One way to avoid back-button problems is to use timestamps. The page saves two copies of a timestamp obtained via the Now function: one in view state, the other in session state.

- The IsExpired function tests the view state and session state timestamps to make sure they are the same. If they aren't, the user has posted a page that has been retrieved from the browser's cache.

Note

- Some developers prefer to use random numbers rather than timestamps. Either technique will work.

Figure 21-14   How to use timestamps to avoid the back-button problem

Perspective

This chapter has presented three types of enhancements that you can add to an application once you've got the basic functions working right. In practice, most serious applications use both email and custom error pages to make an application more user friendly and less error prone.

In contrast, many serious applications ignore the back-button problem on the theory that the users should be smart enough to avoid that problem themselves. As a result, clicking on the Back button and re-posting a page will cause a problem on many e-commerce sites. That's why you may want to use the techniques in this chapter to handle that problem on your own web site.

Terms

Simple Mail Transfer Protocol (SMTP)
Post Office Protocol (POP)
Multipurpose Internet Message Extension (MIME)
mail client
mail server
attachment
UUEncode
Base64 encoding
back-button problem

22

How to use web parts to build portals

Portals are web pages that display modular content that can be customized by the user. In the past, developing a portal was a difficult proposition that involved writing a lot of code. But now, with ASP.NET 2.0, you only need to write a few lines of code to be able to develop a portal.

To make this possible, ASP.NET 2.0 provides a built-in portal framework that's conceptually similar to the framework that's used by Microsoft SharePoint. In addition, Visual Studio 2005 provides full support for building portals, and the .NET Framework exposes an API that can be used to work with portals.

An introduction to the portal framework

The topics that follow introduce you to the ASP.NET 2.0 portal framework that allows you to easily develop *portals*, which are web pages that provide modular content that can be customized by each user of the page. To start, you'll see five screens that illustrate some of the features for a portal that might be used by a salesperson employed by the company that runs the Halloween Store web site. Then, you'll learn how portal configurations are stored, and you'll learn how the ASP.NET portal framework compares with the Microsoft SharePoint portal framework. Finally, you'll learn about the types of controls that can be used as *web parts*, which are the controls that provide modular content that can be used by a portal.

A portal that uses web parts

Each portal page contains one or more web parts. In part 1 of figure 22-1, for example, the Sales Portal page contains three web parts: Order Calculator, Days to Halloween, and Product List. In the first screen, the user has pulled down the control menu for the Product List part and is about to minimize it. In the second screen, the Product List has been minimized. As a result, only its title bar is displayed. In addition, the user is about to click on a radio button to switch to another display mode that allows the user to move web parts.

A portal page that displays three web parts

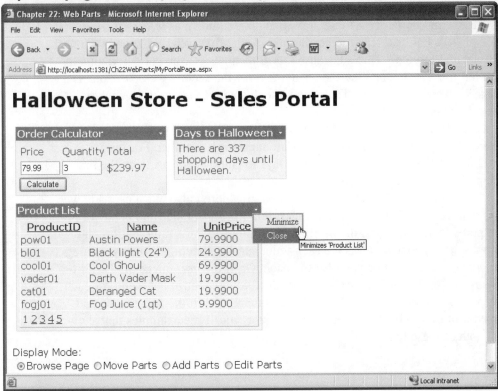

The same page after one web part has been minimized

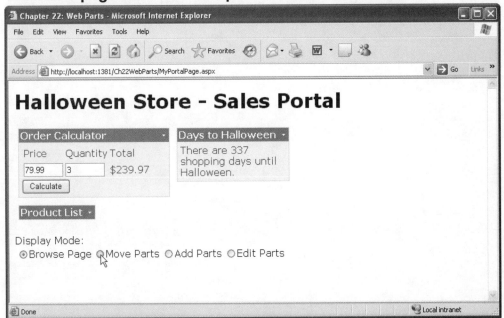

Figure 22-1   A page that uses web parts (part 1 of 3)

In part 2 of figure 22-1, the user has switched to the mode that allows the user to move web parts between different areas of the page. This causes the header text and borders for these areas, which are known as *web part zones*, to be displayed. For example, the header text for the first web part zone is "Zone 1 – Horizontal Layout." That's because this zone lays out web parts horizontally from left to right. In contrast, the header text for the second web part zone is "Zone 2 – Vertical Layout." That's because this zone lays out the web parts vertically from top to bottom.

Once the user has switched to the mode that allows the web parts to be moved, the user can drag a web part from one zone to another. For instance, in part 2 of this figure, the user drags the Days to Halloween part from the first web part zone to the second one.

Although this figure doesn't illustrate it, this portal also lets a user add web parts to a web part zone, and it lets a user edit the appearance and behavior of web parts. If, for example, the user clicks on the Add Parts radio button, the page displays a zone that lets the user add a part by selecting it from a catalog that contains all available parts for the page. Or, if the user clicks on the Edit Parts radio button, an Edit command is added to the control list menu for each web part. Then, the user can select this command to edit the appearance and behavior of this web part. Later in this chapter, you'll see examples that show how both of these features work.

The same page as a web part is being moved

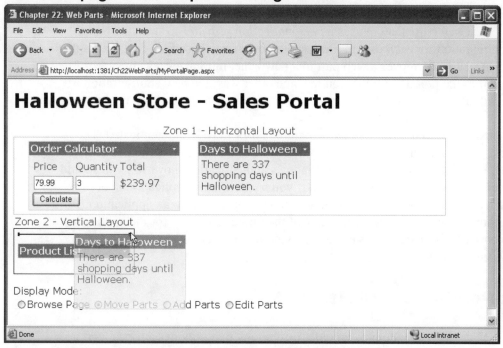

The same page after the move has been completed

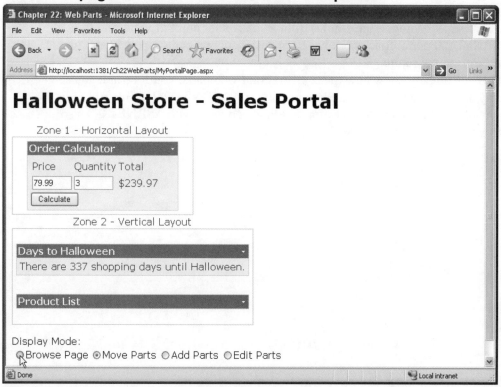

Figure 22-1   A page that uses web parts (part 2 of 3)

How user configurations are stored

The web parts feature uses a *personalization provider* to store the portal configuration for each user in the AspNetDb.mdf database file. That means that whenever a user moves a web part to a new zone, minimizes a web part, or modifies the portal configuration in some other way, the new configuration is saved in this database. That way, the customized page can be displayed the next time the user visits the site.

Note that to use the web parts feature, a user must be authenticated. The best way to authenticate a user is to use forms-based authentication as described in chapter 18. If you want to use Windows authentication, however, you should know that you'll run into a problem if you try to run the application under IIS. That's because, by default, IIS allows anonymous access to an application. Although you can change a property of the virtual directory for the application to correct this problem, it's easiest to avoid the problem by creating a file-system web site.

SharePoint and ASP.NET 2.0

Microsoft SharePoint is an older technology that provides a robust portal framework that can, among other things, be used to develop web parts. Although the ASP.NET 2.0 portal framework can also be used to develop web parts, web parts aren't interchangeable between these two technologies. However, these technologies are similar from a conceptual point of view, and the ASP.NET 2.0 portal framework has been designed so it can support SharePoint web parts in the future.

If you already know how to use SharePoint web parts, you'll be able to use many of the same skills for building portals with ASP.NET 2.0. Conversely, many of the skills that you learn for building web parts with ASP.NET 2.0 also apply to building web parts with SharePoint.

The same page after the minimized part has been restored

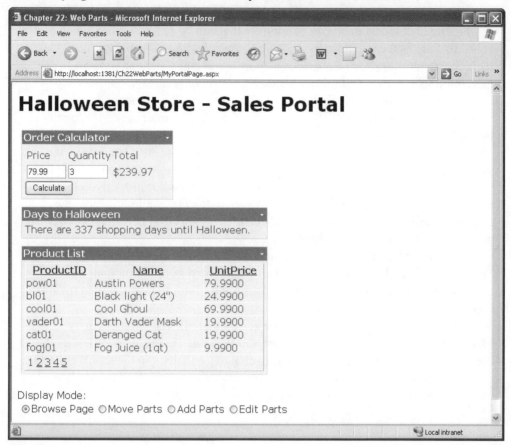

Description

- ASP.NET 2.0 comes with a built-in portal framework that allows you to easily develop *portals*, which are web pages that can be customized by users. To customize a portal, a user must be authenticated.

- A *web part* is a special type of control that can be displayed within a *web part zone*. Most portals let the user customize the appearance of the portal by minimizing, restoring, closing, and moving the web parts. In addition, most applications let the user add web parts to the page, and some applications let the user edit the properties of the web parts.

- The portal configuration for each user is stored in the AspNetDb.mdf database. To accomplish that, the web parts feature uses a *personalization provider*.

Figure 22-1   A page that uses web parts (part 3 of 3)

Types of controls that can be used as web parts

Figure 22-2 shows the types of controls that can be placed within a web part zone. To start, you can place any ASP.NET control within a web part zone. This includes standard ASP.NET controls such as Label and Calendar controls, it includes user controls, and it includes custom server controls. When you add one of these controls to a web part zone, the control will automatically be wrapped by the GenericWebPart class at runtime. This class allows the control to behave like a web part.

The advantage of this approach is that you can use the ASP.NET skills that you're already familiar with to quickly develop controls that can be used as web parts. The disadvantage is that the GenericWebPart class doesn't let you take advantage of several advanced features of web parts. For example, when you use the GenericWebPart class, you can't create a connection between two web parts and share data between them.

If you need to use any of the advanced features, you can develop custom WebPart controls that inherit the WebPart class. Keep in mind, though, that custom WebPart controls are significantly more difficult to develop than the user controls that are used in this chapter.

The WebPart hierarchy in this figure shows that all web parts begin by inheriting the Panel class. Then, the Part and WebPart classes provide additional members that can be used to work with web parts. Finally, the GenericWebPart class provides the functionality that's necessary to wrap ASP.NET controls so they can appear and behave as WebPart controls at runtime.

Types of controls that can be used as web parts

ASP.NET controls that can be placed in a web part zone

- Standard controls (such as the Label control in figure 22-3)
- User controls (such as the ProductList control in figure 22-4)
- Custom server controls

Custom WebPart controls

- Custom WebPart controls (such as the HalloweenCounter control in figure 22-10)

The WebPart hierarchy

```
Panel
    Part
        WebPart
            GenericWebPart
```

Description

- When you add an ASP.NET control such as a user control to a web part zone, the control is automatically wrapped by the GenericWebPart class. This class allows ASP.NET controls to behave like web parts.

- A custom WebPart control inherits the WebPart class. As a result, custom WebPart controls let you take advantage of several advanced web part features that aren't available for standard ASP.NET controls. However, custom WebPart controls are significantly more difficult to develop than user controls.

- You can learn how to develop user controls and custom server controls in chapters 24 and 25. In this chapter, then, you can just focus on how you use these controls as web parts.

Figure 22-2   Types of controls that can be used as web parts

How to use web parts

Now that you have a general idea of what web parts are and how they work, you're ready to learn how to use Visual Studio to create portals that use web parts. As you'll see in a moment, you only need to write a few lines of code to create a fully functional portal.

How to create a page that uses web parts

Figure 22-3 shows how to create a page that uses two web part zones and three web part controls. To start, you open the page in Design view, go to the WebParts group of the Toolbox, and drag a WebPartManager control onto the page. This control manages the web parts and zones, and each portal page must include one of these controls.

Once you've added a WebPartManager control to a page, you can add WebPartZone controls by dragging them from the Toolbox onto the page. To keep things simple, the page in this figure contains only two zones, but it's common to place several web part zones on a page. Often, these web part zones are added within a table. Then, you can add a web part zone to each cell of the table to give the user more flexibility for how the page can be organized.

Once you've added the WebPartZone controls to the page, you can add web parts to the web part zones. In this figure, for example, two Label controls have been added to the first web part zone, and one Label control has been added to the second web part zone. These controls are coded within the ZoneTemplate element of the WebPartZone controls. This template specifies the web parts that are displayed the first time a user accesses the portal. However, if the user closes or moves these web parts, the user's changes will be stored in the database, and the changes will be displayed the next time the user accesses the portal.

Any control that's placed within a WebPartZone control is automatically wrapped by the GenericWebPart class so it can behave like a web part. As a result, for the Label controls in this figure, you can set any attributes that are available to the GenericWebPart class. Of these attributes, the Title attribute is commonly used to set the title of a web part. This attribute is stored in the Part class, which is ultimately inherited by the GenericWebPart class.

A page that contains two web part zones and three web parts

The tags for the page

```
<h1>Halloween Store - Sales Portal</h1>

<asp:WebPartManager ID="WebPartManager1" runat="server">
</asp:WebPartManager>

<asp:WebPartZone ID="WebPartZone1" runat="server"
    LayoutOrientation="Horizontal"
    HeaderText="Web Part Zone 1 - Horizontal Layout">
    <ZoneTemplate>
        <asp:Label ID="Label1" runat="server" Title="Part 1 Title"
            Text="Part 1 Content"></asp:Label>
        <asp:Label ID="Label2" runat="server" Title="Part 2 Title"
            Text="Part 2 Content"></asp:Label>
    </ZoneTemplate>
</asp:WebPartZone><br />

<asp:WebPartZone ID="WebPartZone2" runat="server"
    HeaderText="Web Part Zone 2 - Vertical Layout">
    <ZoneTemplate>
        <asp:Label ID="Label3" runat="server" Title="Part 3 Title"
            Text="Part 3 Content"></asp:Label>
    </ZoneTemplate>
</asp:WebPartZone>
```

Figure 22-3   How to create a page that uses web parts (part 1 of 2)

If necessary, you can use the HeaderText attribute of a WebPartZone control to specify the header text for the web part zone. Then, this text will be displayed above the control in Design view, and it will be displayed above the control at runtime whenever the portal enters certain modes such as the mode that allows the user to move web parts between zones.

You may also want to set the LayoutOrientation attribute of a WebPartZone control to specify the layout orientation. In this figure, for example, the first web part zone specifies a horizontal orientation, so the web parts are displayed from left to right. In contrast, the second web part zone doesn't specify a layout orientation, so the default orientation is used to display the web parts vertically.

When you run a page like the one in this figure, the default features provide a lot of built-in functionality. For example, the control menu for each web part will contain Minimize and Close commands for any parts that haven't been minimized and Restore and Close commands for any parts that have been minimized. So, if you use the Minimize command to minimize a web part, you can use the Restore command to restore that web part. However, if you select the Close command, the web part will be removed from the page. In that case, there's no way for the user to add that part back to the page unless the page provides for it as described in figure 22-6.

The page when it's displayed in a browser

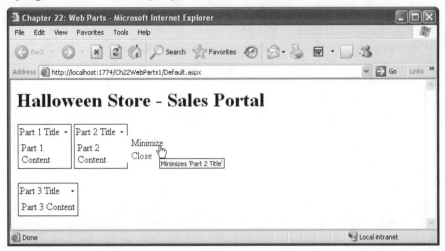

Description

- In the Toolbox, all of the controls for working with web parts are stored in the WebParts group.

- Each portal must have one (and only one) WebPartManager control. This control manages the web parts and zones on the page.

- Most portals have two or more WebPartZone controls that define the web part zones that are available on the page. These controls are often coded within a table that specifies the number of rows and columns to be used for the page.

- The ZoneTemplate element of a WebPartZone control specifies the web parts that are displayed the first time a user accesses the portal. When you add a control to a web part zone from Design view, the control is added within a ZoneTemplate element.

- The HeaderText attribute of a WebPartZone control specifies the header text that's used for the zone when it's displayed in Design view. This text is also displayed at runtime when the portal enters certain modes such as the mode that allows the user to move web parts between zones.

- The Title attribute can be added to any control in a web part zone. That's because each control added to a web part zone is automatically wrapped by the GenericWebPart class, which provides access to the Title attribute of the Part class. Because the controls aren't wrapped until runtime, however, the Title attribute isn't available from the Properties window or from the IntelliSense completion list.

Figure 22-3   How to create a page that uses web parts (part 2 of 2)

How to add a user control to a web part zone

Although figure 22-3 shows how to add a standard Label control to a web part zone, it's more common to add a user control to a web part zone as shown in figure 22-4. Then, this user control will automatically be wrapped by the GenericWebPart class so it behaves like a web part.

In chapter 24, you can learn how to develop user controls. To do that, you (1) add a user control (ascx file) to the project, (2) use the User Control Designer to design the control, and (3) use the Code Editor to write any code that's necessary to get the control to work.

In this figure, for example, a user control file named ProductList.ascx has been added to the project. This user control contains a SqlDataSource control that specifies the connection string and the Select statement needed to retrieve the data for the user control. In addition, it contains a GridView control that displays a list of the products that are retrieved by the SqlDataSource control.

The ProductList user control in Design view

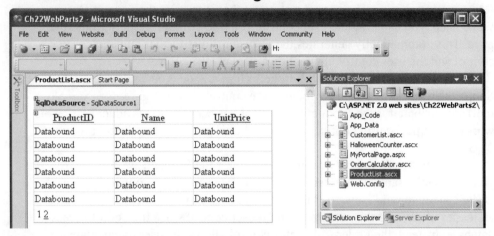

The ProductList control in Source view

```
<%@ Control Language="VB" AutoEventWireup="false" CodeFile="ProductList.ascx.vb"
            Inherits="ProductList" %>

<asp:SqlDataSource ID="SqlDataSource1" runat="server"
    ConnectionString="Data Source=localhost\SQLExpress;
        Initial Catalog=Halloween;Integrated Security=True"
    SelectCommand="SELECT ProductID, Name, UnitPrice
        FROM Products ORDER BY Name">
</asp:SqlDataSource>

<asp:GridView ID="GridView1" runat="server" DataSourceID="SqlDataSource1"
     AllowPaging="True" AllowSorting="True" AutoGenerateColumns="False"
     PageSize="6" Width="400px">
    <Columns>
        <asp:BoundField DataField="ProductID" HeaderText="ProductID"
            ReadOnly="True" SortExpression="ProductID" />
        <asp:BoundField DataField="Name" HeaderText="Name"
            SortExpression="Name" />
        <asp:BoundField DataField="UnitPrice" DataFormatString="{0:c}"
            HeaderText="UnitPrice" SortExpression="UnitPrice" />
    </Columns>
</asp:GridView>
```

Description

- In chapter 24, you can learn how to create a user control. In brief, you add a user control (ascx file) to the project, use the User Control Designer to design the control, and use the Code Editor to write any code that's necessary to get the control to work.

Figure 22-4   How to add a user control to a web part zone (part 1 of 2)

Once you've created a user control and added it to your project, you can add it to your portal page. The easiest way to do that is to view the page in Design view. Then, you can drag the user control from the Solution Explorer onto the page. This automatically generates the Register directive that registers the control and the user control element that displays the control.

Once you add the user control to the web part zone, you can switch to Source view and add a Title attribute to the control. In this figure, for example, the Title attribute for the ProductList control has been set to "Product List." This works the same for user controls as for the Label controls described in figure 22-3.

Although this figure only shows the code for the ProductList user control, you can use the same coding techniques to create other user controls such as the Order Calculator and Days to Halloween controls. In many ways, these controls are easier to develop than the ProductList user control since they don't access a database. Instead, the Order Calculator control allows the user to calculate a total based on quantity and price, and the Days to Halloween control calculates the number of days to Halloween and displays the result within a label.

A page that includes three user controls

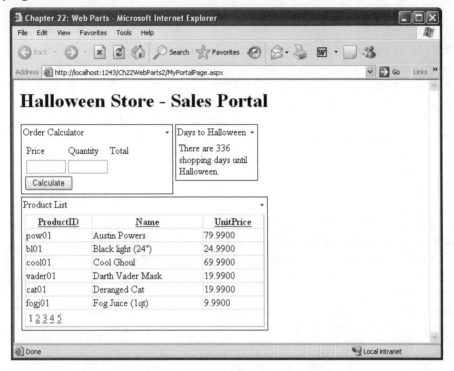

The code that registers a user control for a page

```
<%@ Register Src="ProductList.ascx" TagName="ProductList" TagPrefix="uc1" %>
```

The code that adds a user control to a web zone

```
<asp:WebPartZone ID="WebPartZone2" runat="server"
    HeaderText="Web Part Zone 2 - Vertical Layout">
    <ZoneTemplate>
        <uc1:ProductList ID="ProductList1" runat="server" Title="Product List">
        </uc1:ProductList>
    </ZoneTemplate>
</asp:WebPartZone>
```

Description

- In Design view, you can register a user control and add it to the page by dragging it from the Solution Explorer onto the page.

- In Source view, you can register a user control and add it to the page by coding the Register directive and by coding the element for the user control.

Figure 22-4 How to add a user control to a web part zone (part 2 of 2)

How to let the user move web parts between zones

By default, a page that contains web parts runs in *browse display mode*. In this mode, you can only minimize, restore, and close web parts. Then, if you want to let the user move web parts between zones, you must switch into *design display mode*. In this mode, which is shown in figure 22-5, the header text and borders appear for each web part zone, and the user can move web parts between zones by dragging them from one zone to another. In this figure, the user is moving the Days to Halloween web part from the first web part zone to the second web part zone.

To switch between display modes in the code-behind file for a page, you set the DisplayMode property of the WebPartManager class equal to one of the DisplayMode constants that are available from that class. In this figure, for example, the page includes a RadioButtonList control that lets the user choose between browse display mode and design display mode. If the user chooses the second option, the page enters design display mode so the user can move web parts between zones. Then, when the user is done moving web parts, the user can select the first option. This will cause the page to enter browse display mode, which is the optimal mode for browsing the data that's displayed on a page.

A page that lets the user move web parts between zones

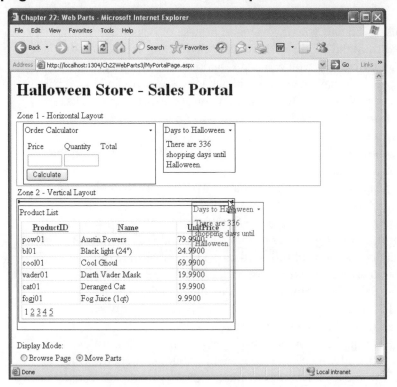

A radio button list that switches between display modes

```
<asp:RadioButtonList ID="rdoDisplayMode" runat="server" AutoPostBack="True"
    RepeatDirection="Horizontal">
        <asp:ListItem Selected="True">Browse Page</asp:ListItem>
        <asp:ListItem>Move Parts</asp:ListItem>
</asp:RadioButtonList>
```

The event procedure for the radio button list

```
Protected Sub rdoDisplayMode_SelectedIndexChanged(ByVal sender As Object, _
    ByVal e As System.EventArgs) _
    Handles rdoDisplayMode.SelectedIndexChanged
    If rdoDisplayMode.SelectedIndex = 0 Then
        WebPartManager1.DisplayMode = WebPartManager.BrowseDisplayMode
    ElseIf rdoDisplayMode.SelectedIndex = 1 Then
        WebPartManager1.DisplayMode = WebPartManager.DesignDisplayMode
    End If
End Sub
```

Description

- You can use the DisplayMode property of the WebPartManager class to switch between display modes. To do that, you can set this property equal to any of the constant values stored in the WebPartManager class such as BrowseDisplayMode and DesignDisplayMode.

Figure 22-5   How to let the user move web parts between zones

How to let the user add web parts to a zone

If a user closes a web part when working in browse or design display mode, the part is removed from the page and there's no way for the user to add the web part back to the page. However, you can add functionality to the page that lets the user add web parts that have been closed back to the page and add web parts that aren't on the page by default. To do this, you must perform three tasks.

First, you must provide a way for the user to switch to the *catalog display mode* that's shown in figure 22-6. To do that, you can extend the RadioButtonList control shown in figure 22-5 so it includes a third option that lets the user switch into catalog display mode.

Second, you must add a CatalogZone control to the page. To do that, you can drag the CatalogZone control from the Toolbox onto the page.

Third, you must add one or more of the CatalogPart controls within the CatalogZone control. In this figure, for example, the CatalogZone control contains a PageCatalogPart control followed by a DeclarativeCatalogPart control. The DeclarativeCatalogPart control includes a WebPartsTemplate element that declares any web parts that aren't on the default page but should also be available. In this example, the CustomerList part is the only part in this catalog, but you can include as many parts as you need.

When the page is running in browse display mode, the catalogs of available web parts that are defined by the CatalogZone and CatalogPart controls aren't displayed. However, if the user switches to catalog display mode, the catalog is displayed. In this figure, for example, the CatalogZone control is displayed in the bottom half of the page, starting with the heading (Catalog of Web Parts) that's provided by the HeaderText attribute.

After the heading, the CatalogZone control displays "Select the catalog you would like to browse" and a menu that lets you switch between the CatalogPart controls within the zone. In this figure, the choices are Page Catalog and Declarative Catalog, and the user has selected Page Catalog. This displays a list of all the web parts that were on the page by default, but were closed by the user (this list includes just the Product List part). In contrast, if the user selects Declarative Catalog, the list displays all of the web parts in that catalog. The number in parentheses after each menu item for the catalog zone indicates the number of items in each list (one each).

Under the catalog list, the CatalogZone control generates controls for adding a selected web part. Here, the user is using the drop-down list to specify the zone that the selected web part should be added to. Then, when the user clicks the Add button, the selected part is added to that zone.

By default, the CatalogZone control also displays a Close link in its header and a Close button next to the Add button. This provides the user with a way to close the CatalogZone control and exit catalog display mode. However, this also causes the display mode to get out of synch with the RadioButtonList control. As a result, the Visible attribute of the HeaderCloseVerb and CloseVerb elements has been used to hide these elements. (When working with web parts, the term *verb* is used to refer to the actions that are executed by the buttons, links, and menu items that are available from a web part.)

A page that lets the user add web parts to a zone

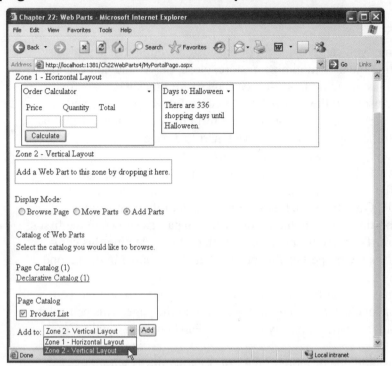

The asp tags for the catalog

```
<asp:CatalogZone ID="CatalogZone1" runat="server"
    HeaderText="Catalog of Web Parts">
    <ZoneTemplate>
        <asp:PageCatalogPart ID="PageCatalogPart1" runat="server" />
        <asp:DeclarativeCatalogPart ID="DeclarativeCatalogPart1" runat="server">
            <WebPartsTemplate>
                <ucl:CustomerList ID="CustomerList1" runat="server"
                    Title="Customer List"/>
            </WebPartsTemplate>
        </asp:DeclarativeCatalogPart>
    </ZoneTemplate>
    <HeaderCloseVerb Visible="False" />
    <CloseVerb Visible="False" />
</asp:CatalogZone>
```

The code that switches to catalog display mode

```
WebPartManager1.DisplayMode = WebPartManager.CatalogDisplayMode
```

Description

- To let the user add web parts to a page, you must (1) provide a way to switch to *catalog display mode*,
  (2) add a CatalogZone control to the page, and (3) place one or more of the CatalogPart controls
  within the CatalogZone control. (The CatalogPart controls are the PageCatalogPart,
  DeclarativeCatalogPart, and ImportCatalogPart controls.)

Figure 22-6   How to let the user add web parts to a zone

How to let the user edit the properties of a web part

Most of the time, you can provide all of the customization that's necessary for a portal by letting the user minimize, restore, close, move, and add web parts as described in the last three figures. However, there are times when you may also want to let the user edit the properties that control the appearance and behavior of a web part. To do this, you must perform three tasks that are similar to the three tasks for letting the user add a web part to a page.

First, you must provide a way for the user to switch to the *edit display mode* that's shown in figure 22-7. To do that, you can extend the RadioButtonList control shown in figure 22-5 so it includes a fourth option that lets the user switch to this mode. Once the switch has been made, an Edit command is included in the drop-down control menu for each web part as shown in the first screen in this figure. Then, the user can edit a web part by selecting this command, which displays the properties that can be edited, as shown in the second screen.

Second, you must add an EditorZone control to the page. To do that, you can drag the EditorZone control from the Toolbox onto the page. This control is a container control that works similarly to the WebPartZone and CatalogZone controls.

Third, you must add one or more of the EditorPart controls within the EditorZone control. In this figure, for example, the EditorZone control contains just one EditorPart control, the AppearanceEditorPart control. But you could add other EditorPart controls such as the BehaviorEditorPart, LayoutEditorPart, or PropertyGridEditorPart control.

By default, the EditorZone control displays a Close link in its header. This lets the user close the EditorZone control, which hides this control and any subordinate EditorPart controls, but doesn't exit edit display mode. As a result, the Edit command is still available from each of the web parts on the page.

A page that lets the user edit web parts

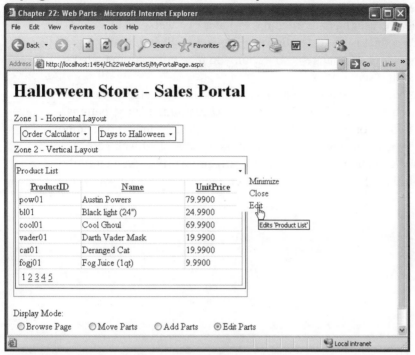

An editor zone for the Product List part

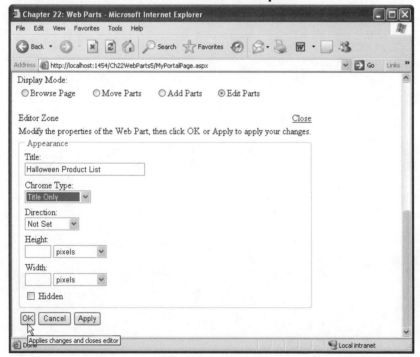

Figure 22-7   How to let the user edit the properties of a web part (part 1 of 2)

Although the EditorPart controls let the user modify the properties of a web part, most of these properties only provide for minor cosmetic changes. In this figure, for example, the user has modified the Product List web part by changing the title from "Product List" to "Halloween Product List" and by turning off the border. Since this type of change is so trivial, you may not want to bother with this type of editing support.

When working with web parts, the term *chrome* is used to refer to the non-content area of a web part such as the border, title bar, minimize/close buttons, and so on. In this figure, for example, the user can use the Chrome Type combo box to change the type of chrome that's used for the Product List web part. In the next figure, you'll see how you can use the PartChromeStyle element of the WebPartZone control to change the style of the chrome for each web part within a web part zone.

A page after the appearance of the product list part has been edited

The asp tags for the editor zone

```
<asp:EditorZone ID="EditorZone1" runat="server">
    <ZoneTemplate>
        <asp:AppearanceEditorPart ID="AppearanceEditorPart1" runat="server" />
    </ZoneTemplate>
</asp:EditorZone>
```

The code that switches to EditDisplayMode

```
WebPartManager1.DisplayMode = WebPartManager.EditDisplayMode
```

The EditorPart controls

```
AppearanceEditorPart
BehaviorEditorPart
LayoutEditorPart
PropertyGridEditorPart
```

Description

- To let the user edit the web parts on a page, you must (1) provide a way to switch to *edit display mode*, (2) add an EditorZone control to the page, and (3) place one or more of the EditorPart controls within the EditorZone control.

- When a page enters edit display mode, an Edit command becomes available from the drop-down control menu for each web part. When a user selects this command, the properties of the web part are displayed so the user can edit them.

- When working with web parts, the term *chrome* is used to refer to the non-content area of a web part such as the border, title bar, minimize/close buttons, and so on.

Figure 22-7   How to let the user edit the properties of a web part (part 2 of 2)

How to apply formatting to web parts

So far, the examples in this topic haven't included any formatting. That's why they appear as white controls with black borders. However, for a typical portal, each web part should be formatted in a way that's appropriate for that portal. Most of the time, that means applying formatting that gives the portal a professional and pleasing appearance as shown in figure 22-8.

The easiest way to apply formatting to all of the web parts in a web part zone is to use the AutoFormat feature. To do that, select the AutoFormat command from the web part zone's smart tag menu and then choose a scheme from the dialog box that's displayed. When you do, you'll be able to pick from a variety of schemes and the appropriate attributes and elements will be added to the WebPartZone tag. Then, if necessary, you can edit these tags. In this figure, for example, I applied the Professional scheme to the first web part zone. Then I modified the attributes and elements slightly to make them more appropriate for the application.

If you want to apply the same formatting to multiple web part zones, you can store the formatting for the WebPartZone control in a skin file within a theme as described in chapter 11. To get the formatting for a web part zone into a skin file, you can copy the tag for the WebPartZone control from the aspx file into the skin file. Then, you can delete any attributes or elements that aren't used to control the formatting of web parts such as the ID attribute, the LayoutOrientation attribute, the HeaderText attribute, and the ZoneTemplate element. When that's done, you end up with a WebPartZone element like the one in this figure that only contains the attributes and elements that apply formatting. Then, this formatting can automatically be applied to all web part zones on the page or to all web part zones in the entire application.

As you might expect, you can use similar techniques to apply formatting to the CatalogZone and EditorZone controls, which will change the appearance of the CatalogPart and EditorPart controls within these zones. For example, you can use the AutoFormat feature to automatically apply formatting to a catalog or editor zone. Although the tags that apply this type of formatting aren't shown in this figure, you can see them in the application for this chapter that you can download from our web site.

A page after formatting has been applied to the web parts

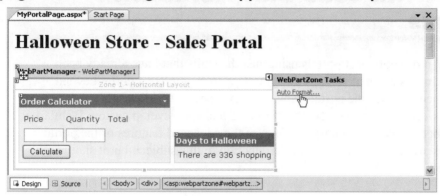

The asp tags that apply formatting to a web part zone

```
<asp:WebPartZone runat="server"
    BorderColor="#CCCCCC"
    Font-Names="Verdana"
    Padding="6">
    <PartChromeStyle
        BackColor="#F7F6F3"                 BorderColor="#E2DED6"
        Font-Names="Verdana"                ForeColor="White" />
    <MenuLabelHoverStyle                    ForeColor="#E2DED6" />
    <MenuLabelStyle                         ForeColor="White" />
    <MenuVerbHoverStyle
        BackColor="#F7F6F3"                 BorderColor="#CCCCCC"
        BorderStyle="Solid"                 BorderWidth="1px"
        ForeColor="#333333" />
    <HeaderStyle
        ForeColor="#CCCCCC"                 HorizontalAlign="Center" />
    <MenuVerbStyle
        BorderColor="#5D7B9D"               BorderStyle="Solid"
        BorderWidth="1px"                   ForeColor="White" />
    <PartStyle
        ForeColor="#333333" />
    <TitleBarVerbStyle
        Font-Underline="False"              ForeColor="White" />
    <MenuPopupStyle
        BackColor="#5D7B9D"                 BorderColor="#CCCCCC"
        BorderWidth="1px"/>
    <PartTitleStyle
        BackColor="#5D7B9D"                 Font-Bold="True"
        ForeColor="White" />
</asp:WebPartZone>
```

Description

- You can use the AutoFormat feature to automatically format all of the parts in a web part zone, catalog zone, or editor zone. To do that, select the AutoFormat command from the zone's smart tag menu and then choose a scheme from the dialog box that's displayed.

- You can use a theme to apply formatting to all of the zones on a page (or to the entire web site). For more information about themes, see chapter 11.

Figure 22-8   How to apply formatting to web parts

How to write code that works with web parts

You can develop most portals using just the skills that have already been presented in this chapter. However, if you need to customize a portal beyond what has been shown, the portal framework exposes an API that lets you write code that works with web parts. This API also lets you develop custom WebPart controls that can take advantage of some of the advanced features of the portal framework. What follows is just an introduction to this subject, but it should get you started.

Classes for working with web parts

Figure 22-9 shows some of the classes that are commonly used to work with web parts. Of these classes, the WebPartManager class is the one that's most commonly used to work with portals. As you learned earlier in this chapter, you can use this class to switch between display modes. In addition, you can use this class to access a collection of WebPart and WebPartZone objects that correspond to the web parts and zones available from the page. And you can use this class to respond to the events that occur on a web portal such as switching display modes or adding or removing a web part or zone.

In general, the classes described in this figure correspond with the controls that are available from the WebParts group in Visual Studio's Toolbox. Most of the time, you can use Visual Studio to set the properties for these controls at design time. Whenever necessary, though, you can write code that uses these classes to work with these controls at runtime. To do that, you often need to get a more complete description of the class for the control by looking it up in the documentation for the .NET Framework class library.

Classes for working with web parts

Class	Description
WebPartManager	Can be used to work with all of the zones and web parts on the page, to change display modes for the page, and to respond to events that are raised by the zones and web parts on the page.
WebPartZone	Can be used to modify the properties of a web part zone. Many of these properties control the appearance of the web parts within this zone.
CatalogZone	Can be used to modify the properties of a catalog zone. Many of these properties control the appearance of the catalog parts within this zone.
EditorZone	Can be used to modify the properties of an editor zone. Many of these properties control the appearance of the editor parts within this zone.
ConnectionsZone	Can be used to work with connections between custom WebPart controls.
WebPartVerb	Can be used to work with a *verb*, which is a button, link, or menu item in the title bar of a web part.
WebPart	Can be used to work with web parts at runtime, or it can be overridden to create a custom WebPart that takes advantage of the advanced features of the portal framework (see figure 22-10).
GenericWebPart	Can be used to work with user controls and custom server controls within a web part zone. Many of its properties are inherited from the Panel and Part classes. The ASP.NET 2.0 portal framework automatically uses this class whenever it needs to wrap web parts that are created from ASP.NET controls such as standard controls, user controls, and custom server controls.
PageCatalogPart	Can be used to work with the web parts in the page catalog, including parts that a user has closed.
DeclarativeCatalogPart	Can be used to work with the web parts in the declarative catalog.
ImportCatalogPart	Can be used to import a catalog of web parts.
BehaviorEditorPart	Can be used to apply behavior changes to an associated web part.
AppearanceEditorPart	Can be used to apply appearance changes to an associated web part.
LayoutEditorPart	Can be used to apply layout changes to web parts.
PropertyGridEditorPart	Can be used to change the property grid of a web part.

Description

- For a complete description of each class, including its constructors, properties, methods, and events, look up the class in the documentation for the .NET Framework class library.

Figure 22-9   Classes for working with web parts

How to develop and use a custom WebPart control

To show you how to develop a custom WebPart control, figure 22-10 presents the HalloweenCounter class. This class defines a custom WebPart control that displays a message that indicates the number of shopping days until Halloween. To start, this class inherits the WebPart class. Since this WebPart class inherits the Panel class and the Part class, the HalloweenCounter class inherits these classes too.

Next, the constructor for the HalloweenCounter class sets the Title property to "Days to Halloween." This is possible because the Title property is available from the Part class, which is inherited by the WebPart class and the HalloweenCounter class.

Then, the HalloweenCounter class overrides the RenderContents method of the WebControl class. Like all web server controls, the Panel class inherits the WebControl class. Because the Part class inherits the Panel class, the RenderContents method is available from the HalloweenCounter class. This method is called by the web page whenever the page needs to display the control. The code within this method calculates the number of shopping days to Halloween, creates a message that includes the results of this calculation, and uses the HtmlTextWriter object to write that message to the page.

Since the message doesn't include any HTML tags, this HalloweenCounter class causes plain text to be displayed as the content of the web part. However, you can include HTML tags in the message if you want to format it. Also, if you know how to render controls as HTML, you can create complex controls using this method. In this regard, the skills for developing a custom WebPart control are similar to the skills for developing a custom server control, as you will see in chapter 25.

The last two statements in this figure show how to register a custom WebPart control and place it on the page. First, you code a Register directive that specifies the namespace for the control and a prefix for the control's tag. Then, you code the tag for the control, using the prefix followed by the name of the class that defines the control. Once you do that, the page will display the custom WebPart control just as it would display a user control that was wrapped in the GenericWebPart class.

The code that defines the custom WebPart control

```
Imports Microsoft.VisualBasic

Namespace murach

    Public Class HalloweenCounter
        Inherits WebPart

        Public Sub New()
            Me.Title = "Days to Halloween"
        End Sub

        Protected Overrides Sub RenderContents _
                (ByVal writer As HtmlTextWriter)
            Dim dtmToday As Date = Date.Today
            Dim dtmHalloween As Date = New Date(Date.Today.Year, 10, 31)
            If dtmToday > dtmHalloween Then
                dtmHalloween = dtmHalloween.AddYears(1)
            End If

            Dim tsSpan As TimeSpan = dtmHalloween - dtmToday
            Dim sContent As String = "There are " & tsSpan.Days _
                & " shopping days until Halloween."

            writer.Write(sContent)
        End Sub

    End Class

End Namespace
```

Code that registers a custom WebPart control for a page

```
<%@ Register TagPrefix="mma" Namespace="murach" %>
```

Code that places a custom WebPart control on a page

```
<mma:HalloweenCounter ID="HalloweenCounter1" runat="server" />
```

Description

- To develop a custom WebPart control, code a class that inherits the WebPart class. Then, override the RenderContents method of the WebControl class to render the contents of the web part.
- To use a custom WebPart control, code a Register directive that specifies the namespace for the control and a prefix for the control's tag. Then, code the tag for the control using the prefix followed by the name of the class that defines the control.

Figure 22-10   How to develop and use a custom WebPart control

Perspective

Now that you've finished this chapter, you should have the skills you need to develop portals with web parts. In particular, you should be able to develop a portal that lets the user move web parts between zones, add web parts to a page, and even edit the properties of a web part. You should also be able to develop some custom WebPart controls.

Of course, there's more to developing portals than has been presented in this chapter. In chapters 24 and 25, for example, you can learn how to develop the user controls and custom server controls that you need for your portals. Also, if you want to do something like share data between web parts, you're going to have to dig into the documentation for the classes that let you work with web parts. For many portals, though, this chapter should provide all of the skills that you're going to need.

Terms

portal
web part
web part zone
personalization provider
browse display mode
design display mode
catalog display mode
verb
edit display mode
chrome

23

How to configure and deploy ASP.NET 2.0 applications

This chapter presents the ways that ASP.NET 2.0 applications can be configured and deployed, including the new features that help you do that. After this chapter presents two new tools for configuring an application, it presents three general ways to deploy an application. Then, it presents four specific deployment techniques.

How to configure an ASP.NET 2.0 application

As with previous versions of ASP.NET, the web.config file controls the configuration of an ASP.NET 2.0 application. As a result, you usually need to change this file not only during the development of an application but also when it is deployed. For example, you need to create a connection string to access the application's database when you develop the application. But if you move the database to another server when the application is deployed, you need to adjust the connection string to point to the correct database.

With previous versions of ASP.NET, you had to manually edit the web.config file whenever you wanted to change an application's configuration. But now, ASP.NET 2.0 provides two new GUI tools that let you change the settings in this file. These tools are presented in the topics that follow.

How to use the Web Site Administration Tool

As figure 23-1 shows, the Web Site Administration Tool is a web-based editor that lets you specify certain configuration options. This tool uses a tabbed interface that lets you switch between the home page and the pages that configure security, application, and provider settings.

The Security and Provider tabs let you configure the ASP.NET authentication and provider features. You can refer to chapter 18 for more information on using the Security tab. And if you ever create your own custom providers, you shouldn't have any trouble using the Provider tab.

The Application tab lets you create custom application settings that appear in the appSettings element of the web.config file and can be accessed in code by using the System.Configuration.ConfigurationManager class. In chapter 17, for example, you saw how to add a setting that specifies the path for an application. To enter this infomation using the Web Site Administration Tool, you can click the Create Application Settings link on the Application tab. Then, you can use the page that's displayed to enter the key and value for the setting.

The Application tab also lets you configure a web site to work with an SMTP server so it can send and receive email. You saw how this works in chapter 21. It also lets you configure debugging options for the site. And it lets you start and stop the site.

When you use the Web Site Administration Tool, you need to remember that it has two limitations. First, it doesn't let you set all of the configuration options that are available via the web.config file. For example, you can't use it to change the connection strings stored in the file or specify custom error pages. To edit these configuration settings, you must manually edit the web.config file or use the IIS Management Console that's described in the next figure.

The second limitation is that you can only use the Web Site Administration Tool from within Visual Studio 2005. As a result, you can't use this tool for a web site that's been deployed to a production server unless you can open the web site in Visual Studio 2005.

The home page of the Web Site Administration Tool

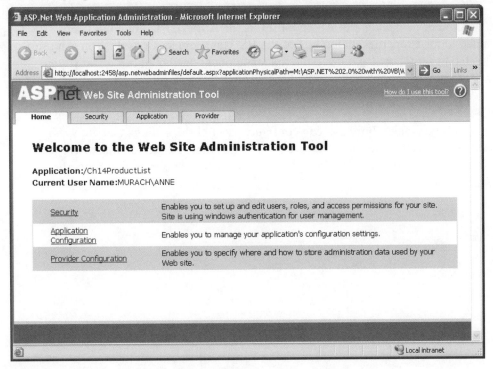

The four tabs of the Web Site Administration Tool

- **Home:** Displays the home page.
- **Security:** Lets you configure security features. For more information, see chapter 18.
- **Application:** Lets you create custom application settings, configure SMTP email support (see chapter 21), control debugging and tracing settings, and start or stop the application.
- **Provider:** Lets you configure providers for features such as membership and profiles.

Description

- The Web Site Administration Tool lets you configure certain web.config settings using a browser-based interface.
- To start the Web Site Administration Tool, open the project in Visual Studio 2005 and choose Website→ASP.NET Configuration.

Figure 23-1   How to use the Web Site Administration Tool to configure an ASP.NET 2.0 application

How to use the IIS Management Console

Another new feature of ASP.NET 2.0 is the ASP.NET tab that has been added to the Properties dialog box of the IIS Management Console. You can use this tab to set the ASP.NET version that an application should run under if you want to run a 1.x application with the ASP.NET 2.0 web server. In addition, this tab provides an Edit Configuration button that displays the dialog box in figure 23-2.

With this dialog box, you can configure most of the settings that are specified via the web.config file. However, to use this dialog box, you must have the authorization to run the IIS Management Console on the server that hosts the application.

The ASP.NET Configuration Settings dialog box

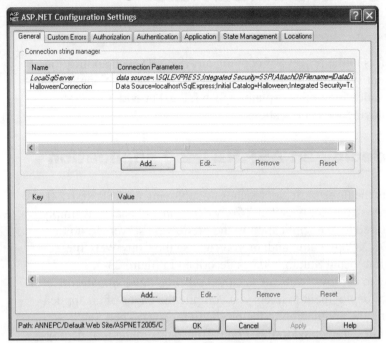

The seven tabs of the ASP.NET Configuration Settings dialog box

- **General:** Creates connection strings and application settings.
- **Custom Errors:** Configures custom error pages.
- **Authorization:** Creates authorization rules.
- **Authentication:** Specifies the authentication mode and configures membership and role providers.
- **Application:** Configures application settings such as the default master page and theme.
- **State Management:** Configures session state settings.
- **Locations:** Adds Location elements to the web.config file that let you apply configuration settings to specific parts of the application.

Description

- The IIS Management Console includes an ASP.NET Configuration Settings dialog box that lets you configure the web.config file for an ASP.NET application.
- The ASP.NET Configuration Settings dialog box lets you configure more web.config settings than the Web Site Administration Tool, but it only works for IIS-based applications.
- To open the ASP.NET Configuration Settings dialog box, open the IIS Management Console, right-click the web site, and choose Properties. Then, click the ASP.NET tab and click the Edit Configuration button.

Figure 23-2   How to use the IIS Management Console to configure an ASP.NET 2.0 application

How to deploy an ASP.NET 2.0 application

Deployment refers to the process of copying an ASP.NET web application from the development system to the production server on which the application will be run. As the following topics explain, ASP.NET 2.0 provides several alternatives for deploying web applications.

Three ways to deploy an ASP.NET 2.0 application

Figure 23-3 lists the three basic approaches to deploying an ASP.NET 2.0 application. The first is commonly called *XCopy deployment* because it simply copies the files required by the application to the production server. To do that, you can use the DOS XCopy command, or you can use the Copy Web Site command from within Visual Studio 2005 as described in figure 23-4.

The second way to deploy a web site is called *precompiled deployment*. This is a new type of deployment that lets you compile the pages of an application before deploying the application to the production server. Then, the precompiled assemblies are copied to the server. To use this method of deployment, you can use the Publish Web Site command from within Visual Studio 2005 as shown in figure 23-5. Or, you can use the aspnet_compiler command from a command prompt as shown in figure 23-6.

The third way to deploy a web application is to develop a Web Setup project that creates a Windows *Setup program* for the application. Then, you can run this Setup program on the production server to install the application. This approach is described in figures 23-7 and 23-8.

Which of these deployment alternatives is the best choice depends on the particular needs of each application. XCopy deployment is the easiest, and is often used during development to create copies of an application on different servers for testing purposes. For small applications, XCopy deployment may also be the best choice for production deployment.

Precompiled deployment has several advantages over XCopy deployment. For example, precompiled deployment provides better performance for the first users that access the site. In addition, it provides increased security because you don't have to copy the application's source files to the server.

For applications that are deployed to one or just a few servers, precompiled deployment is usually the best choice. However, if you're distributing an application to many different servers, you should consider creating a Setup program for the application. Although creating this program can involve considerable work, the effort will be repaid each time you use the program to install the application.

XCopy deployment

- To manually copy the files of an ASP.NET web site to a server, you can use the XCopy command from a command prompt. Then, you can use the IIS Management Console to create a virtual directory that's mapped to the directory that you copied the web site to.

- To automate the deployment, you can create a batch file for the XCopy command. Then, you can run the batch file any time you make changes to the application and want to deploy the updated code.

- You can also do XCopy deployment from Visual Studio 2005 by using the Copy Web Site command (see figure 23-4).

Precompiled deployment

- Deploys precompiled assemblies to the specified server.

- Lets you deploy the web site with or without the source files.

- Can be done from within Visual Studio using the Publish Web Site command (see figure 23-5) or from a command prompt using the aspnet_compiler command (see figure 23-6).

Setup program deployment

- Uses a Web Setup project to build a Windows Setup program that can be run to deploy a web application to a server (see figures 23-7 and 23-8).

- Useful if you want to distribute a web application to multiple servers.

- Can be used to deploy precompiled assemblies and can be configured to include or omit the source files.

- An application that's installed by a Setup program can be removed by using the Add or Remove Programs dialog box that can be accessed from the Control Panel.

Description

- There are three general methods for deploying ASP.NET 2.0 applications: *XCopy deployment*, *precompiled deployment*, and *Setup program* deployment.

- The method you should use for deployment depends on how often the application will need to be deployed and whether you want to include the source code with the deployed application.

Figure 23-3   Three ways to deploy an ASP.NET 2.0 application

How to use the Copy Web Site command for XCopy deployment

Although previous versions of Visual Studio have provided a Copy Project command, figure 23-4 shows that this command has been replaced in Visual Studio 2005 with the more powerful Copy Web Site command. This command lets you copy a web site to a file system, local IIS, FTP, or remote IIS web site. In addition, it lets you copy all of the files in the web site or just selected files, and you can use it to synchronize web sites so that both sites have the most recently updated versions of each file.

To use this command, open the web site you want to copy and start the command to display the dialog box shown in this figure. Here, the Source Web site section lists the files in the current web site. Next, click the Connect button to display an Open Web Site dialog box that lets you pick the location you want to copy the web site to. If you're copying to a local or remote IIS system, you can also use this dialog box to create a virtual directory on the server if the virtual directory doesn't already exist.

Once you select the remote web site, its files will appear in the Remote Web site section of the dialog box. You can then select the files you want to copy in the Source Web Site list and click the right-arrow button that appears between the lists to copy the files from the source web site to the remote web site. You can use the other buttons to copy files from the remote web site to the source web site, to synchronize files in the web sites, or to stop a lengthy copy operation.

The Copy Web Site dialog box

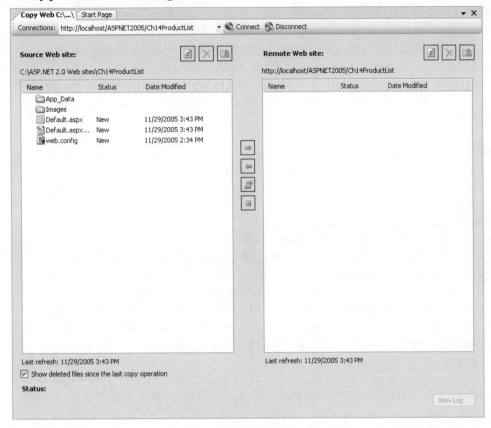

How to use the Copy Web Site command

1. In Visual Studio, open the web site you want to deploy and choose the Website→Copy Web Site command.
2. Click the Connect button to display an Open Web Site dialog box that lets you choose the destination you want to copy the web site to.
3. Select the files you want to copy. (Press Ctrl+A to select all of the site's files.)
4. Click the → button to copy the files from the source web site to the remote web site.

Description

*   You can use the Copy Web Site command to deploy an ASP.NET 2.0 application with XCopy deployment.

Figure 23-4   How to use the Copy Web Site command for XCopy deployment

How to use the Publish Web Site command for precompiled deployment

The new Publish Web Site command that's available with Visual Studio 2005 lets you precompile an ASP.NET 2.0 application and copy the precompiled assemblies to a target server. This is the easiest way to use the new precompiled deployment feature, and figure 23-5 shows how to use this command.

As this figure indicates, there are three main advantages to using precompiled deployment. First, because all of the pages are compiled before the web site is deployed to the server, this avoids the delays that can be encountered by the first visitors to the web site. In contrast, when precompiled deployment isn't used, each page is compiled by the ASP.NET runtime the first time the page is accessed by a user. As a result, the first user to retrieve each page will encounter a delay while the page is compiled.

A second advantage is that any compiler errors will be found before the application is deployed. Although unlikely, it's possible for pages in a production web site to become out of sync when the application is deployed. For example, a supporting class might be accidentally omitted. Then, when a page that uses that class is first accessed by a user, a compiler error will occur. By precompiling the entire application, though, you can eliminate the chance of users encountering these errors.

A third advantage is that you can deploy a precompiled application without the source files. This can be useful for two main reasons. First, it avoids the security risk that's inherent when you place your application's source code on the production server because there's always the possibility that a hacker might exploit a vulnerability in IIS and access your code. Second, if you develop a commercial application and don't want your customers to be able to access your source code, this makes that possible.

To omit the source code from a precompiled application, you uncheck the Allow This Precompiled Site to be Updateable box. Then, the source files won't be copied to the production server. Instead, dummy files with the same names as the source files will be copied to the server. If you open one of these files, you'll find that it contains a single line with the following text:

```
This is a marker file generated by the precompilation tool,
and should not be deleted!
```

Although these dummy files are required for the application to work, their contents are ignored by the ASP.NET runtime.

The Publish Web Site dialog box

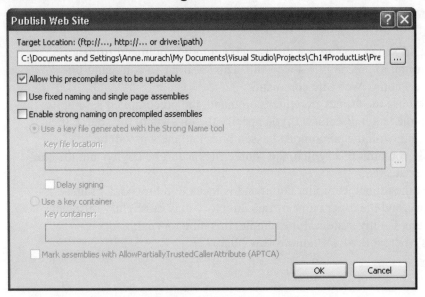

Advantages of precompiling a web site

- Avoids delays caused by compiling web pages when they are first accessed by a user.
- Finds compile errors before the site is deployed.
- Can copy just the executable files and not the source files to the server.

Description

- The Build→Publish *web site* command compiles all of the files that make up an ASP.NET 2.0 application, then deploys the compiled assemblies to the server you specify.
- If you check the Allow This Precompiled Site To Be Updateable box, the source files are deployed to the server along with the executable files. If you leave this box unchecked, the source files aren't copied to the server.

Figure 23-5   How to use the Publish Web Site command for precompiled deployment

How to use the aspnet_compiler command for precompiled deployment

Figure 23-6 shows how to use the aspnet_compiler command from a command prompt to precompile a web site. This is simply a command-line version of the Publish Web Site command.

When you use the aspnet_compiler command, the precompiled assemblies are copied to the target directory. If you specify the –u switch, the source files are copied along with the precompiled assemblies and the site will be updateable. If you omit this switch, the source files won't be copied and the site will not be updateable.

Note that the aspnet_compiler command is located in the .NET Framework directory, and the exact name of this directory may be slightly different on your system. On my system, for example, this directory is C:\Windows\Microsoft.NET\Framework\v2.0.50727.

The syntax of the aspnet_compiler command

```
aspnet_compiler -v virtual-directory [-u] [-d] [-f] [target-directory]
```

Switches

Switch	Description
-v	Precedes the name of the virtual directory of the existing web site to be precompiled.
-u	The precompiled web site will be updateable.
-d	Debug information will be included in the compiled assemblies.
-f	Overwrites the target directory if it already exists.

Examples

Precompiles an existing web site

```
aspnet_compiler -v Ch05ProductList c:\Deploy\Ch05ProductList
```

Precompiles a web site in place

```
aspnet_compiler -v Ch05ProductList
```

Creates an updateable precompiled web site with debugging info

```
aspnet_compiler -v Ch05ProductList -u -d c:\Deploy\Ch05ProductList
```

Description

- You can use the aspnet_compiler command to precompile a web site from a command prompt.
- If you specify a target directory, the precompiled web site is stored in the directory you specify. If you don't specify a target directory, the web site is precompiled in place.
- If the target directory isn't the final destination for an application, you can use XCopy deployment to move the precompiled web site to that destination.

Note

- The aspnet_compiler command is located in the .NET Framework directory, which is %systemroot%\Microsoft.NET\Framework\v2.0.xxxxx, where *xxxxx* is the five-digit build number. This location may vary depending on the release of ASP.NET 2.0 that you're using.

Figure 23-6   How to use the aspnet_compiler command for precompiled deployment

How to create a Web Setup project

Another way to deploy a web application is to develop a *Web Setup project* that creates a standard Windows *Setup program* that you can use to install the web application on an IIS server. As figure 23-7 shows, you start by adding a Web Setup project to an existing web site. Then, you configure the Web Setup project so it installs the files required by the web application. You can also use the setup editors to configure many custom options that control how the application will be installed.

You can use the File System Editor shown in this figure to add files and folders to the setup project. To add a Readme file, for example, you can right-click the Web Application Folder in the left pane of the File System Editor and then select Add→File. Note that the Web Application Folder represents the virtual directory where the web application will be installed, and it has properties that define that virtual directory. The two properties you're most likely to change are VirtualDirectory, which specifies the name of the virtual directory, and DefaultDocument, which specifies the page that's displayed by default.

You can use the Registry Editor to specify the keys and values that should be added to the registry on the target computer. And you can use the File Types Editor to establish a file association between a file extension and an application on the target computer. Since most web applications don't need to adjust registry settings or create file type associations, you shouldn't need either of these editors. However, the other three editors can be useful.

The User Interface Editor lets you customize the dialog boxes that are displayed when you run the Setup program to install a web application. For example, you can change the BannerBitMap property of any dialog box to display your company's logo in that dialog box. This editor also lets you add your own dialog boxes to those that are displayed by the Setup program.

The Custom Actions Editor lets you add actions to those that are performed by the Setup program. For example, you can use a custom action to create a SQL Server database when the application is installed. Before you can add a custom action to a Setup project, though, you must first develop a batch file, a script, or an executable program that implements the action.

Finally, the Launch Conditions Editor lets you set conditions that must be met before the application can be installed. For example, you can use a launch condition to check the operating system version or to see if a particular file exists on the target system. If the condition isn't met, the Setup program aborts the installation.

In addition to using the setup editors, you can set properties of the setup project. Some of those properties provide support information and are displayed in the Support Info dialog box. The user can display this information by opening Add or Remove Programs in the Control Panel, selecting the application, and clicking the Click Here for Support Information link for the application. Other properties provide additional information about the application, such as the icon that's displayed for the application in the Add or Remove Programs dialog box and the product name that's displayed by the Setup program and in the Add or Remove Programs dialog box.

A web setup project with the File System Editor displayed

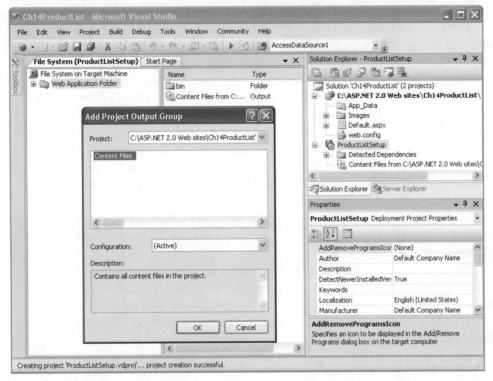

How to create a Setup project

- Choose the File→Add→New Project command to display the Add New Project dialog box. Then, choose Setup and Deployment in the Other Project Types list, select Web Setup Project as the template, enter a name for the Web Setup project, and click OK.

- In the Solution Explorer, right-click the Web Setup project and choose the Add→Project Output command to display the Add Project Output Group dialog box. Then, click OK to add the content files from your web site to the Web Setup project.

- Use the buttons that are displayed at the top of the Solution Explorer when the Web Setup project is selected to access setup editors that let you customize various aspects of the Web Setup project.

Description

- A *Web Setup project* creates a standard Windows *Setup program* that installs the web application on an IIS server. To create a Web Setup project, add a Web Setup project to the web site you want to deploy and then configure it using the setup editors.

- You can set project properties that provide support and other information for the application. You can also set properties that provide information about the virtual directory where the application will be installed, which is represented by the Web Application Folder in the File System Editor shown above.

Figure 23-7   How to create a Web Setup project

How to create and use a Setup program

Once you've configured the Web Setup project, you can create the Setup program and install the application as described in figure 23-8. To start, you should choose whether you want to create a debug or release version of the application. Because the debug version contains symbolic debugging information that you don't typically need in a production application, and because this version isn't optimized, you'll usually create a release version. On the other hand, you may want to create a debug version during testing. To determine which version is created, you can use the Configuration Manager.

Next, you build the Setup project. This creates the setup files (Setup.exe and Setup.msi) in the Debug or Release folder of the Web Setup project, depending on whether a debug or release version is created. Then, in most cases, you'll copy these files to a network server or burn them to a CD or DVD. Finally, you can install the application by running the Setup.exe program from the server that will host the application.

Note that the Setup program itself is a standard Windows application, not a web application. As a result, the Setup.exe and Setup.msi files aren't found in the same directory as the web application. Instead, you'll find these files in the project directory for the Web Setup project, which you can find under My Documents\Visual Studio 2005\Projects by default.

When you run a Setup program to install the web application on the host server, it steps you through the installation process. In this figure, for example, you can see the screen for one of the steps of a typical Setup program. Here, the application will be deployed to the default web site in a virtual directory named HalloweenProductList.

The Select Installation Address step of a typical Setup program

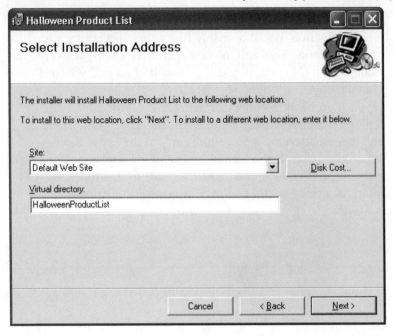

Description

- To create a setup program, right-click the setup project in the Solution Explorer and then use the Build command. When you do, Visual Studio creates files named Setup.exe and Setup.msi. Setup.exe is the file you will run to install the application, and Setup.msi contains all of the files to be installed.

- The Setup.exe and Setup.msi files are stored in the Web Setup project's Debug or Release folder, depending on whether Visual Studio is configured to create a debug or release version of the setup project. In most cases, you'll want to create a release version because it's fully optimized and contains no debugging information.

- To change the version of the setup program that Visual Studio creates, use the Build➔Configuration Manager command. Then, use the Configuration drop-down list for the web setup project to select the version you want to create.

- To install the web application, copy the Setup.exe and Setup.msi files to a network server or burn them to a CD or DVD. Then, run the Setup program on the server that will host the application.

Figure 23-8   How to create and use a Setup program

Perspective

As you develop a web application, you'll probably find yourself working with both the new Web Site Administration Tool and the new ASP.NET Configuration dialog box of the IIS Management Console. In addition, you'll often find yourself editing the web.config file directly.

As for deployment, you'll probably spend a surprising amount of time developing procedures for deploying even relatively small applications. So for a large application, I recommend that you develop a procedure early in the application's development cycle. Then, you can use this procedure to install the application on multiple servers during testing, and you can use that experience to fine-tune the procedure as you go along. As a side benefit, you may discover installation issues that affect the application's design.

Terms

deployment
XCopy deployment
precompiled deployment
Web Setup project
Setup program

Section 5

Developing reusable code

This section consists of three chapters that show you three different ways to develop reusable code. In chapter 24, you'll learn how to create and use user controls. User controls are easy to develop and are typically reused within a single web application. In chapter 25, you'll learn how to create and use custom server controls. Custom server controls are more difficult to develop and are typically reused within multiple web applications. Finally, in chapter 26, you'll be introduced to web services. Web services allow you to write methods that can be used by any web application, even by web applications that are running under a different web server such as Apache. Web services can also be used by Windows applications.

If you're working in a large development shop, you may never need to develop user controls, custom server controls, or web services. That's because senior developers are usually given the responsibility for developing controls and services that are used across applications. In that case, though, you still need to know how to use these controls and services. And to do that, it never hurts to know what's going on behind the scenes.

24

How to develop user controls

In this chapter, you'll learn how to develop user controls and use them in the web forms you develop. As you'll see, user controls make it possible to group multiple elements into a single user control. Then, instead of recreating these elements on each page that needs them, you can include the user control. Later, if you modify the user control, the changes will be reflected on all pages that contain the user control.

An introduction to user controls

A *user control* is a special type of ASP.NET page that can be added to other pages. In figure 24-1, for example, you can see a web page that contains three user controls, along with a procedure for creating and using user controls.

A web page that contains three user controls

Figure 24-1 presents a new page of the Halloween Store application called the Featured Products page. This page uses three user controls. The first two controls are ProductDisplay controls that contain information about a product. In addition to this information, these controls also include an Add to Cart button that adds the product to the cart and a View Cart button that lets the user view the cart. The third control is a DaysUntil control that displays a message that includes the number of days until Halloween.

As you decide what to include in each user control, keep in mind that the major benefit of user controls is that they are reusable. That means that you want to design a user control so it can be used in two or more places within a web site. For example, the ProductDisplay control is used twice on the Featured Products page. Although it's not shown here, it's also used on the Order page. Similarly, the DaysUntil control could be used on almost any page of the Halloween Store web site.

If you need to, you can change all the pages that contain a user control by changing the user control. In contrast, if you don't use a user control, you have to change each page separately.

A procedure for creating and using user controls

Figure 24-1 also presents a procedure for creating and using user controls. To start, you add a new user control to the web site. Then, you can use the User Control Designer that's displayed to design the control. As you'll see, this designer works much like the Web Forms Designer you use to design web forms.

Next, you add any code that's necessary to implement the control. For instance, the code for the DaysUntil control in this figure must create the message that's displayed. This code is added to the code-behind file for the user control. This works the same as adding code to the code-behind file for a form.

After you create a user control, you can add it to any form in the project. Then, if necessary, you can set its properties, and you can add code for working with the control to the form.

A Featured Products page that contains three user controls

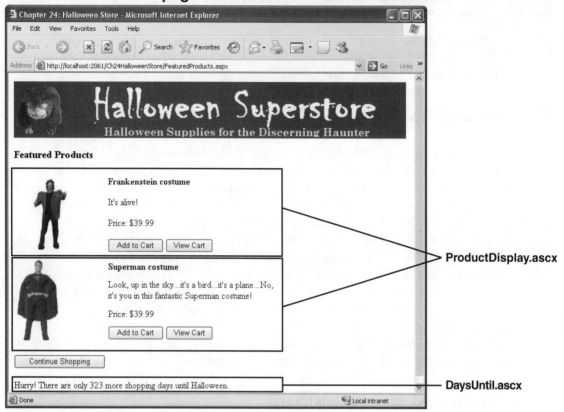

ProductDisplay.ascx

DaysUntil.ascx

Concepts

- A *user control* is a special type of ASP.NET web page that has been converted to a control. A user control is stored in a separate file so that it can be added to any form in a project.

- User controls are typically used to develop page elements that can be used in multiple places within a web site.

- Like an ASP.NET web page, a user control can handle Page events such as the Load event. You code the procedures for handling those events in the code-behind file for the control.

A procedure for creating and using user controls

1. Add a new user control to the project.
2. Design the user control using the User Control Designer.
3. Add the code to implement the control using the Code Editor.
4. Add the control to any form in the project.
5. If necessary, set any properties of the user control using the Properties window.
6. If necessary, add code to the form that contains the user control using the Code Editor.

Figure 24-1   An introduction to user controls

How to create user controls

Now that you know the basic procedure for creating user controls, the topics that follow present the details. As you'll see, the techniques you use are similar to the techniques you use to create a web form.

How to add a user control to a project

To add a user control to a project, you use the Website→Add New Item command to display the Add New Item dialog box. Then, you select the Web User Control template and enter a name for the control.

After you create a user control, it will appear in the Solution Explorer as shown in figure 24-2. The user control shown here is the DaysUntilHalloween control, which is a simplified version of the DaysUntil control you saw in the previous figure. Note that the file extension for a user control is *ascx*.

This figure also shows the code in the ascx file that Visual Studio generated for the DaysUntilHalloween control. This code begins with a Control directive that's similar to the Page directive for a web form. In particular, it includes a CodeFile attribute that associates the control with its code-behind file. In addition, it includes an Inherits attribute that provides the name of the class in the code-behind file that the control will inherit at runtime.

How to design a user control

After you add a user control to a project, it appears in the *User Control Designer* shown in figure 24-2. Then, you can add ASP.NET controls to the control by dragging them from the Toolbox. In this figure, for example, I added a label to the user control. Then, I set the ID property of the label to lblDaysUntilHalloween, and I set the Text property of the label so it contains some text that approximates what the control will look like at runtime.

You can also add HTML elements to a control by typing the appropriate tags directly into Source view. Note, however, that a user control shouldn't contain a Body or Form element. That's because the control will be added to a form, which already contains these elements.

A user control displayed by the User Control Designer

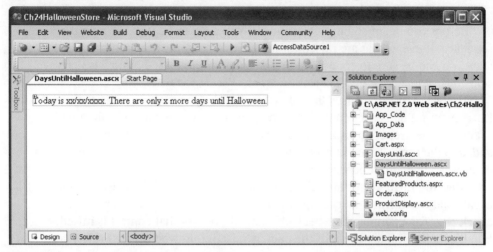

The ascx code for the user control

```
<%@ Control Language="VB" AutoEventWireup="false"
CodeFile="DaysUntilHalloween.ascx.vb" Inherits="DaysUntilHalloween" %>

<asp:Label ID="lblDaysUntilHalloween" runat="server">
    Today is xx/xx/xxxx. There are only x more days until Halloween.
</asp:Label>
```

Description

- To add a user control to a project, use the Website→Add New Item command to display the Add New Item dialog box. Then, use the Web User Control template to create a user control with the name you specify.

- When you add a user control, it will appear in the Solution Explorer with an extension of *ascx*.

- You can use the *User Control Designer* to add ASP.NET controls and HTML elements to the control. A user control should not include a Body or a Form element.

- The ascx code for a user control begins with a Control directive that's generated by Visual Studio when you create the user control. This directive includes Language, AutoEventWireup, CodeFile, and Inherits attributes just as the Page directive of a page does.

Figure 24-2   How to design a user control

How to code a user control

Before you begin coding user controls, you need to be familiar with the sequence of events that are raised for a page that contains user controls. That way, you can be sure to code the user control appropriately. Figure 24-3 presents this sequence of events.

To start, ASP.NET raises the Load event of the page. Then, it raises the Load event for each user control that the page contains. By default, the Load events for the user controls are raised in the order in which the controls are added to the form. To avoid problems, however, you should code your user controls so they don't depend on other user controls.

After the Load events are raised and processed, ASP.NET raises the control events that result from the user interacting with the page. If the user selects a check box, for example, the CheckedChanged event of that control is raised. Finally, the PreRender event of the page is raised, followed by the PreRender event of each user control.

This figure also presents the code for the DaysUntilHalloween user control. The first thing you should notice here is that the class that defines the control inherits the System.Web.UI.UserControl class. Because this class provides many of the same properties, methods, and events as the System.Web.UI.Page class, the code you use to implement a user control is similar to the code you would use to implement the same function in a web form. For example, you can use the Load event to execute code each time the control is loaded.

The UserControl class also provides many of the same properties as the Page class. For example, you can use the Request and Response properties to work with the HttpRequest and HttpResponse objects, and you can use the Session property to work with the HttpSessionState object. You can also use the IsPostBack property to determine whether the page that contains the user control is being displayed for the first time or if it's being posted back to the server. This is illustrated in the procedure for the Load event shown here. As you can see, the code in this procedure is executed only if the page is being displayed for the first time. Then, the label that the user control contains is formatted so that it displays the current date and the number of days until Halloween.

In addition to the properties, methods, and events a user control inherits from the UserControl class, you can add your own properties, methods, and events to a user control. Then, you can access those properties, methods, and events from the page that contains the control. You'll learn how to expose properties, methods, and events in the next figure, and you learn how to work with those properties, methods, and events later in this chapter.

The sequence of events that are raised for a page with user controls

1. The Load event for the page.
2. The Load event for each user control.
3. Control events caused by user interaction with the page.
4. The PreRender event for the page.
5. The PreRender event for each user control.

The Visual Basic code for the DaysUntilHalloween user control

```
Partial Class DaysUntilHalloween
    Inherits System.Web.UI.UserControl

    Protected Sub Page_Load(ByVal sender As Object, _
            ByVal e As System.EventArgs) Handles Me.Load
        If Not IsPostBack Then
            lblDaysUntilHalloween.Text = "Today is " & DateTime.Today
            lblDaysUntilHalloween.Text &= ". There are only "
            lblDaysUntilHalloween.Text &= Me.DaysUntilHalloween
            lblDaysUntilHalloween.Text &= " more shopping days until Halloween."
        End If
    End Sub

    Private Function DaysUntilHalloween() As Integer
        Dim dtmHalloween As Date = New DateTime(DateTime.Today.Year, 10, 31)
        If DateTime.Today > dtmHalloween Then
            dtmHalloween = dtmHalloween.AddYears(1)
        End If
        Dim tsTimeUntil As TimeSpan = dtmHalloween - DateTime.Today
        Return tsTimeUntil.Days
    End Function

End Class
```

Description

- You can use the Code Editor to add code to the code-behind file that's generated for a user control. The code-behind file should only contain code that's directly related to the user control. It shouldn't contain code that depends on code in other controls.

- You can define properties and methods within a user control and then access them from the page that contains the control. You can also define and raise events within a user control and then respond to them from the page that contains the control. See figures 24-4 and 24-7 for details.

- The class for a user control inherits the System.Web.UI.UserControl class. This class includes many of the same properties as a page, including IsPostBack, Request, Response, Server, and Session. This class also contains a Page property that refers to the Page object that contains the control.

Figure 24-3   How to code a user control

How to expose properties, methods, and events

Figure 24-4 presents the Visual Basic code for the DaysUntil user control that you saw in figure 24-1. This control exposes four properties. The first two properties let the developer change the text that's displayed before and after the number of days until a specified date. And the second two properties let the developer specify the date by setting the month and the day. As a result, you could display a message that indicates the number of days until Christmas or any other day of the year. This makes the control more flexible and increases the chance that it will be reused.

The values of the four properties are stored in the private variables that are declared at the beginning of the class. Notice that these variables are assigned default values that are used if the developer doesn't set the corresponding properties. As a result, this control works similarly to the DaysUntilHalloween control by default.

After the variable declarations is the code that declares the four public properties. Each property begins with a *designer attribute* that's coded in angle brackets. This attribute determines how the property will be displayed in the Web Forms Designer. In this figure, all four properties include a Category attribute that specifies the category in the Properties window where the property will appear. Here, all four properties will be displayed in the Appearance category.

To use designer attributes like this, a user control must import the System.ComponentModel namespace as shown here. Then, the control can use any of the attributes defined by this namespace. Since you're more likely to use attributes like this with custom server controls, you can learn more about them in the next chapter. Note, however, that these attributes don't always work the same way for user controls as they do for custom server controls.

The Visual Basic code for the DaysUntil control   **Page 1**

```vb
Imports System.ComponentModel

Partial Class DaysUntil
    Inherits System.Web.UI.UserControl

    Dim sTextBefore As String = "There are only"
    Dim sTextAfter As String = "days until Halloween"
    Dim iMonth As Integer = 10
    Dim iDay As Integer = 31

    <Category("Appearance")> _
    Property TextBefore() As String
        Get
            Return sTextBefore
        End Get
        Set(ByVal Value As String)
            sTextBefore = Value
        End Set
    End Property

    <Category("Appearance")> _
    Property TextAfter() As String
        Get
            Return sTextAfter
        End Get
        Set(ByVal Value As String)
            sTextAfter = Value
        End Set
    End Property

    <Category("Appearance")> _
    Property Month() As Integer
        Get
            Return iMonth
        End Get
        Set(ByVal Value As Integer)
            iMonth = Value
        End Set
    End Property

    <Category("Appearance")> _
    Property Day() As Integer
        Get
            Return iDay
        End Get
        Set(ByVal Value As Integer)
            iDay = Value
        End Set
    End Property
```

Figure 24-4   How to expose properties, methods, and events (part 1 of 2)

On page 2 of the code listing for the DaysUntil control, you can see the event procedure for the Load event of this control. This procedure creates an appropriate message and assigns it to the Text property of the label named lblDaysUntil. To do that, it uses the four properties declared by the control.

To start, the value of the TextBefore property is assigned to the label, followed by a space. Then, the value returned by the DaysUntilDate method is appended to the label. This method uses the Month and Day properties to get the number of days until the specified date. Finally, a space and the value stored in the TextAfter property are appended to the label.

Although the DaysUntil control only exposes properties, it could also expose methods or events. To expose a method or event, you just code it with the Public keyword like any other method or event. You can also expose a field by declaring it with the Public keyword. However, you're more likely to use public properties since public fields aren't displayed in the Properties window of the Web Forms Designer.

The Visual Basic code for the DaysUntil control Page 2

```vb
Protected Sub Page_Load(ByVal sender As Object, _
        ByVal e As System.EventArgs) Handles Me.Load
    lblDaysUntil.Text = TextBefore & " "
    lblDaysUntil.Text &= Me.DaysUntilDate
    lblDaysUntil.Text &= " " & TextAfter
End Sub

Private Function DaysUntilDate() As Integer
    Dim dtmTargetDate As Date _
        = New DateTime(DateTime.Today.Year, Month, Day)
    If DateTime.Today > dtmTargetDate Then
        dtmTargetDate = dtmTargetDate.AddYears(1)
    End If
    Dim tsTimeUntil As TimeSpan = dtmTargetDate - DateTime.Today
    Return tsTimeUntil.Days
End Function

End Class
```

Description

- A user control can include public properties, methods, and events that you can work with from any page that contains the control.

- If you want to be able to set the properties of a user control at design time, you need to code a *designer attribute* that indicates how the control is used by the Web Forms Designer. Each property of the DaysUntil control includes a Category attribute that indicates the category that the property appears under in the Properties window.

- Although you can also include public fields in a user control, you're more likely to use private fields that can be accessed through public properties of the user control.

Figure 24-4   How to expose properties, methods, and events (part 2 of 2)

How to use user controls

After you design and code a user control, you can add it to any form in the web site that needs it. Then, if necessary, you can use the Web Forms Designer to set the properties for the control, and you can use the Code Editor to add code that works with the control. You'll learn how to do that in the topics that follow. You'll also see the aspx code that's generated for a user control when you add it to a form so you have a better understanding of how user controls are implemented by ASP.NET.

How to add a user control to a web form

Figure 24-5 shows how you add a user control to a web form. To do that, you simply drag the control from the Solution Explorer to the location where you want it displayed on the form. Then, ASP.NET generates a tag that registers the control so it can be used on the form. In addition, it generates a tag that displays the control. You'll see these tags in the next figure.

The form shown here is the Featured Products form. As you can see, it consists of the three user controls you saw back in figure 24-1. In this figure, the DaysUntil control at the bottom of the form is selected, and you can see the custom properties that are exposed by this control in the Properties window. Notice that all four of these properties—Day, Month, TextAfter, and TextBefore—are listed in the Appearance category of this window. That's because "Appearance" was specified for the Category attribute of each property.

In addition to the custom properties for a user control, you can also set some of the properties that are defined by the UserControl class that all user controls inherit. In this figure, for example, you can see the EnableTheming property. In addition to this property, you can set the EnableViewState, Visible, ID, and Runat properties.

The Featured Products page with user controls

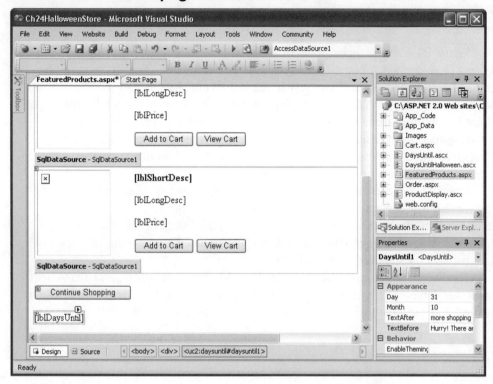

Description

- To add a user control to an ASP.NET page, drag it from the Solution Explorer onto the page. The Web Forms Designer automatically generates all of the tags necessary to register the user control and insert it into the page.

- To set a public property of a user control, select the control in the Web Forms Designer and use the Properties window to set the property. Any custom properties you have defined for the control appear in this window, along with some of the properties provided by the UserControl class.

Figure 24-5   How to add a user control to a web form

The aspx code that's generated when you add a user control to a form

Figure 24-6 shows an example of the aspx code that's generated by the Web Forms Designer when you add user controls to a web form. This is the code for the Featured Products form you saw in the last figure. As you can see, it starts with two Register directives that register the two user controls. Each Register directive includes three attributes: Src, TagName, and TagPrefix. The Src attribute specifies the name of the ascx file that defines the user control. The TagName attribute associates a name with the control. And the TagPrefix attribute associates a prefix with the control.

The values of the TagPrefix and TagName properties are used in the opening tag for the user control to identify the control. For example, the opening tag for each ProductDisplay user control starts with uc1:ProductDisplay. Each opening tag also includes a Runat attribute and an ID attribute. These attributes work just like they do for standard ASP.NET controls.

The DaysUntil control also includes Day, Month, TextBefore, and TextAfter attributes. These attributes correspond to the properties that are defined by this control and are added when you set the values of these properties.

The aspx code for the Featured Products form that uses user controls

```
<%@ Page Language="VB" AutoEventWireup="false" CodeFile="FeaturedProducts.aspx.vb"
Inherits="FeaturedProducts" %>

<%@ Register Src="ProductDisplay.ascx" TagName="ProductDisplay" TagPrefix="uc1" %>
<%@ Register Src="DaysUntil.ascx" TagName="DaysUntil" TagPrefix="uc2" %>

<!DOCTYPE html PUBLIC "-//W3C//DTD XHTML 1.0 Transitional//EN"
"http://www.w3.org/TR/xhtml1/DTD/xhtml1-transitional.dtd">

<html xmlns="http://www.w3.org/1999/xhtml" >
<head runat="server">
    <title>Chapter 24: Halloween Store</title>
</head>
<body>
    <form id="form1" runat="server">
    <div>
        <img src="Images/banner.jpg" alt="No image found."/><br />
        <br />
        <h3>Featured Products</h3>
        <uc1:ProductDisplay id="ProductDisplay1" runat="server"
            ProductID="frankc01">
        </uc1:ProductDisplay>
        <uc1:ProductDisplay id="ProductDisplay2" runat="server"
            ProductID="super01">
        </uc1:ProductDisplay>
        <br />
        <asp:Button ID="btnContinue" runat="server"
            PostBackUrl="~/Order.aspx" Text="Continue Shopping" /><br />
        <br />
        <uc2:DaysUntil ID="DaysUntil1" runat="server"
            Day="31" Month="10"
            TextBefore="Hurry! There are only" />
            TextAfter="more shopping days until Halloween."
        </div>
    </form>
</body>
</html>
```

Description

- Visual Studio adds two elements to a page when you add a user control. The Register directive appears before the Html element and registers the user control. The user control element appears within the Form element to place the control on the form.

- The Register directive specifies a tag prefix, which is uc1 by default for the first user control that's added to the form. The number on this tag is incremented by one for each different user control that's added.

- The Register directive also specifies a tag name that corresponds to the class name for the user control.

- The user control element identifies the control by combining the tag prefix and the tag name from the Register directive.

Figure 24-6   The aspx code that's generated when you add a user control to a form

How to write code that works with properties, methods, and events

Figure 24-7 shows how to write code that works with the properties of a user control. The first code example shows how you can use the Load event procedure of the page to set a property of a user control. Specifically, it shows how you can set the ProductID property of the ProductDisplay control named ProductDisplay1 to the product ID that's selected in the drop-down list named ddlProducts. (You'll see the code for this user control in just a minute.) This code is used by the Order page of the Halloween Store application. Since the Load event of the page is executed before the Load event of the user control, the Load event procedure for the user control can retrieve the appropriate value from this property.

Although this figure only shows a code example for working with properties, the same principles apply to working with methods or events. For example, if the class for a user control defines a public method, you can call it from the Load event procedure of the page. In addition, if the class for a user control defines and raises a public event, the page that contains the control can contain an event procedure to handle that event.

For this to work, you should know that, like other controls that you add to a form, the ASP.NET runtime automatically generates a declaration for a user control when the page that contains it is requested. For example, the second code example in this figure shows the declaration for the ProductDisplay control used by the first example. Notice that this declaration includes the WithEvents keyword. That's what makes it possible to respond to the events defined by the control.

Code that sets a property of the control from the page that contains it

```
Protected Sub Page_Load(ByVal sender As Object, _
        ByVal e As System.EventArgs) Handles Me.Load
    If Not IsPostBack Then
        ddlProducts.DataBind()
    End If
    ProductDisplay1.ProductID = ddlProducts.SelectedValue
End Sub
```

The declaration that's automatically generated for a user control

```
Protected Dim WithEvents ProductDisplay1 As ProductDisplay
```

Description

- You can use code to work with the properties, methods, and events of a user control just as you would the properties, methods, and events of any other control.

- You typically set user control properties from the event procedure for the Load event of the page. That way, the value will be set before the control's Load event procedure is executed.

- When a user requests a page of an ASP.NET 2.0 application, the ASP.NET runtime generates a partial class that contains a declaration for each of the controls on the page. This declaration includes the WithEvents keyword as shown above. As a result, you can code event procedures that respond to any events that are raised by the control.

Figure 24-7   How to write code that works with properties, methods, and events

The ProductDisplay user control

The remaining topics in this chapter present the ProductDisplay user control that you saw in figure 24-1. As you'll see, this control is more complex than the DaysUntil control, but it's still relatively easy to create and use.

The design

Part 1 of figure 24-8 shows the design of the ProductDisplay user control. This control uses a table to align an image control, three label controls, and two button controls. It also includes a SqlDataSource control that's used to get the data that's displayed by the control.

The ascx file

Part 1 of figure 24-8 also shows the ascx code for this control. Notice that the Select statement specified by the data source includes a ProductID parameter that determines what product is retrieved by this statement. Also notice that the Parameter element for this parameter doesn't indicate where the value of this parameter comes from. In a minute, you'll see how this value is set in code.

The code-behind file

Parts 2 and 3 of figure 24-8 present the code-behind file for the ProductDisplay user control. Two private variables are used by this class. The sProductID variable will hold the product ID of the product that's displayed by the control, and the Product variable will hold the Product object for that product.

The property named ProductID provides access to the value that's stored in the sProductID variable. This property includes a designer attribute that makes this property available to the developer at design time. As a result, the developer can set this property to specify the product that the control should display.

The Page_Load event procedure uses the control's GetProduct method to get a Product object from the database. Notice that the first statement in the GetProduct method sets the value of the ProductID parameter to the ProductID property. That way, only the row with that product ID is retrieved. Then, the rest of the method creates the Product object if a row with the specified ID is found.

If the GetProduct method returns a Product object, the data for that object is displayed in the user control. Otherwise, the image and button controls are hidden, and a message that indicates that the product ID was not found is displayed by the labels in the control.

Finally, the btnAdd_Click event procedure updates the shopping cart. This code is similar to the code you've seen elsewhere in this book, so you shouldn't have any trouble understanding how it works. The only difference is that a quantity of one is always assumed.

The design of the ProductDisplay user control

The ascx code for the ProductDisplay user control

```
<%@ Control Language="VB" AutoEventWireup="false"
    CodeFile="ProductDisplay.ascx.vb" Inherits="ProductDisplay" %>
<table id="Table1" border="0" cellpadding="5" cellspacing="0"
        style="width: 542px">
    <tr>
        <td rowspan="4" style="width: 123px; height: 140px;" valign="top">
            <asp:Image ID="imgProduct" runat="server" Height="140px" /></td>
        <td style="width: 300px">
            <asp:Label ID="lblShortDesc" runat="server" Font-Bold="True"
                    Font-Size="Medium"></asp:Label></td>
    </tr>
    <tr>
        <td style="width: 300px">
            <asp:Label ID="lblLongDesc" runat="server"></asp:Label></td>
    </tr>
    <tr>
        <td style="width: 300px">
            <asp:Label ID="lblPrice" runat="server"></asp:Label></td>
    </tr>
    <tr>
        <td style="width: 300px">
            <asp:Button ID="btnAdd" runat="server" Text="Add to Cart" />
            <asp:Button ID="btnViewCart" runat="server" Text="View Cart"
                PostBackUrl="~/Cart.aspx" /></td>
    </tr>
</table>
<asp:SqlDataSource ID="SqlDataSource1" runat="server"
    ConnectionString="<%$ ConnectionStrings:HalloweenConnectionString %>"
    SelectCommand="SELECT [ProductID], [Name], [ShortDescription],
        [LongDescription], [UnitPrice], [ImageFile]
        FROM [Products]
        WHERE ([ProductID] = @ProductID)">
    <SelectParameters>
        <asp:Parameter Name="ProductID" Type="String" />
    </SelectParameters>
</asp:SqlDataSource>
```

Figure 24-8   The ProductDisplay user control (part 1 of 3)

The code-behind file for the ProductDisplay user control

```
Imports System.ComponentModel
Imports System.Data

Partial Class ProductDisplay
    Inherits System.Web.UI.UserControl

    Private sProductID As String
    Private Product As Product

    <Category("Appearance")> _
    Public Property ProductID() As String
        Get
            Return sProductID
        End Get
        Set(ByVal Value As String)
            sProductID = Value
        End Set
    End Property

    Protected Sub Page_Load(ByVal sender As Object, _
            ByVal e As System.EventArgs) Handles Me.Load
        Product = GetProduct()
        If Product Is Nothing Then
            imgProduct.Visible = False
            lblShortDesc.Text = "ProductDisplay control"
            lblLongDesc.Text = "ProductID not found."
            lblPrice.Text = "Make sure to set ProductID property."
            btnAdd.Visible = False
            btnViewCart.Visible = False
        Else
            lblShortDesc.Text = Product.ShortDescription
            lblLongDesc.Text = Product.LongDescription
            lblPrice.Text = "Price: " & FormatCurrency(Product.UnitPrice)
            imgProduct.ImageUrl = "Images\Products\" & Product.ImageFile
        End If
    End Sub

    Private Function GetProduct() As Product
        SqlDataSource1.SelectParameters("ProductID").DefaultValue = ProductID
        Dim dvProductTable As DataView = CType( _
            SqlDataSource1.Select(DataSourceSelectArguments.Empty), DataView)
        If dvProductTable Is Nothing Then
            Return Nothing
        Else
            Dim drvProductRow As DataRowView = dvProductTable(0)
            Product = New Product()
            Product.Name = drvProductRow("Name").ToString
            Product.ShortDescription = drvProductRow("ShortDescription").ToString
            Product.LongDescription = drvProductRow("LongDescription").ToString
            Product.UnitPrice = CDec(drvProductRow("UnitPrice"))
            Product.ImageFile = drvProductRow("ImageFile").ToString
            Return Product
        End If
    End Function
End Function
```

Figure 24-8   The ProductDisplay user control (part 2 of 3)

The code-behind file for the ProductDisplay user control

```
Protected Sub btnAdd_Click(ByVal sender As Object, _
        ByVal e As System.EventArgs) Handles btnAdd.Click
    Dim CartItem As New CartItem
    Dim ShoppingCart As SortedList
    If Session("Cart") Is Nothing Then
        ShoppingCart = New SortedList
    Else
        ShoppingCart = Session("Cart")
    End If
    If ShoppingCart.ContainsKey(Me.ProductID) Then
        CartItem = ShoppingCart(Me.ProductID)
        CartItem.Quantity += 1
        ShoppingCart(Me.ProductID) = CartItem
    Else
        CartItem.Product = Product
        CartItem.Quantity = 1
        ShoppingCart.Add(Me.ProductID, CartItem)
    End If
    Session("Cart") = ShoppingCart
    Response.Redirect("Cart.aspx")
End Sub
End Class
```

Figure 24-8   The ProductDisplay user control (part 3 of 3)

Perspective

Now that you've completed this chapter, you should be able to develop user controls whenever you need them for your own applications. This is one way to write code once and reuse it on more than one page. Another way to reuse code is to create custom server controls, which you'll learn how to do in the next chapter.

Terms

user control
User Control Designer
designer attribute

25

How to develop custom server controls

In this chapter, you'll learn how to create custom server controls. Custom server controls are similar to user controls, but they're more powerful. They're also more difficult to develop than user controls.

Since custom server controls are an advanced feature, you can't use the Standard Edition of Visual Studio or the Express Edition of Visual Web Developer to develop them. As a result, you may want to skip this chapter if you're using one of these editions.

An overview of custom server controls

Before I show you how to create and use custom server controls, you need to understand what these controls are and how you work with them. That's what you'll learn in the topics that follow.

An introduction to custom server controls

Figure 25-1 presents an introduction to *custom server controls*. These controls are similar to the server controls that come with ASP.NET. Because you create custom server controls yourself, however, they can include features that aren't available with the standard web server controls.

For example, the form shown at the top of this figure includes four custom server controls. The first two, called CaptionedBox controls, are similar to a TextBox control but include a caption to the left of the text box. The second control, called a DateDDL control, consists of three drop-down lists that let the user select a month, day, and year. Like the CaptionedBox control, the DateDDL control also includes a caption. The third control, called a DaysUntil control, calculates the number of days until a specified date. In addition, text can be displayed before and after the calculated days.

When you create a custom server control, you base it on the WebControl class or a class that's derived from this class. That way, the control inherits the properties, methods, and events of that class. For example, the DaysUntil control is based on the WebControl class. In contrast, the CaptionedBox control is based on the TextBox class so it has access to the additional properties, methods, and events defined by that class. And the DateDDL control is based on the CompositeControl class. You'll learn about this class later in this chapter.

In addition to the properties, methods, and events that are inherited from the base class, a custom server control can define its own custom properties, methods, and events. For example, the DaysUntil control has properties that let you set the month and day that's used in the calculation, as well as properties that let you specify the text that's displayed before and after the calculated number of days. You can also override the properties, methods, and events defined by the base class.

Custom server controls are typically stored in a *web control library*. Then, if you add the web control library to a web site as shown in this figure, the custom server controls become available from the Toolbox. To use a control, you simply drag it to a web form just as you would any other control. When you do, the control is displayed in the Web Forms Designer window.

Although custom server controls are easy to use, they can be difficult to develop. That's because Visual Studio doesn't provide a designer interface to help you create them. Instead, you have to develop custom server controls entirely in code. As a result, you can't see how the control will appear until you build it and add it to a web form.

Four custom server controls displayed in the Web Forms Designer

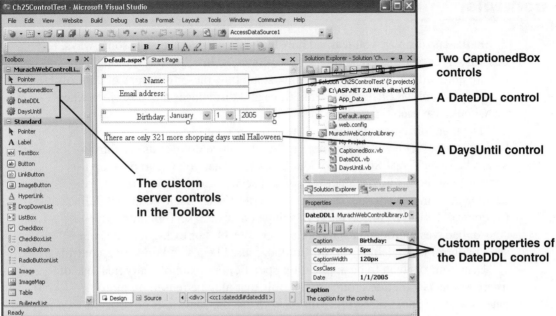

Two CaptionedBox controls

A DateDDL control

A DaysUntil control

The custom server controls in the Toolbox

Custom properties of the DateDDL control

How custom controls are created

- A *custom server control* is a class that inherits the WebControl class or a class that derives from this class.
- Visual Studio doesn't have a designer to help you create custom server controls. As a result, you must create them using code.
- The Professional Edition of Visual Studio includes a Web Control Library template you can use to create libraries of custom server controls. You can then distribute the library to other developers.

How custom server controls work with designers

- Custom server controls work just like the server controls that come with ASP.NET, but they can be customized with additional features.
- If you add a web control library to a web site, the custom server controls in that library are added to the Toolbox automatically. Then, you can add a custom server control to a web form by dragging it from the Toolbox just like any other ASP.NET control.
- Custom server controls have a visual interface you can use to work with them when you add them to an ASP.NET web form. For example, you can set the properties of a custom server control by selecting it in the designer and then using the Properties window.

Figure 25-1   An introduction to custom server controls

How custom server controls compare with user controls

In the last chapter, you learned how to create user controls. In some ways, custom server controls are similar to user controls. In other ways, though, they're quite different. To help you understand how these two types of controls compare, figure 25-2 lists their similarities and differences and describes when you should use each type.

The main difference between custom server controls and user controls is that custom server controls are more difficult to develop than user controls. That's because Visual Studio provides a designer that you use to develop user controls, but there's no designer for custom server controls. As a result, to develop custom server controls, you must write Visual Basic code that defines the control. However, once you've developed a custom server control, the control behaves more like a standard server control. For example, a custom server control is available from the Toolbox, just like a standard server control.

User controls tend to be application-specific. For example, a typical use of user controls is to define groups of controls that may be reused on multiple pages of a web site. Since you're unlikely to use the same user controls in another application, you usually store them in the same folder as the forms for the rest of the web site.

Custom server controls usually provide more general-purpose functions than user controls. For example, the CaptionedBox and DateDDL user controls shown in the previous figure could be useful in a variety of applications. To make them available to other applications, custom server controls are usually created in a separate Web Control Library project. Then, if you add the Web Control Library project to a web site, Visual Studio adds the controls in the library to the Toolbox so they're available to all of the forms of the web site.

Custom server controls...

- Are best used to create general-purpose controls you want to reuse in several applications.
- Are more difficult to develop than user controls.
- Are created entirely in code and consist of a single vb class file.
- Are usually created in Web Control Library projects.
- Are available from the Toolbox.

User controls...

- Are best used when you want to create elements you can reuse on several pages within the same application.
- Are easier to develop than custom server controls.
- Are created with the User Control Designer and consist of an ascx file that defines the control's user interface along with a code-behind file.
- Aren't available from the Toolbox.

Figure 25-2   How custom server controls compare with user controls

Three types of custom server controls

Figure 25-3 describes the three basic types of custom server controls. As you'll learn in this chapter, you implement each of these controls using different programming techniques. Keep in mind as you learn these techniques, however, that they're not mutually exclusive. In other words, you can use one or more of these techniques within the same custom server control.

A *rendered control* is a control that contains code that generates all or most of the HTML that's used to render the control. The rendered control shown in this figure is the DaysUntil control you saw in figure 25-1. Rendered controls are usually based on the WebControl class, which provides the basic functionality of an ASP.NET Server control. Then, the custom control overrides the Render method of this class to generate its own HTML. You'll see how that works in just a minute.

A *superclassed control* is a control that adds functionality to an existing web server control. The CaptionedBox control you saw in figure 25-1, for example, adds a caption to a TextBox control. Because this control is based on the TextBox class rather than the WebControl class, it has all the properties, methods, and events of a standard TextBox control.

A *composite control* is a control that's made up of two or more web server controls. For example, the DateDDL control consists of three DropDownList controls. Composite controls are based on the CompositeControl class. Then, the *child controls* that make up the control are added to the collection of controls defined by the CompositeControl class.

Note that a control can sometimes be implemented using more than one of the control types. For example, you could implement the DaysUntil control using any three of the control types. To implement it as a superclassed control, you would base it on a Label control. Then, you would calculate the days remaining until the target date and assign the result to the Text property of the control, along with the text you want to display before and after the calculated days. To implement this control as a composite control, you could use three Label controls: one for the text you want to display before the calculated value, one for the calculated value, and one for the text you want to display after the calculated value. Before you create a control, then, you should consider which type will provide the greatest flexibility and ease of use.

A rendered control that calculates the days until a specified date

There are only 321 more shopping days until Halloween.

Two superclassed controls that add a caption to a text box

Name: [   ]
Email address: [   ]

A composite control that consists of three drop-down lists with a caption

Birthday: [January ▼] [1 ▼], [2005 ▼]

Description

- A *rendered control* is a control that inherits the WebControl class and handles the details of rendering its own HTML.

- Rendered controls are the most flexible type of custom control because they aren't bound by the predefined behavior of any existing controls. However, they can also be the most difficult to create.

- A *superclassed control* inherits the class for an existing control, such as a text box, and adds additional features, such as a caption.

- A *composite control* is made up of two or more standard control types. Composite controls inherit the CompositeControl class and add *child controls* to the collection of controls for that class.

- A custom server control can sometimes be implemented as two or more of the control types. In that case, you'll need to decide which type works best.

Figure 25-3   Three types of custom server controls

How to create a rendered control

In the topics that follow, you'll learn how to create a simple rendered control. First, I'll describe the default class that provides a template for creating a custom control. Then, you'll learn how to override the Render or RenderContents method in this class so you can control the HTML that's generated when the control is rendered. Finally, you'll see the design and code for the DaysUntil control.

The default class for a custom server control

When you add a custom server control to a project, Visual Studio creates a class like the one shown in figure 25-4. This class inherits the WebControl class and contains a single property named Text that gets and sets the value of a variable that's stored in the view state of the page. This class also contains a procedure named RenderContents that overrides the RenderContents method of the WebControl class.

As it is, the default class doesn't provide a useful function. However, it does provide a good starting point for building useful controls. Before you use this class, though, you need to understand how it works. If you've created your own class files using Visual Basic, you shouldn't have much trouble understanding most of this code. However, a few of the details might be confusing.

To start, notice the code within the angle brackets at the beginning of the Class and the Property statements. This code defines *designer attributes* that supply the Web Forms Designer with information about the control when it's used on a web form. You'll learn more about these designer attributes later in this chapter.

Next, notice that the class overrides the RenderContents method of the WebControl class that it inherits. That way, it can generate the HTML needed to display the control. In this case, the RenderContents method uses the Write method of the HtmlTextWriter object that's passed to it to write the value of the Text property to the control's HTML output stream. You'll learn more about the Write method and the other methods of the HtmlTextWriter class later in this chapter.

You should realize that because the RenderContents method in the default class overrides the RenderContents method of the WebControl class, the properties of the WebControl class that the default class inherits, such as ID, Height, Width, and BorderStyle, never get rendered. To render these properties, you have to call one of the Render methods of the WebControl class. You'll learn how to do that in the next figure.

The starting code for a custom server control

```
Imports System
Imports System.Collections.Generic
Imports System.ComponentModel
Imports System.Text
Imports System.Web
Imports System.Web.UI
Imports System.Web.UI.WebControls

<DefaultProperty("Text"), _
ToolboxData("<{0}:WebCustomControl1 runat=server></{0}:WebCustomControl1>")> _
Public Class WebCustomControl1
    Inherits WebControl

    <Bindable(True), Category("Appearance"), _
    DefaultValue(""), Localizable(True)> _
    Property Text() As String
        Get
            Dim s As String = CStr(ViewState("Text"))
            If s Is Nothing Then
                Return String.Empty
            Else
                Return s
            End If
        End Get

        Set(ByVal Value As String)
            ViewState("Text") = Value
        End Set
    End Property

    Protected Overrides Sub RenderContents(ByVal output As HtmlTextWriter)
        output.Write(Text)
    End Sub

End Class
```

Description

- The code that appears within angle brackets (< and >) before the Class and Property statements defines *designer attributes* that specify how the control and its properties work with the Web Forms Designer. See figure 25-11 for more information.

- The designer attributes are a part of the declaration for the class or property they apply to. If you want to place the Class or Property statement on a separate line, be sure to use a continuation character after the attribute's closing bracket as shown above.

- A class like the one above is created by default when you add a control to a project using the Web Custom Control template or when you create a new Web Control Library project. It defines a simple rendered control that exposes a property named Text.

- The RenderContents method receives an argument named output that's declared as an HtmlTextWriter object. This object is created by ASP.NET when it receives a request for a page. You can use it to write output to the HTML document for the web page.

Figure 25-4   The default class for a custom server control

How to override the Render or RenderContents method for a custom control

Every web server control has a Render or RenderContents method that's responsible for generating the HTML that's sent to the browser to display the control. In a custom server control, you usually override one of these methods so you can generate the HTML that renders the control. Figure 25-5 shows how you do that.

When ASP.NET receives a request for a web page, it creates an HtmlTextWriter object that's used to write HTML to the output stream. This object is passed to the Render and RenderContents methods, and you can use it within these methods to write the HTML that renders the control.

The first example shows how to override the RenderContents method to add content to the HTML element for the base class. Here, the Write method of the HtmlTextWriter object adds the value of the Text property between the start and end tags that are generated automatically for the base class. The start tag that's generated includes attributes that correspond to any control properties you set as you work with the control in the designer. As a result, you can use the RenderContents method to render the properties the custom control inherits from its base class.

The second example shows how to override the Render method to add content to the HTML element for the base class. The Render method is similar to the RenderContents method, but it renders the start and end tags as well as the content. Because of that, when you override this method to add content to the HTML element, you must use the RenderBeginTag and RenderEndTag methods of the base class to render the start and end tags for the control. To access methods from the base class, you can use the MyBase keyword as illustrated in this example.

The third example shows how to override the Render method to add additional HTML elements before or after the element for the base class. Here, the first statement calls the Write method of the HtmlTextWriter object to add an HTML element before the element for the base class. This statement sends a string that includes an HTML element for the caption to the browser. Then, the second statement calls the Render method of the base class. This method generates the HTML necessary to the render the base class, including the start and end tags, and sends it to the browser. In this case, the class is based on the TextBox class. As a result, calling the Render method of the base class renders an HTML element for a text box and sends it to the browser.

Methods of the WebControl class for rendering controls

Method	Description
`RenderContents(output)`	Renders the contents of the control to the specified HtmlTextWriter object, but does not include its start and end tags.
`Render(output)`	Renders the HTML for the control to the specified HtmlTextWriter object, including the start and end tags.
`RenderBeginTag(output)`	Renders the begin tag for the control to the specified HtmlTextWriter object.
`RenderEndTag(output)`	Renders the end tag for the control to the specified HtmlTextWriter object.

A RenderContents method that adds text content to a control

```
Protected Overrides Sub RenderContents(ByVal output As HtmlTextWriter)
    output.Write(Text)
End Sub
```

A Render method that adds text content to a control

```
Protected Overrides Sub Render(ByVal output As HtmlTextWriter)
    MyBase.RenderBeginTag(output)
    output.Write(Text)
    MyBase.RenderEndTag(output)
End Sub
```

A Render method that adds a caption to a superclassed control that's based on a text box

```
Protected Overrides Sub Render(ByVal output As HtmlTextWriter)
    output.Write(sCaptionHTML)
    MyBase.Render(output)
End Sub
```

Description

- A custom control can inherit the System.Web.UI.WebControls.WebControl class, or a more specific class such as the TextBox class.

- If a custom control inherits the WebControl class and renders a single element, you should override the RenderContents method of the WebControl class. Then, you can use the Write methods of the HtmlTextWriter class to add content between the start and end tags for the element, which are rendered automatically.

- If a custom control renders more than one element, you should override the Render method of the base class. Then, you can use the Write methods of the HtmlTextWriter class to add elements before or after the base class, and you can call the Render method of the base class to render the base class. To add content between the start and end tags for the base class, you can use the RenderBeginTag and RenderEndTag methods of the base class and then write the content between these tags.

Note

- Web controls also have a RenderControl method, but you shouldn't execute this method from your overridden Render or RenderContents method.

Figure 25-5   How to override the Render or RenderContents method

The design of the DaysUntil control

Figure 25-6 presents the design of the DaysUntil control you saw earlier in this chapter. As you'll recall, this control displays the number of days remaining until the target date specified by the Month and Day properties. Note that the default values for the Month and Day properties are 10 and 31, which means that this control displays the number of days until Halloween by default.

In addition to the Month and Day properties, the DaysUntil control includes TextBefore and TextAfter properties. These properties let you specify text that's displayed before and after the number of days. Because these properties don't have default values, no text is displayed by default.

The screen in this figure shows how you could use the DaysUntil control on the Order page of the Halloween Store application. Here, I left the Month and Day properties at their default values so the control will display the number of days until Halloween. In contrast, I set the TextBefore and TextAfter properties so the control appears as shown here.

This figure also shows the aspx code that's generated for the control. This code includes ID and Runat attributes just as it would for any web server control. In addition, the tag for this control uses a prefix of cc1. As you'll see later in this chapter, this is the prefix that's generated by default when you add a custom server control to a web form.

The code for the DaysUntil control

Figure 25-7 presents the complete code for the DaysUntil control. The first thing you should notice is that this control inherits the WebControl class. That means that it can use any of the properties, methods, and events of that class.

This class starts with the four properties of the control. Here, each property consists of simple Get and Set routines that retrieve and set the value of a variable that's stored in view state.

This class finishes with the overridden RenderContents method. This method uses the HtmlTextWriter object to write the value of the TextBefore property, followed by the number of days remaining until the target date, followed by the value of the TextAfter property. To calculate the number of days remaining until the target date, the RenderContents method calls the DaysUntilDate function. Because you saw code like this in previous chapters, you shouldn't have any trouble understanding how it works.

The DaysUntil control on the Order page of the Shopping Cart application

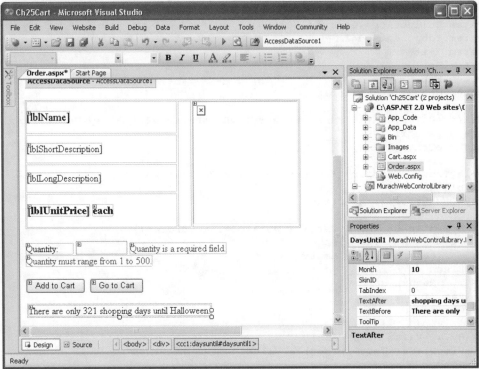

The aspx code for the DaysUntil control

```
<cc1:DaysUntil ID="DaysUntil1" runat="server"
    TextAfter="more shopping days until Halloween."
    TextBefore="There are only"/>
```

Properties of the DaysUntil control

Property	Description
Month	The target date's month. The default is 10.
Day	The target date's day. The default is 31.
TextBefore	The text that's displayed before the days until the target date.
TextAfter	The text that's displayed after the days until the target date.

Description

- The DaysUntil control is a rendered control that displays the number of days remaining until a target date and, optionally, text before and after the days remaining. The target date is specified by the Month and Day properties.

- By default, the Month and Day properties are set to display the number of days until Halloween. If that's not what you want, you can change these properties after you add the control to a web form.

Figure 25-6   The design of the DaysUntil control

The Visual Basic code for the DaysUntil control

```vb
Imports System
Imports System.Collections.Generic
Imports System.ComponentModel
Imports System.Text
Imports System.Web
Imports System.Web.UI
Imports System.Web.UI.WebControls

<ToolboxData("<{0}:DaysUntil runat=server ID=DaysUntil1></{0}:DaysUntil>")> _
Public Class DaysUntil
    Inherits WebControl

    <Bindable(True), Category("Appearance"), DefaultValue(""), _
    Localizable(True)> _
    Property TextBefore() As String
        Get
            Dim s As String = CStr(ViewState("TextBefore"))
            If s Is Nothing Then
                Return String.Empty
            Else
                Return s
            End If
        End Get

        Set(ByVal Value As String)
            ViewState("TextBefore") = Value
        End Set
    End Property

    <Bindable(True), Category("Appearance"), DefaultValue(""), _
    Localizable(True)> _
    Property TextAfter() As String
        Get
            Dim s As String = CStr(ViewState("TextAfter"))
            If s Is Nothing Then
                Return String.Empty
            Else
                Return s
            End If
        End Get

        Set(ByVal Value As String)
            ViewState("TextAfter") = Value
        End Set
    End Property
```

Figure 25-7   The code for the DaysUntil control (part 1 of 2)

The Visual Basic code for the DaysUntil control   **Page 2**

```vbnet
<Bindable(True), Category("Appearance"), DefaultValue(""), _
Localizable(True)> _
Property Month() As Integer
    Get
        Dim s As String = CStr(ViewState("Month"))
        If s Is Nothing Then
            Return 10
        Else
            Return CInt(ViewState("Month"))
        End If
    End Get

    Set(ByVal Value As Integer)
        ViewState("Month") = Value
    End Set
End Property

<Bindable(True), Category("Appearance"), DefaultValue(""), _
Localizable(True)> _
Property Day() As Integer
    Get
        Dim s As String = CStr(ViewState("Day"))
        If s Is Nothing Then
            Return 31
        Else
            Return CInt(ViewState("Day"))
        End If
    End Get

    Set(ByVal Value As Integer)
        ViewState("Day") = Value
    End Set
End Property

Protected Overrides Sub RenderContents(ByVal output As HtmlTextWriter)
    output.Write(TextBefore & " ")
    output.Write(DaysUntilDate.ToString)
    output.Write(" " & TextAfter)
End Sub

Private Function DaysUntilDate() As Integer
    Dim dtmTargetDate As Date _
        = New DateTime(DateTime.Today.Year, Month, Day)
    If DateTime.Today > dtmTargetDate Then
        dtmTargetDate = dtmTargetDate.AddYears(1)
    End If
    Dim tsTimeUntil As TimeSpan = dtmTargetDate - DateTime.Today
    Return tsTimeUntil.Days
End Function

End Class
```

Figure 25-7   The code for the DaysUntil control (part 2 of 2)

How to create and test a web control library

Now that you've seen the basic coding requirements for custom server controls, you're ready to learn how to create and use them in Visual Studio. To do that, you can create a Web Control Library project that contains one or more custom server controls. Then, you can add this project to any web site to test these controls.

Figure 25-8 presents a procedure for creating and testing a web control library. You'll learn the details of each step in this procedure in the topics that follow.

Step 1: Create a web control library

The first step is to create a new Web Control Library project. To do that, you display the New Project dialog box as described in figure 25-8. Then, you select the Web Control Library template and enter a name and location for the project. In this figure, for example, you can see a web control library named MurachWebControlLibrary.

When you create a Web Control Library project, the project is created with a control named WebCustomControl1 by default. This control contains the starting code you saw in figure 25-4.

Step 2: Create the custom server controls

After you create a new Web Control Library project, the next step is to create the custom server controls you want to include in the library. To create the first control, you can modify the WebCustomControl1.vb file that's generated by default. Alternatively, you can delete this file and add a new file for each custom control.

To add a custom server control to a web control library, right-click on the project and select the Add→New Item command to display the Add New Item dialog box. Then, select the Web Custom Control template and enter a name for the control. In figure 25-8, for example, you can see that the library contains the DaysUntil, CaptionedBox, and DateDDL controls.

After you add a new control to a web control library, you need to add the code that implements the control. You'll see examples of that throughout this chapter.

Step 3: Build the web control library

The next step is to build the web control library. To do that, just right-click the project and select the Build command. Then, Visual Studio creates the files you'll need to use the web control library in a web site.

A solution with a Web Control Library project

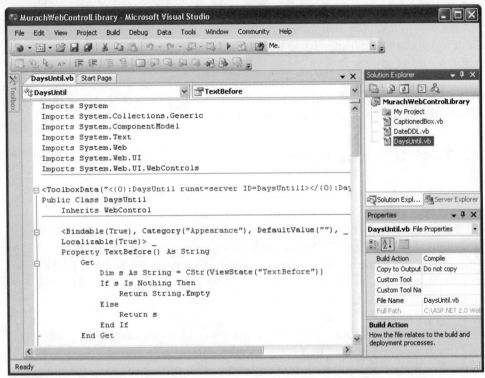

A procedure for creating and testing custom server controls

1. Create a new Web Control Library project using the Web Control Library template.
2. Create the custom server controls in the library.
3. Build the Web Control Library project.
4. Add the Web Control Library project to a solution that contains a web site.
5. Use the Toolbox to add the controls to a web form so you can test them.

Description

- A *web control library* consists of one or more custom server controls. You can build this library into a DLL that you can distribute to other developers.

- To create a project for a web control library, display the New Project dialog box (File→New Project). Then, select the Web Control Library template that's available from the Windows group of the Visual Basic group, and enter a name and location for the project. By default, a Web Control Library project is stored in the Visual Studio projects location directory.

Figure 25-8   How to create a web control library

Step 4: Add the library to a web site

One way to test your custom server controls is to add the web control library to a new or existing web site. To do that, create or open the web site and then use the File→Add→Existing Project command to display the Add Existing Project dialog box. Then, locate and select the project file for the web control library. In figure 25-9, for example, the MurachWebControlLibrary project shown in the previous figure has been added to a web site.

Step 5: Test the controls

When you add a Web Control Library project to a web site, Visual Studio automatically adds the custom controls in the library to the Toolbox. The controls are included in a group with the same name as the web control library. This is illustrated by the MurachWebControlLibrary group shown in figure 25-9.

At this point, you can test a control by dragging it from the Toolbox to the form. The first time you add a custom control to a form, Visual Studio creates a Bin folder like the one shown here. This folder contains the dll, pdb, and xml files for the web control library.

After you add a custom control to a form, you can set the control properties using the Properties window. In this figure, for example, you can see three DaysUntil controls with different property settings. Note that to create the third control, I set not only the custom properties of the control, but also the Font-Italic property that this control inherits from the WebControl class.

If you find that a control doesn't look or work the way you want it to, you can change its code and then rebuild the web control library that contains it. You may also need to rebuild a form that uses a custom control or refresh the custom controls on a form if you change the code or properties for the control. To rebuild a form, just, right-click on it in the Solution Explorer and select the Build Page command. To refresh a control, right-click on it in the form and select the Refresh command.

When you test your custom controls, you should realize that coding errors sometimes manifest themselves in strange ways. Because of that, they can be difficult to debug. For example, if a control generates invalid HTML, it won't display correctly in the Web Forms Designer. Typically, the designer will simply display the name of the control in brackets. In other cases, the control will appear correctly in the designer, but it won't display properly when you run the application. And in still other cases, the control will throw an exception when you run the application.

Fortunately, you can use the debugger to help you determine the cause of an error. If a control isn't rendered properly, for example, you can set a breakpoint in the Render or RenderContents method. Then, you can review variable values and monitor program execution to determine the cause of the problem.

If the control displays in the browser but doesn't appear or work the way it should, you can also look at the HTML that's generated to be sure it's correct. To do that, use the View→Source command in your browser's menu.

Three instances of the DaysUntil control in the Web Forms Designer

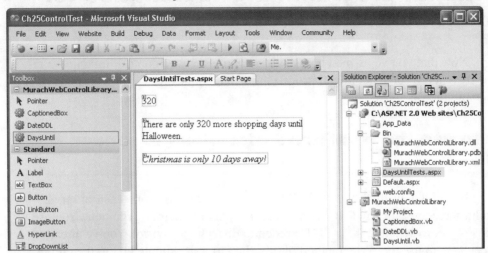

The aspx code for these three controls

```
<%@ Register Assembly="MurachWebControlLibrary"
    Namespace="MurachWebControlLibrary" TagPrefix="cc1" %>
    .
    .
<cc1:DaysUntil ID="DaysUntil1" runat="server" />
<br /><br />
<cc1:DaysUntil ID="DaysUntil2" runat="server"
    TextAfter="more shopping days until Halloween."
    TextBefore="There are only" />
<br /><br />
<cc1:DaysUntil ID="DaysUntil3" runat="server"
    Day="25" Font-Italic="True" Month="12" TextAfter="days away!"
    TextBefore="Christmas is only" />
```

Description

- To test a custom control, add it to a form in your web site. To do that, just drag it from the Toolbox. When you do, Visual Studio will generate a Register directive that registers the web control library, and it will generate a tag for the control with a default prefix of cc1.

- After you add the control to a form, you can set its properties in the Properties window to be sure that it appears as it should in the designer. You can also run the project to be sure that the control works properly at runtime.

- If you make changes to a control, make sure to rebuild the control library. To do that, you can right-click on the library in the Solution Explorer and select Build from the resulting menu. Then, the changes are applied to any controls you've added to a web form.

- Because the DaysUntil control inherits the WebControl base class, you can set properties of this class as illustrated by the Font-Italic attribute of the third control shown above.

Figure 25-9   How to test controls in a web control library

Additional programming techniques for custom controls

Now that you've learned how to create and test a web control library, you're ready to learn some additional programming techniques for creating custom server controls.

How to use the HtmlTextWriter class to render HTML

As you know, the Render and RenderContents methods of a custom server control receive an HtmlTextWriter object named output as an argument. You use this object to generate the HTML needed to display the control. You've already seen how to use the Write method of this class to write simple text to the output stream. You can use this method to render all of the HTML for a custom server control by carefully constructing the HTML using Visual Basic's string handling features. However, figure 25-10 presents some additional methods of the HtmlTextWriter class that make it easier to generate HTML output.

The methods shown in this figure simplify the process of creating valid HTML. For example, the WriteBeginTag method writes an HTML start tag using the element name you supply. Note, however, that this method doesn't write the closing bracket for the start tag. That way, you can use the WriteAttribute method to add attributes to the tag. Then, you can use the Write method to add the closing bracket for the tag by specifying HtmlTextWriter.TagRightCharacter for the string value.

You can also use the Write method to add content after the start tag. Then, you can use the WriteEndTag method to write the end tag. This is illustrated in the example in this figure. This code creates a Td element with a Style attribute that specifies the width and alignment of the content between the start and end tags.

If an element doesn't include any content, you can code the start tag as a *self-closing tag*. To do that, you use the HtmlTextWriter.SelfClosingTagEnd field to close the start tag instead of HtmlTextWriter.TagRightCharacter. This constant adds the characters "/>" to the output stream, which indicates the end of the element. Then, you can omit the end tag.

Common methods of the HtmlTextWriter class

Method	Description
`Write(string)`	Writes the specified string to the HTML output.
`WriteBeginTag(tagname)`	Writes the start tag for the specified HTML element. This method does not write the closing bracket (>) for the start tag. That way, you can include attributes within the tag.
`WriteAttribute(attribute, value)`	Writes the specified attribute and assigns the specified value. This method should be coded after the WriteBeginTag method but before the Write method that adds the closing bracket for the start tag.
`WriteEndTag(tagname)`	Writes the end tag for the specified HTML element.

Common fields of the HtmlTextWriter class

Field	Description
TagRightChar	The closing bracket of an HTML tag (>).
SelfClosingTagEnd	The closing slash and bracket of a self-closing HTML tag (/>).

A procedure that renders a Span element with text

```
Private Sub RenderCaption(ByVal output As HtmlTextWriter)
    output.WriteBeginTag("td")
    Dim sStyle As String
    sStyle = "width: " & CaptionWidth.ToString() & ";"
    sStyle &= "text-align: right;"
    output.WriteAttribute("Style", sStyle)
    output.Write(HtmlTextWriter.TagRightChar)
    output.Write(Caption)
    output.WriteEndTag("td")
End
```

Description

- You can use the Write methods of the HtmlTextWriter class to create HTML for a custom control.

- To add the closing bracket for a start tag, you use the Write method and specify HtmlTextWriter.TagRightChar.

- If an element doesn't include any content, you can code the start tag as a *self-closing tag*. A self-closing tag ends with the characters />. To add these characters, use the HtmlTextWriter.SelfClosingTagEnd field.

Figure 25-10 How to use the HtmlTextWriter class to render HTML

How to use designer attributes

Figure 25-11 presents some of the designer attributes you can use with custom control classes and properties. The only two *class attributes* you'll typically use are the ones that are added by default to a custom control. As its name implies, the DefaultProperty attribute identifies the default property for the control. This attribute is set to Text by default since this is the only property that's defined for a control when you first create it. If you delete the Text property or change its name, you should delete the DefaultProperty attribute or change it to another property.

The second class attribute, ToolboxData, provides information that Visual Studio uses when you add the control to a form. Specifically, it provides the name of the tag that's used for the control. By default, this is the class name that you specify when you create the web control, which is usually what you want.

The *property attributes* provide the Web Forms Designer with additional information about the custom properties you define. For example, the attributes that are included on the Text property of a custom server control by default specify that the property can be used for binding, that the property should be listed in the Appearance category of the Properties window, that the property has no default value, and that the property can be localized to use a specific user's language and culture. You can modify or delete any of these attributes or add any of the other attributes.

One property attribute you're likely to add is Description. The value you specify for this attribute is displayed in the Description pane at the bottom of the Properties window when you select the control in the designer window and then select the property. In this figure, you can see the description that's specified for the Month property of the DaysUntil control.

Common attributes for custom control classes

Attribute	Description
`DefaultProperty(name)`	The name of the default property for the control.
`ToolboxData(tagName)`	The name of the tag that's generated when the control is added to a web form from the Toolbox.

Common attributes for custom control properties

Attribute	Description
`Bindable(boolean)`	Specifies whether the property is typically used for binding.
`Browsable(boolean)`	Specifies whether the property should be visible in the Properties window. The default is True.
`Category(string)`	The category the property should appear under in the Properties window.
`DefaultValue(string)`	The default value for the property.
`Description(string)`	A description for the property.
`DesignOnly(boolean)`	Specifies whether the property is available only at design time. The default is False.
`Localizable(boolean)`	Specifies whether the property can be localized so that it uses the user's language and culture.

A property definition with property attributes

```
<Bindable(True), Category("Appearance"), DefaultValue("") _
Description("The month used to determine the target date.")> _
Property Month() As Integer
    Get
        Dim s As String = CStr(ViewState("Month"))
        If s Is Nothing Then
            Return 10
        Else
            Return CInt(ViewState("Month"))
        End If
    End Get

    Set(ByVal Value As Integer)
        ViewState("Month") = Value
    End Set
End Property
```

Description

- You can use *class attributes* and *property attributes* to add information to a control class or property that makes the class or property easier to use in the Web Forms Designer.

- Class attributes are coded at the beginning of a Class statement, and property attributes are coded at the beginning of a Property statement. The entire attribute list must be enclosed in angle brackets (<>).

- An attribute list consists of one or more attributes, separated by commas. Each attribute consists of an attribute name, followed by a value enclosed in parentheses.

Figure 25-11   How to use designer attributes

How to raise events in a custom control

In addition to defining custom properties, a custom server control can raise custom events. For example, the DateDDL control you saw earlier in this chapter raises an event named DateChanged whenever the user selects a different month, day, or year. A web form that uses this control can then include a handler for this event to provide special processing when the user changes the date.

At the top of figure 25-12, for example, you can see a page that includes a DateDDL control that has been named ddExpirationDate. To test the event that has been defined by the DateDDL class, the code for this page includes an event handler that displays a label that contains an appropriate message whenever the DateChanged event occurs. You can see this message on the form.

To define an event for a custom server control, you use an Event statement as shown in this figure. On this statement, you code the name of the event along with the definitions of any arguments you want to pass to the procedure that handles the event when it's raised. Then, to raise the event, you code a RaiseEvent statement. On this statement, you name the event you want to raise and you provide values for its arguments.

In this figure, you can see the Event statement that defines the DateChanged event and a Raise statement that raises the event. Notice that the Event statement defines two arguments. The first argument is an object named sender, and the second argument is an EventArgs object named e. Most events raised by custom controls should pass these two arguments. Then, the RaiseEvent statement should pass the control itself (Me) or a child control it contains as the sender argument so that the event handler can refer to this control. The event handler shown in this figure, for example, uses the ID property of the sender argument to display the name of the control.

For the e argument, the RaiseEvent statement typically passes a new EventArgs object. Because this object doesn't contain any event data, it serves no useful purpose to the event handler. If you develop more sophisticated controls, however, you can pass an event argument object that's based on the EventArgs object and that contains useful state information.

A page that tests the DateChanged event of the ddExpirationDate control

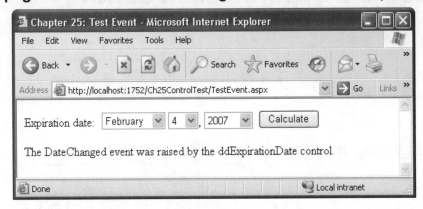

The syntax of the Event statement

```
[Public] Event name[(argumentlist)]
```

The syntax of the RaiseEvent statement

```
RaiseEvent name[(argumentlist)]
```

Code that defines the DateChanged event in the DateDDL class

```
Public Event DateChanged(ByVal sender As Object, ByVal e As EventArgs)
```

Code that raises the event in the DateDDL class

```
RaiseEvent DateChanged(Me, New EventArgs)
```

The event handler for the event in the web form

```
Protected Sub ddExpirationDate_DateChanged(ByVal sender As Object, _
        ByVal e As System.EventArgs) Handles ddExpirationDate.DateChanged
    lblMessage.Text _
        = "The DateChanged event was raised by the " _
        & sender.ID & " control."
End Sub
```

Description

- To declare an event for a custom control, you code a Public Event statement at the class level. Then, you use a RaiseEvent statement in any method of the class to raise the event.

- The RaiseEvent statement for a control event should pass two arguments to the event handler: sender and e.

- The value of the sender argument should be the control that's raising the event (Me) or a child control that it contains. The event handler can use this argument to retrieve information about the control.

- The value of the e argument should be an EventArgs object. This is a base class that contains no event data and is used by events that don't need to pass state information to the event handler. You can use the New keyword to create an EventArgs object.

Figure 25-12   How to raise events in a custom control

How to create a superclassed control

As you know, a superclassed control is a control that inherits a specific ASP.NET server control rather than the generic WebControl class. The programming techniques for creating a superclassed control are similar to the techniques for creating a rendered control. However, you should be aware of a few coding details.

How to code a superclassed control

Before you create a superclassed control, you should carefully consider which control it inherits. In general, you'll want it to inherit the control that most resembles the appearance and function of the custom control you're creating. For example, if the primary purpose of the custom control is to display text, it should inherit the Label control. On the other hand, if the primary purpose of the control is to accept text input from the user, it should inherit the TextBox control.

When you create a superclassed control, you typically use the Render method to render its HTML. How you code this method depends on how you're extending the base control. If you're simply adding some HTML before or after the control, or if you're just changing some of the base control's property values, your Render method can call the Render method of the base class to render the entire base control. If your enhancements are more substantial, however, you may need to use the RenderBeginTag and RenderEndTag methods so you can render additional HTML between the control's start and end tags.

The design of the CaptionedBox control

To help you understand how superclassed controls work, figure 25-13 presents the design of the CaptionedBox control. This control adds a caption to a standard text box. Because it must provide all the standard features of a text box, it's based on the TextBox class.

To define the caption, this control uses four properties. The Caption property specifies the text to be displayed, the CaptionWidth property specifies the width of the caption, and the RightAlignCaption property determines whether the caption is right-aligned. Finally, the CaptionPadding property specifies how much space appears between the caption and the text box that follows it.

If you take a moment to consider the design for the CaptionedBox control, I think you'll agree that it can be quite useful for aligning text boxes on a form. The web page in this figure illustrates how this works. As you can see, this page contains two CaptionedBox controls. To align the text box portions of these controls, the CaptionWidth and CaptionPadding properties of both controls are set to the same values. In addition, the RightAlign properties of the controls are set to True so that they appear as shown. This can be easier than using tables to align text boxes as you've seen throughout this book. However, as you'll see in a moment, the CaptionedBox control itself uses a table to align its elements.

A web page with two CaptionedBox controls

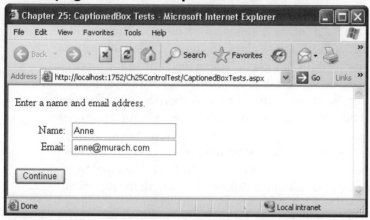

Properties of the CaptionedBox control

Property	Description
Caption	The text that's displayed to the left of the text box.
CaptionWidth	The width of the control's caption area.
CaptionPadding	The width of the area between the caption and the text box.
RightAlignCaption	Determines whether the caption text is right-aligned. The default is False.

The aspx code for the two CaptionedBox controls

```
<cc1:captionedbox id="CaptionedBox1" runat="server" Caption="Name:"
    CaptionPadding="10px" CaptionWidth="75px" RightAlignCaption="True">
</cc1:captionedbox>
<cc1:captionedbox id="CaptionedBox2" runat="server" Caption="Email:"
    CaptionPadding="10px" CaptionWidth="75px" RightAlignCaption="True">
</cc1:captionedbox>
```

Description

- The CaptionedBox control is a superclassed control that adds a text caption to the left of a text box. This control makes it easy to align text boxes without using tables.

Figure 25-13   The design of the CaptionedBox control

The code for the CaptionedBox control

Figure 25-14 presents the code for the CaptionedBox control. To start, you can see that the control inherits the TextBox class. In addition, you can see the custom properties that are defined for this class. Notice that, unlike the properties for the DaysUntil control, each of these properties includes a Description attribute that describes the property. In addition, these properties simply get and set the values of class variables. Because that simplifies the code for the properties, we prefer this technique over saving the properties in view state.

Also notice that the CaptionWidth and CaptionPadding properties and the class variables that hold their values are declared with the Unit data type. In case you aren't familiar with this data type, it represents a length measurement that consists of both the length and the unit of measure. By default, the unit of measure is a pixel, which is usually what you want.

The Visual Basic code for the CaptionedBox control

```vb
Imports System
Imports System.Collections.Generic
Imports System.ComponentModel
Imports System.Text
Imports System.Web
Imports System.Web.UI
Imports System.Web.UI.WebControls

<DefaultProperty("Caption"), _
ToolboxData("<{0}:CaptionedBox runat=server></{0}:CaptionedBox>")> _
Public Class CaptionedBox
    Inherits TextBox

    Dim sCaption As String
    Dim uCaptionWidth As Unit
    Dim uCaptionPadding As Unit
    Dim bRightAlignCaption As Boolean

    <Category("Appearance"), _
    Description("The caption displayed to the left of the text box.")> _
    Public Property Caption() As String
        Get
            Return sCaption
        End Get
        Set(ByVal Value As String)
            sCaption = Value
        End Set
    End Property

    <Category("Appearance"), _
    Description("The width of the caption.")> _
    Public Property CaptionWidth() As Unit
        Get
            Return uCaptionWidth
        End Get
        Set(ByVal Value As Unit)
            uCaptionWidth = Value
        End Set
    End Property

    <Category("Appearance"), _
    Description("The space between the caption and the text box.")> _
    Public Property CaptionPadding() As Unit
        Get
            Return uCaptionPadding
        End Get
        Set(ByVal Value As Unit)
            uCaptionPadding = Value
        End Set
    End Property
```

Figure 25-14   The code for the CaptionedBox control (part 1 of 2)

The overridden Render method uses an HTML table that contains a single row with three columns to align the caption and the text box. To accomplish this, this method uses the Write methods of the HtmlTextWriter object to write the tags and attributes necessary to render the table as HTML. Notice that, within the Table element, the CellPadding and CellSpacing attributes specify 0 pixels of padding and spacing.

Within the Td element for the first column, the Style attribute specifies the width of the caption using the CaptionWidth property. Notice that the ToString method is used to convert the length and unit of measure of this property to a string value. If the caption width is set to 10 pixels, for example, the result is 10px. In addition, if the RightAlignCaption property is set to True, the Style attribute also specifies that the text should be right-aligned. The start tag for the first Td element is followed by its content, which is the value of the Caption property. The content is then followed by an end tag for the Td element.

Next, the Render method renders the Td element for the second column. This Td element creates the space between the caption and the text box. To do that, it includes a Style attribute that specifies the value of the CaptionPadding property as the width of the element.

Finally, the Render method renders the Td element for the third column. This column contains the text box. To render the text box, the shaded statement executes the Render method of the base class. Since this class is based on the TextBox class, this renders the TextBox control.

The Visual Basic code for the CaptionedBox control

```vb
    <Category("Appearance"), _
    Description("Determines if the caption is right-aligned.")> _
    Public Property RightAlignCaption() As Boolean
        Get
            Return bRightAlignCaption
        End Get
        Set(ByVal Value As Boolean)
            bRightAlignCaption = Value
        End Set
    End Property

    Protected Overrides Sub Render _
        (ByVal output As System.Web.UI.HtmlTextWriter)
        'begin writing table
        output.WriteBeginTag("table")
        output.WriteAttribute("cellpadding", "0")
        output.WriteAttribute("cellspacing", "0")
        output.Write(HtmlTextWriter.TagRightChar)

        'begin writing row
        output.WriteBeginTag("tr")
        output.Write(HtmlTextWriter.TagRightChar)

        'write first column
        output.WriteBeginTag("td")
        Dim sStyle As String = "width: " _
            & CaptionWidth.ToString() & ";"
        If RightAlignCaption Then
            sStyle &= "text-align: right;"
        End If
        output.WriteAttribute("Style", sStyle)
        output.Write(HtmlTextWriter.TagRightChar)
        output.Write(Caption)
        output.WriteEndTag("td")

        'write second column
        output.WriteBeginTag("td")
        sStyle = "width: " & CaptionPadding.ToString() & ";"
        output.WriteAttribute("Style", sStyle)
        output.Write(HtmlTextWriter.TagRightChar)
        output.WriteEndTag("td")

        'write third column
        output.WriteBeginTag("td")
        output.Write(HtmlTextWriter.TagRightChar)
        MyBase.Render(output)
        output.WriteEndTag("td")

        'finish writing row
        output.WriteEndTag("tr")

        'finish writing table
        output.WriteEndTag("table")
    End Sub

End Class
```

Figure 25-14   The code for the CaptionedBox control (part 2 of 2)

How to create a composite control

A composite control is a control that includes two or more child controls. Because of that, a composite control can be more difficult to create than rendered controls and superclassed controls. In the topics that follow, you'll learn the basic techniques for creating composite controls, and you'll see the design and code for the DateDDL control.

How to code a composite control

A composite control typically inherits the CompositeControl class as shown by the first code example in figure 25-15. This class inherits the WebControl class and adds functionality to that class. In particular, it ensures that all the child controls defined by the composite control are created before they're accessed.

The CompositeControl class also implements the INamingContainer interface. In case you're not familiar with interfaces, they define properties, methods, and events just like classes. Unlike classes, however, an interface doesn't include the details of how the properties, methods, and events are implemented. That's left to the classes that use them.

The INamingContainer interface is unusual in that it doesn't define any properties, methods, or events. Instead, it simply identifies a control as a container control, which ensures that its child controls will be unique. That way, you can include two or more instances of the control on the same page.

To work with the collection of child controls in a composite control, you use the Controls property of the CompositeControl class. To add a control to the collection, for example, you can use the Add method of the control collection object, and to remove all of the controls from the collection, you use the Clear method. This is illustrated by the second example in this figure. This procedure starts by clearing the controls collection. Then, it creates an instance of the Label class and an instance of the TextBox class and adds them both to the controls collection.

Notice that these statements are coded within a procedure named CreateChildControls. As you can see by the procedure declaration, this procedure overrides the CreateChildControls method of the base class. ASP.NET calls this method automatically to create the child controls of the base control, if it has any. To create a composite control, then, you need to override this method to create the child controls you want to include in the composite control.

The last example in this figure shows how to add literal text to the controls collection. To do that, you use a literal control that specifies the text value you want to include. In this example, the literal control contains a single space ( ). Note that when you use a literal control, you can't apply a style to the text it contains. If you need to do that, you'll want to use a Label control instead.

A property and method of the CompositeControl class used with child controls

Property	Description
`Controls`	Accesses the collection of controls contained by the web control.

Method	Description
`CreateChildControls()`	Called automatically by ASP.NET when a page is posted back or before it's rendered.

Common methods of control collection objects

Method	Description
`Add(control)`	Adds the specified child control.
`Remove(control)`	Removes the specified child control.
`Clear()`	Removes all child controls.

The start of a class for a typical composite control

```
Public Class DateDDL
    Inherits CompositeControl
```

Code that adds a label and a text box to the collection of child controls

```
Public Overrides Sub CreateChildControls()
    Controls.Clear()
    Dim lbl As New Label()
    lbl.Text = sLabelText
    Controls.Add(lbl)
    Dim txt As New TextBox()
    Controls.Add(txt)
End Sub
```

Code that adds a literal control with a space to the controls collection

```
Controls.Add(New LiteralControl(" "))
```

Description

- A composite control has two or more child controls that are stored in a ControlCollection object, which you access through the Controls property.

- A composite control inherits the System.Web.UI.WebControls.CompositeControl class, so it has access to all the properties and methods of that class.

- The CompositeControl class inherits the WebControl class and overrides the Render method of that class to ensure that all the child controls are created before they're accessed.

- The CompositeControl class also implements the INamingContainer interface, which ensures that the ID attributes of all the child controls are unique.

- When you create a composite control, you must override the CreateChildControls method to create the child controls it contains.

Figure 25-15   How to code a composite control

The design of the DateDDL control

Figure 25-16 presents the design of the DateDDL control. This control includes three drop-down lists that let the user select a month, day, and year. When the control is displayed, the Month drop-down list is populated with the names of the months, the Day drop-down list is populated with the numbers 1 through 31, and the year drop-down list is populated with the 10 years that begin with the current year. This control also includes a caption just like the CaptionedBox control. In the page that's displayed at the top of this figure, you can see how this control is used to accept an expiration date from the user.

In addition to the Caption, CaptionWidth, CaptionPadding, and RightAlignCaption properties that are used to implement the caption, the DateDDL control has four properties that store date information. The first one, Date, stores the entire date. This property is updated any time the user selects a different month, day, or year. The other properties, Month, Day, and Year, store just the month, day, and year portion of the date and are updated any time the user changes that portion of the date. The last property, AutoPostBack, lets you specify whether the page that contains the control should be posted back to the server when the user selects a different month, day, or year.

The DateDDL control also raises an event named DateChanged whenever the user selects a different month, day, or year. As you'll see, however, the Month, Day, and Year properties for this control are coded so that this event is raised only once each time the page is posted.

The code for the DateDDL control

Figure 25-17 presents the complete source code for the DateDDL control. Because this code is a bit complicated, you may have to study it awhile before you understand how this control works. I'll just describe some of the key portions of the code here.

First, the five child controls that are included in this control are declared at the beginning of the class with the WithEvents keyword. That way, this class can use any of the events that these controls are based on. For example, this class uses the SelectedIndexChanged event of each of the three DropDownList controls.

Second, the Date property shown on page 2 of the code listing is a read-only property that consists of just a Get routine. As you can see, this routine returns a formatted date that's constructed using the Month, Day, and Year properties. Because you can't set the value of this property, it doesn't include any designer attributes.

Also notice that the name of the Date property is enclosed in brackets. These brackets indicate that Date is an *escaped identifier*. Escaped identifiers provide a way to use Visual Basic keywords as identifier names. If these brackets weren't used, this class would not compile, and an error message would be displayed indicating that Date is a keyword.

A web page that uses a DateDDL control

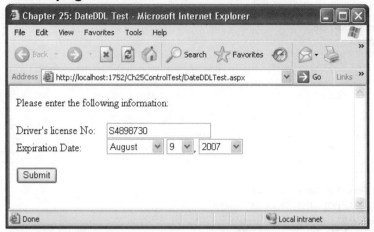

Properties of the DateDDL control

Property	Description
Caption	The text that's displayed to the left of the drop-down lists.
CaptionWidth	The width of the control's caption area.
CaptionPadding	The width of the area between the caption and the drop-down lists.
RightAlignCaption	Determines whether the caption is right-aligned. The default is False.
Date	The date selected by the user.
Month	An integer representing the month (1 to 12).
Day	An integer representing the day of the month (1 to 31).
Year	An integer representing the year.
AutoPostBack	Determines whether the page should be posted when the user selects a different month, day, or year. The default is False.

Event raised by the DateDDL control

Event	Description
DateChanged	Raised when the user selects a different month, day, or year.

The aspx code for the DateDDL control

```
<cc1:DateDDL ID="ddExpirationDate" runat="server" Caption="Expiration Date:"
    CaptionPadding="10px" CaptionWidth="140px"></cc1:DateDDL>
```

Description

- The DateDDL control is a composite control. It uses one label to display the caption to the left of the date, another label to provide spacing between the caption and the date, and three drop-down lists to let the user select a date.

Figure 25-16   The design of the DateDDL control

The Visual Basic code for the DateDDL control   **Page 1**

```vb
Imports System
Imports System.Collections.Generic
Imports System.ComponentModel
Imports System.Text
Imports System.Web
Imports System.Web.UI
Imports System.Web.UI.WebControls

<DefaultProperty("Caption"), _
ToolboxData("<{0}:DateDDL runat=server></{0}:DateDDL>")> _
Public Class DateDDL
    Inherits CompositeControl

    Dim WithEvents lblCaption As New Label
    Dim WithEvents lblCaptionPadding As New Label
    Dim WithEvents ddlMonth As New DropDownList
    Dim WithEvents ddlDay As New DropDownList
    Dim WithEvents ddlYear As New DropDownList

    Dim sCaption As String
    Dim uCaptionWidth As Unit
    Dim uCaptionPadding As Unit
    Dim bRightAlignCaption As Boolean

    Dim iMonth As Integer
    Dim iDay As Integer
    Dim iYear As Integer
    Dim bAutoPostBack As Boolean
    Dim bDateChangedEventRaised As Boolean

    Public Event DateChanged(ByVal sender As Object, ByVal e As EventArgs)

    <Category("Appearance"), Description("The caption for the control.")> _
    Public Property Caption() As String
        Get
            Return sCaption
        End Get

        Set(ByVal Value As String)
            sCaption = Value
        End Set
    End Property

    <Category("Appearance"), Description("The width of the caption.")> _
    Public Property CaptionWidth() As Unit
        Get
            Return uCaptionWidth
        End Get
        Set(ByVal Value As Unit)
            uCaptionWidth = Value
        End Set
    End Property
```

Figure 25-17   The code for the DateDDL control (part 1 of 5)

The Visual Basic code for the DateDDL control   Page 2

```vb
<Category("Appearance"), _
Description("The space between the caption and the text box.")> _
Public Property CaptionPadding() As Unit
    Get
        Return uCaptionPadding
    End Get
    Set(ByVal Value As Unit)
        uCaptionPadding = Value
    End Set
End Property

<Category("Appearance"), Description("Determines if the caption " _
    & "is right-aligned.")> _
Public Property RightAlignCaption() As Boolean
    Get
        Return bRightAlignCaption
    End Get
    Set(ByVal Value As Boolean)
        bRightAlignCaption = Value
    End Set
End Property

Public ReadOnly Property [Date]() As Date
    Get
        Return CDate(Month & "/" & Day & "/" & Year)
    End Get
End Property

<Category("Misc"), Description("Gets or set the month.")> _
Public Property Month() As Integer
    Get
        iMonth = ddlMonth.SelectedIndex + 1
        Return iMonth
    End Get
    Set(ByVal Value As Integer)
        iMonth = Value
        ddlMonth.SelectedIndex = iMonth - 1
        If Not bDateChangedEventRaised Then
            RaiseEvent DateChanged(Me, New EventArgs)
            bDateChangedEventRaised = True
        End If
    End Set
End Property
```

Figure 25-17   The code for the DateDDL control (part 2 of 5)

At the bottom of page 3, you can see the Render method for this control. It simply calls the Render method of the base class to render the control and the child controls it contains.

On page 4 of this listing, you can see the overridden CreateChildControls method. This method is responsible for creating the two Label controls and the month, day, and year drop-down lists and adding them to the controls collection. To do that, it starts by executing the private MakeCaption and MakeCaptionPadding procedures to initialize the caption and the spacing between the caption and the drop-down lists. Then, it executes the private MakeMonthList, MakeDayList, and MakeYearList procedures to initialize the drop-down lists. Next, it clears the controls collection and adds the controls. Notice that literal controls that contain a space are added between the drop-down lists so that these lists don't appear right next to each other when they're displayed.

When the user selects a different month, day, or year from a drop-down list, the event handler for the SelectedIndexChanged event of that control is executed. The code for these event handlers is shown on page 5 of this listing. They simply set the Month, Day, and Year properties to the selection made by the user, and then call the AdjustDay procedure. If you look at the Set routines for these properties in parts 2 and 3, you can see that they in turn raise the DateChanged event. Notice that a Boolean variable is used to keep track of whether the DateChanged event has already been raised to make sure it isn't raised more than once.

The AdjustDay procedure that's called by the SelectedIndexChanged procedures prevents the date from being set to an invalid date. If the user selects April 31, for example, this procedure adjusts the date to April 30 since April only has 30 days. Or, if the user selects February 29 and it isn't a leap year, this procedure adjusts the date to February 28 since February only has 29 days in a leap year.

Although this is the simplest solution to the problem, it's probably not the best solution. Another solution would be to post the page any time the user selected a different month and then load the appropriate days for that month into the Day drop-down list. Still another solution would be to raise an event or throw an exception if the user selects an invalid date. These are the types of coding decisions you'll need to make as you design your custom controls.

The Visual Basic code for the DateDDL control

```
<Category("Misc"), Description("Gets or sets the day.")> _
Public Property Day() As Integer
    Get
        iDay = ddlDay.SelectedIndex + 1
        Return iDay
    End Get
    Set(ByVal Value As Integer)
        iDay = Value
        ddlDay.SelectedIndex = iDay - 1
        If Not bDateChangedEventRaised Then
            RaiseEvent DateChanged(Me, New EventArgs)
            bDateChangedEventRaised = True
        End If
    End Set
End Property

<Category("Misc"), Description("Gets or sets the year.")> _
Public Property Year() As Integer
    Get
        iYear = ddlYear.SelectedValue
        Return iYear
    End Get
    Set(ByVal Value As Integer)
        iYear = Value
        ddlYear.SelectedValue = iYear
        If Not bDateChangedEventRaised Then
            RaiseEvent DateChanged(Me, New EventArgs)
            bDateChangedEventRaised = True
        End If
    End Set
End Property

<Category("Misc"), _
Description("Determines whether a postback occurs " _
& "when the selection is changed."), DefaultValue(False)> _
Public Property AutoPostBack() As Boolean
    Get
        Return bAutoPostBack
    End Get
    Set(ByVal Value As Boolean)
        bAutoPostBack = Value
    End Set
End Property

Protected Overrides Sub Render _
        (ByVal output As System.Web.UI.HtmlTextWriter)
    MyBase.Render(output)
End Sub
```

Figure 25-17   The code for the DateDDL control (part 3 of 5)

The Visual Basic code for the DateDDL control

```vb
Protected Overrides Sub CreateChildControls()
    Me.MakeCaption()
    Me.MakeCaptionPadding()
    Me.MakeMonthList()
    Me.MakeDayList()
    Me.MakeYearList()
    Controls.Clear()
    Controls.Add(lblCaption)
    Controls.Add(lblCaptionPadding)
    Controls.Add(ddlMonth)
    Controls.Add(New LiteralControl(" "))
    Controls.Add(ddlDay)
    Controls.Add(New LiteralControl(", "))
    Controls.Add(ddlYear)
End Sub

Private Sub MakeCaption()
    lblCaption.Text = Caption
    lblCaption.Width = CaptionWidth
    If bRightAlignCaption Then
        lblCaption.Style.Item("text-align") = "right"
    End If
End Sub

Private Sub MakeCaptionPadding()
    lblCaptionPadding.Width = CaptionPadding
End Sub

Private Sub MakeMonthList()
    ddlMonth.Width = Unit.Pixel(85)
    ddlMonth.Items.Clear()
    ddlMonth.Items.Add("January")
    ddlMonth.Items.Add("February")
    ddlMonth.Items.Add("March")
    ddlMonth.Items.Add("April")
    ddlMonth.Items.Add("May")
    ddlMonth.Items.Add("June")
    ddlMonth.Items.Add("July")
    ddlMonth.Items.Add("August")
    ddlMonth.Items.Add("September")
    ddlMonth.Items.Add("October")
    ddlMonth.Items.Add("November")
    ddlMonth.Items.Add("December")
    ddlMonth.SelectedIndex = Month - 1
    ddlMonth.AutoPostBack = bAutoPostBack
End Sub
```

Figure 25-17   The code for the DateDDL control (part 4 of 5)

The Visual Basic code for the DateDDL control

```
    Private Sub MakeDayList()
        ddlDay.Width = Unit.Pixel(40)
        ddlDay.Items.Clear()
        Dim i As Integer
        For i = 1 To 31
            ddlDay.Items.Add(i)
        Next
        ddlDay.SelectedValue = Day
        ddlDay.AutoPostBack = bAutoPostBack
    End Sub

    Private Sub MakeYearList()
        ddlYear.Width = Unit.Pixel(65)
        ddlYear.Items.Clear()
        Dim i As Integer
        For i = DateTime.Today.Year To DateTime.Today.Year + 10
            ddlYear.Items.Add(i)
        Next
        ddlYear.SelectedValue = Year
        ddlYear.AutoPostBack = bAutoPostBack
    End Sub

    Private Sub ddlMonth_SelectedIndexChanged(ByVal sender As Object, _
            ByVal e As System.EventArgs) Handles ddlMonth.SelectedIndexChanged
        Month = ddlMonth.SelectedIndex + 1
        Me.AdjustDay()
    End Sub

    Private Sub ddlDay_SelectedIndexChanged(ByVal sender As Object, _
            ByVal e As System.EventArgs) Handles ddlDay.SelectedIndexChanged
        Day = ddlDay.SelectedValue
        Me.AdjustDay()
    End Sub

    Private Sub ddlYear_SelectedIndexChanged(ByVal sender As Object, _
            ByVal e As System.EventArgs) Handles ddlYear.SelectedIndexChanged
        Year = ddlYear.SelectedValue
        Me.AdjustDay()
    End Sub

    Private Sub AdjustDay()
        Select Case Month
            Case 4, 6, 9, 11
                If Day = 31 Then Day = 30
            Case 2
                If Year Mod 4 = 0 Then
                    If Day > 29 Then Day = 29
                Else
                    If Day > 28 Then Day = 28
                End If
        End Select
    End Sub

End Class
```

Figure 25-17   The code for the DateDDL control (part 5 of 5)

Perspective

In this chapter, you've learned the basics of creating custom server controls. You should realize, however, that there's a lot more to developing custom controls than what's presented in this chapter. For example, if you want to distribute a library of custom server controls that you've developed, you may want to include a bitmap that can be used as the icon for the control when it's displayed in the Toolbox. Or you may want to specify the default prefix that's used for the controls in the library. You may also want to bind data to custom controls, or you may want to create templated controls that work like the GridView control you saw in chapter 14. Although this chapter doesn't show how to accomplish these tasks, the programming techniques you've learned in this chapter should give you a good start toward developing your own custom server controls.

Terms

custom server control
web control library
rendered control
superclassed control
composite control
child control
designer attribute
self-closing tag
class attribute
property attribute
escaped identifier

26

An introduction to web services

In addition to web applications, you can use Visual Studio 2005 to create web services. Web services allow you to store common processing routines on a web server, where they're available to other programmers who need to use the routines in their applications. In other words, web services provide another way to reuse code. In this chapter, you'll learn the basic concepts and skills you need to create and use web services.

Basic concepts and terms

Simply put, a *web service* is a class that resides on a web server and can be accessed via the Internet or an intranet. As a result, ASP.NET applications or other types of web applications can access the web service from any computer that's connected to the Internet or an intranet.

What web services are used for

Web services are becoming an integral part of web development. One use of web services is to develop *distributed web applications* in which portions of an application can reside on different servers. For example, you might implement the business logic and database processing code for an application as a web service that runs on one server. Then, the user interface portion of the application can run on another server and call on the web service whenever business logic or database features are needed. It's even possible to provide two interfaces to the same web service: a web interface provided by an ASP.NET application that can be run from any computer that has a browser and Internet access, and a Windows interface provided by a Windows application that's installed on the user's computer.

Another use for web services is to allow applications developed by different companies or organizations to interact with one another. For example, the United States Postal Service has web services that let you calculate shipping rates, correct addresses, and track packages. You can use web services like these to incorporate the features they provide into your applications. Similarly, the popular search site Google offers web services that let you incorporate Google searches into your applications. As more companies create web services and publish them on the Internet, applications that use these services will become more popular.

How web services work

Figure 26-1 illustrates how web services work. As you can see, the web service is accessed from a web page running on a web server. In this example, the web service and the application's web pages reside on two different web servers. Although that doesn't have to be the case, this arrangement illustrates how web services can be used to create distributed applications. The server that hosts the web service must have both IIS and the .NET Framework installed.

Notice that the web page and the web service communicate using XML. Actually, web services use a rather complicated collection of protocols that are built on XML. These protocols include *WSDL*, which stands for *Web Services Description Language,* and *SOAP*, which stands for *Simple Object Access Protocol*. Fortunately, all of this is taken care of for you when you create and use a web service. As a result, you don't usually have to deal directly with XML, WSDL, or SOAP.

The operation of a distributed ASP.NET web application

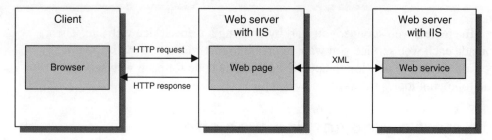

Description

- A *web service* is a class that resides on a web server and can be accessed by web applications or other web services to implement distributed ASP.NET web applications. A web service can also be accessed by Windows applications.

- Web services typically contain business logic that's coded as a collection of public methods.

- Like web applications, web services must reside on a web server with IIS. Although they can reside on the same server as the web applications that use them, they can also reside on a separate server.

- Information is passed between a web page and a web service using XML. Each web service must contain an XML document written in the *Web Services Description Language* (*WSDL*) that describes how the web service works and how clients can interact with it.

- If the web page and web service reside on the same server, the XML is passed as part of an HTTP request or response. If the web service resides on a different web server, the *Simple Object Access Protocol*, or *SOAP*, is used to facilitate the HTTP request and response.

- Since web services use a standard XML protocol to pass data between servers, they allow different types of servers to be able to communicate with each other. For example, a web application that's running on an IIS web server can use a web service that's running on an Apache web server. Conversely, a web application that's running on an Apache web server can use a web service that's running on an IIS web server.

Figure 26-1   How web services work

How to create a web service

To create a web service, you start by creating a web service web site. Then, you add each web service you want to create to this web site. Finally, you use the Code Editor to develop the public and private code for each web service. The following topics show you how.

How to start a web service web site

Figure 26-2 shows the New Web Site dialog box for creating a web service web site. From this dialog box, you identify the location of the web server and the name of the directory where the web service web site will reside just as you do for a regular web site. Then, all of the files for the web site are stored in that directory on the web server, and the solution file is stored in a directory with the same name within the projects location for Visual Studio directory.

How to add a web service

When you first start a web service web site, it contains a single web service named Service. In most cases, you'll want to delete this web service and add your own. In the next figure, for example, you'll see a web site with a web service named DaysUntil. To add a web service like this, you use the Add New Item dialog box shown here.

The New Web Site and Add New Item dialog boxes

Description

- To start a web service web site, display the New Web Site dialog box and select the ASP.NET Web Service template. Then, select HTTP from the Location drop-down list and identify the IIS server and the directory where you want the web site stored. Visual Studio creates this directory in the Inetpub\wwwroot directory of the IIS server by default.

- Visual Studio also creates a directory with the name you specify in the projects location for Visual Studio and stores the solution file there.

- By default, a web service web site consists of a single web service named Service. In most cases, you'll delete this web service and add your own. To add a web service, display the Add New Item dialog box, select the Web Service template, and enter a name.

Figure 26-2   How to start a web service web site and add a web service

How to develop the code for a web service

When you create a web service, two files are added to the web site. The first one has an extension of *asmx* and is the file you use to call the methods that you add to the web service. Like the aspx extension that's used for web pages, the asmx extension tells IIS that the file should be processed by ASP.NET.

The second file for a web service has a *vb* extension and is stored in the App_Code folder. This file contains the methods and other code that defines the web service. The starting code in this file is displayed by default when you create a web service. You can see this code in figure 26-3.

You'll want to note several things about the code in this figure. First, like everything else that's built on the .NET Framework, a web service is implemented as a class. In this case, the class inherits the WebService class, which provides the web service with access to the ASP.NET objects commonly used by web services.

Second, notice the WebService *attribute* that precedes the class definition. An attribute is similar to a keyword (like Public or Private) that provides information as to how the code should be used. In this case, the WebService attribute identifies the namespace that will contain the web service. The default is tempuri.org, which is a temporary namespace that you can use during development of a web service. If you publish a web service so it's available to other users, however, you'll want to change this name to something unique. That way, if someone else publishes a web service with the same name, the two can be distinguished by the namespace that contains them.

The WebService attribute can also contain a description of the web service. If you publish a web service, you'll want to include this information to provide potential users of the service with information about what it does. You'll see an example of how you code this information in the next figure.

To code a method that's accessible from outside the web service, you use the Public keyword, and you precede the method with the WebMethod attribute. This is illustrated by the HelloWorld function that's included in the starting code for a web service. As its name implies, the WebMethod attribute identifies a public method as a *web method*. Aside from the WebMethod attribute, you code a web method just as you would any other method. In addition, you can include private variables and procedures that are used by the web method.

One key difference between a web service and a regular Visual Basic class is that a web service can't have properties. You can define public variables, but those variables aren't accessible to clients that use the web service. As a result, web methods are the only interface a client has to a web service.

You can still implement the equivalent of properties using web methods, though. For example, to retrieve the value of a property, use a web method that's coded as a function that returns the value of the variable for the property. And to set the value of a property, use a Sub procedure that accepts the value of the property and assigns it to a variable.

By the way, you can also add components such as datasets to a web service. To do that, you display the Component Designer window as described in this figure. Then, you can drag components from the Toolbox to this window.

The starting code for a web service

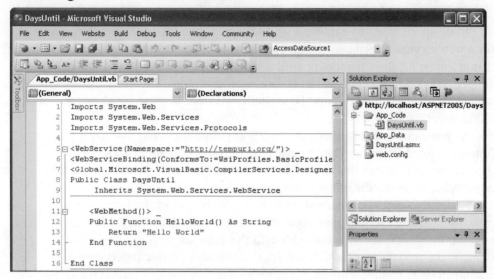

Description

- A web service is made up of two files. The file with the *asmx* extension is the file that you use to call the web service methods. The file with the *vb* extension in the App_Code folder contains the code for the web service. The code file is displayed by default when you start a new web service.

- A web service is implemented as a class that inherits the WebService class of the System.Web.Services namespace. This class provides the basic functionality for all web services.

- You develop the code for a web service by coding *web methods*. A web method is a Public procedure with the WebMethod *attribute* (<WebMethod()>). A web service can also include private code that's not available from outside the service.

- Web services don't support property declarations or public variables. Instead, you can use public functions to get the values of private variables, and you can use public Sub procedures to set the values of private variables.

- You can use the WebService attribute (<WebService()>) to identify the namespace for a web service. The default namespace is http://tempuri.org. If a web service is made public, it must have a unique namespace to distinguish it from other web services with the same name.

- The WebService attribute can also include a description of the web service. This description is displayed on the help and service description pages for the service.

- If you need to add a component such as a dataset to a web service, you can do that by dragging the component from the Toolbox to the Component Designer window. To display the Component Designer window, highlight the code file and then click the View Designer button at the top of the Solution Explorer.

Figure 26-3   How to develop the code for a web service

The code for the DaysUntil web service

To illustrate how you can use a web service, figure 26-4 presents the code for a web service named DaysUntil. This service contains three web methods that calculate the days remaining until a specified date. The first method, named simply DaysUntil, accepts the target date as an argument. The other methods, named DaysUntilHalloween and DaysUntilChristmas, assume 10/31 and 12/25 as the target date.

As you can see, the methods are coded as public functions that use a private function named DaysUntilDate to calculate the days remaining until the target date. Since you've seen this calculation earlier in this book, you shouldn't have any trouble understanding how it works.

Notice that each web method starts with a WebMethod attribute. In this case, the attribute is coded on a separate line that's continued to the line that contains the Function statement. Although this attribute isn't required, it can improve the readability of a web service that contains private procedures in addition to web methods. So we recommend that you use this format for all your web services.

You should also notice that the Date argument that receives the date used by the DaysUntil method is enclosed in brackets. These brackets indicate that Date is an *escaped identifier*. Escaped identifiers allow you to use Visual Basic keywords for the names of variables, procedures, and properties.

Finally, notice the WebService attribute at the beginning of the web service. This attribute identifies the namespace for the web service as

`http://murach.com/`

This namespace is used to uniquely identify the web service. Although it isn't required, it is common practice to use an Internet domain name to help ensure that the namespace is unique.

The WebService attribute in this example also includes a brief description of the web service. You'll see one way this information is used in the next figure.

The Visual Basic code for the DaysUntil web service

```vb
Imports System.Web
Imports System.Web.Services
Imports System.Web.Services.Protocols

<WebService(Namespace:="http://murach.com/", _
    Description:="Calculates the number of days until a given date")> _
<WebServiceBinding(ConformsTo:=WsiProfiles.BasicProfile1_1)> _
<Global.Microsoft.VisualBasic.CompilerServices.DesignerGenerated()> _
Public Class DaysUntil
    Inherits System.Web.Services.WebService

    <WebMethod()> _
    Public Function DaysUntil(ByVal [Date] As Date) As Integer
        Return DaysUntilDate([Date].Month, [Date].Day)
    End Function

    <WebMethod()> _
    Public Function DaysUntilHalloween() As Integer
        Return DaysUntilDate(10, 31)
    End Function

    <WebMethod()> _
    Public Function DaysUntilChristmas() As Integer
        Return DaysUntilDate(12, 25)
    End Function

    Private Function DaysUntilDate(ByVal Month As Integer, _
            ByVal Day As Integer) As Integer
        Dim TargetDate As DateTime
        TargetDate = DateTime.Parse(Month.ToString & "/" & _
            Day.ToString & "/" & DateTime.Today.Year)
        If DateTime.Today > TargetDate Then
            TargetDate = TargetDate.AddYears(1)
        End If
        Dim tsTimeUntil As TimeSpan = TargetDate - DateTime.Today
        Return tsTimeUntil.Days
    End Function

End Class
```

Note

- The Date argument used by the DaysUntil method is enclosed in square brackets to distinguish it from the Date keyword. This construct, called an *escaped identifier*, lets you use a Visual Basic keyword as a variable, procedure, or property name.

Figure 26-4   The code for the Days Until web service

How to test a web service

After you develop a web service, you can test it without having to create a client program that uses it. To do that, you simply build and run the web service in your default browser or in a Browse window just as you would a web application. When you do that, a *Web Service help page* like the first one shown in figure 26-5 is displayed.

The Web Service help page identifies the web service and displays the description you specified in the WebService attribute. It also includes a link to the *service description* for the web service. This is the XML document you learned about in figure 26-1 that contains the Web Services Description Language (WSDL) that describes the web service. If you're interested in what this document looks like, you can click on this link to display it.

Finally, the Web Service help page lists the web methods that are available from the web service. If you click on the link for one of these methods, a help page for that method is displayed. The second screen in this figure, for example, is the help page for the DaysUntil method.

If a method requires arguments, the help page for that method lists them by name and lets you enter values for them. Then, when you click the Invoke button, the method is executed and the XML that's generated as a result is displayed. In this figure, for example, you can see the XML that's generated when the DaysUntil method is executed using 4/13 as the value of the Date argument. If you're familiar with XML, you can see that the actual result of the calculation is contained within <int> and </int> tags. These tags are generated based on the return type of the method.

Although you can't see it in this figure, the help page for that method also contains sample SOAP and HTTP requests and responses. If you're interested in what this code looks like, you may want to scroll down so you can see it. In general, though, you don't need to worry about how it works.

When you test a web service in your browser as shown in this figure, you can use the Visual Studio debugging tools you learned about in chapter 4 to debug it. To do that, just set one or more breakpoints before you run the web service. Then, the web service will enter break mode before it executes a statement that has a breakpoint, and you can use the tools that are available from break mode to debug the web service.

Help pages for the DaysUntil web service

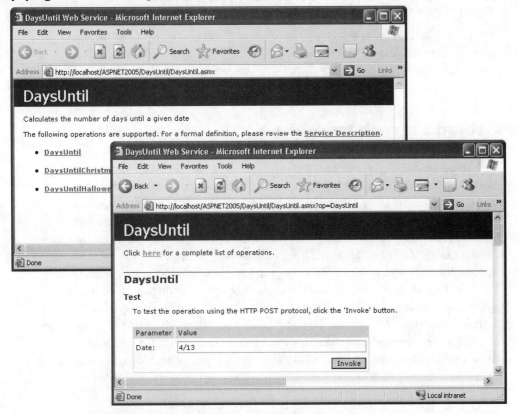

XML output for the DaysUntil web method

Description

- To test a web service in your default browser, click the Start button in the Standard toolbar. A *Web Service help page* like the first one shown above is displayed.

- To test a web method, click the link for that method. Then, enter any required parameters in the help page that's displayed and click the Invoke button. A page that shows the XML output for the method is displayed.

- When you use your browser to test a web service, you can set breakpoints and debug the web service just as you do for a web application.

Figure 26-5   How to test a web service

How to consume a web service

After you build and test a web service, you can use it from any application that requires the services it provides. To do that, you first have to add a reference to the web service. Then, you can create an instance of it and use it like any other class.

How to add a web reference

To add a web reference to a web site, you use the Add Web Reference dialog box shown in figure 26-6. From this dialog box, you can enter the address of the asmx file for the web service into the URL box. You can also locate a web service using the links that are available from this dialog box. If the service is on your local server, for example, you can click the Web Services on the Local Machine link and a list of all the web services on the local server will be listed. Then, you can click the link for the web service you want to add.

After you identify the web service, its description is displayed in the left pane of the dialog box. This is the same information that's displayed in the Service help page you saw in the last figure. You can use it to test or review the available web methods or to display the service description for the web service. When you're sure you've located the web service you want, you can click the Add Reference button to add a reference to the service to the web site.

The dialog box for adding a web reference

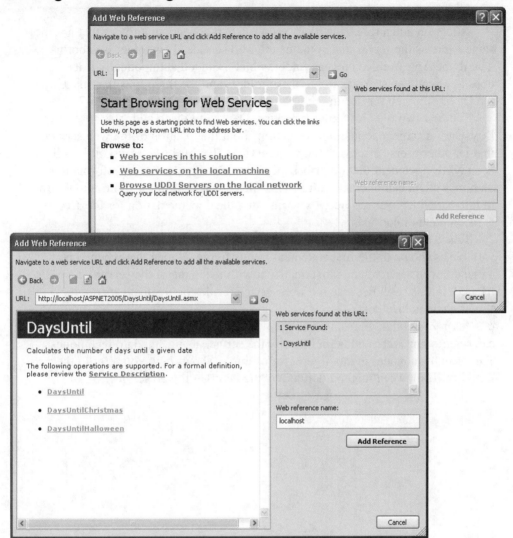

Description

- To add a reference to a web service to a web site, right-click the web site in the Solution Explorer and select the Add Web Reference command from the shortcut menu to display the Add Web Reference dialog box.

- To locate a web service, enter the address of its aspx file in the URL box and press Enter, or select the URL from the drop-down list. Then, information about the service is displayed, and you can click the Add Reference button to add a reference to the web service to your web site.

- You can also use the links in the Add Web Reference dialog box to locate web services in the current solution, on your local machine, or on a local network.

Figure 26-6   How to add a web reference

How to use a web service

After you add a reference to a web service, it appears in a folder that has the same name as the server that contains the web service. This folder is subordinate to the App_WebReferences folder, which is added automatically if it doesn't already exist. You can see these folders and the three files that make up the DaysUntil web service in the Solution Explorer shown in figure 26-7.

The first two files for the web service, DaysUntil.disco and DaysUntil.discomap, contain information about the location of the web service that let other users "discover" the web service. The third file, DaysUntil.wsdl, is an XML document that describes the web service and contains information on how a client can interact with it. This file can be helpful for figuring out how to interact with a web service if you find that the documentation for the service is incomplete or confusing.

To use a web service, you create an instance of it and assign it to an object variable as shown in the first statement in this figure. Notice that when you name the web service, you must qualify it with the name of the server where it's located. In this case, because the web service resides on the local server, the server name is localhost.

After you assign an instance of the web service to an object variable, you can refer to any web method defined by the service using standard techniques. The second statement in this figure, for example, shows how you refer to the DaysUntilHalloween method defined by the DaysUntil web service.

The Solution Explorer with a web service reference

A statement that creates an instance of the DaysUntil web service

```
Private DaysUntil As New localhost.DaysUntil
```

A statement that executes the DaysUntilHalloween method of this web service

```
iDaysUntilHalloween = DaysUntil.DaysUntilHalloween
```

Description

- When you add a reference to a web service to a web site, a folder with the name of the server where the web service is located is created under the App_WebReferences folder in the Solution Explorer.

- Three files are included for the web service. The *disco* and *discomap* files contain information about the location of the web service. The *wsdl* file contains a description of the web service.

- To use a web service in an application, you can create an instance of it using a declaration statement with the New keyword like the one shown above. The reference to the web service must include the name of the server where it resides.

- After you create an instance of a web service, you can execute its web methods using the same techniques you use to execute a method of any object.

Figure 26-7   How to use a web service

Perspective

Although the web service presented in this chapter is trivial, it demonstrates the techniques you can use to develop more substantial web services. As a result, the basic skills you've learned here are enough to get you started developing your own web services. In addition, you'll be prepared to learn the more complicated aspects of web services programming when the need arises.

* * *

In this book, we've done our best to present all of the skills that you need for developing e-commerce web applications. Now, if you've read all 26 chapters of this book, we hope you feel that you're adequately prepared for doing that. You should also feel like you have the concepts, skills, and perspective to learn whatever else you need to know as you develop web applications. If that's the case, this book has done its job. And we thank you for reading it.

Terms

web service
distributed web application
WSDL (Web Services Description Language)
SOAP (Simple Object Access Protocol)
attribute
web method
escaped identifier
Web Service help page
service description

Appendix A

How to install and use the software and downloadable files

To develop ASP.NET 2.0 applications, you need to have Visual Studio 2005 or Visual Web Developer Express Edition installed on your PC. Both of these products include a development web server that you can use to run your applications. However, because of the limitations of this server, you'll also want to test your applications using IIS. The easiest way to do that is to install IIS on your own PC.

This appendix shows you how to install both Visual Studio and IIS. It also shows you how to download, install, and use the applications and databases that are available from our web site. And it shows you how to work with web applications from within IIS.

Basic techniques for working with the software and downloadable files

The topics that follow present the basic techniques for installing and using the downloadable files for this book and for installing the software you need to develop applications like those presented in this book. We recommend you read these topics before you start developing your first web application so you can be sure that you have all the software and files you need.

How to download and install the files for this book

Throughout this book, you'll see complete applications that illustrate the material presented in each chapter. To help you understand how these applications work, you can download the source code and databases for these applications from our web site at www.murach.com. Then, you can open and run them in Visual Studio. These files come in a single download, as summarized in figure A-1. This figure also describes how you download and install these files.

When you download the single install file and execute it, it will install all of the files for this book in the Murach\ASP2VB folder on your C drive. Within this folder, you'll find a folder named Apps that contains all the applications in this book. You can open and run these applications in Visual Studio as file-system applications as described in figure A-4. The exception is the application for chapter 17, which must be run under IIS because it requires a digital secure certificate. The procedure for running a file-system web site under IIS is also presented in figure A-4. For more information on digital secure certificates, see chapter 17.

The download also includes Access and SQL Server Express versions of the Halloween database used by many of the applications. Since the Access database is small, we've included it in the App_Data folder of each application that uses it so you can run these applications without any trouble. Before you can run the applications that use the SQL Server database, however, you must attach this database to SQL Server Express, and you must grant ASP.NET access to this database.

To attach the database to SQL Server Express, you can use Windows Explorer to find and run the db_attach.bat file in the C:\Murach\ASP2VB\Database directory. This batch file runs a SQL Server script named db_attach.sql that attaches the database to your local server.

To grant ASP.NET access to the SQL Server database, you can run the db_grant_access.bat file in the Database directory. But first, you must modify the db_grant_access.sql file that this batch file runs so it uses the name of your computer. To do that, open the file in a text editor, and replace each occurrence of [machineName] with the name of your computer. Then, save and close this file, and run the db_grant_access.bat file to grant ASP.NET access to the Halloween database.

What the downloadable application file for this book contains

- The source code for all of the applications presented in the book
- Access and SQL Server Express versions of the Halloween database used in these applications
- Files you can use to work with the SQL Server Express version of the Halloween database
- A Readme file that contains additional information about working with the SQL Server database and the applications

How to download and install the files for this book

- Go to www.murach.com, and go to the page for *Murach's ASP.NET 2.0 Web Programming with VB 2005*.
- Click on the link for "FREE download of the book applications." Then, download "All book files." This will download one file named asp2vb_allfiles.exe to your C drive.
- Use Windows Explorer to find the downloaded file on your C drive. Then, double-click on this file and respond to the dialog boxes that follow. This installs the files in folders that start with C:\Murach\ASP2VB.

How to install the SQL Server database

- Use Windows Explorer to navigate to the C:\Murach\ASP2VB\Database directory.
- Double-click the db_attach.bat file to run it. This will attach the Halloween database to the SQL Server Express database server on your local machine.
- Right-click the db_grant_access.sql file and select Edit to open it in a text editor. Then, replace all occurrences of [machineName] with the name of your computer. When you're done, save the file.
- Double-click the db_grant_access.bat file to run it. This will grant a user named ASPNET owner access to the Halloween database.

Description

- You can download the sample applications and databases for this book from www.murach.com.
- The Access version of the Halloween database is included in the App_Data folder of each application that uses it.
- For more information on the db_attach.bat, db_attach.sql, db_grant_access.bat, and db_grant_access.sql files, please see the Readme file for this download.

Figure A-1   How to download and install the files for this book

If you run into any trouble attaching the Halloween database or granting ASP.NET access to it, you can read the Readme file that's included with this download. This file describes alternate techniques you can use that can help you troubleshoot the cause of a problem. It also describes the other batch and script files that are included in this download.

How to install IIS

When you run an ASP.NET web application from Visual Studio, it runs under the built-in development server by default. Because of that, you don't have to have IIS installed to develop the applications in this book or to run the applications that you download from our web site (with the exception noted in the previous topic). Keep in mind, however, that the built-in server has some limitations, which you'll learn about in chapter 4. Because of that, you'll want to install IIS so that you can thoroughly test the applications you develop. (Note that you can't install IIS if you're using Windows XP Home Edition. In that case, IIS isn't available to you, and you'll have use the development server or you'll have to have access to a separate web server.)

Figure A-2 shows how to install IIS. To start, you display the Add/Remove Programs dialog box and then click the Add/Remove Windows Components button at the left side of the dialog box that's displayed. When you do, the Windows Components Wizard starts and the first dialog box shown in this figure is displayed. This dialog box lists all the available Windows components. The components that are currently installed have a check mark in front of them. To install another component (in this case, IIS), just check it, click the Next button, and complete the dialog boxes that are displayed.

In chapter 4, you'll learn how to create remote IIS web sites, and you'll learn how to use IIS as an FTP server. To use either of these features, you must install components of IIS that aren't installed by default. To install these components, select IIS in the Windows Components Wizard and then click the Details button to display the Internet Information Services (IIS) dialog box shown here. Then, if you want to use IIS as an FTP server, select the File Transfer Protocol (FTP) Service component. And, if you want to create remote IIS web sites, select the FrontPage 2000 Server Extensions component. When you're done, click OK and then continue with the Windows Components Wizard.

The Windows Components Wizard

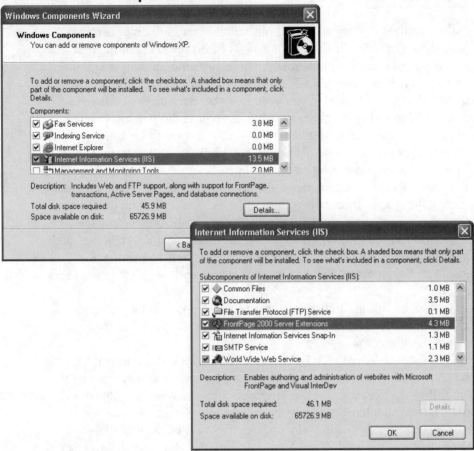

How to install IIS

1. Double-click Add or Remove Programs in the Control Panel. Then, click on Add/Remove Windows Components to display the Windows Components Wizard, and select Internet Information Services (IIS) from the list of components that are displayed.

2. If you want to install FPSE, or if you want to configure IIS as an FTP Server, click the details button, select the appropriate options from the Internet Information Services (IIS) dialog box that's displayed, and click OK.

3. Click the Next button to complete the installation.

Description

- If you want to run applications from a local IIS server, install IIS before you install Visual Studio.

- To create or access an IIS web site on a remote computer, that computer must have FPSE installed. To use IIS as an FTP server, the FTP Service must be installed.

Figure A-2   How to install IIS

How to install Visual Studio 2005

If you've installed Windows applications before, you shouldn't have any trouble installing Visual Studio 2005. You simply insert the DVD or the first CD and the setup program starts automatically. This setup program will lead you through the steps for installing Visual Studio as summarized in figure A-3. If you're using Windows XP, though, you need to install Service Pack 2 before you start. If you don't, the Visual Studio 2005 setup program will alert you to the fact that the service pack hasn't been installed, and it won't let you continue.

When you click the Install Visual Studio 2005 link, the setup program starts loading the installation components it needs. Then, after you click the Next button and accept the license agreement, the program displays a dialog box that lets you select the type of installation. In most cases, you'll perform a default installation so the most commonly used features are installed, including the .NET Framework, Visual Studio, Visual Basic, the development web server, and SQL Server Express. Later, in the Default Environment Settings dialog box, you can choose Web Development Settings so your menus will be like the ones in this book.

After you install Visual Studio, you can install the documentation for Visual Studio and all of the products that come with it. To do that, just click the Install Product Documentation link.

If you're using the Visual Web Developer 2005 Express Edition, you have to download and install Web Developer 2005 and SQL Server Express separately. But if you follow the directions on the Microsoft web site when you download these products, you shouldn't have any trouble installing them.

The final setup step is to apply any updates that have become available since the product was released. If you don't perform this step, though, you can check for updates from within Visual Studio by using the Help→Check for Updates command. In fact, you should use this command periodically to be sure that Visual Studio is up-to-date.

If you have installed IIS as described in the previous topic, you'll want to register ASP.NET 2.0 with IIS after you install Visual Studio. Although the setup program may indicate that it has done that for you, I found that not to be the case. To register ASP.NET with IIS, just run the aspnet_regiis program as described in this figure.

To find the build number that you need for doing that, you can first enter a cd\ command to return to the root directory of the C drive. Then, you can run this command to identify the Windows root directory:

```
C:\>cd %systemroot%\Microsoft.NET\Framework
C:\Windows\Microsoft.NET\Framework>
```

This shows you what the root directory is so you can use Windows Explorer to find the last build number in the Framework directory. To complete the registration, you can run these commands (assuming the build number is 50727):

```
C:\Windows\Microsoft.NET\Framework>cd v2.0.50727
C:\Windows\Microsoft.NET\Framework\v2.0.50727>aspnet_regiis -i
```

The Visual Studio 2005 Setup program

How to install Visual Studio 2005

1. Insert the DVD or Disc 1 of the CDs. The setup program will start automatically.

2. Click the Install Visual Studio 2005 link and follow the instructions. When the Options page is displayed, you can accept the Default option unless you have special requirements. When the Default Environment Settings dialog box is displayed, you can select the Web Development Settings.

3. To install the documentation for Visual Studio and the related products (Visual Basic, ASP.NET, etc.), click the Install Product Documentation link.

4. To install any updates that are available, click the Check for Service Releases link.

How to register ASP.NET with IIS

- After you install IIS and Visual Studio 2005, you need to register ASP.NET 2.0 with IIS. To do that, open a command prompt and use the cd command to change the directory to %systemroot%\Microsoft.NET\Framework\v2.0.xxxxx, where %systemroot% is the root directory for Windows and xxxxx is the last .NET build number. Then, enter the command aspnet_regiis –i.

- To find the last .NET build number, use the Windows Explorer to go to the Framework directory and look for the build numbers in the subdirectories.

Description

- The Visual Studio 2005 Setup program installs not only Visual Studio, but also the .NET Framework, the development web server, and SQL Server Express.

- If you're using Visual Web Developer 2005 Express Edition, you have to download and install SQL Server Express separately. To download and install these products, just go to the Microsoft web site and follow the directions on the download pages.

Figure A-3   How to install Visual Studio 2005

How to use the downloaded web applications

You can use two techniques to run the downloaded web applications for this book. First, you can open the applications in Visual Studio and then run them using the built-in development server. Second, you can run them under a local IIS server. Figure A-4 describes both of these techniques.

Before you can run an application with a local IIS server, you must create a virtual directory for the application within IIS. A virtual directory is a directory that contains a pointer to the directory that actually contains the files for a web site. To create a virtual directory, you can use the procedure shown in this figure. Then, you can run the application from within Visual Studio just as you would a file-system application.

Once you create a virtual directory for a web application, you can also run the application from outside of Visual Studio. To do that, open a browser window and specify //localhost/ followed by the virtual directory name and the starting page. For example, if the virtual directory name is Ch03Cart and the starting page is Order.aspx, you can run the application by entering //localhost/Ch03Cart/Order.aspx in the browser's address bar.

The IIS Management Console

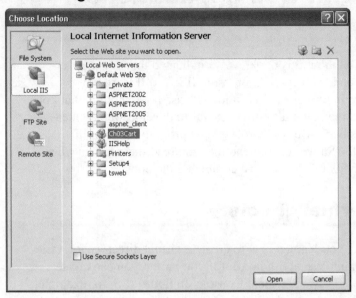

How to run a file-system web site under the development web server

1. Start Visual Studio and open the web site using the File→Open Web Site command.
2. Right-click the starting page for the application and select Set As Start Page.
3. Run the application using the Debug→Start Debugging command.

How to run a file-system web site under IIS

1. Start Visual Studio and display the New Web Site dialog box using the File→New Web Site command.
2. Select HTTP for the location, then click the Browse button to display the Choose Location dialog box.
3. Select the Local IIS button at the left side of the dialog box, select the Default Web Site node from the tree that's displayed, and then click the Create New Virtual Directory button near the upper right corner of the dialog box. This displays the New Virtual Directory dialog box.
4. Enter the name for the virtual directory you want to create, enter the path where the files for the web site are stored, and click OK to return to the Choose Location dialog box.
5. Select the virtual directory you just created, and click Open to return to the New Web Site dialog box.
6. Click OK. A warning will be displayed indicating that there is already a web site at the location you specified. Select the Open the Existing Web Site option, and click OK.
7. Right-click the starting page for the application and select Set As Start Page.
8. Run the application using the Debug→Start Debugging command.

Figure A-4   How to use the downloaded web applications

How to work with web applications using IIS

In several places throughout this book, we've indicated that you can perform certain operations on a web application using IIS. You'll learn how to perform those operations in the topics that follow. Please note, though, that you don't need to understand the material in these topics to develop web applications as described in this book. But as a professional programmer, you'll probably need these skills. So we recommend that you read these topics when we refer to them in the book or after you've completed the book.

How to create a virtual directory

In the previous topic, you learned how to create a virtual directory for a file-system web site from within Visual Studio. But if you prefer, you can create a virtual directory from the IIS Management Console. In figure A-5, for example, you can see two of the dialog boxes for creating a virtual directory named Ch03Cart that points to the web site stored in the C:\ASP.NET 2.0 Web sites\Ch03Cart directory.

After you create a virtual directory, it will appear under the Default Web Site node in the IIS Management Console. Then, you can use Visual Studio to open the web site from this directory so you can run the application under IIS. You can also run the application from outside of Visual Studio.

The dialog boxes for creating a virtual directory in IIS

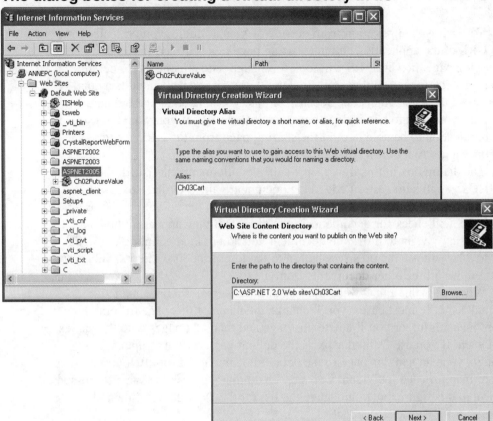

How to create a virtual directory for a file-system web site

1. Open the Control Panel, and make sure it's displayed in Classic View rather than Category View. Then, double-click Administrative Tools, and double-click Internet Information Services to open the IIS Management Console.

2. Use the tree to locate the Default Web Site node, right-click Default Web Site, and choose New→Virtual Directory to start the Virtual Directory Creation Wizard.

3. Enter the name you want to use for the virtual directory on the Virtual Directory Alias page of the wizard, enter the path for the directory that contains the web site on the Web Site Content Directory page, and accept the defaults on the Access Permissions page.

Description

- In chapter 4, you can learn how to create a virtual directory for a new or existing web site using Visual Studio. You can also create a virtual directory for a web site from IIS. Then, you can use Visual Studio to open the web site from the virtual directory, and you can run the web site under IIS.

Figure A-5   How to create a virtual directory

How to set the default page for a web site

To run a web application from outside of Visual Studio, you typically enter the URL of the application and the starting page in a browser. If you don't enter a starting page, however, IIS will look for a page with a name in the default document list for the application. By default, this list doesn't include a document with the aspx extension. Because of that, you'll need to add the name of the page you want to be displayed by default to this list if you want the users of the application to be able to omit the starting page from the URL for the application. Figure A-6 shows how you do that.

The dialog box in this figure shows the default document list for the Ch03Cart application after I added the document named Order.aspx. Note that when you add a document to the list, it's displayed at the end of the list. Because IIS will check for documents in the order that they appear in the list, you'll usually want to move the document you add to the beginning of the list. To do that, you use the up arrow button to the left of the list. Alternatively, you can remove all the other documents from the list.

When you start a new web site, Visual Studio creates a page named Default.aspx. In most cases, you'll change the name of this page to something more meaningful, or you'll delete this page and then add pages with the names you want. If you use Default.aspx as the default page for your applications, though, you can add this page to the default document list for all your web sites rather than for each individual web site. To do that, you use the same technique shown in this figure, but you change the list for the Default Web Site node instead of for a specific web site.

The Documents tab of the Properties dialog box

How to work with the list of default documents for a web site

- To display the list of default documents for a web site, display the IIS Management Console, and locate the web site. Then, right-click on the web site, select Properties from the shortcut menu, and click the Documents tab in the Properties dialog box that's displayed.

- To add a document to the list of default documents, click the Add button, enter the document name in the dialog box that's displayed, and click OK.

- To change the order in which IIS looks for the documents, use the up and down arrow buttons to the left of the document list.

- To remove a document from the list, select the document and click the Remove button.

Description

- By default, if you run a web application from a browser outside of Visual Studio and you don't include the name of the page you want to display in the URL, IIS looks for a document with the name Default.htm, Default.asp, index.htm, or iisstart.asp. If you want IIS to look for a document with a different name, you can use the procedure above to add that document to the list of default documents.

- You can also add a document to the list of default documents for all your web sites. To do that, use the procedure above, but right-click the Default Web Site node instead of a specific web site. For example, you might want to add Default.aspx to the list since this is the file that's created by default when you start a new web site in Visual Studio.

Figure A-6   How to set the default page for a web site

How to force a page to use a secure connection

In chapter 17, you can learn how to secure a web application. One aspect of securing an application that's covered in that chapter is how to be sure that a page that should always use a secure connection can't be displayed without one. The technique shown in that chapter involves adding code to the Load event of the page. That way, if a user tries to bypass the navigation features provided by an application and access a page directly, the page will still be secured. Another way to provide that security is to use the IIS Management Console as shown in figure A-7.

In most cases, you'll only secure the pages of a web site that contain confidential information. If you need to, however, you can secure all the pages in a folder within the web site or all of the pages within the web site. To do that, you use the same technique shown in this figure, but you display the properties of the folder or the web site.

Appendix A *How to install and use the software and downloadable files* **819**

The dialog boxes for securing a web page

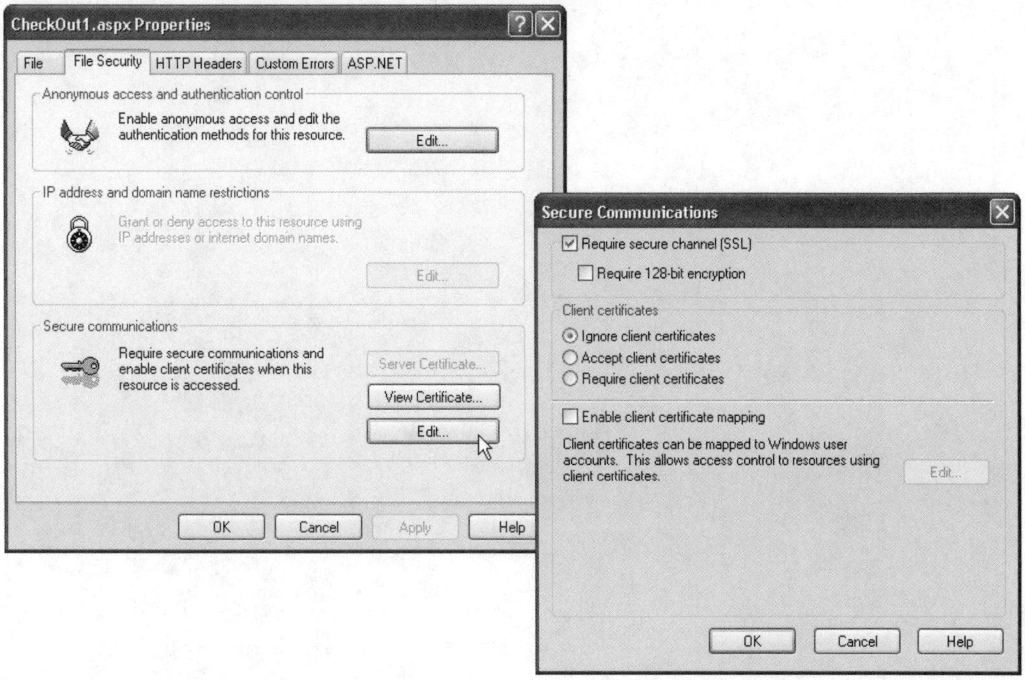

How to set the security for a web page

1. Display the IIS Management Console, locate the web site that contains the page you want to secure, and select the web site or the folder within the web site that contains the page.

2. Right-click the page (.aspx) in the right pane of the IIS Management Console, select the Properties command from the shortcut menu, and display the File Security tab of the Properties dialog box that's displayed.

3. Click the Edit button in the Secure Communications section to display the Secure Communications dialog box. Then, select the Require Secure Channel (SSL) option. If you want the page to be displayed only if 128-bit encryption is used, select the Require 128-bit Encryption option.

Description

- In chapter 17, you can learn how to add Visual Basic code to a page to be sure that it uses a secure connection. Another way to do that is to set IIS security properties for the page.

- You can also set the security for all the pages within a folder of a web site or for all the pages of a web site. To do that, display the properties for the folder or web site, display the Directory Security tab, and then set the appropriate options.

Figure A-7 How to force a page to use a secure connection

Index

TextChanged event, 193
  text box, 58, 59
TextMode attribute (text box), 202, 203
Theme attribute
  Page directive, 338, 339, 340, 341
  Pages element, 328, 329, 340, 341
Theme property (page), 338, 339, 340, 341
Themes, 323-343
  applying to a page, 338, 339
  applying to an application, 328, 329
  making available to an application, 328, 329
  removing, 340, 341
Tilde operator, 86, 87
Timeout attribute (sessionState element), 268, 269
Title (form), 50
  modifying, 48, 49
Title attribute
  Page directive, 296
  Part class, 682, 685
  siteMapNode element, 309
Title element, 158, 159
Title property (custom WebPart control), 702, 703
Title tag, 22
TitleStyle element (calendar control), 228
To property (MailMessage class), 648, 649
TodayDayStyle element (calendar control), 228
Toolbox, 32, 33
ToolboxData attribute (Class statement), 768, 769
ToolTip property (web server control), 47
Top attribute (RectangleHotSpot element), 226
Tr element, 180, 181
Trace attribute (Page directive), 142, 143, 160, 161
Trace feature, 142-145
  size of view state, 258, 259
Trace messages (custom), 144, 145
Trace output, 142, 143
Trace property (page), 144, 145
Tracepoint, 132, 133
Transact-SQL, 356
Transfer method (HttpServerUtility class), 82, 83
  query strings, 282, 283
TreeView control, 306, 307, 312, 313
Trial certificate, 526, 527
Try...Catch block (custom error handling), 656, 657, 658, 659
Two-dimensional positioning, 170, 171
Two-way binding, 398, 399, 438
Type attribute
  ControlParameter element, 385
  Input element, 156, 157

Link element, 174, 175
  profile property, 588, 589, 594, 595
Type property
  compare validator, 240, 241
  range validator, 54, 55, 242, 243
TypeName attribute (ObjectDataSource control), 488, 489, 490

U

Unique constraint, 348
Unique key, 348, 349
Unique key constraint, 348, 349
Unlock method (HttpApplicationState class), 273
Update method
  data access class, 498, 499, 502, 503
  SqlDataAdapter class, 368, 369
Update statement (SQL), 91, 360, 361
  SqlDataSource control, 380
UpdateCommand attribute (SqlDataSource control), 402, 403
UpdateCommand property (SqlDataAdapter class), 368, 369
UpdateImage attribute (CommandField element), 424
UpdateMethod attribute (ObjectDataSource control), 488, 489, 498
UpdateParameters element (SqlDataSource control), 402, 403
UpdateText attribute (CommandField element), 424
UpdateUser method (Membership class), 577, 578
URL (Uniform Resource Locator), 8, 9
  coding, 86, 87
Url attribute (siteMapNode element), 309
URL encoding, 282, 283
Url property (HttpRequest class), 532, 533
User Control Designer, 728, 729
User controls, 725-745
  adding to web forms, 736, 737
  adding to web part zones, 686, 687
  compared to custom server controls, 750, 751
  creating, 728-735
  working with from web form, 740, 741
User Interface Editor (web setup project), 718
UserControl class, 730, 731
Username property (MembershipUser class), 579
Users, 550, 551
Users attribute (Deny and Allow elements), 574, 575
UUEncode format, 652, 653

For more on Murach products, visit us at
www.murach.com

For professional developers

Murach's ASP.NET 2.0 Web Programming with VB 2005	$52.50
Murach's ASP.NET 2.0 Web Programming with C# 2005	52.50
Murach's ASP.NET 2.0 Upgrader's Guide: C# Edition	39.50
Murach's ASP.NET 2.0 Upgrader's Guide: VB Edition	39.50
Murach's C#	49.50
Murach's Beginning Visual Basic .NET	49.50
Murach's ASP.NET Web Programming with VB.NET	49.50
Murach's VB.NET Database Programming with ADO.NET	49.50
Murach's SQL for SQL Server	49.50
Murach's Beginning Java 2, JDK 5	$49.50
Murach's Java Servlets and JSP	49.50
Murach's OS/390 and z/OS JCL	$62.50
Murach's Mainframe COBOL	59.50
Murach's CICS for the COBOL Programmer	54.00
DB2 for the COBOL Programmer, Part 1 (Second Edition)	45.00

Prices and availability are subject to change. Please visit our web site or call for current information.

Our unlimited guarantee...when you order directly from us

You must be satisfied with our books. If they aren't better than any other programming books you've ever used...both for training and reference...you can send them back within 90 days for a full refund. No questions asked!

Your opinions count

If you have any comments on this book, I'm eager to get them. Thanks for your feedback!

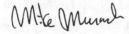

To comment by

E-mail: murachbooks@murach.com
Web: www.murach.com
Postal mail: Mike Murach & Associates, Inc.
             3484 W. Gettysburg, Suite 101
             Fresno, California 93722-7801

To order now,

 Web: www.murach.com

 Call toll-free:
1-800-221-5528
(Weekdays, 8 am to 4 pm Pacific Time)

 Fax: 1-559-440-0963

 Mike Murach & Associates, Inc.
Professional programming books

What software you need for this book

- Any full edition of Microsoft Visual Studio 2005 or the inexpensive Visual Web Developer Express Edition.

- These editions include everything you need for developing ASP.NET 2.0 applications, including .NET Framework 2.0, ASP.NET 2.0, Visual Basic 2005, a built-in web server, and a scaled-back version of SQL Server called SQL Server Express.

- If you want to use IIS (Internet Information Services) instead of the built-in web server to run web applications on your own PC, you also need to install IIS. You need to do this to test some aspects of web applications, and IIS comes with Windows 2000 or XP (except the XP Home Edition).

- To learn more about installing these products, please read appendix A.

The downloadable files for this book

- The source code for all the applications presented in this book.

- Access and SQL Server Express versions of the Halloween database used by these applications.

- Files you can use to work with the SQL Server Express version of the Halloween database.

- A Readme file that contains additional information about working with the SQL Server database and the applications.

- To learn more about downloading and installing these applications and databases, please read appendix A.

The C# edition of this book

- If this book looks interesting but you're a C# developer, please see *Murach's ASP.NET Web Programming with C# 2005*. It covers all of the same features but uses C# coding examples.

New .NET 2.0 books

- During the next several months, we'll be publishing new books on .NET 2.0 subjects like Visual Basic 2005, C# 2005, and database programming.

- So please check our web site periodically for information about our new .NET books.

www.murach.com